Lecture Notes of the Institute for Computer Sciences, Social Informatics and Telecommunications Engineering 675

The LNICST series publishes ICST's conferences, symposia and workshops.
LNICST reports state-of-the-art results in areas related to the scope of the Institute.
The type of material published includes

- Proceedings (published in time for the respective event)
- Other edited monographs (such as project reports or invited volumes)

LNICST topics span the following areas:

- General Computer Science
- E-Economy
- E-Medicine
- Knowledge Management
- Multimedia
- Operations, Management and Policy
- Social Informatics
- Systems

Robert C. Qiu · Xiang Chen · Vasilis Friderikos ·
Zhiyong Tao
Editors

IoT as a Service

10th EAI International Conference, IoTaaS 2024
Wuhan, China, November 22–24, 2024
Proceedings

 Springer

Editors
Robert C. Qiu
Huazhong University of Science
and Technology
Wuhan, China

Vasilis Friderikos
King's College London
London, UK

Xiang Chen
Sun Yat-sen University
Guangdong, China

Zhiyong Tao
Wuhan Research Institute of Posts
and Telecommunications
Wuhan, China

ISSN 1867-8211   ISSN 1867-822X (electronic)
Lecture Notes of the Institute for Computer Sciences, Social Informatics
and Telecommunications Engineering
ISBN 978-3-032-14680-9   ISBN 978-3-032-14681-6 (eBook)
https://doi.org/10.1007/978-3-032-14681-6

This Springer imprint is published by the registered company Springer Nature Switzerland AG
The registered company address is: Gewerbestrasse 11, 6330 Cham, Switzerland

If disposing of this product, please recycle the paper.

Preface

We are delighted to introduce the proceedings of EAI IoTaaS 2024, The 10th International Conference on IoT as a Service. This conference, held from November 22–24, 2024 in Wuhan, China, aimed to bring together researchers and industry experts to present state-of-the-art research work on the challenges and developments related to IoT systems. This conference built a domestic and international exchange and docking platform in the field of IoT, which plays an important role in absorbing the essence of the latest research achievements. At the same time, the conference promoted the integration of overseas talents and domestic scientific and technological forces, carried out high-level cooperative research and academic exchanges, and sped up the rapid development of technology in IoT and communications.

The technical program of IoTaaS 2024 consisted of 34 full papers in oral presentation sessions. The topics covered Cellular Vehicle-to-Everything (C-V2X), Industrial IoT, Artificial Intelligence for AIoT, Security and Privacy for Smart IoT, and Intelligent Sensing Technology. These papers were selected from 95 submissions. Each submission was reviewed following a single-blind process with a minimum of 5 reviews per paper. Aside from the high-quality technical paper presentations, the technical program also featured three keynote speeches. The speakers were Shanzhi Chen from China Information and Communication Technology Group, Ziqin Sang, Vice Chair of IoT and Smart Cities Working Group, ITU-T, and Tao Wen, General Manager of Wuhan Fiberhome Fuhua Electric Co., Ltd.

Coordination with the steering chairs Huaglory Tianfield and Ren Ping Liu were essential for the success of the conference. We sincerely appreciate their constant support and guidance. It was also a great pleasure to work with such an excellent organizing committee team for their hard work in organizing and supporting the conference. In particular, the Technical Program Committee, led by our TPC Co-Chairs, Robert C. Qiu, Xiang Chen, Vasilis Friderikos, and Xingpeng Jiang, completed the peer-review process of technical papers and made a high-quality technical program. We are also grateful to Conference Manager, Zhiyong Tao for his support and to all the authors who submitted their papers to IoTaaS 2024.

We strongly believe that EAI IoTaaS 2024 provided a good forum for all researchers, developers, and practitioners to discuss all science and technology aspects that are relevant to IoT as a Service. We also expect that future IoTaaS conferences will be as successful and stimulating, as indicated by the contributions presented in this volume.

Robert C. Qiu
Xiang Chen
Vasilis Friderikos
Zhiyong Tao

Organization

Steering Committee

Ren Ping Liu — University of Technology Sydney, Australia

Huaglory Tianfield — Glasgow Caledonian University, UK

Organizing Committee

General Chair

Zhiyong Tao — Wuhan Research Institute of Posts & Telecommunications, China

General Co-chairs

Xingpeng Jiang — Wuhan Vocational College of Software and Engineering, China

Zhenyu Liao — Huazhong University of Science and Technology, China

TPC Chairs and Co-chairs

Robert C. Qiu — Huazhong University of Science and Technology, China

Xiang Chen — Sun Yat-sen University, China

Vasilis Friderikos — King's College London, UK

Xingpeng Jiang — Wuhan Vocational College of Software and Engineering, China

Tao Lu — Wuhan Institute of Technology, China

Qiong He — Wuhan Vocational College of Software and Engineering, China

Sponsorship and Exhibit Chair

Shan Wu — Wuhan Research Institute of Posts & Telecommunications, China

Local Chairs

Yue Wu	Wuhan Research Institute of Posts & Telecommunications, China
Qi Li	Wuhan Vocational College of Software and Engineering, China
Bingxiao Tian	Wuhan Research Institute of Posts & Telecommunications, China

Workshops Chair

Xuefang Zhang	Wuhan Research Institute of Posts & Telecommunications, China

Publicity and Social Media Chairs

Wen Cheng	Wuhan Research Institute of Posts Telecommunications, China
Lai Soon Wong	Universiti Tunku Abdul Rahman, Malaysia

Publications Chair

Shangjing Lin	Beijing University of Posts and Telecommunications, China

Web Chair

Yu Ling	Wuhan Research Institute of Posts & Telecommunications, China

Posters and PhD Track Chair

Jingjing Geng	Wuhan Vocational College of Software and Engineering, China

Panels Chair

Zhen Cao	Wuhan Research Institute of Posts & Telecommunications, China

Demos Chair

Zhiqiang Fan Wuhan FiberHome International Technology Co., Ltd, China

Tutorials Chair

Wei Wang Huazhong University of Science and Technology, China

Technical Program Committee

Caixiao Ouyang Wuhan Vocational College of Software and Engineering, China
Fan Rao Jianghan University, China
Hafiz Tiomoko Ali Samsung Research UK, UK
Hao Yang Huazhong University of Science and Technology, China
Huaglory Tianfield Glasgow Caledonian University, UK
Hui Lan Jianghan University, China
Jiaming Wang Wuhan Institute of Technology, China
Jie Gong Sun Yat-sen University, China
Jie Wen Huazhong University of Science and Technology, China
Jie Zhang Syneos Health, USA
Jing Xiao Wuhan City Polytechnic, China
Joel Reginald Dodoo McGill University, Canada
Jun Liu Wuhan Institute of Technology, China
Kun Zhang Huazhong University of Science and Technology, China
Lansu Dai University of Ottawa, Canada
Minjie Cao University of Ottawa, Canada
Ramayah Thurasamy Universiti Sains Malaysia, Malaysia
Renping Liu University of Technology Sydney, Australia
Rozitaa Gholami Ferdowsi University of Mashhad, Iran
Shangjing Lin Beijing University of Posts and Telecommunications, China
Songtao Li Jianghan University, China
Tao Lu Wuhan Institute of Technology, China
Taoyu Wu University of Ottawa, Canada
Vasilis Friderikos King's College London, UK

Wenbo Huang	Huazhong University of Science and Technology, China
Xi Hu	Jianghan University, China
Xi Wang	Huazhong University of Science and Technology, China
Xiang Chen	Sun Yat-sen University, China
Xiang Gao	New York Medical College, USA
Xiaojing Wang	Wuhan Vocational College of Software and Engineering, China
Xijun Wang	Sun Yat-sen University, China
Xin Xiong	Jianghan University, China
Xinghua Sun	Sun Yat-sen University, China
Xuehui Dong	Huazhong University of Science and Technology, China
Yun Zhu	Wuhan Vocational College of Software and Engineering, China
Zhengyu Wang	Huazhong University of Science and Technology, China
Zhenyu Liao	Huazhong University of Science and Technology, China
Zhiming Zhan	Jianghan University, China
Zhiqing Luo	Huazhong University of Science and Technology, China

Contents

A Novel Hotspot Strategies Based on Big Data and Its Application in Studying a Case of Miami State, U.S.A.

Hewen Wei[1]([envelope]) and Zhuoxian Wei[2]

[1] School of Artificial Intelligence, Jianghan University, Wuhan, China
395629936@qq.com
[2] School of Science, The University of Queensland, Brisbane, Australia

Abstract. With the increasing number of car owners in the following years, Traffic accidents have become an important issue in urban traffic management. However, the analysis of hotspot areas in traffic accidents still lacks sufficient attention for further improving traffic safety. This paper firstly researches traffic accident hotspots using point density and random forest model. Secondly, this paper visualizes hotspot areas in traffic accidents and discusses the corresponding strategies for solving the problem of urban traffic management. Finally, these corresponding strategies are discussed and some useful suggestions are given, which provide a new method for the prediction and management of hotspots in traffic accidents.

Keywords: traffic accident · hot spot analysis · random forest model · point density

1 Introduction

As urbanisation accelerates, the problem of traffic congestion is becoming more prominent, which leads to an increased risk of traffic accidents. The World Health Organization's first Global Status Report on Road Safety shows that 1.27 million people worldwide die each year from road traffic accidents [1].

Currently, frequent traffic accidents has caused great pressure on the society, which threaten people's life safety and bring significant economic losses [1, 2]. For better solving the phenomenon, hotspot areas in traffic accidents have become the focus of research, including around schools, near hospitals, and construction zones.

The analysis of hotspots in traffic accidents is a necessary to reduce the occurrence of traffic accidents, to improve the efficiency of road use and to ensure the safety of people's lives and property [3–5]. It involves technical challenges, as well as an in-depth understanding of urban development and planning.

Existing works focus on the analysis in [6] have proposed a spatial statistics and traditional statistical methods for Accurate identification of accident hotspots. However, the above-mentioned works lack of the analysis of hotspots in traffic accidents, which may suffer from several limitations in the following aspects.

R. C. Qiu et al. (Eds.): IoTaaS 2024, LNICST 675, pp. 1–10, 2026.
https://doi.org/10.1007/978-3-032-14681-6_1

1. High Complexity: The approach involves multiple statistical and mathematical models, making the data processing and analysis procedures complex. It may require advanced professional knowledge and substantial computational resources.
2. High Data Demand: The method relies heavily on large volumes of traffic and spatial data, necessitating high-quality and comprehensive datasets, which may pose challenges in data acquisition.
3. High Time Cost: The Delphi method requires multiple rounds of expert opinion collection and analysis, potentially consuming a significant amount of time.
4. Limited Applicability: The method may be difficult to apply in regions with insufficient or low-quality data, affecting its generalizability and broader applicability.

This paper firstly researches traffic accident hotspots based on point density and random forest model. Secondly, this paper visualizes hotspot areas in traffic accidents and discusses the corresponding strategies for solving the problem of urban traffic management. Finally, these corresponding strategies are discussed and some useful suggestions are given, which provide a new method for the prediction and management of hotspots in traffic accidents.

The main contributions of our study is as follows.

1. High Accuracy: Random Forest models improve prediction accuracy by aggregating the results of multiple decision trees. Each tree's prediction is combined through voting or averaging, reducing the error of individual models.
2. Handling High-Dimensional Data: Random Forest can handle datasets with a large number of features, which is crucial in traffic accident prediction since accident data often involve various factors such as weather, time, road conditions, and vehicle characteristics.
3. Reduction of Overfitting: Random Forest reduces the risk of overfitting by using random sampling and multiple trees. Each tree is trained on a subset of the data and features, improving the model's generalization ability.
4. Feature Importance Evaluation: Random Forest provides feature importance scores, helping to identify the most critical factors for accident prediction. This is useful for traffic management authorities to take targeted measures to improve road safety.

The rest of this paper is arranged as follows. In Sect. 2, a brief overview of Hotspot identification in traffic accidents is presented. Section 3 analyzes the traffic accident causation.

2   Hotspot Identification in Traffic Accidents

In this study, point density heat map is used to visualize and identify traffic accident hotspots [6]. Taking the above processed Miami city traffic accident dataset as the data, using the latitude and longitude coordinates of each traffic accident data occurrence point in the data, the geographic coordinates of each data point are mapped into the canvas area.

2.1 Heat Map

Heat map can be intuitive, explicit web page traffic data distribution through different colors, to the website adjustment and optimization to provide a strong reference basis, convenient to improve the user experience. The realization principle of heat map in [3] can be generally summarized as the following steps: geographic mapping, impact factor calculation, generating circles, weight value superposition, image colorization.

2.2 Traffic Accident Hotspot Identification Results

In the process of traffic accident hotspot identification, potential high accident areas can be effectively revealed by point density analysis. The traffic accident data in the study area were subjected to point density calculation, and the distribution of accident density in different areas was obtained. Figure 1 shows the hot spots of traffic accidents in some areas of Miami. The closer the color is to red, the higher the number of accidents at that location, and the closer the color is to blue, the higher the number of accidents at that location, the higher the number of accidents at that location, and the higher the number of accidents at that location, the higher the number of accidents at that location.

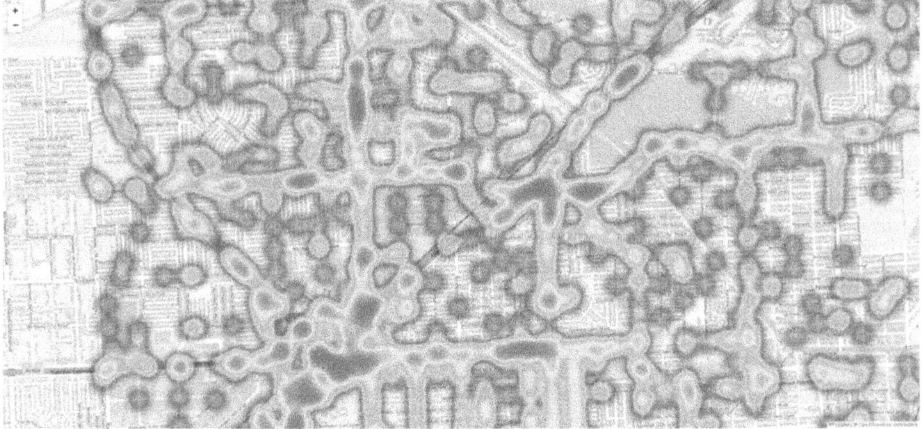

Fig. 1. Regional hotspot map

Through point density analysis, we found some important traffic accident hotspots, which are often closely related to road traffic conditions, population density, transportation planning and other factors. In further research, we will combine the random forest model to explore the causative factors behind these hotspots, which will provide a scientific basis for the development of effective traffic accident prevention strategies.

3 Traffic Accident Causation Analysis

Traffic accident causation analysis is essential to widely use in urban traffic management [4]. This paper applies random forest model in traffic accident causation analysis and then analyze the results of traffic accident hotspot causation.

3.1 Application of Random Forest Model in Traffic Accident Causation Analysis

In order to better establish the model, it is necessary to transform the data in the category type data into numerical data, and to separate the characteristics and target variables. And the purpose of this modeling is to predict the severity of traffic accidents (Severity) rather than whether there is a traffic accident or not, in which the severity of the accident is divided into levels 2 and 4, which are shown in the results as 2 and 4, and the higher the level, the more serious the traffic accident is, i.e., the level 4 traffic accidents are more serious than the level 2 traffic accidents. Here is the beginning of the modeling:

1) Divide the data set. Divide the dataset into test set and training set in the ratio of 8:2. And set a random seed to ensure that the same randomized division results are obtained every time the code is run, which helps the reproducibility of the results. The division and selection of data are completely random, but the training set and test set after random selection are subsequently kept unchanged to ensure the consistency of personal loan data and the reproducibility of the prediction results in the process of subsequent optimization of the random forest model and comparative analysis of different models.

2) Establish the initial random forest model. The Random Forest Classifier class in the sklearn library in Python language is used to build the initial random forest model, and the training set of the divided traffic accident data is imported, and all the parameters of the initial model are taken by default, and the random forest model containing 100 decision trees is constructed, and the model is trained by using the training set in order for the model to be able to learn how to accurately predict the target variable.

3) Model Evaluation. By calling the predict function, the model will predict the feature data of the test set and get the prediction results. These predictions will be used to compare with the real target variables. The classification report function is then called, passing in the real target variable and the model's predictions as parameters. Use the classification_report function to calculate and output a report containing various classification metrics such as accuracy, recall, F1 score, etc. These metrics help us to evaluate the performance of the model on the test set now, including the model's prediction accuracy for different categories. The prediction results of this model are shown in Fig. 2.

From the evaluation indexes in the table, it can be seen that the accuracy of the random forest model for traffic accident prediction reaches 99%, which means that about 99% of the data in the test set of traffic accidents are correctly classified and predicted; at the same time, the precision rate, the recall rate and the F1-score value of the initial model prediction are all close to 1. Combined with the above analysis of prediction indexes, the random forest model has achieved a good effect in the prediction of traffic accidents. The prediction of the random forest model on traffic accidents has achieved a better effect.

3.2 Analysis Results of Traffic Accident Hotspot Causation

Firstly, the performance criteria of analysis results of traffic accident hotspot causation is introduced in this paper, which is presented in Table 1.

```
Accuracy: 0.9981700216270172
                 precision      recall    f1-score     support

             2      1.00        1.00        1.00        24009
             4      0.00        0.00        0.00           35

      accuracy                              1.00        24044
     macro avg      0.50        0.50        0.50        24044
  weighted avg      1.00        1.00        1.00        24044
```

Fig. 2. The results of model evaluation

Table 1. Performance criteria of analysis results of traffic accident hotspot causation (类似下面图这样)

The criteria of the MAPE measure	
MAPE (%)	Forecasting power
<10	Excellent
10–20	Good
20–50	Reasonable
>50	Incorrect

Finally, the importance ranking of the feature variables of the Random Forest Model in traffic accident prediction is outputted, and the influencing factors of traffic accidents are analyzed. The principle process of ranking the importance of feature variables:

1) Find a trained model.
2) Disrupt the values in a single column and use the generated dataset to make predictions.
3) Use these predictions and the true target values to calculate the effect of the shuffling on the loss function. This deterioration in performance measures the importance of the variable you just scrambled.
4) Return the data to its original order (undoing the scrambling in step 2). Now repeat Step 2 for the next column in the dataset until the importance of each column is calculated.

The results of the feature variable importance ranking visualization are shown in Figure 3:

From Figure 3, it can be seen that: pressure (Pressure), air temperature (Temperature), humidity (Humidity), wind speed (Wind_Speed), weather (Weather_Condition) and other factors have a greater impact on traffic accidents. Among them, pressure (Pressure) has the greatest impact, generally bad weather conditions, such as storms,

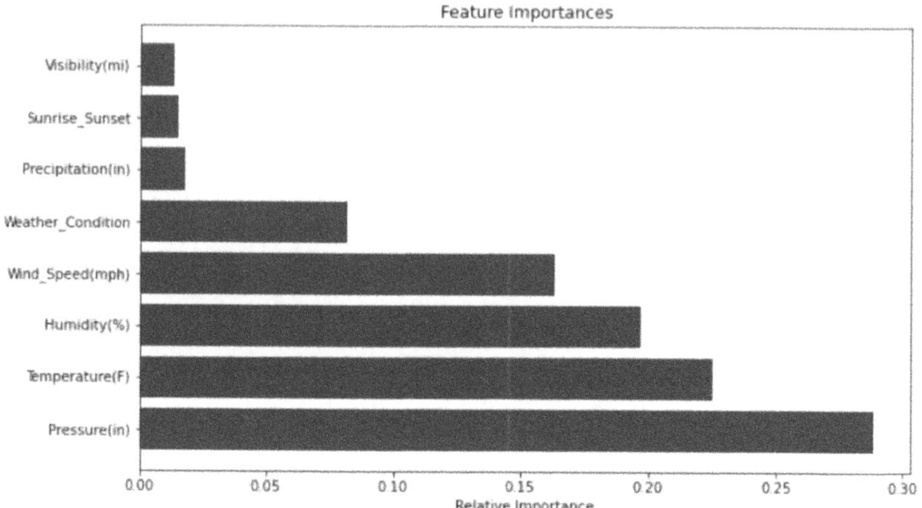

Fig. 3. Importance ranking of feature variables

heavy rain, high winds, etc. will cause pressure (pressure) changes, this weather not only affects visibility, but also lead to slippery roads and reduce vehicle handling performance, increasing the probability of accidents. And pressure (pressure) on the importance of local traffic accidents accounted for such a high proportion of the reason is that although the city of Miami is in the plains, but the climate is subtropical, warm and humid throughout the year, the summer is the rainy season, the winter is relatively dry and less rainy, often subject to hurricanes and typhoons, the arrival of hurricanes lead to local pressure changes dramatically, while the hurricanes of the terrible has also led to serious traffic accidents.

Secondly, the temperature (Temperature) of the significant changes in half accompanied by climate change, such as high temperatures in the summer, winter cold road icing. According to information learned in [7], "bomb cyclone" cold wave hit the United States, due to the impact of global warming in recent years, resulting in cold air southward, the United States "Bomb cyclone" more and more frequently, the destructive power of the winter cold wave gradually increased, suchweather conditions, road icing and freezing, shortening the braking distance of vehicles, car tires skidding phenomenon is serious, resulting in traffic accidents.

In addition, the amount of traffic accidents was visualized for different weather conditions, with the intention of finding the impact of different weather on the probability of traffic accidents. As shown in Figure 4:

From Fig. 4, it can be seen that the highest number of traffic accidents occurs under Fair (clear days with good visibility) weather conditions, followed by Mostly Cloudy (cloudy) conditions, followed by Partly Cloudy (partly cloudy) conditions, followed by Cloudy (cloudy) and Light Rain (light rain) weather conditions. It is reasonable to assume that in good weather conditions, the travel base is significantly more than in bad weather, and the traffic base is large thus leading to a high probability of traffic

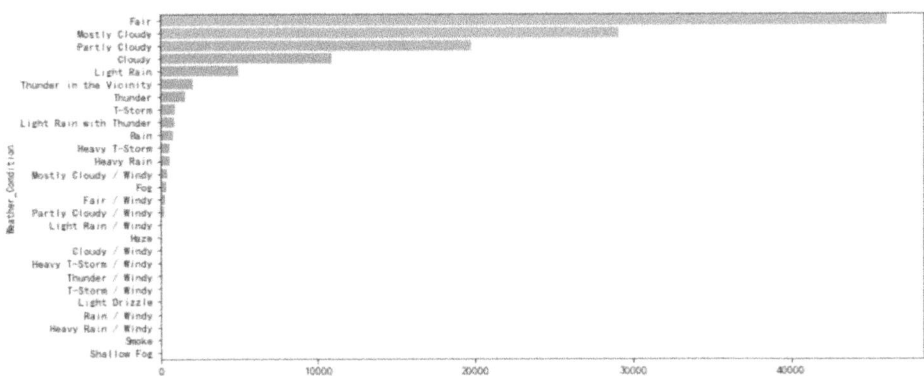

Fig. 4. The No. of accidents based on weather conditions

accidents, thus presenting the results of the data analysis in which the number of traffic accidents in good weather conditions is significantly greater than the number of bad weather conditions.

4 Strategies for Preventing Hotspots of Traffic Accidents [5]

4.1 Construction of Traffic Safety Awareness of Relevant Personnel

According to relevant figures, the human factor in traffic accidents is more than 90% Road traffic accidents in-depth investigation of the current situation analysis and future development concept, so the road education for relevant personnel to prevent traffic accidents is crucial. Therefore, road education for relevant people is crucial to prevent traffic accidents. Education for relevant people can be carried out from improving safety awareness and supervision and management.

(1) Improve public safety awareness. This can be done by carrying out traffic safety knowledge popularization activities, holding traffic safety lectures and training courses, supplemented by new media such as short videos and live broadcasts, etc., to raise the awareness and consciousness of drivers and passengers about traffic safety.
(2) Traffic road supervision and management. Traffic supervision is one of the important means to ensure traffic safety. First of all, it can be carried out through strict law enforcement, crack down on traffic violations, strengthen the punishment for violations, and improve the overall importance of society to road traffic safety. At the same time, traffic flow management and traffic signal control are carried out through big data systems in order to reduce traffic congestion and traffic accidents, improve transportation efficiency, and reduce traffic congestion and transportation costs

4.2 Road Infrastructure Construction

Traffic accident prevention can also start from road infrastructure construction, such as road maintenance, traffic monitoring system, protective isolation measures, etc.

(1) Conduct road maintenance.
(2) Improve the traffic monitoring system.

4.3 Vehicle Technology Quality Construction

A good vehicle can ensure the life safety of the occupants when an accident occurs, and in terms of vehicles, it will be expressed through the two aspects of vehicle performance quality and the application of new technological innovation.

In general, the future research direction should pay more attention to the all-round analysis of traffic accident hotspots and multi-factor exploration, combined with the era of emerging technology means, to provide more powerful data support for the traffic safety management department, more targeted decision-making suggestions and more effective measures and means, and jointly promote the reduction of traffic accidents and the stable development of road traffic safety.

5 Numerical Experiments

5.1 Data Overview

In this paper, we use the US Accidents (2016–2023) [1, 2] dataset (US Accidents (2016–2023) [1, 2]) obtained from the kaggle website (www.kaggle.com) as data for hotspot identification and causation analysis of traffic accidents. This is a national crash dataset covering 49 states in the U.S. Traffic data captured by a variety of entities, including U.S. and state departments of transportation, law enforcement agencies, traffic cameras, and traffic sensors within the roadway network. The time frame of the crash data is from February 2016 through March 2023. This sample data records a total of 7,728,393 traffic accidents and contains 46 eigenvalues such as accident severity, accident longitude, accident latitude, accident street, weather conditions, rainfall, wind direction, and more. This data has a very high degree of rigor and feasibility. Due to the large volume of directly imported data and its inability to meet the needs of the study, the data need to be screened and preprocessed.

5.2 Data Screening

Through reasonable data attribute screening, data attributes related to the purpose of the study can be better screened to provide reliable data support and basis for the hot spot analysis of traffic accidents and strategy research. The criteria for data screening in this paper are as follows:

1) Take each city in the United States as a unit, sort the number of traffic accidents in each city, and select the city with the most traffic accidents. The sorting results are shown in Table 2, and this paper selects the city Miami as the research object. The city of Miami is densely populated, with high vehicle flow and high traffic pressure, which is a typical city with heavy traffic and frequent traffic accidents. In the city, the main traffic sections include highways, main roads and side roads.

2) In order to narrow down the research data and make the results more current, this paper selects the traffic data occurring from January 1, 2021 to the deadline of data statistics as the research object. There are some fields within the eigenvalues that may be too complex to contribute significantly to the study. By removing these fields, the goal was to simplify the dataset and make it more centralized and efficient to analyze. The filtered data has a total of 12,876 entries and 38 columns of features.

Table 2. Traffic accident sorting

	City	Cases
0	Miami	128627
1	Orlando	71727
2	Los Angels	66000
3	Houston	56210
4	Dallas	55086
5	Charlotte	505572
6	Releigh	34285
7	Nashville	31874

5.3 Data Preprocessing

Data preprocessing can improve the quality and usability of data and provide a better basis for subsequent data analysis and modeling. Traffic accident data are collected from different traffic sensors and recording systems, and different recording methods may lead to missing values, outliers, duplicated values, etc. in the data, so the data need to be cleaned. In this data, the missing parts are small in number relative to the dataset as a whole and cannot be filled in due to their specificity, so deletion is directly applied to them. The data volume is reduced from 12876 to 120267. The visualized box line diagram of the data in this paper is shown in Fig. 5(a). Upon inquiry, the outliers were found to be due to the fact that another area named "Miami" was incorrectly included in the data, and the latitude and longitude of the accident location was not within the city of Miami, so it could not be used as an object of study, and therefore the outliers were deleted.

Therefore, the outliers were selected for deletion. The outliers were removed using the 3σ principle, and Fig. 5(b) shows the box plots after the removal of the outliers, which shows that the outliers have disappeared from the data.

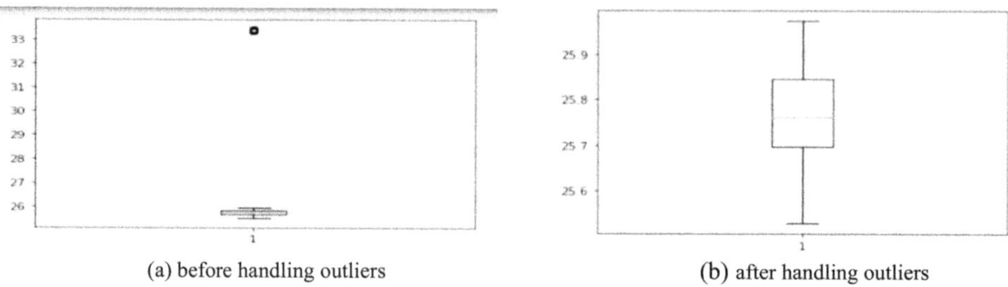

(a) before handling outliers(b) after handling outliers

Fig. 5. Boxplot

6 Conclusion

For further improving traffic safety, this paper has analyzed hotspot areas in traffic accidents. This paper has firstly researched traffic accident hotspots based on point density and random forest model. Secondly, this paper has visualized hotspot areas in traffic accidents and discusses the corresponding strategies for solving the problem of urban traffic management. Finally, these corresponding strategies are discussed and some useful suggestions have been given, which have provide a new method for the prediction and management of hotspots in traffic accidents.

References

1. Moosavi, S., Samavatian, M.H., Parthasarathy, S., Ramnath, R.: A Countrywide Traffic Accident Dataset (2019)
2. Moosavi, S., Samavatian, M.H., Parthasarathy, S., Teodorescu, R., Ramnath, R.: Accident risk prediction based on heterogeneous sparse data: new dataset and insights. In: proceedings of the 27th ACM SIGSPATIAL International Conference on Advances in Geographic Information Systems, ACM (2019)
3. Berhanu, Y., Schroeder, D., Teklu, B., Alemayehu, E.: Spatial analysis of road traffic accidents: identifying hotspots for improved road safety in Addis Ababa, Ethiopia. Cogent Eng. **10**(2), 1–23 (2023)
4. Du, Y.: Research on hotspot identification and causation of bus accident under the perspective of spatio-temporal features. Chang'an University (2023)
5. Yue, Y., Cheng, S.: Screening the causes of road traffic accidents in China and countermeasure suggestions. Sci. Innov. **04**, 21–24 (2021)
6. Pirdavani, A., Brijs, T., Wets, G.: A multiple criteria decision-making approach for prioritizing accident hotspots in the absence of crash data. Transp. Rev. **30**(1), 97–113 (2010)
7. "Bomb cyclone" cold front hits the U.S.A.: Temperatures plummet to minus 48 degrees, many freeze to death in cars
8. https://m.163.com/dy/article_cambrian/HPN42L720553WHJN.html

Approaches To Managing Licensees Across International Borders

Yingrui Yang$^{(\boxtimes)}$, Jingjing Geng, and Qi Li

Wuhan Vocational College of Software and Engineering, Wuhan, China
973054226@qq.com

Abstract. The increasing number of radiocommunication technologies and the Cross-border Interference (CBI) caused by ionospheric and tropospheric scatter, multipath reflection and diffraction are deteriorating the lack of spectrum re sources in border areas. Sharing spectrum seems to be the only way to reduce the chance of such harmful interference and increase the efficiency of the usage of spectrum. However, spectrum sharing in border areas can be tricky because incumbents and spectrum operators from different countries may have different goals for each frequency band. Take Canada and the US as an example, USA has employed CBRS with centralized control on 3500 MHz frequency band however, Canada is pursuing exclusive licensing. This paper is going to propose a new spectrum sharing mechanism that can be used in Canada-US border areas. We first study the existing cross-border frequency management solutions including the Harmonized Calculation Method (HCM) agreement, the Licensed Shared Access (LSA) dynamic spectrum sharing system and its advanced evolution Cross border LSA (CBLSA). We explore the advantage and disadvantage of the existing solutions. We then explore a recent research direction related to non-cooperative Game Theory and Nash Equilibrium to overcome the disadvantages. We go through several researches which use non-cooperative Game Theory to model the spectrum management issues between operators in different countries, and the primary users and secondary users in general. We list some of their results to show that this is indeed a possible way to solve the spectrum management issues in the border areas between Canada and the US. We finally conclude the non cooperative Game Theory approach with its Technology Readiness Level (TRL) to indicate its progress towards a final solution to the problem and the future work that needs to be done.

Keywords: Satellite Frequency Management · Frequency band regulations

1 Introduction

The radiofrequency (RF) spectrum is a national limited resource just like land, water, natural gas, and minerals. However, as the number of radiocommunication technologies increasing in the past decade, the lack of spectrum resource is getting more serious. This problem is even worse in border areas because spectrum

© ICST Institute for Computer Sciences, Social Informatics and Telecommunications Engineering 2026
Published by Springer Nature Switzerland AG 2026. All Rights Reserved
R. C. Qiu et al. (Eds.): IoTaaS 2024, LNICST 675, pp. 11–28, 2026.
https://doi.org/10.1007/978-3-032-14681-6_2

operators from different countries may follow different policies and have different goals for each frequency band. These frequency conflicts may introduce harmful interference and thus degrade the efficiency of the usage of spectrum. Take the Canada-US border as an example, several important frequency bands are not harmonized including 800 MHz frequency block, the L-band (1427–1518 MHz) and 3500 MHz block. In Canada, the 800 MHz frequency block contains 2 parts. The first part (806–821/851–866 MHz) is used for fixed point-to-point and land mobile systems, and the second part (821–824/866–869 MHz) is designated for exclusive use by public safety systems. However, 800 MHz frequency bands are used for commercial mobile broadband services and are currently being used to deploy LTE networks in the US. For the L-band, as an important band for future 5G deployments in Canada, the Innovation, Science and Economic Development (ISED) wants to release it for flexible fixed and mobile use, but it is currently operating aeronautical mobile telemetry in the US. The other key band for the development of 5G services, the 3500 MHz block (3450–3650 MHz) is currently reserved for aeronautical and maritime radars and will be subject to a near future consultation for mobile use in Canada whereas in the US, it has been made for flexible use on a shared basis through a database supported authorization system, also known as the Citizen Broadband Radio Service (CBRS) [1].

Apparently, there is potential harmful interference in the above scenarios and the frequency bands need to be harmonized in border areas. Moreover, it is obvious that the coordination between organizations from different country will be much harder than between regional departments. For example, if Canada wants to coordinate the 3500 MHz block in the Canada-US border, it will be very hard for Canadian spectrum operators to get in touch with the relevant organizations in the US because such information exchange needs to be proved by both governments as well. The coordination process gets more complicated when more cities or states are involved in the border coordination issue. Fortunately, not like natural gas and minerals, the RF spectrum is a renewable resource, it can be allocated and reallocated, and it can be shared. Spectrum operators can harmonize frequency bands by sharing the spectrum where two or more users are allowed to use the same frequency range under a defined sharing agreement. In fact, back in 2011, researchers in Europe had realized the Radio Regulation provided by ITU-R in 2008 was not efficient in resolving international interference management and were seeking better ways of harmonizing international spectrum [9]. As stated in European Commission's report in 2012, all spectrum sharing agreements in border areas were facing the following challenges, a way of managing harmful interference and a way of creating an agreement with sufficient incentives to all interested parties [15]. In the following years, there has been some very effective solutions coming out including the Harmonized Calculation Method (HCM) used in Croatia and its neighboring countries and the Licensed Shared Access (LSA), a dynamic spectrum sharing system widely used in Europe. The HCM consists of an agreement which defines general rules and coordination parameters such as coordination scope, coordination zone etc. and a mechanism which calculates the interference filed strength and makes coordination procedures accordingly [6]. The LSA on the other hand regulates the shared spectrum by assigning and reassigning spectrum to users on a per-need basis. It has a repository that can store each members' preferential frequency bands and the maximum accepted interference level and a controller that switching spectrum resources between users while compensating them with lower price or higher Quality of Services [5].

However, these solutions do not completely overcome the challenges stated in 2012. Some countries may not be incentive enough because having the agreement will not improve their payoff significantly [9]. For example, if one side of the border only covers a small area or has low population density, there is a small chance that this country will sacrifice part of their sovereign right of regulating its own spectrum resources to make an agreement with its neighbor [12]. In fact, as stated in [6], one of the greatest limitations of HCM is the fact that not all European countries are signatories, meaning that the agreement is not incentive enough. An agreement that is guaranteed incentive to any border area is still under investigation. Our goal in this paper is going to collect the ongoing researches and trying to graph a general picture of how a future solution would look like.

Talking about the incentive to do something is the same as determining whether it is worth to do so. Naturally, the Game Theory which checks and balances the payoff be tween decisions has become a new direction to approach the international spectrum sharing problem. If a system based on Game Theory can always ensure spectrum operators' payoff over time by compensating valuable things such as money or Quality of Service when their decisions lead to a lower payoff, then it is surely incentive to both sides of any border. Researches have been made trying to collaborate Game Theory with spectrum management since 2010. In 2010, mathematicians have listed several Game Theory models that would possibly be used in spectrum management applications in [4]. These models were evaluated by engineers and it was found that the non-cooperative Game is the closest model to describe an international spectrum sharing scenario where spectrum operators on each side of the border are selfish and non-cooperative [2]. Moreover, researchers have found that the non-cooperative Game model is guaranteed to converge to a Nash Equilibrium where all players' payoff is maximized through their own and each other's decisions [10]. With the positive results from these current researches, we think of an agreement that is similar to IICM with a controlling and information exchanging system equipped with non-cooperative Game Theory would be a possible future solution.

The remaining chapters of this paper is as follow: Sect. 2, details of existing solutions; Section 3, strengths and limitations of existing solutions; Section 4, current research directions; and Sect. 5, conclusion of this paper.

2   Existing Solutions

In this chapter, we give a basic tutorial on HCM and LSA/CBLSA we mentioned in Sect. 1.

Before going straight into the solutions, we studied a little bit more on the history of international spectrum management. Back in 2005, researchers had studied an auto mated interference analysis system trying to calculate the interference power limit at border areas [10]. They approached the issue with the following steps: establishing the interference scenario; establishing the sharing objectives and sharing criteria; selecting an adequate interference analysis algorithm; selecting an adequate propagation model and finally executing the interference analysis and determining the sharing possibility [10]. Note that the researchers are strictly following an ITU-R's recommendation on bilateral or multilateral agreements used in international spectrum management and the first four steps are essentially confirming the coordination parameters of such an agreement. In 1995 ITU-R released a recommendation containing the methods of mutual frequency coordination between neighboring countries in border areas [13]. The recommendation recommends that neighboring administrations should establish coordination agreements which should include the following: the exchange of appropriate spectrum management data from a national database; a means of resolving instances of unexpected harmful interference; procedural mechanisms such as the establishment of a Coordination zone where the coordination agreement applies and a Coordination perimeter which is a line establishing the agreed limit of the Coordination zone [13]. In determining Coordination zone, the agreement may include components such as: frequency range to be covered in the agreement; authorized bandwidth of service; modulation system; effective antenna height; limiting the service area of transmitters to the area required to be covered; the pertinent information to be exchanged; a method for collating, standardizing and exchanging information; a method for identifying stations requiring coordination; and the point in the process at which coordination is affected [13]. Within the Coordination zone administrations should consider some frequency sharing options including allotted frequencies which are designated to an individual administration on an exclusive or preferential basis (preferential frequencies); shared frequencies which are shared by administrations; and Coordinated frequencies which can be assigned only after successful coordination [13]. And finally, to determine the Coordination perimeter, mutual agreement on a number of factors is required: the maximum permitted interference filed strength for each service/frequency band; the maximum values of transmitter power, effective antenna height and gain allowed or a method of including these in the calculations; an agreed method of prediction calculation; and methods for allowing each administration to verify the correct or accepted use of the model on a case-by-case basis [13].

Not surprisingly, about 10 years later, HCM used a similar approach as the researchers did in 2005. HCM also followed the ITU-R's recommendation strictly in the main body of its multilateral agreement. For example, the main body states the frequency classification corresponding to the spectrum sharing options stated in the recommendation. The classification includes frequencies requiring coordination, preferential frequencies, frequencies for planned radio networks and frequencies used on the basis of geographical network plans [6]. The last two types of frequencies are listed in article 1.3.4 and 1.3.5 of the HCM Agreement and they are not applied in most of the cases in fixed and mobile services. Therefore, we only focus on the first two types here. The frequencies requiring coordination contains all frequency bands that need extra coordination. The preferential frequencies, also stated in the recommendation from ITU-R as allotted frequencies, are commonly used as the essence of multilateral agreements. It enables the exclusive usage of pre-defined channels which minimizes the management cost and maximizes the flexibility in network planning. Other than the definition of frequency categories, the main body contains other definitions like the frequency ranges for fixed and mobile service. It also contains other parts except for definitions such as the general coordination procedure of every frequency categories mentioned above and the technical provisions which should be followed when a request for coordination of a station or the evaluation of this request is needed.

After the main body, there are two major annexes, annex 1 related to Mobile Service and annex 9 related to Fixed Service. The two annexes corresponding to the means of calculating and resolving harmful interference in the recommendation, explain different calculation methods for interfering filed strength of fixed services and mobile services. Annex 1 for mobile services states that the basic criteria for decision if some station can be put into operation are maximum permissible interference field strength and maximum cross-border range of harmful interference. More specifically, the transmitters of certain frequency range cannot exceed permissible interference filed strength at the maximum cross-border range of harmful interference or coordination procedures will be triggered. Annex 9 for fixed services on the other hand, states that the criteria for fixed services is based on the Threshold Degradation because fixed radio links are used to transmit large set of data and the major problem is to preserve the same Bit Error Rate (BER) at the threshold level in presence of interfering signals. The term Threshold Degradation refers to the difference between the increased threshold level value due to interference, and the threshold value without interference. The coordination procedures will be triggered if for a given BER, the permissible Threshold Degradation exceeds 1 dB at the coordination distance for each frequency range. By establishing and calculating these basic criteria such as maximum permissible interference field strength and threshold degradation, HCM is able to quickly identify potential interfering transmitters and make coordination accordingly. There are other annexes in HCM defining and describing more information about the coordination. Annex 2A and 2B states the data exchange in the land mobile and fixed services respectively. Annex 3A states the determination of the correction factor for the permissible interference filed strength at different frequency bands in land mobile services. Annex 3B states the determination of the masks discrimination and the net filter discrimination in fixed services. Annex 4, 5, 6 state the propagation curves, the determination of the interference field strength, and the coding instructions for antenna diagrams in land mobile services respectively. Annex 7 states the provisions on measurement procedures in both fixed services and land mobile services. Annex 8A and 8B state the method for combining the horizontal and vertical antenna patterns in land mobile and fixed services respectively. Annex 10 states the determination of the basic transmission loss in fixed services. And finally, annex 11 states the trigger for coordination in fixed services.

Again, as stated by European Commission back in 2012, in order to re-use the spectrum resources more efficiently, more advanced technology is needed. An appropriate regulatory mechanism which authorizes shared spectrum access to a frequency band seemed to be another way out in the international spectrum sharing issue [15].

As mentioned in the previous chapter, the main purpose of LSA is to provide additional spectrum resources by establishing a sharing platform between native spectrum operators. A main system architecture is shown in Fig. 1 below.

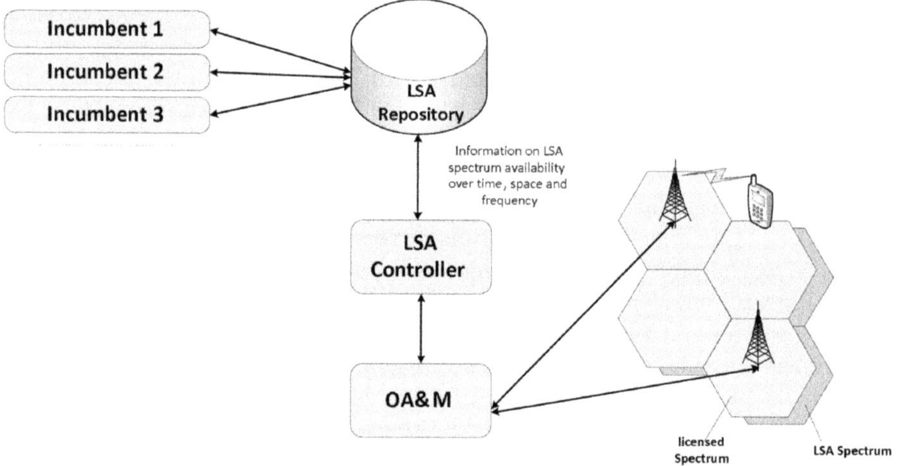

Fig. 1. Licensed Shared Access System Architecture. (from [5], p2).

To briefly discuss the structure, the incumbents are usually spectrum owners who have achieved sharing agreement with cellular operators. Incumbents are able to access the LSA spectrum which will not be used by other stakeholders without prior notification or negotiation through the LSA repository [5]. Incumbents are also able to request exclusion zones where the cellular operators have no access to any LSA spectrum re sources, and protection zones where a maximum interference level is guaranteed to incumbents. The LSA repository is a large database that stores the schedule of the distribution of LSA spectrum in near future. It stores the future intended requests for vacating LSA bands which can be triggered by incumbents. It also stores the information related to exclusion zones and protection zones defined by incumbents. The LSA controller can access the data in the repository and allocate free spectrum to cellular operators in a specific area for a specific period of time. It exploits all available information and identifies the best available spectrum for concerned cellular operator, taking the information provided by the incumbents to the repository as well. The operation, ad ministration, and management (OA&M) unit is the interface of LSA controller for cellular operators to interact with the controller to get access to specific LSA bands over a specific area in a specific period of time.

However, LSA is not enough to coordinate the spectrum conflict in border areas where incumbents from different countries may have different policies. Because there might be conflicting data or requirement from incumbents stored in the repository and thus the whole coordination system would fail. In order to accommodate the special case in border areas, researchers have proposed an advanced evolution of LSA called Cross-Border LSA or CBLSA. A general system architecture is shown in Fig. 2 below.

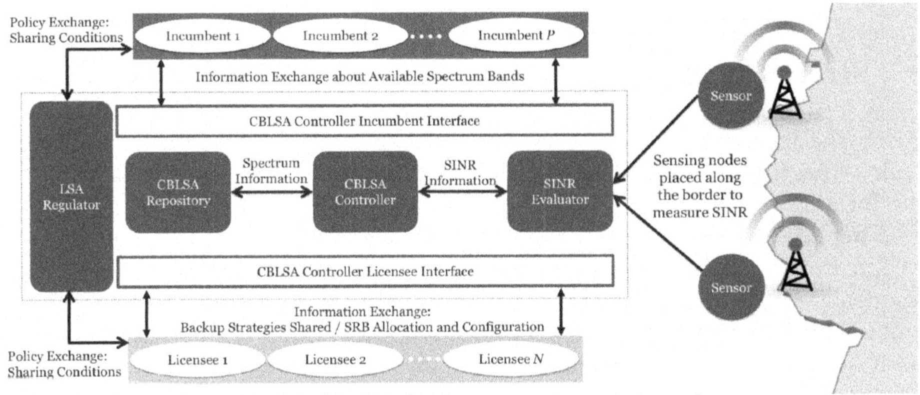

Fig. 2. CBLSA System Architecture. (from [2], p2)

As can be seen that the main upgrade from the previous architecture is the sensors placed along the border which measure signal to interference plus noise ratio (SINR) and feed it back to SINR evaluator in the system. The evaluator then evaluates the SINR along with its geographic information, the interference level, and the corresponding affected Spectrum Resource Blocks (SRBs) and sending these data back to the controller. Therefore, with the update, the CBLSA system can now reallocate the LSA bands to the licensees who have their SRBs affected by the interference caused by foreign incumbents from the neighboring country. Moreover, licensees can choose if they need a reallocation of SRBs for a higher price or still use the affected SRBs but with a lower price depending on different amount of SINR before they signed the LSA sharing agreement with the domestic incumbents [2]. The spectrum reallocation will be repeated to find the best fit SRB for a specific licensee according to their strategies negotiated in the sharing agreement.

The above two existing solutions are based on the possibility of making an agreement to share the spectrum or to coordinate the use of spectrum in border areas. How ever, in some cases, making an agreement is impossible or extremely hard because of different international standing or diplomatic issues. Researchers have also looked into some effective techniques to minimize the CBI without any coordination such as man aging transmitted power (Power Control), adjusting antenna height and tilt, and placing appropriate type of antenna in an appropriate manner. However, results from [3] shows that the most effective way of reducing CBI remains to be the coordination methods. An example is found in the border between Pakistan and India. The source of interference, two CDMA operators in India has severely degraded the QoS of a GSM operator in Pakistan whereas the cross-technology interference impacts GSM only (Pakistan side). Therefore, India has no incentive at all to coordinate with Pakistan to resolve the CBI [8]. Pakistan operators have used the techniques mentioned above trying to reduce the CBI and the results indicated a significantly improved network performance for the GSM system in Pakistan.

3   Strengths and Limitations

Given the basic tutorial on the existing solutions, we will discuss more about their strengths and limitations in this chapter to see what can be improved in the future.

First, the HCM has a total of 17 member administrations (Signatories) all within Europe. It allows the co-existence of different technologies in the same frequency bands and uninterrupted operation of networks in cross-border areas among the Signatories. The application of HCM has led to reproducible results on both sides of each border among the Signatories. Very low interference cases have been found in recent years and investigation showed that most cases were caused by deviating data between coordination database and real transmit parameters [14]. Moreover, the HCM is a living document which means all signatories can contribute to the further development of it. This makes the HCM an evolving agreement which may suit better among the Signatories and have the potential to attract more members.

However, the HCM also has limitations such as not all European countries are signatories, which means that not all countries have their policies in compliance with the provisions of HCM and they do not have enough incentive in signing the agreement [5]. This is true because international spectrum sharing issues are highly depending on geographic situations. In the previous chapter we mentioned the case between India and Pakistan where there is no room for any agreement. It can be the same in some of the European countries where signing the agreement only brings more restrictions but less interest. Furthermore, the emerging technologies such as preferential channels which is one of the advantages of LSA seems to be a more appropriate option compared to generic agreements like HCM in dynamic spectrum sharing [5].

Moving on to the LSA system, it provides more spectrum resources by assigning and reassigning frequency bands to spectrum operators according to their preferential frequencies [5]. LSA enables primary license holders to grant the spectrum resources to limited number of secondary users to ensure a predictable QoS to all spectrum users. Unlike many other dynamic spectrum access systems, where secondary users try to find vacant frequency channels themselves to avoid interfering with primary users, LSA provide a tight control of spectrum allocation by automatically assigning vacant frequency bands to secondary users with the consideration of their preferential frequencies. In a coordinated manner using centralized control, spectrum sharing between multiple operators is most likely to be implemented [11].

However, it also has several challenges such as determining the interference level at protection zones where incumbents have guaranteed spectrum quality, and the performance degradation in spectrum entering and vacating where the spectrum resource is transferring from one licensee to another [5]. The most important one is the management of cross-border issues. In order to let the LSA function, either a separate LSA repository and related management entities are established on each side of the border or a common LSA repository is needed containing spectrum usage information for stakeholders on both sides of the border [5]. In general, spectrum usage information can be too sensitive to share with another country especially with military incumbents. Therefore, the latter solution is generally impossible, and the former solution may re quire more manual coordination between two countries in order to exchange spectrum usage information. Indeed, in order to overcome the disadvantage of LSA in border areas, researchers have proposed CBLSA system which is equipped with sensors and a SINR evaluator to determine the interference level and evaluate SINR at border areas, so that less information exchange is required when repositories are separated.

For both existing solutions, the common major problem is that they cannot provide enough incentive for all countries in the world because of geographic situations, inter national relationships, and privacy. There is no compensation method for those countries who do not benefit from the agreement too much. The compensation can be either lower cost of spectrum resources or higher Quality of Service. With the compensation, not only the existing members can find more interest in sharing the spectrum but also can attract more countries to join the agreement because the loss by signing the agreement can be compensated somehow now. However, when there is a compensation, there will be some countries loss more because the whole spectrum resource is limited. Therefore, a dynamic equilibrium is needed in order to be fair to every member. The dynamic equilibrium should at least maintain all the members' interest and at least have one member's interest increased, which is also known at Pareto Optimality in Game Theory.

Another common problem can be the difficulty in information exchange either be cause of too complicated coordination process or sensitive spectrum information (privacy). The members want to keep those sensitive data as much as possible but at the same time they want to coordinate and share the spectrum as much as possible in order to use the spectrum more efficiently. It seems contradictory at the first glance but again Game Theory has a branch which studies exactly where players are non-cooperated and selfish meaning that each player does not have the information about other players' strategy, called non-cooperative Game Theory.

With the above discussion, Game Theory seems to be a possible future research direction for the international spectrum management issue.

4   Current Research Topics

4.1   Why Game Theory and Its Basics

In order to overcome the limitations of existing solutions mentioned in the previous chapter, researchers have investigated in various new technologies and ideas. Among them, Game Theory has become one of the most promising future directions to approach the problem.

Game theory is a mathematical tool which analyzes strategic interactions among multiple decision makers also known as players. In the context of spectrum sharing, spectrum operators make intelligent decisions on their spectrum usage and operating parameters based on spectrum dynamics and other operators' actions. Moreover, operators from different country who are competing spectrum resources may have no incentive to cooperate with each other and instead behave selfishly. Therefore, Game Theory has naturally become a new perspective to study the intelligent behaviors and interactions made by selfish spectrum operators. To describe a general Game model, Game Theory has three major components, a finite set of players, a set of actions for each player, and the outcome for each player according to their own and others' actions (payoff) [4]. To be more focused, researchers have studied the non-cooperative Game Theory where players in the game are selfish and will not cooperate with each other when making decisions, enabling dynamic spectrum sharing in border areas with only local information. The non-cooperative game theory approach is even more desirable when centralized control is not possible or self-organization is necessary [4].

Talking about non-cooperative game theory, the Nash Equilibrium (NE) can be a key concept to understand it better. The NE is generally an outcome of such a game where every player's payoff is maximized according to their best strategy when taking others' decisions into account as well [4]. It is called an equilibrium because players will not deviate their decisions in order to maintain the maximum payoff. However, NE itself only tells us what the final outcome of the game will be, it does not tell us how we are going to get there. The latter problem is much more concerned in the context of spectrum sharing than the former one. Spectrum operators as players have no global information to directly get to the equilibrium state but instead, they need to start from arbitrary strategies and update their strategies according to the consequence or payoff of that decision and finally converge to an NE [4]. Therefore, we will get to the NE of the game eventually if such an equilibrium exists for the game. 'Will the desired Nash Equilibrium always exist?' could be the next problem that needs to be addressed. Fortunately, mathematicians have already proved that for a well-defined strategic game, there is always a mixed strategy NE where players in the game adopt mixed strategies rather than deterministic ones [4]. The mixed strategy can be interpreted as a probability distribution among the set of action for each player. If an action/decision can provide more gain, then it has a higher probability to be chosen compared to the others. In fact, this is exactly how the spectrum operators behave. The decision which leads to a better outcome, either lower price or higher Quality of Services will have higher possibility to be chosen by operators. Therefore, the existence of NE for the game in the context of spectrum sharing will not be a problem at all.

Besides the existence, the uniqueness of an equilibrium is another desirable property when we are managing spectrum resources. Because we may predict the equilibrium strategy of all players and the resulting performance of the whole sharing system if we know the unique NE [4]. In this way, governments can manipulate the behavior of spectrum operators towards efficient spectrum sharing at the equilibrium. However, the uniqueness of NE only holds for several special cases and it can be tricky. For example, if the payoff function of every player is strictly convex, there exists a unique equilibrium of the game. Researchers have put effort in finding ways to ensure the uniqueness of NE in recent years and some of them did success, but their solutions are only valid in their specific cases, no general method has been found.

If the uniqueness of NE cannot be guaranteed, what happens when we have multiple NE for the game? In this case, players will have to manually select those NEs that are superior to others according to some equilibrium selection criteria. In [4], authors have introduced Pareto optimality, or Pareto efficiency to find the optimal solutions so that at least one player's payoff is improved while maintaining the others'.

4.2   Researches on Non-cooperative Game Theory in Spectrum Management

Non-cooperative Game Theory in Power Control Analysis
In fact, researchers tried to use non-cooperative Game Theory in spectrum management and CBI coordination long ago. Back in 2007, researchers have used non-cooperative Game Theory to model a two-player competitive power control game [7]. They set up the power control game and have its set of players and set of actions well defined. The purpose of the research is to analyze the outcome of the game when single player is strategic meaning that only one player takes intelligent actions and when both players are strategic to see if players have the incentive to be strategic or more specifically, to coordinate their pilot power of their base stations. The research shows that when only one player is strategic, that player's payoff can easily reach a unique maximum point by adjust his pilot signal power. When both players are strategic, both player's payoff can reach to a slightly lower maximum point compared to the previous case but there is surely an NE where there is no motivation for players to keep increasing their pilot power so that their relative maximum payoff can be maintained [7]. The

research also shows that for a high user density, the NE achieved in the latter case would be more efficient than using the standard pilot powers (around 2W), which again suggests that the operators do have an incentive to be strategic in the game. The NE pilot power for different user densities is shown in Fig. 3 below.

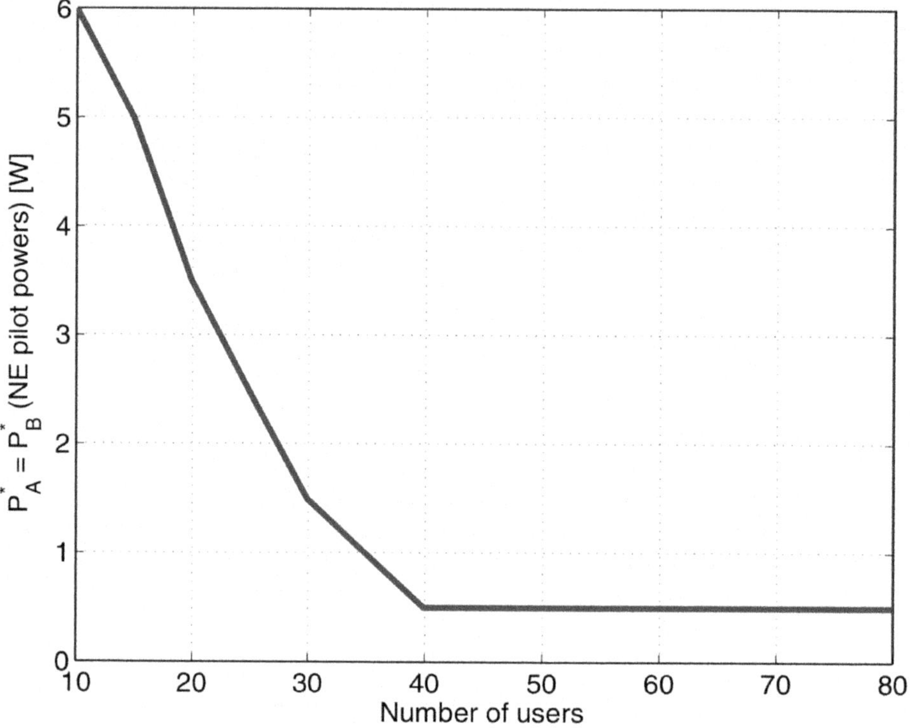

Fig. 3. Nash equilibrium pilot power values as a function of the user density. (from [7], p6)

Non-cooperative Game Theory with CBLSA

A recent research on the CBLSA also reflects the unique position of Game Theory in international spectrum management [2]. Researchers equipped their CBLSA system mentioned in Sect. 2 with a non-cooperative game model. The game is a multiplayer, tri-strategy spectrum sharing game. Each players' payoff depends on their SINR category along with the offered price and bandwidth, meaning that the more high-quality (lower SINR) SRBs a player get, the higher its payoff will be [2]. After the game starts, the CBLSA controller keeps updating the SINR information for each SRB and categorizes them into high to low quality categories accordingly. When there exist conflicts in spectrum sharing, the controller provides three strategies for all players, Maintain, Reduce and Switch

[2]. 'Maintain' means that the player requests to retain the SRBs irrespective of price; 'Reduce' means that the player agrees to withdraw a fixed number of SRBs but expecting lower cost on the remaining ones. 'Switch' means that the player authorizes CBLSA controller to perform a re-allocation to maximize its payoff in given SRBs by adjusting price, bandwidth and SINR category [2]. Researchers have provided a two-player example, explaining what will happen in every combination of their decisions. If one player chooses to Maintain and the other one chooses to Reduce, the former player maintains its SRBs because CBLSA has enough high quality SRB availability whereas the latter player suffers a degraded outcome due to SRB reduction. If one player chooses to Maintain and the other one chooses to Switch, the former player again maintains its SRBs because of the enough availability and the latter player authorizes the CBLSA controller to maximize its payoff by balancing between price and QoS. If one player chooses to Reduce and the other one chooses to Switch, the former player suffers a degraded outcome and the latter one asks the controller to maximize its payoff. If both players choose to Maintain, then there is a deadlock because CBLSA controller does not have enough SRBs availability for both players. Instead, the controller will reduce the SRBs allocated to both players according to previous sharing ratio and in creases spectrum cost to discourage this situation. If both players choose to Reduce meaning that both agree to reduce their SRB request, the outcome of both players will be degraded but the cost will be reduced to compensate the loss of QoS. Finally, if both players choose to Switch, the controller reallocates the SRBs for both players based on SINR information to maximize their payoff again by balancing price and QoS. A table from [2] shows the above combinations in a more intuitive way in Fig. 4.

Player 2 / Player 1	Maintain (M) *Licensee requests to retain the SRBs irrespective of price*	Reduce (R) *Licensee agrees to withdraw a fixed number of SRBs, expecting lower cost*	Switch (S) *Licensee authorizes CBLSA controller to take an allocation decision to maximize its payoff in given situation by adjusting price, bandwidth and SINR category*
Maintain (M)	Neither player compromises and reduces SRB request - deadlock. CBLSA reduces SRBs allocated to both players according to previous sharing ratio, and increases spectrum cost to discourage this choice.	P1 maintains its SRBs provided CBLSA has enough SRB availability. P2 agrees to reduce, and suffers a degraded outcome as its payoff is reduced due to SRB reduction.	P1 maintains its SRBs provided CBLSA has enough SRB availability. P2 authorizes CBLSA to maximize its payoff as fairly possible by adjusting price/QoS.
Reduce (R)	P2 maintains its SRBs provided CBLSA has enough SRB availability. P1 agrees to reduce, and suffers a degraded outcome as its payoff is reduced due to SRB reduction.	Both players agree to reduce their SRB request. This combination results in a degraded outcome for both players, as their payoff is reduced due to SRB reduction.	P1 agrees to reduce SRBs request, and suffers a degraded outcome as its payoff is reduced due to SRB reduction. P2 authorizes CBLSA to maximize its payoff as fairly possible by adjusting price/QoS.
Switch (S)	P2 maintains its SRBs provided CBLSA has enough SRB availability. P1 authorizes CBLSA to maximize its payoff as fairly possible by adjusting price/QoS.	P2 agrees to reduce SRBs request, and suffers a degraded outcome as its payoff is reduced due to SRB reduction. P1 authorizes CBLSA to maximize its payoff as fairly possible by adjusting price/QoS.	P1 and P2 authorize CBLSA to reallocate the SRBs based on updated SINR information and maximize their payoff by adjusting price/QoS.

Fig. 4. Non-Cooperative Strategy selection combinations (from [2], p3).

The proposed game converges to an NE when no player would deviate from the current strategy given other players have adopted an NE strategy already [2]. To be more general, changing strategy for an individual player does not improve its payoff any further. Just like we stated earlier in this chapter, the players do not have a global vision on others' strategy of making decisions. Therefore, the players can only choose arbitrary strategies initially and constantly evolving their strategies by evaluating their payoff and eventually learn their best responses and converge to the NE as the game progresses. The study also shows that by optimizing the game parameters, the game will converge to a particular equilibrium. For example, by appropriate designing the payoff functions for the players, a rational strategic plan can lead to a more efficient spectrum sharing as the game evolves towards the proposed equilibrium. Again, just like we stated earlier in this chapter, the payoff function can be optimized manually to make the game converge to a unique NE. The result of their research shows that the best strategy for the two-player game model proposed is when both players choose to Switch. In this case, the controller can maintain the payoff for each player and improve it for some players to compensate their possible degraded outcome brought by their previous bad strategies. Moreover, the averaged normalized payoff for each player at the equilibrium is increasing with the total number of players increased. This is similar to the result of the previous research mentioned above where in both cases, the NE is even more efficient when the total number of users is large. The Fig. 5 below shows this in a more intuitive way.

Non-cooperative Theory in Power Management Between Primary and Secondary Users

Another recent research on using non-cooperative Game Theory is for collaborative spectrum sharing between primary and secondary network users. Sharing the limited spectrum resources between the primary network users (PUs) and secondary network users (SUs) poses similar challenges just like in border areas. The two main challenges are the harmful interference to the primary network operation caused by SUs and the real-time delays caused by excessive signaling overhead for information exchange be tween systems [10]. To address these challenges, researchers have designed a non-co operative game where network nodes act as players rather than spectrum operators, and each node adjusts its transmit power automatically adapting to the interference measurement provided [10]. They have designed a game parameter, dynamic price coefficient as the weight of the price of the transmit power, which can be modified by primary network nodes dynamically to make sure the interference level under a predefined threshold. To be more specific, the dynamic price coefficient can be regarded as the penalty to an individual Base Station that has excessively high transmit power. Unlike researches before them, which used a static price coefficient to adjust the weight of the price of the transmit power, they used the dynamic price coefficient to ensure that the interference power constraint is always met as the received interference at PUs' Base Station will be minimized adaptively. After fine-tune the dynamic price coefficient, their simulation results showed that by adjusting the dynamic price coefficient, the PUs are able to achieve their target throughput at minimum level and maintain their QoS. They have also proposed a dual-mode solution which ensures that the game converges to a unique NE without further coordination and also reduces the real-time signaling overhead.

They implemented the non-cooperative game with two modes: the initialization-mode where the Base Stations exchange parameter information and the iteration mode where the Base Stations iteratively change their transmit powers until an equilibrium is reached. To be more specific, during the initialization-mode, the game controller collects interference information from all Base Stations and compute necessary parameter values such as initial transmit power, minimum target SIR etc. During the iteration-mode, each Base Station will get a unique dynamic price coefficient based on the parameters calculated in initialization-mode and it will be updated in every iteration. By using these values in the iteration-mode, all Base Stations can choose their optimal powers iteratively to suit the traffic conditions until the transmit powers of all Base Stations are stabilized and converged to the unique NE. A more detailed execution process is illustrated in Fig. 5 below. Notice the equations and symbols are not included here so please refer to [10].

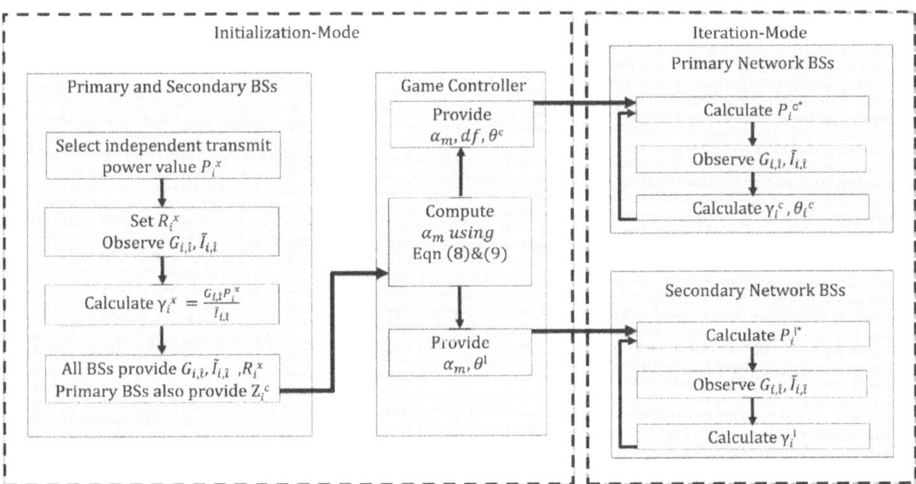

Fig. 5. Sequence of tasks executed in the initialization and iteration modes of the game. (from [10], p7)

4.3   Conclusion on the Game Theory Approach

As can be seen in the above researches, Game Theory has proved its unique position in spectrum management. It has been used for transmitting power control to ensure the interference level below certain threshold and it has been equipped to CBLSA spectrum sharing system to coordinate international spectrum sharing issues. Moreover, the performance of the non-cooperative Game Theory model is getting better when the number of players increases. This gives extra incentive to new players to join the sharing system. However, it is still far from the ultimate solution that can solve all international spectrum sharing problems because these problems are highly dependent on geographic situations and international situations. For instance, in all of the above cases, the players are the same type of agents from different organization or countries. However, as mentioned in Sect. 1, in the border between US and Canada, the USA deployed CBRS for 3500 MHz whereas Canada has decided to release this band for exclusive mobile use in the near future. Not only there are only two players in this case, which limits the performance of the Game Theory model, but different type of agents and licensing is also making the international spectrum management even trickier since the information exchange between them is extremely time-consuming and we will have an asymmetric game which is not covered in any of the above researches. Therefore, to conclude the recent researches on Game Theory in spectrum management, it is still not sufficient to solve all international spectrum sharing issues such as the places where you have different type of agents or polices across the border. Additional work needs to be done to address this type of issues.

5   Conclusion

To conclude this paper, we investigated the spectrum management problem in border areas. We collected existing solutions including bilateral or multilateral agreements like HCM and dynamic spectrum sharing systems like LSA/CBLSA. We made critical re view on the existing solutions and reveal the challenges they are facing. We explored a current research direction which equips non-cooperative Game Theory to automated spectrum sharing systems along with its simulation results.

We realized that international spectrum management is an important topic for future radiocommunication filed especially for 5G deployments however, it has been excessively underestimated by most of the large countries in the world. Large countries often have a small portion of its territory and low population density along the border, which makes them concern more about spectrum management inside the border but less about the international management. Moreover, they do not have enough incentive to share the spectrum in border areas. Instead of sharing the spectrum, dividing the spectrum into pieces for exclusive use is much more likely because large countries usually have dominating position while managing the spectrum with their neighbors. A perfect sup port is that most of the international spectrum management researches are conducted in Europe where countries are small and close enough to each other so that the problem is inevitable and serious enough to get governments' attention. However, unlike other large countries, Canada has a large population density along the border and is suffering a lot from the cross-border interference. Canada as a leading and large country can initiate the act of resolving international spectrum management among other large countries so that more countries can participate in resolving the problem but not just the countries suffered from it.

We also found that the existing solution like HCM and LSA/CBLSA are not enough to deal with the problem outside Europe because they depend too much on geographic situations. Large neighboring countries cannot benefit too much from them and the agreements associated with them are not appealing enough. Once again, as a large country that suffers from CBI, Canada should raise the awareness of the importance of international spectrum sharing among other large countries, not only for themselves but also for a worldwide spectrum harmonization.

Lastly, we evaluated the Game Theory approach with the simulation results from recent researches. We rated this new direction with the Technology Readiness Level (TRL) as TRL4 which stands for the highest level in 'Research to prove Feasibility' block. Because the simulation results demonstrated a very promising system, but it is still in research phase and far from the real technology.

References

1. Spectrum Outlook - 2018–2022. ISED, Ottawa, 43 p. (2018)
2. Saadat, A., Fang, G., Dutkiewicz, E., Mueck, M., Srikanteswara, S.: Enhanced QoS for domestic licensees in border areas through game theory based licensed shared access. In: 2016 16th International Symposium on Communications and Information Technologies (ISCIT) (2016)
3. Haq, T.U., Iqbal, A., Mahmood, H., Farooq, U., Asad, M.U.: Effective techniques to reduce cross border interference in cellular networks. In: 2010 Second International Conference on Computer Engineering and Applications (2010)
4. Wang, B., Wu, Y., Liu, K.R.: Game theory for cognitive radio networks: an overview. Comput. Netw. **54**(14), 2537–2561 (2010)
5. Mueck, M.D., Frascolla, V., Badic, B.: Licensed shared access—State-of-the-art and current challenges. In: 2014 1st International Workshop on Cognitive Cellular Systems (CCS) (2014)
6. Duković, V., Mucalo, A.K.: Principles and prospects of cross-border coordination for fixed and mobile services. In: Proceedings ELMAR-2013, Zadar, pp. 311–314 (2013)
7. Felegyhazi, M., Cagalj, M., Dufour, D., Hubaux, J.: Border games in cellular networks. In: IEEE INFOCOM 2007 - 26th IEEE International Conference on Computer Communications, Barcelona, pp. 812–820 (2007). https://doi.org/10.1109/INFCOM.2007.100
8. ul Haq, T., Iqbal, A.: Mitigation of external interference on an EGSM network. In: XXXth URSI General Assembly and Scientific Symposium, Istanbul, pp. 1–4 (2011). https://doi.org/10.1109/URSIGASS.2011.6050725
9. Louis, J.: International radio spectrum management beyond service harmonisation. In: 2011 Fourth International Conference on Emerging Trends in Engineering and Technology, Port Louis, pp. 116–120 (2011). https://doi.org/10.1109/ICETET.2011.14.
10. Saadat, A., Ni, W., Vesilo, R.: Collaborative spectrum sharing through non-collaborative gaming for next-generation small cells. IEEE Access **5**, 10182–10192 (2017). https://doi.org/10.1109/ACCESS.2017.2712129
11. Umar, R., Sheikh, A.U.H., Deriche, M., Shoaib, M., Hadi, M.: Multi-operator spectrum sharing in next generation wireless communications networks: a short review and roadmap to future. In: International Symposium on Wireless Systems and Networks (ISWSN), Lahore, pp. 1–5 (2017). https://doi.org/10.1109/ISWSN.2017.8250015

12. Cross-border coordination issues for fixed and mobile services, WORKSHOP from ITU-R
13. A method of spectrum management to be used for aiding frequency assignment for terrestrial services in border areas. https://www.itu.int/dms_pubrec/itu-r/rec/sm/R-REC-SM.1049-1-199510-I!!PDF-E.pdf. Accessed 4 Aug 2024
14. ITU Workshop. Cross-border Frequency Coordination, Bangkok (2017)
15. European Commission: Promoting the shared use of radio spectrum resources in the internal market (2012). https://ec.europa.eu/digital-single-market/sites/digital-agenda/files/com-ssa.pdf. Accessed 4 Aug 2024

Resolving Catastrophic Forgetting
in Continual Semantic Segmentation
with Dual Distillation

Yuan Luo, Jun Liu[✉], and Shuqi Zeng

School of Computer Science and Engineering, Wuhan Institute of Technology, Wuhan
430205, China
`liujun@wit.edu.cn`

Abstract. While deep neural networks are widely used across various
domains, particularly in the field of image processing, and have demonstrated impressive performance, they still encounter crucial and unresolved challenges. The problem of catastrophic forgetting is a typical
issue faced by most deep learning models at present. This implies that
when a model needs to be updated due to changes in its task or to
adapt to external conditions by acquiring new training data for new categories, it necessitates retraining for the new phase. However, the old
training data is no longer accessible. In recent years, a series of solutions and incremental learning frameworks have been proposed in the
academic field to address the issue of catastrophic forgetting caused by
the need for continuous updates to current models. However, these solutions largely focus on classification and detection tasks and have shown
some effectiveness. In this paper, we aim to tackle this issue within the
context of semantic segmentation, which involves addressing pixel-level
classification problems. We concern the issue of background shift caused
by the unavailability of labels for old classes in the new training phase,
and have utilized a modified cross-entropy loss function. Simultaneously,
we employ dual distillation on intermediate features and outputs to capture the knowledge learned by the old model, thereby constraining the
training process of the new model.

Keywords: Semantic Segmentation · Continual Learning ·
Catastrophic Forgetting

1 Introduction

Semantic segmentation is a crucial challenge in computer vision with broad
applications. The extensive utilization of deep convolutional neural networks
in the field of image processing, along with the availability of large, manually
annotated datasets [12,35], has resulted in notable breakthroughs and advancements [6,18,19,32,33] in this domain. The current prevalent approach involves
employing static data-driven fully convolutional neural networks (FCNs) [19]

R. C. Qiu et al. (Eds.): IoTaaS 2024, LNICST 675, pp. 29–40, 2026.
https://doi.org/10.1007/978-3-032-14681-6_3

to extend the original image-level classification problem to a pixel-level classification problem. This is accomplished by assigning a unique category to each pixel in the image based on the output of the fully convolutional neural network, thereby obtaining segmentation masks for each category to segment the original image. However, most existing methods [7,10] are based on static datasets, implying that the model is initially designed to recognize only the categories predetermined by humans. When presented with new category training data, the model cannot adaptively update its internal classification model, thus imposing significant limitations on incremental learning. This significantly hampers the model's ability to swiftly adapt to continuously updating data and evolving environments in the real world. Using the general approach of forcefully training new category data on an old model typically leads to severe catastrophic forgetting [16] in the majority of cases. In the context of semantic segmentation, where extensive, dense pixel-level predictions are required, this exacerbates the model's tendency to forget previously learned knowledge. In recent years, many advanced incremental learning methods have achieved exciting achievements in the field of continual semantic segmentation: The ILT [22], for the first time, introduced incremental learning behavior in the context of semantic segmentation, and proposed a standard continual semantic segmentation model training framework, that is, freezing the model of the previous stage and extracting the learned knowledge from it, but they still use fully annotated datasets when training in the new stage, which is contrary to the definition of continual semantic segmentation; The MiB [3], for the first time, uses an incompletely annotated dataset that meets the definition of continuous semantic segmentation, and considers the background shift in the continual learning environment and models them to extract the knowledge by the old model to prevent catastrophic forgetting. This method has achieved a milestone performance breakthrough, but they Only focusing on the background shift at the final outputs, while ignoring the correlation between the new and old models at the intermediate feature dimension; PLOP [11], this method focuses on the distillation of intermediate features, proposes an effective distillation method for feature blocks, and takes into account the global and local dependencies, but they use the segmentation mask generated by the old model as a pseudo-label to supervise the training of the current model, which is undoubtedly irrational, because in multiple stages of iterative training, the output results of the old model will gradually distort; The RCIL, proposes to use parallel convolutions in the network, so that one of them contains the convolution parameters from the old model, and finally merges the parallel convolutions into one. Although this method has achieved certain results, it costs nearly twice the memory overhead, which is not worth it. We propose a method based on the dual distillation mechanism, which takes into account both intermediate features and final outputs, does not cause additional memory overhead, and achieves significantly higher performance than existing methods.

2   Relative Work

2.1   Semantic Segmentation

Semantic segmentation is a fundamental task in artificial intelligence for image processing. In recent years, a significant number of groundbreaking methods [6,18,19,32,33] have emerged, excelling at solving this problem. For instance, the emergence of fully convolutional neural networks (FCNs) [1,19] has been pivotal. These networks extract contextual semantic information using various strategies and make pixel-level predictions, such as employing multi-scale fusion strategies [4–6,18,32,33] and modeling spatial dependencies [5,13]. Subsequently, the encoder-decoder structure [6] emerged, reducing the coupling of various components in the model. Dilated convolutions [21] were introduced to obtain a larger range of global information, while attention mechanisms [27,30,31] established contextual relationships within images, both making outstanding contributions to this field. In the current year, Transformer architectures [29,34] have demonstrated excellent performance in the field of semantic segmentation. They emphasize both multi-scale feature fusion and the aggregation of contextual features.

2.2   Continual Learning

Continual learning primarily aims to empower models to distinguish newly added classes while mitigating substantial performance degradation caused by catastrophic forgetting [16]. This objective has been extensively researched in the context of image classification tasks [8]. So far, a substantial amount of work can be categorized into the following aspects: replay-based [15,24,28] regularization-based [9,17], and parameter isolation-based methods [20,25]. In replay-based methods [15,24,28], samples from previous classes are either stored or obtained through generative networks. These samples are then replayed when learning new classes, incurring additional overhead. In parameter isolation-based methods [20,25], a parameter subset is allocated for each class to prevent forgetting. Many methods explore the use of regularization to retain previous knowledge, including techniques such as knowledge distillation and adversarial training. Some approaches center on the neural network's structure, proposing to expand the network's architecture while learning new classes. Additionally, they suggest improving feature representations by combining self-supervised feature extractors.

2.3   Continual Semantic Segmentation

In response to the gradual inclusion of new classes in practical applications, scholars have introduced continual learning and applied it to semantic segmentation tasks. However, continuous semantic segmentation remains a highly challenging endeavor, primarily due to the unresolved issue of catastrophic forgetting. In this context, several pioneering works have made significant progress: research into replay-based methods for revisiting prior knowledge [36]; the MiB

[3], which addresses background shift during the training of new classes by studying the relationship between background and categories; the PLOP [11] method, which applies knowledge distillation strategies to the intermediate features of the model; SDR [23], which achieves potential spatial feature consistency constraints through prototype matching; and a focus on dynamic network expansion, decoupling feature learning for old and new classes.

3   Method

3.1   Preliminary

Before delving into the details of the continual semantic segmentation problem, we first review the work of semantic segmentation. We denote the entire input space as $\mathcal{X}$ (the image space). So, for any image x in the dataset, $x \in \mathcal{X}$. The set of pixels in x is denoted as $\mathcal{I}$, and the number of pixels in the set is represented as $|\mathcal{I}| = N$. Next, we denote the output space of the model as $\mathcal{Y}^N$, where $\mathcal{Y}^N$ represents the label set $\mathcal{Y}$ independently corresponding to the each pixels. For a given image x, the goal of semantic segmentation is to assign a label $y_i \in \mathcal{Y}$ to each pixel $x_i (i \in \mathcal{I})$ within the image x, where $y_i \in \mathcal{Y}$ represents the semantic information of the pixel. For pixels that do not belong to any specific class, we assign them to the background class $\mathcal{B}$, thus it follows that $mathcalB \in \mathcal{Y}$. We represent the training set as $\mathcal{T} \subset \mathcal{X} \times \mathcal{Y}^i$, and by training a network model f_θ, where θ represents the model's parameters, we map the input image x from the input space $\mathcal{X}$ to a pixel-wise probability vector space of classes $f_\theta : \mathcal{X} \rightarrow \mathbb{R}^{N \times |\mathcal{Y}|}$. Finally, we obtain the segmentation mask through the formula $y^* = \{\arg\max_{c \in \mathcal{Y}} f_\theta(x)[i, c]\}_{i=1}^N$, where $f_\theta(x)[i, c]$ represents the probability that pixel i belongs to class c.

Continual Semantic Segmentation (CSS) is training a semantic segmentation model continuously over T stages. At the current stage t, a training set $\mathcal{T}_t$ can be used, where only the currently trained class $\mathcal{C}_t$ is annotated, and the rest of the classes (including previously learned classes $\mathcal{C}_{1-(t-1)}$ and future classes to be learned $\mathcal{C}_{(t+1)-T}$) are annotated as background. The purpose of our work is making the model able to predict all classes $\mathcal{C}_{1-T}$ after all training stages T.

3.2   Continual Semantic Segmentation Frame

At learning step t, we directly train the predictor f_{t-1} on a new training set while reducing the learning rate to fine-tune the model, which is the simplest way to achieve continuous semantic segmentation. However, this approach leads to catastrophic forgetting. In fact, in the new learning step, the model can no longer sample from the old dataset. Due to this issue, the predictions of all networks will shift towards the new categories, gradually impairing the predictions for the old categories. Furthermore, as the old categories are no longer visible, the network cannot learn the differences between the new and old categories, ultimately resulting in the model forgetting the old categories and not effectively learning the new ones. Therefore, we need to extract knowledge from the old model f_{t-1} to assist the learning of the new model. Inspired by some method [3,11], we re-minimize a loss function:

$$\mathcal{L}\left(\theta^t\right) = \frac{1}{|\mathcal{T}^t|} \sum_{(x,y)\in\mathcal{T}^t} \left(\ell_{ce}^{\theta^t}\left(x,y\right) + \lambda\ell_{kd}^{\theta^t}\left(x\right) + \mu\ell_{pod}^{\theta^t}\left(x\right)\right) \ . \tag{1}$$

where $\ell_{ce}^{\theta^t}$ is the Cross-Entropy Loss, $\ell_{kd}^{\theta^t}$ the outputs distillation loss, and $\ell_{pod}^{\theta^t}$ the intermediate loss.

3.3   Modify Cross-Entropy Loss

In Eq. 1, ℓ_{ce} is the computed standard cross-entropy loss over all image pixels.

$$\ell_{ce}^{\theta^t}\left(x,y\right) = -\frac{1}{|\mathcal{I}|} \sum_{i\in\mathcal{I}} \log q_x^t\left(i,y_i\right), \tag{2}$$

where $q_x^t\left(i,y_i\right)$ represents the probability that, for a given input image x, the model outputs the corresponding true label.

However, the challenge with employing this formula is that the new training set solely encompasses information regarding the current class. The background class anticipated by the new model may have been previously identified as an old class in the former model. We contend that without adequate consideration of this matter, catastrophic forgetting in the new model will exacerbate. Hence, we task the old model with predicting the new training data and leverage the prediction results to fine-tune our cross-entropy loss function:

$$\ell_{ce}^{\theta^t}\left(x,y\right) = -\frac{1}{|\mathcal{I}|} \sum_{i\in\mathcal{I}} \log \tilde{q}_x^t\left(i,y_i\right), \tag{3}$$

where:

$$\tilde{q}_x^t\left(i,c\right) = \begin{cases} q_x^t\left(i,c\right) & \text{if } c \neq \mathcal{B} \\ \sum_{k\in\mathcal{Y}^{t-1}} q_x^t\left(i,k\right) & \text{if } c = \mathcal{B} \end{cases} \tag{4}$$

In this way, when the new model learns examples labeled as background class, it reduces the loss by adding the probabilities with the old class, preventing catastrophic forgetting.

3.4   Modify Distillation Loss

In the context of incremental learning, distillation is a common strategy to transfer knowledge from the old model $f_{\theta_{t-1}}$ to the new model to prevent catastrophic forgetting. The standard form of the distillation loss ℓ_{kd} is:

$$\ell_{kd}^{\theta^t}\left(x,y\right) = -\frac{1}{|\mathcal{I}|} \sum_{i\in\mathcal{I}} \sum_{c\in\mathcal{Y}^{t-1}} q_x^{t-1}\left(i,c\right) \log \tilde{q}_x^t\left(i,c\right), \tag{5}$$

The fundamental principle behind ℓ_{kd} is that f_{θ_t} should generate activations that closely resemble those produced by $f_{\theta_{t-1}}$. This regularization process anchors the parameters θ_t to solutions utilized for identifying pixels of the previous classes, i.e., θ_{t-1}. However, the traditional distillation strategy overlooks the fact that the background class predicted by the old model is highly likely to be the class we are currently learning. Therefore, we modify a portion of the formula as follows:

$$\tilde{q}_x^t\,(i,c) \begin{cases} q_x^t\,(i,c) & \text{if } c \neq \mathcal{B} \\ \Sigma_{k \in \mathcal{C}^t}\, q_x^t\,(i,k) & \text{if } c = \mathcal{B} \end{cases} \tag{6}$$

This modification is crucial. During distillation with the old model, the probabilities of all new classes in the new model are summed into the background class before computing the distillation loss with the old model, as the old model treats unseen classes as background.

3.5   Intermediate Feature Distillation

Drawing inspiration from [11] we can distill the intermediate features of the network model's output. We denote an intermediate tensor of size $H \times W \times C$ as $\mathbf{x}$. We can extract a POD embedding $\mathbf{x}$ from it with the following equation:

$$\Phi\,(\mathbf{x}) = \left[\frac{1}{W} \sum_{w=1}^{W} \mathbf{x}\,[:, w, :] \,\middle\|\, \frac{1}{H} \sum_{h=1}^{H} \mathbf{x}\,[h, :, :] \right] \in \mathbb{R}^{(H+W) \times C} \tag{7}$$

We obtain the POD loss by calculating the L2 distance of the intermediate features POD between the new and old models.

$$\ell_{\text{pod}}\,(\theta^t) \;=\; \frac{1}{L} \sum_{l}^{L} \left\| \Phi\,\left(f_l^t\,(x)\right) - \Phi\,\left(f_l^{t-1}\,(x)\right) \right\|^2, \tag{8}$$

where $f_l^t\,(x)$ is the tensor generated from the lth layer of f. Subsequently, we partition each tensor $\mathbf{x}$ into 4 local tensors of size $\frac{W}{2} \times \frac{H}{2} \times C$, and then calculate their POD loss. Due to its ability to constrain spatial statistics rather than raw pixel values, and establish both global and local dependencies of features between the new and old models, thus meeting the high spatial accuracy requirements for continuous semantic segmentation (Fig. 1).

4   Experiment

We compared our method with recent advanced methods for continuous semantic segmentation such as ILT, Mib, and PLOP. To ensure the objectivity and fairness of the comparison, the dataset, relevant settings, performance metrics, and reference standards all followed [3].

4.1   Pascal VOC2012

Pascal VOC2012 [12] is a widely utilized standard public dataset in the field of computer vision, encompassing 20 manually annotated foreground object

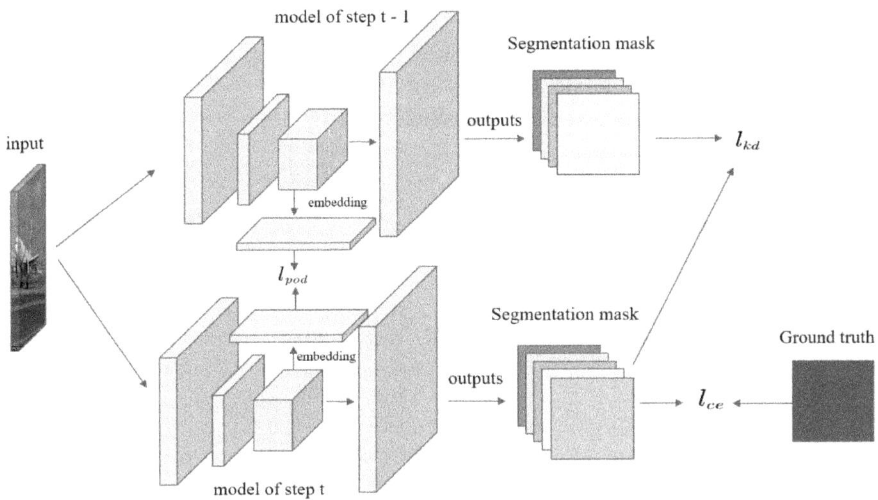

Fig. 1. overview of the dual distillation mechanism.

classes. Based on [22,26], we employed two distinct sampling configurations to build an augmented dataset. Based on [22], we established a disjoint incremental dataset, wherein each training set image in every experimental stage contains pixels belonging only to classes that are either current or have already been learned. However, unlike in [22], the classes that have already been learned will be labeled as background in the current learning stage. The other configuration is overlapped dataset following [26], where each training set image in every experimental stage contains at least one pixel of the current class and only the pixels of the current class are annotated. It's important to note that this incremental dataset configuration may exhibit intersections at each stage of the experiment, mirroring typical real-world scenarios, where some pixels in an image belong to classes that will be learned in the future but are currently labeled as background. Following the previous work in [3], we conducted three different experiments, namely: adding one class (19-1), adding five classes (15-5), and continuously adding five classes (15-1).

4.2 Implementation Details

For all methods in the experiment, we use Deeplab-v3 architecture [5] with a Resnet-101 [14] as the backbone and the stride of the output is 16. Since memory cost is an important problem in semantic segmentation, we use in-place activated batch normalization proposed in [2]. The backbone ResNet-101 we use is ImageNet pretrained model, which is from [2]. We train the network with SGD, using the same learning rate policy, momentum and weight decay as [5]. In the first stage we use the learning rate 10^{-2}, and in others we use 10^{-3}, as in [3] We train the model with a batch-size of 16 for 30 epoch in every experiment step.

We crop the images to a size of 512×512 during both training and testing, and perform the same data augmentation as in [2]. For setting the hyper-parameters of each method, we employed the incremental learning protocol defined in [8], using 20% of the training set as validation. The final test use the standard validation set of the datasets.

Table 1. Mean IoU on the Pascal-VOC 2012 dataset for different method.

Method	19-1						15-5						15-1					
	disjoint			overlapped			disjoint			overlapped			disjoint			overlapped		
	1–19	20	all	1–19	20	all	1–15	15–20	all	1–15	15–20	all	1–15	15–20	all	1–15	15–20	all
FT	4.8	10.4	8.2	4.4	8.3	7.6	0.8	32.1	11.8	0.6	33.8	12.0	0.3	2.0	4.0	0.1	1.8	3.8
PI	4.9	10.3	8.2	4.5	8.3	7.7	1.0	32.1	11.9	0.6	33.8	12.0	0	1.7	3.7	0	1.6	3.7
RW	4.9	10.3	8.2	4.5	8.3	7.7	0.9	32.0	11.8	0.6	33.8	12.0	0.2	5.2	4.7	0	4.2	4.2
EWC	4.8	10.4	8.2	4.5	8.3	7.7	0.8	32.1	11.8	0.6	33.8	12.0	0.1	4.5	4.5	0	3.2	4.0
LwF	52.8	7.1	52.3	49.3	6.6	49.0	58.5	36.7	54.8	57.2	35.3	53.5	1.1	4.6	5.8	0.3	4.0	5.0
LwF-MC	50.5	7.0	49.9	47.9	9.0	47.5	54.1	27.3	49.1	49.2	33.0	46.8	0.8	4.5	5.0	0.3	3.8	4.4
ILT	67.8	11.2	66.1	63.1	8.2	61.7	62.2	37.0	57.6	67.4	40.3	62.0	2.4	6.6	7.1	3.8	7.3	8.1
MIB	67.9	16.5	66.4	70.5	12.9	68.6	73.1	44.1	67.0	75.6	49.2	70.0	34.5	15.1	32.3	37.5	13.6	34.0
PLOP	74.1	23.4	72.5	75.7	23.6	73.7	66.3	39.1	61.0	74.5	48.7	69.1	50.4	11.8	42.6	65.6	15.6	54.5
RCIL	**75.1**	19.1	73.2	**76.5**	17.1	**74.3**	72.2	29.1	62.8	**78.1**	49.3	71.8	51.0	15.5	44.1	62.8	19.2	53.3
ours	74.8	**24.8**	**73.2**	75.7	**24.2**	74.0	**75.3**	**46.3**	**69.1**	77.0	**52.8**	**71.9**	**57.6**	**17.1**	**49.2**	**67.6**	**21.0**	**57.2**
Joint	77.7	77.0	78.4	77.7	77.0	78.4	78.8	74.2	78.4	78.8	74.2	78.4	78.8	74.2	78.4	78.8	74.2	78.4

4.3   Addition of One Class (19-1)

In this experiment, we have two learning steps. In the first step, our model learns the first 19 classes. And then in the second, it learns the 20th class(tv-monitor). Results are in Table 1. Clearly, incremental learning methods such as PI, RW, EWC, used in the classification domain, are not applicable to semantic segmentation tasks, all falling to the performance lower bound consistent with fine-tuning. However, LwF and LwF-MC significantly outperformed them. The ILT method and its subsequent approaches can achieve further performance improvements. Our method can also achieve results that are no less effective than theirs.

4.4   Single-Step Addition of Five Classes (15-5)

In this setting, similar to the 19-1, we observe the first 15 classes, then we add the remaining 5 classes: plant, sheep, sofa, train, tv-monitor. Results are in Table 1. The final experimental results exhibit a strong consistency with the previous '19-1' experiment: Incremental learning methods based on classification tasks perform poorly. Subsequent methods show significant performance improvements, and our method also achieves very good results.

4.5   Multi-step Addition of Five Classes (15-1)

This experimental setting differs from the 15-5 in that, after the initial learning step, the remaining five classes are continuously added in five subsequent steps, one by one. From Table 1, we can observe that performing multiple steps poses a challenge: old methods perform poorly in this setting, with mIoU on both old and new classes falling below 7%. Even under significant challenges, our method is capable of achieving a certain degree of resilience against catastrophic forgetting (Fig. 2).

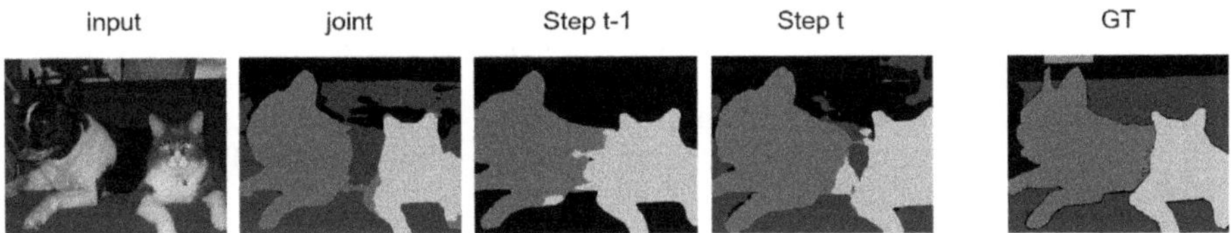

Fig. 2. Outputs of models at different stages of continual semantic segmentation. "joint" represents the output of the offline training model. The model at "step t - 1" can recognize cats and dogs. The "step t" model can learn new knowledge - sofa category.

5   Conclusion

This paper study the critical issue of catastrophic forgetting within the domain of semantic segmentation, which involves pixel-level classification challenges. To address this, we introduce a modified cross-entropy loss function to manage background shift resulting from the unavailability of labels for old classes in new training phases. Additionally, we employ dual distillation on intermediate features and outputs to capture knowledge from the old model, thereby constraining the training process of the new model. Our method demonstrates effectiveness in both typical and high-challenge scenarios. This approach provides an innovative solution for catastrophic forgetting in semantic segmentation, offering new insights for continual learning and model updates.

References

1. Badrinarayanan, V., Kendall, A., Cipolla, R.: Segnet: a deep convolutional encoder-decoder architecture for image segmentation. IEEE Trans. Pattern Anal. Mach. Intell. **39**(12), 2481–2495 (2017)
2. Bulo, S.R., Porzi, L., Kontschieder, P.: In-place activated batchnorm for memory-optimized training of DNNs. In: Proceedings of the IEEE Conference on Computer Vision and Pattern Recognition, pp. 5639–5647 (2018)

3. Cermelli, F., Mancini, M., Bulo, S.R., Ricci, E., Caputo, B.: Modeling the background for incremental learning in semantic segmentation. In: Proceedings of the IEEE/CVF Conference on Computer Vision and Pattern Recognition, pp. 9233–9242 (2020)
4. Chen, L.C., Papandreou, G., Kokkinos, I., Murphy, K., Yuille, A.L.: DeepLab: semantic image segmentation with deep convolutional nets, atrous convolution, and fully connected CRFs. IEEE Trans. Pattern Anal. Mach. Intell. **40**(4), 834–848 (2017)
5. Chen, L.C., Papandreou, G., Schroff, F., Adam, H.: Rethinking atrous convolution for semantic image segmentation. arXiv preprint arXiv:1706.05587 (2017)
6. Chen, L.-C., Zhu, Y., Papandreou, G., Schroff, F., Adam, H.: Encoder-decoder with atrous separable convolution for semantic image segmentation. In: Ferrari, V., Hebert, M., Sminchisescu, C., Weiss, Y. (eds.) ECCV 2018. LNCS, vol. 11211, pp. 833–851. Springer, Cham (2018). https://doi.org/10.1007/978-3-030-01234-2_49
7. Chen, L.Z., Lin, Z., Wang, Z., Yang, Y.L., Cheng, M.M.: Spatial information guided convolution for real-time RGBD semantic segmentation. IEEE Trans. Image Process. **30**, 2313–2324 (2021)
8. De Lange, M., et al.: Continual learning: a comparative study on how to defy forgetting in classification tasks, **2**(6), 2. arXiv preprint arXiv:1909.08383 (2019)
9. Dhar, P., Singh, R.V., Peng, K.C., Wu, Z., Chellappa, R.: Learning without memorizing. In: Proceedings of the IEEE/CVF Conference on Computer Vision and Pattern Recognition, pp. 5138–5146 (2019)
10. Ding, H., Jiang, X., Shuai, B., Liu, A.Q., Wang, G.: Semantic segmentation with context encoding and multi-path decoding. IEEE Trans. Image Process. **29**, 3520–3533 (2020)
11. Douillard, A., Chen, Y., Dapogny, A., Cord, M.: Plop: learning without forgetting for continual semantic segmentation. In: Proceedings of the IEEE/CVF Conference on Computer Vision and Pattern Recognition, pp. 4040–4050 (2021)
12. Everingham, M., Van Gool, L., Williams, C., Winn, J., Zisserman, A.: The pascal visual object classes challenge 2012 (voc2012) results (2012). http://www.pascal-network.org/challenges. In: VOC/voc2012/workshop/index. html (2012)
13. Ghiasi, G., Fowlkes, C.C.: Laplacian pyramid reconstruction and refinement for semantic segmentation. In: Leibe, B., Matas, J., Sebe, N., Welling, M. (eds.) ECCV 2016. LNCS, vol. 9907, pp. 519–534. Springer, Cham (2016). https://doi.org/10.1007/978-3-319-46487-9_32
14. He, K., Zhang, X., Ren, S., Sun, J.: Deep residual learning for image recognition. In: Proceedings of the IEEE Conference on Computer Vision and Pattern Recognition, pp. 770–778 (2016)
15. Hou, S., Pan, X., Loy, C.C., Wang, Z., Lin, D.: Learning a unified classifier incrementally via rebalancing. In: Proceedings of the IEEE/CVF Conference on Computer Vision and Pattern Recognition, pp. 831–839 (2019)
16. Kirkpatrick, J., et al.: Overcoming catastrophic forgetting in neural networks. Proc. Natl. Acad. Sci. **114**(13), 3521–3526 (2017)
17. Li, Z., Hoiem, D.: Learning without forgetting. IEEE Trans. Pattern Anal. Mach. Intell. **40**(12), 2935–2947 (2017)
18. Lin, G., Milan, A., Shen, C., Reid, I.: Refinenet: multi-path refinement networks for high-resolution semantic segmentation. In: Proceedings of the IEEE Conference on Computer Vision and Pattern Recognition, pp. 1925–1934 (2017)
19. Long, J., Shelhamer, E., Darrell, T.: Fully convolutional networks for semantic segmentation. In: Proceedings of the IEEE Conference on Computer Vision and Pattern Recognition, pp. 3431–3440 (2015)

20. Mallya, A., Davis, D., Lazebnik, S.: Piggyback: adapting a single network to multiple tasks by learning to mask weights. In: Ferrari, V., Hebert, M., Sminchisescu, C., Weiss, Y. (eds.) ECCV 2018. LNCS, vol. 11208, pp. 72–88. Springer, Cham (2018). https://doi.org/10.1007/978-3-030-01225-0_5
21. Mehta, S., Rastegari, M., Caspi, A., Shapiro, L., Hajishirzi, H.: ESPNet: efficient spatial pyramid of dilated convolutions for semantic segmentation. In: Ferrari, V., Hebert, M., Sminchisescu, C., Weiss, Y. (eds.) ECCV 2018. LNCS, vol. 11214, pp. 561–580. Springer, Cham (2018). https://doi.org/10.1007/978-3-030-01249-6_34
22. Michieli, U., Zanuttigh, P.: Incremental learning techniques for semantic segmentation. In: Proceedings of the IEEE/CVF International Conference on Computer Vision Workshops (2019)
23. Michieli, U., Zanuttigh, P.: Continual semantic segmentation via repulsion-attraction of sparse and disentangled latent representations. In: Proceedings of the IEEE/CVF Conference on Computer Vision and Pattern Recognition, pp. 1114–1124 (2021)
24. Ostapenko, O., Puscas, M., Klein, T., Jahnichen, P., Nabi, M.: Learning to remember: a synaptic plasticity driven framework for continual learning. In: Proceedings of the IEEE/CVF Conference on Computer Vision and Pattern Recognition, pp. 11321–11329 (2019)
25. Rusu, A.A., et al.: Progressive neural networks. arXiv preprint arXiv:1606.04671 (2016)
26. Shmelkov, K., Schmid, C., Alahari, K.: Incremental learning of object detectors without catastrophic forgetting. In: Proceedings of the IEEE International Conference on Computer Vision, pp. 3400–3409 (2017)
27. Tao, A., Sapra, K., Catanzaro, B.: Hierarchical multi-scale attention for semantic segmentation. arXiv preprint arXiv:2005.10821 (2020)
28. Wu, C., Herranz, L., Liu, X., Van De Weijer, J., Raducanu, B., et al.: Memory replay GANs: learning to generate new categories without forgetting. In: Advances in Neural Information Processing Systems, vol. 31 (2018)
29. Xie, E., Wang, W., Yu, Z., Anandkumar, A., Alvarez, J.M., Luo, P.: Segformer: simple and efficient design for semantic segmentation with transformers. In: Advances in Neural Information Processing Systems, vol. 34, pp. 12077–12090 (2021)
30. Yuan, Y., Chen, X., Wang, J.: Object-contextual representations for semantic segmentation. In: Vedaldi, A., Bischof, H., Brox, T., Frahm, J.-M. (eds.) ECCV 2020. LNCS, vol. 12351, pp. 173–190. Springer, Cham (2020). https://doi.org/10.1007/978-3-030-58539-6_11
31. Zhang, H., et al.: Resnest: split-attention networks. In: Proceedings of the IEEE/CVF Conference on Computer Vision and Pattern Recognition, pp. 2736–2746 (2022)
32. Zhang, Z., Zhang, X., Peng, C., Xue, X., Sun, J.: ExFuse: enhancing feature fusion for semantic segmentation. In: Ferrari, V., Hebert, M., Sminchisescu, C., Weiss, Y. (eds.) ECCV 2018. LNCS, vol. 11214, pp. 273–288. Springer, Cham (2018). https://doi.org/10.1007/978-3-030-01249-6_17
33. Zhao, H., Shi, J., Qi, X., Wang, X., Jia, J.: Pyramid scene parsing network. In: Proceedings of the IEEE Conference on Computer Vision and Pattern Recognition, pp. 2881–2890 (2017)
34. Zheng, S., et al.: Rethinking semantic segmentation from a sequence-to-sequence perspective with transformers. In: Proceedings of the IEEE/CVF Conference on Computer Vision and Pattern Recognition, pp. 6881–6890 (2021)

35. Zhou, B., Zhao, H., Puig, X., Fidler, S., Barriuso, A., Torralba, A.: Scene parsing through ade20k dataset. In: Proceedings of the IEEE Conference on Computer Vision and Pattern Recognition, pp. 633–641 (2017)
36. Zhu, L., Chen, T., Yin, J., See, S., Liu, J.: Continual semantic segmentation with automatic memory sample selection. In: Proceedings of the IEEE/CVF Conference on Computer Vision and Pattern Recognition, pp. 3082–3092 (2023)

Adaptive Batch Processing and Resource Allocation for LLM Inference in Edge Computing

Lei Yang[1,2] (ID), Shuying Gan[2], Xijun Wang[2(✉)], Jing Liu[1], and Xiang Chen[2]

[1] Shenzhen University, Shenzhen, Guangdong 518060, China
[2] Sun Yat-sen University, Guangzhou, Guangdong 510006, China
`wangxijun@mail.sysu.edu.cn`

Abstract. Large Language Models (LLMs) have revolutionized artificial intelligence, showcasing unprecedented capabilities across a wide range of tasks and significantly enhancing edge computing. However, deploying LLMs on edge devices presents challenges due to the distributed nature of users across edge nodes and the complexity of request types. To address these challenges, this paper first establishes an LLM inference model within an edge computing system and formulates an optimization problem aimed at maximizing the number of requests processed per unit time while satisfying user demands. To solve this problem, we model the system as a Semi-Markov Decision Process (SMDP) and employ reinforcement learning methods to propose the Dynamic Inference Separable Proximal Policy Optimization (DISPPO) algorithm. This algorithm dynamically adjusts the order of the prefill and decode stages. We evaluate the performance of DISPPO in edge-based LLM inference by comparing it with traditional inference methods. Simulation results demonstrate that DISPPO outperforms traditional methods in LLM inference scenarios. Additionally, we explore the algorithm's performance across different batch sizes.

Keywords: large language models · edge computing · reinforcement learning

1   Introduction

In recent years, the emergence of Large Language Models (LLMs) such as GPT-4 [1] and LLaMa [2] has propelled rapid advancements in the field of generative AI. These models have showcased remarkable capabilities across a wide range of applications, fundamentally transforming Internet services and profoundly influencing various aspects of human life and work. The growth of these large models is driven by the Scaling Law[3], which posits that model performance improves with increases in model size, data volume, and computational resources. Consequently, the pursuit of higher intelligence and enhanced performance has led to the development of increasingly larger LLMs. Current LLMs, consisting of hundreds of millions of parameters, place substantial demands on computation and

© ICST Institute for Computer Sciences, Social Informatics and Telecommunications Engineering 2026
Published by Springer Nature Switzerland AG 2026. All Rights Reserved
R. C. Qiu et al. (Eds.): IoTaaS 2024, LNICST 675, pp. 41–52, 2026.
https://doi.org/10.1007/978-3-032-14681-6_4

storage [4], forcing service providers to allocate extensive GPU resources. However, the varying resource demands from users often lead to significant GPU idle time, resulting in resource inefficiencies. As the deployment of LLM inference services continues to expand, these challenges have become even more pronounced.

Edge intelligence presents a viable solution to the challenges faced by LLMs by enabling dynamic decision-making through AI models deployed at the network edge [5,6]. By performing LLM inference closer to the data source, edge intelligence can significantly reduce latency and improve response times. Moreover, since user data is distributed across edge nodes rather than being centrally stored on servers, the risk of privacy breaches is significantly mitigated.

LLM inference presents unique challenges for resource-constrained edge nodes due to several distinctive characteristics. Firstly, unlike conventional neural network models, where inference time is typically fixed based on the model and hardware, LLM inference involves multiple iterations. Each iteration generates an output token, which is appended to the input to produce the next output token in subsequent iterations. As iterations progress, the computational complexity of the model gradually increases, resulting in extended inference times. Existing inference service solutions [7,8] rely on precise time analysis for scheduling. Still, this approach is insufficient for addressing the progressively increasing computational demands during LLM inference. Secondly, LLMs utilize self-attention mechanisms, wherein each output token must be computed based on all previously generated tokens. This necessitates the retention of all generated tokens until the output sequence is complete, substantially increasing memory requirements [9]. Finally, when requests are uploaded, they undergo a communication phase before being processed for inference. If a request arrives early during the inference phase, it occupies memory until processing is completed. To optimize GPU utilization under stringent inference latency constraints [10], it is essential to schedule inference time and allocate computational resources efficiently. Although various algorithms have been proposed in Mobile Edge Computing (MEC) for joint task scheduling [11] and optimizing GPU usage [12], research on applying these solutions to LLMs remains limited.

To address the challenge of efficiently processing user requests while maximizing the number of requests handled per unit time [13], this paper establishes a Semi-Markov Decision Process (SMDP) framework and introduces a request buffer. We develop a method that dynamically separates the prefill and decode stages of a batch of requests, optimizing GPU resource utilization. This approach allows for faster and more efficient handling of user requests. Additionally, we compare this method with traditional LLM inference techniques, demonstrating its effectiveness in improving request processing efficiency.

The rest of this paper is organized as follows. Section 2 presents the system model and problem formulation. Section 3 introduces the DISPPO algorithm. In Sect. 4, we provide simulation results and performance analysis. Finally, the conclusions are drawn in Sect. 5.

2   System Model and Problem Formulation

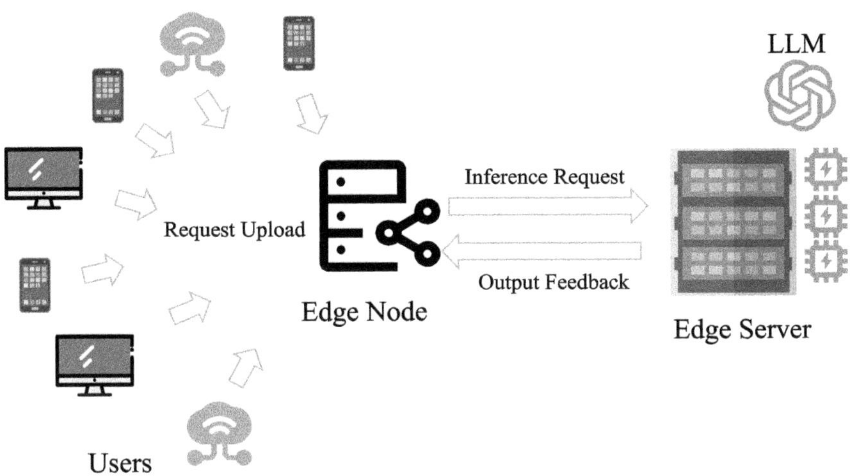

Fig. 1. Edge Inference System.

As illustrated in Fig. 1, we consider an edge inference system where an edge node receives user requests and manages their transmission in batches. The edge server, equipped with three GPUs, is responsible for processing the uploaded requests. Due to the limited computational resources of the GPUs, it is crucial to process incoming requests in batches to efficiently manage the workload.

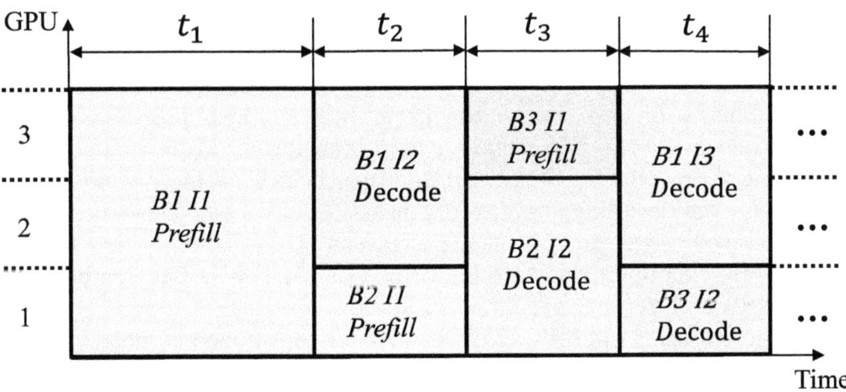

Fig. 2. Request processing.

Due to the uncertainty in LLM computation time, which varies depending on the stage and the number of tokens, we consider each computation phase as a time slot and establish a system with non-uniform time slots. At the beginning of each time slot, user requests arrive following a Poisson distribution with parameter λ. The request from the ith user arriving at time t is defined as $y_{i,t} = \{H, E, D\}$, where H represents the number of input tokens for the request, E represents the number of output tokens following a uniform distribution $E \sim U(\alpha_1, \alpha_2)$ with parameters $\alpha_1 = 50$ and $\alpha_2 = 200$, and D denotes the request's deadline. If the request is not processed before the deadline, it will be discarded, resulting in a penalty of p.

After the requests in each time slot are successfully uploaded, the edge server processes them in real-time based on the current batch's information and adjusts GPU allocation accordingly. Unprocessed requests are stored in an infinitely large buffer. Upon completion of the request upload, the edge server generates a decision variable γ, which contains information about the utilization of each GPU, including the requests occupying the GPUs and their current stage—whether in the prefill or decode stage. The edge server leverages this decision variable γ, to manage GPU allocations, updating it after each stage of a request is completed. Once processing is finished, the server selects new requests from the buffer for further processing, guided by the updated decision variable.

Figure 2 illustrates the request processing procedure, where each batch of requests must undergo a prefill stage before proceeding to the decode stage. The notation (B_i, I_j) represents the jth iteration of the ith batch of requests. During this process, due to the differing computational complexities of the prefill and decode stages, the same batch of requests may occupy varying amounts of GPU resources at different stages. The edge server updates its decisions based on the latest feedback at each stage transition and uses the updated γ to determine the next steps.

2.1   Inference Model

During the generation process of a typical LLM generative inference task, three key elements must be stored: weights, activations, and the key-value (KV) cache. The task consists of two stages: the prefill stage, which processes a prompt sequence to generate the KV cache for each transformer layer of the LLM, and the decoding stage, which utilizes and updates the KV cache to generate tokens iteratively. In the decoding stage, the generation of each token depends on the tokens generated in the previous steps.

Assume that all operations are performed on the GPU. The symbols related to the model's architecture are listed in Table 1.

Since the attention operation utilizes specially optimized kernels, we will first focus on other matrix multiplications in the prefill stage, specifically the QKV linear transformations, attention output, FFN input, and FFN output. All of these operations are related to σ and are compute-bound. Therefore, we can model the latency of these operations in total seconds as follows:

$$T_1 = K_1 \cdot \frac{4\sigma h^2 + 2\sigma h f}{g_m}. \tag{1}$$

Table 1. Notation and Definitions

Symbol	Definition
h	Hidden size
L	Number of layers in the model
e	Number of heads
z	Head size ($h = e \cdot z$)
f	FFN intermediate size
B	Batch size
σ	Number of tokens in the batch ($\sigma = \sum_{i=0}^{B-1} L_i$)
σ_2	Squared sum of the input lengths ($\sigma_2 = \sum_{i=0}^{B-1} L_i^2$)
b	Block size in the attention kernel
g_m	GPU FLOPs per second for matrix multiplication
b_m	GPU FLOPs per second for batched matrix multiplication

Next, we discuss the prefill attention operation optimized with FlashAttention. Since attention operates only among tokens within the same request, current implementations launch attention kernels for each request within the same batch. For a single attention head and a request containing L tokens, the attention kernel needs to perform a total of $2zL + 3zL \cdot (L/b) \approx 3zL \cdot (L/b)$ memory reads and writes, along with $2zL^2 + zL(L/b) \approx 2zL^2$ FLOPS. Therefore, the latency for the entire attention layer (including all requests and all heads) can be modeled as:

$$T_2 = K_2 \cdot \frac{3h\sigma_2}{b \cdot b_m}. \tag{2}$$

So the latency of the prefill phase can be modeled as:

$$T_{pre} = T_1 + T_2. \tag{3}$$

Then, we use profiling and interpolation to determine the values of K_1 and K_2.

Similarly, we focus on the following GEMMs in the decoding phase: These calculations are all related to B. Since B is constrained by the GPU memory size and stringent latency requirements, these operations in existing serving scenarios are memory-bound. Consequently, the decode stage is also memory-bound. The total memory reads and writes amount to $8Bh + 4h^2 + 2hf + 2Bf$. Thus, we can model the latency as follows:

$$T_3 = K_3 \cdot \frac{8Bh + 4h^2 + 2hf + 2Bf}{g_m}. \tag{4}$$

Regarding the decoding attention operation, for a single attention head and a request with L generated tokens, it needs to perform $3zL$ memory reads and writes, along with $2zL$ FLOPs. Therefore, we can model the latency of the decoding attention as follows:

$$T_4 = K_4 \cdot \frac{3h\sigma}{b_m}. \tag{5}$$

Summing up, the latency of the decoding phase is:

$$T_{gen} = T_3 + T_4. \tag{6}$$

Similarly, we use profiling and interpolation to figure out the values of K_3 and K_4.

Then the following constraints describe the calculation of total latency:

$$T^I = T_{pre} \cdot L + T_{gen} \cdot (\sigma - 1) \cdot L. \tag{7}$$

2.2   Problem Formulation

The objective of this study is to maximize the number of requests processed per unit time while ensuring that user requests are handled promptly. The optimization problem can thus be formulated as follows:

$$\max_{a_i(t),d(t)} \quad \lim_{T \to \infty} \frac{1}{T} \sum_{t=0}^{T} \beta \left(x(t) - \mu \cdot p \right) \tag{P1}$$

$$\text{s.t.} \quad t(a_i(0)) \le t(a_i(1)), \forall i \in N \tag{P1a}$$

Constraint P1a specifies the order of request processing, requiring that the requests within the same batch must undergo the prefill stage before proceeding to the decode stage.

Problem P1 is a complex optimization problem involving multiple variables, such as GPU scheduling, request processing order, and resource allocation, all of which are interdependent. This complexity makes it challenging to solve using traditional optimization methods. However, by modeling it as a SMDP, we can effectively incorporate the temporal dependencies and randomness inherent in the problem. This approach enables a more systematic decision-making process in a multi-variable context, ultimately leading to the optimal solution.

State **S**: The system state st includes the usage status of each GPU $Q(t) = \{q_i\}$ at time t, where $i \in \{1, 2, 3\}$ represents whether the GPU is unoccupied, in the prefill stage, or in the decode stage. It also includes the total number of requests being processed in batch i, denoted as k_i, and the cumulative number of requests completed by time t, denoted as $X(t) = \sum_{\tau=0}^{t} x(\tau)$, where $x(\tau)$ represents the number of requests completed at time τ. Additionally, the state includes the current processing status of each request, characterized by the number of input tokens H, the number of output tokens E, and the request deadline D.

Action $\mathbf{A}$: The action $\mathbf{a}$ includes making decisions at time t regarding the current batch of requests i, specifically whether to proceed with prefill, decode, or temporarily delay processing, denoted as $a_i(t)$. Additionally, it includes the decision $d(t)$ on whether to accept new requests.

Reward $\mathbf{R}$: The ultimate goal is to maximize the number of requests processed per unit time while meeting user demands. Therefore, the reward function is defined as:

$$R = \frac{\beta}{t} \sum_{\tau=0}^{t} (X(\tau) - \mu \cdot p), \tag{8}$$

where t represents the current time, β and μ are constants representing different reward coefficients, and p represents the penalty associated with discarded requests.

3 Dynamic Inference with Separable Prefill and Decode Using PPO Algorithm

This paper integrates the theory of LLM inference within MEC scenarios and proposes a dynamic inference algorithm with separable prefill and decode stages, based on Proximal Policy Optimization (PPO) [14] and resource allocation strategies (DISPPO). This algorithm effectively addresses the challenge of timely and efficient processing of user requests in edge environments. The detailed algorithm is presented in Algorithm 1.

The DISPPO algorithm leverages the PPO framework to dynamically adjust policy and value networks in response to changes in the environment. Unlike traditional single-network approaches, DISPPO incorporates a dual-stage optimization process that separates the prefill and decode phases. This separation allows for more precise control over resource allocation, particularly in complex scenarios where tasks exhibit different computational demands.

In the DISPPO algorithm, the policy, parameterized by θ, dynamically selects actions, including prefill actions a_t^{prefill} and decode actions a_t^{decode}. The prefill stage optimizes resource distribution to efficiently handle incoming requests, while the decode stage focuses on completing inference tasks with minimal latency.

The DISPPO algorithm updates the policy using the PPO-Clip objective, formalized as:

$$\theta_{k+1} = \arg \max_{\theta} \mathbb{E}s, a \sim \pi\theta_k \left[L(s, a, \theta_k, \theta) \right], \tag{9}$$

where the loss function $L(s, a, \theta_k, \theta)$ is defined as:

$$L(s, a, \theta_k, \theta) = \min \left(\frac{\pi_\theta(a|s)}{\pi_{\theta_k}(a|s)} A^{\pi_{\theta_k}}(s, a), \text{clip}\left(\frac{\pi_\theta(a|s)}{\pi_{\theta_k}(a|s)}, 1 - \epsilon, 1 + \epsilon \right) A^{\pi_{\theta_k}}(s, a) \right), \tag{10}$$

where $\frac{\pi_\theta(a|s)}{\pi_{\theta_k}(a|s)}$ represents the ratio of the new policy to the old policy, and A_t is the advantage function, which quantifies the benefit of taking a specific action

---

Algorithm 1. DISPPO: Dynamic Inference Separable PPO Algorithm

---

Input: Available resources and requests
Output: Trained policy network parameters θ

1. Initialize policy network parameters θ, value network parameters ϕ
2. Reset environment to initialize the simulation
3. **for** $i = 1$ **to** EPISODES **do**
4.   Reset environment and obtain initial state s_0
5.   Initialize the total reward for the episode to zero
6.   **while** not end of episode **do**
7.   Select action a_t based on the current policy $\pi_\theta(s_t)$ using softmax selection
8.   Execute action a_t
9.   Observe next state s_{t+1}, reward r_t, and check if episode is done
10.   Store transition $(s_t, a_t, r_t, s_{t+1}, \text{done})$ in memory
11.   Update the current state to s_{t+1}
12.   Accumulate reward r_t to the total reward for the episode
13.   **end while**
14.   Update policy and value network parameters using the PPO algorithm:
15.   For each epoch, compute advantages and update θ and ϕ based on:
16.   Advantage estimation and the clipped surrogate objective
17.   Log accumulated rewards and prepare for the next episode
18. **end for**
19. **Output:** Trained policy network parameters θ

---

compared to the expected value. This approach typically involves multiple steps (often small batches) of SGD to maximize the objective.

To further enhance the adaptability of the DISPPO algorithm in MEC environments, the reward function R_t is carefully designed to balance resource utilization and task completion time. The value function $V(s_t)$, which estimates the expected return from state s_t, is iteratively updated based on the observed rewards and the DISPPO function. The value functions for both the prefill and decode stages can be computed similarly:

$$V(s_t) = R_{t+1} + \gamma V(s_{t+1}). \tag{11}$$

By decoupling the prefill and decode stages, and using separate value functions for each, DISPPO achieves a higher degree of precision and efficiency in resource management, leading to superior performance in MEC scenarios.

4   Simulation Results

The simulation results validate the superiority of this algorithm. In terms of parameter settings, the hidden layer size is 64, the number of layers in the model is 12, the number of heads is 8, the head size is 8, the FFN intermediate size is 256, and the batch size is 8, indicating that each batch can contain up to eight requests. The block size in the attention kernel is 32, and the values for gm and bm are assigned according to the actual GPU performance.

In the PPO network, both the policy network and the value network adopt a two-layer fully connected neural network architecture. The number of neurons in the hidden layer is 128. The first layer of the policy network is a fully connected layer with an input dimension equal to the state size and an output dimension equal to the hidden layer size. The activation function is ReLU. The second layer is also a fully connected layer with an input dimension of 128 and an output dimension equal to the action space size, The output is normalized using the Softmax function to generate a probability distribution over actions. The first layer of the value network is also a fully connected layer with ReLU as the activation function. The second fully connected layer estimates the value of the state. The policy network and the value network are optimized using the Adam optimizer. The discount factor is set to 0.95 to compute the present value of future rewards. The λ parameter for Generalized Advantage Estimation is 0.95. The PPO clipping parameter is 0.2 during optimization. When using the PPO algorithm, the advantage function is compared with the probability ratio of the old policy, and clipping is applied to limit the extent of policy updates.

To validate the effectiveness of the proposed method, we primarily compared the following approaches: 1) our method, which penalizes unprocessed requests and allows the prefill and decode stages of each batch to be handled separately; 2) simple parallel processing, where other settings are the same as in our method, but the prefill and decode stages must be processed consecutively; and 3) sequential processing, where requests must be processed in order, and the prefill and decode stages must be handled consecutively.

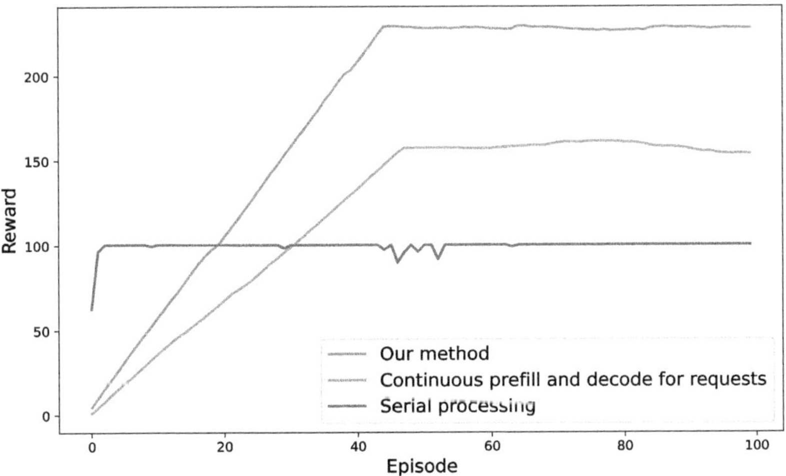

Fig. 3. Comparison of Our Algorithm with Traditional LLM Inference Methods.

As illustrated in Fig. 3, our proposed method exhibits significant advantages by enabling the decoupling of the prefill and decode stages, which ensures the timely processing of user requests. This decoupling allows for a more flexible and effective allocation of computational resources, particularly in scenarios where the demands between the prefill and decode stages vary substantially. Consequently, our method rapidly achieves and sustains a high reward level, demonstrating superior adaptability and efficiency in dynamic environments. In contrast, the second method, which mandates the consecutive execution of the prefill and decode stages, encounters challenges in handling requests with differing resource requirements across these stages. This constraint leads to suboptimal resource utilization, thereby limiting the performance of this approach relative to ours. The third method, which processes requests in a strictly sequential manner, exacerbates inefficiencies due to its inability to decouple these stages, resulting in poor GPU resource scheduling and the lowest overall rewards. These findings underscore the superiority of our approach, which not only optimizes resource allocation but also maximizes processing efficiency and reward accumulation under varying operational conditions.

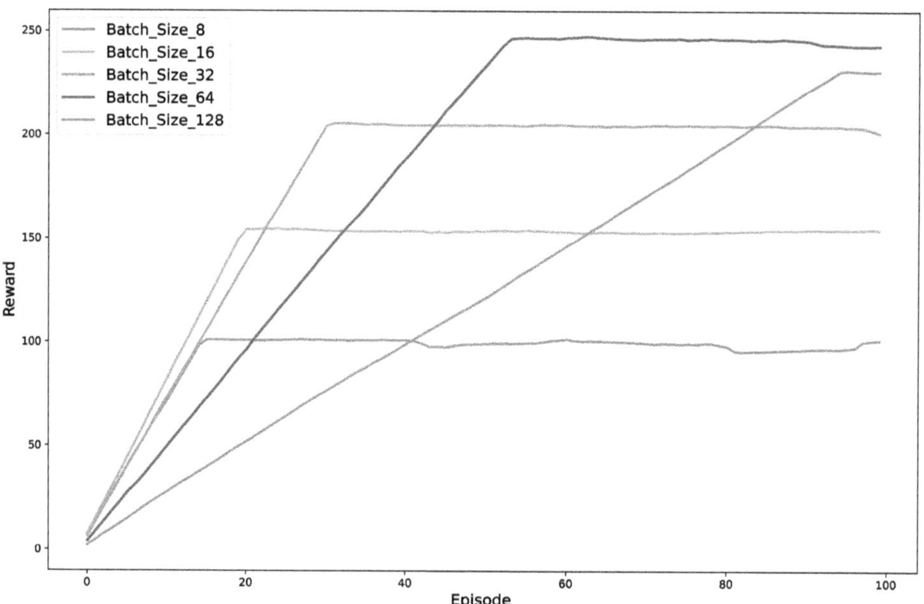

Fig. 4. Impact of Different Batch Sizes on Algorithm Performance.

Figure 4 compares the performance of processing requests with different batch sizes. The analysis reveals several key insights. First, when the batch size is less than 128, increasing the batch size generally leads to higher rewards. However, the reward does not increase proportionally with the doubling of the batch size. This may be because as the number of requests within a batch increases, the inference process becomes more complex, thereby affecting the overall efficiency and resulting in a nonlinear growth in rewards. Additionally, the gradual increase in batch size leads to a slower convergence rate of the training process, further supporting the notion that larger batch sizes introduce greater complexity into the inference process. Finally, when the batch size reaches 128, the reward decreases compared to when the batch size is 64. This indicates that larger batch sizes do not always yield better performance. If the batch size exceeds the maximum capacity that the edge server can handle, it may lead to a deterioration in inference results. Therefore, it is essential to explore the optimal batch size to balance inference efficiency and system capacity.

5   Conclusion

This paper focuses on the resource allocation problem in LLM inference within edge environments. To address the challenges of large volumes of user requests that cannot be processed promptly and the significant differences in resource demands during the inference process, we propose a DRL approach based on the PPO algorithm that separates the prefill and decode stages. Simulation results demonstrate the effectiveness and superiority of the proposed algorithm, and we also study the impact of batch size on the inference process. Future research will further explore the application of this method in more complex scenarios, such as in edge environments with higher dynamics and uncertainties. Additionally, we will investigate how to integrate multi-agent systems to better coordinate resource allocation across different edge nodes, thereby further improving inference efficiency and system robustness.

References

1. OpenAI. GPT-4 Technical report (2023)
2. Touvron, H., Lavril, T., Izacard, G,. et al.: Llama: open and efficient foundation language models. arXiv preprint arXiv:2302.13971 (2023)
3. Kaplan, J., McCandlish, S., Henighan, T., et al.: Scaling laws for neural language models. arXiv preprint arXiv:2001.08361 (2020)
4. Aminabadi, R.Y., et al.: Deepspeed-inference: enabling efficient inference of transformer models at unprecedented scale. In 2022 SC22: International Conference for High Performance Computing, Networking, Storage and Analysis (SC), pp. 646–660. IEEE Computer Society (2022)
5. Zhou, Z., Chen, X., Li, E., Zeng, L., Luo, K., Zhang, J.: Edge intelligence: paving the last mile of artificial intelligence with edge computing. Proc. IEEE **107**(8), 1738–1762 (2019)
6. Jang, S.Y., Kostadinov, B., Lee, D.: Microservice-based edge device architecture for video analytics. In: Proceedings of IEEE/ACM Symposium on Edge Computing (SEC), Los Alamitos, CA, USA, pp. 165–177 (2021)
7. Gujarati, A., et al.: Serving DNNs like clockwork: performance predictability from the bottom up. In: USENIX OSDI (2020)
8. Zhang, H., Tang, Y., Khandelwal, A., Stoica, I.: 2023. SHEPHERD: Serving DNNs in the Wild (2023)

9. Vaswani, A., et al.: Attention is all you need. In: NeurIPS 17, vol. 30, Long Beach, CA. Curran Associates, Inc., USA (2017)
10. Shi, W., Zhou, S., Niu, Z., Jiang, M., Geng, L.: Multiuser CoInference With batch processing capable edge server. IEEE Trans. Wirel. Commun. **22**(1), 286–300 (2023)
11. Zeng, L., Chen, X., Zhou, Z., Yang, L., Zhang, J.: CoEdge: cooperative DNN inference with adaptive workload partitioning over heterogeneous edge devices. IEEE/ACM Trans. Netw. **29**(2), 595–608 (2021)
12. Lu, B., Yang, J., Xu, J., Ren, S.: Improving QoE of deep neural network inference on edge devices: a bandit approach. IEEE Internet Things J. **9**(21), 21:409–21:420 (2022)
13. Yao, Z., Li, C., Wu, X., Youn, S., He, Y.: A comprehensive study on post-training quantization for large language models. arXiv preprint arXiv:2303.08302 (2023)
14. Schulman, J., Wolski, F., Dhariwal, P., et al.: Proximal policy optimization algorithms. arXiv preprint arXiv:1707.06347 (2017)

Intelligent Production Line Design of Photoelectric Display Devices Based on Industrial Internet of Things Technology

Yan Huang[1,2(✉)], Bin Xiao[1], Xiang Chen[3], and Qiang Wu[4]

[1] Wuhan Vocational College Software and Engineering, Wuhan 430205, China
Huoyanyanyi137@126.com
[2] Hubei Engineering Research Center for Intelligent Detection and Identification of Complex Parts, Wuhan, China
[3] TCL China Star Optoelectronics Technology, Wuhan 430000, China
[4] Hunan Anna Intelligent Technology Co., LTD, Changsha 410000, China

Abstract. According to the production process of photoelectric display devices, a set of intelligent production line based on industrial Internet of Things technology is designed. Various processes and key data in the production process are collected, and transmitted to the Iot platform through the industrial IoT gateway with the edge computing. There are many key parameters which can control the process of the manufacturing. The industrial Internet of Things platform can complete production data analysis and equipment management, and display it through data analysis and report system. The intelligent production line can not only improve production efficiency, but also reduce the waste of resources and error rate caused by poor information transmission. The system can be extended the production of photoelectric display devices, to promote flexible production and digital twin black light factory.

Keywords: Industrial Internet of Things · LCD manufacturing · Intelligent production line · Data analyse

1 Introduction

On December 22,2020, the Ministry of Industry and Information Technology, PRC issued the Action Plan for Industrial Internet Innovation and Development (2021–2023), [1] which mentioned that to build a characteristic industrial Internet platform for key industries and regions. Focusing on key industries with a good digital foundation and strong driving effect, we will build an industrial Internet platform with industry characteristics, and promote the accumulation of industry knowledge and experience on the platform. In modern intelligent factory, through the industrial Internet of things, sensors, controllers, embedded systems and gateway communication and the manufacturing process, realizes the interconnection between equipment and information sharing, simulates and records the modern production of main industrial data and main scenarios, to realize equipment

R. C. Qiu et al. (Eds.): IoTaaS 2024, LNICST 675, pp. 53–65, 2026.
https://doi.org/10.1007/978-3-032-14681-6_5

interconnection, production automation, control real-time, configuration optimized intelligent production lines, and can be widely used in flexible production and digital twin black lamp factory.

2   Design and Architecture of the Production Line of Photoelectric Display Devices

The 14th Five-Year Plan of Hubei province is planning put forward to build "Photonics, Chips, Displays, Devices, and Networks" industrial cluster [2], the new displays as one of the key development directions of strategic emerging industries, encourage and support the construction of a new display industry innovation center at the provincial level, promote the localization of core materials and key equipment, will show the gripper, promote the construction of low temperature polysilicon (LTPS) panel production line, at the same time actively cultivate and the introduction of industry chain upstream and downstream enterprises, accelerate the industrialization of new display technology such as OLED [3].

To broaden the application scope of the new display technology, develop more application scenarios, improve the local industrial supporting facilities, and promote industrial upgrading, more manpower and material resources are needed to achieve this. Based on the industrial Internet of Things technology to build the photoelectric display intelligent production line, aiming to upgrade all link of the photoelectric display production line through the industrial Internet of Things technology, improve production efficiency, optimize product quality, and reduce resource consumption [4].

2.1   Introduction to the Manufacturing Process of Photoelectric Display Devices

The Manufacturing Process of Photoelectric Display Devices. Taking liquid crystal display devices as an example, the production and manufacturing process mainly involves the array process, color film process, box process, and module process.

The front array process mainly includes "thin film, yellow light, etching and peeling film" four parts, the main role is to deposit a layer of transparent and conductive indium tin oxide (ITO), used to make electrodes, on the glass substrate by lithography, etching microelectronics process form thin film transistor (TFT) array, as a key component of the control of liquid crystal molecular rotation.

The color film process is the process of making a color filter, which is used to give each pixel three basic colors: red, green, and blue. This usually involves forming RGB color patterns on a glass substrate by photography or inkjet printing, and adding a black matrix (Black Matrix) to improve contrast and color purity.

The boxed process is to align and package the array substrate with the color filter substrate together, and inject the liquid crystal material in the middle. A closed space is formed between the two substrates, in which the liquid crystal molecules can change the arrangement of the electric field to control the amount of light passing through. This process also includes the polarizer and coating layer and sealing at the edges to maintain the sealing and stability of the internal environment.

In the module assembly stage, the completed LCD panel (Cell) will be further processed into a directly usable display module. This includes connecting a flexible printed circuit board (FPC) or COF/COG to deliver electrical signals, installing a backlight ((e.g. LED strip), polarizer, brightening film (if required), and a possible touch screen layer (e.g. TP). Finally, all components are accurately assembled and functionally tested to ensure that the display is flawless and then packaged.

LCD device production process involves more than 40 processes, the process is complex, and each process also needs some key parameters for intelligent control, in the process of intelligent production line transformation, through the perception of all kinds of sensors, controllers, and mobile communication, intelligent analysis technology, the combination of industrial Internet of things of production line each link of real-time monitoring, data collection, and analysis. Industrial Internet of Things technology can be deeply integrated into every link of the photoelectric display production line, which can greatly improve manufacturing efficiency, improve product quality, and reduce production costs and resource consumption [5].

Main Manufacturing Process and Key Parameters of the Module Process. Taking the module process of the liquid crystal display device as an example, the key parameters required for collection in the intelligent production line are introduced.

The purpose of the module process is to bind IC, FPC, and PCBA to the LCD panel through anisotropic conductive adhesive (ACF) to form an open panel, and then assemble the backlight module, plate gold, screw and so on the open panel, to complete a display module (Fig. 1.).

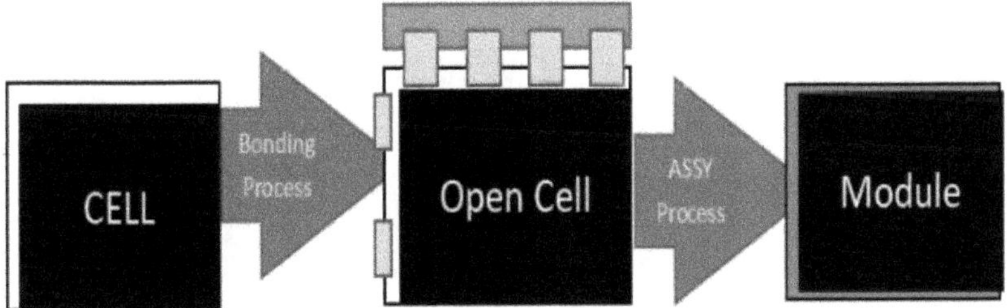

Fig. 1. Module manufacturing process diagram

The main two manufacturing processes in the module process are COG (chip on glass) and FOG (FPC on glass), and the main purpose is to connect IC and FPC with the cell through ACF using thermal pressure, as shown in Fig. 2. To ensure the uniformity and reliability of the thermal pressure, the heat conduction and buffer protection of the buffer material Teflon are also used in the manufacturing process. As shown in Fig. 2.

In the actual production process, the COG process includes cleaning and loading, ACF attachment, COG prepressing, COG primary pressure, detection, and unloading. The process of FOG process includes loading, ACF attachment, FOG precompression, sealing, and UV curing, detection and packaging. Materials are transferred in each production line by AGV car, and the four-dimensional manipulator is responsible for the

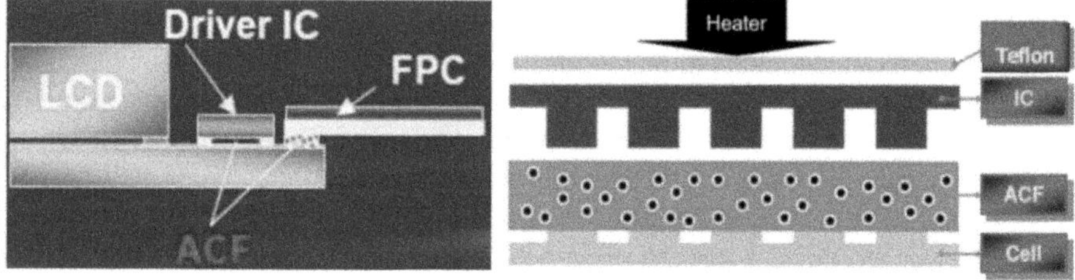

Fig. 2. The purpose of the COG and FOG and the COG process with Teflon

loading and unloading process of raw materials. The design of the overall production line is shown in Fig. 3.

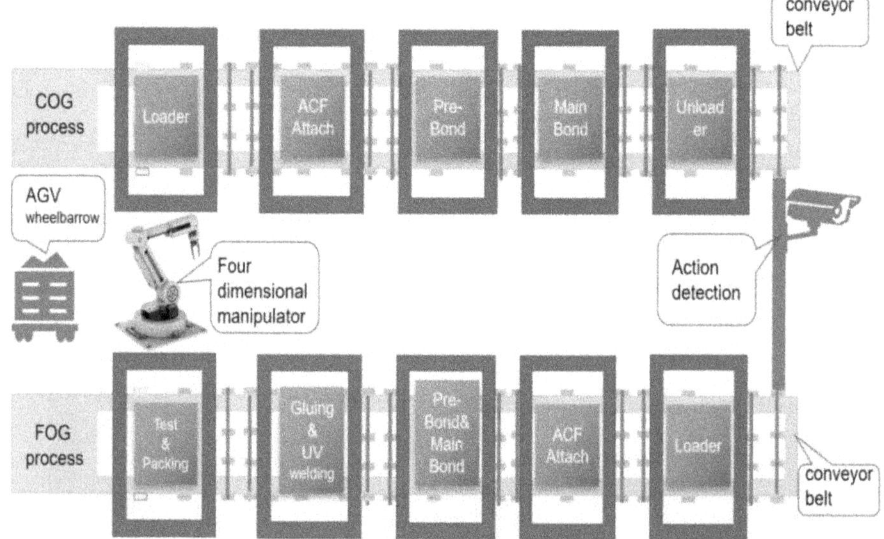

Fig. 3. Automatic production line of COG and FOG process diagram

Due to the module processing process, involves the product negative pressure adsorption, product alignment, ACF and Teflon material winding, as well as the thermal pressure, temperature, and time control, these parameters are particularly important in the automatic processing process, so in the process of design photoelectric display device automatic production line, these parameters are must collected [6].

2.2 Data Collection of the Production Line of Photoelectric Display Devices

In the design process of the intelligent production line, it is necessary to use a variety of sensors to complete the conversion and record of various physical quantities to the processing of digital information in the production system, which is the key component of the intelligent production line to realize the automation, monitoring, control and data analysis system [7].

The production system introduced in this paper is based on the automatic control of PLC and industrial Internet of Things (IIOT) data collection, gateway data communication, and has the functions of industrial Internet of Things data docking. It can realize the intelligent production line, the collection of the main industrial data, the automation of typical industrial scenarios, and the industrial Internet of Things fusion application (Fig. 4).

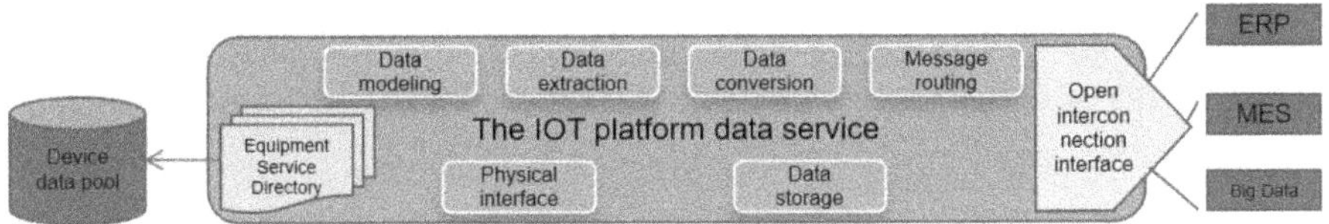

Fig. 4. The IOT Platform equipment service bus

Functional Structure of the Production Line of Photoelectric Display Devices. Basic sensors: proximity switches, photoelectric sensors, temperature sensors, current sensors, magnetic sensors, pressure sensors, CCD cameras, and other common different types of industrial sensors. Collect the work piece status of production line, environment, and other parameter data to PLC and gateway, finally transmitted to the cloud platform.

The execution part of the production line: the stepper motor realizes the production line conveyor belt work, and completes the transportation of the workpiece from the four-dimensional manipulator to the COG production line to the FOG production line and then to the final unloading warehouse area, with a total of 10 stations.

PLC control system: supports 4AD interface with 4100K high-speed output, use industrial industrial control configuration touch screen, touch screen display, can control the vacuum negative pressure switch in the production line, product grab, precision workbench shift and other work [8].

Data Acquisition and Implementation Method

The Conveyor Belt Control. The production line of photoelectric display device manufacturing can realize the processing process of small-size panels in the assembly line, with a total of 10 stations. The transmission wire body is driven by the magnetic transmission wheel, and the whole wire body is driven by the speed-regulating motor to move the product. The tension detection sensor HSZ-P detects the tension of the synchronous band. The LCD panel is transmitted by the conveyor belt between various stations, the stepper motor receives by the PLC which can set abnormal warning and information feedback and upload to the industrial Internet of Things gateway [9].

Temperature Detection and Control. In the pre-pressure process and this pressure process, use the heating pipe in the equipment to heat the product, and the temperature and humidity in the module are monitored by the temperature and humidity sensor RS-WS-N01-8 in actual time, and fed back to the upper machine.

Product Counterpoint Detection: The product alignment detection passes the LED lamp irradiation to the processed liquid crystal module, and the TES1334A monitors the light brightness and light energy lamp parameters in the process. Through the CCD visual system to detect whether the product has cracks or other defects, abnormal warnings and information feedback can be set.

Pressure Detection Module. In the process of pre-pressure and this pressure, drive the pressure sensor LUR-A-500NSA1 through the servo rod components, conduct a pressure test on the product at a certain pressure value, and set the appropriate pressure value according to the processing needs, and give abnormal warning and information feedback [10].

Material Capture Module. XZ manipulator built by four-axis manipulator by vacuum suction products and transfer, in the process by ACC375 to monitor the process of acceleration, jitters, by GT-H10 to monitor the product thickness, and electrostatic detector for product static quantity, and feedback to the upper machine, can set an abnormal alarm.

Other Collected Data. Some stations are equipped with blowing and suction devices to prevent pollution, and are equipped with negative pressure monitoring, VOC monitoring, airflow monitoring, exhaust flow monitoring, and feedback to the upper machine, which can set abnormal warning and information feedback.

The Connection of the Industrial Internet of Things Gateway. PLC programmable logic controller uses controlled 2N series PLC, which functions as the logic control of switching quantity. It is used for data reading control and distribution of multiple devices. Currently, multiple devices are connected through two 485 data acquisition ports, and the circuit logic is controlled through switching quantity acquisition and output. PLC485 Port 1 connects with the corresponding modules and reads their data and issues control; PLC485 Port 2 connects with the D520 gateway module and uploads the collected data to the gateway module. The analog quantity module, the main function is to collect the 4~20 mA current output by part of the sensor, and convert it into a numerical signal to PLC [11].

The industrial IoT gateway can collect data from PLC, sensors, meters, and other devices. It supports a variety of industrial communication protocols (such as MODBUS, OPC UA, CANopen, etc.), and converts the data of these different protocols into a unified format to facilitate subsequent data processing and transmission. Industrial IOT gateway supports wireless connectivity of traditional and remote industrial devices to the next-generation intelligent infrastructure, suitable for critical systems and industrial environments that acquire data using sensor nodes or I/O devices. IOT gateways can be configured with a range of different protocols that allow them to communicate with these terminal sensor nodes or I/O devices. The connection mode of the industrial Internet of Things gateway is shown in Fig. 5. The device and the gateway can realize high-speed and reliable LAN data transmission through the RJ 45 interface and the standard TCP/IP protocol. It can also be connected via the RS-232 or RS-485 serial interface. The

RS-232 is commonly used for point-to-point communication, and the RS-485 supports multi-point communication, suitable for long-distance and multi-device connections, and is commonly used in industrial control systems. The gateway connection mode with the main console generally adopts wireless WIFI or 4G / 5G mobile communication connection to ensure a high data transmission rate.

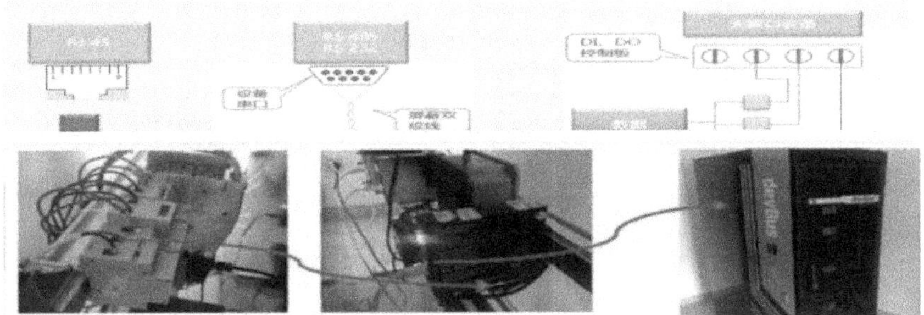

Fig. 5. The interface of Industrial Internet of Things gateway and connections

Design of the Man-Machine Interface. Stepper motor controller interface and sensor data acquisition interface are designed. The stepping motor controller interface (as shown in Fig. 6) has four indicator lights, respectively representing the three stations of the production line. The touchscreen button controls the stepping motor to reverse, start and stop.

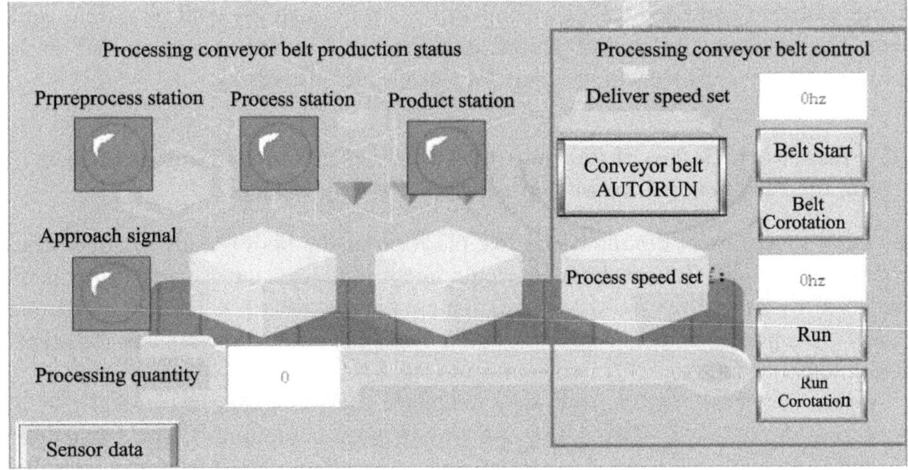

Fig. 6. The interface of Stepper motor controller

The sensor data acquisition interface (Fig. 7) is mainly used to collect and display the data collected by each sensor.

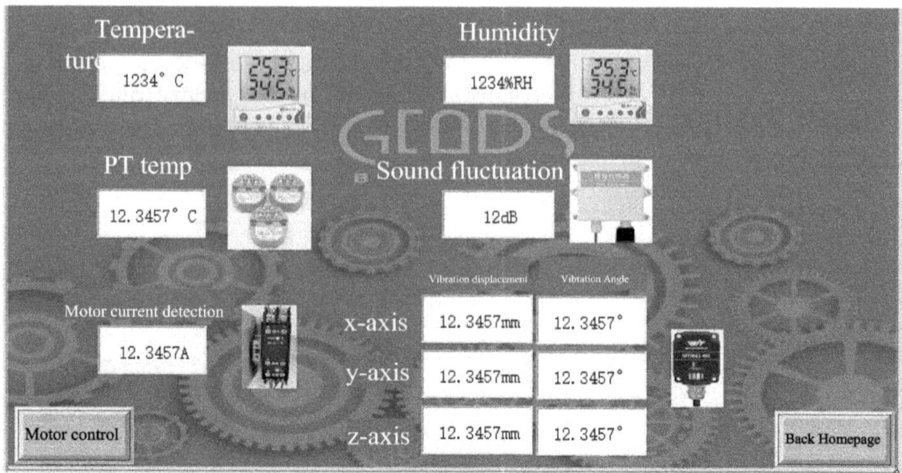

Fig. 7. The interface of Sensor data acquisition

3 Platform Architecture of Industrial Internet of Things

The industrial Internet of Things platform adopts a B/S architecture system, docker container deployment, and micro-service architecture, mainly used for data collection, processing, visualization and equipment management. The Industrial IoT platform enables device connectivity through the industry-standard IoT protocols MQTT, CoAP, and HTTP, and supports cloud and local deployment, with scalability, fault tolerance, and superior performance. The production equipment connects to the industrial Internet of Things platform and conducts data communication through the control system equipment. The industrial Internet of Things platform can transfer equipment data to data analysis and reporting system products for storage and processing.

3.1 Framework Design of the Industrial Internet of Things Platform Based on the Production Line of Photoelectric Display Devices

The main functions of the industrial IoT platform of the photoelectric display device production line are data analysis and equipment management. The platform is also connected with three functional groups, namely device sensing access, intelligent data processing report system, and Internet of Things applications, to complete the efficacy of the industrial Internet of Things platform (Fig. 8).

Various devices communicate, data exchange, device management, and message processing through IoT SDK. Using the way of edge computing (Edge Computing), the data processing, application execution and service deployment from the centralized cloud center or core network to the edge of the network nodes to optimize the data processing efficiency and transmission speed, reduce the distance and time delay of data transmission, improve the response speed, enhance the real-time and effectiveness of data processing [12].

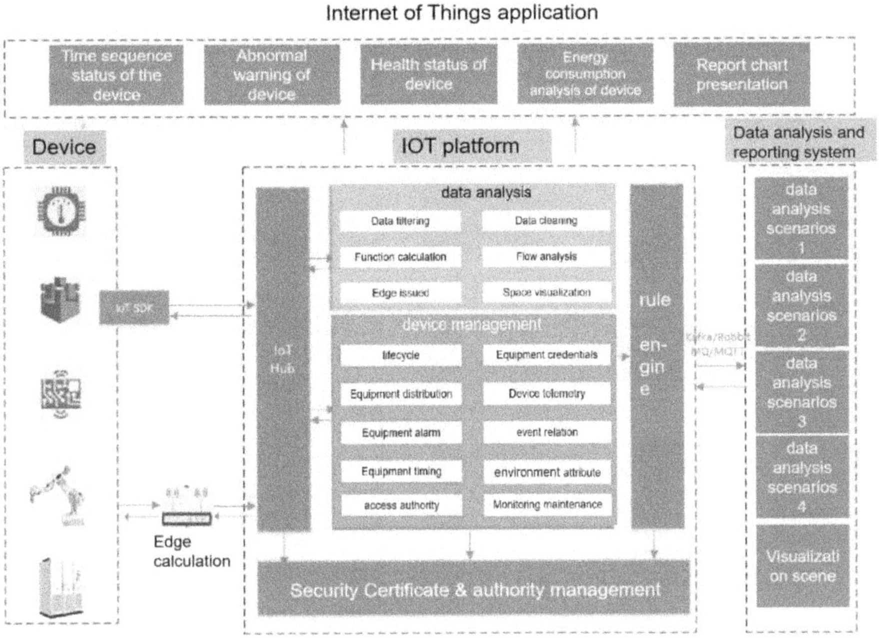

Fig. 8. Function of the industrial Internet of Things platform

The industrial Internet of Things platform receives data processing and equipment management after receiving various equipment data and information through the industrial Internet of Things gateway. The data management functions of the platform include data filtering, data cleaning, function calculation, flow analysis, edge distribution and function visualization functions. Equipment management needs to manage the equipment life cycle, equipment credentials, equipment distribution, equipment telemetry, equipment alarm, equipment timing, equipment attributes, event relationship, access rights, monitoring and maintenance, etc.

The intelligent data processing report system mainly summarizes data and reports output according to different data scenarios and visualization scenarios. For example, all the measured values of the corresponding detectors, whether they exceed the rating value, alarm records, etc.

At the same time, the industrial Internet of Things platform is output through the Internet of Things application, including equipment running status, equipment abnormal warning, equipment health status, equipment energy consumption analysis, report and chart display.

3.2 System Function Design of the Industrial Internet of Things Platform

The core functions of the industrial Internet platform system include home page design, rule chain setting, customer permission setting, equipment management, component library, edge instance, edge management, dashboard library, version control, audit log,

API statistics and system settings (Fig. 9). The following mainly introduces the related content of customer permission setting and equipment management design.

Fig. 9. Interface of Industrial Internet of Things platform system operation

Customer Permission Setting of Industrial IOT Platform.

Click the [Customer Management] button of the platform system to enter the customer management list interface. Customer management is based on multi-tenant users, which can be classified as customer management.

Customer Management List. Which can complete the operation of adding new users, managing customer assets, managing customer equipment, managing customer instrument management and deleting customers.

The Asset Management Function Includes the New Assets. Whether the assets are open, allocating the assets to customers, and deleting the assets.

Equipment Management Design of Industrial Internet of Things platform

Click the [Equipment] Button of the Platform System to Enter the Equipment Management Interface. The managed equipment can be added and deleted, while managing the equipment vouchers.

Set the Server-Side Attributes. Client attributes, and shared attributes of the device.

Equipment data telemetry, and equipment data is collected using MQTT, CoAP or HTTP protocol [13].

Store Time Numbers in Cassandra. (efficient, scalable, fault-tolerant NoSQL database).

Visualize Timing Data Using Configurable and Configurable Widgets and Instrument. For example, the need to set the visual interface of real-time temperature at the station, the appropriate instrument can be found in the instrument library, and associated to the actual equipment. The visual interface of this function can be realized by matching the temperature output in the instrument with the temperature value collected by the industrial Internet of Things gateway (Fig. 10).

Using the Rule Engine to Filter and Analyze the Data. You can form a bar chart or a line chart for macro analysis and data analysis for a period of time.Event alarms can be triggered based on the collected data.

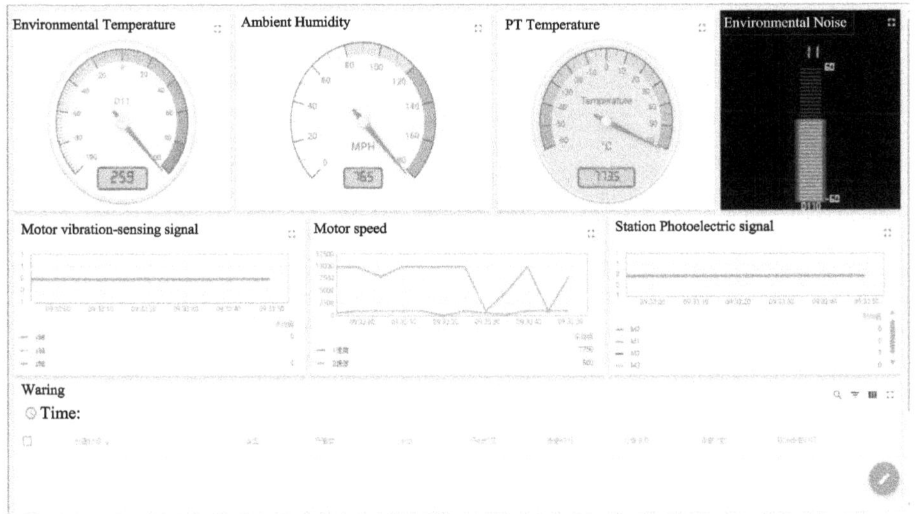

Fig. 10. The visual interface for device management

4 Data Analysis and Report Form System Design

The data output of the industrial Internet of Things platform is integrated through data analysis and report systems. The main functions include data management, data analysis, Echar5.0 dynamic chart of various application scenarios, bar chart, line diagram, box chart output, industrial scene self-developed chart components, etc. The chart components can connect SQL dynamic data, static data, excel data, interface data, data analysis process, and other scenario analysis, to realize the whole process from data access, data analysis to data visualization [14].

To analyze the right pressure temperature data of COG press for example, first set the data type to WebSocket data, find the interface address and input the interface address into ws: / / 10.80.2.31:8280 / api / ws / plugins / telemetry; find the WebSocket transfer data and enter the code editing program. Click the network button in the development tool to find the data named "deviceId", and confirm whether the following code is the COG this press code. Copy the data path to complete the data collection [15].

Considering that the right pressure temperature of the COG press should be observed for a period of time, the display is made by line diagram. Select the line chart in the component bar, set the data type to dynamic data, and output the line chart by entering the newly copied data path of the press in the interface data. In this way, the data collection and report reality on each station can be completed, and a complete system data analysis and report map such as Fig. 11 [16].

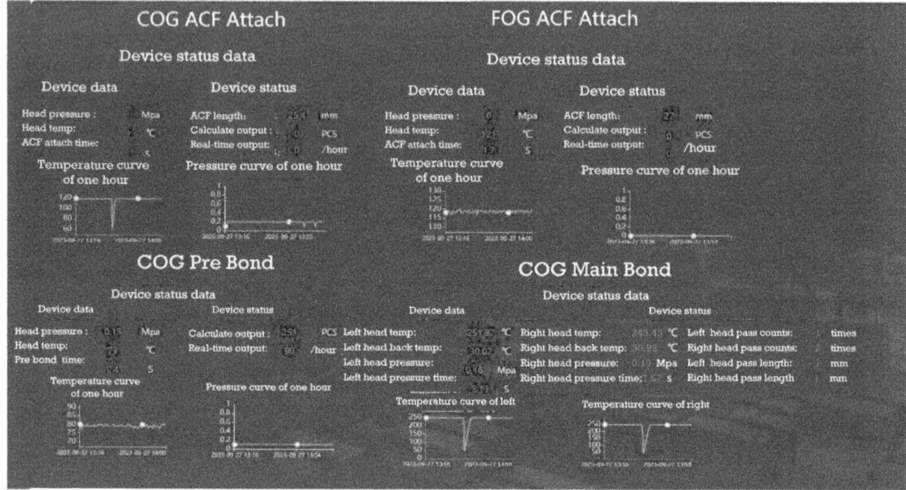

Fig. 11. Visualization interface for data analysis and reporting system

5 Conclusion

In the design process of intelligent production line design of photoelectric display devices, the following aspects are focused on:

Sensor selection and data communication, industrial Internet platform function design, data processing and analysis, late will also establish data processing center, the collected data cleaning, integration and analysis, use of big data and artificial intelligence technology, mining valuable information in the data, provide decision support for production line optimization, build intelligent control system, automation control and management of production line equipment.

The intelligent production line of photoelectric display devices based on industrial Internet of Things technology can seamlessly connect various equipment, workstations and management systems on the production line, and can flexibly respond to various changes, including the switch of product types, the adjustment of production batch and the change of production plan. Through modular design and reconfigurable technology, the production line layout and equipment configuration can be easily adjusted to meet different production needs and realize flexible manufacturing. Through the industrial Internet of Things technology, the real-time information sharing and collaborative operation are realized. This can not only improve production efficiency, but also reduce the waste of resources and error rate caused by poor information transmission. In the later stage, it can also be promoted to various kinds of black lamp factories through digital twin technology.

Acknowledgments. The authors acknowledged the Hubei Engineering Research Center for Intelligent Detection and Identification of Complex Parts (Grant No. GCZX-XN-202408).

References

1. The Ministry of Industry and Information Technology. PRC issued the Action Plan for Industrial Internet Innovation and Development (2021–2023). https://www.miit.gov.cn/jgsj/xgj/gzdt/art/2021/art_ecb6ec1ddbf748eebe05ac69c086339d.html. Accessed 13 Jan 2021
2. Hubei Provincial Development and Reform Commission. The 14th five-year Plan for national economic and social development of Hubei Province and the two-three five-year Vision goal outline. https://fgw.hubei.gov.cn/fbjd/xxgkml/ghjh/lsgh/145/202104/t20210413_3467299.shtml. Accessed 13 Apr 2021
3. Interpretation of the Press Conference of the "14th Five-Year Plan for the development of strategic emerging industries in Hubei Province".http://www.hubei.gov.cn/hbfb/xwfbh/202108/t20210817_3707100.shtml. Accessed 17 Aug 2021
4. Mourtzis, D., Vlachou, E.: A cloud-based cyber-physical system for adaptive shop-floor scheduling and condition-based maintenance. J. Manuf. Syst. **2018**(47), 179–198 (2018)
5. Wei, X., Liu, H.: A cloud manufacturing resource allocation model based on ant colony optimization algorithm. Int. J. Grid Distrib. Comput. **8**(1), 55–66 (2015)
6. Ying, W., Pee, L.G., Jia, S.: Social informatics of intelligent manufacturing ecosystems: a case study of KuteSmart. Int. J. Inf. Manag. **42**(Oct.), 102–105 (2018)
7. Giallanza, A., Aiello, G., Marannano, G.: Industry 4.0: smart test bench for shipbuilding, industry. Int. J. Interact. Des. Manuf. (IJIDeM) **14**(4), 1525–1533 (2020)
8. Serpanos, D., Wolf, M.: Industrial Internet of Things. Internet-of-Things (IoT) Systems, pp. 37–54. Springer, Cham (2018)
9. Ding, G., Lu, H., Bai, J., et al.: Development of a high precision UWB/vision-based AGV and control system. In: 2020 5th International Conference on Control and Robotics Engineering (ICCRE), pp. 99–103. IEEE (2020)
10. Dares, M., Kai, W.G., Ye, S.K., et al.: Development of AGV as test bed for fault detection. In: 2020 6th International Conference on Control, Automation and Robotics (ICCAR), pp. 379–383. IEEE (2020)
11. Wahab, O.A., Mourad, A., Otrok, H., et al.: Federated machine learning: survey, multi-level classification, desirable criteria and future directions in communication and networking systems. IEEE Commun. Surv. Tutor. **23**(2), 1342–1397 (2021)
12. Brunton, S.L., Noack, B.R., Koumoutsakos, P.: Machine learning for fluid mechanics. Annu. Rev. Fluid Mech. **52**(1), 477–508 (2020)
13. Tao, F., Cheng, J., Qi, Q., et al:. Digital twin-driven product design, manufacturing and service with big data. Int. J. Adv. Manuf. Technol. **94**(9–12), 3563–3576 (2018)
14. Karniadakis, G.E., Kevrekidis, I.G., Lu, L., et al.: Physics-informed machine learning. Nat. Rev. Phys. **3**(6), 422–440 (2021)
15. Lei, R., Lin, Z., Lihui, W., et al:. Cloud manufacturing: key characteristics and applications. Int. J. Comput. Integr. Manuf. **30**(6), 501–515 (2014)
16. Lo Bello, L., Steiner, W.: A perspective on IEEE time-sensitive networking for industrial communication and automation systems. Proc. IEEE **107**(6), 1094–1120 (2019)

Research on the Integrated Sensing and Communication System Based on OPA LiDAR

Jing Huang[1,2]([✉]), Yan Huang[1,2], and Tingting Ren[1,2]

[1] School of Electronic Engineering, Wuhan Vocational College of Software and Engineering, Wuhan, China
99478465@qq.com
[2] Hubei Engineering Research Center for Intelligent Detection and Identification of Complex Parts, Wuhan, China

Abstract. LiDAR has become the focus of domestic research due to its advantages of small size, fast scanning speed, reliable performance and low-cost manufacturing. The TOF-based LiDAR ranging solution is suitable for fast ranging scenarios with low accuracy requirements under a large measurement range, and is very suitable for application in OPA LiDAR ranging system. On the premise of detailed modeling of laser communication channels, it is of great research value to explore the integrated communication and sensing system based on OPA architecture, which can provide effective technical support for the realization of urban security monitoring, smart city construction and other application scenarios, and accelerate the realization of the overall goal of 6G "intelligent connection of all things".

Keywords: Integrated Sensing And Communication (ISAC) · Free Space Optical Communications (FSOC) · Light Detection And Ranging (LiDAR) · Optical Phased Array (OPA)

1 Introduction

With the popularization of various mobile communication devices and advanced connected sensors, people's demand for high-speed and large-connection communication is increasing. In the face of limited spectrum resources, the idea of "spectrum sharing between radar and communication" was first proposed. Spectrum sharing between radar and communication systems is realized by multiplexing radar frequency bands, thereby improving spectrum utilization. The development of technology has made the hardware structure of radar system and communication system more similar and have the same functional modules (such as transmitter, receiver, antenna and signal processing unit), so "radar communication integration" has emerged. Compared with the mutual interference of radar signals and communication signals in the traditional separate radar and communication systems, the radar and communication signals in the integrated mode not only

R. C. Qiu et al. (Eds.): IoTaaS 2024, LNICST 675, pp. 66–77, 2026.
https://doi.org/10.1007/978-3-032-14681-6_6

do not interfere with each other, but can also share advantages and promote each other. The goal of 6G "Intelligent Connectivity of Everything" corresponds to the potential requirements of massive connections, ultra-reliability, low latency, and large throughput, and requires the integration of independent technical architectures such as communication, sensing, and computing into a unified overall network framework. Therefore, the "integrated sensing and communication" (ISAC) technology, which enables radar and communication to work in the same system, is attracting the attention of researchers, and it is also a key technology towards 6G.

The integration of communication and perception has broad application prospects, such as AI machine learning, unmanned driving, automated robots, smart home, Internet of Vehicles, smart medical care, public safety and environmental monitoring, smart city, etc. These emerging fields require target identification, positioning, detection, tracking, and early warning; Real-time acquisition of external attributes and status information such as weather, images, and temperature; Connect to the network resource library to obtain the required information and learn independently; Single-agent adaptive control and multi-agent mutual recognition and coordination work; Human-computer interaction and collaborative work between intelligent systems. Their further need for information acquisition and processing has driven communication-sensing integration as a major technology and dominant trend in 6G, giving 6G networks the ability to freely connect the physical and digital worlds. The integrated communication and perception technology first sends wireless communication signals, and then collects the reflected, scattered and direct signals of these signals, and obtains object information through analysis, so as to complete functions such as positioning, tracking, ranging, imaging and recognition, so as to realize the perception of the physical world. This kind of communication and perception are integrated into the design of a system: on the one hand, with the help of the communication system, the perception service can improve the accuracy and timeliness, combine multiple sensors to provide more comprehensive perception information, and also solve the problem of massive data transmission and realize the mutual perception between network nodes. On the other hand, with the help of the perception results, the transmission system parameters can be adjusted in real time, thus providing higher quality communication services. In addition, the integration of communication and perception can also make full use of wireless resources, reduce the size of equipment, and have the advantages of large bandwidth, no electromagnetic interference, high efficiency, and low cost of modification to the existing network architecture.

The perception function in the integration of communication and perception is realized by radar. Compared with traditional radars that emit microwaves or radio waves and receive reflected waves to detect the information of the DUT, lidar emits and receives pulsed laser signals. Mature miniaturized diode lasers and smaller geometrical transceiver antennas required for shorter operating wavelengths have led to a reduction in the size and production cost of lidar devices. Compared with traditional microwave radar, lidar based on higher frequency laser beams has faster measurement speed, higher resolution and stronger reliability. Therefore, in the integrated communication and perception technology, lidar is preferred to provide perception functions. The communication function in the integration of communication and perception is realized by wireless space communication. The current wireless communication system is mainly traditional microwave wireless communication and free-space laser communication. Free-space laser communication uses laser as the carrier and the atmosphere as the transmission channel for communication, and the bandwidth is tens of thousands of times that of traditional wireless communication using microwaves, and it is rich in resources, and there is no need to apply for frequency or pay frequency band usage fees in advance, which reduces the construction cost. Compared with traditional wireless communication technology, laser communication has the advantages of high speed, large capacity, high directionality and energy concentration, and its confidentiality is stronger, the transmission distance is longer, there is no electromagnetic interference, and the power consumption is lower. Therefore, free-space laser communication has more advantages in the integrated technology of communication and perception with space communication as the main application scenario.

The integrated technology of communication and perception with free-space laser communication and lidar as the core has been paid attention to by all walks of life in China. The U.S. Department of Defense has established the "Terahertz and Perception Fusion Technology Research Center". European companies and universities have joined forces to form the Hexa-X project. China's Huawei and the China Mobile Research Institute also initiated meetings and discussions. In addition, 3GPP and IEEE have also established relevant standards.

This project plans to adopt an optical array-based lidar architecture to achieve the goal of communication and perception integration at the same time. The schematic diagram of the transmitter and receiver board used to realize laser communication and sensing is shown in the Fig. 1. The realization of the ISAC is mainly due to the transmission of pulse signals with integrated ranging and communication, which is based on the modulation mode of DPIM, which can use the frequency domain analysis algorithm of echo signals based on short-time Fourier transform (STFT) to achieve high ranging accuracy when transmitting communication signals with high efficiency.

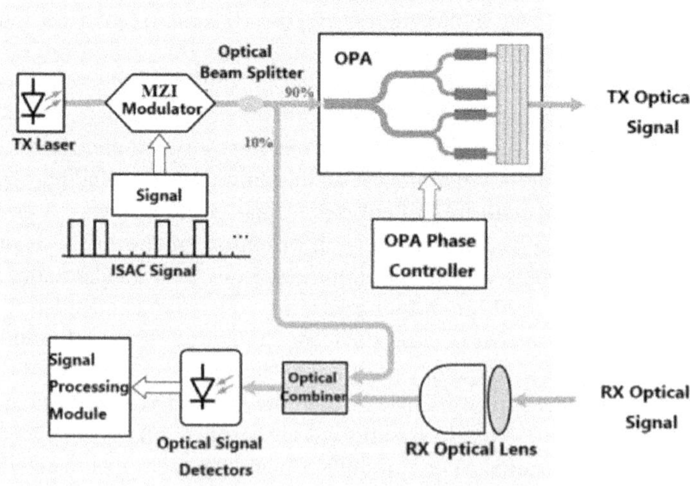

Fig. 1. The framework of ISAC

2 Research Status and Development Trends of ISAC

2.1 Research Status and Development Status of Laser Communication

In 1968, the National Aeronautics and Space Administration (NASA) built the first optical heterodyne communication system based on frequency modulation in the space flight center, and completed the laser communication experiment based on free space optical transmission for the first time. In 1970, Japan's NEC established the world's first commercial wireless laser link, thus starting the research and application of free-space optical communication. Since then, countries such as the United States, the European Union, and Japan have begun to invest heavily in research related to laser communications, and have formulated a number of R&D plans for satellite communications and deep space communications as strategies. In 2000, JPL and NASA jointly completed the Optical Communication Demonstrator (OCD) program, which mainly used array detection and windowing technology to realize the communication between low-orbit satellites and the ground, with a rate of 500 Mbps and 2.5 Gbps. In 2008, the European Space Agency (ESA) cooperated with the United States to carry out the first inter-satellite communication experiment, realizing the inter-satellite coherent laser communication experiment based on the light capture method, with a transmission rate of 5.6 Gbps and a transmission distance of more than 3000 km. In the following years, ESA launched a series of satellites to test and debug the performance of the second-generation inter-satellite laser communication terminal. In 2013, the Massachusetts Institute of Technology (MIT) and NASA cooperated to carry out a lunar laser communication experiment, realizing the lightweight device communication between the moon and the earth, with downlink and uplink transmission rates of 622 Mbps and 20 Mbps respectively, using PPM signals as the modulation format, and the communication link length reached 400,000 km. In 2019, in order to develop a next-generation spacecraft data backhaul system for deep space missions, NASA Laboratories launched the enhanced laser communication research and development program, and first completed the test on the ground, with an estimated communication rate of 250 MHz and a total weight of less than 28 kg. The project is expected to be officially launched in 2023, and the actual communication distance will be greater than 630 million kilometers.

The research in the direction of laser communication in China started late, but it has developed rapidly. There have been many breakthroughs in key technologies such as the development of laser communication terminals. In 2011, the research team of Harbin Institute of Technology developed the first laser communication terminal in China, which was carried on a satellite and successfully realized an inter-satellite laser communication experiment with a rate of 504 Mbps. In 2013, Changchun University of Science and Technology successfully realized a laser communication experiment between two aircraft 144 km apart, and its transmission rate reached 2.5 Gbps. In 2020, the laser terminal developed by the China Academy of Space Technology completed the in-orbit experimental verification of China's first high-order high-speed laser communication system on the "Shijian-20" satellite, realizing 10 Gbps signal communication between the satellite and the ground, and its technical indicators have reached the international advanced level.

In recent years, the space light-based vehicle-mounted communication system has received extensive attention, and many related research works have been reported at home and abroad. Initially, the vehicle-mounted space optical communication system was mainly based on LED light sources. In 2012, R. Corsini et al. from Italy realized the spatial light information transmission between vehicles of 31 m based on LED, and used PIN photodetectors at the receiving end for detection, with a communication rate of 115.2 kbps and a bit error rate of less than 10e−4 [1]. In 2014, Isamu Takai from Japan realized spatial light workshop communication based on camera receivers, using LEDs as light sources, with a communication rate of up to 10 Mbps [2]. However, although the LED light source has the advantages of large divergence angle, long life and low cost, its transmission distance is relatively close, most of which is not more than 35 m. Compared with LED light sources, laser light sources can provide higher power efficiency and larger modulation bandwidth, which can provide longer transmission distances. In 2016, a research team from the United States proposed an integrated system of vehicle communication and ranging based on lidar, and the ranging and communication functions are time-sharing, but the efficiency of this scheme is low, and the signal transmission cannot be completed at the same time as the distance measurement [3]. In 2018, Zhang Yufei and others from the Shanghai Institute of Optics and Mechanics proposed an integrated communication and perception system, which realizes the communication and ranging functions at the same time by comparing the optical flight time of the transmission sequence and the echo sequence, and realizes the communication and ranging functions within the range of 3.7 km, with a communication rate of 10 kbps, a bit error rate of less than 10e−5, and a ranging accuracy of 1 m. With the continuous development of laser communication technology in on-board systems, it will gradually be popularized in application scenarios such as building smart cities.

2.2 Research Status and Development Trend of LiDAR

At present, lidar can be divided into two main categories according to its scanning method, one is mechanical lidar, and the other is solid-state lidar. Among them, mechanical lidar mainly uses mechanical structure for scanning control, and the rotation of the mirror is controlled by the motor to realize the scanning of the beam. However, the lidar structure of this structure is complex, the integration is low, and the scanning speed is slow, which is not conducive to further improvement of performance. Solid-state lidar overcomes these shortcomings. At present, there are three main types of solid-state lidar: Flash lidar, MEMS lidar and OPA lidar. Among them, OPA lidar has become the focus of domestic research due to its advantages of small size, fast scanning speed, reliable performance and low-cost manufacturing.

OPA LiDAR uses OPA scanning technology and uses OPA chips for beam pointing control. As the core device, the OPA chip determines the performance of LiDAR. The OPA chip is an optical phased array, each chip contains a number of transmitting units that can be phase controlled, and the phase of each output waveguide can be controlled individually, and the output combination of the whole beam is changed by adjusting the phase of each output wall, and the combination at the far end forms a beam with different deflection angles. In 1997, the University of California successfully prepared an array waveguide structure on a silicon wafer, which can control the beam direction by adjusting the wavelength of the light wave, and realized the basic function of the OPA chip. Later, in 2009, the University of Ghent in Belgium realized the first two-dimensional beam scanning of OPA chips. On this basis, the performance improvement of OPA chips is mainly studied at home and abroad. In 2013, the Massachusetts Institute of Technology (MIT) realized the integration of 4096 (64 × 64) grating transmitting antennas on an SOI chip, and the whole structure is divided into 8 × 8 combinations, using 1550 nm wavelength and using embedded phase control to adjust, so that the optical coherence between different modules can obtain the desired far-field radiation mode, and can be dynamically controlled. In 2015, the California Institute of Technology (Caltech) implemented a 4 × 4 phased array using a diode-based phase tuner using carrier injection. This electro-optic effect-based refractive index modulation effect is very fast compared to the thermo-optical effect, thus achieving a tuning bandwidth of 200 MHz and fast beam steering. In 2022, the University of Shanghai for Science and Technology conducted relevant research on the grating suppression of OPA lidar, and used non-equal-spacing optical phased array chips to achieve the best grating lobe suppression effect in the wavelength range of 1500–1600 nm.

The biggest advantage of OPA lidar is high integration, so how to further reduce the size of OPA chips, improve the overall integration, and give full play to the advantages of high integration is the top priority of OPA chip design, and reducing the chip size has also become a research hotspot in recent years. For the optimization of the spectroscopic structure, in 2020, the Polytechnic University of Valencia achieved a reduction in the size of the OPA chip with the same resolution and field of view. They replaced the traditional power division devices with a star-coupler that is traditionally an AWG component and an array waveguide as a beamsplitter, and a grating coupler as a beam emitter to achieve the OPA structure. The scheme takes advantage of the phase shift characteristics of different input ports of AWG, and uses multiple input ports to achieve a multiplication of resolution on a single AWG structure, and the magnification is the number of input ports. At the same size, the resolution and field of view are increased by a factor of eight, the field of view is 15° × 2.8°, the output beam width is 0.36° × 0.175°, and the input can be integrated with a 1 × 8 optical switch to further reduce the size of the device.

2.3 Research Status of Laser Ranging Based on OPA

The most widely used laser ranging scheme in the existing commercial LiDAR OPA is the pulsed direct detection ranging method based on time-of-flight (TOF), which has been developed very maturely. In addition, due to the defects of pulse ranging that are prone to interference and lack of accuracy, the continuous wave coherent detection and ranging method based on frequency modulated continuous wave (FWCW) is becoming more and more important.

The TOF-based laser ranging method uses a laser pulse with high peak power as the detection signal to obtain the distance information of the target by accurately measuring the flight time of the reflected light pulse. In the TOF measurement, a high-frequency counting clock is first used to fill in the real flight time interval and make a rough measurement of the TOF. Obviously, the accuracy of the rough measurement will improve as the frequency of the high-frequency counting clock increases. Due to the limitations of the development of electronic devices, the counting clock frequency is limited, so more refined time measurement methods are needed to measure the time residues that cannot be fully filled by the counter, and the TOF can be obtained by combining the two. TOF is relatively simple and straightforward, the measurement speed is fast, and the circuit structure used is simple. At the same time, for pulsed laser transmission, reception and signal processing, there are corresponding mature module components and special processing chips. However, the measurement ambiguity between the various pulses of the lidar is easy to cause, and this interference will produce ghosting in the signal processing process, resulting in the low accuracy of TOF-based laser ranging, usually cm-level accuracy. In summary, the TOF-based LiDAR ranging scheme is suitable for fast ranging scenarios with low requirements for accuracy under a large measurement range, and is very suitable for application in OPA LiDAR ranging system.

In 1991, Maatta et al. from the University of Oulu, Finland, used a laser diode as a light source to measure a target of 15–20 m, and obtained a millimeter-level ranging resolution by averaging the measurement results many times [4]. In 2005, Russia plans to mount an inter-satellite laser navigation communication system on the GLONASS-K satellite and conduct in-orbit tests. The GLONASS-K satellite has established the world's first inter-satellite laser link, and the pulsed laser system is used to achieve high-precision inter-satellite ranging, with a ranging accuracy of 10 cm [5]. Subsequently, in 2009, Jan et al. from the University of Oulu proposed a method to eliminate the measurement wandering error by using the pulse front moment discrimination to solve the problem of pulse laser echo moment identification, and the experiment achieved a ranging accuracy of ±5.5 mm in the measurement range of 10 m [6]. In 2013, the US LLCD system used a 5 GHz high-precision clock to sample the edge of the downlink laser pulse at the ground station, and the ranging accuracy of a single sampling was 6 cm, and the ranging accuracy was better than 1 cm through multiple measurements, which fully verified the potential of the laser link in high-precision ranging in deep space [7]. The laser ranging system of the relevant timing chip in China has also achieved good results, which can achieve the ranging accuracy of cm or even mm. In 2013, researchers from the Institute of Semiconductors of the Chinese Academy of Sciences used the TDC-GP1 timing chip of the German ACAM company to realize pulsed laser ranging in combination with DSP chip control. Experiments show that the measurement accuracy of the system for single pulse can be controlled within 100 ps, and the ranging error is only 0.01 m under the experimental condition of 25 °C. In 2016, Zhang Binbin and others from North University of China used two TDC-GP2 timing chips to verify the timing accuracy of 1ns and the timing resolution of 100ps under FPGA coordination. In 2018, Wang Jiajia of Shanghai Institute of Technology and Materials used the TDC-7201 timing chip to complete the pulsed laser ranging experiment, and achieved a time measurement accuracy of 4.1 ps in the time range of 12 ns–100 s (Fig. 2).

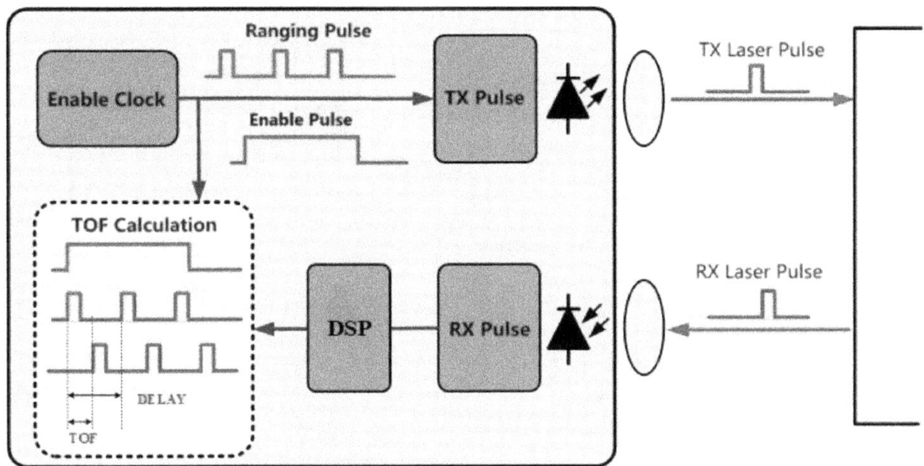

Fig. 2. The principle of TOF ranging

Laser ranging based on FMCW usually uses an electro-optical modulator to modulate the frequency of the emitted laser to generate a linear frequency modulation laser, and uses a beam combiner to coherent the echo beam and the emitted beam, and compares the instantaneous frequency difference between the reflected light signal and the local oscillator signal to obtain the target distance information, and can also detect the velocity information, which can achieve high-resolution and high-sensitivity detection. Compared with TOF, FWCM has strong anti-interference and high detection accuracy, which can reach mm-level accuracy. However, FMCW requires a large number of optical components, which requires high precision of optical components and complex optical systems, so the measurement speed is slow. In 1987, researchers in the Netherlands used the LFMCW radar for the first time in the field of air detection, and conducted preliminary research on its related theoretical problems [8]. In 2007, Kim Min Joon et al. from South Korea proposed a frequency correction algorithm for improving range resolution. The simulation results show that the distance resolution can reach 0.5 mm under the radar measurement range of 35 m. In 2021, Dong Yongkang et al. from Harbin Institute of Technology proposed and demonstrated an FWCM optical detection and ranging system. The system uses a combination of bilateral band modulation and injection locking to produce a triangular chirp light source. The fiber laser with MZM is used to modulate the fiber laser as the main laser to generate two first-order sidebands with a tuning range of 8~14 GHz, one of which is extracted and amplified by the distributed feedback laser. A carrier rejection ratio of up to 20 dB is achieved. The experimental results show that the spatial resolution of the lidar is 2.5 cm [9] (Fig. 3).

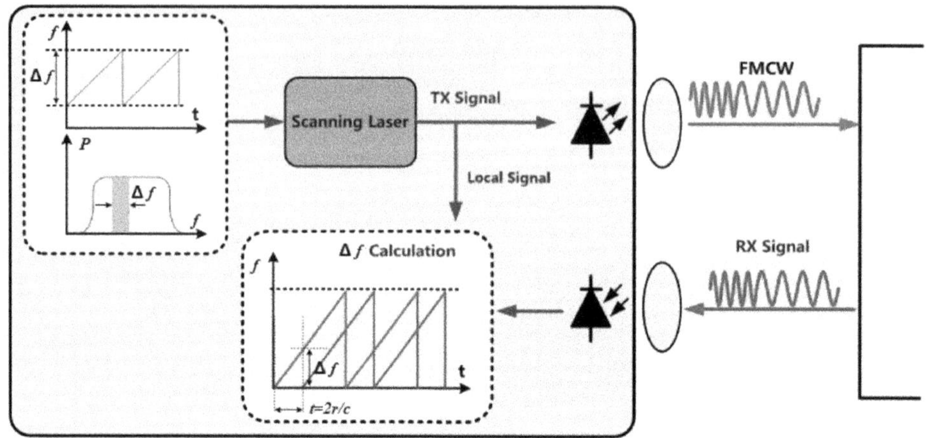

Fig. 3. The principle of FWCW ranging

2.4 Research Status and Development Trend of Laser Communication Channel Modeling

Free-space laser communication (FSO) uses a laser as the carrier and the atmosphere as the transmission channel. FSO technology has the advantages of wide frequency band, strong confidentiality and anti-electromagnetic interference, which has attracted extensive attention in wireless communication and has become the focus of attention in the construction of next-generation wireless mobile communications and smart cities. However, there are still a number of key challenges to the practical use of high-capacity FSO systems, one of which is the complexity of the atmospheric channel. The atmosphere is a mixture of large amounts of water vapor, a variety of gas molecules, and dust, with particles of various forms and compositions. Due to the existence of temperature differences, the atmosphere is in a state of motion for a long time, and its composition and density are constantly changing. The main effects of gas on laser are atmospheric absorption, atmospheric scattering and atmospheric turbulence, which will lead to problems such as signal energy attenuation, power jitter, and change of propagation direction. In order to achieve high-speed FSO, it is necessary to model the space laser communication channel completely, accurately and effectively, and analyze its characteristic mechanism. This is the basis for evaluating the communication performance of the FSO and provides a reliable theoretical basis for the design of the actual system. In FSO channels, atmospheric turbulence is the main factor causing the deterioration of FSO communication performance.

Atmospheric turbulence is a key feature of FSO channels: unlike fiber-based systems, the received optical signal is subject to random power fluctuations, a phenomenon often referred to as optical scintillation. To accurately describe this effect, the researchers proposed and validated several statistical models, including the lognormal distribution, Gamma-Gamma distribution, K distribution, and Malaga (M) distribution.

In 1971, V. I. Tatarskii et al. proposed a Lognormal distribution model based on the Rytov approximation theory of atmospheric turbulence [10]. Subsequently, G. PARRY (1981) found that in the case of weak turbulence, the probability distribution function

(PDF) of the received light intensity normalized after the laser beam passes through the atmosphere usually conforms to the Lognormal distribution model [11]. This shows that the Lognormal distribution model is suitable for weak turbulence situations. In order to cope with the situation of strong turbulence, L. C. Andrews and R. L. Phillips et al. proposed an I-K distribution model based on the generalized K distribution in 1985, which can be consistent with the experimental results under a wide range of turbulence intensities [12]. In addition, E. Jakeman and P. Jakeman and P. Jakeman Pusy also proposed a K-distribution model in 1978 to describe the fading of received light intensity under strong turbulence [13]. In 2001, M. A. Al-Habash et al. proposed a Gamma-Gamma distribution model based on the improved Rytov theory, which is directly derived from the physical characteristics of the atmospheric channel, which is suitable for strong turbulence and has become a commonly used light intensity probability density distribution model for FSO systems [14]. Since then, many scholars have further studied the characteristics of the Gamma-Gamma model. In 2014, Liu Min et al. from the Naval Institute of Aeronautical and Astronautical Engineering studied the influence of the waveform conditions and wavelength, transmission distance, aperture size, turbulence intensity, and internal and external dimensions of Gamma-Gamma beams on the characteristics of the Gamma-Gamma distribution model through simulation. In 2020, Minghua Cao et al. from Lanzhou University of Technology deduced the average bit error rate and average capacity expressions of the super-Nyqist FSO system under the Gamma-Gamma distribution model, and studied the effects of parameters such as turbulence intensity and transmission distance on the system performance. In 2021, DanChen et al. from Xi'an University of Technology proposed to use the Maximum Likelihood (ML) method to estimate the channel parameters of the Gamma-Gamma distribution model, and derived the ML estimation expression for calculating the unknown parameters based on Expected Maximization (EM), and experimentally proved that the method has good estimation performance for the fading parameters of the atmospheric turbulence channel [15]. The above discrete distribution models can effectively cope with each corresponding independent scenario, but there is still a lack of a unified distribution model. To this end, A. Jurado-Navas et al. (2011) proposed a generalized Malaga (M) distribution model, which unifies multiple classical models, such as Lognormal distribution, Gamma-Gamma distribution, K distribution and other models by adjusting the parameters of M distribution, and the distribution model is in good agreement with the experimental data in all turbulence cases [16–20].

It can be seen that researchers have proposed and validated many effective distribution models for atmospheric turbulence. Among them, the Lognormal distribution model and the Gamma-Gamma distribution model are the classical models in the case of weak turbulence and strong turbulence, respectively. Based on these two models, many researchers have conducted in-depth explorations to study the influence of channel parameters on FSO transmission performance. However, most of the current atmospheric turbulence models are still aimed at individual weak turbulence and strong turbulence cases, and there is still a lack of universal atmospheric turbulence models to cope with FSO transmission in complex atmospheric scenarios. At the same time, in the face of transmission signals with different modulation formats, it is necessary to further study the existing FSO channel models to explore the internal relationship between transmission performance and channels.

3 Conclusion

In summary, the integration of communication and perception is the only way to move towards 6G to realize the "intelligent connection of all things", which is widely used in machine learning, smart home, smart healthcare, Internet of Vehicles, public safety and other fields. Its core technologies, free-space laser communication and lidar sensors, are not only the theoretical support for the development of key industries in the future, but also the technical support for improving urban safety monitoring and building smart cities, and they also have high research value. In view of these two technologies, it is believed that the current technological breakthrough lies in increasing the communication rate of free-space laser communication to 1 Gb/s, so that the detection distance of the lidar sensor can reach more than 100 m, the horizontal detection range exceeds 200°, and the measurement accuracy can be improved to the order of cm.

Acknowledgments. The authors acknowledged the Hubei Engineering Research Center for Intelligent Detection and Identification of Complex Parts (Grant No. GCZX-XN-202408).

References

1. Corsini, R., et al.: Free space optical communication in the visible bandwidth for V2V safety critical protocols. In: 2012 8th International Wireless Communications and Mobile Computing Conference (IWCMC), Limassol, Cyprus, pp. 1097–1102 (2012)
2. Takai, I., Harada, T., Andoh, M., Yasutomi, K., Kagawa, K., Kawahito, S.: Optical vehicle-to-vehicle communication system using LED transmitter and camera receiver. IEEE Photon. J. **6**(5), 1–14 (2014)
3. Lipson, A., Scheim, K.J.: Lidar with optical communication: U.S. Patent 10,281,581. 2019-5-7
4. Määtta, K., Kostamovaara, J., Myllylä, R.: Profiling of hot surfaces by pulsed time-of-flight laser range finder techniques. Appl. Opt. **32**(27), 5334–5347 (1993)
5. Pasynkovvv, V., Sadovnikovma, M., Sumerinvv, V., et al.: The concept and preliminary results of use of satellite laser ranging for GLONASS accuracy improvement. In: The 18th International Workshop on Laser Ranging. Fujiyoshida,Japan ILRS (2013)
6. Nissinen, J., Nissinen, I., Kostamovaara, J.: Integrated receiver including both receiver channel and TDC for a pulsed time-of-flight laser rangefinder with cm-level accuracy. IEEE J. Solid-State Circuits **44**(5), 1486–1497 (2009)
7. Borosondm, R.: The lunar laser communication demonstration: NASA's first step toward very high data rate support of science and exploration missions. Space Sci. Rev. **185**, 115–128 (2014)
8. Lighthart, L.P., Nieuwkerk, L.R.: System aspects of a solid-state FM-CW weather surveillance radar. In: Conference Proceeding, IEEE International Radar Conference 87, London, UK, 19–21, vol. 10, pp. 112–115 (1987)
9. Dong, Y., Zhu, Z., Tian, X., et al.: Frequency-modulated continuous-wave LIDAR and 3D imaging by using linear frequency modulation based on injection locking. J. Lightwave Technol. **39**(8), 2275–2280 (2021)

10. Tatarskii, V.I.: The effects of the turbulent atmosphere on wave propagation. Jerusalem: Israel Program Sci. Transl. **1971** (1971)
11. Parry, G.: Measurement of atmospheric turbulence induced intensity fluctuations in a laser beam. Optica Acta: Int. J. Opt. **28**(5), 715–728 (1981)
12. Andrews, L.C., Phillips, R.L.: I-K distribution as a universal propagation model of laser beams in atmospheric turbulence. JOSA A **2**(2), 160–163 (1985)
13. Jakeman, E., Pusey, P.N.: Significance of K distributions in scattering experiments. Phys. Rev. Lett. **40**(9), 546 (1978)
14. Al-Habash, A., Andrews, L.C., Phillips, R.L.: Mathematical model for the irradiance probability density function of a laser beam propagating through turbulent media. Opt. Eng. **40**(8), 1554–1562 (2001)
15. Chen, D., Hui, J.: Parameter estimation of Gamma-Gamma fading channel in free space optical communication. Opt. Commun. **488**, 126830 (2021)
16. Jurado-Navas, A., Garrido-Balsells, J.M., Paris, J.F., et al.: A unifying statistical model for atmospheric optical scintillation. Numer. Simul. Phys. Eng. Process. **181**(8), 181–205 (2011)
17. Saber, M.J., Hasna, M.: Security analysis of integrated HAP-based FSO and UAV-enabled RF downlink communications. IEEE Open J. Commun. Soc. **5**, 5427–5435 (2024)
18. Ara, R., Lee, I.E., Ghassemlooy, Z., Chung, G.C.: Outage performance of free-space optical links over turbulence channels with pointing errors. In: 2024 14th International Symposium on Communication Systems, Networks and Digital Signal Processing (CSNDSP), pp.1–6 (2024)
19. Ishida, T., Naila, C.B., Okada, H., Katayama, M.: Performance analysis of IRS-assisted multi-link FSO system under pointing errors. IEEE Photon. J. **16**(4), 1–10 (2024)
20. Abou-Rjeily, C.: A distance-aware buffer-aided relaying protocol for cooperative FSO communications. IEEE Wirel. Commun. Lett. **13**(8), 2275–2279 (2024)

Research on Misshapen Mango Recognition Algorithm Based on Improved YOLOv7

Yuanqiao Bi, Qihui Xia, Jiahao Zhu, Peng Zhao, and Yuxi Yang[✉]

Jianghan University, Wuhan 430056, China
15337705177@163.com

Abstract. A misshapen mango recognition algorithm which is named YOLOv7-AIFI based on improved YOLOv7 (You Only Look Once version 7) is proposed to improve the recognition accuracy of misshapen mango. Firstly, the AIFI (Attention-based Intra-scale Feature Interaction) module is introduced into this algorithm to reduce computational redundancy on the basis of the YOLOv7 model. Secondly, three CBAM (Convolutional Block Attention Modules) are introduced to enhance the model's generalization capability. Finally, the MPD-IOU (Maximized Position-Dependent Intersection over Union) loss function is selected to optimize the calculation method and reduce the computational load. Experiments were conducted on the self-built mango data set to verify that the improvement of YOLOv7-AIFI can effectively improve the performance of the model and make it lightweight. Compared to YOLOv7, the accuracy of YOLOv7-AIFI identifying ripe mangoes and misshapen mangoes is improved by 5.9% and 0.17% respectively, the F1-Score is increased by 0.13%, the mean average precision (mAP) is increased by 3.34%, and the model weight is reduced by 2.7MB. Moreover, the mAP and F1-Score of YOLOv7-AIFI surpass other commonly used models comprehensively. Experimental results demonstrate that the proposed YOLOv7-AIFI model can effectively improve the accuracy and efficiency of misshapen mango recognition, providing a new idea for the recognition of misshapen mango.

Keywords: Misshapen mango recognition · Yolov7 · Feature interaction · Attention mechanism

1 Introduction

Mango, as a popular tropical fruit, is loved by people all over the world, with its production and trade volume increasing annually. However, mangoes are susceptible to natural pests, diseases, and environmental factors during their growth,

Supported in part by the 2022 Ministry of Education Industry-Academia Collaboration Coordinated Education Project under Grant 220901576203216; in part by the 2023 National College Student Innovation and Entrepreneurship Training Program under Grant 202311072013; in part by the 2023 Provincial College Student Innovation and Entrepreneurship Project under Grant S202311072038.

resulting in misshapen fruits. Misshapen mangoes cannot be sold normally and compete for the nutrients required by normal mangoes. Therefore, it is of great significance to accurately recognize misshapen mangoes for improving mango quality and reducing economic losses for farmers.

Robot picking mangoes based on Internet of Things (IOT) technology is the development trend in the future, the key of which is the recognition of misshapen mangoes. Currently, research on the recognition of misshapen mangoes mainly focuses on the fields of image processing [1] and machine learning. Zhou Shuo et al. [2] achieved good results by extracting two-dimensional image information and three-dimensional point cloud information on the surface of mango for detection. Zhang Dejun et al. [3] used deep transfer learning models to train and test mango image data, improving the recognition accuracy. Zhang Lihua et al. [4] studied various low-level processing methods such as determining image processing windows, noise removal, image segmentation, and image enhancement to meet the requirements for further improving the detection and classification of mango surface defects.

In recent years, deep learning technology has developed rapidly, and an increasing number of researchers are applying deep learning in agriculture. Ahmed F et al. [5] and Li Chao et al. [6] successfully used the YOLOv7 model in agriculture. Yu Chuntao et al. [7] improved the accuracy of the model for soybean hypocotyls by adding CARAFE [8] feature upsampling operators, SE attention mechanism modules, and WIOU position loss functions based on YOLOv7. Zhang Wanzhi et al. [9] increased the accuracy of the improved model by 4.2% by adding CT self-attention mechanism on the basis of YOLOv7, incorporating InceptionNeXt modules, and changing the bounding box loss function to NWD. Tang Zhezheng et al. [10] enhanced the feature learning capability of the model by adding the SiLU function to the original model, introducing the C3 module at the small target layer, and increasing the recognition speed of the original model by 26.3%. Hua Chunjian et al. [11] improved the mAP of the network by 1.2% by adding the coordinate attention mechanism CA to the original model and changing the loss function to Focal-EIOU Loss. Wang Yu et al. [12] achieved good results by inserting a parameter-free attention mechanism into the YOLOv7 model to distinguish between normal and abnormal growth of bell pepper fruits.

However, there are still some challenges in applying the YOLOv7 model network to the recognition of misshapen mangoes. Firstly, misshapen mangoes exhibit various forms in mango images, with diverse shapes, colors, sizes, and varieties, which makes it difficult to recognize misshapen mangoes. Secondly, the growth environment of misshapen mangoes is complex, making them not easily recognizable. Existing studies generally optimize the model by adding or reducing the model network. However, excessive simplification of the model network leads to a decrease in accuracy or an increase in excessive network structures. While improving accuracy, it significantly increases the computational complexity and model size, failing to lightweight the model.

To address the above issues, an improved method is proposed to simplify the model while ensuring recognition accuracy. Firstly, an AIFI module is added on the basis of the original YOLOv7 model to reduce computational complexity. Secondly, three CBAM attention mechanism modules are added to the head of the YOLOv7 model to enhance feature point extraction capability, ensuring recognition accuracy while lightweighting the model. Finally, the original CIOU loss function is replaced with the MPD-IOU loss function, which has a smaller computational overhead, to reduce the computational complexity of the model.

2   Data Set Creation

2.1   Data Acquisition

The experimental data were captured at the Yongxiang mango plantation. The mangoes captured were of the Huangyan variety, and the shooting took place from 9:00 a.m. to 5:00 p.m. The OPPO K10 smartphone was used as the shooting device, with the rear camera (64-megapixel resolution) utilized. The shooting distance for mangoes ranged from 40 to 60 cm. To enhance the diversity of images, mango pictures in four different states such as ripe mango, mango at veraison stage, unripe mango, and misshapen mango, were captured as shown in Fig. 1(a)–(d), totaling 1208 images. The types and number of images are shown in Table 1.

<table>
<tr><td>(a) ripe mango</td><td>(b) turning-stage mango</td></tr>
<tr><td>(c) unripe mango</td><td>(c) deformed mango</td></tr>
</table>

Fig. 1. Different mango images captured under various conditions.

2.2   Building the Dataset

In order to construct the data set, the collected images were annotated using the LabelImg tool. Ripe mangoes and mango at veraison stage, with yellow

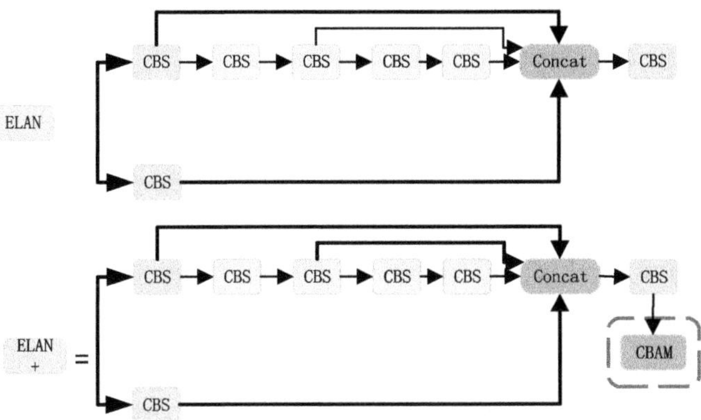

Fig. 4. ELAN module and ELAN+ module.

3.3   AIFI Module

The AIFI [15] module aims to enhance the intra-scale and inter-scale feature interaction capabilities in object detection models. Traditional object detection models require attention computation when processing features at multiple scales, which consumes considerable computational resources. However, AIFI introduces a mechanism for intra-scale feature interaction, which enhances interaction between features at different scales without introducing additional computations. This improves the model's performance, reduces computational complexity, and achieves the goal of lightweighting the model. By replacing the SPPCSPC module in the YOLOv7 model with the AIFI module, the model's intra-scale and inter-scale feature interaction capabilities are strengthened, while addressing issues such as high computational cost associated with attention computation across multiple scales. This replacement can contribute to model lightweighting.

3.4   Replacing CIOU with the MP-DIOU Function

MP-DIOU [16] is an improved IOU loss function designed to enhance the generalization ability of object detection models. Compared to CIOU, MP-DIOU has a simpler computation process. Additionally, due to the incorporation of scale-awareness and dense sampling concepts, MP-DIOU can better capture the similarity between bounding boxes and ground truth boxes, thereby improving model accuracy. By replacing the original CIOU with MP-DIOU, precision can be maintained while reducing computational complexity. The formula for computing the MP-DIOU loss function is shown as

$$Loss_{MPDIOU} = 1 - MPDIOU$$

$$MPDIOU = IOU - \frac{d_1^2}{w^2 + h^2} - \frac{d_2^2}{w^2 + h^2} \tag{1}$$

Meanwhile, d_1^2 and d_2^2 represent the Euclidean distances between two bounding boxes, and their calculation formula is shown as

$$d_1^2 = (x_1^{prd} - x_1^{gt})^2 + (y_1^{prd} - y_1^{gt})^2$$
$$d_2^2 = (x_2^{prd} - x_2^{gt})^2 + (y_2^{prd} - y_2^{gt})^2$$

(2)

The structure diagrams of the CIOU loss function and the MPD-IOU loss function are shown in Fig. 5. Compared to the traditional CIOU loss function, the MPD-IOU loss function exhibits better convergence speed and stability, making it more adept at handling complex and irregular segmentation tasks. Additionally, it effectively addresses the issue of significant discrepancies between model predictions and target segmentation, thereby enhancing the model's predictive accuracy and robustness.

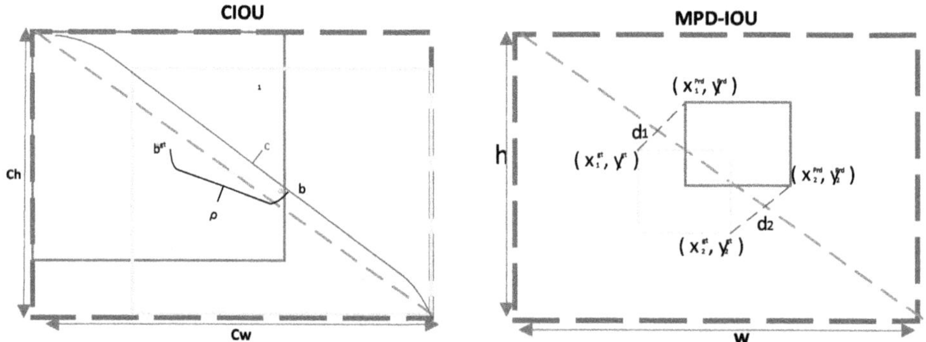

Fig. 5. The computational structure diagrams for CIOU and MPD-IOU.

4   Model Training

4.1   Evaluation Criteria

A confusion matrix is proposed based on the model's classification results, as shown in Table 2. Meanwhile, TP represents the number of normal mature mangoes and mangoes in the color-changing stage that are recognized as 'Normal', FP represents the number of unripe mangoes and misshapen mangoes incorrectly identified as 'Deformed', FN represents the number of ripe mangoes and mangoes in the color-changing stage incorrectly identified as 'Deformed' or 'Immature', and TN represents the number of unripe mangoes and misshapen mangoes correctly identified as 'Immature' and 'Deformed'.

Based on the confusion matrix, the model's performance is evaluated using evaluation metrics such as Precision, Recall, F1-Score, mAP, weights, and recognition speed. Precision, abbreviated as P, is calculated as shown in (3); Recall,

Table 2. Confusion matrix.

Predicted	Actual	
	Positive	Negative
Positive	True Positive (TP)	False Positive (FP)
Negative	False Negative (FN)	True Negative (TN)

abbreviated as R, is calculated as shown in (4); F1-Score is calculated as shown in (5); and mAP is calculated as shown in (6). Weights represent the model size, measured in MB, and recognition speed is the time required to recognize one image.

$$P = \frac{TP}{TP + FP} \times 100\% \tag{3}$$

$$R = \frac{TP}{TP + FN} \times 100\% \tag{4}$$

$$F1 - Score = 2 \times \frac{PR}{P + R} \times 100\% \tag{5}$$

$$mAP = \frac{1}{C} \sum_{i=1}^{C} \int_{0}^{1} P(R)d(R) \tag{6}$$

4.2 Experimental Environment and Training Parameters

The experimental operating system uniformly used Windows 11. The computer's CPU is 12th Gen Intel(R) Core(TM) i5-1240P 1.70 GHz, with 16 CB of RAM, and an Intel(R) Iris(R) Xe Graphics card with 8GB of VRAM. The programming platform used was PyCharm, and the programming language was Python 3.7. The PyTorch version is 2.0.0. The input image size for model training was set to 640×640. Based on hardware limitations and multiple experimental experiences, the batch size was set to 4, and the number of epochs was set to 300.

5 Experiments and Results

5.1 Training Loss Comparison

The training loss curves of the YOLOv7 model and the YOLOv7-AIFI model are compared in this paper, with the results shown in Fig. 6. According to Fig. 6, it can be observed that the loss value of the YOLOv7-AIFI model decreases rapidly within the first 20 epochs, indicating strong learning capability and rapid model fitting. Subsequently, from the 50th epoch to the 300th epoch, the loss value of the YOLOv7-AIFI model decreases slowly, stabilizing around 0.030. Compared with the YOLOv7 model, the improved YOLOv7-AIFI model converges faster, with smaller and more stable fluctuations, resulting in a smaller loss value.

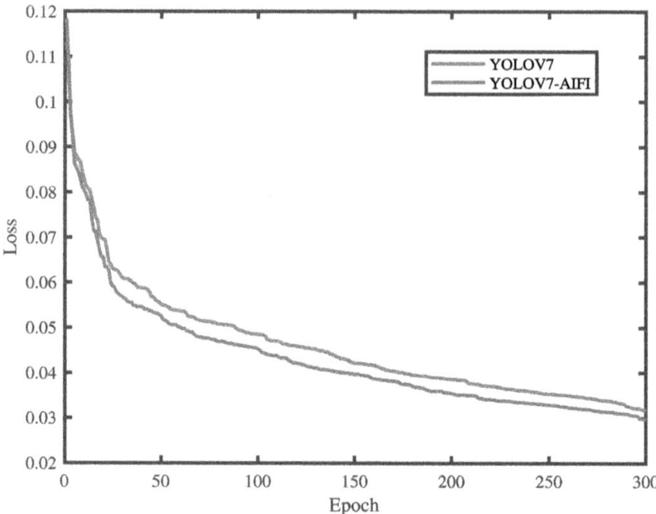

Fig. 6. Training loss curves before and after model improvement.

5.2   Comparative Experiment

The performance comparison between the YOLOv7 model and the improved YOLOv7-AIFI model is shown in Table 3 and Table 4. From Table 3 and Table 4, compared with YOLOv7, the accuracy of the improved YOLOv7-AIFI model for mature mangoes and malformed fruits has increased by 5.9% and 0.17% respectively, the F1-Score has increased by 0.13%, and the mAP has increased by 3.34%. Meanwhile, the model weight of YOLOv7-AIFI is reduced by 2.7MB, and the recognition speed is slightly reduced.

Table 3. Comparative experimental results.

Model	P%		R%		F1-Score	mAP(%)	Weights(MB)
	Normal	Deformed	Normal	Deformed			
YOLOv7	88.29	92.30	91.20	92.30	92.30	85.90	71.3
YOLOv7-AIFI	94.19	92.47	93.10	92.40	92.43	89.24	68.60

As shown in Fig. 7, 'Normal Precision', 'Deformed Precision', 'Normal Recall', 'Deformed Recall', and 'F1-Score' respectively represent the precision of normal mangoes, the precision of misshapen mangoes, the recall of normal mangoes, the recall of misshapen mangoes, and the F1-Score. Compared to the original YOLOv7 model, the improved YOLOv7-AIFI has improved performance. Meanwhile, the accuracy of the improved YOLOv7-AIFI model for mature mangoes and misshapen mangoes has increased by 5.9% and 0.17% respectively, and the F1-Score has increased by 0.13%, mAP increased by 3.34%.

Table 4. Experimental Results of Recognition Speed Comparison.

Model	Recognition Speed(FPS)
YOLOv7	59.8
YOLOv7-AIFI	60.2

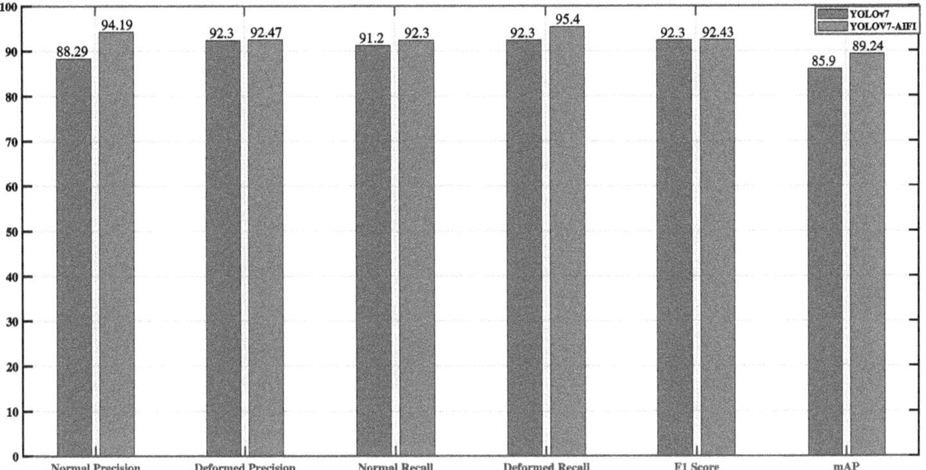

Fig. 7. Comparative experimental results.

5.3   Ablation Experiment

A series of ablation experiments were conducted to investigate the impact of each improvement on the original model's performance. Based on the YOLOv7 model, the MPD-IOU function, AIFI module, and CBAM module were sequentially introduced to assess their effects on model performance. Evaluation metrics consisted of mAP, accuracy, and model weight. The experimental results are presented in Table 5. According to Table 5, it is evident that the adoption of the MPD-IOU loss function leads to an increase in model accuracy, resulting in a 0.32% improvement in mAP. Furthermore, the inclusion of the CBAM attention mechanism module further enhances mAP by 3.53%. Finally, replacing the SPPCSPC module in the YOLOv7 model with the AIFI module reduces the model weight by 5.2MB while maintaining model accuracy.

It can be concluded that adding the MPD-IOU loss function, AIFI module and CBAM attention mechanism module to the YOLOv7 model can effectively improve the model recognition accuracy while reducing model weight.

5.4   Comparative Experiments with Other Algorithms

In order to validate the superior performance of the proposed YOLOv7-AIFI model, experiments were designed to compare YOLOv7-AIFI with the current

Table 5. Comparative experimental results.

Improved			mAP(%)	Weights(MB)
MPD-IOU	AIFI	CBAM		
			85.90	71.3
✓			86.22	71.3
	✓		81.51	68.0
		✓	89.30	71.8
✓	✓		85.72	68.0
✓		✓	89.75	73.80
	✓	✓	88.10	68.60
✓	✓	✓	89.24	68.60

mainstream object detection algorithms on the same platform, same devices, and the same dataset. The selected object detection models mainly include: Faster R-CNN, YOLOv5, YOLOv7-X, YOLOv7-Tiny, and YOLOv8m. This experiment compares the precision, recall, average precision (AP), F1-Score, mAP, and model weight of each model when recognizing the same targets. The experimental results are shown in Table 6.

Table 6. Comparative experiments of different models.

Model	P%		R%		F1-Score	mAP(%)	Weights(MB)
	Normal	Deformed	Normal	Deformed			
Faster R-CNN	68.00	61.34	79.57	87.95	72.27	79.00	118.20
YOLOv5	78.60	77.62	74.90	80.94	79.25	81.60	82.90
YOLOv7-Tiny	94.05	91.30	89.77	95.45	93.32	85.60	71.60
YOLOv7	88.29	92.30	91.20	92.30	92.30	85.90	71.30
YOLOv7-X	94.32	83.87	87.37	93.98	88.64	81.80	71.40
YOLOv8-M	96.87	86.67	89.42	92.86	89.66	87.00	49.60
YOLOv7-AIFI	94.19	92.47	93.10	92.40	92.43	89.24	68.60

According to Table 6, the average precision (mAP) and F1-Score of the improved YOLOv7-AIFI model are higher than those of Faster R-CNN, YOLOv5, YOLOv7, and YOLOv7-X models, respectively 10.24%, 20.16%; 7.64%, 13.18%; 3.34%, 0.13%; 7.44%, 3.79%. The model weights of YOLOv7-AIFI are reduced by 49.6MB, 14.3MB, 2.7MB, and 2.8MB, respectively. Compared to YOLOv7-Tiny, the F1 score of YOLOv7-AIFI is slightly lower, but its weight and mAP are better. Although the weight file of YOLOv7-AIFI is larger than YOLOv8-M, the F1-Score and recognition rate for misshapen mangoes of

YOLOv7-AIFI are higher by 2.77% and 5.80%, respectively. Comparative experimental results indicate that the YOLOv7-AIFI model outperforms other models in recognizing misshapen mangoes.

6   Conclusion

An improved lightweight model based on YOLOv7 which is named YOLOv7-AIFI is proposed to more accurately identify misshapen mangoes. Compared to the traditional YOLOv7 model, YOLOv7-AIFI has the following advantages:

(1) By replacing the CIOU loss function with the faster and more accurate MPD-IOU loss function, the precision of the model is improved and the computational load is reduced. Additionally, three attention mechanism modules are introduced in the head to enhance the model's capability to extract target features. Compared to YOLOv7, the accuracy of YOLOv7-AIFI identifying ripe mangoes and misshapen mangoes is improved by 5.9% and 0.17% respectively, the F1-Score is increased by 0.13%, the mean average precision (mAP) is increased by 3.34%.
(2) The SPPCSPC module in the YOLOv7 was replaced with an AIFI module that has better performance and lower computational consumption. Compared with the original model, YOLOv7-AIFI has a model weight reduction of 2.7MB, successfully lightweighting the model while ensuring accuracy.

Compared to traditional models such as Faster R-CNN, YOLOv5, YOLOv7, and YOLOv7-X, the improved YOLOv7-AIFI model achieves a respective increase in precision for ripe mangoes of 7.74%, 5.14%, 0.84%, and 4.94%. Additionally, the mAP is increased by 20.16%, 13.18%, 0.13%, and 3.79%, respectively. Moreover, the weight of model is reduced while improving recognition accuracy.

Although the optimization of model weight and accuracy has been achieved, there is an increase in training time and recognition time. In the future, we will further reduce model weights and speed up model recognition.

References

1. Ni, Y., Yang, J., Wen, H.: Lightweight mango fruit surface defect detection based on machine vision. Food Mach. **39**(03), 91–95+240 (2023)
2. Zhou, S., Song, F., Li, Z.: Discrimination of mango pose and volume mass prediction based on 3D structured light. J. Electron. Measur. Instrum. **36**(2) (2022)
3. Dejun, Z., Xuecheng, Z., Xudong, Y.: Recognition of mango fruit diseases based on image processing and deep transfer learning. J. South China Agric. Univ. **42**(4), 113–124 (2021)
4. Zhang, L.: Research on Mango Surface Defect Detection Method Based on Computer Vision. Guangxi University (2006)
5. Ahmed, F., Ahad, M.T., Emon, Y.R.: Machine Learning-Based Tea Leaf Disease Detection: A Comprehensive Review. arXiv preprint arXiv:2311.03240 (2023)

6. Chao, L., Yueyue, N., Teng, H.: Research on target detection for mechanized harvesting of cantaloupes. Agric. Eng. **9**, 56–60 (2023)
7. Yu, C., Li, J., Shi, W.: Hybrid soybean seedling stage radicle color detection model based on improved YOLOv7. J. China Agric. Univ. **(29)** (2024)
8. Wang J., Chen K., Xu R.: Carafe: content-aware reassembly of features. In: Proceedings of the IEEE/CVF International Conference on Computer Vision, pp. 3007–3016 (2019)
9. Wanzhi, Z., Hongyi, Z., Shufeng, L.: Potato seed bud detection based on improved YOLOv7 model. Trans. Chin. Soc. Agric. Eng. **39**(20), 148–158 (2023)
10. Tang, Z., Wu, Y., Xu, X.: Research on mature strawberry recognition model based on improved YOLOv7-Tiny. Acta Agriculturae Universitis Jiangxiensis 1–17
11. Hua, C., Sun, M., Jiang, Y.: Surface defect detection of apples using improved YOLOv7-tiny with multispectral imaging. Laser Optoelectron. Prog. 1–15
12. Wang, Y., Yao, X., Li, B.: An algorithm for identifying deformed bell peppers based on improved YOLO v7-tiny. Trans. Chin. Soc. Agric. Mach. **54**(11), 236–246 (2023)
13. Wang, C.Y., Bochkovskiy, A., Liao, H.Y.M.: YOLOv7: trainable bag-of-freebies sets new state-of-the-art for real-time object detectors. In: Proceedings of the IEEE/CVF Conference on Computer Vision and Pattern Recognition, pp. 7464–7475 (2023)
14. Woo, S., Park, J., Lee, J.Y.: CBAM: convolutional block attention module. In: Proceedings of the European Conference on Computer Vision (ECCV), pp. 3–19 (2018)
15. Lv, W., Xu, S., Zhao, Y.: Detrs beat yolos on real-time object detection. arXiv preprint arXiv:2304.08069 (2023)
16. Siliang, M., Yong, X.: MPD-IOU: a loss for efficient and accurate bounding box regression. arXiv preprint arXiv:2307.07662 (2023)

Research on Underwater Diver Recognition Algorithm Based on Improved YOLOv9

Peng Zhao, Shuangsheng Liang, Mingcong Ge, Jiahao Zhu,
Qihui Xia, and Yuanqiao Bi(✉)

Jianghan University, Wuhan 430056, China
13100709560@163.com

Abstract. In response to issues such as the low recognition accuracy of small objects and low-resolution images in traditional diver machine recognition algorithms, a underwater diver recognition algorithm which is named IM-YOLOv9 based on improved YOLOv9 (You Only Look Once version 9) is proposed to enhance the precision and reliability of diver recognition for applications in marine resource development. The algorithm introduces SPD-Conv (Spatial Depth Conversion Convolution) for image processing, incorporates the SENetV2 (Squeeze and Excitation Networks Version 2) module, adds the MPDIoU (Multi-Path Distance Intersection over Union) loss function, and includes the SCINet (Self-Calibrating Illumination Network) module. These modifications aim to improve recognition accuracy without affecting the model's operating speed. Results indicate that the improved IM-YOLOv9 model outperforms the original YOLOv9 model, with a 3.88% increase in precision, a 4.35% increase in recall, a 2.56% improvement in the F1 score, and a 4.76% increase in mean average precision (mAP). These enhancements make the improved model better suited for underwater diver recognition.

Keywords: Underwater diver recognition · YOLOv9 · Spatial depth conversion convolution · Self-calibrating illumination network

1 Introduction

The global diving industry is growing rapidly with the popularity of adventure sports, driven by tourism and infrastructure investments, as well as advances in e-commerce and technology. In particular, North America, Europe, and Asia Pacific are witnessing significant market growth, with technological advancements such as innovations in diving computers and eco-friendly equipment further enhancing the diving experience. At the same time, the concern of sustainable development and marine protection and exploitation of marine resources

Supported in part by the 2023 National College Student Innovation and Entrepreneurship Training Program under Grant 202311072013; in part by the 2023 Provincial College Student Innovation and Entrepreneurship Project under Grant S202311072038.

R. C. Qiu et al. (Eds.): IoTaaS 2024, LNICST 675, pp. 91–103, 2026.
https://doi.org/10.1007/978-3-032-14681-6_8

has also attracted more diving activities. The global diving equipment market is expected to continue to grow between 2023 and 2028 with an average annual growth rate of 4.53%, showing a good development trend.

Although the diving industry is well developed, the complexity of the marine environment has brought some safety hazards in diving activities, such as low visibility under water, strong currents, marine life and potentially dangerous substances, and limited perspective of divers, which threaten the safety of divers. When developing offshore fields, for example, divers are often required to handle leaking pipelines and touch the crude oil. Their hot suits and umbilical cords are often covered with crude oil containing dissolved H2S, leading to many H2S deaths among divers. Therefore, to ensure the safety of divers has become an important factor in the development of the diving industry.

Meanwhile, artificial intelligence (AI) technology and Internet of Things (IoT) technology are also rapidly developing and widely applied in the diving industry. For example, Yuval M. et al. [1] have developed an automated framework that combines remote sensing, computer vision, and deep learning, achieving efficient and accurate 3D measurement and semantic segmentation of marine benthic habitats through tag-enhanced technology. Nikolaev V. P. et al. [2] studied the nature of decompression sickness; the biophysical basis of the simulation process triggered its initiation, including easily computable main parameters, and compared the effectiveness of different decompression and recompression modes under certain initial conditions. Houston A. I. [3] characterizes the proximity to the aerobic diving limit (ADL) by the fraction of the maximum stored oxygen used during diving. Among these, machine recognition is particularly important for the diving industry, as it can identify divers in complex marine environments and ensure their safety. However, diver machine recognition still faces some challenges, such as poor performance in detecting small objects and sensitivity to low contrast and noise, which affects the development of the diving industry. By improving the accuracy of diver machine recognition, the safety of divers can be effectively guaranteed, thereby promoting the rapid development of the diving industry. Therefore, researching diver machine recognition has significant practical significance.

In recent years, there has been a significant focus on research into underwater identification algorithms to ensure the safety of divers. Traditional edge detection and hand-crafted feature-based machine learning methods have gradually been replaced by deep learning models, particularly convolutional neural networks (CNNs), which have significantly improved underwater object recognition performance. The YOLO series models, with their efficiency in single-stage detection, have been widely applied in underwater scenarios. Notably, in the iterations from YOLOv3 to YOLOv9, multi-scale feature extraction and real-time performance have been continuously optimized.

Currently, the main method used in diver detection by machine learning is the YOLOv8 and YOLOv9 object detection algorithm. The YOLOv8 algorithm has the advantages of high efficiency, one-stage detection, end-to-end training, high accuracy, multi-scale detection, strong generalization ability, and flexibility, which makes it widely used in fields such as autonomous driving, security monitoring, and drone vision. However, it also faces problems such as lighting changes, object occlusion, scale changes, class imbalance, real-time requirements, insufficient generalization ability, high density scenarios, and noise interference in actual applications. YOLOv9 optimizes YOLOv8 and has higher accuracy, enhanced multi-scale feature extraction, higher efficiency, improved generalization ability, and stronger robustness, making it more suitable for deployment on various hardware platforms. However, the disadvantages of increased model complexity, higher demand for high-quality data, higher computational resource requirements, increased difficulty in tuning, and the possibility of introducing new problems also arise. Therefore, it is imperative to propose an improved YOLOv9 diver detection algorithm.

Focusing on some common problems of the current main object detection algorithms for diver machine recognition, such as poor detection performance of small objects, sensitivity to low contrast and noise, this study proposes an underwater diver detection algorithm based on improved YOLOv9. SCINet is added to preprocess the image to enhance the discrimination of low light environment, so as to improve the detection accuracy. The SPD-Conv spatial depth conversion convolution is added to the network to replace the original Conv convolution, and the upsampling times of the network in the model are increased to improve the ability of the model to detect smaller diver targets. SENetV2 were added to improve model training efficiency, enhance feature extraction ability, and integrate into the existing network architecture. The improved YOLOv9 has higher accuracy and recall rate, and has excellent effect on underwater diver detection.

2 Improved Algorithm

YOLOv9 is the latest version of the YOLO family of object detection models, inherits and improves on the advantages of previous generations, aiming to provide higher detection accuracy and speed. YOLOv9 introduces a new feature extraction module and a deeper network layer, which can better capture the details of the target, and by optimizing the multi-scale detection mechanism, it is more accurate in detecting objects of different sizes. The application of advanced data augmentation techniques also improves the generalization ability and adaptability of the model to various scenarios.

However, YOLOv9 also has some shortcomings. Compared with some lightweight models, it still requires high computational resources, especially in the training phase, which may limit its application on devices with very limited resources. In addition, the training process is more complex than that of earlier versions, requiring more tuning parameters and larger datasets to achieve the best results. Despite the improvement in detecting small objects, its performance may still be inferior to some models that specialize in small object detection. In order to fully exploit the advantages of YOLOv9, a large amount of high-quality labeled data is usually required, which may affect the model performance for application scenarios without large-scale datasets.

In order to timely and accurately identify divers underwater low illumination and improve the detection performance of the network, this paper improves the YOLOv9 model and adds SCINet to preprocess the image. The SPD-Conv spatial depth convolution was used to replace the original Conv convolution. SENetV2 were added to improve the model training efficiency and enhance the feature extraction ability. The improved structure of IM-YOLOv9 is shown in Fig. 1.

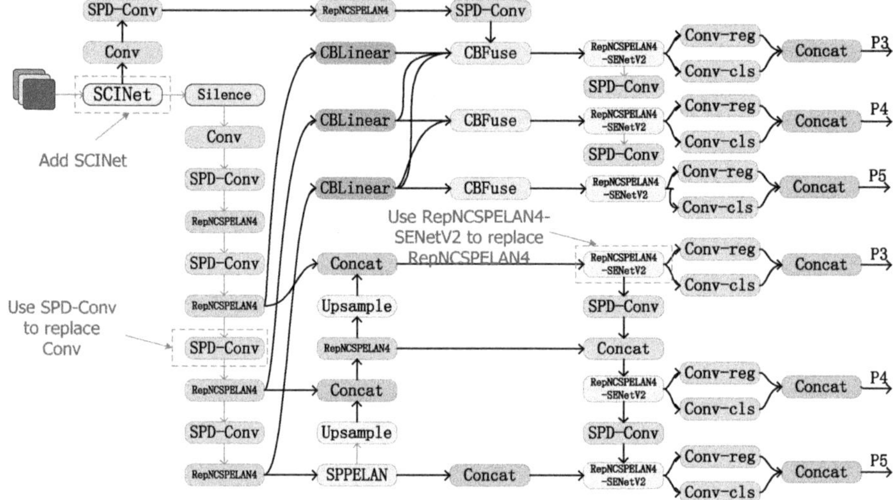

Fig. 1. The improved architecture diagram of YOLOv9.

By implementing these enhancements, the improved YOLOv9 model aims to overcome the challenges posed by underwater low-light conditions and achieve more accurate and timely diver detection.

2.1 SPD-Conv Spatial Depth-Transforming Convolution

SPD-Conv [4] is an innovative spatial encoding technique that improves the performance of deep learning models by processing image data more efficiently. As a technology that can convert image spatial information into depth information, SPD-Conv was used to replace the original Conv of the model, so that the Convolutional Neural Network (CNN) could learn image features more effectively.

SPD-Conv (Space to Depth Convolutional) improves the performance of traditional convolutional neural networks (CNN) in dealing with small objects and low-resolution images. SPD-Conv consists of two key components: the SPD layer and the non-stride convolutional layer. First, the SPD layer converts the spatial dimensions of the feature map into depth dimensions, thereby retaining more information. Second, the non-stride convolutional layer with a stride of 1 reduces the number of channels while keeping the spatial dimensions unchanged. SPD-Conv replaces the traditional step-size convolution and pooling layers to avoid information loss, thereby improving the effect of the feature extraction stage and enhancing the recognition ability of complex tasks and small objects. The principle of SPD-Conv is shown in Fig. 2.

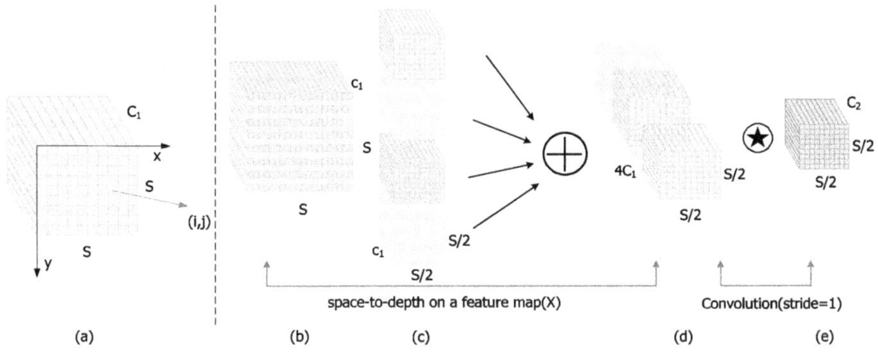

Fig. 2. The schematic diagram of SPD-Conv.

The working steps of SPD-Conv are as follows:

Step 1. Feature Map (a): Traditional feature map with channel number C1, height, and width.

Step 2. Spatial-to-Depth Transformation (b): By spatial-to-depth operation, spatial blocks of pixels are rearranged into depth/channel dimension, increasing the channel number to 4C1, while reducing spatial dimension by half.

Step 3. Channel Concatenation (c): Different channel groups are concatenated along the channel dimension.

Step 4. Addition Operation (d): The merged feature map undergoes addition operation with other processed feature maps.

Step 5. Non-Stride Convolution (e): Convolution with stride 1 is applied to the resulting feature map, reducing the channel dimension to C2 while maintaining spatial resolution, which remains half of the original size.

In this study, when SPD-Conv is applied to YOLOv9 model, part of the traditional step convolutional layers and pooling layers are replaced by SPD layers to retain more information and improve the processing ability of small objects and low-resolution images [5]. At the same time, a non-step convolutional layer with step size 1 is used to keep the spatial dimension of the feature map unchanged, optimize the number of channels, and finally ensure the overall performance improvement by fine-tuning the model [6].

2.2 Squeeze and Excitation Unit SENetV2

SENetV2 is an improved network architecture that improves the training performance of RepNCSPELAN4 by introducing global channel relationships and a new SaE module, which upgrades it to RepnCSpelan4-SENetV2. SENetV2 is similar to channel-type attention mechanism but improves on a global scale. By adding squeeze and excitation operations to traditional convolutional networks, SENetV2 shows significant classification accuracy gains in object detection tasks with only a slight increase in model parameters [7]. The comparative diagram of network modules ResNeXt, SENet, and SENetV2 is as shown in Fig. 3.

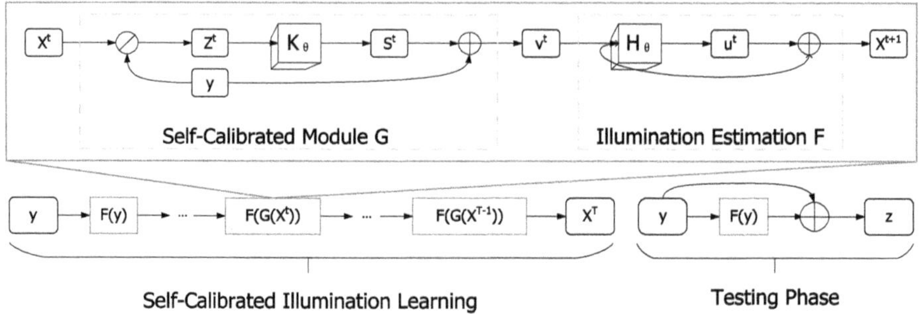

Fig. 3. The comparative diagram of network modules ResNeXt, SENet, and SENetV2.

(a) ResNeXt module: a multi-branch CNN structure is used, and the feature maps of each branch are merged after convolution operation and subjected to additional convolution processing.
(b) SENet module: After standard convolution operation, the features are compressed using global average pooling, then the channel weights are calculated by two 1x1 size fully connected layers and Sigmoid activation function, and finally the convolutional features are scaled.
(c) SENetV2 module: It combines the characteristics of ResNeXt and SENet, and uses a multi-branch fully connected layer to perform compression and excitation operations, and finally performs feature scaling. The design of SENetV2 aims to further improve the fineness of feature representation and the ability to integrate global information through the multi-branch structure [8]. The internal principle is shown in Fig. 4.

In this study, when SENetV2 is applied to YOLOv9, by integrating SENetV2 module in the feature extraction part, adjusting the channel weight allocation of the convolutional layer, and fine-tuning the model training, the channel relationship modeling ability is effectively enhanced, and the classification accuracy and overall detection performance are improved [9].

2.3   MPDIoU Boundary Loss Function

Bounding Box Regression (BBR) is crucial to the accurate positioning and recognition of the model, which is the key to achieving efficient and accurate object

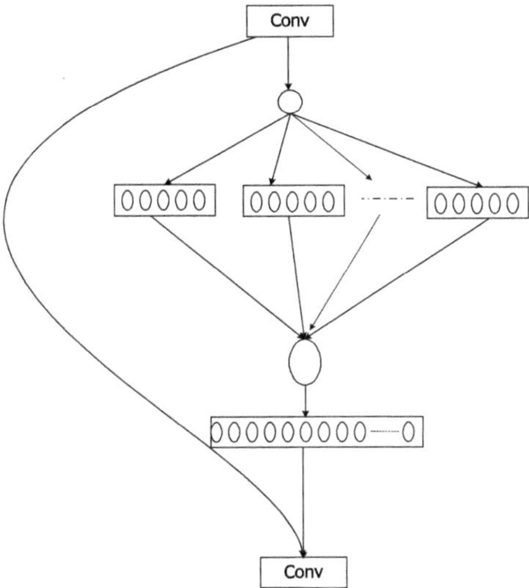

Fig. 4. The internal workings of SENetV2.

detection. At present, most BBR loss functions are divided into N-norm based loss functions and Intersection over Union (IoU) based loss functions [10]. The traditional BBR loss function does not perform well when the predicted box and the actual labeled box have the same aspect ratio [11]. The MPDIoU loss function improves the efficiency and accuracy of regression by minimizing the distance between the top-left and bottom-right corners of the predicted box and the true box, especially when distinguishing bounding boxes with the same aspect ratio but different sizes or positions. MPDIoU provides a more accurate loss measure. The MPDIoU calculation formula is shown in (1)

$$MPDIoU = 1 - IoU + \frac{c^2}{d^2} \tag{1}$$

where IoU is the ratio of the intersection of two bounding boxes to the Union [12]; d is the Euclidean distance between the centers of the two bounding boxes; c is the average of the diagonal lengths of the two bounding boxes. The closer MPDIoU are to 1, the more similar the two bounding boxes are; the closer MPDIoU are to 0, the more different the two bounding boxes are. The MPDIoU bounding box similarity measure method is shown in Fig. 5.

2.4   Improving Low-Light Object Detection with Enhanced Image Enhancement Network SCINet

In the underwater low-light environment, adding SCINet to preprocess the images can effectively improve the accuracy of diver detection. SCINet is a framework specifically designed for low-light image enhancement. It optimizes

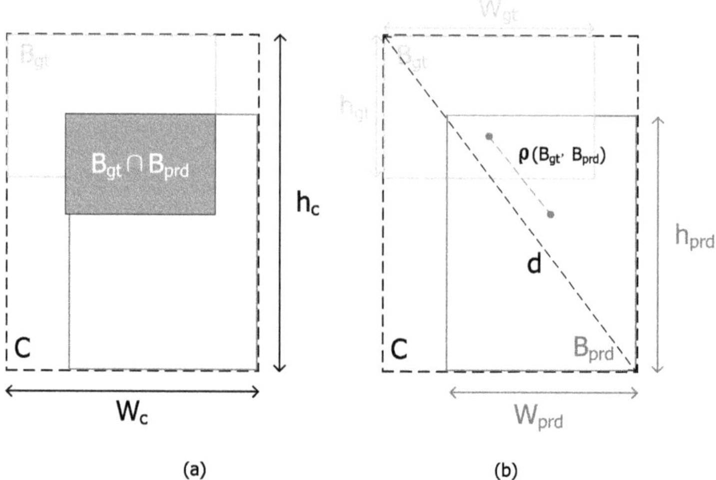

Fig. 5. The MPDIoU method for bounding box similarity measurement.

image quality through cascading illumination learning and weight sharing mechanism, and its self-correction module reduces the computational burden and improves the stability of results. SCINet also has adaptability to simple operational settings and universality to enhance existing lighting enhancement performance [13].

The core principles of SCINet include the following key aspects: First, it adopts cascading illumination learning with weight sharing to optimize lighting components for efficient model design by sharing weights at different stages and ensuring that only a single base block is used at each stage. Secondly, SCINet introduces an unsupervised training loss to limit the output of the self-calibration module at each stage, so that the model can better adapt to various scenarios and improve its generalization ability. Cascade illumination learning and weight sharing is one of the core features of SCINet, which mainly includes cascade process, weight sharing, self-calibration module, computational efficiency and performance improvement. The overall framework of SCINet is shown in Fig. 6, including the illumination estimation and self-correction modules.

In the training phase for the dataset, the output of the self-correcting module is added to the original low-light input as the input for the illumination estimation in the next stage. These two modules share parameters throughout training. In the testing phase, only a single illumination estimation module is used. This is closely related to the first and second points of the SCINet rationale, namely the cascading illumination learning process and weight sharing and the self-correcting module design to reduce the computational burden and improve the stability of the results [14]. In this study, when the low-light image enhancement network SCINet is applied to YOLOv9, SCINet is first integrated in the input pipeline of YOLOv9 to preprocess the low-light image. Secondly, the

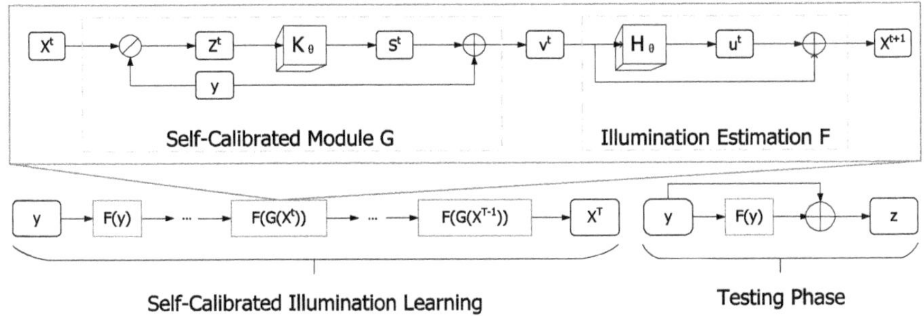

Fig. 6. Overall Framework Diagram of SCINet.

model is optimized through joint training to ensure that it performs well when processing images enhanced by SCINet. Finally, we evaluate the overall model performance and make necessary adjustments to ensure that the collaboration between SCINet and YOLOv9 achieves the best results [15].

In this study, the low-light image enhancement network SCINet is applied to YOLOv9. Firstly, SCINet is integrated into the input pipeline of YOLOv9 to preprocess low-light images. Secondly, the model is jointly trained to optimize its performance, ensuring good performance when handling images enhanced by SCINet. Lastly, the overall model performance is evaluated, and necessary adjustments are made to ensure optimal collaboration between SCINet and YOLOv9.

3 Model Training

3.1 Dataset Construction

The experimental data set in this paper is self-built, and the image data is obtained through a web crawler and labeled according to VOC format. The entire dataset contains 1242 photos. In the experiment, we divided the dataset into training set, validation set and test set according to the ratio of 6:2:2. Specifically, 744 images were randomly selected as the training set, 248 images were randomly selected as the validation set and 250 images were randomly selected as the test set. Figure 7 illustrates a sample of the underwater image dataset. In addition, the above image enhancement method is used to improve the quality of the original underwater data set, and experiments are carried out on the original and enhanced underwater image data sets to verify the effectiveness of the proposed method. Part of the dataset picture is shown in Fig. 7.

3.2 Experimental Setup and Evaluation Criteria

Windows11 operating system was used as the experimental operating system, the CPU of the computer was 12th Gen Intel(R) Core(TM) i5-1240P 1.70 GHz, and the running memory was 16 GB. The programming platform is PyCharm

Fig. 7. The images and annotations of diver underwater.

2021.2.4, the programming language is Python3.8, and the number of training and testing rounds is 300.

Model checking performance evaluation is a multi-dimensional process. In this paper, the performance and robustness of the model will be verified from three aspects of model accuracy, detection speed and model complexity through the model training underwater data set. On the underwater image dataset, the accuracy of the model's prediction is evaluated by a number of key metrics, It includes, Precision (P), Recall (R), Average Precision (AP), and Mean Average Precision (mAP). The formula for calculating Precision (P) is shown in (2), the formula for calculating Recall (R) is shown in (3), and the formula for calculating mAP is shown in (4), and the harmonic mean ($F1$) of precision and recall is shown in (5).

$$P = \frac{TP}{TP + FP} \times 100\% \tag{2}$$

$$R = \frac{TP}{TP + FN} \times 100\% \tag{3}$$

$$mAP = \frac{1}{C} \sum_{i=1}^{C} \int_{0}^{1} P(R)d(R) \tag{4}$$

$$F1 = \frac{2PR}{P + R} \tag{5}$$

where TP is the number of true examples, FP is the number of false positive examples and FN is the number of false negative examples.

3.3   Model Training and Comparison

In order to evaluate the performance of the improved YOLOv9 algorithm, we conduct a comparison experiment with the original YOLOv9 algorithm on the same experimental equipment and data set. The experimental results are shown in Table 1 below.

Table 1. Experimental results.

Models	P(%)	R(%)	F1(%)	mAP(%)
YOLOv9	79.80	92.00	78.00	79.90
IM-YOLOv9	82.90	96.00	80.00	83.70

Compared with YOLOv9, the improved IM-YOLOv9 algorithm has improved in accuracy, recall rate, F1 index and mean average precision. The accuracy is 82.90%, which is 3.88% higher than YOLOv9. The recall rate is 96.00%, which is 4.35% higher than that of YOLOv9. The F1 index (harmonic mean of precision and recall) is 80.00%, which is 2.56% higher than that of YOLOv9. mAP is 83.70, which is 4.76%higher than that of YOLOv9. The comparison of P, R, F1 and mAP is shown in Fig. 8.

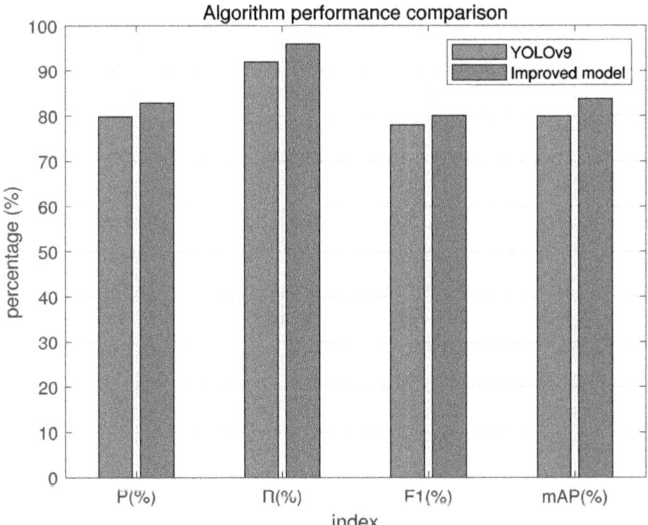

Fig. 8. Comparison of experimental results between YOLOv9 and the improved model.

Figure 9 shows the comparison of the loss function of the YOLOV9 algorithm and the improved algorithm on the training set. The loss function curve of the improved IM-YOLOv9 algorithm is smoother and more stable than that of the YOLOv9 algorithm, and the loss value is lower.

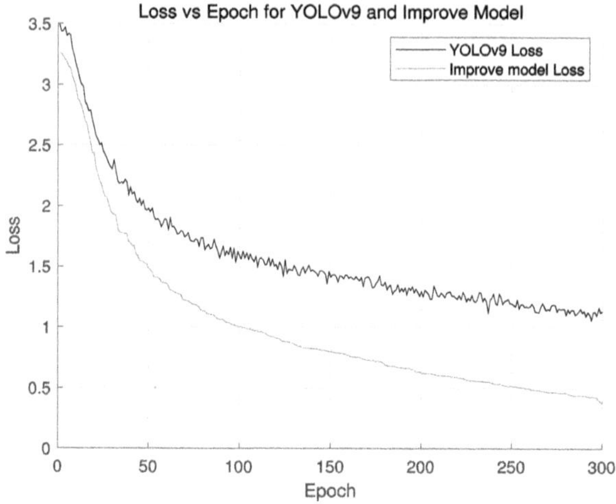

Fig. 9. Comparison of loss values between YOLOv9 and the improved model.

4   Conclusion

Aiming at the problem that the traditional diver machine recognition algorithm has poor recognition ability for small objects and low-resolution images, in order to improve the recognition accuracy and reliability and promote its application in the development of marine resources, this study proposes an underwater diver recognition algorithm based on improved YOLOv9. The SPD-Conv spatial depth conversion convolution is introduced to process images, the SENet V2 module is added, the MPDIoU loss function is introduced, and the SCINet is used to improve the image quality while maintaining the speed, flexibility and stability of the model. The improved IM-YOLOv9 has achieved significant performance improvement in underwater diver recognition tasks. The experimental results show that compared with the original YOLOv9 algorithm, The accuracy of the improved IM-YOLOv9 algorithm is increased by 3.88%, the recall rate is increased by 4.35%, the harmonic mean of accuracy and recall rate is increased by 2.56%, and the mean average precision is increased by 4.76%, which effectively improves the detection ability of underwater divers. This paper provides a new idea for improving YOLOv9.

Although the improved IM-YOLOv9 model has achieved significant advancements in recognition accuracy, its increased complexity also brings higher computational resource demands. This poses a challenge, especially in resource-constrained environments such as embedded systems or edge devices. Future research will focus on addressing these computational resource limitations by further optimizing the model's lightweight design, such as exploring more efficient network architectures and weight compression techniques to reduce computational overhead.

References

1. Yuval, M., Alonso, I., Eyal, G., et al.: Repeatable semantic reef-map** through photogrammetry and label-augmentation. Remote Sens. **13**(4), 659 (2021)
2. Liu, J., Zhao, G., Liu, S., et al.: New progress in intelligent picking: online detection of apple maturity and fruit diameter based on machine vision. Agronomy **14**(4), 721 (2024)
3. Nikolaev, V.P., Grigoriev, A.I.: Problems of prevention and treatment of decompression sickness in divers. Her. Russ. Acad. Sci. **85**(6), 504–509 (2015). https://doi.org/10.1134/S1019331615060040
4. Houston, A.I.: Optimal diving and oxygen use. Anim. Behav. **182**, 189–193 (2021)
5. Ali, E.S., Saeed, R.A., Eltahir, I.K., et al.: A systematic review on energy efficiency in the internet of underwater things (IoUT): recent approaches and research gaps. J. Netw. Comput. Appl. **213**, 103594 (2023)
6. Li, R., Zeng, X., Yang, S., et al.: ABYOLOv4: improved YOLOv4 human object detection based on enhanced multi-scale feature fusion. EURASIP J. Adv. Signal Process. **2024**(1), 6 (2024)
7. Sunkara R., Luo T.: No more strided convolutions or pooling: a new CNN building block for low-resolution images and small objects. In: Joint European Conference on Machine Learning and Knowledge Discovery in Databases, pp. 443–459. Springer, Cham (2022)
8. Narayanan M.: SENetV2: aggregated dense layer for channelwise and global representations. arxiv preprint arxiv:2311.10807 (2023)
9. Zhao, P., Li, Z., You, Z., et al.: SE-U-lite: milling tool wear segmentation based on lightweight U-Net model with squeeze-and-excitation module. IEEE Trans. Instrum. Measur. (2024)
10. Zhang, L., Zhang, X., Liu, M.: Lightweight convolutional neural network for fast visual perception of storage location status in stereo warehouse. J. Intell. Manufact. 1–21 (2024)
11. Panuntun, I.A., Jamaluddin, I., Chen, Y.N., et al.: LinkNet-spectral-spatial-temporal transformer based on few-shot learning for mangrove loss detection with small dataset. Remote Sens. **16**(6), 1078 (2024)
12. Gao, X., Zhao, K., Han, L., et al.: BézierCE: low-light image enhancement via zero-reference Bézier curve estimation. Sensors **23**(23), 9593 (2023)
13. Ma, L., Ma, T., Liu, R., et al.: Toward fast, flexible, and robust low-light image enhancement. In: Proceedings of the IEEE/CVF Conference on Computer Vision and Pattern Recognition, pp. 5637–5646 (2022)
14. Konstantinidis, F.K., Myrillas, N., Tsintotas, K.A., et al.: A technology maturity assessment framework for industry 5.0 machine vision systems based on systematic literature review in automotive manufacturing. Int. J. Prod. Res. 1–37 (2023)
15. Yang, Z., Ma, W., Lu, J., et al.: The application status and trends of machine vision in tea production. Appl. Sci. **13**(19), 10744 (2023)

Low Bit-Rate Speech Coding Based upon GMD-LPCNet

Chunlin Zhang and Ke Wang[✉]

Beijing University of Posts and Telecommunications, Beijing 100876, China
{zhangchunlin,wangke}@bupt.edu.cn

Abstract. With the rise of direct-to-satellite mobile services, communication between high-orbit satellites and ground devices is becoming increasingly common. However, due to the increased communication distance, the rate of satellite voice calls has decreased. LPCNet encoders have become increasingly popular due to their effectiveness and high quality in speech synthesis. In this work, we propose a Gaussian mixture distribution LPCNet, where speech excitation employs a mixture of Gaussian distributions, predicting multiple consecutive excitation values independently at once, suitable for low bit-rate speech coding. We conducted tests on three open-source Chinese speech samples. Through subjective MUSHRA scoring, the improved approach showed a 5% increase in subjective listening ratings compared to the original LPCNet.

Keywords: Gaussian mixture distribution LPCNet · Low bit-rate speech coding · MUSHRA scoring

1 Introduction

The traditional speech coding methods are roughly divided into waveform coding, parameter coding, and hybrid coding. The higher the bit rate of the coding, the higher the quality of the synthesized speech corresponding to the three coding methods. The most widely used waveform coding is Pulse Code Modulation (PCM), generally divided into A-law and μ-law. Parameter coding, also known as vocoder, is based on the model generation of speech signals, extracting and coding speech signal feature parameters, including Sinusoidal Transform Coding (STC) and Mixed Excitation Linear Prediction Coding (MELP) [1]. Hybrid coding also extracts speech signal feature parameters, but the standard for extraction is that the reconstructed speech signal should closely match the original speech signal in waveform, including Code Excited Linear Prediction (CELP) [2]. Codec2 [3] is a low bit-rate coding scheme, including 450 bps, 700 bps, 1.2 kbps, 1.3 kbps, 1.4 kbps, 1.6 kbps, 2.4 kbps, and 3.2 kbps, with synthesized speech quality better than the MELP algorithm. However, the low-quality synthesized speech generated by traditional speech coding methods makes it difficult for listeners to understand the speech content clearly.

With the rise of deep learning, they are now also being applied to tasks such as Text-to-Speech (TTS) synthesis. Neural network-based vocoders directly map acoustic features to speech waveforms, resulting in high-quality synthesis. Transformer TTS [4]

© ICST Institute for Computer Sciences, Social Informatics and Telecommunications Engineering 2026
Published by Springer Nature Switzerland AG 2026. All Rights Reserved
R. C. Qiu et al. (Eds.): IoTaaS 2024, LNICST 675, pp. 104–113, 2026.
https://doi.org/10.1007/978-3-032-14681-6_9

is a solution for the backend of the neural TTS pipeline. For vocoders, the first successful neural network-based model is WaveNet [5], with better experimental results and less computational complexity running on high-end GPUs. WaveNet mainly employs an expanded causal convolution module, which extends the range of the receptive field, ensuring that the model can continuously monitor the long-term correlation between speech samples. WaveNet's synthesis quality reaches state-of-the-art levels, outperforming the wave concatenative speech synthesis methods. However, this architecture has some drawbacks. For example, noise causes continuous interference with synthesized speech, leading to significant distortion in the higher frequency band. Moreover, due to WaveNet's autoregressive nature, the model is not suitable for real-time speech synthesis. Other architectures, such as ClariNet [6], achieve parallel synthesis through the concept of flows: a series of simple distributions are modeled using reversible trainable transformations, producing distributions similar to real speech sample signals. There are also architectures like WaveRNN [7] that use a large number of complex sampling and compression techniques to reduce the autoregressive vocoder.

All these neural network models can generate high-quality speech without using classical speech synthesis techniques. However, recent research has shown that combining machine learning methods with traditional Source-Filter speech generation models (e.g. [8,9]) results in higher-quality speech. The Source-Filter model is based on the independence assumption of "source" consisting of unvoiced sound of the periodic glottal excitation modeled with white noise as well as voiced sound modeled with pulse trains, and "filter" corresponding to the vocal tract shape. This simplification benefits efficient algorithms and hardware implementations for speech coding and synthesis. The core idea of LPCNet [10] is that Linear Predictive Coding (LPC) filter coefficients can be calculated from feature-generated neural network outputs. Another neural network can solve the remaining part. Due to the high quality and efficiency of synthesized speech, it has become very popular.

We propose a modified version of LPCNet that further enhances processing efficiency without compromising the quality of synthesized speech. Despite being conceptually similar, our modifications feature two significant architectural differences from the original LPCNet design described in the paper, this model architecture is called as GMD-LPCNet. Firstly, we design the modified LPCNet to predict the weights, means, and covariance parameters of a Gaussian mixture distribution $\lambda(\omega_t, \mu_t, \Sigma_t)$ to achieve 16-bit sampling, eliminating the need for softmax layer outputting classification distributions. This allows us to address the issue of signal embedding matrices required by the original LPCNet, as each of the 256 possible signal values is represented as a separate class. The second distinction is the independent sampling of multiple consecutive excitation values, generating multiple samples in a single inference. While this approach assumes conditional independence among multiple consecutive excitation values, empirical evidence shows that it does not affect the quality of the generated speech. Meanwhile, it significantly improves the processing speed of synthesized speech.

The structure of our article is as follows: in Sect. 2, we outline the LPCNet model; in Sect. 3, we describe our proposed improved LPCNet; in Sect. 4, we describe the experimental process and compare the performance of the original LPCNet and GMD-LPCNet in terms of quality and efficiency; in Sect. 5, we provide conclusions.

2   LPCNET

This section introduces the original LPCNet model, an improvement on WaveRNN. LPCNet analyses and synthesises speech signals using an all-pole LPC filter model with linear predictive coding [11]. Figure 1 provides an overview of its architecture, which will be further elaborated upon in this section. The excitation is predicted by a combination of encoder and decoder neural networks. It includes a sampling rate network operating at 16 kHz and a frame rate network processing non-overlapping 10-ms frames (160 samples), but the neural network model we modified has a sampling rate of 8 kHz. In the original LPCNet network, the input vector for speech synthesis consists of 20 features including 18 Bark-scale [12] cepstral coefficients and 2 pitch parameters (period and correlation). The sampling rate network is based on a two-layer gated recurrent unit RNN (GRU), predicting the excitation e_t from previous speech signal s_{t-1}, previous excitation e_{t-1}, current linear prediction p_t and acoustic feature vector f provided by the encoder. For low bit-rate encoding, pitch and cepstral parameters are quantised.

2.1   Linear Prediction Coding

LPC can accurately estimate speech parameters, with the basic idea being that a speech sample can be approximated by a linear combination of past speech samples. In the LPC model, the speech signal is considered to be composed of several resonant peaks and the outputs of corresponding band-pass filters. The LPC algorithm evaluates the coefficients of the linear filters, which can approximate the spectral envelope of the signal, and these coefficients are called Linear Predictive Coefficients (LPCs). They are generally used to describe the characteristics of these band-pass filters, including their bandwidth, gain, and position. Encoding of sound waveforms is transformed into parameter encoding, greatly reducing the amount of audio data; at the decoding end, the synthesizer reconstructs speech, which is a time-varying linear filter representing a model of the human speech generation system. Linear analysis prediction parameters include LPCs, PARCOR, and LSP, among other parameters, which can be converted into each other.

2.2   LPCNet Algorithm

LPCNet combines low complexity with high synthesis quality. This vocoder predicts the source of the Source-Filter part using a neural network, while the filter part is calculated using DSP methods. The transfer function $H(z)$ of an all-pole filter is as follows:

$$H(z) = \frac{1}{1 - \sum_i^M \alpha_i s_{t-i}}. \tag{1}$$

Each sampling point s is calculated by the filter prediction p and the excitation e, where the excitation e is predicted using a neural network.

$$s_t = e_t + p_t, \tag{2}$$

$$s_t = \sum_{i=1}^{M} \alpha_i s_{t-i},\tag{3}$$

where M is the order of LPC analysis, α_i are the LPC coefficients, s_t is the speech signal, $P(s_t)$ is its linear prediction, and e_t is the excitation or residual signal.

The excitation of LPCNet is predicted by a combination of two neural networks: encoder and decoder. The encoder network operates on non-overlapping 10-millisecond frames and processes an input vector consisting of 18 Bark-scale cepstral coefficients and 2 pitch parameters (period and correlation). It is based on two layers of Gated Recurrent Units (GRU) and operates based on acoustic feature vector f from the encoder and predicted excitation e_t, corresponding to the current frame, previous excitation e_{t-1}, previous signal value s_{t-1}, and current linear prediction p_t. The algorithm is summarized in Fig. 1.

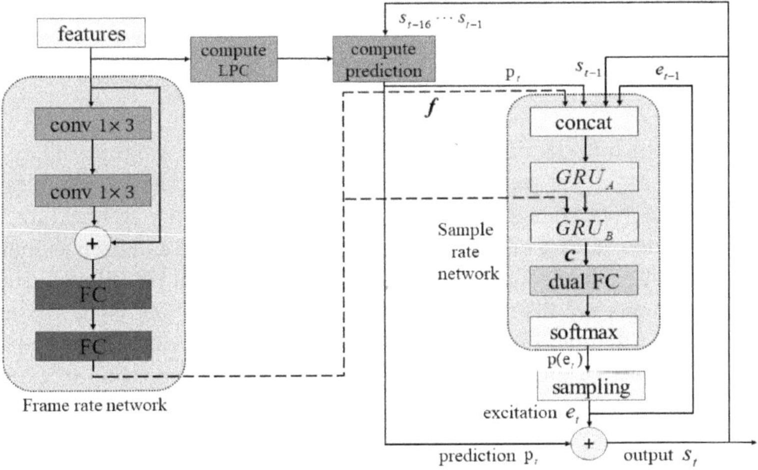

Fig. 1. Original LPCNet algorithm [10]. The compute prediction block predicts the sample at time t based on previous samples and on the linear prediction coefficients.

The LPCNet network model consists of a frame rate network and a sampling rate network, with the sampling rate network being particularly important. This part comprises two layers of GRUs and a dual-channel fully connected layer. The calculation formula for the GRUs in the LPCNet model is shown in the following equations:

$$u_t = \sigma(W_u h_t + v_{s_{t-1}}^{(u,s)} + v_{p_{t-1}}^{(u,p)} + v_{e_{t-1}}^{(u,e)} + g^{(u)}),\tag{4}$$

$$r_t = \sigma(W_r h_t + v_{s_{t-1}}^{(r,s)} + v_{p_{t-1}}^{(r,p)} + v_{e_{t-1}}^{(r,e)} + g^{(r)}),\tag{5}$$

$$h_{ot} = \tanh(r_t \circ (W_h h_t) + v_{s_{t-1}}^{(h,s)} + v_{p_{t-1}}^{(h,p)} + v_{e_{t-1}}^{(h,e)} + g^{(h)}),\tag{6}$$

$$h_t = u_t \circ h_{t-1} + (1 - u_t) \circ h_{ot}, \tag{7}$$

$$P(e_t) = soft\max(dual\_fc(GRU_B(h_t))). \tag{8}$$

Since the second GRU layer, GRU_B is significantly smaller than the first layer GRU_A (16 units compared to 384 units), weight pruning is only applied to GRU_A. The purpose of pruning this layer is to achieve a specific sparse structure for efficient vectorization. We also focus on modifying the output distribution. When activations are directly sampled from the output distribution, the resulting noise level in the speech signal is too high. To address this issue, the authors suggest altering the output distribution: the probability of each class given by the *softmax* layer is multiplied by some frame-level constant (dependent on the pitch correlation in that frame), thereby reducing the temperature of the speech frame sampling process. Then, the class probabilities are normalized to form an effective probability distribution, avoiding outliers in the activation sampling process.

3   GMD-LPCNET

As mentioned in the introduction, the modified LPCNet has two significant differences: it operates on 16-bit signal samples and predicts multiple excitation samples at once. This primarily involves changes in the neural network model's architecture, with the output of the previous GRU_B being embedded with excitations and used as input for the subsequent prediction layer. Additionally, whereas the original LPCNet's linear prediction p_t used a categorical distribution, our model employs a Gaussian mixture distribution. By training the modified LPCNet on speech signals without pre-emphasis, we found that the quality of the modified model has improved according to experimental results.

3.1   Parallelized Sampling

The essence of parallelised sampling is to enable the sampling rate network to generate multiple samples in one inference pass, thereby reducing the number of times it needs to run and significantly decreasing the computational cost. SampleRNN [13], as an efficient autoregressive model, employs different clock rates at the higher and lower levels of its neural network architecture to enhance throughput. Bunched LPCNet [14] maintains the autoregressive nature of LPCNet while increasing the capacity of the RNN, ensuring the quality of the synthesised speech.

The architecture of our proposed GMD-LPCNet model is depicted in Fig. 2. The decoder section features clustered sampling sharing GRU layers, and each prediction in a bundle has its own prediction layer and fully connected layer. The input to the prediction layer for the first excitation depends solely on the output of the GRU_B, $e_{t+1} \sim p(e_t|c)$; for the subsequent ones, it also relies on the previous excitation within the bundle, $e_{t+S} \sim p(e_{t+S-1}|c, e_t, \ldots, e_{t+S-2})$, via embedded feeds. This approach enables the sampling of multiple consecutive samples in parallel, greatly enhancing the speed of

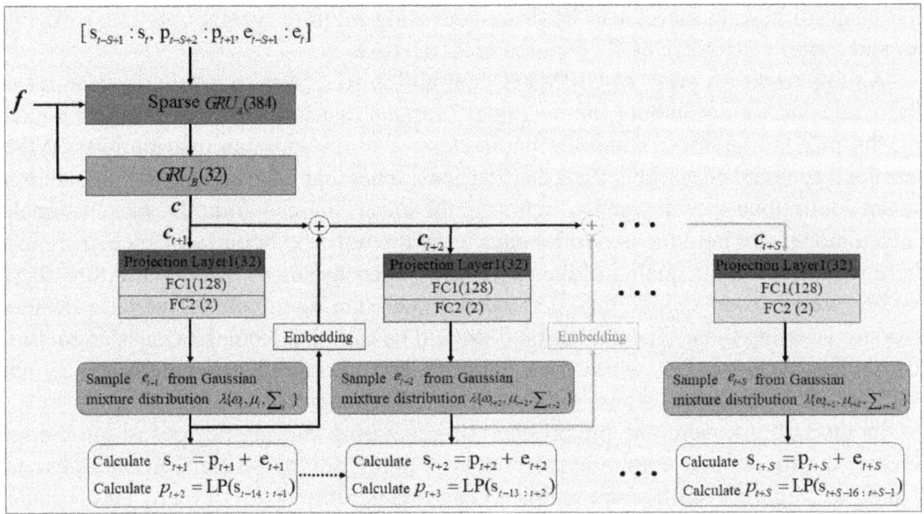

Fig. 2. Gaussian mixture distribution LPCNet decoder. 32-dimensional GRU_B output vector is denoted by c. LP denotes calculating linear prediction based on frame-level LPC coefficients. $E(\cdot)$ means 128-dimensional signal embedding.

speech decoding. We have demonstrated that, while maintaining the quality of the synthesised speech, the improved LPCNet can provide more than double the acceleration compared to the baseline.

3.2 Gaussian Mixture Distribution for Prediction

The research on Gaussian LPCNet [15] has shown that the original LPCNet's output excitation distribution exhibits both unimodal and multimodal characteristics. However, the excitation distribution of the original LPCNet is categorical, with too many categories. Using only a single Gaussian distribution to simulate excitation fails to capture all the characteristics of the input speech. Therefore, our model adopts a mixture of Gaussian distributions, which is more suitable for generating 16-bit samples.

The Gaussian Mixture Model (GMM) [16] is essentially a multi-dimensional probability density function, used to represent linear combinations of multiple Gaussian distributions. In a GMM λ with K-components of L-dimensions, if we assume the observation vector is x, then the likelihood of x under this GMM is given by:

$$p(x|\lambda) = \sum_{t=1}^{K} \omega_t f_t(x), \tag{9}$$

$$f_t(x) = \frac{1}{(2\pi)^{L/2}|\Sigma_t|^{1/2}} \exp\left\{-\frac{1}{2}(x-\mu_t)^T \Sigma_t^{-1}(x-\mu_t)\right\}. \tag{10}$$

In the above expression, ω_t is a mixture of weighted values, $f_t(x)$ is an L-dimensional Gaussian function, μ_t is the mean vector, and Σ_t is the covariance matrix. The entire

Gaussian mixture model λ can be described using mixture weights ω_t, mean vectors μ_t, and covariance matrices Σ_t, denoted as $\lambda(\omega_t, \mu_t, \Sigma_t)$.

An important property of GMMs is their ability to capture overlapping features of the data, which is something that a single Gaussian distribution cannot do. By adjusting the mixing parameters and the parameters of each Gaussian distribution, GMMs can flexibly adapt to various data distributions. They can also model the characteristics of continuous speech signals, capturing the uncertainties within the speech signals. Such a model can help the network better learn the intrinsic features of speech signals, thereby improving the quality of the synthesised speech. Since Gaussian mixture distributions are easier to sample than generalized Gaussian distributions, we have decided to continue using them. The excitation e_t should be sampled from the Gaussian mixture distribution $\lambda(\omega_t, \mu_t, \Sigma_t)$, while the GMD-LPCNet uses predicted parameters μ_t and $\ln(\Sigma_t)$ to avoid situations where the network predicts negative values.

In addition, to overcome the problem of generating varying degrees of click noise directly in process that employing the network prediction parameters produces excitation e_t, we slightly modified the sampled Gaussian mixture distribution by least-squares optimal estimate. The output distribution is modified in the following equation, which allows the model to get rid of variance outliers:

$$\sum_{ot}(x-\mu_t) = \min\left\{\sum_t (x-\mu_t), \sum_{t-1}(x-\mu_{t-1}), \ldots, \sum_{t-M+1}(x-\mu_{t-M+1})\right\},$$

$$(11)$$

where M is the hyperparameter tuned on the validation set. During the experiments, setting $M = 10$ yielded better results. Generally, it is difficult to predict variance accurately, leading to occasional errors in the model. When the network model predicts an excessively large variance, clicking sounds are produced, which is why we need to avoid variance outliers corresponding to large values. We did this by analysing the characteristics of the excitation signals and in many cases the excitation was homoscedastic over the 10-ms frame period. Therefore, it is easy to correct errors in the variance by performing some robust aggregation of previous variance values.

4   Evaluation

4.1   Complexity

The complexity of the original LPCNet model consists of the GRU and the dual-channel fully connected layer, as well as the other parts that are ignored (bias, conditional networks, activation functions, etc.), and it has a total computational complexity of about 2.8 GFLOPS. Whereas, the complexity of the modified LPCNet model we propose mainly stems from two GRUs, projection layer and fully connected layers. For each generated sample, it is given by the following equation:

$$C = (3dN_A^2 + 3N_B(N_A + N_B) + 2N_B Q) \cdot 2F_S, \tag{12}$$

where N_A and N_B are the sizes of the two GRUs, d is the density of the sparse GRU, Q is the number of levels in the μ-law, and F_s is the sampling rate. The original LPCNet operates at a sampling rate of 16 kHz, whereas the modified low bit-rate speech coding operates at 8 kHz. As a result, the complexity of the modified LPCNet model, adjusted using the above mentioned formula, is approximately halved compared to its previous state, with a total computational complexity of 1.4 GFLOPS.

4.2   Quality Evaluation

Our experiments directly compute the network's feature parameters from input speech samples. The training data consists of only 3 h of speech from a Chinese speech database, excluding the speaker's speech used in testing. Each network undergoes training for 120 epochs with a batch size of 128. Training is conducted on servers with Nvidia 3080T_i GPU and optimized using CuDNN GRU implementation. We input Chinese audio from ITU-T P.501 into the modified LPCNet network, and after encoding and decoding, the spectrogram of the generated audio compared to the original Chinese audio is shown in Fig. 3. From the chart, it can be observed that the speech consists of two speech segments, with the energy of the speech concentrated in the low-frequency part. Firstly, our codec can indeed estimate and synthesize the original speech well, especially in the low-frequency part, although there is some energy loss in the high frequencies. Even in the low bit-rate coding region, the cepstral model still captures well.

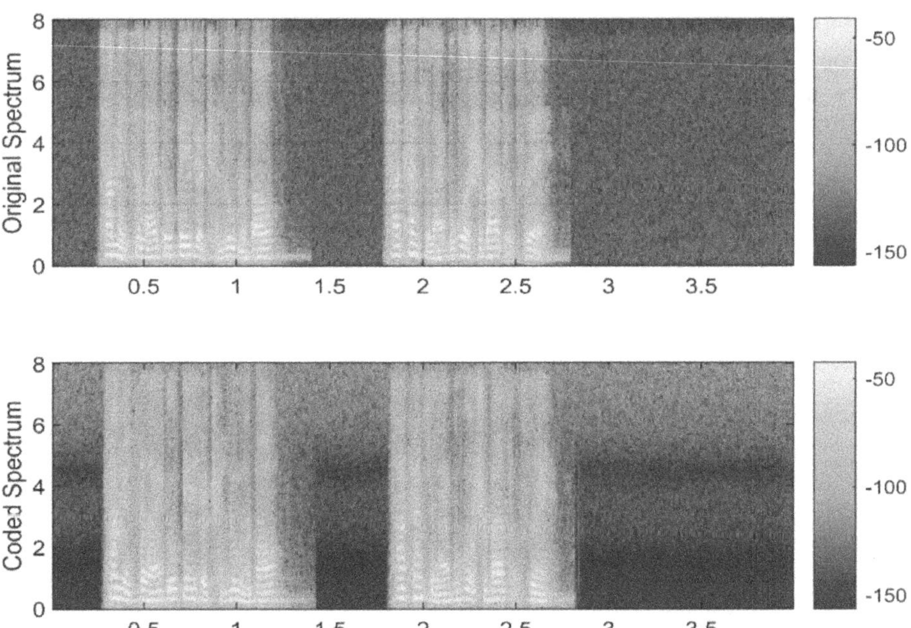

Fig. 3. The image above shows the original spectrum, pictures below displays the coded spectrum. The depth of the yellow color of the resonance peaks shows the strength of the speech energy. (Color figure online)

As reported in [17], objective quality metrics like PESQ and POLQA are unable to reflect some typical distortions and cannot adequately evaluate non-waveform neural vocoders. We conducted subjective listening tests using the MUSHRA method [18]. The subjective scores for the two LPCNet algorithms are shown in Table 1, with MUSHRA scores as the target metric. The original and modified LPCNet models were trained on three different Chinese audio datasets representing various speech contents and speakers: THCH-30, AISHELL-3, and SHALCAS22A. The SHALCAS22A dataset comprises 60 speakers, each with different short-duration audio samples downsampled to the 8 kHz sampling rate. Each resulting audio was evaluated by 30–60 listeners. Participants were asked to rate speech quality on a five-point scale, categorizing recordings as "Bad" (1 point), "Poor" (2 points), "Fair" (3 points), "Good" (4 points), or "Excellent" (5 points). Listeners were instructed to focus on overall clarity, the presence of background noise, and the correctness and naturalness of speech articulation.

Table 1. MUSHRA Scores for speech synthesized with two LPCNet.

Dataset	Language	Duration	Listeners	Original LPCNet	GMD-LPCNet
THCH-30	Chinese	33h	30	4.23 ± 0.06	**4.51 ± 0.05**
AISHELL-3	Chinese	85h	60	4.37 ± 0.04	**4.65 ± 0.03**
SHALCAS22A	Chinese	72h	50	4.34 ± 0.05	**4.63 ± 0.04**

Table 1 reports MUSHRA scores and 95% confidence intervals. The results indicate that the GMD-LPCNet model synthesizes speech of roughly the same quality as the original. Additionally, it can be concluded that the modified LPCNet performs better when trained on datasets with longer overall duration and higher quality, showing improved performance.

The speech samples used in the subjective evaluation can be found at open source websites https://www.openslr.org/resources.php.

5   Conclusion

In this work, we propose a Gaussian mixture distribution LPCNet, which features a more optimized structure and enhanced parallelised sampling process, resulting in higher-quality synthesized speech. The GMD-LPCNet generates speech signals by predicting multiple excitation samples at once, greatly improving the efficiency of the algorithm and making it more suitable for hardware processing capabilities of terminal chips connected to satellites, which makes it easier for most terminal manufacturers to adapt their devices to mobile direct-to-satellite services. Furthermore, through training and testing on Chinese audio datasets, the vocoder product becomes more flexible for applications in the domestic satellite communication market. Additionally, the dataset can be expanded to include mainstream international languages, opening up the international satellite communication application market. Future work for the GMD-LPCNet includes handling more diverse speech datasets to make the model applicable on a wider range of speech synthesis scenarios.

References

1. Unno, T., Barnwell, T.P., Truong, K.: An improved mixed excitation linear prediction (MELP) coder. In: Proceedings of International Conference on Acoustics, Speech, and Signal Processing (ICASSP), vol. 1, pp. 245–248 (1999)
2. Miki, S., Mano, K., Moriya, T., Oguchi, K., Ohmuro, H.: A pitch synchronous innovation CELP (PSI-CELP) coder for 2–4 kbps. In: Proceedings of International Conference on Acoustics, Speech, and Signal Processing (ICASSP), vol. 2, pp. 113–116 (1994)
3. Rowetel, D.: Techniques for Harmonic Sinusoidal Coding. Ph.D. thesis (1997)
4. Li, N., Liu, S., Liu, Y., Zhao, S., Liu, M.: Neural speech synthesis with transformer network. In: AAAI (2018)
5. van den Oord, A., et al.: WaveNet: a generative model for raw audio. In: Proceedings of 9th ISCA Speech Synthesis Workshop, p. 125 (2016)
6. Ping, W., Peng, K., Chen, J.: ClariNet: Parallel Wave Generation in End-to-End Text-to-Speech, CoRR vol. abs/1807.07281 (2018)
7. Jin, Z., Finkelstein, A., Mysore, G.J., Lu, J.: FFTNet: a real-time speaker-dependent neural vocoder. In: Proceedings of International Conference on Acoustics, Speech, and Signal Processing (ICASSP) (2018)
8. Juvela, L., Bollepalli, B., Yamagishi, J., Alku, P.: GELP: GAN-Excited Linear Prediction for Speech Synthesis from Mel-spectrogram (2019)
9. Song, E., Byun, K., Kang, H.-G.: ExcitNet vocoder: a neural excitation model for parametric speech synthesis systems (2018)
10. Valin, J., Skoglund, J.: LPCNet: improving neural speech synthesis through linear prediction. In: Proceedings of International Conference on Acoustics, Speech, and Signal Processing (ICASSP), pp. 5891–5895 (2019)
11. Makhoul, J.: Linear prediction: a tutorial review. Proc. IEEE **63**(4), 561–580 (1975)
12. Moore, B.C.J.: An introduction to the psychology of hearing. Brill, 5th edn (2012)
13. Soroush, M., et al.: SampleRNN: an unconditional end-to-end neural audio generation model. In: Proceedings of ICLR (2017)
14. Vipperla, R., et al.: Bunched LPCNet: Vocoder for Low-cost Neural Text-To-Speech Systems, arXiv preprint arXiv:2008.04574 (2020)
15. Popov, V., Kudinov, M., Sadekova, T.: Gaussian LPCNet for multisample speech synthesis. In: Proceedings of International Conference on Acoustics, Speech, and Signal Processing (ICASSP), pp. 6204–6208 (2020)
16. Cho, K., Van Merrienboer, B., Bahdanau, D., Bengio, Y.: On the properties of neural machine translation: encoder-decoder approaches. In: Proceedings of Eighth Workshop on Syntax, Semantics and Structure in Statistical Translation (SSST-8) (2014)
17. Kleijn, W.B., et al.: WaveNet based low rate speech coding. In: Proceedings of International Conference on Acoustics, Speech, and Signal Processing (ICASSP), pp. 676–680 (2018)
18. ITU-R BS.1534-3–MUSHRA, Assessment of sound quality for multiple systems (2015)

Design of IoT Information Security System Based on Data Mining

Yuling Gu$^{(\boxtimes)}$ and Daming Li

Wuhan Vocational College of Software and Engineering, Wuhan 430025, China
gyl5212021@163.com

Abstract. With the rapid development of Internet of Things (IoT) technology, network security has become increasingly prominent, especially in the security issues of data transmission, storage, and other links. This article intends to use data mining methods to conduct in-depth analysis and mining of the transmission characteristics of data in the Internet of Things, in order to improve the level of information security management in the Internet of Things. This article establishes a data flow model for the Internet of Things, and uses methods such as association rule learning and abnormal behavior detection in data mining to identify security risks in the Internet of Things. By using machine learning and other methods, deep mining of data in the network can be carried out, and real-time monitoring of abnormal behavior in the network can be carried out to cope with various security attacks and threats. In addition, this article can also introduce technologies such as cryptography and access control to ensure the security and integrity of data in transmission, storage, and other aspects. The detection speed of various types of malware varies, but most of them are between 30 s and 70 s, indicating that the system has a fast response ability to different types of malware. The research results of this article have important theoretical significance and application value for ensuring the security of IoT information, maintaining network stability, and protecting the privacy of user information.

Keywords: Data Mining · IoT Information Security System · Fast Response Capability · Detection Speed

1 Introduction

With the rapid development of Internet of Things technology, devices around the world are constantly interconnected. From smart homes to industrial automation and other fields, the Internet of Things has gradually penetrated into human

Supported by The project of production, teaching and research in municipal universities of the Education Bureau of Wuhan, Development of full stack system for industrial Internet teaching and application, Subject number: CXY202216.

R. C. Qiu et al. (Eds.): IoTaaS 2024, LNICST 675, pp. 114–123, 2026.
https://doi.org/10.1007/978-3-032-14681-6_10

daily life. However, at the same time, the rapid development of this technology has also raised higher requirements for network security, especially in areas such as data transmission and storage. Meanwhile, in the coming years, as more and more mobile phones emerge, the security threats to the Internet of Things can multiply. Therefore, researching methods to enhance information security in the Internet of Things is an important aspect of the current development of computer science and information technology. This article intends to use data mining methods to construct a new Internet of Things information security system, which can effectively discover and resist potential security risks, and improve the overall security protection level of the system. It has significant theoretical and practical significance for ensuring network security.

The research work of this article is based on data mining technology and investigates information security in the Internet of Things. This article intends to use advanced data mining methods to conduct real-time analysis of data flow in the Internet of Things environment, and combine machine learning and other methods to identify and predict security risks in the Internet of Things environment, in order to achieve effective protection of Internet of Things devices. It establishes a data mining model, uses statistics and algorithms to process and analyze massive data, and extracts possible abnormal patterns and threats from it. On this basis, this article explores the introduction of the aforementioned key technologies into a unified IoT security system to enhance the overall security level of the Internet of Things. It verified the effectiveness of the adopted scheme through experiments and compared and analyzed it with existing security schemes.

This article intends to conduct research from the following aspects: Firstly, it can clarify the data security requirements in the Internet of Things environment, conduct indepth analysis of existing security issues and technical difficulties, and lay a theoretical foundation for future research on the Internet of Things. Secondly, a detailed explanation was provided on the data mining, machine learning and other methods used, as well as their applications in IoT security. Finally, this article conducts a series of experiments to test the proposed scheme and evaluate its responsiveness and protection effectiveness against various attack situations. This article focuses not only on the implementation of key technologies, but also on how to combine them with actual business to form a complete and reliable IoT information security solution.

2   Related Work

s has important practical significance, but with the widespread use of terminal devices and the continuous expansion of application scope, security issues have become a bottleneck that restricts the further development of this technology. Researching and improving information security systems in the Internet of Things can effectively prevent risks such as data leakage and malicious device manipulation, ensuring user privacy and sensitive information of enterprises. Luo Siyuan studied the information security threat analysis and protection technology of IoT systems [1]. Zheng Yaowen studied the security threats and security models of the Internet of Things [2]. Yang Ting studied a multi-task scheduling algorithm for heterogeneous information security in the power Internet of Things [3]. Zheng Yi explored the network security technology of smart power IoT in the context of ubiquitous IoT [4]. Wang Dan studied a hospital doctor privacy information security storage and control system based on the Internet of Things [5]. Although a large amount of research has been conducted on the security issues of the Internet of Things, current research often lacks indepth analysis of data flow and real-time requirements in the network, making it unable to effectively respond to high dynamic IoT environments. The research on information security in the Internet of Thing

Studying the information security of the Internet of Things can not only improve the security protection level of devices themselves, but also provide users with a more secure and reliable network service environment. Especially in the era driven by big data, ensuring the integrity and privacy of data is an important means of making business decisions based on big data. Shao Jiagen discussed information security issues in the Internet of Things environment [6]. SudhaK conducted a review of privacy requirements and application layer security in the Internet of Things [7]. Li B studied the physical layer security technology in the spatial information network of the Internet of Things [8]. Hansaraj D utilized IoT and artificial intelligence technology to prevent security attacks on cloud medical data [9]. Miloslavskaya N studied information security event management solutions in the Internet of Things ecosystem [10]. However, current research often overlooks the diverse and distributed characteristics of IoT terminals, making it difficult for existing security strategies to be applicable to diverse IoT environments. It is urgent to seek a new optimization approach from aspects such as architecture, security mechanisms, and implementation.

3   Method

3.1   Data Processing and Feature Selection

The data collection module can be embedded into the front-end of IoT devices to collect device status, network traffic, and operation logs. By using data purification methods, noisy data is removed and transformed into a format suitable for analysis using data transformation techniques.

This article adopts a combination of statistics and machine learning methods to extract features from raw data [11]. On this basis, feature selection algorithms such as decision trees and random forests can be used to identify the most efficient feature set, reduce algorithm complexity, and improve algorithm performance.

3.2   Model Construction and Training

This article uses classification methods such as SVM (Support Vector Machine), neural networks, and deep learning to establish a network oriented security threat recognition model. In the context of the Internet of Things, abnormal behavior recognition technology based on data mining is the core of building an information security system for the Internet of Things. It can utilize data mining methods to preprocess and extract massive sensor data, perform feature analysis on it, and then normalize its identification. On this basis, various machine learning methods such as SVM, random forest, and deep learning are used to model abnormal behavior and potential threats in the network. Meanwhile, by combining with time series analysis, continuous and sudden anomaly detection can be achieved. On this basis, the feedback mechanism is used to dynamically update and optimize the model, improve the accuracy and real-time performance of IoT monitoring, and ensure the safe and stable operation of the IoT.

The anomaly detection threshold $S(x)$ can be calculated by the following formula:

$$S(x) = \frac{|x - \mu|}{\sigma},\tag{1}$$

x is the observed value, μ and σ are the mean and standard deviation of normal behavior data, respectively. The threshold is usually set based on system security requirements.

3.3 System Integration and Deployment

At the same time, training can be provided on the deployment and maintenance of the system to ensure that the system administrator manages and maintains the security system.

In IoT devices, entropy is used to measure the uncertainty and randomness of network traffic or device behavior, and it is a useful indicator for detecting potential security events. Entropy can be calculated using the following formula:

$$H(X) = \sum_{i=1}^{n} p(x_i) \log p(x_i),\tag{2}$$

Among them, $p(x_i)$ is the probability of event x_i occurring, and n is the total number of possible events.

3.4 Performance Evaluation and Optimization

This article analyzes the efficiency and accuracy of safety accident response by collecting system operation information. On this basis, this article continuously improves the system based on the risk assessment results to ensure that the system can effectively respond to potential security threats in the future.

In the feature selection process, information gain helps determine which features are most useful for classifying attack patterns. The information gain can be calculated by comparing the entropy before and after segmentation:

$$IG(T, a) = H(T) - \sum_{v \in \text{Values}(a)} \frac{|T_v|}{|T|} H(T_v),\tag{3}$$

Among them, T is the dataset, a is a certain feature, and T_v is a subset when the value of feature a is v.

4   Results and Discussion

4.1   Experimental Setup

In order to verify the effectiveness of the IoT information security system based on data mining, this study designed and implemented a series of experiments by simulating practical application scenarios.

Experimental environment settings:

The experimental environment consists of various IoT devices, including smart home devices, industrial control system devices, and intelligent transportation vehicles, which are connected in a simulated network environment. Each device is equipped with a data acquisition module that can send real-time data to the central monitoring system. The experimental hardware includes high-performance computers and multiple routers, and the software environment is Linux operating system. Python language is used for data processing and model development.

Evaluation indicators:

The evaluation of system performance is mainly based on the following indicators:

Accuracy: The proportion of accurate predictions among all predictions.

Recall rate: The proportion that is correctly predicted as positive among all actual positive samples.

Precision: The proportion of samples that are actually positive among all predicted positive samples.

F1 score: The harmonic mean of precision and recall, used to measure the stability of the model.

4.2   Experimental Exploration Results of Design

The detection results of DDoS (Distributed Denial of Service) attacks are shown in Fig. 1.

During the period from time 1 to time 3, the packet rate (pps) gradually increases, and its amplitude and absolute value are within the normal range, indicating flow fluctuations during normal system operation. Starting from 4 h, the packet rate significantly increased, from 5000 pps to 10000 pps at 5 h, and maintained at 8000 pps at 6 h. This sharp change is a typical feature of DDoS attacks, where attackers exhaust the resources of the target system by sending a large number of packets. At 7 h, the packet rate decreased slightly but still exceeded the normal level, which may indicate that the attack intensity is being adjusted or that the system has taken partial mitigation measures. From 8 h to 9 h, the packet rate rapidly decreases and returns to normal levels, indicating that the attack has stopped or been successfully defended.

From time 1 to time 3, the number of source IP (Internet Protocol) slightly increases with the increase of packet rate, belonging to the normal traffic mode. Starting from 4 h, the number of source IPs increases sharply, matching the increase in packet rate. In DDoS attacks, a large number of packets typically

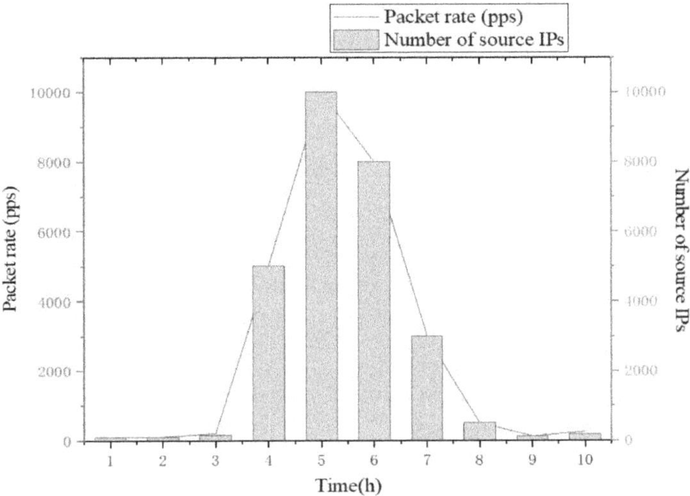

Fig. 1. DDoS attack detection results.

come from different IP addresses to conceal the source of the attack and increase defense difficulty. The number of source IPs began to decrease after 5 h and returned to normal levels from 8 h to 10 h.

Based on the above analysis, it can be reasonably inferred that during the period from 4h to 7h, the system may have suffered from DDoS attacks, and the sharp increase in packet rate and source IP number is a typical feature of this type of attack. The detection system should be able to identify this abnormal traffic pattern and trigger alerts or defense mechanisms, such as detecting DDoS attacks through threshold settings (such as sudden increase in packet rate exceeding a certain threshold) or using machine learning algorithms (identifying changes in traffic patterns).

Malicious software injection data is shown in Table 1. Table 1 records the malicious software injection events at various time points on October 1, 2023, covering the injection time, type of malicious software, and injection method. The data shows that there are various types of malware, including worms, Trojans, ransomware, botnets, and spyware. The injection methods are diverse, such as network downloads, email attachments, and illegal website downloads. This indicates that the network security situation is extremely severe, and it is necessary to strengthen protective measures and enhance user security awareness to cope with various network attacks. Especially the frequent appearance of worms and ransomware reminds people to pay high attention to these threats and adopt corresponding defense strategies.

For various types of malicious programs, the detection speed varies, but most of them are around 30–70 seconds, indicating that the system has a fast response speed to various types of malicious programs. In the testing, the testing performance of the worm virus was particularly excellent, with testing speeds of 30 s

Table 1. Malicious software injection data

SN	Injection time	Malicious software types	Injection method
1	2023-10-01 08:00:00	Worm-type virus	Network download
2	2023-10-01 08:15:00	Trojan horse	Email attachments
3	2023-10-01 08:30:00	Ransomware	Illegal website download
4	2023-10-01 08:45:00	Botnet	Remote command
5	2023-10-01 09:00:00	Spyware	USB (Universal Serial Bus) driver
6	2023-10-01 09:15:00	Vulnerability exploitation	File sharing
7	2023-10-01 09:30:00	Worm variant	Bluetooth transmission
8	2023-10-01 09:45:00	Unknown virus	Network download
9	2023-10-01 10:00:00	Worm-type virus	Cloud storage synchronization
10	2023-10-01 10:15:00	Ransomware	Social media links
11	2023-10-01 10:30:00	Botnet	Software updates
12	2023-10-01 10:45:00	Spyware	Known vulnerabilities

and 25 s, indicating that the system has a relatively mature detection method. The exploration results of the system's ability to protect against malware and viruses are shown in Fig. 2.

The simulation time, threat type, and leakage data type under different serial numbers are shown in Table 2. Table 2 records a series of security threat events from October 1 to October 2, 2023, including various types of data tampering, illegal access, and malicious code execution, involving sensitive customer data, product design drawings, and financial data. This indicates that the company needs to strengthen its security strategy, enhance its awareness of prevention, to cope with increasingly complex security challenges, and ensure data integrity and confidentiality. At the same time, timely response and handling of these security threats are crucial for protecting company assets and reputation.

Attempting data deletion (15MB) and illegal access (10MB) are the two largest threats to data leakage, indicating that once these threats succeed, they can lead to serious data loss. In terms of detection time, most types of threats have shorter detection times, indicating a faster system response to security issues. Among them, unauthorized data access (0.8 min) has the shortest detection time, reflecting the system's high alertness to such threats. However, the detection time for malware uploads (3.5 min) is relatively long, and further optimization of the detection system is needed. In terms of response time, most types of threats have response times within an acceptable range (3 to 7 min), but malicious software uploads have the longest response time (8 min). This may be due to the complex processing of malware, which requires more time for analysis, isolation, and removal. Overall, the table provides an overview of the different types of threats faced by the company and their impacts. For threats with large leaks and long response times, the company needs to strengthen security strategies and response measures to ensure data security and integrity. The amount

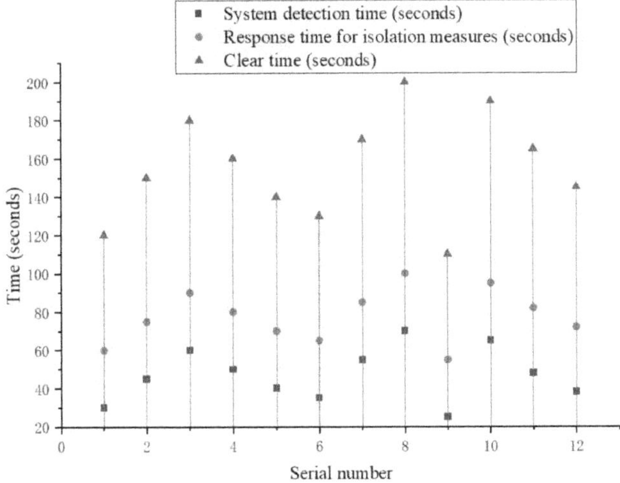

Fig. 2. Exploration results of the system's ability to protect against malware and viruses.

Table 2. Simulation time, threat type, and leakage data type under different serial numbers

SN	Simulation time	Threat type	Leakage data type
1	2023-10-01 09:00	Data tampering	Sensitive customer data
2	2023-10-01 10:15	Illegal access	Product design drawings
3	2023-10-01 11:30	Malicious code execution	Financial data
4	2023-10-01 13:00	Illegal copying	Employee salary information
5	2023-10-01 14:15	Leakage of sensitive documents	Contract agreement
6	2023-10-01 15:30	Attempting data deletion	Sales records
7	2023-10-02 08:45	Unauthorized data access	Customer contact information
8	2023-10-02 10:00	Attempting to bypass security policies	Research and development code
9	2023-10-02 11:15	Illegal data export	Supplier Information
10	2023-10-02 12:30	Malicious software upload	Internal company applications

of leaked data with different serial numbers, detection time, and response time for response measures are shown in Fig. 3.

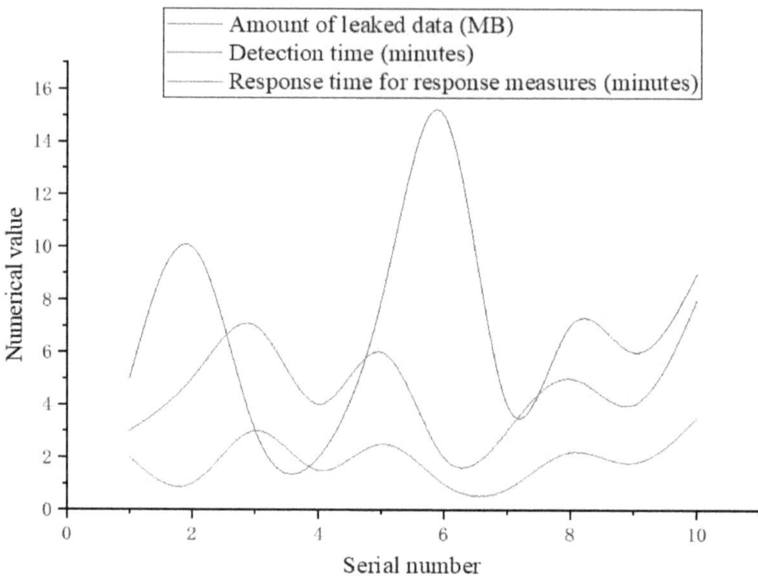

Fig. 3. Leakage data volume, detection time, and response time of response measures for different serial numbers.

5   Conclusion

This article focuses on the increasing security risks in the Internet of Things and adopts an IoT information security system based on data mining technology. The research focuses on data collection and preprocessing, feature extraction and selection, model construction and training, abnormal event detection and response, and other aspects. The research objective of this article is to enhance the ability of IoT terminals to respond to various types of network attacks and internal threats. The effectiveness of this method has been demonstrated through a series of experiments. This system can monitor and respond in real-time to various security threats such as DDoS attacks, malicious program injection, and data leaks. The experiment shows that this method has good recognition performance in different testing environments. In addition, the system has undergone performance testing on multiple terminals, and the results show that the system has good compatibility and integration. Although there have been some achievements, there are still shortcomings. Firstly, the current system largely depends on the quality and quantity of data, thus placing higher demands on data collection and processing. Secondly, it is still difficult for the system to effectively identify new or unknown attacks, as the learning of the model requires modeling of known attack patterns. Finally, relevant research was conducted to address issues such as the diversification of IoT terminals and insufficient adaptive capabilities for multiple application scenarios. In the future, more effective data collection and preprocessing methods can enhance the robustness of the system under low-quality conditions. Secondly, further research can be conducted on machine learning models based on deep learning to improve their ability to identify new and unknown attacks. On this basis, it can further expand to a wider range of IoT terminals and more complex application scenarios to verify the universality and scalability of this method.

References

1. Luo, S., Wang, Z., He, D.Q.: Research on information security threat analysis and protection technology of IoT system. Internet Things Technol. **13**(8), 111–114 (2023)
2. Zheng, Y., Wen, H., Cheng, K., et al.: Internet of things security threats and security models. J. Inf. Secur. **8**(5), 81–95 (2023)
3. Yang, T., Cai, S., Yan, P., et al.: A multitasking scheduling algorithm for heterogeneous information security of the power internet of things. Power Syst. Autom. **46**(15), 162–170 (2022)
4. Zheng, Y., Wang, L., Hu, Z., et al.: Exploration of network security technology of smart power internet of things in the context of ubiquitous IOT. Inf. Secur. Technol. **011**(012), 65–72 (2020)
5. Wang, D., Peng, Q.: A secure storage and control system for private information of hospital doctors based on the internet of things. Autom. Technol. Appl. **42**(9), 119–122 (2023)
6. Shao, J.: Discussion on information security issues in the internet of things environment. China Manag. Informatiz. **26**(10), 97–99 (2023)
7. Sudha, K.S., Jeyanthi, N.: A review on privacy requirements and application layer security in internet of things (IoT). Cybern. Inf. Technol. **21**(3), 50–72 (2021)
8. Li, B., Fei, Z., Zhou, C., et al.: Physical-layer security in space information networks: a survey. IEEE Internet Things J. **7**(1), 33–52 (2020)
9. Hansaraj, D., Wankhede, S., Gowri, N.V., et al.: An internet of things for prevention of security attack on cloud medical data using artificial intelligence. Int. J. Grid Distrib. Comput. **14**(1), 1143–1161 (2021)
10. Miloslavskaya, N., Tolstoy, A.: IoTBlockSIEM for information security incident management in the internet of things ecosystem. Clust. Comput. **23**(3), 1911–1925 (2020). https://doi.org/10.1007/s10586-020-03110-5
11. Badillo, S., Banfai, B., Birzele, F., et al.: An introduction to machine learning. Clin. Pharmacol. Ther. **107**(4), 871–885 (2020)

Research on the Application of Continuous Phase Modulation in 6G Satellite-Terrestrial Integrated Network

Xiufang Sun[1], Kai Jiang[2], Zhanjie Yang[3], and Yinzhen Wei[1(✉)]

[1] Wuhan Vocational College of Software and Engineering (Wuhan Open University), Wuhan 430205, Hubei, China
`wyz_gs@163.com`
[2] Wuhan Technical College of Communications, Wuhan 430065, Hubei, China
[3] Wuhan Zhongyuan Electronics Group Co., Ltd., Wuhan 430205, Hubei, China

Abstract. As a constant envelope modulation method, continuous phase modulation has high bandwidth and power utilization, and strong anti-interference ability, which is very suitable for the physical layer waveform design of Satellite-Terrestrial Integrated Network in 6G full coverage scenarios with nonlinear power and limited bandwidth. However, the complexity and real-time requirements of CPM demodulation algorithms are high, and most of the research focuses on algorithm performance evaluation and simulation, and lacks engineering application implementation. Therefore, based on the real-time high-speed data processing capability of Digital Signal Processing (DSP), a practical CPM modulation and demodulation system is designed, in which the data at the sender is first obtained coding gain by Trellis Coded Modulation (TCM), and then CPM modulation is carried out to form a constant envelope modulation signal, and the Viterbi algorithm (VA) is used at the receiver. The demodulation of CPM signals is realized. The effectiveness of the proposed system has been verified through simulation evaluation and practical testing in high-speed narrowband frequency hopping data transmission radios, indicating that the system has good stability and practicality, providing support for the application of CPM in 6G Satellite-Terrestrial Integrated.

Keywords: Continuous phase modulation · Trellis coding modulation · Satellite-Terrestrial Integrated Network · 6G

Supported by

1. Educational Science Planning of Wuhan (No.: 2022C151).

2. Wuhan Vocational College of Software and Engineering (No.: KYQDJF2023007).

3. National Social Science Foundation (No. 21BTQ074).

4. National Research Association for Basic Computer Education in Colleges and Universities (No. 2024-AFCEC-610).

5. Wuhan Technical College of Communications (Z2024002).

6. The Doctoral Team Technology Innovation Platform Project (No. 06) of Wuhan Vocational College of Software and Engineering.

1   Introduction

In the field of wireless communication, with the acceleration of 6G research, the demand for communication is no longer limited to data exchange between people. Data exchange between people and things, as well as between things and people, has gradually become the mainstay of communication. The Internet of Things communication represented by the Internet of Things technology will be greatly expanded in terms of space and communication content, especially with the active promotion of network technology, the NB-IoT, narrow band Internet of things will cover towns, mountains, deserts, oceans, deep ground, sky, space and other broader areas, forming an Satellite-Terrestrial Integrated Network, providing ubiquitous, intelligent, collaborative, and collaborative network for various network applications in wide area space. Efficient Information Assurance [1]. So, one of the core technologies in the progress of 6G research is to construct a seamless connection between satellite and ground networks at any position after deep fusion, in order to achieve full coverage of application scenarios [2]. The basic requirement of the Satellite-Terrestrial Integrated Network in this application scenario is to form an integrated space-ground network with seamless three-dimensional coverage of the world based on the terrestrial mobile network and supported by the orbital satellite network [3]. Therefore, the physical layer waveform design, as the basic work for the realization of satellite-ground convergence network, determines the information transmission performance of Satellite-Terrestrial Integrated Network [4]. Signal modulation and demodulation is one of the key technologies to achieve high-speed data transmission [5], and in the face of this kind of Satellite-Terrestrial Integrated Network with limited frequency band resources, the bandwidth of the continuous phase modulation signal is compact, the main lobe energy of the power spectrum is concentrated, the side-lobe fading is rapid, and the interference to the critical frequency signal is small. CPM modulation has been evaluated as a C-band navigation signal modulation method in China's Beidou system, and its good frequency band utilization can meet the strict compatibility requirements of navigation signals [6]. As a class of constant envelope phase continuous modulation signals, the CPM modulation signal has a constant envelope compared with other modulated signals, which is insensitive to the nonlinear characteristics of the power amplifier and is easy to amplify [7].

In general, however, the higher the bandwidth and power efficiency of a CPM modulated signal, the higher the complexity of the receiver implementation [8]. At present, the optimal solution for the receiver of CPM modulated signals is the Maximum Likelihood Sequence Detection (MLSD) algorithm [9], which is difficult to implement in engineering and requires a simplified algorithm to reduce the demodulation complexity. There are two general directions, one is to reduce the difficulty of demodulation by reducing the number of mesh states, mainly including the Reduced State Sequence Detection (RSSD) algorithm [10] and Frequency Pulse Truncation (FPT) [11], and the other is to reduce the demodulation complexity by reducing the number of matching filters, mainly including Walsh decomposition algorithm [12], Singular Value Decomposition (SVD)

[13], Pulse Amplitude Modulation (PAM) Decomposition [14], State Space Partitioning (SSP) Algorithm [15], etc. These algorithms significantly reduce the complexity of the receiver's demodulation implementation by simplifying the way in which the demodulation algorithm sacrifices part of the demodulation performance. In order to compensate for the demodulation performance, TCM modulation is performed first before CPM modulation of the data [16,17], and the TCM is designed to jointly design coding and modulation, and compared with the traditional uncoded multi-level modulation, a significant coding gain of 3 6db is obtained by expanding the signal collection of multi-level phases without expanding the bandwidth [16,18]. According to the MLSD algorithm, the probabilities corresponding to most of the sequences generated by the sender can often be ignored, and it is not necessary to calculate the likelihood probabilities of all possible sequences when calculating the desired step. In practical engineering applications, the Viterbi algorithm can be used to perform the desired step [19] to obtain the probability of a set of surviving paths, calculate the expected value of the log-likelihood function, and realize the demodulation of CPM modulated signals [20].

With the continuous deepening of research, scholars have achieved positive results in the study of CPM modulation signal demodulation techniques applied in star-ground fusion networks. However, there are still some limitations in the existing research. First of all, the optimal solution algorithm is difficult to realize; the optimal solution for CPM modulated signal is the maximum likelihood sequence detection (MLSD) algorithm, but in engineering practice, the MLSD algorithm is difficult to realize because it requires extremely high computational complexity. In addition, the performance sacrifice of the simplified algorithm is not negligible. In order to reduce the demodulation complexity, researchers have proposed various simplified algorithms such as reduced state sequence detection (RSSD), frequency pulse truncation (FPT), Walsh decomposition, singular value decomposition (SVD), pulse-amplitude modulation (PAM) decomposition, and State Space Partitioning (SSP). These algorithms reduce the implementation complexity but sacrifice some of the demodulation performance.

To address the above limitations, this study is dedicated to the following work contributions: 1) Modulated signal generation method. At the transmitter side, the article proposes and implements a joint modulation signal generation method of TCM (Trellis Coded Modulation) and CPM (Continuous Phase Modulation), which provides a new way to improve the power efficiency and bandwidth efficiency of signal transmission. At the receiver side, the article adopts the Viterbi algorithm to demodulate the CPM signals, which is an effective simplified algorithm that can reduce the complexity of demodulation while guaranteeing the performance. 2) Theoretical analysis and simulation study. The article provides a detailed theoretical analysis of the two modulation and demodulation methods, 4CPM (4-Level Continuous Phase Modulation) and 4CPTCM (4-Level Continuous Phase Trellis Coded Modulation), and a MATLAB simulation tool is used for the Comparative study, which provides empirical evidence to understand the characteristics and performance of different modulation methods. 3) Program debugging and hardware implementation. The article uses TI's high-speed DSP (Digital Signal Processor) data processing chip for program debugging, and the algorithm is successfully ported to an actual narrowband high-speed digital radio, which demonstrates the potential of the research results for practical application. 4) Performance test and scenario applicability. Through practical tests, the article proves that the two modulation methods have stable and reliable performance and high success rate of digital transmission, especially in the 6G full coverage Satellite-Terrestrial Integrated Network, which is a scenario with limited bandwidth and energy, to meet the application requirements, and provide an important reference for the design of future communication systems. Overall, the contribution of the work in the article is to propose an efficient modulation and demodulation scheme, and to demonstrate its applicability and superior performance in specific constrained scenarios through theoretical analysis, simulation validation, and practical testing.

2 Theoretical Analysis of TCM-CPM Modulation and Demodulation

2.1 Description of CPM Modulated Signals

The CPM-modulated signal represents:

$$S(t) = \sqrt{\frac{2E}{t}}\cos[2\pi f_c t + \Phi(t, \bar{I}) + \phi_0] \tag{1}$$

$$\Phi(t, \bar{I}) = 2\pi h \sum_{-\infty}^{n} I_k q(t - kT)\, nT \le t \le (n+1)T \tag{2}$$

$$q(t) = \int_0^t g(\tau)d\tau \tag{3}$$

where f_c is the carrier frequency, $\Phi(t, \bar{I})$ is the carrier phase, ϕ_0 is that the initial phase can be 0, In this case, it does not affect the generality of the discussion, E is the signal energy in the period of a symbol, I_k is the symbol of the information to be modulated in the base of M, The value ranges from the following values: $\{\pm1, \pm3, \pm5, ...\pm(M-1)\}$, $h = \frac{k}{p}$ is the modulation index. k, pare prime numbers with each other, $g(\tau)$ where is the pulse function, $q(t)$ is a phase response function, It is the integral of the impulse function, The continuity of $q(t)$ determines the continuity of the phase of the modulation signal $\Phi(t, \bar{I}) + \phi_0$.

Parameter L is introduced, When $g(\tau) = \left\{ \begin{smallmatrix} non0 & 0 \le t \le LT \\ 0 & others \end{smallmatrix} \right.$, L=1. The modulated signal is a full-response signal. When L > 1, The modulated signal is a partially responsive signal, L is the associated length. Therefore, CPM modulation parameters mainly include M, h, L, $g(\tau)$, where $g(\tau)$ can be any one of the pulse functions of 1REC, 1RC, or GMSK. Here are three commonly used pulse forms:

1) LREC represents a rectangular pulse with a duration of LT

$$g_{LREC}(t) = \frac{1}{2LT} \tag{4}$$

$$g_{LREC}(t) = \frac{t}{2LT} \tag{5}$$

2) LRC represents a rising cosine pulse with a duration of LT

$$g_{LRC}(t) = \frac{1}{2LT}[1 - \cos(\frac{2\pi t}{LT})] \tag{6}$$

$$g_{LRC}(t) = \frac{t}{2LT} - \frac{1}{4\pi}\sin(\frac{2\pi t}{LT}) \tag{7}$$

3) GMSK is a Gaussian frequency shift keying pulse with a bandwidth parameter of B, and B represents the bandwidth of -3 db of Gaussian pulse

$$g_{GMSK}(t) = \frac{1}{2T}Q[2\pi B_b \frac{t - \frac{t}{2}}{\sqrt{In2}}] - \frac{1}{2T}Q[2\pi B_b \frac{t - \frac{t}{2}}{\sqrt{In2}}] \tag{8}$$

$$Q(t) = \int_t^{\infty} \frac{1}{\sqrt{2\pi}}e^{-\frac{T^2}{2}} d\tau \tag{9}$$

The calculation is as follows:

$$\Phi(t, \bar{I}) = 2\pi h \Sigma_{k=-\infty}^{n} I_k q(t - kT) \tag{10}$$

$$\Phi(t, \bar{I}) = 2\pi h \Sigma_{k=-\infty}^{n-L} I_k q(t - kT) + 2\pi h \Sigma_{k=n-L+1}^{n} I_k q(t - kT) \tag{11}$$

$$\Phi(t, \bar{I}) = \pi h \Sigma_{k=-\infty}^{-L} I_k q(t - kT) + 2\pi h \Sigma_{k=n-L+1}^{n} I_k q(t - kT) \tag{12}$$

$$\Phi(t, \bar{I}) = \phi_n + \phi(t, \bar{I}) \tag{13}$$

The modulation block diagram of CPM modulation signal is shown in Fig. 1.

2.2   TCM Signal Description

TCM is essentially a search for codes that maximize the minimum Euclidean distance for different modulation schemes. The modulation used in this paper is a combination of convolutional code and multilevel multiphase modulation. In the modulation structure, the signal mapping is based on the principle of set segmentation, which divides a signal set into smaller subsets one after another, and maximizes the minimum spatial distance in the segmented subsets. Each split splits a large signal set into two smaller subsets, with the smallest distance within the subset being the largest. Therefore, TCM is actually a kind of convolutional coding, which was first proposed by Elias in 1955, and Viterbi proposed the maximum likelihood decoding algorithm in 1967, which has been widely used in the field of communication since then. Convolutional coding encodes k-bit information segments into n-bit code groups, but the n-long code sets are not

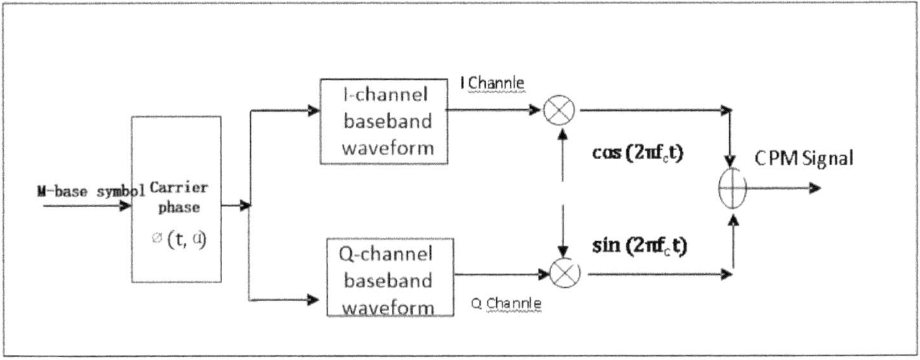

Fig. 1. Modulation block diagram of a CPM modulated signal.

only related to the current k-bit information segments, but also to the preceding $(N-1)$ information segments. Convolutional codes are often referred to as (n, k, N) convolutional codes, with an encoding efficiency of $R_c = \frac{k}{n}$, where N is the constraint length of the convolutional code.4CPTCM encoding adopts the maximum free-distance convolutional code encoding method with a constraint length of 3. Figure 2 is a block diagram of 4CPTCM encoding.

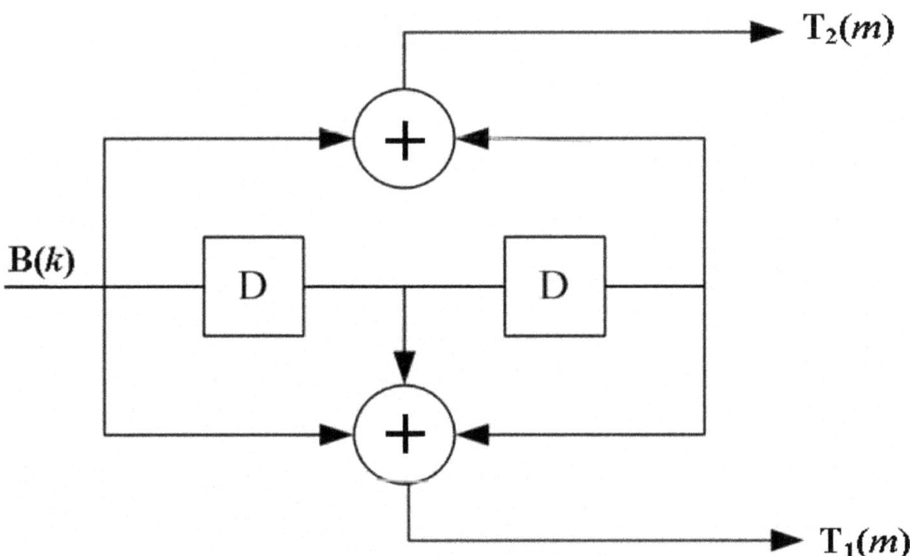

Fig. 2. Block diagram of 4CPTCM encoding.

2.3   TCM Signal Description

The resulting polynomial for T2(m) is:

$$g_2(x) = x^2 + 1 \tag{14}$$

The resulting polynomial for T1(m) is:

$$g_1(x) = x^2 + x + 1 \tag{15}$$

2.4   TCM-CPM Modulation Block Diagram

The TCM-CPM modulation process block diagram is shown in Fig. 3, where the TCM coding block diagram is shown in Fig. 2 and the CMP modulation block diagram is shown in Fig. 1.

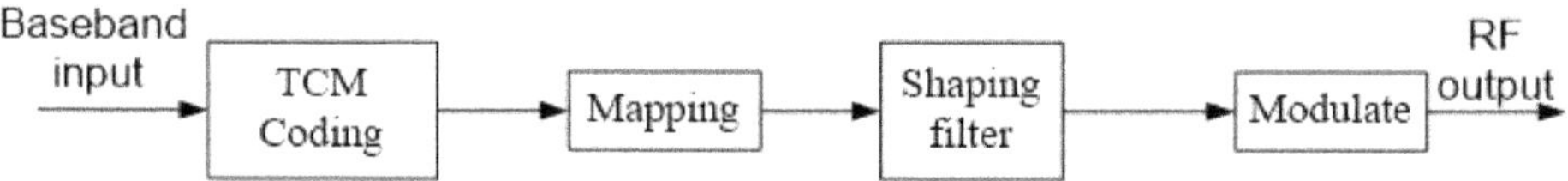

Fig. 3. Block diagram of TCM-CPM modulation process.

2.5   Demodulation of CPM Signals

CPM can be used as a grid plot to represent the possible transmission signals, and its optimal demodulation method is to use maximum likelihood sequence detection. However, due to the smoothing of the phase impulse response, the increase in the set of modulated signals, and the decrease in the modulation index, the detection of the maximum likelihood sequence, which is commonly used, becomes complex and difficult to achieve in engineering. Therefore, differential detection and Viterbi decoding are generally used to demodulate the CPM signal according to the parameters of the CPM signal. In practical engineering implementation systems, in order to ensure the reliability of transmission during the synchronization phase, a fully responsive CPM signal with small base number and high modulation index is generally used. In this case, differential detection can be used, which is a simple detection method and easy to implement with DSP. In the data transmission stage, in order to improve spectrum utilization, it is necessary to use partially responsive CPM signals with high base numbers and low modulation indices. At this time, Viterbi algorithm is needed for demodulation. In this paper, we discuss that the synchronization information applied to high-speed data transmission radio stations adopts the modulation method of 2CPM, and the demodulation method adopts the method of differential demodulation. 4CPTCM and 4CPM modulation were used for data modulation, and Viterbi algorithm was used for demodulation.

Differential Detection. Let the input CPM signal be: $S(t) = \sqrt{\frac{2E}{t}}$ $\cos[2\pi f_c t + \Phi(t, \bar{I}) + \phi_0]$, $\phi_0 = 0$, The carrier phase at time $K-1$ is ϕ_{k-1}, The carrier phase at time k is ϕ_{k-1}, The input sequence at time k is I_k, then

$$\Phi_k - \Phi_{k-1} = \pi h I_k \tag{16}$$

The differential detection block diagram is shown in Fig. 4.

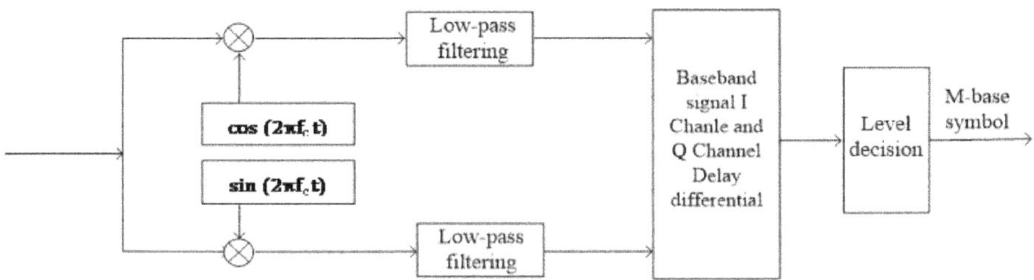

Fig. 4. Differential Detection Block Diagram

Among them $I_k = \frac{1}{2}\sin\phi_k$, $Q_k = \frac{1}{2}\cos\phi_k$ then

$$I_k Q_{k-1} - I_{k-1} Q_k = \frac{1}{2}(\sin\phi_k \cos\phi_{k-1} - \cos\phi_k \sin\phi_{k-1}) = \frac{1}{2}\sin\pi h I_k \tag{17}$$

The input sequence I_k can then be determined by setting the corresponding level to the discriminator.

Viterbi Decoding. Viterbi decoding algorithm is a sequential grid search algorithm used to perform ML sequence detection. At each moment, each path into the grid node has its own metric. The Viterbi algorithm compares the metrics of each path and stores the path with the smallest metric (called the surviving path) so that the optimality of the grid search is not lost. Each new signal received from the demodulator, at each level of the grid search, the Viterbi algorithm calculates the path metric that enters each node, stores one surviving path and discards the others, and then extends the surviving path Reach to the next state. It can be seen that the computational comparison of metrics is the key to the Viterbi algorithm. The Viterbi decoding block diagram is shown in Fig. 5.

In the AWGN channel, the ML criterion can be simplified to a signal with a minimum Euclidean distance from the received signal r. The following formula is used to estimate the sending sequence:

$$\alpha = argmax Pr\{r(t)|s(t,\alpha)\} = argmin\|r(t) - s(t,\alpha)\|^2 \tag{18}$$

where $r(t) = s(t,\alpha) + n(t)$ is the received signal and $s(t,\alpha)$ is the transmitted signal. Further, since the CPM signal has equal energy, the above criterion and

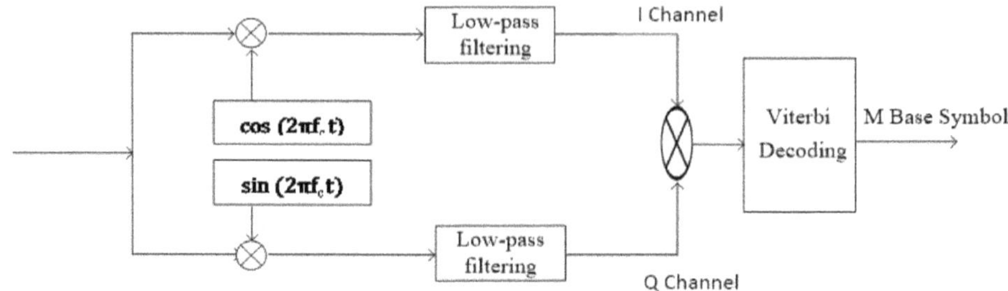

Fig. 5. Viterbi decoding block diagram.

the selection assume that the signal $\widetilde{\alpha}$, $s(t, \widetilde{\alpha})$ has the greatest correlation value with the received signal is equivalent.

$$\widetilde{\alpha} = argmax Re\{\langle r(t), s(t, \widetilde{\alpha})\rangle\} \tag{19}$$

In the Viterbi algorithm, this correlation value is iteratively calculated, and decisions are made based on the path metric for sequences merged into the same state. After the sign interval n, $t \in [nT, (n+1)T]$, the path metric becomes:

$$PM_n(\alpha) = Re\{\int_{-\infty}^{(n+1)T} r(t)s^*(t, \alpha)dt\} = PM_{n+1}(\alpha) + CM_n(\alpha) \tag{20}$$

where CM_n represents the additional metric caused by the signal within the $nT \ll t \ll (n+1)T$ time interval:

$$CM_n(\alpha) = Re\{\int_{-\infty}^{(n+1)T} r(t)s^*(t, \alpha)dt\} \tag{21}$$

The signal has M^L possible symbol sequences $\alpha = \{\alpha_n, \alpha_{n-1}......\alpha_{n-L+1}\}$ and P (or 2p) possible phase states, Thus pM^L (or $2pM^L$) different CM_n values are calculated at each signal interval, each of which is used as an increment corresponding to the surviving sequence metric in the previous signal transmission interval.

For each state in the Viterbi decoding process, the number of surviving sequences is pM^{L-1} (or $2pM^{L-1}$). For each surviving sequence, there are M new increments CM_n, which are appended to the existing metrics, resulting in M^L (or $2pM^L$)) sequences with M^L (or $2pM^L$) metrics. However, the number of these sequences is reduced back to pM^{L-1} (or $2pM^{L-1}$) surviving sequences with corresponding metrics, due to the selection of the most likely sequence among the M sequences converging at each node of the grid and discarding the other M − 1 sequences.

3 TCM-CPM Modulation and Demodulation Performance Simulation

In the actual project, combined with the test requirements of CPM modulation in high-speed data transmission radio stations and the data transmission index requirements of modems, and considering the complexity of demodulation, M=4, h=1/4, L=1, 1RC and so on were selected for 4CPTCM and 4CPM simulations. The bit error rate curves of 4CPTCM and 4CPM are shown in Fig. 6. It can be seen from Fig. 6 that the modulation and demodulation performance of 4CPTCM is significantly better than that of 4CPM under the same SNR. Simulation results show that the proposed TCM-CPM modulation scheme has high spectral efficiency and bit error rate performance, When the bit error rate is 1×10^{-4}, 4CPTCM achieves 4db encoding gain compared with traditional CPM modulation, so 4CPTCM modulation can be used for data transmission at a lower rate to ensure transmission distance and transmission reliability.4CPM modulation is used for higher rate data transmission to improve data transmission capacity, but the transmission distance and transmission reliability are reduced.

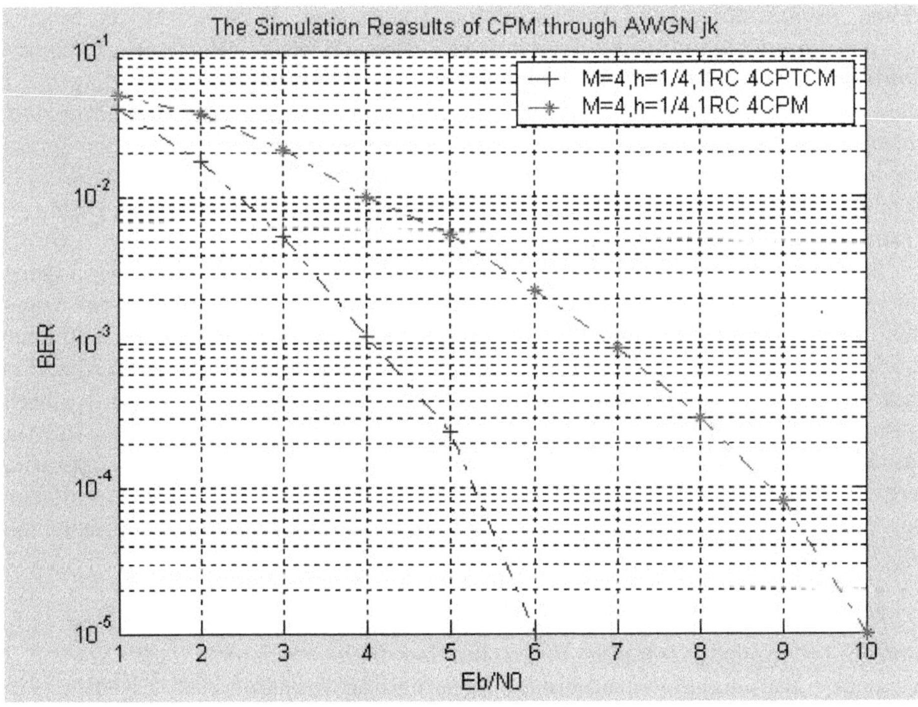

Fig. 6. Simulation BER curves of 4CPTCM and 4CPM.

The combined analysis and simulation results show that the CPM parameters have a great influence on the modulation performance in the multi-base CPM modulation technology. It mainly includes the following parameters: modulation index h, correlation length L, and multi-base number M. The effects of each parameter on the performance of the modulation system are as follows: The modulation index h affects the spectrum characteristics of CPM, and the smaller the h, the higher the frequency band utilization; The larger the number M, the greater the number of bits carried by each message symbol, which can improve the bit rate of information transmission, but will bring about a decline in bit error rate performance. When used in practical environments with limited bandwidth and power, the physical layer waveform design can consider using a low 2CPM modulation method for the synchronization information channel to ensure the correct transmission and extraction of synchronization information, while the data transmission channel can consider using a high 4CPM modulation method to meet the high-speed data transmission requirements.

4   4TCM-CPM Modulation and Demodulation Test and Results

When programming and implementing the actual TCM CPM modulation scheme, based on the above analysis, the physical layer waveform adopts two modulation methods:4CPTCM and 4CPM, The modulation block diagram is shown in Fig. 3. When the DSP is programmed at the sending end, the 1RC waveform pulse, I waveform and Q waveform form are taken as the corresponding lookup table to improve the generation speed of the modulated signal. The receiving end uses Viterbi demodulation, and the block diagram of DSP programming is shown in Fig. 7 below.

According to the above analysis, In the actual TCM-CPM modulation transmission test, a high-speed data transmission radio station is used as the transmission carrier. The two operating modes of the radio station are fixed frequency mode and frequency-hopping mode, and the channel bandwidth is 25 Khz. The test was completed in the laboratory, and the test equipment included two high-speed data transmission stations, among which radio 1 was the data transmitter, radio 2 was the data receiver, a power synthesizer, an RF signal source operating frequency of 15.025 Mhz, an attenuator, and several test cables. The modulation and demodulation test of CPM was carried out according to the instrument test platform shown in Fig. 8 below.

The test process is as follows:

Radio working mode: frequency hopping (FH:177.777hop/s), sending radio station 1: frequency hopping meter number 04005, receiving radio station 2: frequency hopping meter number 05005, mixing frequency: 15.025 MHz. Frequency hopping table number 04005, 05005 operating frequency is 30.025Mhz-87.975Mhz random frequency composed of frequency hopping table.

Radio working mode: fixed frequency.

The test results of 4CPTCM are shown in Table 1 below.

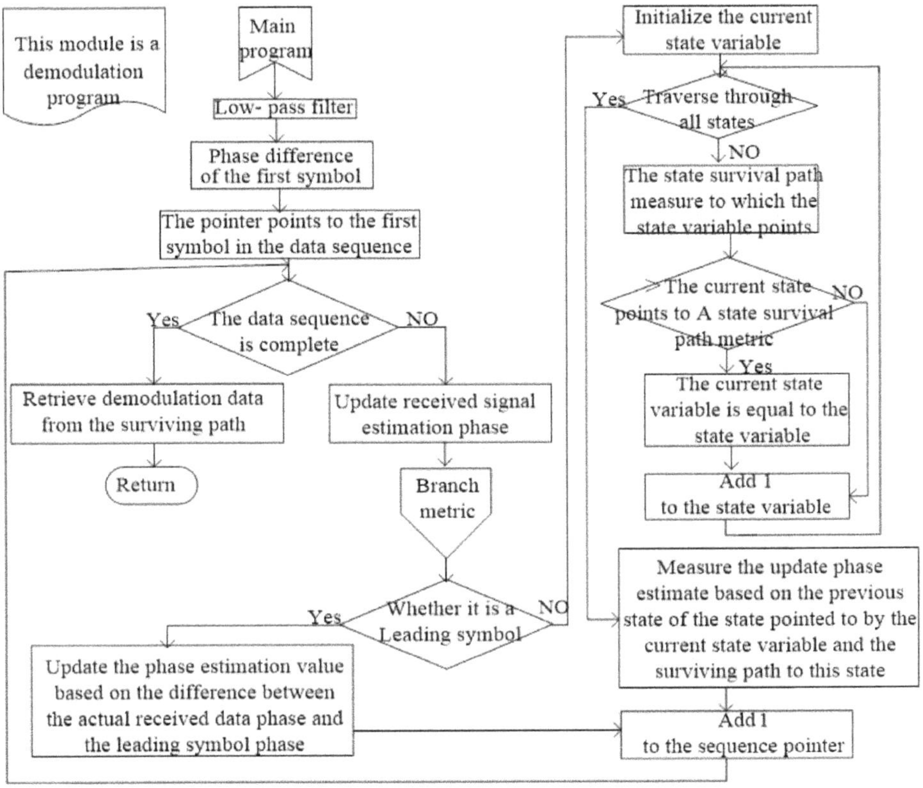

This module is a demodulation program

Main program

Low-pass filter

Phase difference of the first symbol

The pointer points to the first symbol in the data sequence

The data sequence is complete — Yes / NO

Retrieve demodulation data from the surviving path

Return

Update received signal estimation phase

Branch metric

Whether it is a Leading symbol — Yes / NO

Update the phase estimation value based on the difference between the actual received data phase and the leading symbol phase

Initialize the current state variable

Traverse through all states — Yes / NO

The state survival path measure to which the state variable points

The current state points to A state survival path metric — NO / Yes

The current state variable is equal to the state variable

Add 1 to the state variable

Measure the update phase estimate based on the previous state of the state pointed to by the current state variable and the surviving path to this state

Add 1 to the sequence pointer

Fig. 7. Block diagram of Viterbi demodulation.

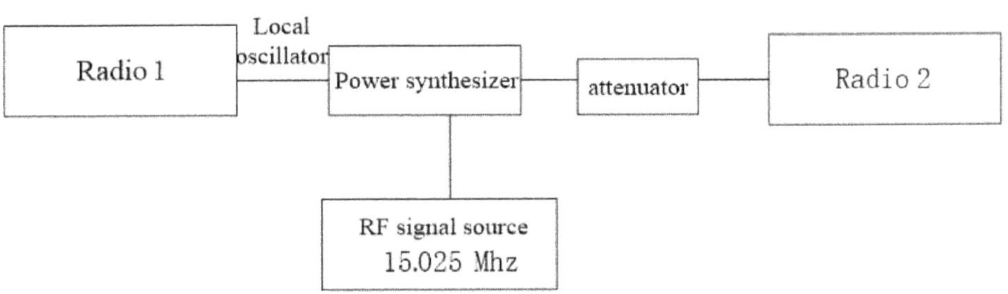

Fig. 8. Test schematic diagram.

Table 1. CPM modulation test results of 4CPTCM

Data rate	Sending Frequency	Receiving frequency	Data transmission success rate
1.2 kbps	FH04005, 30.025 Mhz	FH05005, 45.050 Mhz	−116 dbm, 95%
2.4 kbps	FH04005, 45.050 Mhz	FH05005, 60.075 Mhz	−116 dbm, 95%
4.8 kbps	FH04005, 36.425 Mhz	FH05005, 51.450 Mhz	−116 dbm, 95%
9.6 kbps	FH04005, 55.000 Mhz	FH05005, 70.025 Mhz	−116 dbm, 95%

Table 2. CPM modulation test results of 4CPM

Data rate	Sending Frequency	Receiving frequency	Data transmission success rate
19.2 kbps	FH04005, 30.025 Mhz	FH05005, 45.050 Mhz	-111 dbm, 95%
28.8 kbps	FH04005, 45.050 Mhz	FH05005, 60.075 Mhz	-111 dbm, 95%

The test results of 4CPM are shown in Table 2 below.

From the actual test results of the radio station, it can be seen that in a narrowband channel of 25 Khz, 4CPTCCM modulation is suitable for medium to low speed data transmission at speeds of 1.2 kbps, 2.4 kbps, 4.8 kbps, 9.6 kbps, etc. Under small signals, the success rate of data transmission is greater than or equal to 95% at -116 dbm, ensuring stable data transmission. In 25 Khz narrowband channel, 4CPM modulation, suitable for high-speed data transmission rates of 19.2 kbps, 28.8 kbps. Under small signal -111 dbm, the success rate of data transmission is greater than or equal to 95%, and the data transmission is stable and reliable. It can be seen that the demodulation performance of 4CPTCM is about 4 db higher than that of 4CPM, which is consistent with the simulation results. From the simulation performance and measured results. The practical test results of 4CPM and 4CPTCM modulation and demodulation are consistent with the theoretical analysis results, and the performance of modulation and demodulation is stable. Furthermore, after transmission tests in narrowband high-speed data transmission radios, it can be seen that their operation is stable and reliable. Therefore, the CPM modulation method can be applied in the scenario of limited bandwidth and power of satellite-terrestrial integrated network in engineering implementation.

5   Conclusion

When faced with the application scenario of limited bandwidth and limited power in 6G full-coverage satellite-terrestrial integrated network, the constant envelope of CPM modulation signal is the key to realize the waveform design of physical layer. In this paper, the general principle of CPM modulation and demodulation is analyzed. Aiming at the problem of high complexity of CPM receiver demodulation algorithm, TCM joint design strategy is combined to make up for the performance degradation caused by simplified demodulation algorithm. Two modulation schemes of 4CPTCM and 4CPM are simulated and successfully applied in narrowband high speed data transmission radios. The experimental results show that the combination of TCM and CPM modulation technology is stable, reliable, low demodulation complexity, easy to implement in engineering, and is more suitable for the application of narrow-band high-speed channels with limited power and bandwidth.

References

1. Shen, X.M., Cheng, N., Zhou, H.B., et al.: Space-air-ground integrated networks: review and prospect. Chin. J. Internet Things **4**(3), 3–19 (2020)
2. You, X.H., Wang, C.X., Huang, J., et al.: Towards 6G wireless communication networks: vision, enabling technologies, and new paradigm shifts. Sci. China Inf. Sci. **64**(1), 1–74 (2020)
3. Liu, J., Du, X.Q., Cui, J.H., et al.: Task-oriented intelligent networking architecture for the space–air–ground integrated network. IEEE Internet Things J. **7**(6), 5345–5358 (2020)
4. Pan, Z., Xie, C., Wang, H., Guo, D.: Research status of CPM for satellite-terrestrial integrated network. Space-Integrated-Ground Inf. Netw. **4**(1) (2023)
5. Ssimbwa, J., Lim, B., Lee, J.H., et al.: A survey on robust modulation requirements for the next generation personal satellite communications. Front. Communi. Netw. **3**, 850781 (2022)
6. Ni, Y.D., Zou, L., Liu, R.H., et al.: C-band navigation signal modulation mode and performance evaluation of BeiDou system. Syst. Eng. Electron. **44**(12), 3800–3810 (2022)
7. Chamaa, M.E., Lankl, B.: Noncoherent symbol detection of short CPM bursts in frequency-selective fading channels. IEEE Trans. Wirel. Commun. **19**(2), 771–782 (2020)
8. Xi, Z.P., Zhu, J., Fu, Y.M.: Low-complexity detection of binary CPM with small modulation index. IEEE Commun. Lett. **20**(1), 57–60 (2016)
9. Lang, A., Lankl, B.: A comprehensive study of CPM trellis initialization methods. In: 2022 IEEE Military Communications Conference (MILCOM), pp. 78–83. IEEE, Rockville (2022)
10. Sun, J., Li, J., Jin, L., et al.: Noncoherent reduced state differential sequence detection of continuous phase modulation. In: 2004 IEEE 15th International Symposium on Personal, Indoor and Mobile Radio Communications, Barcelona, pp. 780–784. IEEE (2004)
11. Svensson, A., Sundberg, C., Aulin, T.: A class of reduced-complexity Viterbi detectors for partial response continuous phase modulation. IEEE Trans. Commun. **32**(10), 1079–1087 (1984)
12. Fu, M., Wade, G., Ning, J., et al.: On Walsh filtering method for decoding of CPM signals. IEEE Commun. Lett. **8**(6), 345–347 (2004)
13. Chen, S., Yang, Y., Wei, K., et al.: Time-varying frequency-modulated component extraction based on parameterized demodulation and singular value decomposition. IEEE Trans. Instrum. Meas. **65**(2), 276–285 (2015)
14. Perrins, E., Rice, M.: A new performance bound for pam-based CPM detectors. IEEE Trans. Commun. **53**(10), 1688–1696 (2005)
15. Larsson, T.: Optimal design of CPM decoders based on state-space partitioning. In: IEEE International Conference on Communications, pp. 123–127. IEEE, Geneva (1993)
16. Ungerboeck, G.: Channel coding with multilevel/phase signals. IEEE Trans. Inform. Theory **28**(1), 55–67 (1982)
17. Divsalar, D., Simon, M.K.: Multiple trellis coded modulations. IEEE Trans. Commun. **36**(4), 410–419 (1988)
18. Chen, X., Yang, X., Tong, Z., et al.: 150 m/500 Mbps under water wireless optical communication enabled by sensitive detection and the combination of receiver-side partial response shaping and TCM technology. J. Lightwave Technol. **39**, 4614–4621 (2021)

19. Bin, L., Shiping, S., Xiren, X.: Demodulation of CPM with noncoherent detection and Viterbi algorithm. In: Proceedings of 1992 International Conference on Communication Technology, CIE, CIC, Tsinghua University, vol. 2 (1992)
20. Nguyen, H., Levy, B.C.: Blind and semi-blind equalization of CPM signals with the EMV algorithm. IEEE Trans. Signal Process. **51**(10), 2650–2664 (2003)

Research on Intelligent Garbage Classification Algorithm Based on Improved YOLOv9

Gang Cao, Qihui Xia, Mingcong Ge, Shuangsheng Liang, Yuxi Yang, and Bin Wang(✉)

Jianghan University, Wuhan 430056, China
caogang0411@jhun.edu.cn, wangbin93@outlook.com

Abstract. Garbage classification can reduce pollution, promote resource circulation, and is the key to sustainable development. An intelligent garbage classification algorithm based on the improved YOLOv9, which is named MC-YOLOv9, is proposed to address the challenges of classification and resource utilization in the current garbage management field. Building upon the original YOLOv9 algorithm, MC-YOLOv9 introduces the Dual Convolution (DualConv) module, Multi-Scale Dilated Attention (MSDA) mechanism, and innovates on the loss function. A multi-class garbage dataset is constructed to train and optimize the MC-YOLOv9 model, aiming to enhance its accuracy and efficiency in garbage classification, and is compared with other common classification methods. Experimental results demonstrate that the improved MC-YOLOv9 model maintains the original accuracy of YOLOv9 while reducing GFLOPs by 9% and increasing recognition speed by 45.9%. Compared with traditional models such as YOLOv7, YOLOv7-Tiny, YOLOv5, and Faster R-CNN, the improved MC-YOLOv9 model achieves speed increases of 10.6%, 1.80%, 13.90%, and 54.9%, respectively. The experimental results indicate that the improved MC-YOLOv9 model can effectively enhance the recognition speed of garbage classification, providing new insights for the application of deep learning technology in the field of garbage management.

Keywords: Garbage classification · Yolov9 · Dual Convolution module · Multi-Scale Dilated Attention mechanism

1 Introduction

With the continuous advancement of urbanization and improvement of living standards, garbage management has become a significant challenge in today's

Supported in part by the 2023 National College Student Innovation and Entrepreneurship Training Program under Grant 202311072013; in part by the 2023 National College Student Innovation and Entrepreneurship Training Program under Grant 202311072007; in part by the 2023 Provincial College Student Innovation and Entrepreneurship Project under Grant S202311072038.

R. C. Qiu et al. (Eds.): IoTaaS 2024, LNICST 675, pp. 139–152, 2026.
https://doi.org/10.1007/978-3-032-14681-6_12

society. The massive generation and accumulation of garbage not only cause severe environmental pollution but also threaten human health and ecological balance. Garbage classification can reduce the pollution of soil, water sources, and air, facilitate resource recovery and recycling, maximize environmental protection, and promote sustainable development. However, traditional manual garbage classification methods are inefficient and susceptible to subjective factors, making it difficult to achieve large-scale automation and intelligent processing.

In recent years, with the development of the Internet of Things [1–3] and machine vision technology [4,5], the use of computer vision and deep learning techniques for intelligent garbage classification has become a research hotspot. Li Y et al. [6] overcame overfitting by introducing Dropout, used Adagrad to fine-tune parameters, and applied ReLU to address gradient vanishing problems, achieving centralized processing and feature extraction of garbage images. Liang G et al. [7] constructed the FConvNet model for garbage classification, achieving an accuracy rate of 95%. Yang Z et al. [8] addressed low precision caused by light and shadow interference by adopting an adaptive image brightening algorithm to average background brightness and using a threshold replacement method to reduce shadow noise, optimizing the neural network based on the MLH-CNN model, resulting in simple and efficient outcomes. Tested on a self-built dataset, the CNN model achieved an accuracy of 96.77%. Gao Xia et al. [9] improved the activation function of ShuffleNet v2 by replacing the original ReLU function with the LeakyReLU function after pre-training multiple convolutional neural networks on the large Imagenet database, which improved recognition accuracy by 0.3%. Li X et al. [10] introduced the CBAM attention mechanism to extract key features by spatially and channel-weighting the output features, used the LeakyReLU function as the activation function, and constructed the loss function using label smoothing to mitigate the error impact of sample imbalance, achieving better nonlinear transformation effects. Tests on ordinary garbage images and infrared imaging technology-based garbage images showed that the proposed GScbamKL-Net exhibited excellent classification performance while maintaining a lightweight nature.

Existing research has improved model accuracy by optimizing model structures. However, the pursuit of higher accuracy is often accompanied by significant increases in computational load and model size. Deeper network layers and more parameters can capture richer feature information and improve detection accuracy, but they also increase computational complexity and memory usage. This poses a significant challenge for applications that need to run on embedded or mobile devices.

YOLOv9 has demonstrated excellent performance in object detection, showcasing remarkable detection accuracy and speed. It introduces a series of innovative techniques, including deeper network structures, improved feature extraction methods, and optimized loss functions, achieving state-of-the-art detection results on multiple benchmark datasets. However, due to the complexity and large number of parameters in the model, the application of YOLOv9 is limited in resource-constrained environments, preventing full utilization of its advanced detection capabilities. Therefore, this study first replaces the original Conv convolution in the YOLOv9 model with an improved DualConv convolution to significantly reduce computational parameters, thereby lightening the model. Secondly, a lightweight multi-scale dilated attention module is added at the detection head to ensure model accuracy. Finally, the original loss function is replaced with InnerCIOU to accelerate model convergence and enhance model generalization capability.

2 Introduction to the Improved MC-YOLOv9

2.1 Model Improvement

YOLOv9 [11] is mainly composed of three parts: Head, Neck, and Backbone. Although it has high accuracy, it is slightly lacking in feature extraction for small objects and recognition speed. To address these issues, improvements are made to the YOLOv9 model, as shown in Fig. 1, where the dashed box represents the improved part.

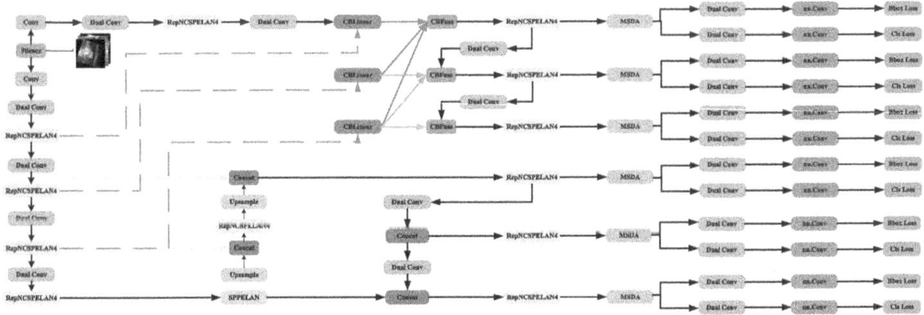

Fig. 1. The network structure diagram of MC-YOLOv9.

Firstly, to enhance the model's ability to extract features from small objects, an MSDA module is added before each detection head to strengthen the model's perception of small objects, thereby improving recognition efficiency. Secondly, to accelerate the model's recognition speed, the original convolution operations are replaced with more lightweight DualConv convolutions. These convolution operations have higher computational efficiency, effectively reducing the model's computational load and thus improving recognition speed. Through these improvements, the model's ability to extract features from small objects is enhanced while accelerating the model's recognition speed, making it more efficient and reliable in practical applications.

2.2 DualConv Convolution

In improving the YOLOv9 model, an innovative network structure called Dual Convolution (DualConv) [12] was adopted to achieve model lightweighting while enhancing feature extraction capabilities and optimizing computational efficiency. In DualConv, 3×3 and 1×1 convolutional kernels simultaneously process the same input feature map channels. The 3×3 convolutional kernel is responsible for capturing local spatial information and detailed features, providing a larger receptive field, which helps the model understand complex patterns and structures. Meanwhile, the 1×1 convolutional kernel is used for linear transformations between channels, reducing the dimensionality of the feature maps, thereby decreasing the computational load and the number of parameters. This design combines classic techniques from convolutional neural networks (CNNs) by using two consecutive convolutional layers in each convolutional block to improve feature extraction capabilities.

In the improved model, the DualConv module replaces the original Conv convolution, enhancing the model's ability to extract features from small objects and accelerating the computation process by reducing the number of parameters and computational load. To further optimize computational efficiency, the model also incorporates Grouped Convolution technology. Grouped Convolution divides the input feature maps into groups and performs convolution operations independently within each group, significantly reducing computational load. Compared to traditional fully connected convolutions, Grouped Convolution maintains efficient feature extraction while effectively lowering model complexity and the number of parameters, thus improving model speed and resource utilization.

When image information enters the DualConv convolution, the 3×3 convolutional kernel first captures local spatial information and detailed features, while the 1×1 convolutional kernel performs linear transformations between channels, reducing the dimensionality of the feature maps. Then, during the Grouped Convolution stage, the feature maps are divided into groups and processed independently within each group, further reducing computational load. Throughout this process, the model efficiently extracts and processes image features, ultimately generating high-precision detection results.

By parallel use of 3×3 and 1×1 convolutional kernels, along with Grouped Convolution technology, the improved model achieves faster recognition speed and lower computational cost while maintaining high accuracy.

2.3 MSDA Attention Mechanism

Multi-Scale Dilated Attention (MSDA) [13] is an advanced attention mechanism designed to enhance the feature extraction capabilities of convolutional neural networks (CNNs), particularly when handling complex scenes and multi-scale objects. By incorporating the concepts of multi-scale and dilated convolutions, MSDA effectively captures feature information across different scales and receptive fields, thereby improving the model's robustness and accuracy. Its structural diagram is shown in Fig. 2.

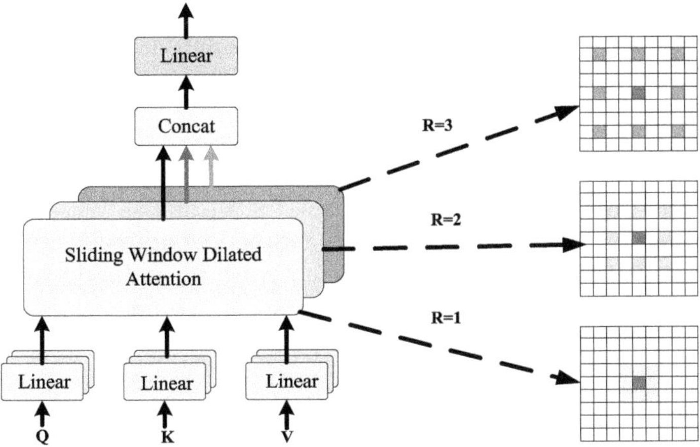

Fig. 2. The structural diagram of MSDA attention mechanism.

Firstly, MSDA uses dilated convolutions to increase the receptive field. Dilated convolutions introduce gaps (i.e., skip some pixels) between the convolutional kernels, expanding the receptive field without increasing the number of parameters and computational load. This allows the network to focus on a broader range of contextual information at the same layer, aiding in capturing both global features and fine details.

Secondly, MSDA operates on multiple scales. Specifically, the model applies dilated convolutions to feature maps at different scales to capture feature information of varying sizes. Multi-scale processing enables the model to simultaneously attend to large and small objects, as well as complex structures at different scales, enhancing its adaptability to diverse scenarios.

In MSDA, the attention mechanism calculates the attention weights of the feature maps to selectively enhance important features. Attention weights are allocated based on the importance of features, enabling the model to focus more on key areas while ignoring irrelevant or redundant information. The combination of multi-scale dilated convolutions and the attention mechanism gives the model strong feature selection and enhancement capabilities across different scales, thereby improving overall performance.

The key improvement in the YOLOv9 model involves the introduction of the MSDA module. This enhancement significantly boosts the model's ability to recognize complex scenes and multi-scale objects. By integrating the MSDA module into the feature extraction phase and detection head of the model, YOLOv9 can better capture the features of objects at different scales and positions, thereby increasing detection accuracy. For example, when processing various objects in urban street scenes or natural environments, MSDA enables the model to simultaneously focus on pedestrians, vehicles, and small distant objects, improving overall detection performance.

Additionally, the use of dilated convolutions does not significantly increase computational costs, allowing the model to maintain efficient operation while possessing stronger feature extraction and attention allocation capabilities.

2.4 Loss Function

The traditional Intersection over Union (IoU) is a commonly used loss function for object detection models, which directly reflects the degree of overlap between the predicted bounding box and the ground truth bounding box. The formula for calculating IoU is as follows:

$$IoU = \frac{Area\_of\_Overlap}{Area\_of\_Union} \tag{1}$$

where $Area\_of\_Overlap$ is the area of the intersection area of the predicted bounding box and the real bounding box, and $Area\_of\_Union$ is the area of the union region of the predicted bounding box and the real bounding box.

The traditional IoU only considers the area overlap between the prediction box and the real box, and ignores the center point position relationship between the two boxes. This can lead to poor performance of the model when dealing with complex scenes and small object detection with less bounding box overlap or large shape differences.

In order to solve these problems of IoU, InnerCIoU [14] (Inner Center Intersection over Union) is proposed to replace the traditional IoU. On the basis of IoU, InnerCIoU combines the evaluation index of the distance from the center point, so that the loss function can consider both the area overlap and the position relationship, and the calculation formula of InnercIoU is shown in (2).

$$CIoU = IoU - \frac{d^2}{S} - a \times p \tag{2}$$

where d is the Euclidean distance between the center point of the predicted frame and the center point of the real frame, and the calculation formula is shown in (3).

$$d = \sqrt{(x_1 - x_2)^2 + (y_1 - y_2)^2} \tag{3}$$

where (x_1, y_1) is the center point coordinate of the prediction box, (x_2, y_2) is the center point coordinate of the real box. a is the minimum area of the circumscribed rectangle containing the prediction box and the real box, as shown in (4).

$$\alpha = width \times height \tag{4}$$

where $width$ is the width of the minimum circumscribed rectangle and $height$ is the height of the minimum circumscribed rectangle. p is the aspect ratio item, which predicts the difference between the aspect ratio of the bounding box and the aspect ratio of the actual bounding box, as shown in (5).

$$p = \frac{w_1}{h_1} - \frac{w_2}{h_2} \tag{5}$$

where w_1 and h_1 represent the width and height of the predicted box, while w_2 and h_2 represent the width and height of the real box.

The structure diagrams of IoU loss function and InnerCIoU loss function are shown in the figure. Compared to IoU, InnerCIoU not only focuses on the overlap between bounding boxes but also considers the consistency within their internal regions. By taking into account the intersection of internal regions, InnerCIoU can better handle complex scenes, improve detection accuracy, and enhance robustness. Additionally, InnerCIoU can more accurately distinguish overlapping objects, reducing false positives and false negatives, and improving the detection rate of small objects.

3   Dataset Production

3.1   Data Acquisition

The experimental data were collected in different urban and suburban areas, covering various types of garbage, including recyclables, kitchen garbage, hazardous garbage, and other non-recyclable garbage. As shown in Fig. 3, the data were captured using a Nikon D3100 camera, totaling 5245 images.

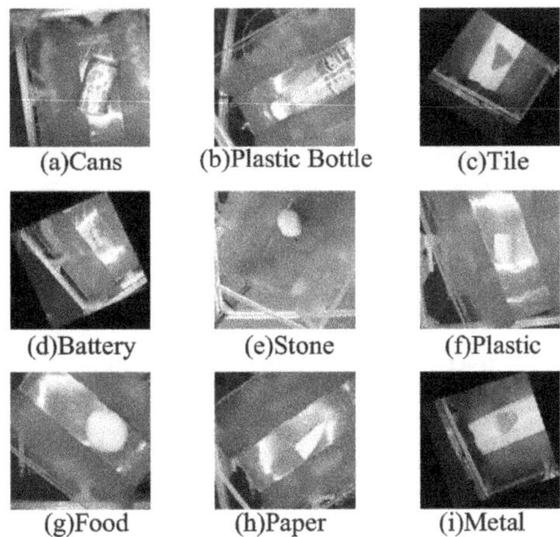

Fig. 3. Pictures of different types of garbage.

3.2   Dataset Construction

The dataset was constructed using the collected images and annotated using the LabelImg tool software. The annotation labels are as shown in Table 1, and the data were further categorized according to the "Household garbage Classification System" into Recyclables (REC), Hazardous garbage (HW), Food garbage (FW), and Other Garbage (OG).

Table 1. Type and quantity of garbage.

Types	Quantity
Cans	420
Plastic Bottle	370
Tile	500
Battery	690
Stone	930
Plastic	365
Food	520
Paper	810
Metal	640

Table 2. Classification and quantity of garbage.

Label	Contents	Quantity
REC	Cans, Plastic Bottle, Plastic, Paper, Metal	2605
HW	Battery	690
FW	Food	520
OG	Tile, Stone	1430

The label names, corresponding contents, and quantities of the garbage dataset are shown in Table 2.

The garbage dataset is divided into training, validation, and test sets in a ratio of 8:1:1. The respective quantities are shown in Table 3.

Table 3. Data set partitioning.

Dataset	Quantity
Training Set	4196
Validation Set	525
Test Set	524

3.3 Evaluation Criteria

This paper evaluates the model's performance using various metrics including Precision, Recall, Giga Floating Point Operations per Second (GFLOPs), mean Average Precision (mAP), and detection speed (Frames Per Second, FPS). Precision is abbreviated as P, calculated as shown in equation (6); Recall is abbreviated as R, calculated as shown in equation (7); GFLOPs are mainly used to measure the computational complexity of a model or algorithm; mAP is calculated as shown in equation (8); FPS indicates the number of images the model can detect per second, representing the time required to recognize one image.

$$P = \frac{TP}{TP + FP} \times 100\% \tag{6}$$

$$R = \frac{TP}{TP + FN} \times 100\% \tag{7}$$

$$mAP = \frac{1}{C} \sum_{i=1}^{C} \int_{0}^{1} P(R)d(R) \tag{8}$$

3.4 Experimental Environment and Parameter Settings

All experiments in this paper were conducted in the same experimental environment using the same parameter configuration. The relevant configurations and parameter settings are shown in Table 4.

Table 4. Experimental environment.

Hardware Name	Model
Operating System	Windows 11
CPU	AMD Ryzen 7 7735H with Radeon Graphics 3.20 GHz
Memory	8GB
GPU	NVIDIA GeForce RTX 4060 Laptop GPU
VRAM	8GB
Programming Platform	PyCharm
Programming Language	Python 3.8

4 Experiments and Results

4.1 Training Loss Comparison

In this experiment, the training loss curve of the improved MC-YOLOv9 model is compared with that of the original YOLOv9 model. The results are shown in Fig. 4.

According to the data in Fig. 4, the improved MC-YOLOv9 model shows a rapid decrease in loss values within the initial 30 epochs, indicating strong learning ability and fast data fitting capability. Subsequently, between epochs 30 and 300, the loss value decline trend gradually slows down and eventually stabilizes around the level of 0.95, showing a state of minor fluctuation. Compared to the

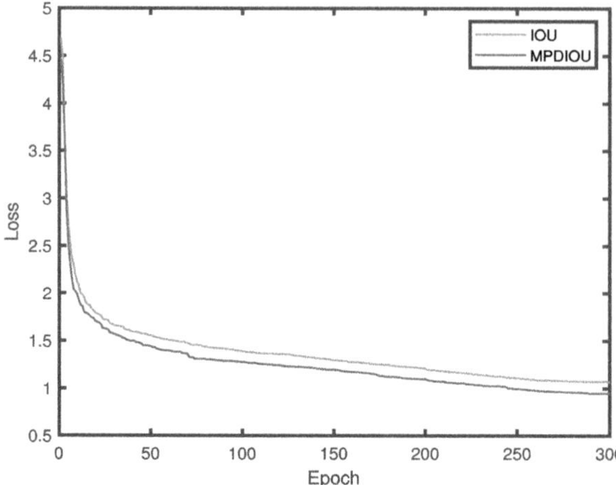

Fig. 4. Loss value curve.

original YOLOv9 model, the improved MC-YOLOv9 model not only converges faster but also exhibits smaller loss value fluctuations, demonstrating higher stability and lower loss values. These improvements indicate that the MC-YOLOv9 model can converge more efficiently during training while maintaining high accuracy and stability.

4.2   Comparison Experiments

The original YOLOv9 model and the improved MC-YOLOv9 model were trained using the same dataset in the same environment. The experimental results are shown in Table 5.

Table 5. Performance comparison between MC-YOLOv9 and YOLOv9.

Model	P%				R%				mPA	GFLOPs	FPS
	REC	HW	FW	OG	REC	HW	FW	OG			
YOLOy9	97.30	98.20	98.30	96.90	98.20	97.20	98.30	97.80	98.20	236.7	34.4
MC-YOLOv9	97.10	98.25	98.60	96.30	98.60	96.80	98.60	98.00	98.12	215.3	50.2

Based on the data analysis, MC-YOLOv9 maintains a high accuracy comparable to YOLOv9 while significantly enhancing recognition speed and reducing computational complexity, demonstrating superior overall performance. In terms of precision and recall, MC-YOLOv9 performs very closely to YOLOv9 across all categories, showing strong recognition capability. Specifically, for food garbage identification, MC-YOLOv9 achieves a precision and recall of 98.60%, slightly surpassing YOLOv9. This indicates that MC-YOLOv9 maintains high accuracy without a noticeable disadvantage in recognizing different categories.

As shown in Fig. 5, MC-YOLOv9 exhibits a significant improvement in computational efficiency, with a computational complexity of only 215.3 GFLOPs, much lower than YOLOv9's 236.7 GFLOPs. This means that MC-YOLOv9 requires fewer computational resources to perform the same tasks, thereby saving costs and improving efficiency. Additionally, MC-YOLOv9 achieves an FPS of 40.2, outperforming YOLOv9's 34.4. This indicates that MC-YOLOv9 can process image data faster within the same timeframe, providing greater potential for real-time or efficient processing. This improvement reflects the advancements in algorithm optimization and computational efficiency in MC-YOLOv9, enabling it to respond more quickly and handle large volumes of image data more effectively in practical applications, thereby enhancing the system's overall performance and usability.

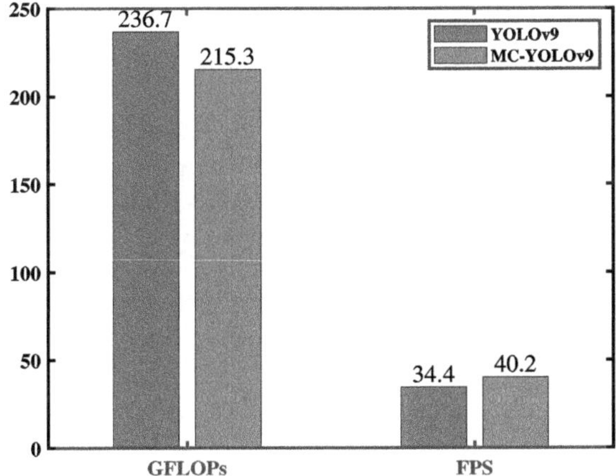

Fig. 5. Comparison of GFLOPs and FPS of MC-YOLOv9 and YOLOv9.

4.3   Comparative Experiment of Different Models

To validate the superior performance of the proposed MC-YOLOv9 model, experiments were designed to compare it with current mainstream object detection algorithms on the same platform, same equipment, and using the same dataset. The selected object detection models include Faster R-CNN, YOLOv5, YOLOv7, and YOLOv7-Tiny. The experiments compared the models based on their precision, recall, average precision (AP), F1 score, mean average precision (mAP), and model weights. The experimental results are shown in Table 6.

From the table, it can be seen that while MC-YOLOv9 is slightly lower than the original YOLOv9 model in average precision on mPA, it improved by 3.70%, 6.20%, 7.10%, and 7.47% compared to YOLOv7, YOLOv7-Tiny, YOLOv5, and

Table 6. Comparative experimental results of different models.

Model	P%				R%				mPA	FPS
	REC	HW	FW	OG	REC	HW	FW	OG		
YOLOv9	97.30	98.20	98.30	96.90	98.20	97.20	98.30	97.80	98.20	34.4
MC-YOLOv9	97.10	98.25	98.60	96.30	98.60	96.80	98.60	98.00	98.12	50.2
YOLOv7	95.40	93.20	93.32	93.41	94.35	94.36	92.35	92.64	94.60	45.4
YOLOv7-Tiny	94.30	91.25	92.36	90.28	92.60	94.61	90.25	91.03	92.35	49.3
YOLOv5	90.50	92.60	94.30	92.38	93.38	92.30	92.60	92.40	91.60	43.20
Faster R-CNN	92.45	91.25	89.56	87.92	90.56	90.32	94.20	93.60	91.30	32.4

Faster R-CNN models, respectively. Additionally, in terms of recognition speed, MC-YOLOv9 achieved 50.2 frames per second. Compared to other models, MC-YOLOv9 improved recognition speed by 10.6%, 1.80%, 13.90%, and 54.9%, respectively. The comparative experiments demonstrate that the improved model excels in recognition speed over other models, though there remains significant room for optimization.

As shown in Fig. 6, the improved MC-YOLOv9 achieved a recognition speed of 50.2 frames per second, significantly higher than the other comparison models. This high-speed recognition capability gives MC-YOLOv9 a distinct advantage in applications that require real-time processing of large amounts of data or demand high efficiency.

5 Experimental Results

To accurately and swiftly classify garbage, an improved lightweight model based on YOLOv9, named MC-YOLOv9, is proposed in this paper. Compared to traditional models, the MC-YOLOv9 model offers the following advantages:

(1) Lightweight Design: The study first replaces the original convolution (Conv) in the YOLOv9 model with an improved DualConv convolution, significantly reducing computational parameters and making the model more lightweight.
(2) Enhanced Feature Extraction for Small Objects: To improve the model's ability to extract features from small objects, an MSDA (Multi-Scale Dilated Attention) module is added before each detection head. This enhances the model's perception of small objects, thereby increasing recognition efficiency. Additionally, a lightweight multi-scale dilated attention module is added at the detection end to ensure model accuracy.
(3) Improved Loss Function: The original loss function is replaced with Inner-CIOU to accelerate model convergence and enhance generalization ability.

Multiple experiments show that the improved MC-YOLOv9 model significantly increases recognition speed. Compared to the original YOLOv9 model, the recognition speed is increased by 45% while maintaining accuracy. GFLOPs

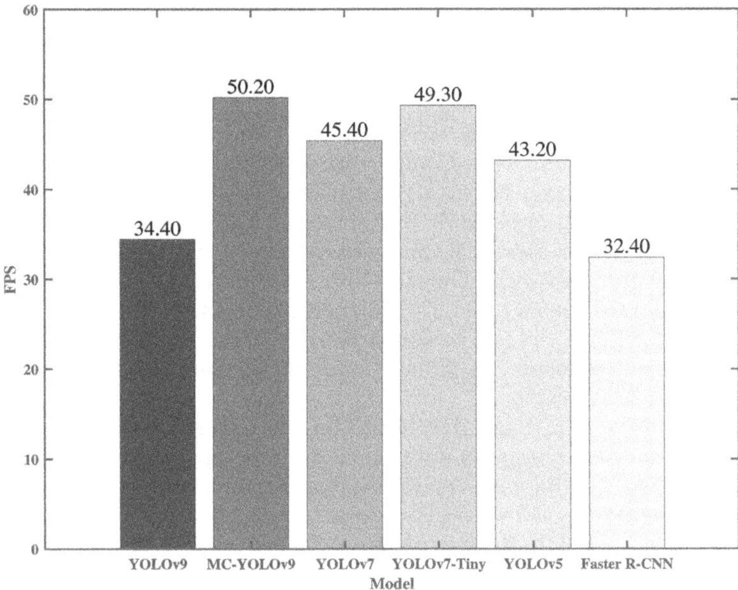

Fig. 6. Recognition speed of different models

are reduced by 9%. When compared to traditional models such as YOLOv7, YOLOv7-Tiny, YOLOv5, and Faster R-CNN, the recognition speed improves by 10.6%, 1.80%, 13.90%, and 54.9%, respectively.

Although the recognition speed has been significantly optimized, the training time has increased. Overall, this improved method shows better results in garbage classification tasks, and there is still room for optimization in the future, such as further compressing model weights through pruning and quantization, and combining hardware acceleration technology to improve actual deployment efficiency.

References

1. Ali, O., Ishak, M.K., Bhatti, M.K.L., et al.: A comprehensive review of internet of things: technology stack, middlewares, and fog/edge computing interface. Sensors **22**(3), 995 (2022)
2. Al-Fuqaha, A., Guizani, M., Mohammadi, M., et al.: Internet of things: a survey on enabling technologies, protocols, and applications. IEEE Commun. Surv. Tutor. **17**(4), 2347–2376 (2015)
3. Kumar, S., Tiwari, P., Zymbler, M.: Internet of Things is a revolutionary approach for future technology enhancement: a review. J. Big Data **6**(1), 1–21 (2019). https://doi.org/10.1186/s40537-019-0268-2
4. Terven, J., Córdova-Esparza, D.M., Romero-González, J.A.: A comprehensive review of yolo architectures in computer vision: from yolov1 to yolov8 and yolo-nas. Mach. Learn. Knowl. Extract. **5**(4), 1680–1716 (2023)

5. Lu, Y., Shen, M., Wang, H., et al.: Machine learning for synthetic data generation: a review. arxiv preprint arxiv:2302.04062 (2023)
6. Li, Y., Liu, W.: Deep learning-based garbage image recognition algorithm. Appl. Nanosci. **13**(2), 1415–1424 (2023)
7. Liang, G., Guan, J.: FConvNet: leveraging fused convolution for household garbage classification. J. Circuits Syst. Comput. 2450140 (2023)
8. Yang, Z., Xia, Z., Yang, G., et al.: A garbage classification method based on a small convolution neural network. Sustainability **14**(22), 14375 (2022)
9. Gao, X., Hong, H.: Research on garbage classification algorithm based on lightweight neural network. J. Guiyang Univ. (Nat. Scie.) **18**(02), 45–50+54 (2023). https://doi.org/10.16856/j.cnki.52-1142/n.2023.02.013
10. Li, X., Li, T., Li, S., et al.: Learning fusion feature representation for garbage image classification model in human–robot interaction. Infrared Phys. Technol. **128**, 104457 (2023)
11. Wang, C.Y., Yeh, I.H., Liao, H.Y.M.: YOLOv9: learning what you want to learn using programmable gradient information. arxiv preprint arxiv:2402.13616 (2024)
12. Zhong, J., Chen, J., Mian, A.: DualConv: dual convolutional kernels for lightweight deep neural networks. IEEE Trans. Neural Netw. Learn. Syst. (2022)
13. Jiao, J., Tang, Y.M., Lin, K.Y., et al.: Dilateformer: multi-scale dilated transformer for visual recognition. IEEE Trans. Multimed. **25**, 8906–8919 (2023)
14. Zhang, H., Xu, C., Zhang, S.: Inner-IoU: more effective intersection over union loss with auxiliary bounding box. arxiv preprint arxiv:2311.02877 (2023)

Task-Oriented Frequency Assignments Scheduling Approach for Geostationary Orbit Radio-Frequency Resources

Zhuojun Dong[1], Zhou Zhang[1(✉)], Yizhu Wang[1], Tongtong Wang[2], and Zhixi Yang[3]

[1] National Innovation Institute of Defense Technology, Beijing 100071, China
qsyjcsxdl2021@163.com
[2] Tianjin Urban Construction Management and Vocation Technology College, Tianjin 300134, China
[3] The 63rd Research Institute, National University of Defense Technology, Changsha 410000, China

Abstract. Radio-frequency resources (RFRs) are strategic and fundamental for the construction and operation of space-based information networks. With the rapid evolution and development of integrated space and ground information networks, competition for RFRs is becoming increasingly intense. Following the International Telecommunication Union (ITU) Radio Regulations, the scarcity of available resources is becoming more evident, and the contradiction between supply and demand is exacerbated by the low utilization efficiency of existing RFRs. To address the current issues, this research investigates scheduling problem in units of frequency assignments (FAs) for multiple tasks, where FAs are basic unit of RFRs defined by the ITU. A multi-task scheduling model is built with dual objectives of maximizing task completion and minimizing aggregate interference for other RFRs in priority. An task oriented FAs scheduling approach based on an improved genetic algorithm is proposed optimizing the dual objectives. Through simulation experiments based on the ITU database, the proposed approach significantly enhances two objectives performance compared to alternative scheduling methods.

Keywords: Radio-frequency Resources · Frequency Assignments · Dual-objective Optimization

1 Introduction

With rapid increase in demand for network capacity, transmission rates and latency for the next generation wireless networks, available RFRs becomes heavily scarce. The integration of space and terrestrial networks is becoming a trend, exacerbating the supply-demand contradiction for RFRs [1]. ITU data statistics indicates that RFRs in popular bands such as Ku and Ka are almost fully occupied. Nevertheless, ITU interference analysis reports show actual interference

© ICST Institute for Computer Sciences, Social Informatics and Telecommunications Engineering 2026
Published by Springer Nature Switzerland AG 2026. All Rights Reserved
R. C. Qiu et al. (Eds.): IoTaaS 2024, LNICST 675, pp. 153–167, 2026.
https://doi.org/10.1007/978-3-032-14681-6_13

disputes in the Ku and Ka bands are less than 10%. As actual satellite systems do not reach the maximum radiation envelope declared in the ITU database, the registered RFRs are under-utilized. Moreover, interference protection thresholds for satellite systems in priority do not consider the cumulative effect of interference over time, making it more difficult to share resources due to over-protection constraints. The dynamic and random nature of actual task demands and user spatial distribution results in large idle time gaps, leading to heavier resource waste. Therefore, efficient RFRs scheduling for dynamic tasks is motivated for relieving RFRs scarcity.

1.1   Related Work

Existing researches primarily investigated communication resources scheduling for in actual satellite communication systems, including satellite transponders, carrier bandwidth, and transmit power [2–9]. Work [2] studied the frequency resource scheduling of satellite transponders for multi-user uplink time division multiple access within the shaped beam coverage area of geostationary satellite communication systems. Based on adaptive threshold user clustering, it proposed a multi-user spectrum scheduling and transmission power control strategy, achieving maximum system uplink aggregated transmission rate. For high-throughput satellite multi-beam communication, authors in [3] investigated interference-aware spectrum resource management problem. By utilizing real-time channel conditions and user demands, an adaptive bandwidth scheduling and power control strategy was designed based on Dinkelbach and successive convex approximations. Moreover, to enhance users quality of service, works [4] and [5] conducted research on traffic-aware multi-user and multi-antenna beamforming. By combining self-supervised learning and deep reinforcement learning methods, they proposed joint optimization strategies for system capacity and channel scheduling, achieving near-optimal throughput. In addition, work [6] studied satellite beam and transponder scheduling for a satellite relay network, which includes multiple high orbit relay satellites and low orbit user nodes. For randomly arrival tasks, it proposed a satellite beam resource dynamic scheduling method based on task execution status and time window information, significantly improving task completion. Based on task conflict assessment and resolution, work [7] further proposed a heuristic scheduling method. For efficient spectrum sharing among multiple heterogeneous orbit satellite systems, works [8] and [9] investigated a cognitive radio enabled spectrum sensing and sharing between a low orbit system and a geostationary satellite system. A joint resource allocation approach was proposed for adaptive power control method based on channel conditions for spectrum sensing and multiple users clustering for beam frequency reuse and transponder scheduling, achieving maximum throughput for low orbit satellite communications.

1.2   Problem Statement and Contributions

As stated above, existing researches mainly focus on communication resources scheduling for satellite transponders, carrier bandwidth, and transmit power of actual satellite communication systems. However, research on scheduling on RFRs is still in the early stage. Different from satellite system resource scheduling, RFRs scheduling presents several challenges: first, modeling scheduling objects is difficult. Since RFRs are based on the ITU database and operate under the ITU Radio Regulations framework, there is no clear association between satellite systems and RFRs, and thus resource representation and modeling is absent based on regulatory knowledge. Secondly, RFRs scheduling involves multi-objective optimization. According to the first-come and first-served principle, later-registered RFRs must ensure non-interference with earlier-registered RFRs with higher priority. Besides task completion, minimizing cumulative interference to higher-priority RFRs is crucial, increase complexity for the resource scheduling optimization process. Thirdly, the randomness and diversity of tasks increases the complexity of resource scheduling. In order to match task types, transmission directions, frequency bands and coverage areas, task completion and resultant interference are influenced by resource bandwidth, beam gain, transponders, ground station power and so on.

To address these challenges, this research investigates task-oriented RFRs scheduling, and the main contributions are listed as follows:

1. A tuple-based representation model for RFRs scheduling is established with fundamental scheduling units as FAs and tasks. The model captures the upper bounds of satellite communication system performance supported by the RFRs.
2. To maximize task completion and minimize the cumulative interference to higher priority systems, the RFRs scheduling problem is formulated as a constrained mixed-integer linear programming problem with dual optimization objectives, which is recognized as NP-hard.
3. Utilizing the dual-objective optimization property, a task-oriented RFRs scheduling approach is proposed based on an improved genetic algorithm, with complexity at $O(M \cdot L_{max} \cdot N_s^2)$, where M denotes the FAs number, N_s denotes the task number and L_{max} denotes the iterations of the proposed scheduling approach. The effectiveness and efficiency of the proposed approach are demonstrated through simulation based on the ITU database.

2   System Model

2.1   Radio-Frequency Resource Model

Under the regulatory framework of ITU, satellite communication systems use RFRs registered in the ITU space service database. Parameters speculated in the database determine major satellite communication parameters, including beam gain, EIRP, transmit power flux density and so on. For the satellite communication, the system is allowed to use the FAs within parameters envelopes. For a

Table 1. Symbols and definitions

Symbol	Definition
$\{R_m\}_{m=1,\ldots,M}$	Frequency assignments
$\{T_i\}_{i=1,\ldots,N_s}$	Tasks to be scheduled
$\{a_{m,i}\}_{m=1,\ldots,M}$	Coverage indicator of FA R_m for task T_i
$\{x_m^i\}_{m=1,\ldots,M}$	Indicator whether task T_i is successfully scheduled on frequency assignments R_m
$\boldsymbol{\phi}_i = [\phi_{i,s}, \phi_{i,e}]$	Scheduled time duration of task T_i
$I_{ul}(\boldsymbol{\phi}_i, x_m^i)$	Total uplink interference from FAs scheduling accumulated from time instant $\phi_{i,s}$ to $\phi_{i,e}$
$I_{dl}(\boldsymbol{\phi}_i, x_m^i)$	Total downlink interference from FAs scheduling accumulated from time $\phi_{i,s}$ to $\phi_{i,e}$
$\Gamma(\boldsymbol{\phi}_i, x_m^i)$	Total task completion reward by scheduling FAs during task time duration

satellite system, the database has a hierarchical structure in four tiers, including satellite beams, transponders, ground stations, and carrier parameters. Based on multi-tier relationships, the available RFRs are represented as a set of FAs, which specifies the parameters at transmitters and receivers of a satellite system wireless link. We denote each FA as a tuple $R_m = \{s_m, d_m, G_m^s, p_m, \mathbf{f}_m, n_m, G_m^e(\theta)\}$ where $m = 1, \ldots, M$, and M denotes the number of FAs. Specifically, s_m represents the service types, including satellite fixed service, satellite mobile service, satellite meteorological service and satellite radio determination service. d_m represents the transmission direction, including uplink and downlink. G_m^s represents the satellite beam gain, p_m represents the satellite transmission power in dBW, $\mathbf{f}_m = [f_{\min,m}, f_{\max,m}]$ represents frequency band, and n_m represents the receiver noise. $G_m^e(0)$ represents the maximum ground station gain, and $G_m^e(\theta)$ represents the ground station off-axis gain, where θ denotes ground station off-axis angle. Table 1 lists the main symbols and definitions.

2.2   Task Model

For FAs scheduling, tasks are represented as tuples $T_i = \{s_i^s, d_i^s, v_i^s, w_i, \mathbf{f}_i^s, \mathbf{t}_i\}$, $i = 1, \ldots, N_s$, where N_s denotes tasks number. Specifically, s_i^s represents the service type of task T_i, d_i^s represents the task transmission direction, v_i^s represents the data quantity, w_i represents the completion reward of task T_i, $\mathbf{f}_i^s = [f_{\min,i}^s, f_{\max,i}^s]$ represents the frequency band, and $\mathbf{t}_i = [t_{i,s}, t_{i,e}]$ represents the time window where the task requires to be completed, respectively.

For tasks dynamics, we use random variables $a_{m,i} \sim B(1, p_s)$ in Bernoulli distributions to represent whether the users of task T_i are located within the coverage of FA R_m. p_s denotes the coverage probability.

2.3   Scheduling Variables and Objective Function

For FAs scheduling, we define decision variables $x_m^i \in \{0, 1\}$ where $m = 1, \ldots, M$ and $i = 1, \ldots, N_s$, indicating whether R_m is allocated to task T_i. Specifically, $x_m^i = 1$ means R_m is allocated to task T_i, and otherwise, R_m is not allocated. Moreover, we define the scheduled time duration of task T_i as $\phi_i = [\phi_{i,s}, \phi_{i,e}]$, where $\phi_{i,s}$ and $\phi_{i,e}$ represent the starting time and ending time, respectively.

Based on these variables, in executing task T_i with R_m, the time aggregated interference in uplink direction can be expressed as

$$I_{ul}(\phi_i, x_m^i) = x_m^i \cdot \text{len}([\phi_{i,s}, \phi_{i,e}]) \cdot p_m \cdot G_r^s \cdot G_m^e(\theta)/L_m^i \tag{1}$$

where $\text{len}(\cdot)$ denotes the time duration length, $G_m^e(\theta)$ represents the off-axis transmitting antenna gain of corresponding ground stations, G_r^s represents the receiving antenna gain of the interfered satellite, and L_m^i denotes the wireless link loss from the users of task T_i to the interfered satellite at FA R_m.

Similarly, the resultant time aggregated interference in downlink direction can be expressed as

$$I_{dl}(\phi_i, x_m^i) = x_m^i \cdot \text{len}(\phi_i) \cdot p_m \cdot G_m^s \cdot G_r^e(\theta)/L_m^i \tag{2}$$

where G_m^s represents the transmitting antenna gain of the satellite, and $G_r^e(\theta)$ represents the off-axis receiving antenna gain of the interfered ground stations.

Therefore, the aggregated interference over all FAs and tasks for both uplink and downlink can be expressed as

$$\sum_{i=1}^{N_s} \sum_{m=1}^{M_1} I_{ul}(\phi_i, x_m^i), \quad \sum_{i=1}^{N_s} \sum_{m=1}^{M_2} I_{dl}(\phi_i, x_m^i)$$

where M_1 and M_2 represent the number of FAs in uplink and downlink direction, respectively.

Moreover, the task completion reward by scheduling FA R_m for task T_i is expressed as

$$\Gamma(\phi_i, x_m^i) = x_m^i a_{m,i} \cdot \mathbb{I}[s_i^s = s_m]\mathbb{I}[\mathbf{f}_i^s \cap \mathbf{f}_m \neq \varnothing]\mathbb{I}[d_i^s = d_m] \cdot w_i. \tag{3}$$

Therefore, the total reward across all tasks and FAs is $\sum_{i=1}^{N_s} \sum_{m=1}^{M} \Gamma(\phi_i, x_m^i)$.

3   Problem Formulation and Scheduling Approach

3.1   Problem Formulation

In this section, based on the two objective functions above, we formulate the task oriented FAs scheduling problem with scheduling variables $\{\phi_i, x_m^i\}_{i=1,\ldots,N_s, m=1,\ldots M}$ as follows.

$$\text{Maximize} \quad F_1 = \sum_{i=1}^{N_s} \sum_{m=1}^{M} \Gamma(\phi_i, x_m^i)$$

$$\text{Minimize} \quad F_2 = \sum_{i=1}^{N_s} \sum_{m=1}^{M_1} I_{ul}(\phi_i, x_m^i) + \sum_{i=1}^{N_s} \sum_{m=1}^{M_2} I_{dl}(\phi_i, x_m^i) \tag{4}$$

s.t. C1, C2, C3

For the optimization problem, there are two optimization goals, maximizing task completion reward F_1 and minimizing the time cumulative interference F_2 resultant to other satellite systems in priority.

Moreover, scheduling variables are subject to following constraints C1, C2 and C3.

C1 imposes a constraint that each task is allocated with at most one FA, expressed as

$$\sum_{m=1}^{M} x_m^i \leq 1, \quad \forall i = 1, \ldots, N_s \tag{5}$$

C2 imposes a constraint that each FA is allocated to up to one task at the same time, expressed as

$$x_m^{i_1} + x_m^{i_2} \leq 1, \quad \text{for} \quad [\phi_{i_1,s}, \phi_{i_1,e}] \cap [\phi_{i_2,s}, \phi_{i_2,e}] \neq \varnothing, \forall i_1 \neq i_2, \forall m = 1, \ldots, M \tag{6}$$

C3 imposes a constraint that the task scheduling time duration must be executed within the valid duration of a task, expressed as

$$[\phi_{i,s}, \phi_{i,e}] \subseteq [t_{i,s}, t_{i,e}], \quad \forall i = 1, \ldots, N_s \tag{7}$$

By analyzing the optimization problem above, it is a Mixed-Integer Linear Programming (MILP) problem and NP-hard [10]. To solve the problem, complexity is in exponential order $O(2^{N_s \cdot M})$, thus infeasible for large M and N_s.

3.2   Enhanced Genetic Algorithm Based Scheduling Approach

In this section, we propose a heuristic FAs scheduling approach based on an enhanced genetic algorithm, solving the optimization problem (4) in efficient manners.

Following the processing flow of classical genetic algorithm, we present a flowchart for the proposed scheduling approach in Fig. 1. In it, the initial population is denoted as $\mathbf{P}_0$, and the lth generation population is denoted as $\mathbf{P}_l$, respectively. After each iteration of population evolution, a new population $\mathbf{O}_l$ is generated. The genetic algorithm has the maximum iterations as L_{max}.

The approach's design idea is illustrated as follows. The FAs scheduling scheme for task set $\{T_i\}_{i=1,\ldots,N_s}$ is regarded as a single chromosome in the genetic algorithm, and the set of different FAs scheduling schemes is regarded as a population, composed of multiple chromosomes. For an FAs scheduling scheme, the scheduled FAs of task T_i refers to the ith gene of the chromosome.

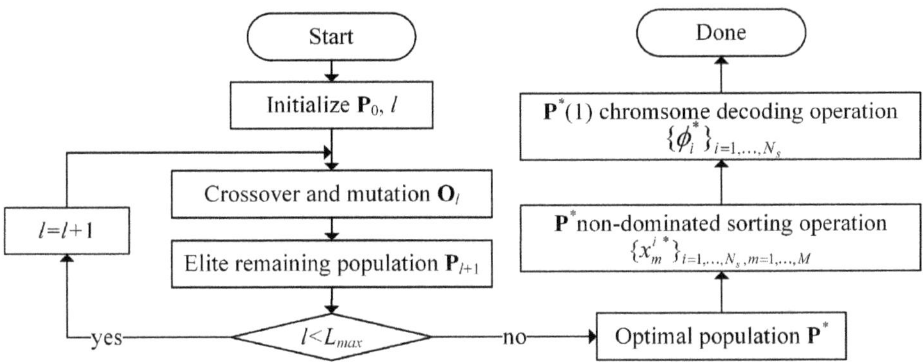

Fig. 1. Flowchart of the proposed heuristic scheduling approach.

Starting from the initial population $\mathbf{P}_0$, an elite population $\mathbf{P}^*$ will be generated through multiple iterations of population evolution based on chromosome fitness and the iterative process of elite remaining. Then, within the population $\mathbf{P}^*$, an optimal chromosome is found, and optimal FAs scheduling solution $\{x_m^{i,*}, \phi_i^*\}, i = 1, \ldots, N_s, m = 1, \ldots, M$ is obtained by running chromosome coding operations.

To enable efficient operation along the flow chart, the proposed FAs scheduling approach is developed in Algorithm 1. In the algorithm, for lth generation population $\mathbf{P}_l$, each chromosome is denoted as $\{\mathbf{P}_l(z)\}_{z=1,\ldots,Z}$, where Z represents the size of population $\mathbf{P}_l$. For population $\mathbf{P}_l$, the chromosome fitness sets with respect to objective function F_1 and F_2 are denoted as $\mathbf{F}_1$ and $\mathbf{F}_2$, respectively. For zth chromosome, the corresponding fitness vector is denoted as $(\mathbf{F}_{1,l}(z), \mathbf{F}_{2,l}(z))$. Moreover, chromosome fitness crowing distance of population $\mathbf{P}$ is denoted as $\boldsymbol{\eta}$, and the crowing distance of zth chromosome is denoted as $\boldsymbol{\eta}(z)$.

For the proposed approach, major operation procedures are described in details below.

Initial Population Generation Operation: Monte Carlo method in [3] is used to generate genes set $\{x_m^i\}_{i=1,\ldots,N_s}$, where for each task $\{T_i\}_{i=1,\ldots,N_s}$ function $randi(M)$ generates a random integer in range $[1, M]$ corresponding to the index of the allocated FA in available FAs $\{R_m\}$, $m = 1, \ldots, M$. By repeating this procedures by Z times, the initial population $\mathbf{P}_0 = \{\mathbf{P}_0(z)\}_{z=1,\ldots,Z}$ is generated.

Chromosome Encoding Operation: Taking chromosome $\mathbf{P}_l(z)$ of population $\mathbf{P}_l$ as input, all the genes are sorted in descending order in terms of the task completion rewards $w_i, i = 1, \ldots, N_s$, and then allocated to FAs $\{R_m\}, m = 1, \ldots, M$ sequentially, obtaining the scheduling variables $\{x_m^i\}, i = 1, \ldots, N_s$ and scheduled time duration $\phi_i = [\phi_{i,s}, \phi_{i,e}]$. Specifically, when the effective time duration $[t_{i,s}, t_{i,e}]$ of task T_i intersects with the available time duration $\mathbf{t}_m$ of R_m, the task is scheduled within the intersection of the two intervals, and R_m is

---

Algorithm 1. The proposed FAs scheduling approach

Input: $\{T_i\}_{i=1,\ldots,N_s}$, $\{R_m\}_{m=1,\ldots,M}$
Output: $\{x_m^{i,*}, \phi_i^*\}$, $i = 1, \ldots, N_s$, $m = 1, \ldots, M$
 1: **Initialize:** μ_{c_0}, μ_{m_0}, $l = 1$
 2: $\mathbf{P}_0 \leftarrow$ Initial population generate operation
 3: **for** $z = 1 : Z$ **do**
 4:    $\{\phi_i^0\}_{i=1,\ldots,N_s} \leftarrow \mathbf{P}_0(z)$ chromosome coding operation
 5:    $(\mathbf{F}_{1,0}(z), \mathbf{F}_{2,0}(z), \boldsymbol{\eta}_0(z)) \leftarrow \mathbf{P}_0(z)$ chromosome decoding operation
 6: $\mathbf{P}_l \leftarrow \mathbf{P}_0$
 7: **while** $l \leq L_{max}$ **do**
 8:    $\mathbf{O}_l \leftarrow \mathbf{P}_l$
 9:    **for** $z = 1 : Z/2$ **do**
10:      **if** $\mu_c(z) \geq rand(0,1)$ **then**
11:        $(\mathbf{O}_l(z), \mathbf{O}_l(2z)) \leftarrow (\mathbf{P}_0(z), \mathbf{P}_0(2z))$ chromosome crossover operation
12:    **for** $z = 1 : Z$ **do**
13:      **if** $\mu_m \leq rand(0,1)$ **then**
14:        $\mathbf{O}_l(z) \leftarrow \mathbf{P}_0(z)$ chromosome mutation operation
15:    **Elite remaining:**
16:    $\mathbf{P}^+ \leftarrow (\mathbf{P}_l \cup \mathbf{O}_l)$ non-dominated sorting operation
17:    $\mathbf{P}_{l+1} \leftarrow \mathbf{P}^+(1 : eZ)$
18:    $\mathbf{P}^- \leftarrow \eta(\mathbf{P}^+(eZ + 1 : 2Z)))$
19:    $\mathbf{P}^- \leftarrow \mathbf{P}^-$ fitness-weighted sorting operation
20:    $\mathbf{P}^- \leftarrow \mathbf{P}^-$ fitness crowding distance sorting operation
21:    $\mathbf{P}_{l+1} \leftarrow \mathbf{P}_{l+1} \cup \mathbf{P}^-((1 - e)Z)$
22:    $l \leftarrow l + 1$
23: **Finding optimal solution:**
24: $\mathbf{P}^* \leftarrow \mathbf{P}_l$ non-dominated sorting operation
25: $\{x_m^{i*}\}_{i=1,\ldots,N_s} \leftarrow \mathbf{P}^*(1)$
26: $\{\phi_i^*\}_{i=1,\ldots,N_s} \leftarrow \mathbf{P}^*(1)$ chromosome coding operation.

---

scheduled to execute the task during $[\phi_{i,s}, \phi_{i,e}]$. Then, the available time $\mathbf{t}_m$ for R_m is updated with $(\mathbf{t}_m - [\phi_{i,s}, \phi_{i,e}])$. On the other hand, when the available time of R_m fails to satisfy task T_i, the scheduling time is set as $[\phi_{i,s}, \phi_{i,e}] = [0,0]$. After re-cursing all genes, the operation outputs the set of scheduling times $\{\phi_i\}$, $i = 1, \ldots, N_s$ corresponding to all genes and the remaining available time $\mathbf{t}_m$, $m = 1, \ldots, M$ for all FAs.

Chromosome Decoding Operation: Taking chromosome $\mathbf{P}_l(z)$ of population $\mathbf{P}_l$ and the associated scheduling time duration $\{\phi_i\}_{i=1,\ldots,N_s}$ as inputs, the operation computes the two fitness values $\mathbf{F}_1(z)$ and $\mathbf{F}_2(z)$ and crowding distance $\boldsymbol{\eta}_l(z)$.

Adaptive Crossover Operation: Taking chromosome $\mathbf{P}(z)$ as input, the operation computes the crossover probability $\mu_c(z)$ as

$$\mu_c(z) = \begin{cases} \mu_{c_0} & \text{if } f(z, \mathbf{P}) \leq f_{\text{avg}}(\mathbf{P}) \\ \mu_{c_0} \left(1 - \frac{\sigma_f(\mathbf{P})}{f_{\text{avg}}(\mathbf{P})}\right) & \text{otherwise} \end{cases} \tag{8}$$

where μ_{c_0} is the initial crossover probability. The fitness-weighted value $f(z, \mathbf{P})$ of chromosome $\mathbf{P}(z)$ is calculated as

$$f(z, \mathbf{P}) = \frac{\mathbf{F}_1(z) - \min(\mathbf{F}_1)}{\max(\mathbf{F}_1) - \min(\mathbf{F}_1)} + \frac{\mathbf{F}_2(z) - \min(\mathbf{F}_2)}{\max(\mathbf{F}_2) - \min(\mathbf{F}_2)} \tag{9}$$

where $f_{\text{avg}}(\mathbf{P}) = \left(\sum_{z=1}^{|\mathbf{P}|} f(z)\right) / |\mathbf{P}|$ denotes the average fitness-weighted value of the population, and $\sigma_f(\mathbf{P})$ denotes the standard deviation. Then, the operation uses function $rand(0, 1)$ to generate uniformly distributed random numbers within $[0, 1]$. And when $\mu_c(z) \geq rand(0, 1)$, the starting point for genes exchange between chromosome $\mathbf{P}(z)$ and chromosome $\mathbf{P}(2z)$ is generated by randomly generating function $randi(N_s)$, and all the genes after the starting point are exchanging between two chromosomes.

Adaptive Mutation Operation: Taking the chromosome $\mathbf{P}(z)$ as input, the mutation probability $\mu_m(z)$ is calculated as

$$\mu_m(z) = \begin{cases} \mu_{m_0} & \text{if } f(z, \mathbf{P}) \geq f_{\text{avg}}(\mathbf{P}) \\ \mu_{m_0} \left(1 - \frac{\sigma_f(\mathbf{P})}{f_{\text{avg}}(\mathbf{P})}\right) & \text{otherwise} \end{cases} \tag{10}$$

where μ_{m0} is the initial mutation probability. After that, the operation uses function $rand(0, 1)$ generating a uniformly distributed random number within $[0, 1]$, and compare it with the mutation probability. When $\mu_m(z) > rand(0, 1)$, an integer mutation point within $[1, N_s]$ is randomly generated by the function $randi(N_s)$, at which the gene is valued a random index $randi(M)$.

Fitness-Weighted Sorting Operation: Taking population $\mathbf{P}$ as input, recurring all chromosome $\mathbf{P}(z)$, $z = 1, .., Z$, it calculates the weighted fitness $f(z, \mathbf{P})$ in (9). Then, population $\mathbf{P}$ is sorted in descending order of the weighted fitness, and the crowding distance $\eta(z, \mathbf{P})$ is calculated as

$$\eta(z, \mathbf{P}) = \begin{cases} \frac{f(z+1, \mathbf{P}) - f(z-1, \mathbf{P})}{f_{\max}(\mathbf{P}) - f_{\min}(\mathbf{P})}, & \text{if } f_{\max}(\mathbf{P}) \neq f_{\min}(\mathbf{P}) \\ +\infty, & \text{otherwise} \end{cases} \tag{11}$$

where $f_{\max}(\mathbf{P})$ and $f_{\min}(\mathbf{P})$ denote the maximum and minimum fitness-weighted values of $\mathbf{P}$, respectively. Based on crowding distances, population $\mathbf{P}$ is sorted in descending order.

Non-dominated Sorting Operation [12]: Taking population $\mathbf{P}$ as input, for chromosome $\mathbf{P}(z)$, $z = 1, .., Z$, number $c(z)$ is calculated in respects to other chromosomes which are Pareto dominant to $\mathbf{P}(z)$ in terms of the fitness vector

$(\mathbf{F}_1(z), \mathbf{F}_2(z))$. The maximum number of $c(z)$ is recorded as c_{max}. Based on the order of the number c_{max}, the operation divides $\mathbf{P}$ into c_{max} groups, denoted as $\mathbf{P}^n = \{P(z)|c(z) = n\}$. Then, each non-empty chromosome group $\mathbf{P}^n$ is sorted through the fitness-weighted value sorting operation and the crowding distance sorting operation. By connecting all non-empty groups in order from $n = 1$ until c_{max}, population $\mathbf{P}$ is non-dominated sorted.

Finding Optimal Solution: After $L_{\max}$ iterations, the optimal population $\mathbf{P}^*$ is obtained. By identifying the optimal chromosome $\mathbf{P}^*(1)$ through a non-dominated sorting operation, the optimal scheduling scheme is found after chromosome coding operation.

3.3   Complexity Analysis

To enable feasibility of the proposed FAs scheduling approach, we analyze the complexity of Algorithm 1. As an initial step, the complexity for generating the initial population is $O(Z)$. For each iteration of the population evolution, the complexity for each operation is analyzed sequentially. Complexities associated with chromosome encoding and decoding operations for all chromosomes are $O(Z \cdot M \cdot N_s)$. Complexities for chromosome crossover and mutation operations are $O(\mu_c \cdot Z)$ and $O(\mu_m \cdot Z)$, respectively. Moreover, complexities for the fitness-weighted sorting operation and fitness crowding distance sorting operation are $O(2Z \cdot \log 2Z)$ and $O(2Z \cdot \log Z)$, respectively. In addition, the non-dominated sorting operation is $O(2Z^2)$. To sum them up, the total complexity for a single iteration is $O(Z \cdot M \cdot N_s^2 + 2Z^2)$.

Taking into account all iterations, the complexity of the proposed FAs scheduling approach is $O(L_{max} \cdot (Z \cdot M \cdot N_s^2 + 2Z^2))$. Notably, while the convergence of the genetic algorithm is guaranteed, the initial population size Z is linear with the number of chromosome genes N_s [14]. Equivalently, to enable proposed approach converging to an optimal solution, the complexity is $O(M \cdot L_{max} \cdot N_s^2)$. Compared to exponential order complexity $O(2^{N_s \times M})$ for solving the MILP problem, the proposed approach significantly decreases the complexity.

4   Performance Evaluation

To verify the effectiveness and efficiency of our proposed FAs scheduling approach, we carry out simulations based on ITU database data. For the simulation setup, we generate different set of tasks randomly for different service of FAs. The sizes of task sets are 200, 400, and 600, respectively. For each task, the service type is randomly selected from 4 types with equal probabilities, i.e. satellite fixed service (TC), satellite broadcasting service (UV), base station service (TY), and satellite meteorological service (TM). The transmission direction is randomly selected from 2 directions, i.e. uplink and downlink. Depending on the service types, data volume in units of Mbs and bandwidth in units of MHz are randomly valued as listed in Table 2. The task completion reward is integer valued and randomly generated by $randi(8)$. In addition, for each task an effective time duration of starting time and ending time is randomly generated within $[0, 25000]$ seconds.

Table 2. Simulation setup for different service types

Service type	data volume in Mbs	Bandwidth in MHz
TC	$[30000, 100000]$	$[0, 200], [2000, 4000],$ $[4000, 8000], [8000, 12000],$ $[12000, 18000], [18000, 26000],$ $[26000, 40000]$
UV	$[200, 10000]$	$[4000, 12000], [18000, 26000]$
TY	$[30000, 100000]$	$[0, 500]$
TM	$[10000, 50000]$	$[0, 2000], [8000, 12000]$

For the RFRs, we select 13 FAs from the ITU database to match the simulated tasks. Major parameters are listed in Table 3.

4.1 Effectiveness of the Proposed Approach

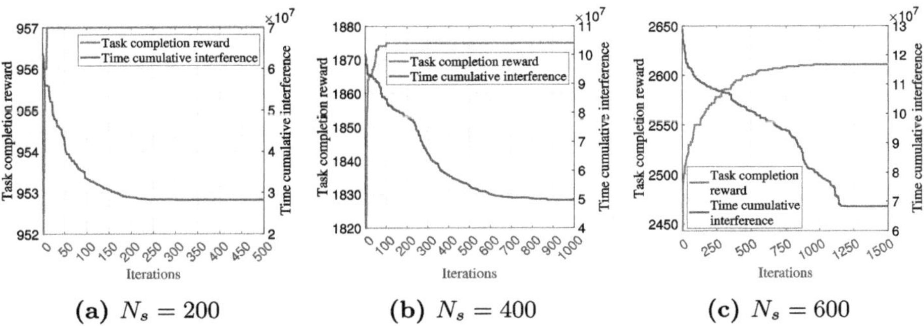

(a) $N_s = 200$ (b) $N_s = 400$ (c) $N_s = 600$

Fig. 2. Objective convergence performance of the proposed scheduling approach.

In this section, we verify the effectiveness of the proposed FAs scheduling approach by analyzing the convergence performance. Figure 2 depicts the FAs scheduling performance of task completion reward objective F_1 and time cumulative interference objective F_2 across different number of iterations when task number N_s is 200, 400 and 600, respectively. In all sub-figures, both objectives converge when iteration number L_{max} increases, verifying effectiveness of the proposed scheduling approach. In Fig. 2a, for task number $N_s = 200$, the task completion reward curve converges when L_{max} is less than 20, while the time cumulative interference curve converges when L_{max} is 200. In Fig. 2b and Fig. 2c,

Table 3. FAs Parameters Values

No.	Frequency Band (MHz)	Power Density (dBW /Hz)	Noise (k)	Direction	Service type	Station Location	Earth Station Antenna Gain	Beam Gain
1	[21400, 22000]	−53.5	300	dl	UV	[116.8, 46.3]	34.4	50
2	[74000, 76000]	−40	190	dl	UV	[100.5, 46.3]	42.1	55
3	[21400, 22000]	−53.5	300	dl	UB	[118, 35.9]	34.8	48.7
4	[345, 351]	−32.8	350	dl	TY	[123.76, 44.5]	17	16
5	[8175, 8215]	−46	770	ul	TM	[98, 40.9]	59	30
6	[1672, 1692]	−60.8	96	dl	TM	[106.4, 27.5]	48.8	18.5
7	[27500, 28600]	−55.4	800	ul	TC	[116.39, 39.9]	69.9	45
8	[10950, 11200]	−51	350	dl	TC	[120.5, 30.4]	58.4	37
9	[27000, 31000]	−40	600	ul	TC	[121, 35]	37.6	45
10	[12200, 12750]	−54.5	135	dl	TC	[119.45, 40.36]	33.7	39
11	[18200, 21200]	−50	110	ul	TC	[115.76, 23.4]	49.3	34
12	[14000, 14480]	−36	870	ul	TC	[108.5, 32.87]	40.2	52
13	[14000, 14480]	−36	870	dl	TC	[108.5, 32.87]	40.2	33

the task completion reward curve converges when $L_{max} \geq 100$ and $L_{max} \geq 800$, while the time cumulative interference curve converges when $L_{max} \geq 700$ and $L_{max} \geq 1200$, respectively. Moreover, it is observed that the required iteration times increase when task number N_s increases. This phenomenon is explained as that when N_s is 200, it is sufficient to schedule the FAs to complete all tasks while managing the interference well. However, when N_s increases to 600, the FAs are not sufficient to complete all tasks, and more iterations for population evolution based on the genetic algorithm are required to find the optimal solutions.

Furthermore, we conduct simulations for a set of 530 tasks and illustrated the FAs scheduling results of the proposed approach when $L_{max} = 500$. Figure 3 presents the Gantt chart showcasing the scheduling solution over the time period ranging from 0 to 25,000 s. The horizontal axis denotes the scheduling time, and the vertical axis corresponds to the scheduled FAs. Each colored block signifies a specific task, with the block's length reflecting the execution time of that task on the respective FA. Based on the scheduling solution, the proposed approach achieves a task completion reward value of 2557 and a cumulative interference value of 9.86×10^7 Joules, reaching a balance between task completion and cumulative interference.

In addition, the proposed scheduling approach shows sequential allocation of tasks with minimal idle times between them, ensuring high utilization of available time slots. This result is particularly evident in the handling of fixed satellite services by FAs R_4 and R_5, which manage the same type of task. It can be observed that the blocks associated with FA R_4 exhibit shorter task duration due to a higher transmission speed, as compared to those of R_5. Consequently, it results in a decreasing cumulative interference for R_4. The scheduling approach also improves the usage of effective time windows, ensuring availability of time duration for future tasks.

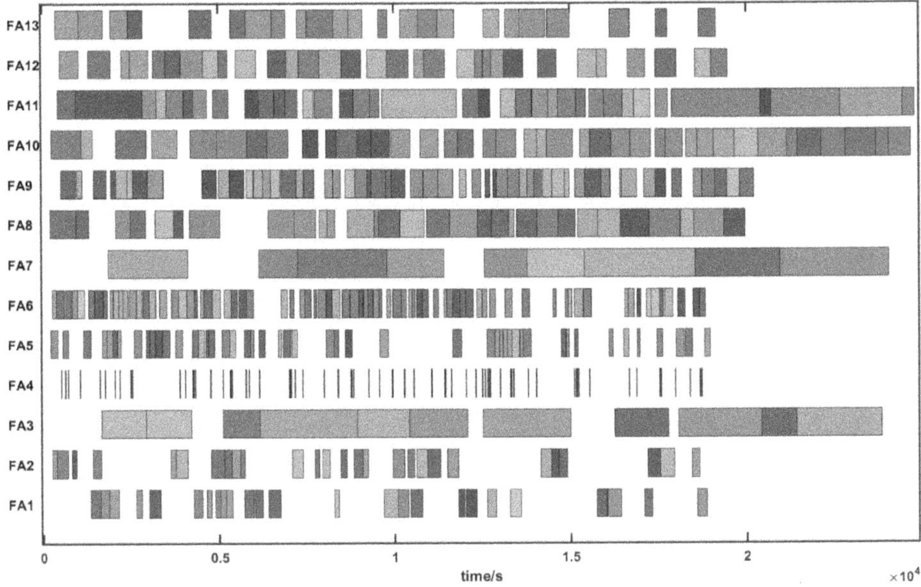

Fig. 3. Gantt chart showcasing the scheduling solution.

4.2 Efficiency Analysis

To verify the efficiency of the proposed FAs scheduling approach, we compare it with two alternative methods: i) traditional genetic algorithm (GA) based scheduling method, and ii) ant colony optimization (ACO) based scheduling method.

Figure 4 depicts the task completion reward and time cumulative interference of the proposed approach and alternative methods across the number of tasks from 200 to 600. The iterations number L_{max} is set as 1000. In Fig. 4a, the proposed FAs scheduling approach outperforms the traditional genetic algorithm (GA) based scheduling method, marked as GA based method and ant colony optimization (ACO) based scheduling method, marked as ACO based method. For instance, for $N_s = 600$, the proposed approach has tasks completion reward advantage 9.5% and 20.5% over the GA based method and ACO based method, respectively. Meanwhile, as illustrated in Fig. 4b, the proposed approach again outperforms the alternative methods.

5 Conclusion

This study investigated radio-frequency resources scheduling problem for multiple tasks, and formulated the task oriented frequency assignments scheduling problem as constrained mixed-integer linear programming problem with dual optimizing objectives. Recognizing the problem as NP-hard, we proposed an

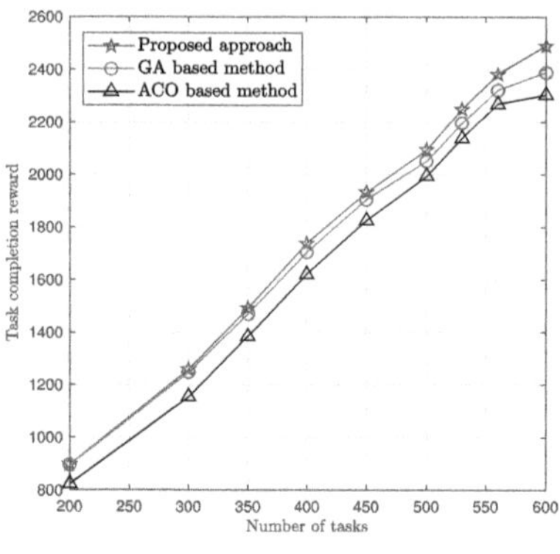

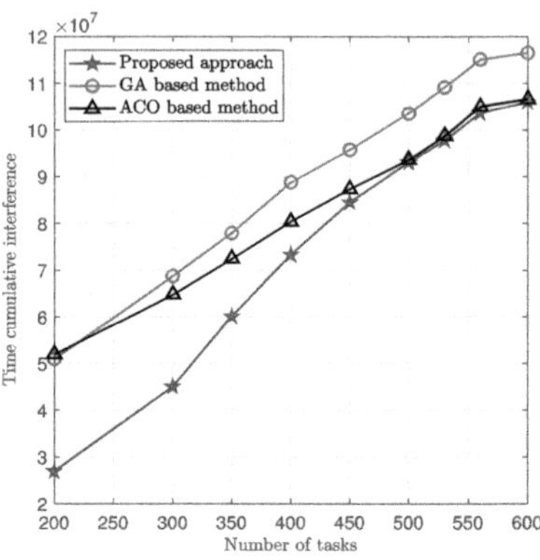

(a) Tasks completion reward   **(b)** Time cumulative interference

Fig. 4. Performance comparison with alternative methods.

enhanced genetic algorithm based frequency assignments scheduling approach, maximizing task completion and minimizing time cumulative interference. The complexity of the proposed approach is at $O(M \cdot L_{max} \cdot N_s^2)$. Effectiveness and efficiency of the proposed approach were verified by simulations based the ITU database. These findings lay the groundwork for the development of novel scheduling designs for radio-frequency resources.

References

1. ITU: Radio Regulations (2020)
2. Abdu, T.S., et al.: Demand and interference aware adaptive resource management for high throughput GEO satellite systems. IEEE Open J. Commun. Soc. **3**, 759–775 (2022)
3. Zhao, D., et al.: Flexible resource management in high-throughput satellite communication systems: a two-stage machine learning framework. IEEE Trans. Commun. **70**(9), 8868–8882 (2023)
4. Abdu, T.S., et al.: Flexible resource optimization for GEO multibeam satellite communication system. IEEE Trans. Wirel. Commun. **20**(12), 7888–7902 (2021)
5. Dai, C.Q., et al.: Dynamic scheduling for emergency tasks in space data relay network. IEEE Trans. Veh. Technol. **70**(1), 795–807 (2020)
6. Wu, G., et al.: Flexible task scheduling in data relay satellite networks. IEEE Trans. Aerosp. Electron. Syst. **58**(2), 1055–1068 (2021)
7. Chen, X., et al.: Task scheduling method for data relay satellite network considering breakpoint transmission. IEEE Trans. Veh. Technol. **70**(1), 844–857 (2020)
8. Wang, C., et al.: A novel dynamic spectrum-sharing method for integrated wireless multimedia sensors and cognitive satellite networks. Sensors **18**(11), 3904 (2018)
9. Vazirani, V.V.: Approximation Algorithms. Springer, Cham (2013)
10. Zhou, D., et al.: Mission aware contact plan design in resource-limited small satellite networks. IEEE Trans. Commun. **65**(6), 2451–2466 (2017)

11. Hofmann, C., et al.: Hybrid Monte Carlo tree search based multi-objective scheduling. Prod. Eng. Res. Devel. **17**(1), 133–144 (2023)
12. Deb, K., et al.: A fast and elitist multiobjective genetic algorithm: NSGA-II. IEEE Trans. Evol. Comput. **6**(2), 182–197 (2002)
13. Carr, J.: An introduction to genetic algorithms. Senior Project **1**(40), 7 (2014)
14. Sohail, A.: Genetic algorithms in the fields of artificial intelligence and data sciences. Ann. Data Sci. **10**(4), 1007–1018 (2023)

Communication Performance of Convex Partially Coherent Flat-Topped Vortex Hollow Beams in Atmospheric Turbulent Links

Qi Li, JingJing Geng$^{(\boxtimes)}$, Caixiao Ouyang, and Yingrui Yang

Wuhan Vocational College of Software and Engineering, Wuhan 430205, China
20815552@qq.com

Abstract. As the application of the Internet of Things (IoT) becomes increasingly widespread, satellite communication systems based on Free-Space Optical Communication (FSOC) play a crucial role in providing more stable communication services for IoT applications. However, wavefront distortion and beam scintillation caused by atmospheric turbulence significantly reduce the communication efficiency of FSOC systems. In this paper, the convex partially coherent flat-topped vortex hollow (CPC-FTVH) beams are employed as beam sources to improve the beam propagation performance under atmospheric turbulence. Using numerical simulation methods, the propagation process of the CPC-FTVH beams under atmospheric turbulence is simulated. The results explain why the CPC-FTVH beams can improve the communication efficiency in turbulence links. Furthermore, we calculated the aperture mean scintillation index and the signal-to-noise ratio (SNR) to evaluate the beam propagation performance and communication potential. The results show that the CPC-FTVH beams have a lower aperture mean scintillation index and provide a significant SNR gain compared to the conventional partially coherent flat-topped vortex hollow (PC-FTVH) beams and Gaussian Schell-model beams. This research provides a new idea for improving FSOC systems and has the potential to increase the reliability of IoT communications.

Keywords: satellite communication · free space optical communication · atmospheric turbulence

1 Introduction

With the development of 5G and 6G networks, the application of the Internet of Things (IoT) has become feasible and is now widely adopted. However, it is a challenge to fulfill the substantial communication requirements of IoT devices, especially in areas with poor ground networks [1–3]. In this condition, satellites play a crucial role in enhancing communication reliability. Free-space optical communication (FSOC) utilizes laser as an information carrier, which can provide an extremely high-bandwidth data transmission between satellites and the ground. A substantial body of research has identified that atmospheric turbulence is currently the greatest obstacle for satellite-to-ground FSOC

R. C. Qiu et al. (Eds.): IoTaaS 2024, LNICST 675, pp. 168–176, 2026.
https://doi.org/10.1007/978-3-032-14681-6_14

systems [4–6]. Atmospheric turbulence results in wavefront distortion and beam scintillation, thereby reducing the communication efficiency of FSOC systems. Consequently, developing methods to mitigate the effects of atmospheric turbulence on FSOC systems is a major focus of current research efforts [7, 8].

Partially coherent beams (PCBs) have been identified to have greater resistant to atmospheric turbulence compared to fully coherent beams. Gaussian Schell-model (Gaussian Schell-model) beams, as the most basic PCBs, have also been widely studied. [9] studied the spreading properties of PCBs propagating through atmospheric turbulence, explaining why PCBs are less affected by atmospheric turbulence than fully coherent laser beams. Using numerical simulations, Wu investigated the transmission performance of PCBs over horizontal links under various distances and turbulence intensities. The results demonstrate that under varying atmospheric conditions, optimal source parameters for PCBs can be identified to achieve superior propagation performance [10]. In addition to conventional Gaussian Schell-model beams, many researchers are also investigating special partially coherent beams to mitigate the effects caused by turbulence, such as partially coherent flat-topped vortex hollow (PC-FTVH) beams [11], partially coherent flat-topped beams [12], and partially coherent Bessel-Gaussian beams [13]. The partial coherence characteristics combined with the special beam provide better transmission performance in turbulent environments compared with Gaussian Schell-model beams.

The convex partially coherent beam (CPCB) is a non-uniform PCBs. Wang has investigated the transmission characteristics of CPCB in horizontal turbulence links, finding that the self-focusing effect of CPCB improves the resistance to atmospheric turbulence. The research demonstrates that, compared to Gaussian Schell-model beams, CPCB is able to effectively reduce beam scintillation and improve the communication efficiency of FSOC systems [14]. In our previous research, we found that partially coherent flat-topped vortex hollow beams exhibit lower scintillation and provide an additional SNR gain over Gaussian Schell-model beams in slant links [15]. This prompted us to consider whether it was possible to generate convex partially coherent flat-topped vortex hollow (CPC-FTVH) beams while maintaining resistance to atmospheric turbulence.

In this paper, a numerical simulation method was used to investigate the propagation and communication performance of the CPC-FTVH beams along horizontal links under atmospheric turbulence. In this method, the CPC-FTVH beams can be modulated by flat-topped vortex hollow beams with convex-shaped coherence phase screens. Further, we calculated the scintillation index and signal-to-noise ratio (SNR) of the CPC-FTVH beams, the PC-FTVH beams, and the Gaussian Schell-model beams under different turbulent intensities and propagation distances. The results show that under specific beam source parameters, the CPC-FTVH beams achieved optimal propagation and communication performance. This research will not only help improve FSOC but will also have a positive effect in the field of IoT.

2 Concept Description

2.1 Partially Coherent Beams Modeling

In our study, the CPC-FTVH beams, the PC-FTVH beams, and the Gaussian Schell-model beams were selected as the beam source. When a fully coherent beam is loaded through uniform random phase screens, the generated beam is a partially coherent beam. When random phase screens are modulated with a specific coherence degree and then loaded on a fully coherent beam, a convex partially coherent beam will be generated [14].

The mathematical expression of a fully coherent FTVH beam in the source plane can be expressed by [16]:

$$U_{10} = \sum_{n=1}^{N} a_n \exp\left[-n\left(\frac{x_0^2 + y_0^2}{\omega^2}\right)\right]\left(\frac{x_0}{\omega} + i\frac{y_0}{\omega}\right)^M \tag{1}$$

where, (x_0, y_0) is the position coordinate in the source plane, N is the beam order, M is the topological charge, ω is the beam width, and the amplitude parameter a_n can be expressed by

$$a_n = \frac{(-1)^{n-1}}{N}\binom{N}{n} \tag{2}$$

here, $\binom{N}{n}$ represents a binomial coefficient.

Then, the PC-FTVH beams and the Gaussian Schell-model beams can be generated by loading uniformly random phase screens on fully coherent FTVH beams and Gaussian beams, respectively. This process can be expressed by [17]:

$$E(r) = E_N(r)\exp[i\varphi(r)] \tag{3}$$

where, $E(r)$ is the fully coherent beam, $E_N(r)$ is the partially coherent beam, $\varphi(r)$ is the random phase screen. The cross-spectral density function of a partially coherent beam can be written as:

$$W_0(r_1, r_2) = S(r_1, r_2)\mu_0(r_1, r_2) \tag{4}$$

where, $S(r_1, r_2)$ is the spectral density, $\mu_0(r_1, r_2)$ is the complex degree of coherence, which can be expressed as:

$$\mu_0(r_1, r_2) = \langle\exp\{i[\varphi(r_1) - \varphi(r_2)]\}\rangle = \exp\left[-\frac{|r_1 - r_2|^2}{l_{c0}^2}\right] \tag{5}$$

where, l_{c0} is the correlation length of the partially coherent phase screen. When l_{c0} is a constant, the phase screen loads a partially coherent beam.

If we apply a spatial modulation function $t(r)$ to the random phase screen, then $\mu_0(r_1, r_2)$ can be written as:

$$\mu_0(r_1, r_2) = \langle\exp\{it(r)[\varphi(r_1) - \varphi(r_2)]\}\rangle = \exp\left[-\frac{|r_1 - r_2|^2}{(l_{c0}/t(r))^2}\right] \tag{6}$$

$$t(r) = \exp\left(-\frac{r^2}{\omega^2}\right) \tag{7}$$

In this condition, the phase screen loads a partially coherent beam with a non-uniform correlation length distribution as $l_{c0}/t(r)$, and the CPC-FTVH beams are generated.

2.2 Simulation for Beam Propagation Under Atmospheric Turbulence

In the numerical simulation, the propagation process of the beam is shown in Fig. 1. Random phase screens are used to generate partially coherent beams. The propagation path of the beam is divided equally by n turbulence phase screens to simulate the atmospheric environment.

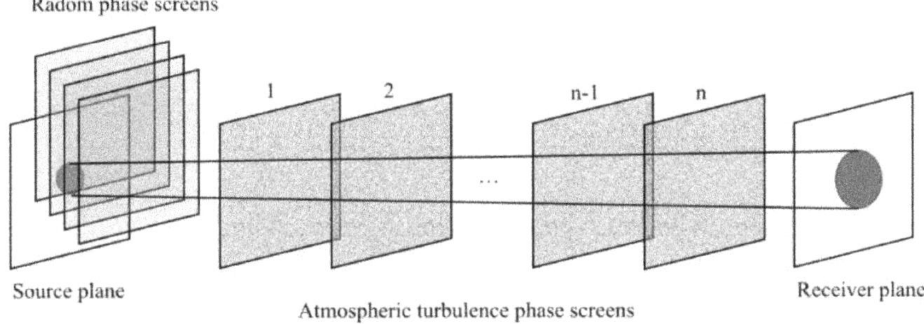

Fig. 1. The simulation process of the beam propagating through turbulence phase screens.

In horizontal links, each turbulence phase screen has the same amplitude. The beam propagation between turbulence phase screens can be described by Fresnel diffraction integral [18]:

$$U_{i+1}(r_{i+1}) = \frac{\exp(jk\Delta z_i)}{i\lambda\Delta z_i} \int U_i(r_i)\exp[j\Psi_i(r_i)] \times \exp\left(\frac{jk}{2\Delta z_i}|r_{i+1} - r_i|^2\right)dr_i \tag{8}$$

where $U_i(r_i)$ and $U_{i+1}(r_{i+1})$ are source plane and receiver plane, respectively, Δz_i is the distance between each phase screen, $k = 2\pi/\lambda$ is wave-number, the turbulence phase screen $\Psi_i(r_i)$ can be obtained by:

$$\Psi_i(r_i) = F^{-1}[G(f_i)\Phi_\Psi^{0.5}(f_i)] \tag{9}$$

$$\Phi_\Psi(f_i) = 0.009729k^2\frac{1}{cos\theta}\int_{Z_i}^{Z_{i+1}} C_n^2 dh \times \frac{\exp(-f^2/f_m^2)}{(f^2/f_0^2)^{11/6}} \tag{10}$$

where, θ is the zenith angle; $Z_i = h_i/cos\theta$, $f_m = 0.92/l_0$, $f_0 = 1/L_0$, and h is the altitude, l_0 and L_0 are turbulence inner and outer scale. C_n^2 is refractive index structure parameter based on Hufnagel-Valley model.

2.3 Scintillation Index and SNR

When a beam propagates through the atmosphere, the wavefront will be distorted by the atmospheric turbulence. This distortion leads to beam scintillation and will reduce the communication efficiency of FSOC systems. The aperture mean scintillation index and the SNR are used to evaluate beam scintillation and communication potential, respectively. The aperture mean scintillation index can be written as follows:

$$\sigma_I^2(R) = \frac{\langle(\int_0^R\int_0^{2\pi} I(r)rdrd\theta)^2\rangle}{\langle\int_0^R\int_0^{2\pi} I(r)rdrd\theta\rangle^2} - 1 \tag{11}$$

where, $I(r)$ is the beam intensity, R is the radius of the aperture on the receiver plane. Based on the aperture mean scintillation index, the SNR can be given as:

$$\langle SNR\rangle = \frac{SNR_0}{\sqrt{\sigma_I^2(R)SNR_0^2 + P_{S0}/\langle P_S\rangle}} \tag{12}$$

where SNR_0 and P_{S0}, respectively, are the SNR and signal power, and $\langle P_S\rangle$ is the average signal power on the receiver plane.

3 Numerical Results and Discussion

Utilizing the optical turbulence propagation model established through the wave optics simulation method in Sect. 2, this section presents a detailed investigation into the propagation characteristics of the CPC-FTVH beams, the PC-FTVH beams, and the Gaussian Schell-model beams in horizontal links under the atmospheric turbulence. The parameter details of the numerical simulation are defined as follows: wavelength is set to 1550nm, the aperture radius on the receiver plane is 50 mm. The propagation process is divided into 20 parts by the turbulent phase screens, and the sampling grid for the source and receiver plane is set to be 512×512, the sampling interval $\Delta x = (\lambda L/N)^{1/2}$, the turbulence structure constant $C_n^0 = 1 \times 10^{-14}m^{-2/3}$, l_0 and L_0 are 5 mm and 5 m, respectively, the realization number of turbulence is 500 in each case.

In vacuum, the central beam intensities of the CPC-FTVH beams with varying parameters and propagation distances are calculated, while l_{c0} set to be 1 cm. Figure 2(a) shows the central beam intensity of the CPC-FTVH beams with different beam order N and topological charge M during propagation. As the propagation distance increases, all CPC-FTVH beams exhibit a self-focusing peak. It can be seen that changing the beam order N and the topological charge M does not significantly affect the self-focusing position. Meanwhile, the CPC-FTVH beam with $N = 1\ M = 1$ demonstrates the highest intensity peak compared to other parameters. Therefore, the CPC-FTVH beams are set to $N = 1\ M = 1$ in the subsequent results. Figure 2(b) illustrates the effect of beam diameter on the position of the self-focusing peak. The simulation results indicate that increasing the beam diameter causes the self-focusing peak position to shift backward while expanding the self-focusing range of the beam.

Further, we studied the effect of turbulence on the central beam intensity during the transmission of the CPC-FTVH beams, the PC-FTVH beams, and the Gaussian

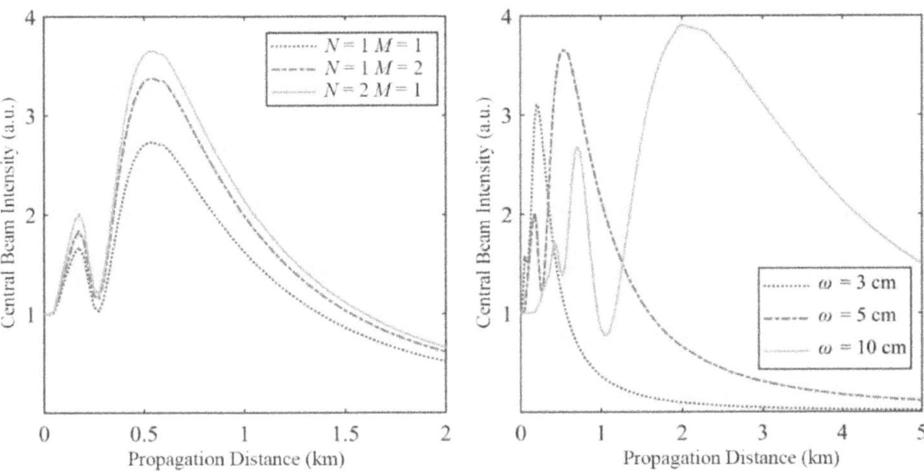

Fig. 2. Influence of beam source parameters on self-focusing effect: (a) the CPC-FTVH beams with $N = 1\ M = 1$, $N = 1\ M = 2$, and $N = 2\ M = 1$, (b) the CPC-FTVH beams with $\omega = 3$ cm, 5 cm, and 10 cm.

Schell-model beams. The beam wide ω_0 is 20 mm, l_{c0} is 1 cm. Figure 3(a) and 3(b) show the central beam intensity of the CPC-FTVH beams, the PC-FTVH beams, and the Gaussian Schell-model beams under different propagation distances under vacuum and atmospheric turbulence conditions, respectively. It can be seen that the CPC-FTVH beams and the PC-FTVH beams both exhibit self-focusing peaks in vacuum or turbulence conditions. However, Gaussian Schell-model beams do not exhibit significant self-focusing characteristics. By comparing the self-focusing peak values in Fig. 3(a) and 3(b), it is obvious that the turbulence has a damaging effect on the self-focusing characteristics. In a vacuum, the intensity peak of the CPC-FTVH beams can reach approximately 2.9 times that of the source plane. However, under turbulent conditions, the peak value is reduced to 1.78 times. The main reason for this phenomenon is the wavefront distortion caused by atmospheric turbulence, which leads to the dispersion of beam intensity. Among the three beam types, the CPC-FTVH beams exhibit the strongest self-focusing peak. This indicates that using CPC-FTVH beams as the beam source can further enhance the beam energy within the receiving aperture and improve the SNR.

The aperture mean scintillation index and the SNR of the CPC-FTVH beams, the PC-FTVH beams, and the Gaussian Schell-model beams are calculated to evaluate the beam scintillation and communication potential of the three beam types. Under the propagation distance of 500 m and 1000 m, the aperture mean scintillation index results of the CPC-FTVH beams, the PC-FTVH beams, and the Gaussian Schell-model beams are shown in Fig. 4. The aperture mean scintillation index for both CPC-FTVH beams and PC-FTVH beams initially decreases and then increases with the rise of l_{c0}, indicating the presence of an optimal l_{c0} that minimizes beam scintillation.

Figure 5 illustrates the effects of l_{c0} on the SNR of the three beams. The results show that, when $z = 1000$ m, the CPC-FTVH beams achieve the highest SNR value. By selecting an appropriate l_{c0}, the CPC-FTVH beams achieve a maximum SNR of

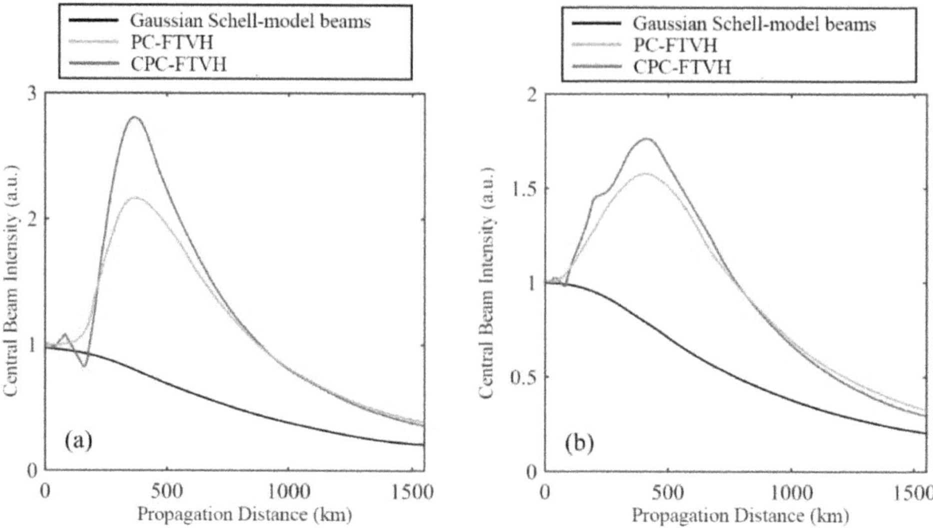

Fig. 3. Central beam intensity of the CPC-FTVH beams, the PC-FTVH beams, and the Gaussian Schell-model beams under different propagation distances under (a) vacuum, (b) atmospheric turbulence conditions.

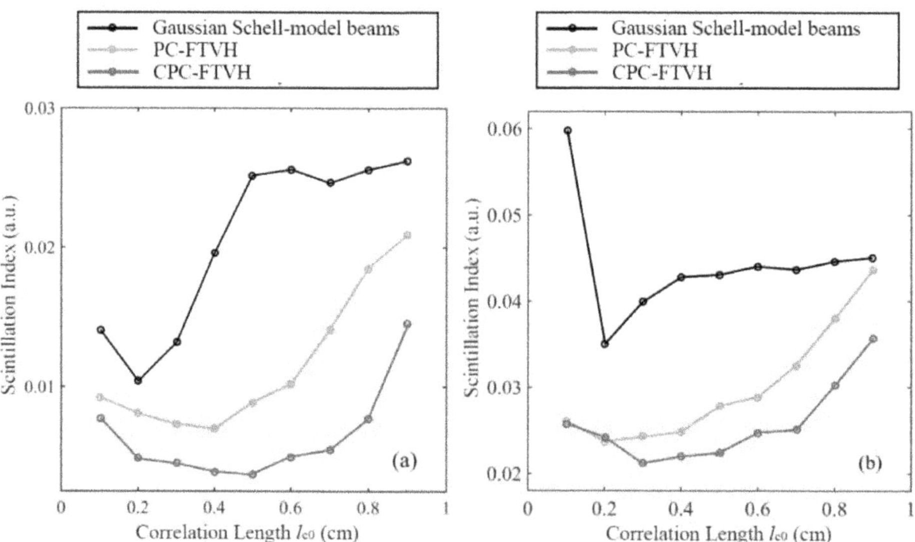

Fig. 4. The aperture mean scintillation index results of the CPC-FTVH beams, the PC-FTVH beams, and the Gaussian Schell-model beams under different propagation distances. (a) $z = 500$ m, (b) $z = 1000$ m.

20.4 dB. The CPC-FTVH beams provide a SNR gain of about 2.1 dB and 3.2 dB compared to the PC-FTVH beams and the Gaussian Schell-model beams, respectively. When the propagation distance increases to $z = 1000$ m, and l_{c0} ranges from 0.1 mm to

0.2 mm, the SNR of the CPC-FTVH beams and the PC-FTVH beams are comparable. As l_{c0} increases further, the SNR of the CPC-FTVH beams becomes higher than that of the other two beam types. The SNR gain advantage of the CPC-FTVH beams is less pronounced at a propagation distance of 1000 m than that at 500 m. This is because the self-focusing advantage of the CPC-FTVH beams gradually decreases as the propagation distance increases.

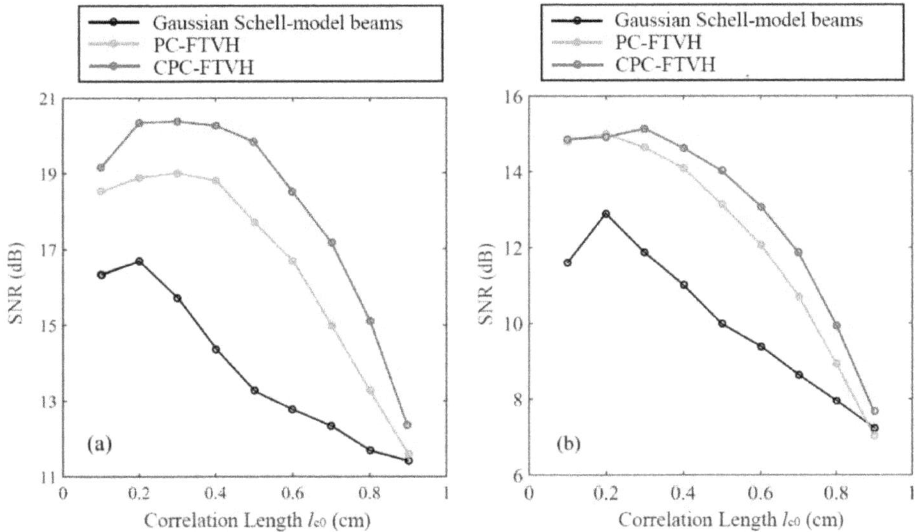

Fig. 5. The SNR results of the CPC-FTVH beams, the PC-FTVH beams, and the Gaussian Schell-model beams under (a) z = 500 m, (b) z = 1000 m.

4   Conclusion

In this paper, the CPC-FTVH beams are proposed to mitigate the negative impacts of atmospheric turbulence on the beams. Using numerical simulations, the propagation performance of the CPC-FTVH beams, the PC-FTVH beams, and the Gaussian Schell-model beams are calculated. As the propagation distance increases, the CPC-FTVH beams exhibit a self-focusing effect. This phenomenon helps enhance the beam energy within the receiving aperture, thereby improving the communication performance of the beams under turbulence. We further calculated the scintillation index and the SNR of the three beams under different l_{c0} values. The results show that there is an optimal l_{c0}, and the CPC-FTVH beams obtain the lowest scintillation index and the highest SNR. By comparing the SNR results under optimal l_{c0}, the CPC-FTVH beams provide an SNR gain of 2.1 dB and 3.2 dB compared to the PC-FTVH beams and the Gaussian Schell-model beams, respectively. According to our research, the CPC-FTVH beams have the potential to enhance the communication performance of FSOC systems and are expected to improve communication reliability for IoT applications.

References

1. Dhar Dwivedi, A., Singh, R., Kaushik, K., et al.: Blockchain and artificial intelligence for 5G-enabled Internet of Things: challenges, opportunities, and solutions. Trans. Emerg. Telecommun. Technol. **35**(4), e4329 (2024)
2. Nguyen, D.C., Ding, M., Pathirana, P.N., et al.: 6G Internet of Things: a comprehensive survey. IEEE Internet Things J. **9**(1), 359–383 (2021)
3. Greengard, S.: The Internet of Things. MIT Press (2021)
4. Wei, T., Feng, W., Chen, Y., et al.: Hybrid satellite-terrestrial communication networks for the maritime Internet of Things: key technologies, opportunities, and challenges. IEEE Internet Things J. **8**(11), 8910–8934 (2021)
5. Kua, J., Loke, S.W., Arora, C., et al.: Internet of things in space: a review of opportunities and challenges from satellite-aided computing to digitally-enhanced space living. Sensors **21**(23), 8117 (2021)
6. Chaudhry, A.U., Yanikomeroglu, H.: Free space optics for next-generation satellite networks. IEEE Consum. Electron. Mag. **10**(6), 21–31 (2020)
7. Guiomar, F.P., Fernandes, M.A., Nascimento, J.L., et al.: Coherent free-space optical communications: opportunities and challenges. J. Lightwave Technol. **40**(10), 3173–3186 (2022)
8. Uysal, Capsoni, Ghassemlooy, et al.: Optical Wireless Communications - An Emerging Technology. Springer, Cham (2016)
9. Shirai, T., Dogariu, A., Wolf, E.: Mode analysis of spreading of partially coherent beams propagating through atmospheric turbulence. JOSA A **20**(6), 1094–1102 (2003)
10. Wu, Z., et al.: Beam properties of a partially coherent beam propagating horizontally in atmospheric turbulence. Photonics **10**(4) (2023)
11. Zhang, Y., et al.: Research on partially coherent flat-topped vortex hollow beam propagation in turbulent atmosphere. Appl. Opt. **56**(10), 2922–2926 (2017)
12. Ge, D., Cai, Y., Lin, Q.: Partially coherent flat-topped beam and its propagation. Appl. Opt. **43**(24), 4732–4738 (2004)
13. Qin, Z., et al.: Propagation of partially coherent Bessel-Gaussian beams carrying optical vortices in non-Kolmogorov turbulence. Opt. Laser Technol. **56**, 182–188 (2014)
14. Wang, M., et al.: Propagation of partially coherent beams with convex-shaped spatial coherence modulation in vertical turbulent links. Opt. Express **26**(24), 32130–32144 (2018)
15. Li, Q.: A numerical study of the partially coherent flat-topped vortex hollow beam and the Gaussian Schell-model beam propagation under atmospheric turbulence. J. Mod. Opt. **68**(21), 1221–1228 (2021)
16. Liu, H., Lü, Y., Xia, J., et al.: Flat-topped vortex hollow beam and its propagation properties. J. Opt. **17**(7), 075606 (2015)
17. Voelz, D.G.: Computational Fourier Optics: A MATLAB Tutorial (2011)
18. Andrews, L.C., Phillips, R.L.: Laser Beam Propagation Through Random Media (2005)

EOST: Research on Enhancing Wi-Fi Direct Detection Rate Based on Environmental Perception

Yan Li[1], Lei Su[2], Guang Hu[3], and Juan Li[1]($\boxtimes$)

[1] Wuhan University of Science and Technology, Wuhan, China
lijuan@wust.edu.cn
[2] Inner Mongolia Branch of CNCERT, Hohhot, China
[3] Huazhong University of Science and Technology, Wuhan, China
huguang@hust.edu.cn

Abstract. Enhancing the detection rate of Wi-Fi Direct networks is essential for assessing network performance in practical applications. This research introduces the EOST (Environmental Optimization for Sniffing Time) algorithm, a novel detection approach for Wi-Fi Direct networks, which dynamically adjusts the sniffing window size for each channel by analyzing environmental characteristics such as the quantity of frames, frame size, and retransmission conditions. Experimental outcomes demonstrate that our algorithm significantly outperforms conventional frequency-hopping listening strategies, achieving a 20.55% improvement in device discovery rates and a 12.01% increase in link discovery rates.

Keywords: Wi-Fi Direct · Detection Rate · Channel Environment · Sniffing Window

1 Introduction

Wi-Fi Direct, predicated on the IEEE 802.11 architecture, facilitates efficient peer-to-peer (P2P) connectivity across both the 2.4 GHz and 5 GHz frequency bands [1]. It has seen an increasing adoption in diverse sectors ranging from digital healthcare and vehicular networking technologies to smart city infrastructures [2]. Capturing Wi-Fi Direct traffic affords a granular comprehension of the network formation process, encompassing key procedural steps such as device discovery, pairing mechanisms, and connection establishment. This process is instrumental not only in identifying and rectifying potential issues that may arise during network assembly but also in optimizing network configurations and delineating network topologies. The capacity to monitor and apprehend the holistic dynamics of the network in real-time, with precision and completeness, during its normal operation is of paramount importance [3].

The majority of packet capture operations are designed to utilize a limited number of sniffers to maximize the volume of packet capture within the 2.4 GHz

R. C. Qiu et al. (Eds.): IoTaaS 2024, LNICST 675, pp. 177–186, 2026.
https://doi.org/10.1007/978-3-032-14681-6_15

and 5 GHz bands, rather than specifically targeting the sniffing of packets from a particular type or device [4–6]. For those operations aimed at capturing specific types of packets, they often demonstrate a certain predictability, as the anticipated signals to be captured can typically be predetermined to occur on specific channels [7,8].

Due to various reasons, detecting wireless communications from specific devices is quite challenging. On one hand, Wi-Fi Direct devices transmit data across different channels, and data packet capturing must configure the sniffer to listen to specific channels [7]. On the other hand, the decentralized nature of Wi-Fi Direct networks and the unique randomness in the network formation process, such as random MAC addresses and random frequency hopping, coupled with the time overhead of network adapters during channel switching [6], all increase the complexity of achieving efficient network detection. To cover as much of the spectrum as possible, frequency-hopping technology can be introduced, where wireless network cards are configured to listen to a channel for a specified switching interval, and then hop to another channel according to the listening strategy. The formulation of frequency-hopping strategies is often closely related to the characteristics of the network.

During the communication process of Wi-Fi Direct devices, the majority of devices quickly disconnect after data transmission is completed. Therefore, for network sniffers, timely tracking when a device enters the discovery or pairing phase is a key strategy to enhance the likelihood of capturing such data. However, determining the optimal tracking duration poses a technical challenge. Some devices may interrupt during the pairing process due to failure or user cancellation, rendering prolonged tracking potentially futile. Moreover, a complex network environment may lead to increased time intervals during the pairing and authentication phases, thereby affecting the efficiency of data capture. According to the Carrier Sense Multiple Access with Collision Avoidance (CSMA/CA) protocol [9], the timing for Wi-Fi Direct devices to transmit key frames is also correspondingly extended, further adding to the uncertainty of the tracking duration.

Wi-Fi channel load can be measured by a single parameter (AP load) [10] or a weighted combination of multiple parameters (throughput and channel occupancy) [11]. Shugo Kajita et al. proposed a method based on actual observable parameters (such as inter-channel distance, RSS, and traffic) to evaluate the relative index of channel quality [12], which may be significantly affected by environmental factors, such as the layout of buildings, physical obstacles, etc. Danielle Saliba et al. grasped the load situation of the channel by analyzing the percentage of channel usage time (i.e., busy and idle time) [13], which relies on the average value of time and may fail to capture short periods of high load. Toni Adame et al. assessed the channel load situation by combining the RSSI obtained from network sites with information related to virtual carrier sensing from parsed frames [14], a method that may be limited by the performance of device hardware, as different devices may have different levels of RSSI measurement accuracy.

In this paper, we propose a detection algorithm model named EOST. This algorithm dynamically adjusts the monitoring window by synthesizing an analysis of channel environmental factors, aiming to more effectively track the critical stages of Wi-Fi Direct until the successful discovery of its network formation. Ultimately, we have designed experiments that use the number of successfully captured devices and the link capture rate as criteria for evaluation, thereby comparing the algorithm's superiority.

The remainder of this paper is organized as follows. The second section introduces preliminary content. The third section provides a detailed system design. The fourth section presents the experimental setup and results, and the fifth section summarizes the paper.

2   Preliminary

2.1   Wi-Fi Direct

Wi-Fi Direct is a Wi-Fi standard defined by the Wi-Fi Alliance for enhancing peer-to-peer communication without the need for a wireless access point (AP) [15]. According to this standard, devices are organized into groups, with one device acting as the Group Owner (GO) and embedding soft AP functionalities similar to those of a traditional AP. Additionally, the GO is responsible for group announcements and routing data through its group. All other devices connect to the GO and act as Group Members (GM).

Two devices can establish a P2P group through various methods, depending on whether they need to negotiate the role of the P2P GO, which are categorized as Standard, Autonomous, and Persistent.

In the Standard scenario, Wi-Fi Direct devices typically initiate with a traditional Wi-Fi scan, either active or passive, enabling them to detect existing P2P groups and Wi-Fi networks. Following this scan, the P2P device selects one of the so-called social channels, specifically channel 1, 6, or 11 within the 2.4 GHz band, as its listening channel. It then alternates between two states: the search state, where the device actively scans by broadcasting probe requests on each social channel; and the listen state, wherein the device listens on its listening channel for probe requests to respond with probe responses. The duration a P2P device spends in each state is stochastically distributed, typically ranging from 100 to 300 milliseconds. Once two P2P devices have located each other, they commence the GO negotiation phase. This is facilitated through a three-way handshake, involving GO Negotiation Request, Response, and Confirmation, where the two devices reach a consensus on which will act as the P2P GO and the channel on which the group will operate, which can be within any 2.4 GHz or 5 GHz band. Upon mutual discovery and agreement on their respective roles, secure communication is established using WPS configuration.

2.2 EOST Model

Given the extensive channel availability in the 2.4 GHz and 5 GHz bands, traditional fixed-frequency detection methods are impractical due to their restricted coverage. Hence, we have introduced a dynamic frequency-hopping detection approach. This method initiates with a preset sniffing time on each channel and dynamically adjusts the dwell time based on the sniffing results within the default interval. During the default sniffing period, our device passively listens for Wi-Fi Direct related frames. Upon detection of these target frames, the device immediately initiates a computational process to determine whether to extend the dwell time on the current channel. The extension duration is calculated based on the characteristics of the detected frames and the current network conditions (see Fig. 1).

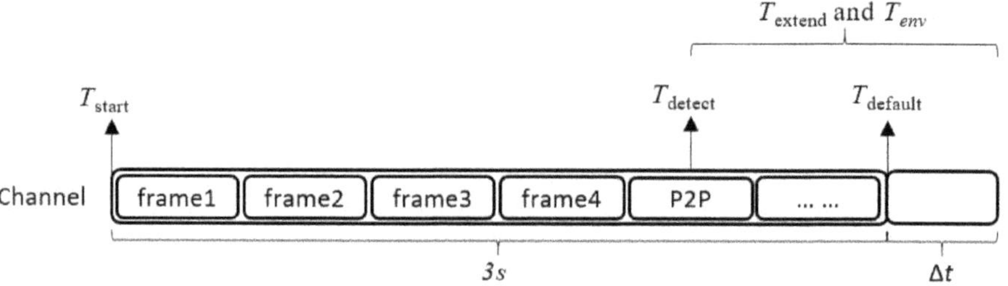

Fig. 1. Channel Dwelling Time Dynamic Adjustment Mechanism.

The adjusted channel dwell time is determined by the following formula:

$$\Delta t = T_{\text{detect}} + T_{\text{extend}} + T_{\text{env}} - T_{\text{default}} \tag{1}$$

T_{detect} represents the arrival time of the target frame, T_{extend} represents the time to decide to extend the channel dwell time upon receiving the frame, T_{default} represents the default sniffing end time, and T_{env} represents the time compensated for the impact of the network environment. Determining T_{extend} for each set of frames and T_{env} for each channel is the focus of our research.

3 System Design

This section elaborates on the methods and techniques employed in this study to enhance the detection rate of Wi-Fi Direct networks, with a particular focus on channel assessment strategies.

3.1 Calculation of T_{extend}

T_{extend} is based on the Distributed Coordination Function (DCF) within the IEEE 802.11 protocol and the transmission rate under the 802.11g standard.

DCF is an access control mechanism for shared channels in wireless networks, with its core being the CSMA/CA, which includes: carrier sensing mechanism, IFS and Random Backoff mechanism.

The official protocol of Wi-Fi Direct dictates that Wi-Fi Direct devices shall not utilize 802.11b for the transmission of data and management frames, indicating that the owner of a P2P group must employ OFDM to transmit signals. Assuming a set of frames for a specific behavior of Wi-Fi Direct devices involves N signal exchanges, the time required for such a set of exchanges between two P2P devices, in the absence of network interference, is defined by the following formula:

$$T_{\text{extend}} = T_{\text{transmit}} + T_{\text{ifs}} + T_{\text{back}} + T_{\text{deal}} \tag{2}$$

In this formula, T_{transmit} represents the time required for N frames to be encapsulated at the physical layer and then modulated for transmission. Calculate T_{transmit} as follows:

$$T_{\text{transmit}} = N \times T_{\text{preamble}} + T_{\text{sym}} \times \sum_{i=1}^{n} \left\lceil \frac{16 + \text{len}_i + 6}{4 \times \text{data rate}} \right\rceil \tag{3}$$

T_{preamble} is the duration of the preamble, T_{sym} is the interval of the OFDM symbol, Ceiling is the ceiling function, len_i is the length of the MPDU part in the ith signaling frame, and "data rate" is the rate at which the data is transmitted.

The T_{ifs} and T_{back} are two processes that must be waited for before signal transmission. The T_{ifs} varies depending on the type of signal, and the T_{back} involves selecting a random number between CW_{min} and CW_{max}. When retransmissions occur, the window interval for CW_{min} and CW_{max} increases. The calculations for T_{ifs} gap and T_{back} are as follows:

$$T_{\text{ifs}} = \sum_{i=1}^{n} T_{\text{ifs}}(i) \tag{4}$$

$$T_{\text{back}} = \text{slot time} \times \sum_{i=1}^{n} k_i \tag{5}$$

Under the 802.11g standard, the "slot time" is set to 10 microseconds by default.

T_{deal} is the processing time required when a device receives a signal, which varies depending on the hardware capabilities and the size and type of the frame. T_{deal} rep resents the processing time for the ith signal:

$$T_{\text{deal}} = \sum_{i=1}^{n} T_{\text{deal}}(i) \tag{6}$$

In this section, we have established a set of exchange times for a group of management frames and set up experiments to measure the T_{deal} or each type of frame. Under conditions free of any interference, we conducted exchanges of various frames in Wi-Fi Direct, taking the time between two frames, for example: probe request and probe response. The time obtained from real-world scenarios is then reduced by the minimum values of T_{transmit}, T_{ifs} and T_{deal}, and finally, T_{deal} is calculated.

3.2   Environmental Assessment

In an interference-free network environment, the efficiency of signal transmission is primarily influenced by the data transmission rate. When retransmissions occur, to ensure the reliability of transmission, the data transmission rate will decrease. Moreover, in a busy network environment, not only will there be signaling from Wi-Fi Direct devices on the channel, but also signals generated by other devices will be mixed in, leading to potential interference during the transmission process.

Given the significant impact of the channel environment on the transmission time of Wi-Fi Direct signaling, this study proposes three key characteristic quantities to predict the optimal solution for T_{env}:

1. Number of frames per unit time: This metric reflects the frequency of channel usage and is a fundamental parameter for assessing network load.
2. Frame size: The size of a frame directly affects the time required for transmission, larger frames require more time to transmit.
3. Retransmission count: In a busy channel environment, frame collisions are exacerbated, leading to an increased number of frames being retransmitted.

To accurately predict the extension time of channel monitoring, we constructed a multiple linear regression model, which takes the number of frames, frame size, and retransmission count as independent variables, and the predicted channel monitoring extension time T_{env} as the dependent variable. The model can be represented as:

$$T_{\text{env}} = \alpha_0 + \alpha_1 x_1 + \alpha_2 x_2 + \alpha_3 x_3 + \varepsilon \tag{7}$$

In the model, x_1, x_2, and x_3 represent the number of frames, frame size, and retransmission count, respectively. α_0 is the intercept, while α_1, α_2, and α_3 are the regression coefficients for each feature, and ε represents the error term.

To collect key data, we fixed the formation and linking of Wi-Fi Direct devices on specific channels and applied load. We monitored the time intervals of frames exchanged during device discovery after the negotiation phase and before authentication, and repeated this process after changing the load conditions. We further analyzed the number of frames per unit time, the average frame size, and the number of retransmissions to assess the impact ratio of these parameters on the frame exchange intervals of this group.

4   Experiments and Evaluation

4.1   Channel Influence Experiment

To assess the influence of channel conditions on Wi-Fi Direct handshakes and link establishment, we employed a pair of Raspberry Pi 4 Model B devices, each equipped with multiple MediaTek CF-926AC V2 wireless network interface cards (NICs), serving as the hardware components for Wi-Fi Direct communication. The software platform for Wi-Fi Direct communication was based on wpa_supplicant. We conducted experiments with three distinct Wi-Fi Direct connection methodologies, each automated and iterated 50 times to ensure statistical significance. Concurrently, to impose stress on the communication channel, a frame emitter was programmed to transmit frames continuously at varying time intervals within the operational channel, thereby simulating a congested channel environment. This methodology is designed to provide insights into the robustness and performance of Wi-Fi Direct under different channel load conditions, which is crucial for its deployment in real-world scenarios.

The results of the experiment can be seen in Fig. 2 below.

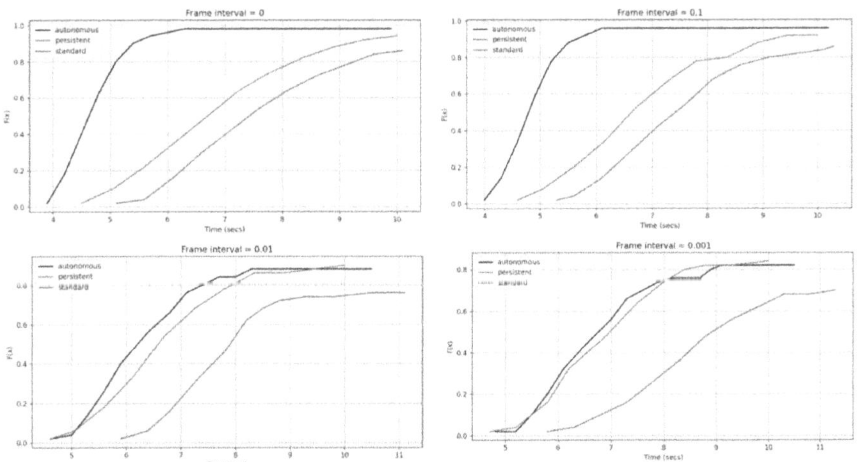

Fig. 2. Influence diagram of channel environment on Wi-Fi Direct communication time.

The experimental results revealed that as the channel pressure increased, the number of data packets appearing within a unit of time in the channel also increased. Each networking method was affected, with the time for each stage of network formation being prolonged, and the success rate of network formation also declined.

4.2   Detection Rate Comparison

To evaluate the detection performance of the algorithm, we replicated the aforementioned communication environment, while continuously conducting random

Wi-Fi Direct handshakes and link establishments in various modes adjacent to the sniffer. Upon successful link establishment, an MP4 file of approximately 1 to 3 MB was transmitted. To accentuate the experimental effects, the initiation of Wi-Fi Direct handshakes and link establishments was fixed within the 2.4G frequency band.

In the experimental setup, we implemented two distinct sniffing strategies. The first strategy employed the conventional channel hopping method, with a fixed monitoring duration of 0.2 s per channel. The second strategy was entirely based on our Enhanced Opportunistic Scheduling Algorithm (EOST), which dynamically adjusts the listening window according to real-time channel conditions. Since EOST is capable of more effectively tracking the behavior of Wi-Fi Direct until network formation is successful, and Wi-Fi Direct devices use interface addresses for data transmission after network formation, we compared the number of information packets captured at different stages and the number of devices post-network formation between the two strategies.

Each set of experiments lasted for one hour, during which between 30 to 40 instances of Wi-Fi Direct communication were established in each group. Link discovery rate comparison can be seen in Fig. 3; Wi-Fi Direct interface address capture count comparison can be seen in Fig. 4.

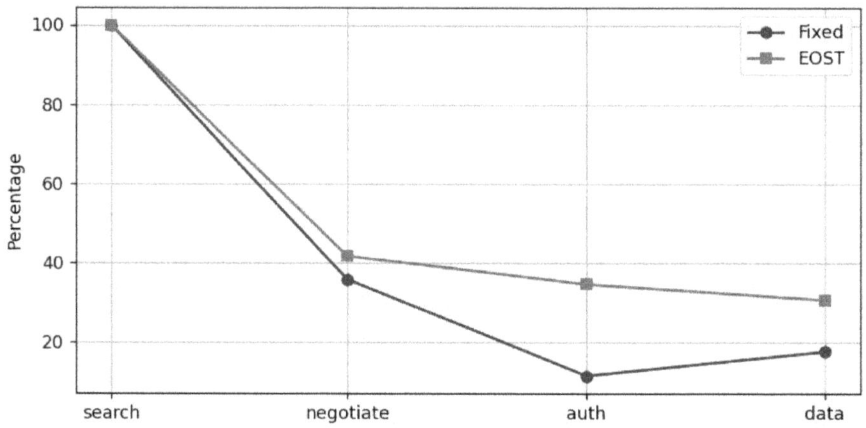

Fig. 3. Comparison plot of the amount of information captured at different stages.

The experimental results indicate that compared to the fixed-time channel-hopping strategy, our EOST algorithm model has achieved significant improvements in both Wi-Fi Direct device discovery and link discovery. The enhancement in link discovery demonstrates the EOST algorithm's notable effect on tracking the behavior of Wi-Fi Direct. Specifically, device discovery improved by 20.55%, and link discovery improved by 12.01%.

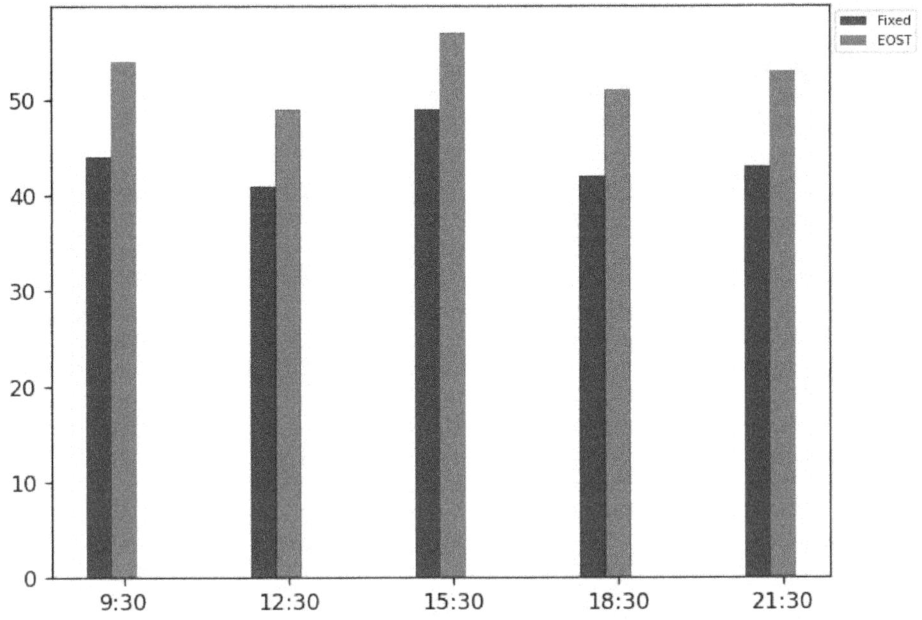

Fig. 4. P2P Device Capture Count.

5   Summarize

In this study, we have focused on improving the detection rate of Wi-Fi Direct networks in resource-constrained environments. We have developed a method for accurately assessing channel congestion, which has been integrated into our Environmental Optimization for Sniffing Time (EOST) algorithm. This integration allows the detection time window to be intelligently adjusted based on real-time channel load conditions. Our system is thus capable of maintaining high efficiency while adapting to fluctuations in network status. Future research will further investigate the impact of channel conditions on the data transmission efficiency of various 802.11 standards (a/g/n/ac) under high-load network conditions, as well as the interference resistance capabilities of each standard, with the aim of enhancing the detection accuracy of Wi-Fi Direct in complex network environments.

References

1. Tan, S., et al.: Performance evaluation of 5G NR traffic offloading onto WiFi direct. In: 2022 IEEE 8th International Conference on Computer and Communications (ICCC), Chengdu, China, pp. 304–308. IEEE (2022). https://doi.org/10.1109/ICCC56324.2022.10065621

2. Jahed, K., Farhat, O., Al-Jurdi, G., Sharafeddine, S.: Optimized group owner selection in WiFi direct networks. In: 2016 24th International Conference on Software, Telecommunications and Computer Networks (SoftCOM), Split, Croatia, pp. 1–5. IEEE (2016). https://doi.org/10.1109/SOFTCOM.2016.7772169

3. Koutras, D., Dimitrellos, P., Kotzanikolaou, P., Douligeris, C.: Automated WiFi incident detection attack tool on 802.11 networks. In: 2023 IEEE Symposium on Computers and Communications (ISCC), Gammarth, Tunisia, pp. 464–469. IEEE (2023). https://doi.org/10.1109/ISCC58397.2023.10218077

4. Arora, P., Szepesvári, C., Zheng, R.: Sequential learning for optimal monitoring of multichannel wireless networks. In: 2011 Proceedings IEEE INFOCOM, Shanghai, China, pp. 1152–1160 (2011). https://doi.org/10.1109/INFCOM.2011.5934892

5. Xu, J., Wang, Q., Zeng, K., Liu, M., Liu, W.: Sniffer channel assignment with imperfect monitoring for cognitive radio networks. IEEE Trans. Wirel. Commun. **15**, 1703–1715 (2016)

6. Le, T., Szepesvári, C., Zheng, R.: Sequential learning for multi-channel wireless network monitoring with channel switching costs. IEEE Trans. Signal Process. **62**(22), 5919–5929 (2014). https://doi.org/10.1109/TSP.2014.2357779

7. Li, Y., Barthelemy, J., Sun, S., Perez, P., Moran, B.: A case study of WiFi sniffing performance evaluation. IEEE Access **8**, 129224–129235 (2020). https://doi.org/10.1109/ACCESS.2020.3008533

8. Song, L., Striegel, A., Mohammed, A.: Sniffing only control packets: a lightweight client-side WiFi traffic characterization solution. IEEE Internet Things J. **8**(8), 6536–6548 (2021). https://doi.org/10.1109/JIOT.2020.3041671

9. Li, L., Dong, Y., Pan, C., Fan, P.: Age of information of CSMA/CA based wireless networks. In: 2022 International Wireless Communications and Mobile Computing (IWCMC), Dubrovnik, Croatia, pp. 530–535 (2022). https://doi.org/10.1109/IWCMC55113.2022.9824704

10. Abusubaih, M., Gross, J., Wiethoelter, S., Wolisz, A.: On access point selection in IEEE 802.11 wireless local area networks. In: Proceedings of the 2006 31st IEEE Conference on Local Computer Networks, Tampa, FL, USA, pp. 879–886 (2006). https://doi.org/10.1109/LCN.2006.322194

11. Gong, H., Nahm, K., Kim, J.: Distributed fair access point selection for multi-rate IEEE 802.11 WLANs. In: 2008 5th IEEE Consumer Communications and Networking Conference, Las Vegas, NV, USA, pp. 528–532 (2008). https://doi.org/10.1109/ccnc08.2007.123

12. Kajita, S., et al.: A channel selection strategy for WLAN in urban areas by regression analysis. In: 2014 IEEE 10th International Conference on Wireless and Mobile Computing, Networking and Communications (WiMob), Larnaca, Cyprus, pp. 642–647 (2014). https://doi.org/10.1109/WiMOB.2014.6962238

13. Saliba, D., Imad, R., Houcke, S.: Wifi channel selection based on load criteria. In: 2017 20th International Symposium on Wireless Personal Multimedia Communications (WPMC), Bali, Indonesia, pp. 332–336 (2017). https://doi.org/10.1109/WPMC.2017.8301833

14. Adame, T., Carrascosa, M., Bellalta, B., Pretel, I., Etxebarria, I.: Channel load aware AP/extender selection in home WiFi networks using IEEE 802.11k/v. IEEE Access **9**, 30095–30112 (2021). https://doi.org/10.1109/ACCESS.2021.3059473

15. "Wi-Fi Alliance", P2P Technical Group Wi-Fi Peer-to-Peer (P2P) Technical Specification v1.9 (2021)

Research on Performance Testing System for Refrigerated Infrared Detectors

Tingting Ren[1,2](✉), Chao Yi[3], and Jing Huang[1,2]

[1] Wuhan Vocational College of Software and Engineering, Wuhan 430205, Hubei, China
rtt_rain@qq.com
[2] Hubei Engineering Research Center for Intelligent Detection and Identification of Complex Parts, Wuhan 430205, Hubei, China
[3] FiberHome Telecommunication Technologies Co., Ltd., Wuhan 430205, Hubei, China

Abstract. Infrared detector is a device that can detect infrared signals on the surface of objects and convert them into electrical signals, which has been widely used in military and industrial fields such as the Internet of Things, communications, guidance, thermal imaging, and surveillance. Using the black body as the calibrator, it can test the parameters of the infrared detector and detect whether the performance indicators of the infrared detector meet the standard. This article describes a test system that uses NI Virtual Instruments and LabVIEW Software to test the performance of infrared detectors. The system provides the bias voltage and signal required for detector performance testing, and data acquisition. At the same time, a method for measuring the DC level, noise, response rate, noise equivalent temperature difference, normalized detection rate and bad pixel of the detector by using the system is given. Finally, the influencing factors of the test results were analyzed to provide reference for related research.

Keywords: Infrared Detector · Performance Testing · Detecting System

1 Introduction

With the development of the Internet of Things and communication technology, people's demand for high-quality data communication is increasing. Infrared signal transmission is an important part of the communication field, and high-quality infrared detector testing systems can accurately evaluate the performance of detectors in high-speed data transmission, such as signal sensitivity and anti-interference ability. Ensure its stable operation in complex communication environments, and open up new paths for 6G to achieve higher transmission rates and lower latency. In the field of the Internet of Things, infrared detectors are widely used for smart device perception. The testing system can verify its detection accuracy and response speed, helping smart homes, industrial Internet of Things, and other industries achieve more intelligent control and monitoring [1]. To ensure accurate perception of human activities in smart homes and reliable detection of device status in industrial IoT.

R. C. Qiu et al. (Eds.): IoTaaS 2024, LNICST 675, pp. 187–196, 2026.
https://doi.org/10.1007/978-3-032-14681-6_16

The basic structure of the infrared detection system (see Fig. 1) mainly includes the optical system, photodetector, signal amplifier, signal processing and display output, and its core is the infrared detector, which can convert the incident radiant energy into a measurable electrical signal [2]. The performance of the infrared detector will directly affect the accuracy and response speed of the infrared temperature measurement system, so the performance indicators of the infrared detector need to be detected before the infrared temperature measurement system is designed.

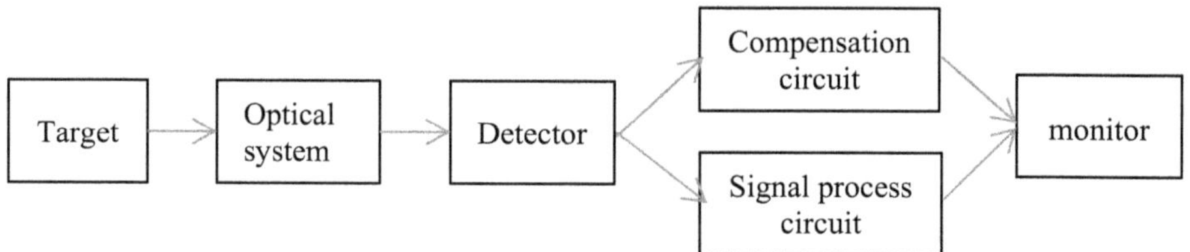

Fig. 1. Structural diagram of infrared temperature measurement system

In this paper, an infrared detector test system was developed based on NI PXI virtual instrumentation and LabVIEW software.

NI Virtual Instruments is a computer-based measurement and control technology with the core idea of "hardware function software", which is more flexible and scalable than traditional hardware instruments to meet different test needs. NI virtual instruments provide complex signal generation and signal processing to meet the individual needs of scientists [3]. At the same time, its powerful data acquisition and analysis functions greatly simplify the design and development process of test equipment, reduce cost and time investment, and improve the accuracy and reliability of test results.

LabVIEW software is a graphical programming environment for the design and implementation of virtual instruments. The LabVIEW language is a formal data flow-driven language. That is, for the node in the program, when the data on its input port becomes valid data, the node is executed immediately, without waiting for other nodes to complete the execution. Which improves the execution speed of the system [4].

2 Testing System Design

The testing system uses the NI-PXIe 8106 chassis as the main hardware device, and works with the NI PXI-6733 high-speed analog I/O card, the NI BNC-2110 shielded junction box, and the NI PXI-1422 data acquisition card to program the instrument for instrument control and data acquisition using LabVIEW software, enabling real-time data processing and results analysis [5].

The NI PXIe-8106 is a high-performance embedded controller for interfacing output and data acquisition cards. The NI PXI-6733 module is a high-speed analog output card that provides eight analog output channels at 1 MS/s each, with 16-bit resolution and digital triggering, for high-speed digital signal generation and detection at 10M word/s. The resulting signal is transmitted to the infrared detector via the NI BNC-2110 shielded junction box. The NI PXI-1422 board enables high-speed, high-capacity, high-resolution digital image acquisition, capable of acquiring data up to 16-bit resolution at 40 MHz clock speeds for a total acquisition rate of up to 80 Mbytes/s. On-board memory (16 MB) provides both a cache for images on the board when capturing large images, as well as continuous real-time acquisition.

The composition of the test system (see Fig. 2) includes a light source, an infrared optical system, an infrared detector assembly, an input signal, an output signal, and a data analysis component. Among them, the infrared radiation of the black-body light source is imaged on the infrared detector array after passing through the infrared optical system [6]. The Dewar bottle in the detector assembly (IDDCA) cools the detector, reads the temperature of the detector through the serial port of the detector assembly, and detects whether it has reached the working temperature; The software controls the bias card of PXI to generate the bias voltage required for detector operation, triggering the required timing signal to ensure stable operation of the detector; Obtain the output data of the infrared detector through a data acquisition card, and process and analyze the data through software [7]. This testing system uses the NI-PXIe 8106 chassis as the main hardware equipment, combined with the NI PXI-6733 high-speed analog input/output card, NI BNC-2110 shielded junction box, and uses LabVIEW software programming to effectively connect the PC and acquisition hardware, becoming a complete instrument control, data acquisition, and analysis system. It completes the performance testing of the refrigeration type infrared detector and can perform real-time data processing and result analysis.

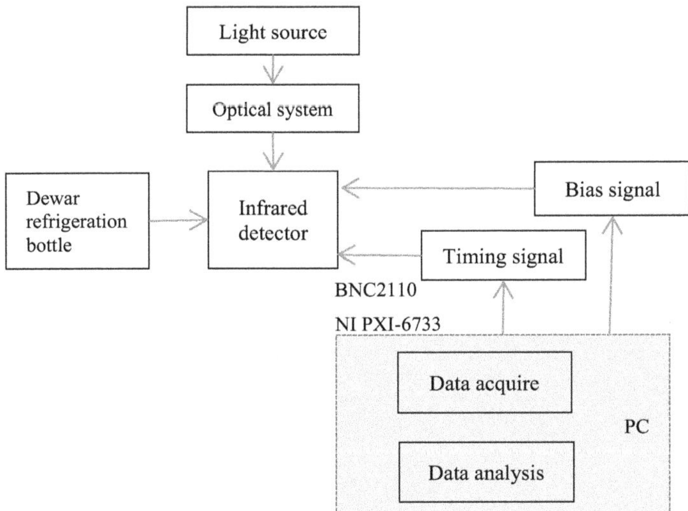

Fig. 2. Block diagram of infrared detector testing system

3 Data Input and Output

Taking a certain model of refrigeration type medium wave infrared detector as an example, the circuit interface of the detector includes the circuit interface of the Dewar bottle refrigeration machine and the circuit interface of the detector driver and data readout. When testing, it is necessary to first start the power supply of the refrigeration unit, and use LabVIEW to write a program to read the temperature value of the detector from the serial port of the refrigeration unit circuit [8]. When the temperature of the focal plane detector drops to about 90 K required for operation, start the detector bias power supply and input a timing signal.

3.1 Bias Signal Output

The main bias voltages of the detector are one 0.7 V and two 5 V voltage outputs.

By using LabVIEW and LabVIEW Signal Express, various bias voltages (see Fig. 3) can be conveniently generated. There are two ways to generate bias voltages in two ways:

- Using the Create Analog Voltage in LabVIEW SignalExpress to generate analog voltage outputs with different amplitudes for each channel of the BNC-2110 through NI PXI-6733.
- Using LabVIEW graphical software design approach to create a bias generator program with a use panel.The LabVIEW program created is a VI file with Front Panel and Block Dialogue.

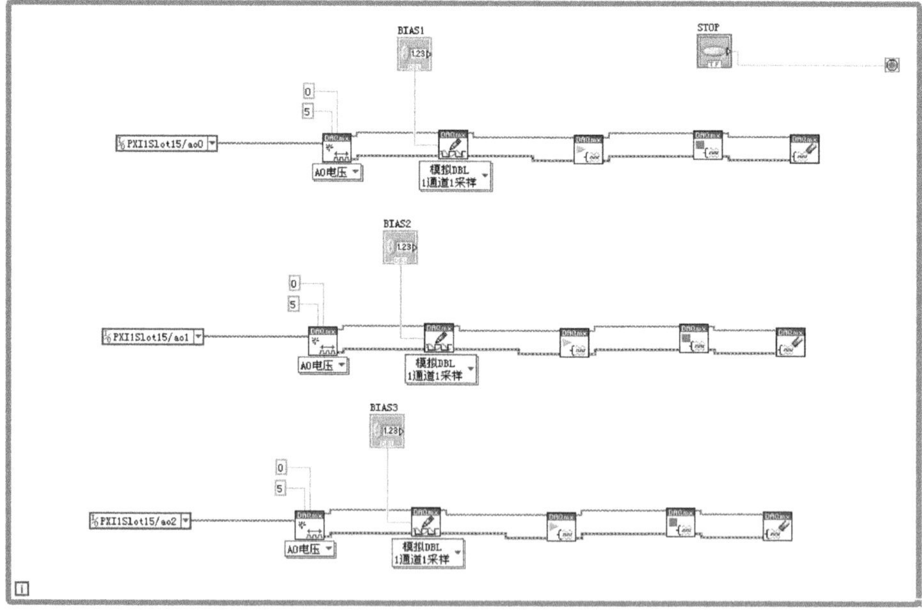

Fig. 3. Bias signal LabVIEW graphical programming window

3.2 Timing Signal Output

In The timing diagram of the detector's readout circuit (see Fig. 4), MC is the main frequency clock, the high level of INT is the integration time, and the high level of DATAVALID is the data readout time. In fact, the only timing required for detector operation is MC and INT [9]. The frequency of the main frequency clock MC is 4 MHz or 6.6 MHz. The rising edge of the INT integration time must be consistent with the rising edge of the MC main frequency, and the falling edge must be consistent with the rising edge of the MC [10].

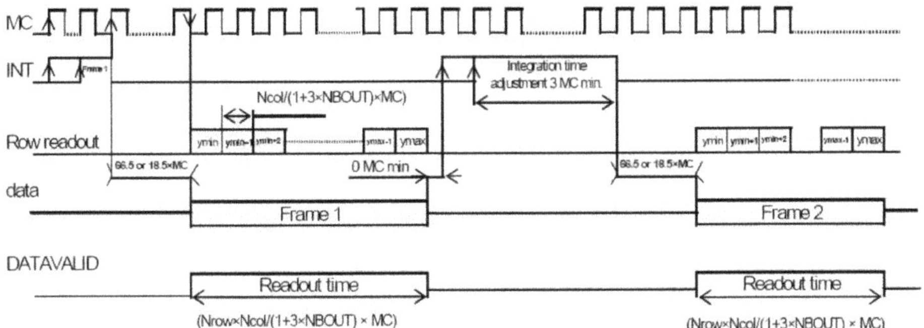

Fig. 4. Timing diagram of the readout circuit of the detector

Similar to the bias program, the generation of timing signals is also programmed by using LabVIEW. Using LabVIEW Measurement&Automation to generate sine wave, square wave, and triangular wave signals of various frequencies. Then output to the detector through NI PXI-6733 and BNC-2110.

There are three commonly used methods to generat temporal signals:

- Status Delay

  LabVIEW software is used to generate a low level of 0~0.8 V, and then output a high level of 2~5 V through the software delay, and the delay process is realized through the wait function, and the delay accuracy is millisecond. MC requires a latency of 250 ns, which is not sufficient.

- Clock Signal Method

  The clock signal generator is used to generate periodic pulse waveforms by using hardware timing, and the delay pulse width accuracy is high. However, most of the clock signal generators of general bias cards have only one or two channels, which cannot meet the function expansion in the future.

- Digital Signal Method

  A pulse signal with a certain pulse width is generated through a pulse pattern, converted into a digital signal, bundled with multiple signals, and output to each digital channel through a DAQ function [11]. The continuous rectangular pulse of the set frequency is used as the clock signal MC by the counter output, and the clock source of the DAQ sampling function is connected to it as the synchronization signal.

Firstly, a certain frequency square wave is generated as the clock signal (see Fig. 5), and secondly, a certain regularity of high and low levels are generated as the integral timing signal (see Fig. 6).

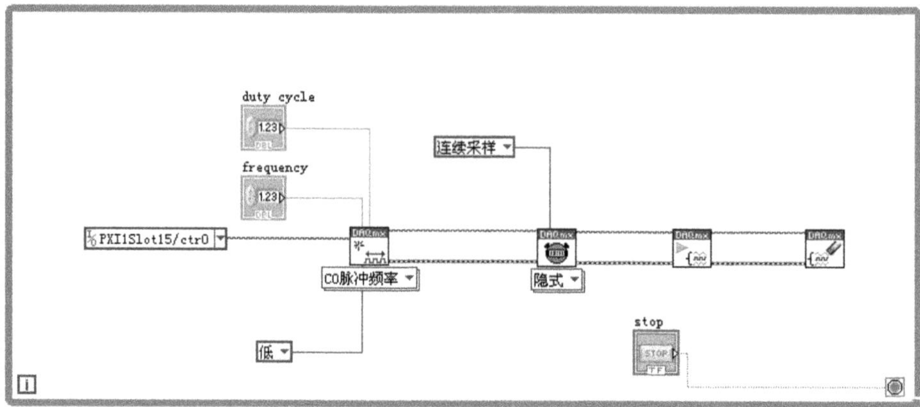

Fig. 5. Clock signal LabVIEW graphical programming window

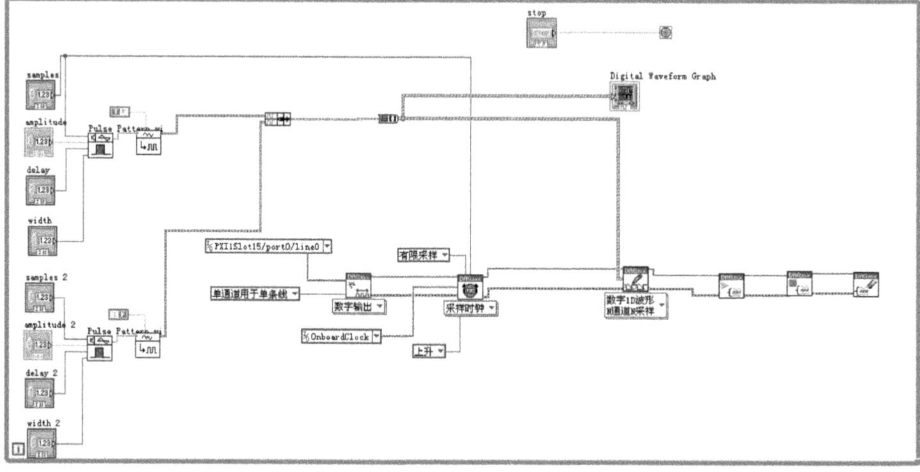

Fig. 6. Timing signal LabVIEW graphical programming window

3.3 Data Acquisition

The data acquisition module collects the output signal of the detector readout circuit ROIC, and uses the LabVIEW DAQ data acquisition system to write a program to control the PXI acquisition card to complete data acquisition [12]. It provides single channel, dual channel, and four channel acquisition modes and can restore the data sequence [13].

The data processing module first calculates the performance parameters of the detector, including DC Uniformity, Noise, Noise Equivalent Temperature Difference (NETD),

300 K Detection Rate (D *), Response Rate, Noise Equivalent Radiation Illumination (NEI), Noise Equivalent Radiation Power (NEP), Bad Pixels, and displays the results in the form of data tables, two-dimensional graphs, three-dimensional graphs, and histograms; Further video process the image data and display the hot image. In this article, SAS software is used to capture images.

The parameters of the infrared detector that the system can test include [4]:

1) DC Uniformity
2) Noise
3) Noise Equivalent Temperature Difference (NETD)
4) 300 K detection rate (D *)
5) Response rate
6) Noise equivalent irradiance (NEI)
7) Noise equivalent radiation power (NEP)
8) Bad Pixels

4 Infrared Detector Testing

After debugging the bias value and correcting the timing, connect the bias and timing according to the following corresponding relationships: interface Vdda connected to Bias1, interface Vddl connected to Bias3, interface Gpol connected to Bias5, interface MC connected to CLK1, interface INT connected to CLK2, and interface GAIN connected to CLK3. After the connection is completed and retested, prepare to cool and power on the detector.

Connect the power cord of the refrigeration unit to the pre-set 24 V power supply, and start the refrigeration unit to focus on the plane for cooling. The cooling time specified for this detector is less than 8 min, and the time needs to be recorded during testing. This cooling time is the primary test parameter for determining whether the detector is qualified [14].

After the detector is successfully cooled, the output image of the detector can be seen in the data acquisition window.

To avoid the grayscale mean of the output image being too small or saturated, the grayscale value should be about half of the maximum value [15]. If the digital signal output by the system is 14 bits, then half of the maximum grayscale value should be:

$$\frac{2^{14}}{2} = 8192 \tag{1}$$

Therefore, the appropriate grayscale mean should be between 7000 and 8000.

After imaging the detector, align the detector probe with the black-body, adjust the black-body temperature to 20 °C (293 K) and 35 °C (308 K), and use SAS software to capture the image (see Fig. 7). The temperature of the black-body is set to 293 K and 308 K respectively, and the performance parameters of the tested detector include DC level, noise, response rate, noise equivalent temperature difference, noise equivalent radiation illuminance, noise equivalent radiation power, normalized detection rate, and bad pixel distribution [16].

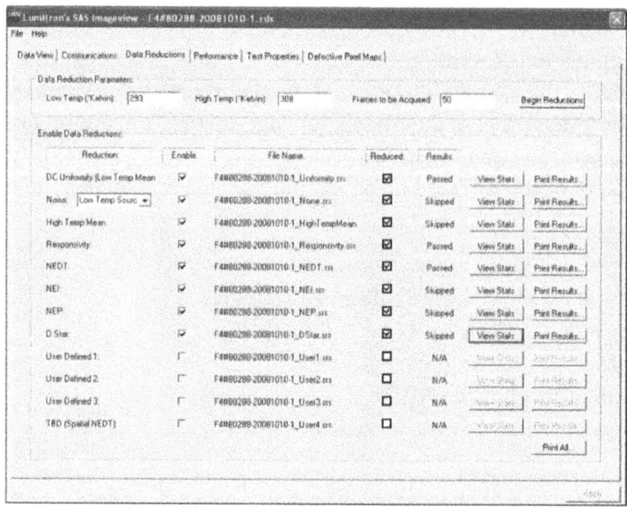

Fig. 7. SAS software testing detector interface

The test results of noise equivalent temperature difference (NETD) (see Fig. 8) are shown in Fig. 6. The histogram shows the distribution of NETD values for all pixels, and the mean NETD of all pixels is 14.59 mK. After removing 104 bad pixels, the mean NETD of effective pixels is 14.53 mK, which meets the requirements of NETD and is not more than 21 mK.

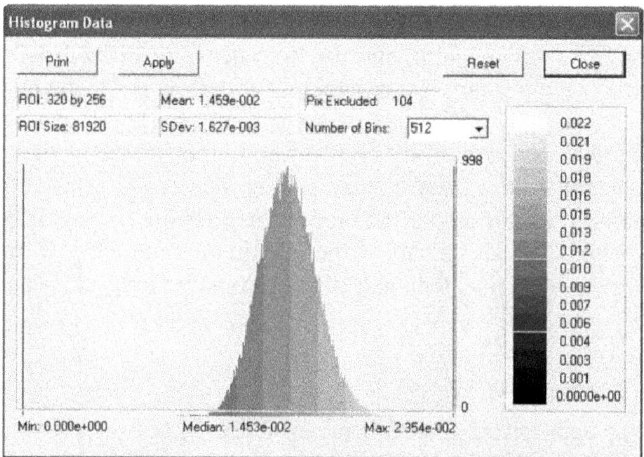

Fig. 8. NETD test results of detector

The test results of the distribution of bad pixels (see Fig. 9) are shown in Fig. 7. Pixels defined as NETD42mK, or pixels with a response rate exceeding 25% above or below the mean of all pixels, or pixels with a DC level exceeding 30% above or below the mean of all pixels, are considered bad pixels.

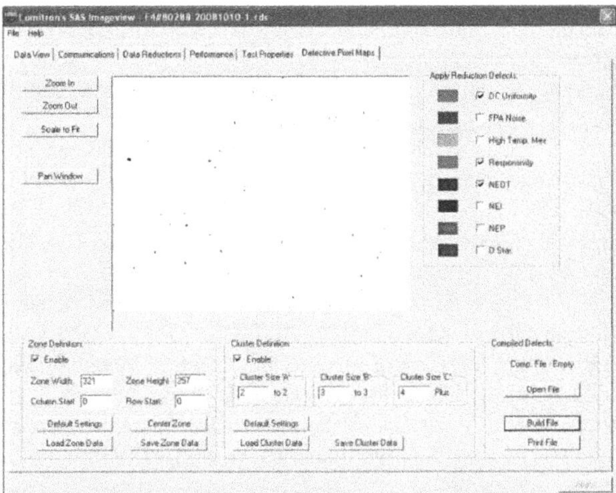

Fig. 9. Test results of detector bad pixels

5   Conclusion

In summary, this testing system is based on NI PXI virtual instruments and LabVIEW software, providing the necessary bias and timing circuits for the operation of refrigeration detectors. Then, use SAS data acquisition software to collect the electrical signals output by the detector, calculate its DC level, noise, response rate, noise equivalent temperature difference, noise equivalent radiation illuminance, noise equivalent radiation power, normalized detection rate, and poor pixel distribution performance parameters. Through testing and comparison, the detection results of the system are consistent with the nominal values of the factory detector, making it an effective method for detecting the performance indicators of infrared detectors and providing a reliable path for accurately evaluating the performance of detectors in high-speed data transmission.

Acknowledgments. The authors acknowledged the Hubei Engineering Research Center for Intelligent Detection and Identification of Complex Parts (Grant No. GCZX-XN-202408) and Wuhan Vocational College of Software and Engineering for Research on Target Classification Algorithms Based on Hyperspectral Imagery (Grant No.SEC2023007).

References

1. Wang, L., Xu, C.: A dark current testing method for tellurium cadmium mercury long wave infrared detectors. Laser Infrared **50**(05), 563–566 (2010)
2. Zhang, S.: Real time imaging software design for infrared focal plane array. Laser Infrared **41**(6), 48–52 (2011)
3. Zhang, N., Wu, H., Zhou, Y.: Design of a non cooled infrared focal plane array testing system based on LabVIEW. Infrared Technol. **33**(5), 66–68 (2011)
4. Sun, B.-C.:Performance test method of InGaAs near infrared detector for astronomical observation. Infrared Millimeter Waves **41**(6), 1002 (2022)

5. Bhan, R.K., Saxena, R.S., Jalwania, C.R., et al.: Uncooled infrared microbolometer arrays and their characterisation techniques. Def. Sci. J. **59**(6), 580–589 (2009)
6. Yu, L., Tang, L., Yang, W., Hao, Q.: Research progress of uncooled infrared detectors. Infrared Laser Eng. **50**(1), 101–106 (2021)
7. Feng, Y.S., Lu, Y., Shen, J.: Mechanism and implementation of bidirectional IR scene simulation system based on the Peltier effect. Int. Soc. Opt. Photonics (2011) https://doi.org/10.1117/12.899659
8. Bowens, R., Viges, E., Meyer, M.R., et al.: The Michigan Infrared Test Thermal ELT N-band (MITTEN), Cryostat (2020). https://doi.org/10.1117/12.2562995
9. Wang, Y., et al.: Photoelectric performance analysis of infrared detector based on image processing. Multimed. Tools Appl. (79), 25–26 (2020)
10. Zou, Q., et al.: Reducing Test Cost of Infrared Detectors: A Machine Learning Approach to Failure Prediction of Infrared Detectors (2018)
11. Jiménez, R., Moreno, M., Torres, A., et al.: Performance characterization of infrared detectors based on polymorphous silicon-germanium (pm-SixGe1x:H) thin films deposited at low temperature. Physica Status Solidi (a) 1700736.10.1002 (2018)
12. Yang, X., Liu, X., Xing, M., et al.: Infrared detectors and test technology of cryogenic camera. In: International Symposium on Optoelectronic Technology and Application. Proceedings of the SPIE (10157) (2016). https://doi.org/10.1117/12.2246503
13. Bhan, R.K., Dhar, V.: Recent infrared detector technologies, applications, trends and development of HgCdTe based cooled infrared focal plane arrays and their characterization. Opto-Electron. Rev. (27), 174–193 (2019)
14. Xiaopei, Z., Zhanhao, H., Zheyao, X.W.: Hiding from infrared detectors in real world with adversarial clothes. Appl. Intell. Int. J. Artif. Intell. Neural Netw. Complex Problem-Solving Technol. **53**(23), 29537–29555 (2023)
15. Li, W., Ni, Z., Wang, J., Li, X.: A front-side microfabricated tiny-size thermopile infrared detector with high sensitivity and fast response. IEEE Trans. Electron Dev. (66), 2230–2237 (2019)
16. Hu, Y., David, M.P., Madalengoitia, J.:Infrared radiation transparent film impact on thermal measurement. In: Intersociety Conference on Thermal and Thermomechanical Phenomena in Electronic Systems. IEEE (2021)

Ransomware Network Traffic Detection Based on Deep Learning

Xuefang Zhang[1], Yanbing Peng[2], and Chengdong Liu[1(✉)]

[1] Wuhan Research Institute of Posts and Telecommunications, Wuhan, China
zhangxuefang@fhxy.net.cn , 1023346913@qq.com
[2] Department of Terminal Development, Naming FiberHome STARRYSKY Co.,
Ltd., Nanjing, China

Abstract. With the continuous development of the Internet in recent years and the continuous expansion of the user base, ransomware attacks have become more frequent, the technologies used have become more diversified, and the purpose of the attack is no longer satisfied with just encrypting the user's files or locking the user's system, but stealing the user's data while encrypting to achieve secondary ransom. How to detect and identify ransomware has become a top priority for Internet security and a hot topic in cyberspace security. This paper uses the 1DCNN+LSTM model with a self-attention mechanism to perform detection and verification on a self-built data set. The experimental results show that the 1DCNN+LSTM algorithm using the self-attention mechanism achieved an accuracy of 97.22% on the self-made ransomware network traffic data set.

Keywords: Ransomware · Network Traffic Detection · Deep Learning · Hybrid Neural Network

1 Introduction

With the development of the times and the transformation and upgrading of a large number of industries, human demand for Internet technology continues to expand. Governments, enterprises, and individuals have moved the processing of affairs to the Internet. In recent years, the concept of a digital economy has been proposed to digitize the economy to improve management efficiency. Excessive dependence on the Internet has created many people who covet their network assets. Endless network intrusions have sprung up like mushrooms after rain. The most representative one is the ransomware virus. Its encrypted ransomware characteristics have made the virus one of the key issues of global network security in recent years. By dynamically analyzing the network communication traffic characteristics of the ransomware virus and using optimized deep learning algorithms to detect the traffic of the ransomware virus, it is possible to achieve early warning of the ransomware virus invasion, so as to achieve the purpose of reducing the losses caused by the ransomware virus invasion.

R. C. Qiu et al. (Eds.): IoTaaS 2024, LNICST 675, pp. 197–206, 2026.
https://doi.org/10.1007/978-3-032-14681-6_17

2 Context

2.1 Ransomware

Ransomware is a destructive malware that can be traced back to the late 1980s. It is usually spread through email attachments, malicious links, online advertisements, and potential software vulnerabilities. Once a user's system is infected with ransomware, it will encrypt the user's files, such as documents, pictures, videos, etc., or lock the user's system so that it cannot be accessed normally. Then, the ransomware will ask the victim to pay a ransom in exchange for a decryption key or a way to unlock the system. Ransomware has different classifications according to different classification standards. According to the different devices targeted, it can be divided into PC ransomware, mobile ransomware, and server ransomware. According to the different intrusion systems, it can be divided into Windows ransomware, Mac ransomware, Linux ransomware, Android ransomware, IOS ransomware, embedded system ransomware, etc. According to the different ransom methods, it can be divided into lock screen ransomware and encryption ransomware.

2.2 Ransomware

The ransomware life cycle refers to the entire process from the infection of a computer system to the completion of the ransomware behavior and the final decryption or re-ransomware. The ransomware life cycle usually includes the following key stages:

Infection Stage: Ransomware infects computer systems through various channels, including phishing emails, malware downloads, vulnerability exploits, remote desktop service attacks, etc. Once the user executes the malware or the user's system is exploited, the virus will begin to perform infection operations and invade the user's system.

File Scanning Phase: After the ransomware successfully infects the computer system, it will scan the computer system to find the files that need to be encrypted. First, it will traverse the file system in the computer system and search for files of the specified type. These file types usually include documents, pictures, videos, databases and other common data files for users.

Encryption Phase: After successfully finding the files to be encrypted, the ransomware will use a powerful encryption algorithm to encrypt the user's files. These files may include important data such as documents, photos, and videos. After encryption is complete, the ransomware may modify the file extension or add a specific mark to indicate that the file has been encrypted, and the user cannot directly access the file content.

Data Processing Stage: After the files are encrypted, the ransomware will establish a communication connection with the attacker's C&C server and transfer the encrypted files to the attacker's server so that the attacker can access and control these files. The ransomware can delete files by completely deleting the files, overwriting the file contents, or renaming the files.

Ransomware Notification Stage: After the data processing is completed, the ransomware will send a ransomware notification to the user, asking the user to pay the ransom to obtain the decryption key. The ransomware notification is usually presented in the form of a pop-up window, text file or desktop background, showing the user the decryption method and payment requirements. After the payment is completed, the corresponding transaction ID or other evidence will be provided to the attacker so that the attacker can confirm the payment and provide the decryption key or tool.

Decryption Stage: After the user pays the ransom, the ransomware attacker will communicate through the contact information provided in the ransom message and provide the user with detailed instructions on the decryption process, including how to use the provided key or tool to perform the decryption operation.

Re-ransom Stage: After receiving the ransom for decrypting the user's local sensitive data, the attacker may send a message again, threatening the user to make the stolen sensitive data public or sell it to a third party, and demanding an additional ransom to prevent data leakage, in order to achieve the purpose of secondary ransom.

2.3   Current Status of Ransomware Network Traffic Detection

Current network-based ransomware detection and analysis methods usually obtain ransomware traffic through various channels and analyze it to design a suitable detection system. Liu et al. [1] analyzed the network behavior of LooCipher ransomware and extracted lightweight packet features in the ransomware interaction traffic to detect LooCipher ransomware. Arivudainambi et al. [2] analyzed the traffic behavior generated by CrptoWall ransomware and used deep learning algorithms to classify the traffic of the ransomware. Kurniawan et al. [3] analyzed the traffic generated by the Cerber ransomware family when attacking internal systems through network forensics, and extracted traffic features to detect Cerber ransomware. Cabaj et al. [4] used software-defined networks (SDN) to analyze the network behavior of the ransomware CryptoWall and proposed a method to mitigate ransomware attacks based on the discovered behavior. Alhawi et al. [5] analyzed the network traffic generated by nine ransomware families and normal samples and used machine learning algorithms to train and detect these 13 traffic features, ultimately achieving a detection accuracy of 97.1%.

3   Method

This paper takes the ransomware on the Windows platform as the research object. Through the method of dynamic analysis of the ransomware, the sandbox is used to extract the network traffic data packets during the dynamic operation of the ransomware, and the network feature data set is constructed in combination with the normal traffic data packets. The 1DCNN+LSTM model optimized based on the self-attention mechanism is used through the deep learning algorithm to detect the network traffic of the ransomware.

3.1   Data Collection

A ransomware dynamic analysis platform based on Cuckoo sandbox [6] is built and a ransomware dataset is constructed based on it. Currently, the source of ransomware samples is single and there is a lack of effective datasets. Therefore, this paper will collect existing ransomware samples, cultivate them through Cuckoo sandbox, observe the communication behavior of the virus in the sandbox environment, and use network traffic capture tools to capture the traffic packets generated by the network communication behavior of the virus in the sandbox, and combine them with normal traffic packets to jointly construct a usable ransomware dataset.

3.2   Feature Extraction and Optimization

In the extraction of network traffic, this paper selected 31 features, including various attributes and characteristics of network traffic, but not all features are equally important for classification tasks. The main purpose of feature screening of data sets is to select the features with the most discriminative and predictive capabilities for classification tasks to improve the performance and generalization of the subsequent model. By reducing the number of features, the complexity and computational cost of the model can be reduced, and the training efficiency of the model can be improved. Selecting features with the greatest discriminative and predictive capabilities can reduce the risk of overfitting of the model and improve the generalization and performance of the model.

The decision tree in the random forest uses Gini impurity to evaluate feature importance. The formula for Gini impurity is shown in the formula.

$$Gini\,(D) = 1 - \sum_{i=1}^{j} p(i)^2. \tag{1}$$

where j is the number of categories and p(i) is the relative frequency of the i-th category in the node.

This method measures the importance of features based on the reduction in Gini impurity when each feature is split at each decision tree node. In a random forest, the feature importance at each node of each decision tree is calculated, and the average is finally taken as the final importance score of the feature.

After feature screening, the 24 features selected in the data set are shown in Table 1 below.

Table 1. Ransomware virus characteristics table.

number	Feature	describe
1	Timestamp	Packet capture time
2	Source IP	The IP address of the device from which the packet originated
3	Destination IP	The IP address of the device to which the packet is destined
4	Source Port	The port number used by the source device
5	Destination Port	The port number used by the target device
6	Protocol	The communication protocol used by the data packet
7	Packet Length	Packet size
8	TCP Flags	Control bits in TCP packets
9	Duration	The time interval between packets
10	Flag	TCP connection status
11	Src Bytes	The number of bytes sent by the source device
12	Avg Length	The average packet length
13	Max Length	Maximum packet length
14	Min Length	Minimum packet length
15	Length Std Dev	Standard deviation of packet length
16	Packet Count	Total number of packets processed
17	ACK Flag	ACK flag of TCP connection
18	TTL	Packet lifetime
19	TCP Window Size	TCP connection window size
20	Packet Order	Whether packets are transmitted in order
21	Flow Duration	Duration of the network flow
22	Flow Size	The size of the network flow
23	Flow Packets	The number of packets in the network flow
24	Inter-arrival Time	The time interval between consecutive packets in the same flow

3.3   Deep Learning Models

A The self-attention mechanism can dynamically assign weights to each element in the sequence, thereby better capturing important information in the sequence and improving the performance and generalization ability of the model. The structure of the 1DCNN+LSTM model based on the self-attention mechanism is shown in Fig. 1 below.

1DCNN Layer: To effectively extract network traffic features, the convolution layer is first applied in the model. The convolution layer extracts feature by sliding the convolution kernel in the input sequence through the convolution operation. The convolution operation can optimize the main features of network traffic and blur the secondary features. By performing convolution operations on the input data, the feature expression of the data can be strengthened and the impact of noise can be effectively reduced.

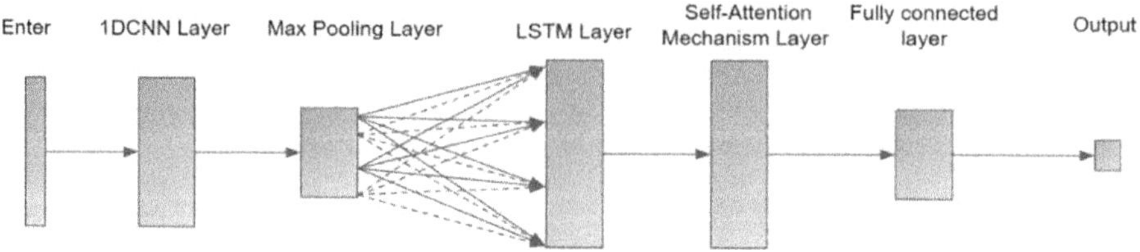

Fig. 1. 1DCNN+LSTM model structure based on self-attention mechanism.

Pooling Layer: The role of the pooling layer in a convolutional neural network is to reduce the spatial size of the feature map while retaining key information. By down sampling the feature map, the pooling layer effectively reduces the computational complexity of subsequent layers and improves the computational efficiency of the model.

LSTM Layer: The LSTM model can fully explore the temporal relationship of network traffic. This layer structure consists of a recurrent neural network model composed of a layer of LSTM, which is used to process time series data. In the sequence model, the time step is regarded as an important part of the sequence, and each time step contains key information in the sequence.

Self-attention Mechanism Layer: Calculate the similarity score for each pair of elements in the sequence. Then use the softmax function to normalize the similarity scores to get the attention weight between each element and other elements. Finally, multiply the attention weight with the representation of the corresponding element and add them together to generate the weighted representation. In this way, the model can obtain a more informative sequence representation, in which the more important parts receive more attention, thus achieving better results.

Fully Connected Layer: The fully connected layer is usually located at the end of the model and is usually used to convert the output of the previous convolutional layer or other feature extraction layer into the final output of the model. dataset.

4 Results

The 1DCNN+LSTM model based on the self-attention mechanism before and after the improvement was trained and tested.

The data set was divided into 80% as a training set and 20% as a test set. This experiment evaluates the model through the following performance indicators:

(1) Accuracy, precision, recall

Accuracy refers to the ratio of the number of samples correctly classified by the model to the total number of samples. It is used to describe the overall performance of the classifier. The calculation formula is shown in formula 2.

$$Accuracy = \frac{TP + TN}{TP + TN + FP + FN} \tag{2}$$

Precision refers to the ratio of the number of samples correctly predicted as positive examples by the classifier to the number of all samples predicted as positive examples. It is used to evaluate the prediction accuracy of the model. The calculation formula is shown in formula 3.

$$Precision = \frac{TP}{TP + FP} \tag{3}$$

The recall rate refers to the ratio of the number of samples correctly predicted as positive examples by the classifier to the number of all samples that are truly positive examples. It is used to evaluate the coverage of the model. The calculation formula is shown in formula 4.

$$Recall = \frac{TP}{TP + FN} \tag{4}$$

(2) F-Score

F-Score is an evaluation indicator that comprehensively considers precision and recall. The calculation formula of F-Score is shown in formula 5.

$$F1 = \frac{2 \times Precision \times Recall}{Precision + Recall} \tag{5}$$

(3) ROC curve

The ROC curve is a performance curve of the evaluation model under different classification thresholds. It plots the curve with the true positive rate as the vertical axis and the false positive rate as the horizontal axis. The calculation formula of the true positive rate (TPR) is shown in formula 6, and the calculation formula of the false positive rate (FPR) is shown in formula 7.

$$TPR = \frac{TP}{TP + FN} \tag{6}$$

$$FPR = \frac{FP}{TN + FP} \tag{7}$$

The ROC curve obtained by the 1DCNN+LSTM model is shown in Fig. 2.

The ROC curve obtained by the improved 1DCNN+LSTM model is shown in Fig. 3.

The accuracy, precision, recall, F1-Score, and average loss of the 20th round of the 1DCNN+LSTM model and the improved 1DCNN+LSTM model are shown in Table 2.

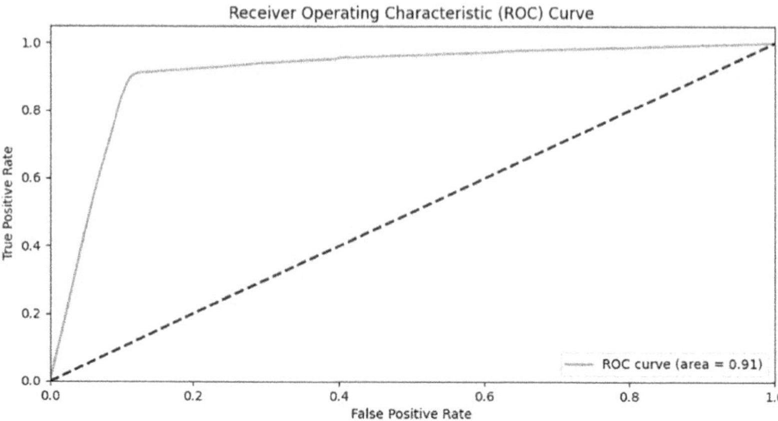

Fig. 2. 1DCNN+LSTM model ROC curve.

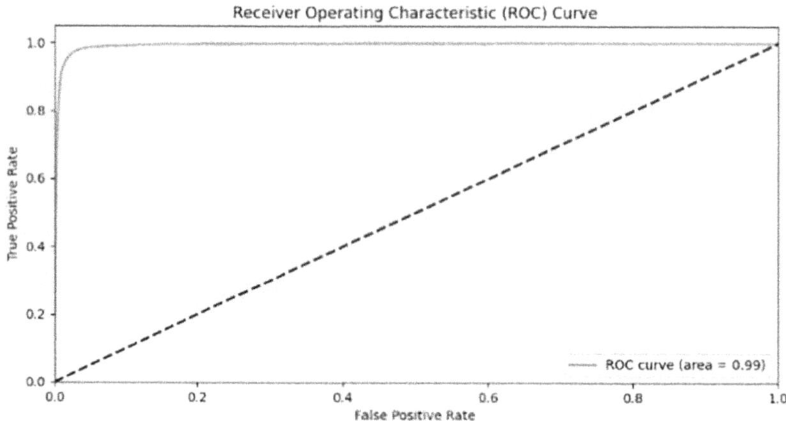

Fig. 3. ROC curve of 1DCNN+LSTM model based on self-attention mechanism.

By comparing the two versions of the 1DCNN+LSTM model, we can see that the performance of the model has been significantly improved after optimization. First, the accuracy rate increased from 88.15% to 97.22%, which means that the model is more accurate in classifying data. Second, the precision rate increased from 0.9222 to 0.9748, which means that among all the samples predicted by the model as positive examples, 97.48% of the samples are indeed positive examples, which is very important in ransomware detection because it means reducing the possibility of false positives. The recall rate increased from 0.8937 to 0.9833, which means that the model can better identify the proportion of all positive samples, so it is more effective in detecting all ransomware samples. F1-Score increased from 0.9077 to 0.9790, which is the harmonic average of precision and recall, combining the accuracy and comprehensiveness of the model.

Table 2. 1DCNN+LSTM model and its optimized model results comparison table.

Model	Accuracy	Precision	Recall	F1-Score	Avg loss
1DCNN+LSTM	88.15%	0.9222	0.8937	0.9077	0.411555
1DCNN+LSTM (optimize)	97.22%	0.9748	0.9833	0.9790	0.329721

In summary, the 1DCNN+LSTM model based on the self-attention mechanism performs better and has higher accuracy and reliability in ransomware detection tasks. To verify the effectiveness of the experiment, this paper adopts a comparative experiment method, selects 1DCNN, Kitsune, and LSTM, three common deep learning network traffic classification algorithms, as the experimental control group, and uses five indicators such as accuracy to comprehensively evaluate the performance of each classification model. The experimental results are shown in Table 3 and Fig. 4.

Table 3. Ransomware network traffic detection model comparison table.

Model	Accuracy	Precision	Recall	F1-Score	Avg loss
1DCNN	56.97%	0.5401	0.4580	0.4209	0.743477
Kitsune	56.57%	0.4985	0.9985	0.6650	0.011236
LSTM	90.04%	0.8859	0.9101	0.8633	0.390344
1DCNN+LSTM	88.15%	0.9222	0.8937	0.9077	0.411555
1DCNN+LSTM (optimize)	97.22%	0.9748	0.9833	0.9790	0.329721

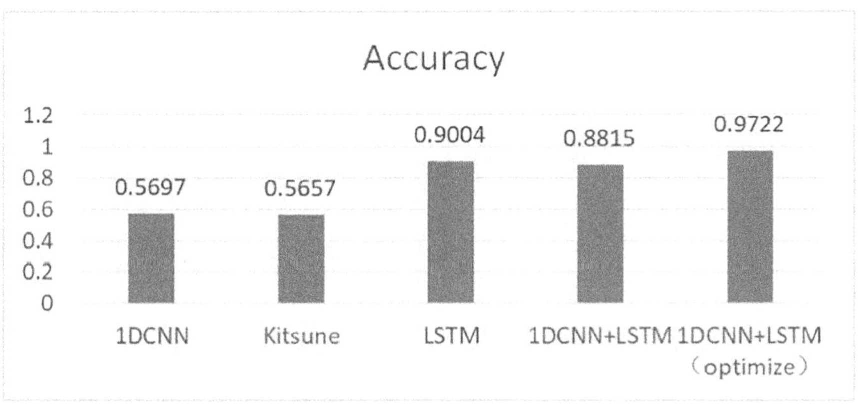

Fig. 4. Accuracy histogram of each model.

5 Conclusion

This paper uses Cuckoo sandbox technology to extract and dynamically analyze the network traffic data packets of the data-stealing ransomware on the Windows platform, constructs a ransomware network traffic dataset belonging to this paper, and combines it with the optimized deep learning classification algorithm to realize the network traffic detection of ransomware. Experiments show that the 1DCNN+LSTM algorithm based on the self-attention mechanism has high effectiveness in the network traffic detection of ransomware. In future research in this direction, the following improvements can be made: First, enrich the data set of ransomware network traffic, and improve the versatility of model detection by collecting more number and family of ransomware network traffic data. Secondly, for the overall ransomware detection, the local detection + network traffic detection method can be used to improve the success rate of ransomware detection. It is hoped that through the above improvements, a safer ransomware detection system can be built in the future.

References

1. Te-Min, L., Da-Yu, K., Yun-Ya, C.: LooCipher ransomware detection using lightweight packet characteristics. Procedia Comput. Sci. **176**, 1677–1683 (2020)
2. Arivudainambi, D., et al.: Ransomware traffic classification using deep learning models: ransomware traffic classification. Int. J. Web Portals (IJWP) **12**(1), 1–11 (2020)
3. Kurniawan, A., Riadi, I.: Detection and analysis cerber ransomware based on network forensics behavior. Int. J. Netw. Secur. **20**(5), 836–843 (2018)
4. Cabaj, K., Mazurczyk, W.: Using software-defined networking for ransomware mitigation: the case of CryptoWall. IEEE Netw. **30**(6), 14–20 (2016)
5. Alhawi, O.M.K., Baldwin, J., Dehghantanha, A.: Leveraging machine learning techniques for windows ransomware network traffic detection. In: Dehghantanha, A., Conti, M., Dargahi, T. (eds.) Cyber Threat Intelligence. AIS, vol. 70, pp. 93–106. Springer, Cham (2018). https://doi.org/10.1007/978-3-319-73951-9_5
6. Cuckoo Sandbox Book. https://cuckoo.readthedocs.io/en/latest

Research on the Optimization of Bidirectional Ranging Schemes Based on Ultra-Wideband (UWB) Technology

Yun Zhu and Xiaojing Wang[✉]

Wuhan Vocational College of Software and Engineering (Wuhan Open University),
117 Guangu Avenue, East Lake New Technology Development Zone, Wuhan, China
56842845@qq.com

Abstract. With the rapid development of wireless communication technology, UWB technology has drawn wide attention for its high-speed transmission and high-precision positioning. This paper focuses on the two-way ranging scheme based on UWB technology, aiming to enhance time synchronization and positioning accuracy through optimization and innovation. It reveals the significant potential of Ultra-Wideband (UWB) in time synchronization and positioning accuracy improvement, and points out the deficiencies in existing schemes and possible ways for improvement. The paper shows how to improve system performance and accuracy by making adjustments and optimizing the asymmetric and symmetric double-sided two-way ranging technologies. It also explores the applicability of UWB in different scenarios and provides strategic guidance for practical deployment. Through comparative analysis and case studies, the importance of technical details and the sensitivity to environmental factors in achieving high-precision synchronization and positioning are revealed.

Keywords: Ultra-Wideband (UWB) technology · Two-Way Ranging · Time of Flight (ToF)

1 Introduction

1.1 Ultra-Wideband (UWB) Technology

Ultra-Wideband (UWB) technology is a high-efficiency, high-speed wireless transmission method that uses short, non-sinusoidal pulses within nanoseconds, covering a broad frequency range. It transmits at low power, reducing energy use. In 2002, the U.S. Federal Communications Commission (FCC) classified devices with a bandwidth over 500MHz or a fractional bandwidth of 20 Ground Penetrating Radar: With Ultra-Wideband (UWB) technology, experts can explore underground structures, from archaeological treasure hunting to geological exploration, with greatly improved accuracy and efficiency [1]. Through-Wall Imaging

R. C. Qiu et al. (Eds.): IoTaaS 2024, LNICST 675, pp. 207–215, 2026.
https://doi.org/10.1007/978-3-032-14681-6_18

Radar: Police and rescue personnel can use Ultra-Wideband (UWB) technology to discover hidden people or objects behind walls or other obstacles, enhancing the safety and success rate of search and rescue and security checks [2]. Vehicle Radar Systems: In modern vehicles, Ultra-Wideband (UWB) technology is used to assist driving and avoid collisions by providing precise ranging and positioning to improve road safety [3]. Measurement and Positioning: In scenarios such as mining operations and sports training, Ultra-Wideband (UWB) technology can provide millimeter-level precise measurement and positioning data. Ultra-Wideband (UWB) technology stands out among many wireless technologies with its wide frequency characteristics, especially suitable for indoor high-speed data communication and positioning systems. This technology is simple in system design, reducing costs, and combines a large bandwidth with high-speed data transmission capabilities. Compared to conventional technologies like Wi-Fi and Bluetooth, Ultra-Wideband (UWB)'s low-power signal causes less interference with other devices, and its excellent wall penetration capability ensures continuous and stable communication [4]. Ultra-Wideband (UWB) is highly adaptable, maintaining signal quality even in changing environments. Its resistance to channel fading and strong anti-multipath interference ensures reliable transmission. Ultra-Wideband (UWB)'s high-precision timestamp technology provides accurate positioning, while its low interceptability enhances security. Ultra-Wideband (UWB) can also coexist with other wireless systems, making it easy to integrate into existing telecom infrastructures. With advantages in speed, accuracy, and system compatibility, Ultra-Wideband (UWB) is becoming the preferred choice for indoor wireless applications.

1.2   Ultra-Wideband (UWB) Positioning Schemes

Common Ultra-Wideband (UWB) positioning schemes are divided into three types: Time Difference of Arrival (TDOA): Time Difference of Arrival technology determines the position of the transmitter by measuring the time difference of the signal's arrival at different receivers. This technology does not require clock synchronization, making it robust in multipath environments [5]. Time of Arrival (TOA: Time of Arrival measurement calculates the distance by precisely measuring the time it takes for a signal to travel from the sender to the receiver [6]. This method requires synchronization of clocks between the sender and receiver) [4]. Angle of Arrival (AOA:) [5] Angle of Arrival uses the receiver's antenna array to measure the angle of incoming radio waves. By using multiple receiving points or multi-directional antennas, the source of the positioning signal can be located through triangulation. This paper mainly introduces various methods of implementing Two-Way Ranging (TWR) schemes between two nodes based on Ultra-Wideband (UWB) technology. This is a variant of TOA, which works by exchanging signals between the sender and receiver and measuring the total round-trip communication time, thereby eliminating the need for clock synchronization.

2   Single-Side Two-Way Ranging (SS-TWR)

Single-side Two-Way Ranging (SS-TWR) measures distance by measuring the round-trip delay time of a message sent from one node to another and then back from that node to the original node. This method involves sending a simple signal or message, waiting for the receiving node to respond to that signal, and then estimating the distance between the two nodes by analyzing the round-trip time. This technique is very useful in wireless communication and positioning systems because it can provide a relatively accurate distance estimate, which is crucial for achieving precise location positioning and tracking [6].

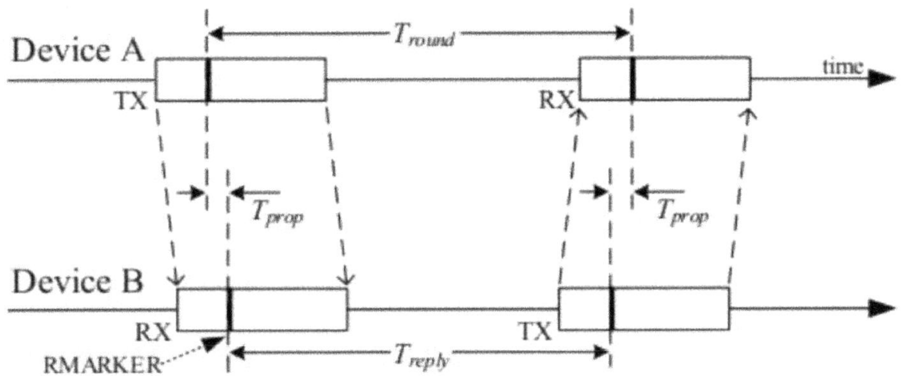

Fig. 1. Single-side Two-way ranging.

In the SS-TWR (Single-Side Two-Way Ranging) process (refer to Fig. 1), Device A commences the exchange of information, to which Device B replies. Throughout this procedure, both devices accurately log the times at which the message frame is sent and received. Through these time records, the round-trip time T_{round} and reply time T_{reply} can be calculated by simple subtraction. Based on these times, the signal propagation time $\hat{T}_{prop}$ (the time required for the signal to propagate from one device to another) can be estimated using Eq. 1. This equation typically takes into account both the round-trip time and reply time to calculate the actual flight time of the signal, thereby estimating the distance between the two devices.

$$\hat{T}_{prop} = \frac{1}{2}\left(T_{round} - T_{reply}\right) \tag{1}$$

In discussing the scenario where Devices A and B perform time measurements, it is important to consider that the local clocks of both devices may have offset errors from their nominal frequencies, denoted as e_A and e_B respectively. These clock offset errors can significantly impact the estimation of the Time of Flight (ToF), which refers to the time required for the signal to transmit from the sending device to the receiving device. In the Single-side Two-Way Ranging (SS-TWR) scheme, Device A sends a signal to Device B, and after receiving the signal, Device B sends a response signal back to Device A after a reply time T_{reply}. It is worth noting that T_{reply} includes not only the turnaround time from receiving to sending the signal at Device B (RX-to-TX turnaround time) but also covers the time length required to send the message. In this approach, the discrepancy in the calculated round-trip time is depicted in Eq. 2.

$$error = \hat{T}_{prop} - T_{prop} \approx \frac{1}{2}(e_B - e_A) \times T_{reply} \tag{2}$$

Therefore, the total measurement error is influenced by the following factors: the clock offset errors of Devices A and B (e_A and e_B), the reply time T_{reply} (which includes the RX-to-TX turnaround time and the time length of the message), and the signal propagation time (the Time of Flight, ToF). To reduce the total measurement error, measures can be taken to minimize the reply time T_{reply} and reduce the clock offset errors as much as possible. This involves using clock synchronization techniques to adjust the clock offsets, or by optimizing the communication protocol to reduce the reply time. Here, we present some typical values (see Table 1).

Table 1. Typical clock induced errors in SS-TWR time of flight estimation.

Clock error	2ppm	5ppm	10ppm	20ppm	40ppm
100us	0.1ns	0.25ns	0.5ns	1ns	2ns
200us	0.2ns	0.5ns	1ns	2ns	1ns
500us	0.5ns	1.25ns	2.5ns	5ns	10ns
1ms	1ns	2.5ns	5ns	10ns	20ns
2ms	2ns	5ns	10ns	20ns	40ns
5ms	5ns	12.5ns	25ns	50ns	100ns

It is observed that with the increase in reply time and clock offset, the error in estimating Time of Flight (ToF) escalates, potentially resulting in highly imprecise estimations. Hence, despite SS-TWR not being widely adopted in certain scenarios, its exploration remains valuable for specific applications involving high-precision clocks and where the communication distance is comparatively limited.

After discussing the impact of clock offset errors and reply time on the accuracy of Time of Flight estimation when Devices A and B perform time measurements, we further explore how these factors affect the measurement results under specific configurations (see Table 2). Based on the IEEE 802.15.4-2011 standard, typical measurement errors under different clock error configurations are presented when using Ultra-Wideband (UWB) frame length for simplified Two-Way Ranging (SS-TWR). These data clearly show the impact of clock error and reply time configurations on the accuracy of Time of Flight estimation, highlighting the importance of optimizing these parameters to improve measurement precision.

Table 2. Typical clock induced error in SS-TWR time-of-flight estimation using actual lEEE80.15,4-2011.

Clock error	2ppm	5ppm	10ppm	20ppm	40ppm
211 us, 6.81 Mbps, 64-symbol preamble	0.2ns	0.5ns	1.1ns	2.1ns	4.2ns
275 us, 6.81 Mbps, 128-symbol preamble	0.3ns	0.7ns	1.4ns	2.8ns	5.5ns
403 us, 6.81 Mbps, 256-symbol preamble	0.4ns	1ns	2ns	4ns	8ns

Note: A discrepancy of 1 ns corresponds to a distance measurement error of approximately 30 cm.

3   Double-Side Two-Way Ranging (DS-TWR)

Double-Side Two-Way Ranging (DS-TWR), building upon the foundational Single-side Two-Way Ranging (SS-TWR), calculates the Time of Flight (ToF) by aggregating the outcomes of two separate round-trip time assessments. A significant feature of this method is that it can effectively reduce errors even in the presence of considerable response delays, thereby improving the accuracy of ranging. DS-TWR optimizes time measurement in this way, maintaining high measurement accuracy even in situations with long delays, which is particularly important for applications requiring high precision positioning and time synchronization [6].

3.1   Using 4 Messages

The operation process of DS-TWR (Double-Side Two-Way Ranging) involves two devices (Device A and Device B) conducting two round-trip time measurements and combining the results of these two measurements to obtain an accurate estimation of the Time of Flight (ToF). This typically involves four messages to complete the two round-trip time measurements (see Fig. 2).

Device A initiates the process by sending a signal to Device B, starting the first round-trip time measurement. After receiving this signal, Device B responds to Device A at an appropriate time, completing the first round-trip measurement. Then, Device B initiates the second round-trip time measurement by sending a signal to Device A. After receiving Device B's signal, Device A responds to Device B, completing the second round-trip measurement. During the entire DS-TWR exchange process, each device precisely marks the times it sends and receives messages.

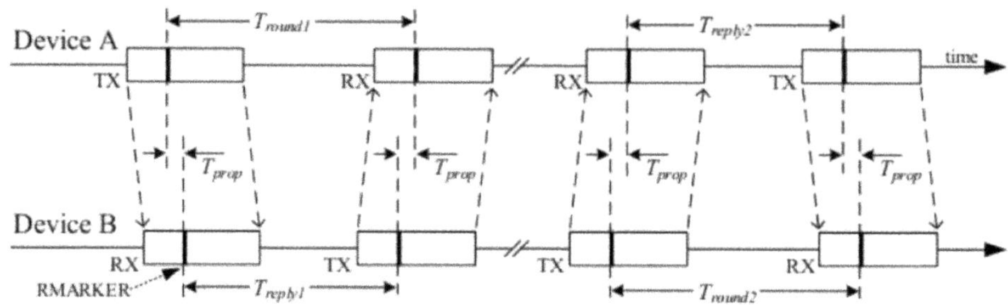

Fig. 2. Double-side Two-way ranging with four messages.

3.2   Using 3 Messages

By utilizing the reply from the first round-trip measurement as the start for the second round-trip in DS-TWR (see Fig. 2), the process can be streamlined from four messages to three (see Fig. 3). This method optimizes the communication process, reduces the number of messages, while maintaining the accuracy of ranging.

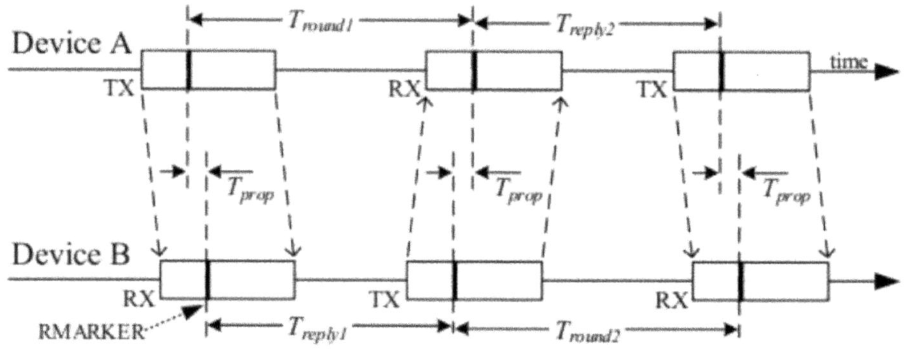

Fig. 3. Double-side Two-way ranging with three messages [7].

Device A sends the first message to Device B, initiating the first round-trip time measurement. After receiving this message, Device B replies to Device A, and this reply also serves as the initiating message for the second round-trip measurement. After receiving Device B's reply, Device A replies to Device B again, completing the entire DS-TWR exchange process. During the DS-TWR process, whether using the three-message or four-message scheme, the estimated Time of Flight (ToF) $\hat{T}_{prop}$ can be calculated using Eq. 3.

$$\hat{T}_{prop} = \frac{T_{round1} \times T_{round2} - T_{reply1} \times T_{relpy2}}{T_{round1} + T_{round2} - T_{reply1} + T_{relpy2}} \tag{3}$$

The two schemes mentioned are described as "asymmetric" because identical reply times for each device are not required.

When discussing network time synchronization or clock synchronization strategies in distributed systems, the "asymmetric" schemes we often refer to do not require the reply times (i.e., the round-trip delays) of each device or node in the network to be consistent. This inconsistency can be caused by various factors, including network congestion, differences in path lengths, and differences between hardware, all of which can lead to different message transmission times.

In these schemes, even when using crystal oscillators with an accuracy of 20ppm, clock-induced errors can be controlled at the low picosecond level (1 picosecond = 10–12 s). This indicates that despite minor inconsistencies in clock frequencies, the induced timing errors are relatively small.

However, in this case, the total propagation time error (Tprop error) includes not only clock errors but also all factors affecting the time it takes for a message to propagate from the sender to the receiver. Therefore, in network communications and distributed systems, ensuring the precision of the arrival time of messages at each receiver is more critical than merely focusing on errors caused by inconsistencies in clock frequencies. This is because the core of ensuring data synchronization and consistency lies in accurately measuring and correcting the propagation time of messages and all other forms of delays, as shown in Eq. 4.

$$error = \hat{T}_{prop} \times \left(1 - \frac{k_a + k_b}{2} \right) \tag{4}$$

Device A and Device B's clocks run at frequencies of ka and kb, respectively, where ka and kb are both close to 1, meaning the clock frequencies of both devices are very close to their nominal frequencies but not exactly the same.

In the worst-case scenario, where the clock frequency error of Devices A and B accumulates to 40ppm (forty parts per million), the values of ka and kb could be 0.99998 or 1.00002, respectively. This minor frequency difference, when measuring Time of Flight (TOF), would only result in a timing error of about 6.7 picoseconds (10–12 s) even under a larger working range (e.g., 100 m), equivalent to a distance error of approximately 2.2 mm. This indicates that very high positioning accuracy can be achieved through precise time synchronization techniques, even in the presence of minor clock frequency differences.

It is worth noting that achieving this high precision in time synchronization does not require the response times of each device to be exactly the same, reflecting the "asymmetric" characteristic considered in designing time synchronization schemes. In fact, at these levels of error, it is more important to accurately determine the time of arrival of messages at each receiver. This means that the key to ensuring data synchronization and consistency in network communications and distributed systems lies not only in resolving minor inconsistencies in clock frequencies but also in being able to precisely measure and correct the propagation time of messages and all other forms of delays.

3.3 Using Symmetric Reply Times

Adopting symmetric reply times. This method is known as Symmetric Double-Side Two-Way Ranging, a special case within Double-Side Two-Way Ranging (DS-TWR) technology, where the response times T_{reply1} and T_{reply2} are constrained to be the same (or as close to the same as possible). In this case, the resulting Time of Flight (ToF) estimation can be calculated using Eq. 5.

$$\hat{T}_{prop} = \frac{T_{round1} - T_{reply1} + T_{round2} - T_{relpy1}}{4} \tag{5}$$

This approach only necessitates four operations: addition, subtraction, and division, making it highly suitable for implementation on low-power microcontrollers. Despite this, it might extend the duration of the entire exchange process beyond initial expectations. Ensuring identical response times across devices remains a challenge due to the varying computational demands of each device. For instance, the concluding message from Device A to Device B often must incorporate timestamps of both sending and receiving within the data packet, enabling Device B to determine the Time of Flight. If symmetric delay times are essential, it might be imperative to prolong the entire round-trip exchange to meet this criterion. When response delays can be varied, the exchange can be executed more rapidly. As the disparity in response times between devices widens, the error margin in the calculated Time of Flight also grows linearly, reaching nearly 30 cm for a discrepancy of 100us in reply times.

4 Conclusion

This paper, through an in-depth analysis of bidirectional ranging schemes based on Ultra-Wideband (UWB) technology, showcases its significant potential in enhancing time synchronization and positioning accuracy. Our research not only deepened the understanding of the core mechanisms of Ultra-Wideband (UWB) technology but also, through a critical evaluation of existing schemes, clearly identified paths for optimization and innovation. Particularly, our analysis highlighted how system performance and accuracy can be effectively improved through minor adjustments and strategic optimization in both asymmetric and symmetric bidirectional ranging technologies. Moreover, this paper explored the applicability and adjustment needs of Ultra-Wideband (UWB) technology in various application scenarios, thereby providing strategic guidance for practical deployment. Through comparative analysis and case studies, this thesis revealed the importance of technical details and the sensitivity to environmental factors in achieving high precision in synchronization and positioning processes.

References

1. Wenchao, L., Xu-Ben, W.: A study of the performance of UWB-GPR. J. Chengdu Univ. Technol. Sci. Technol. Ed. (02), 167–171 (2008)
2. LiangNian, J.: Array design and imaging method for ultra-wideband multiple-input multiple-output through-the-wall radar. J. Electron. Inf. Technol. **34**(07), 1574–1580 (2012)
3. Tao, S., TaoYi, HeMingli, Leiqiang, Z.: Current research and developing trends on vehicle-mounted UWB radar. Electron. Inf. Warfare Technol. **35**(04), 18–22 (2020)
4. Zhiyong, W., Hongwei, Z., Xuhui, B.: TOA localization algorithm of underground mine moving target based on UWB and fingerprint. Mining Res. Dev. **44**(03), 192–200 (2024)
5. Yuhua, Z., et al.: Three-dimensional positioning method of a 5G indoor distribution system based on TDOA and AOA. Power Syst. Protection Control **51**(02), 180–187 (2023)
6. Ma, W., Fang, X., Liang, L., et al.: Research on indoor positioning system algorithm based on UWB technology. Measur. Sens. (33), 101–121 (2024)
7. Yuanlai, W., Jiani, L., Hui, Y., Jiahao, L.: High precision indoor positioning system based on UWB. Changjiang Inf. Commun. (3), 111–114 (2021)

Comprehensive Overview of Intelligent Container Number Recognition Technologies

Xin Wang[1]([envelope]) [iD], Jicheng Zhang[2], and Junjun Xia[2]

[1] College of Posts and Telecommunication of WIT, Wuhan 430074, China
wangxin9189@gmail.com
[2] Yuxi Tieji Logistics Co., Ltd., Yuxi 653202, China

Abstract. Globalization has spurred the rapid expansion of international trade, which in turn demands higher efficiency and accuracy in logistics and shipping. Containers, central to global trade, rely on advanced recognition technology to significantly boost the efficiency of port operations. This review discusses the progression, key innovations, and hurdles in the smart recognition of container numbers, focusing on technologies like Radio Frequency Identification (RFID), video recognition, and Optical Character Recognition (OCR), which dominate the field. It explores methods such as image preprocessing, character segmentation, and feature extraction, highlighting the advantages and challenges of each. Deep learning approaches, especially those utilizing DBN and CNN frameworks, are particularly noted for their precise and robust feature analysis, despite facing issues with real-time processing and durability. Research is moving towards reducing reliance on extensive annotated datasets, enhancing the efficiency of these algorithms, and integrating them more effectively into logistics management systems.

Keywords: Container Recognition · Convolutional Neural Networks (CNN) · Deep Learning · Optical Character Recognition (OCR) · Radio Frequency Identification (RFID)

1 Introduction

Globalization has been a driving force behind the swift expansion of international trade, positioning the logistics and freight sector as a critical support for the global economy and the seamless functioning of supply chains. The surge in global trade has spurred the need for enhanced efficiency at ports and logistics centers, fewer human errors, and quicker cargo processing. Containers, integral to international trade as the primary transport unit, have thus emerged as key subjects in logistics research and technological advancements.

Container Automatic Identification Technology, a pivotal development in computer vision and AI, is a key to overcoming logistical efficiency challenges. This technology utilizes high-resolution cameras to gather container images and integrates cutting-edge image processing, deep learning, and machine learning technologies to auto-detect

R. C. Qiu et al. (Eds.): IoTaaS 2024, LNICST 675, pp. 216–223, 2026.
https://doi.org/10.1007/978-3-032-14681-6_19

essential data, such as ISO codes, container sizes, and ownership details. This automation enhances the accuracy and speed of data processing, as well as significantly reduces labor costs and risks, bolstering the effectiveness of global supply chains.

However, deploying container automatic identification technology is not devoid of challenges. Containers are susceptible to wear, deformation, and contamination through extended use, which can compromise image recognition accuracy. Furthermore, the technology must be exceptionally adaptable and flexible to accommodate the global circulation of containers, ensuring effective recognition across diverse conditions and environments. With the swift expansion of global trade and an exponential increase in container numbers, handling vast amounts of data, enhancing recognition speeds, and ensuring system stability and reliability remain critical technical challenges.

Therefore, considering these above-mentioned factors, this study is dedicated to examining the present status, essential technologies, applications, and challenges of container automatic identification technology, with the goal of proposing effective solutions and suggesting directions for future research. Our goal is to enhance efficiency and decrease errors within the logistics and freight industries, while also provide a thorough technical guide and foundational research resource for scientists in associated fields.

2 Container Intelligent Identification Technology

The development of smart container number recognition technology has significantly advanced alongside the expansion of global trade and improvements in logistics automation. Radio Frequency Identification (RFID), video recognition, and Optical Character Recognition (OCR) are the predominant technologies in this field.

2.1 Radio Frequency Identification (RFID)

RFID technology tags containers using radio frequencies, enabling data transfer and retrieval through wireless communication between the RFID tags, which are affixed to the containers, and readers [1]. These tags record crucial details like container numbers, types, and cargo. As containers pass through locations equipped with RFID readers, the readers automatically extract the data from the tags, facilitating rapid container number identification. This technology's main benefits include the ability to read data without direct visual contact with the tags and the rapid, simultaneous recognition of multiple tags, which greatly enhances both efficiency and accuracy. Additionally, its robust data transmission capabilities ensure stable operation under diverse weather conditions [2]. However, the high installation costs and the requirement for specialized reading equipment limit its widespread adoption.

2.2 Video Recognition Technology

Video recognition technology employs high-definition cameras positioned at ports and loading zones to capture images of containers. These images are then processed by video analysis software to detect container features and identification numbers. This method is effective for real-time monitoring of containers, particularly in settings with high traffic and rapid activities. The primary advantage of video recognition is its capability for ongoing monitoring and delivering instant data. However, it is vulnerable to external environmental influences such as changes in lighting and weather conditions, which can lead to variability in image quality and potentially compromise the accuracy of the recognition process.

2.3 Optical Character Recognition (OCR)

Technology Optical Character Recognition technology utilizes cameras to send images or videos of container numbers to computers, where these visuals are transformed into machine-readable text [3]. Based on its rapid processing and high accuracy, OCR does not rely on specific labels; it merely requires clear imagery for successful recognition. Although OCR technology is advanced and generally provides high recognition rates, it remains susceptible to environmental disturbances, such as lighting, weather, and noise. This calls for powerful back end algorithms that can further refine its accuracy and speed.

3 Research on Optical Image Recognition of Container Number

The methodology of optical image recognition for container numbers involves several key processes - image preprocessing, character segmentation, feature extraction, and the deployment of recognition algorithms.

3.1 Image Preprocessing

In container number recognition research, preprocessing images is vital for enhancing accuracy. Containers endure a range of environmental impacts such as lighting variations, oil contamination, and dust during transit, leading to inconsistent image quality. Various preprocessing techniques have been introduced by researchers to tackle these challenges and improve the reliability of the images.

Pang in [4] introduced a preprocessing algorithm that utilizes morphological operations and edge detection to enhance the quality of container number images. Initially, the method applies morphological erosion and dilation to reduce noise and clarify background details, effectively making character data more prominent. The technique also includes stretching the image to increase contrast, which significantly improves visual quality. Finally, for images affected by uneven lighting and complex backgrounds, the approach involves selecting appropriate thresholds based on simple image statistics and employing the Prewitt edge detection operator for binary processing. This step ensures that character stroke edges are preserved, making the images better prepared for segmentation and recognition.

Li in [5] developed an adaptive binarization strategy that enhances image contrast and suppresses noise by analyzing histograms and grayscale features to determine optimal thresholds. They start by converting color images to grayscale, which simplifies the data and reduces processing complexity since grayscale images lack color information but retain brightness details, aiding further image processing. To lessen noise and improve quality, they employ median filtering, a non-linear technique that effectively removes noise while keeping edges sharp, essential for text recognition within images. They then proceed to binarize the images, converting them to black and white to streamline the data for better handling and analysis. The team uses an adaptive threshold method that adjusts based on local image variations to manage uneven lighting and diverse backgrounds, enhancing the binarization quality. Finally, they introduce a discrete noise point filtering technique to eliminate isolated noise points after binarization.

3.2 Container Number Localization and Segmentation

Character localization uses algorithms to identify targeted number regions within images, a process crucial for the accuracy of subsequent character segmentation and recognition tasks. Common methods include mathematical morphology, edge detection with sliding windows, and multi-feature techniques, as well as optimized ant colony algorithms.

Wang et al. in. [6] introduced a method based on mathematical morphology, utilizing structural elements with predetermined shapes to pinpoint and extract specific shapes within images for container number analysis and recognition. However, this method faces limitations due to its reliance on structural elements whose sizes are fixed based on the container number layout and the image scale, leading to potential inaccuracies when the distance of the camera changes. Additionally, the need for manual adjustment of structural elements for different number layouts limits the method's automation capabilities.

Tan et al. in. [7] proposed a sophisticated algorithm for the localization and segmentation of container number characters in automatic identification systems, using edge detection and mathematical morphology. This two-stage algorithm begins by identifying candidate regions through preprocessing and morphological operations, then finely adjusts its structural elements to accurately locate the number area, effectively managing the diversity of text orientations and complex backgrounds. The subsequent segmentation stage employs morphological techniques to eliminate noise and precisely separate each character, although this requires significant processing power. Meanwhile, Koo K M et al. [8] developed a method that combines edge detection with sliding windows to identify distinct features in number areas, though it struggles with lighting and shadow effects and is computationally intensive.

Huang et al. in. [9] created a multi-feature localization algorithm that merges various characteristics to pinpoint container numbers. However, its complexity results in high computational loads, limiting its practical application.

Sun et al. in. [10] have successfully implemented an optimized ant colony algorithm for container number localization, effectively identifying the edges of numbers against complex backgrounds for precise extraction. However, the method encounters difficulties with numbers that are fragmented or adhered. Zhang et al. in. [11] utilized a deep learning approach, employing a CNN to accurately delineate container number areas from challenging backgrounds. Tu et al. in.[12] crafted a preprocessing technique that reduces computational load and utilized an advanced YOLOv3 network for real-time container number recognition in terminals, achieving 99.6

Character segmentation plays a crucial role in the recognition of container numbers, which can appear in various configurations such as horizontally in single or double rows, or vertically. These formats introduce complexities in segmentation. Researchers have used a range of methods involving projection and feature extraction for accurate character delineation.

Yang in [14] and Ye in [15] successfully implemented vertical projection techniques to separate each character, and used erosion, median filtering, and dilation to effectively handle border removal for characters at the ends of numbers, achieving notable results. Saddami et al. [16] advocated for projection methods for segmenting characters. Chen et al. in [17] developed a recognition strategy that combines template and feature matching with morphological operations and projection to precisely segment container number characters, although they noted that projection segmentation is ideally suited for images with clear backgrounds and minimal noise.

3.3 Container Number Character Recognition

Character recognition for container numbers is a critical component of modern logistics automation, facilitating fast and accurate identification to enhance the overall efficiency and precision of logistics systems. This is achieved by extracting features from segmented characters and employing machine or deep learning algorithms for effective classification and recognition. To ensure reliability, recognized container numbers are verified against specific formatting and regulatory standards. Popular methods in this field include template matching, feature extraction techniques, and neural networks.

Chen et al. in [17] proposed a hybrid algorithm that uses both template and feature matching for enhanced recognition performance. Chen in [18] developed a method using sparse representation for pattern recognition, which has demonstrated high accuracy and rapid processing under typical lighting conditions but faces challenges in accurately recognizing distorted characters under strong lighting.

Chen in [19] in his research on character recognition, integrated various feature extraction methods like grid and contour features along with template matching techniques to boost recognition accuracy. He conducted tests using 56 images, achieving an initial accuracy of 91.

Li in [20] studied container number recognition using the BP algorithm, employing a neural network to provide strong classification capabilities. Song et al. in [21] introduced a container number recognition approach based on Deep Belief Networks, consisting of multiple layers of Restricted Boltzmann Machines and a Back Propagation network, efficiently learning and recognizing high-level image features of container labels. This DBN-based method significantly improves the accuracy and stability of recognition. Cao Lingen and his team enhanced recognition speed and accuracy by combining advanced least squares and gradient descent projection algorithms with a BP neural network, demonstrating substantial performance improvements [22].

With the coming of deep learning, a growing number of scholars are integrating convolutional neural networks (CNN) [23] and recurrent neural networks (RNN) [24] into the recognition of container number characters. This approach is aimed at boosting the recognition systems' accuracy and operational efficiency. Roeksukrungrueang [25] implemented the LeNet convolutional neural network to recognize container numbers, achieving a high recognition rate of 95.41.

Shi in [29] and Xing in [30] developed the CRNN, a comprehensive end-toend framework tailored for sequence recognition within images, which excels at recognizing extended text sequences. This approach has notably outperformed other models in terms of text detection and recognition efficacy. Mei in [31] implemented a container number recognition strategy that harnesses both convolutional neural networks and template matching, securing a recognition accuracy of 91.9

4 The State and Future of Intelligent Container Number Recognition

The field of container number recognition currently grapples with decreased effectiveness in complex scenarios and struggles to fulfill the growing requirements for intelligent technologies. The main challenges are:

i The wide variety of container number characteristics, such as different fonts, sizes, and colors, and issues like dirt and blockages, necessitating algorithms that are both adaptive and robust.

ii As containers are shipped through environments with complex backdropsand fluctuating light, like ports and railway stations, recognition systems must be capable of adjusting to these varying conditions.

iii Exposure to severe weather and environmental degradation during transit often reduces the clarity of number images, increasing the challenges of accurate recognition.

iv Achieving prompt recognition in dynamically moving containers demands algorithms that are both swift and low-latency, posing substantial demands on technological development.

v Acquiring extensive and varied annotated data sets is crucial for improving accuracy but remains a significant challenge, especially in niche areas.

vi The need for real-time processing of extensive image data often stretchesthe capabilities of existing algorithms, which must be both accurate and quick.

vii Incorporating advanced recognition technologies into established container tracking systems necessitates careful consideration of technological compatibility and system scalability and maintenance.

In summary, the evolution of intelligent container number recognition technology is expected to unfold across seven main fronts:

i. Utilizing advanced deep learning models, like CNNs, to boost the recognition of complex images, with an emphasis on creating more effective network designs and training protocols.

ii. Generating a wider array of training data through methods such as dataaugmentation and image synthesis to tackle the challenge of limited datasets.

iii. Improving the robustness of recognition systems under various conditionsby integrating diverse types of sensor data, such as infrared, RGB, and LiDAR.

iv. Enhancing real-time performance through the adoption of edge computing technologies and by refining the underlying hardware.

v. Developing dynamic systems that can adapt to changes and update theirmodels in real-time to handle new scenarios and container number formats.

vi. Increasing focus on safeguarding data privacy and ensuring the securityof systems in line with evolving technological standards and legal requirements.

vii. Integrating intelligent recognition capabilities into existing logistics management frameworks and promoting the standardization of these innovations for broader global implementation.

5 Conclusions

This article provides an overview of leading technologies such as RFID video recognition, and OCR and examines critical technical aspects like image preprocessing, character segmentation, feature extraction, and recognition algorithms. It addresses the challenges confronting intelligent container number recognition and projects future directions for its development. As global trade continues to grow, enhancing logistical efficiencies becomes imperative, and container recognition technology plays a vital role in boosting port operations efficiency. While there are challenges related to image quality, environmental adaptability, and the necessity for real-time processing, the deployment of advanced technologies like deep learning offers promising solutions for boosting recognition accuracy and efficiency. Looking ahead, research will likely prioritize algorithm enhancement, data set enrichment, and system integration to expand the application of container recognition technology, supporting the effectiveness of global supply chains.

References

1. Ngai, E.W., Cheng, T.E., Au, S., Lai, K.H.: Mobile commerce integratedwith RFID technology in a container depot. Decis. Support. Syst. **43**(1), 62–76 (2007)
2. Jin, X.: Research on the Collection Technology of Railway Container Numbers. China Railway 07 (2003)
3. Jin, H., Qu, H.: Application of OCR system in automated shore bridge. Port Handling **03**, 49–52 (2019)
4. Pang, R.: A preprocessing algorithm for container character recognition. Comput. Technol. Dev. **20**(12), 21–24 (2010)
5. Li, F.: Container number recognition based on BP neural network. J. Huaihai Inst. Technol. **19**(1), 24–28 (2010)
6. Wang, Y., He, J.: Fast localization algorithm for container numbers based on mathematical morphology. Comput. Eng. Des. **36**(08), 2162–2166 (2015)
7. Tan, W., Fang, C., Du, J.: An improved algorithm for container number segmentation based on mathematical morphology. Comput. Eng. Appl. **47**(13), 174–177 (2011)
8. Koo, K.M., Cha, E.Y.: A novel container ISO-code recognition method using texture clustering with a spatial structure window. Int. J. Softw. Eng. Appl. **7**(3), 51–62 (2013)
9. Huang, S., et al.: Container number recognition based on computer vision. Port Handling (01), 1–4 (2018)
10. Sun, Y., Li, X.: Application of ant colony optimization algorithm in container number positioning. Modern Comput. (Professional Edition) (13), 54–58 (2018)
11. Zhang, W.: Container number recognition based on deep learning. In: 2017 IEEE International Conference
12. Tu, H., et al.: Real-time container number recognition algorithm based on deep learning. Crane Transp. Mach. (13), 58–63 (2021)

13. Li, L.: Research and Implementation of Container Number Recognition Technology Based on Deep Learning. Donghua University (2021)
14. Yang, L.: Container Number Recognition Technology Based on Convolutional Neural Network. Shanghai Jiao Tong University (2014)
15. Ye, C., Wang, Z.: Research on license plate character segmentation of vehicle cases based on vertical projection method. Inner Mongolia Highway Transp. (01), 48–53 (2018)
16. Saddami, K., Munadi, K., Arnia, F.: A new approach for Jawisub-word segmentation using histogram projection. In: 2016 IEEE Region 10 Conference (TENCON), pp. 1619–1623. IEEE, November 2016
17. Chen, C.: Container number recognition algorithm based on template matchingand feature matching. J. Shanghai Maritime Univ. **40**(1), 65–70 (2019)
18. Chen, Z.: Container Number Recognition Based on Machine Vision. Shanghai Jiao Tong University (2014)
19. Chen, Y.: Research and Implementation of Container Number Recognition Technology. Huazhong University of Science and Technology (2013)
20. Li, X.: Container number recognition using BP algorithm. J. Beijing Inst. Technol. **21**(3), 345–348 (2001)
21. Song, C., Ding, Q., Guo, B.: Container character recognition method based ondeep belief network. Comput. Eng. Des. **37**(03), 742–745 (2016)
22. Cao, L.: Research on container number character recognition algorithm. Comput. Eng. Appl. **57**(15), 178–185
23. Fukushima, K., Miyake, S.: Neocognitron: a self-organizing neural network modelfor a mechanism of visual pattern recognition. Springer, vol. 1982, pp. 267–285 (2021)
24. Mikolov, T., Karafiá't, M., Burget, L., et al.: Recurrent neural network based language model. In: Eleventh Annual Conference of the International Speech Communication Association, pp. 1045–1048 (2010)
25. Roeksukrungrueang, C., Kusonthammrat, T., Kunapronsujarit, N., et al.: An implementation of automatic container number recognition system. In: 2018 IEEE International Workshop on Advanced Image Technology (IWAIT), pp. 1–4 (2018)
26. Verma, A., Sharma, M., Hebbalaguppe, R., et al. Automatic container code recognition via spatial transformer networks and connected component region proposals. In: 2016 15th IEEE International Conference on Machine Learning and Applications (ICMLA), pp. 728–733. IEEE (2016)
27. Chen, L., Li, Y.: OCR for railway container numbers based on dual convolutional neural networks. Comput. Era (06) 1–450 (2019)
28. Zhang, S., et al.: Recognition method for container number images with large-angle perspective deformation. J. Tongji Univ. (Natural Science) **47**(2), 285–290 (2019)
29. Shi, B., Bai, X., Yao, C.: An end-to-end trainable neural network for imagebased sequence recognition and its application to scene text recognition. IEEE Trans. Pattern Anal. Mach. Intell. **39**(11), 2298–2304 (2016)
30. Xing, Q., Zhi, W.W., Tong, C.: Port container number recognition system based on improved YOLO and CRNN algorithm. In: 2020 IEEE International Conference on Artificial Intelligence and Electromechanical Automation, pp. 72–77 (2020)
31. Mei, L., Guo, J., Liu, Q., et al.: A novel framework for container code-character recognition based on deep learning and template matching. In: 2016 IEEE International Conference on Industrial Informatics-Computing Technology, Intelligent Technology, Industrial Information Integration (ICIICII), pp. 78–82 (2016)
32. Liu, Y.: Neural network based container box number recognition system. Shanghai Jiao Tong University (2018)

A New LSTM-GRU Hybrid Model
for Forecasting the Growth of SRDI Enterprises

Lewei Hu[✉]

School of Business, Jianghan University, Wuhan 430056, China
`pedagogical@jhun.edu.cn`

Abstract. This study aims to develop predictive models for key performance indicators of SRDI (Specialized, Refined, Differentiated, and Innovative) enterprises, namely profitability, R&D capabilities, and governance levels, to better understand and support their high-quality development. Utilizing a dataset of 83 A-share listed companies recognized as national-level SRDI "Little Giant" enterprises, we compare traditional time series models (Mean and ARIMA) with advanced deep learning models (LSTM, GRU, and a hybrid LSTM-GRU model). Our results demonstrate that the LSTM-GRU hybrid model significantly outperforms other models. Furthermore, we applied this model to predict key indicators for SRDI enterprises and provided management recommendations based on the predictions.

Keywords: SRDI · LSTM · GRU · High-quality Development · Hybrid LSTM-GRU

1 Introduction

In the context of increasingly complex and volatile international political and economic conditions and the restructuring of global supply chains, the challenges of supply chain risks for domestic enterprises have become increasingly prominent. Despite significant advancements in the overall level and international competitiveness of China's manufacturing industry, there remain high dependencies on foreign imports in key areas such as medical devices, semiconductors, core industrial software, precision machinery, and advanced materials. This reliance directly impacts the stability and security of supply chains.

To address these challenges, following the 2022 Government Work Report, which clearly outlined the need to provide strong support for specialized, refined, differentiated, and innovative (SRDI) small and medium-sized enterprises (SMEs) in terms of funding, talent, and incubation platforms, the 2024 Government Work Report reiterated the importance of promoting the development of SRDI SMEs.

In this environment, the role of SMEs in the industrial chain is particularly critical. These enterprises typically focus on niche markets, and some outstanding ones have achieved high levels of specialization and significant market share in specific products through deep integration of industrial technologies. They have become indispensable

R. C. Qiu et al. (Eds.): IoTaaS 2024, LNICST 675, pp. 224–237, 2026.
https://doi.org/10.1007/978-3-032-14681-6_20

partners in the industrial chain. The flexibility of SMEs allows them to quickly adapt to technological changes and market structure adjustments, fill market gaps, and enhance various segments of the industrial chain. As of the end of June 2024, China has cultivated more than 140,000 SRDI SMEs, including over 12,000 'Little Giant' enterprises. These enterprises hold more than 200,000 invention patents, showcasing promising development.

Growth forecasting of SRDI enterprises is crucial due to their role in driving innovation, economic diversification, and contributing to national GDP and job creation. Accurate forecasts strengthen supply chain resilience, guide strategic resource allocation, and foster innovation and competitiveness. They also help identify risks, enabling businesses and governments to take proactive measures, ensuring sustained growth and long-term economic stability in global markets.

Given this context, this paper aims to explore how to establish a high-quality development forecasting model for SRDI enterprises to evaluate and promote their growth. The model will integrate multiple dimensions, including technological innovation, capital structure, and profitability, to provide more precise development strategies and risk management tools for SMEs. Through analysis of the forecasting model, potential risk points in the industrial chain can be identified, offering decision support for governments and enterprises to mitigate supply chain risks, enhance the autonomous control of the industrial chain, and thereby provide a solid foundation for constructing a new development paradigm.

Specifically, this paper will employ a hybrid LSTM-GRU model, combining time series analysis and deep learning techniques, to forecast the development trends of SRDI enterprises. This model will analyze historical data of enterprises, identify key factors influencing their growth, and predict future development trends. Such forecasts can assist enterprises in promptly adjusting strategies, optimizing resource allocation, and improving responsiveness to market changes, thereby maintaining a competitive edge in a dynamic market environment. Moreover, this model will serve as a reference for policymakers, aiding them in better understanding the role of SMEs in the industrial chain, formulating effective support policies, and promoting the healthy development of the entire industrial chain.

In summary, forecasting the high-quality development of SRDI enterprises not only helps mitigate supply chain risks in China's industrial chain but also provides a scientific basis for enhancing the resilience and competitiveness of the industrial chain. Under the multiple guarantees of policy support, technological innovation, and market responsiveness, SRDI enterprises are poised to play an increasingly important role in future development.

2 Literature Review

2.1 Growth Measurement Metrics for SRDI Enterprises

Profitability, research and development (R&D) capability, and governance level are the three key elements for the high-quality development of specialized and innovative enterprises.

As a direct reflection of a company's financial health, profitability not only demonstrates the enterprise's ability to survive and thrive in market competition but also directly impacts its capital accumulation and reinvestment capabilities. High profitability indicates that a company can utilize resources more effectively, achieving sustainable growth and development [1]. Moreover, enhanced profitability provides the enterprise with more funds for innovation and business expansion, thereby further strengthening its market competitiveness and industry position [2]. Therefore, for SRDI enterprises, maintaining and enhancing profitability is crucial for achieving long-term strategic goals.

SRDI enterprises are renowned for their professionalism and innovation, with R&D capability being the source of their innovation. R&D capability directly enhances a company's innovation ability and market competitiveness, enabling it to respond swiftly to market changes and meet customer needs. Continuous R&D investment can create technological barriers, ensuring the company's long-term sustainable development and enhancing its brand value and market reputation [3]. By improving R&D capability, SRDI enterprises can also achieve diversified development, reducing the risk of reliance on a single market [4]. Thus, R&D capability is a critical factor for SRDI enterprises to maintain a leading position and achieve steady development.

The governance level is also vital for SRDI enterprises. The governance structure affects the decision-making process of the company and directly relates to its innovation capability, risk management, and market competitiveness [5]. SRDI enterprises often rely on highly specialized knowledge and technological innovation, necessitating effective governance mechanisms to ensure the rational allocation of resources and the achievement of strategic goals [6]. Good corporate governance can promote transparency and accountability, attracting investors and partners while reducing agency costs. Furthermore, with the acceleration of globalization and technological changes, specialized and innovative enterprises need to adapt flexibly to market changes, and a strong governance system can provide the necessary organizational support and strategic direction, helping the enterprise maintain a leading position in fierce market competition [7].

Recent advancements in AI-driven models have significantly transformed how enterprises, particularly SMEs, manage their growth and transformation through key aspects like profitability, R&D capability, and governance [8]. These traditionally distinct areas are increasingly integrated through machine learning and AI technologies. For example, profitability is now more accurately predicted using AI models like CNN [9], TCN-LSTM hybrid [10], enabling businesses to forecast financial trends with precision, which helps them make informed reinvestment decisions and allocate resources more effectively, ensuring sustainable growth and competitiveness.

Despite these advancements, a gap remains in the comprehensive integration of AI-driven models. While such as profitability, R&D have each benefited from AI individually, there is still significant room for developing frameworks that fully integrate these critical aspects into a unified model. Such a model would allow enterprises to manage these interconnected areas more effectively, providing strategic insights that align with long-term business objectives. Moreover, research focused on predicting the growth and development of SRDI enterprises remains scarce. These enterprises, with their unique growth drivers, have not been extensively studied in terms of predictive modeling. A comprehensive AI framework tailored to SRDI enterprises would help address this gap, enabling more precise predictions and strategic planning in the context of their specialized growth trajectories.

2.2 Time Series Analysis Methods

Basic Principles and Applications of the Mean Model. The Mean Model is a simple statistical approach that assumes a constant expected value over time in a stable process. It's useful for preliminary analysis and simple forecasting, especially when data shows no significant trends or seasonality. The predicted value is calculated as the average of observed values, making it a common benchmark for comparing more complex models [11].

The Fundamental Principles and Applications of the ARIMA Model. The ARIMA (AutoRegressive Integrated Moving Average) model forecasts time series data by combining autoregressive terms, differencing, and moving average terms, represented as ARIMA(p, d, q).

The ARIMA model incorporates three key components: Autoregressive Terms (AR), which capture relationships between the current observation and previous values; Differencing (I), which ensures stationarity by removing trends and seasonality; and Moving Average Terms (MA), which address random errors by linking the current observation to past error terms.

The ARIMA model is versatile, used in various fields such as economics (predicting GDP and unemployment), business (forecasting stock prices), and meteorology (temperature predictions). It involves data preprocessing, testing for stationarity, and parameter optimization [12].

Deep Learning Methods. Deep learning has shown outstanding performance in time series forecasting, particularly in handling complex and nonlinear data. Compared to traditional statistical models, deep learning models can automatically learn features from data and make efficient predictions. This section will provide a detailed introduction to the basic principles and applications of Long Short-Term Memory (LSTM) and Gated Recurrent Unit (GRU) models.

Principles and Applications of LSTM-based Model. The Long Short-Term Memory (LSTM) model is an improved version of the Recurrent Neural Network (RNN) designed for nonlinear prediction. It effectively captures dependencies between observations in time series, making it widely used for time series forecasting. Compared to the ARIMA model, which performs well when time series trends are evident, the LSTM model is more suitable for modeling and predicting unstable time series with more fixed components. The advent of LSTM has had a profound practical and theoretical impact across multiple fields, including machine translation, speech recognition, and time series prediction [13] (Fig. 1).

An LSTM unit consists of three main gates: the forget gate, the input gate, and the output gate. Each gate is a neural network layer that controls the flow of information via the sigmoid activation function:

Forget Gate: The forget gate receives the hidden state from the previous time step and the current input, and computes the proportion of the cell state from the previous time

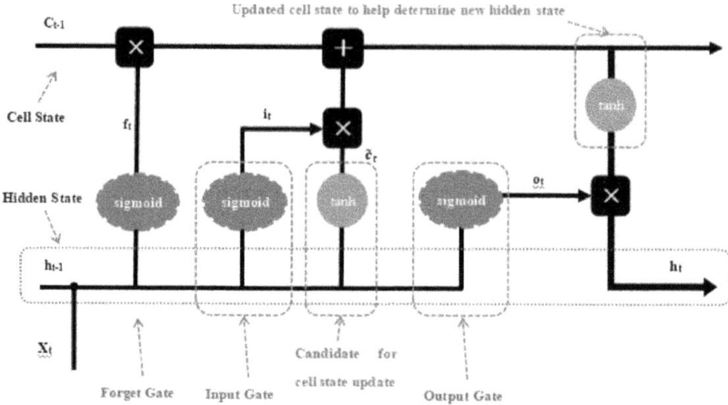

Fig. 1. LSTM Unit Internal Architecture Diagram

step to be retained using the sigmoid function. The computation formula is as follows:

$$f_t = \sigma(W_f \cdot [h_{t-1}, x_t] + b_f) \tag{1}$$

where W_f is the weight matrix of the forget gate, h_{t-1} is the hidden state from the previous time step, x_t is the current input, b_f is the bias term for the forget gate, and σ represents the activation function.

Input Gate: The input gate receives the hidden state from the previous time step and the current input, and outputs the proportion of new information to be written into the cell state using the sigmoid function. The computation formula is as follows:

$$i_t = \sigma(W_i \cdot [h_{t-1}, x_t] + b_i) \tag{2}$$

where W_i is the weight matrix of the input gate, and b_i represents the bias term for the input gate. At the same time, the new candidate memory information for the current time step is obtained through the tanh function. The specific calculation formula is as follows:

$$\tilde{C}_t = tanh(W_c \cdot [h_{t-1}, x_t] + b_c) \tag{3}$$

where W_c is the weight matrix for the candidate memory, and b_c is the bias term for the candidate memory. By combining the retained information from the forget gate with the input from the input gate, an updated cell state C_t for the current time step is formed. The calculation process is as follows:

$$C_t = f_t * C_{t-1} + i_t * \tilde{C}_t \tag{4}$$

Output Gate: The Output Gate receives the Hidden State from the previous time step and the current input, and uses a sigmoid function to output a value between 0 and 1, indicating the proportion of the current Cell State to be output to the Hidden State of the current time step. The formula is as follows:

$$o_t = \sigma(W_o \cdot [h_{t-1}, x_t] + b_o) \tag{5}$$

Finally, the current time step's hidden state is calculated by combining o_t and C_t. The formula is as follows:

$$h_t = o_t * tanh(C_t) \tag{6}$$

Principles and Applications of the GRU-based Model. The GRU (Gated Recurrent Unit) is an improved model based on the RNN and LSTM neural networks. In terms of network structure, the GRU neural network introduces a simpler gating system into the hidden layers. Unlike LSTM, it does not have a separate memory cell. Instead, it uses a reset gate and an update gate to decide what information from the previous hidden state to retain or discard, and how to combine it with the new candidate state information at the current time step [14]. The working principle of the GRU is illustrated in the following figure (Fig. 2):

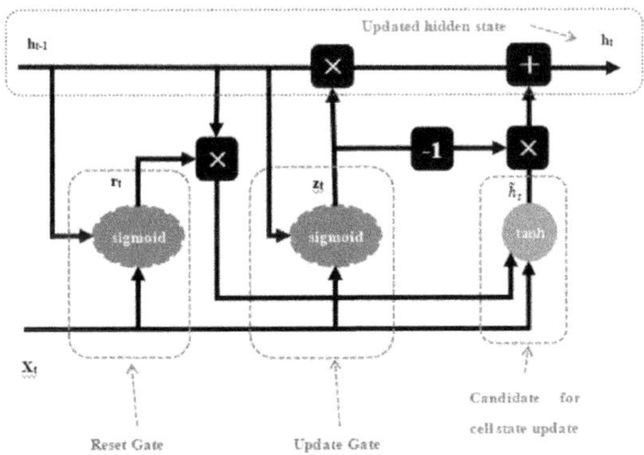

Fig. 2. Diagram of the Internal Structure of a GRU Unit

GRU contains two main gating units: reset gate and update gate. They control the forgetting and updating of information respectively.

Reset Gate: The reset gate controls the extent to which the previous hidden state influences the generation of the candidate hidden state. The calculation formula for the reset gate is as follows:

$$r_t = \sigma(W_r \cdot x_t + U_r \cdot h_{t-1}) \tag{7}$$

where r_t is the output of the reset gate, W_r is the weight matrix from the input to the reset gate, U_r is the weight matrix from previous hidden state to the reset gate, x_t is the input at the current time step, h_{t-1} is the hidden state at the previous time step, and σ represents the sigmoid activation function.

Update Gate: The update gate controls the extent to which the candidate hidden state and the previous hidden state are combined at the current time step. The calculation formula for the update gate is as follows:

$$z_t = \sigma(W_z \cdot x_t + U_z \cdot h_{t-1}) \tag{8}$$

where z_t is the output of the update gate, W_z is the weight matrix from the input to the update gate, and U_z is the weight matrix from the previous hidden state to the update gate.

Candidate Hidden State: The candidate hidden state is generated by combining the current input and the previous hidden state information under the control of the reset gate. The calculation formula is as follows:

$$\tilde{h}_t = tanh(W \cdot x_t + r_t * (U \cdot h_{t-1})) \tag{9}$$

where $\tilde{h}_t$ represents the candidate hidden state at the current time step, W is the weight matrix from the input to the candidate hidden state, U is the weight matrix from the previous hidden state to the candidate hidden state, and tanh represents the tanh activation function.

Final Hidden State: The final hidden state combines the previous hidden state and the candidate hidden state at the current time step, controlled by the update gate. The calculation formula is as follows:

$$h_t = (1 - z_t) * h_{t-1} + z_t * \tilde{h}_t \tag{10}$$

GRU has several advantages, including a simpler structure, fewer parameters, and higher computational efficiency. It can effectively handle long-term dependencies through its gating mechanism, and because it has fewer parameters, it generally trains faster than LSTM. However, in some complex tasks, the applicability of GRU is limited, and LSTM might perform better due to its more parameters and more complex gating mechanisms. In practical applications, choosing between GRU and LSTM requires experimental validation and cannot be generalized. GRU performs excellently in many sequential data processing tasks such as natural language processing, time series forecasting, and speech recognition. For example, in machine translation tasks, GRU is used to model the sequence relationships of the source and target languages. Overall, GRU simplifies the structure of LSTM by introducing reset and update gates while retaining the ability to handle long-term dependencies. Nonetheless, in some specific scenarios, using a combination of GRU and LSTM might be more effective, leveraging the strengths of both to achieve better performance.

3   Methods and Data

3.1   Research Design

In this study, we aim to explore and improve the predictive models for the profitability, R&D capabilities, and governance level of SRDI enterprises. Considering the limitations of traditional time series models and single deep learning models in handling complex nonlinear sequence data, we propose a hybrid LSTM-GRU model, which combines the strengths of both LSTM and GRU to achieve significant improvements in predictive performance. The following outlines the specific design ideas and steps of our research.

Design Concept. Firstly, this study selected the mean model as the benchmark model. At the same time, the ARIMA model was chosen for comparison to provide a more comprehensive analysis.

Secondly, we constructed three different models to achieve accurate predictions of time series data, including: the LSTM model (Long Short-Term Memory), the GRU model (Gated Recurrent Unit), and the LSTM-GRU hybrid model.

The LSTM-GRU hybrid model aims to combine the advantages of both LSTM and GRU by integrating their prediction results through weighted averaging. Specifically, the hybrid model involves training the LSTM and GRU models separately, calculating weights based on their respective prediction errors, and then combining their prediction results through weighted averaging to generate the final prediction. Through this multi-model fusion approach, we aim to achieve superior performance in handling complex time series data.

Furthermore, we used mean squared error (MSE) and runtime as the main evaluation metrics for the models. Additionally, to ensure the stability and generalizability of the models, we adopted cross-validation methods.

Finally, the optimal model was selected to predict the time series data of SRDI enterprises' profitability, R&D, and governance for the next eight time steps, and relevant countermeasures were proposed.

Integration Strategy of the LSTM-GRU Hybrid Model. The hybrid model consists of the following main components: an input layer to receive the raw sequence data; an LSTM layer to process the input sequences and capture long-term dependencies; a GRU layer to further process the sequence data on the basis of the LSTM layer, capturing short-term dependencies and detailed features; and a fully connected layer to integrate the outputs of the LSTM and GRU layers, generating the final prediction results.

In the specific implementation process, the input data is first standardized, then features are extracted sequentially through the LSTM and GRU layers, and finally, the prediction values are output through the fully connected layer. The hybrid model is integrated through the following steps:

Calculate the Prediction Errors of LSTM and GRU: In each fold of cross-validation, compute the prediction MSEs of the LSTM and GRU models, denoted as mse_{lstm} and mse_{gru}, respectively.

Compute the Weights: Calculate the weights of LSTM and GRU models based on their prediction errors. The smaller the error, the larger the weight. The calculation formula is as follows:

$$\begin{cases} w_{lstm} = \dfrac{1}{mse_{lstm}} \\ w_{gru} = \dfrac{1}{mse_{gru}} \end{cases} \tag{11}$$

Then, normalize the weights.

Generate the Hybrid Prediction Results: Calculate the weighted average of the LSTM and GRU prediction results based on the normalized weights. The calculation formula is as follows:

$$y_{combo} = w_{lstm} \cdot y_{ls\_pred} + w_{gru} \cdot y_{gr\_pred} \tag{12}$$

3.2   Data Sources and Preprocessing

Data Sources. The sample data for this study is sourced from the Choice Financial Terminal of East Money, comprising 83 randomly selected A-share listed companies. These companies, recognized as "National-Level SRDI Little Giants" by the Ministry of Industry and Information Technology, represent various high-tech sectors across China's economic regions. To ensure relevance to SRDI SMEs, all companies are listed on the ChiNext Board. The dataset spans from Q1 2015 to Q1 2024, covering 37 time points. The selected indicators and their explanations are provided in the table below (Table 1).

Table 1. Table captions should be placed above the tables.

Indicators	Meaning
Net Profit	The money left after all costs are paid
Total Operating Revenue	The total amount of money a company earns from its core business operations
R&D Expenses	the costs a company incurs while conducting research to develop new products, services, or technologies, as well as improving existing ones
Equity Attributable to Shareholders of the Parent Company	the portion of the company's net assets that belongs to the shareholders of the parent company
Total Invested Capital	The total money invested in a company from both debt and shareholders' equity to run the business

Data Preprocessing. To investigate the profitability, R&D capability, and governance level of 83 SRDI enterprises, this study conducted data preprocessing. Firstly, due to the limited availability of data channels for some enterprises before their listing, there were missing values in indicators such as R&D expenses and equity attributable to shareholders of the parent company. Therefore, observations with missing values were removed from the dataset. Subsequently, the study calculated the required predictive indicators for profitability, R&D capability, and governance level. Specifically, profitability was measured by the ratio of net profit to total operating revenue, covering data from the first quarter of 2015 to the first quarter of 2024, totaling 37 observations. R&D capability was assessed using the ratio of R&D expenses to total operating revenue, with data spanning from the fourth quarter of 2015 to the first quarter of 2024, totaling 33 observations. Governance level was evaluated by the ratio of equity attributable to shareholders of the parent company to total invested capital, covering data from the third quarter of 2018 to the first quarter of 2024, amounting to 23 observations.

3.3   Model Construction and Evaluation

In this study, we utilized Python and various third-party libraries, such as TensorFlow and scikit-learn, to construct multiple time series forecasting models, including the mean model, ARIMA model, LSTM model, and GRU model. These models were evaluated using cross-validation and mean squared error (MSE). Additionally, we constructed an LSTM-GRU hybrid model to combine the strengths of both LSTM and GRU models to enhance forecasting performance.

Model Construction.   Mean Model: In this study, the mean model was used as a baseline

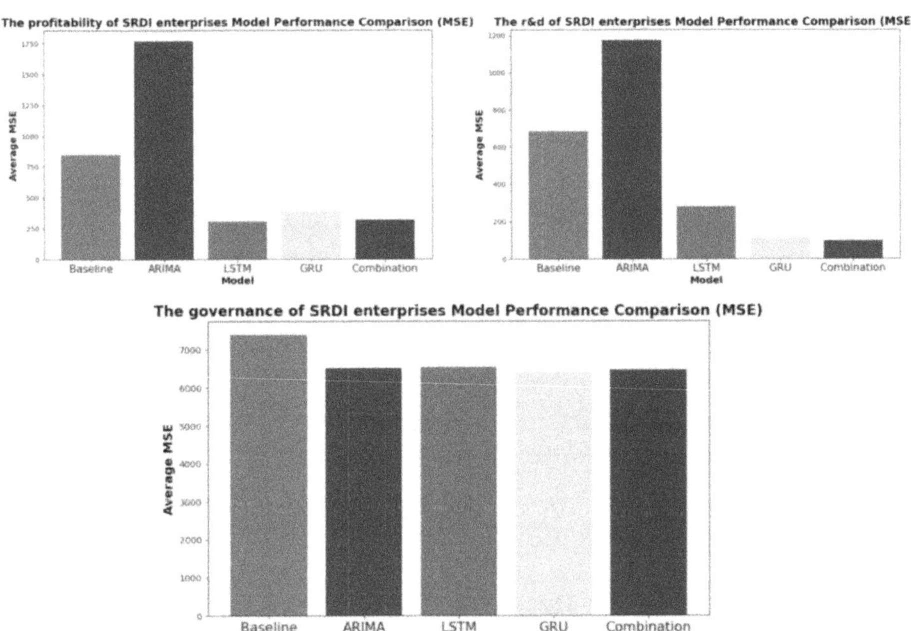

Fig. 3. Comparative Analysis of MSE for Profitability, R&D Capability, and Governance Level Time Series Data Across Five Models

model, predicting future values based on the average of past observations. To ensure the stability of the results, we used K-fold cross-validation (K = 10) for evaluation.

ARIMA Model: We used the auto_arima function from the pmdarima library to automatically select the best parameters for the ARIMA model. This model was also evaluated using K-fold cross-validation (K = 10).

LSTM Model: We employed the LSTM model from the TensorFlow library to construct a neural network for time series forecasting. The hidden layer was set with 50 LSTM cells, and the ReLU activation function was used.

GRU Model: We used the GRU model from the TensorFlow library to construct a neural network for time series forecasting. The hidden layer was set with 50 GRU units, and the ReLU activation function was used.

LSTM-GRU Hybrid Model: The LSTM-GRU hybrid model integrates the forecasting results of LSTM and GRU models through a weighted averaging method. We evaluated each model's MSE using K-fold cross-validation (K = 10) and calculated the weights accordingly.

Model Evaluation. Based on the time series datasets related to the profitability, R&D capabilities, and governance level of SRDI enterprises, this study conducted ten-fold cross-validation for all five models. We obtained the performance results in terms of MSE and runtime for each model, facilitating a comprehensive evaluation and analysis (Figs. 3 and 4).

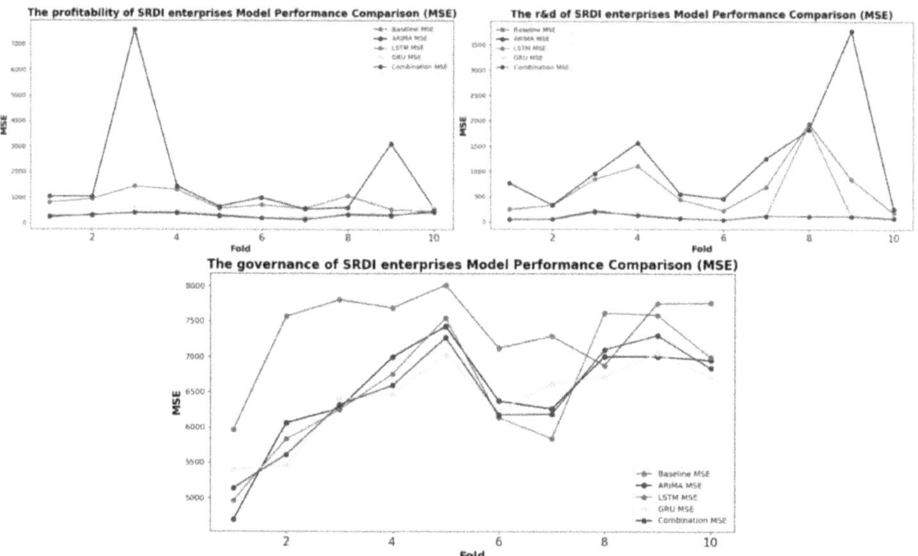

Fig. 4. Line Charts of MSE for Time Series Data on Profitability, R&D Capability, and Governance Level Across Five Models

4 Experimental Results and Analysis

4.1 Model Prediction Performance

From the previous experimental results, we can draw the following conclusions:

First, regarding model performance, the LSTM-GRU hybrid model demonstrates significant advantages. It shows the best performance in predicting profitability and governance levels, achieving the lowest MSE. The GRU model performs best in predicting R&D capabilities, also achieving the lowest MSE. In comparison, traditional models such as the mean baseline model and ARIMA model perform poorly across all datasets, with higher MSE values.

Second, in terms of model runtime, the mean baseline model and ARIMA model have the shortest runtime and the lowest computational cost. The runtime of the LSTM and GRU models is moderate, slightly higher than that of the baseline models. The LSTM-GRU hybrid model has the longest runtime and the highest computational cost. Despite this, the runtime costs of all models are within the same order of magnitude, with no particularly significant differences.

Third, regarding model stability, the LSTM-GRU hybrid model exhibits the smallest MSE fluctuations across all datasets, indicating stable performance. In comparison, other models show varying degrees of instability.

In summary, the LSTM-GRU hybrid model performs best in terms of overall predictive performance, especially in predicting the profitability and governance levels of SRDI enterprises. This model combines the strengths of LSTM and GRU, capturing long-term dependencies in time series data while efficiently handling short-term dependency features. This dual capability makes it particularly effective in dealing with complex and nonlinear time series data. Additionally, the LSTM-GRU hybrid model maintains the lowest MSE across multiple datasets, indicating its ability to provide stable and accurate predictions in various scenarios. Therefore, the LSTM-GRU hybrid model not only holds theoretical advantages but also demonstrates effective practical application.

4.2 Predictive Analysis of the Three Dimensions of SRDI Enterprises

Using the previously trained LSTM-GRU hybrid model, we predict the mean values of profitability, R&D capabilities, and governance levels for 83 sample SRDI enterprises over the next eight time points (2 years). We analyze the trends and patterns within these predictions (Fig. 5).

The forecast trends for SRDI enterprises over the next two years in profitability, R&D capability, and governance level reveal distinct patterns. Profitability shows a significant decline, suggesting potential financial instability or challenges in maintaining market competitiveness. In contrast, R&D capability exhibits a sharp rise, peaking around the seventh time point, indicating strong innovation efforts, possibly driven by investment in new technologies. However, governance level steadily declines, which could signal weaknesses in organizational structures or management practices. To address these issues, SRDI enterprises should focus on enhancing financial resilience through diversified revenue streams and cost optimization. Simultaneously, strengthening governance mechanisms will be crucial to support sustainable growth and capitalize on the rising R&D potential. A balanced approach to managing both innovation and operational efficiency is essential for long-term success.

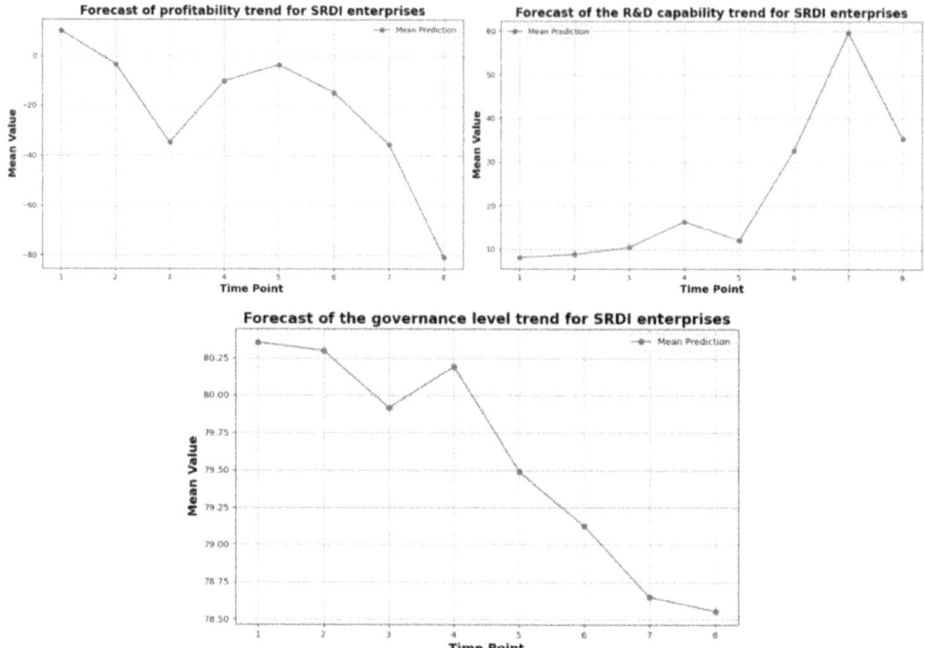

Fig. 5. Trend forecast for the profitability, R&D capability, and governance level of SRDI enterprises

5 Conclusion

5.1 Main Research Findings

This study explores and improves predictive models for the profitability, R&D capabilities, and governance levels of SRDI enterprises. By comparing traditional time series models and advanced deep learning models, we have demonstrated that the LSTM-GRU hybrid model significantly outperforms others in terms of predictive accuracy and stability. Specifically, the LSTM-GRU model exhibits the lowest MSE in predicting profitability and governance levels, while the GRU model excels in predicting R&D capabilities. The findings underscore the importance of utilizing hybrid models to capture both long-term dependencies and short-term features in complex, non-linear time series data.

5.2 Policy Recommendations

Given the demonstrated efficacy of the LSTM-GRU hybrid model in predicting the key performance indicators of SRDI enterprises, policymakers should consider leveraging such advanced predictive models to inform decision-making. By understanding future trends in profitability, R&D, and governance, policies can be tailored to support sustained innovation and growth in these enterprises. It is also crucial to provide ongoing support in terms of funding, talent development, and infrastructure to enhance the resilience and competitiveness of SRDI enterprises amidst global economic uncertainties.

5.3 Future Research Directions

Future research should focus on refining the hybrid model by incorporating additional factors that may influence the performance of SRDI enterprises, such as market dynamics, regulatory changes, and technological advancements. Additionally, expanding the model to include other machine learning techniques and evaluating their performance could provide further insights into optimal predictive strategies. Longitudinal studies tracking the impact of implemented policies on SRDI enterprises will also be valuable in validating and improving the predictive models over time.

Acknowledgment. This research has been supported by University-Level Research Project of Jianghan University 2023KJZX46 and grants from the High-level talent fund of Jianghan University under Grant 1001/08580001 and the National Social Science Foundation of China 72171102.

References

1. Sumaryati, A., Rohman, A.: The influence of sustainability reporting on environmental and financial performance. Qual.-Access Success **20**(171), 131–134 (2019)
2. Zhang, G.B., Wang, T.: Financial budgets of technology-based SMEs from the perspective of sustainability and big data. Front. Public Health **10**, 9 (2022)
3. Toroslu, A., et al.: Value capture in open innovation: a literature review and a research agenda. Ind. Mark. Manage. **114**, 297–312 (2023)
4. Bohnsack, R., et al.: Profiting from innovation when digital business ecosystems emerge: a control point perspective. Res. Policy **53**(3), 20 (2024)
5. Li, P.J., et al.: Indispensable source of risk contagion with big data analysis from a more comprehensive view on shadow banking. J. Glob. Inf. Manag. **32**(1), 29 (2024)
6. Klarner, P., Yoshikawa, T., Hitt, M.A.: A capability-based view of boards: a new conceptual framework for board governance. Acad. Manag. Perspect. **35**(1), 123–141 (2021)
7. Kumar, R.K., Dubey, A.K.: The role of governance in solving the problems of SMEs: a review of the literature using a systematic approach. Int. J. Electron. Govern. Res. **18**(1), 26 (2022)
8. Lu, X.Q., et al.: AI-enabled opportunities and transformation challenges for SMEs in the post-pandemic era: a review and research agenda. Front. Public Health **10**, 11 (2022)
9. Zhong, Y.: E-commerce utilization analysis and growth strategy for smes using an artificial intelligence. J. Intell. Fuzzy Syst. **45**, 7619–7629 (2023)
10. Mahmoud, A., Mohammed, A.: Leveraging hybrid deep learning models for enhanced multivariate time series forecasting. Neural. Process. Lett. **56**(5), 223 (2024)
11. Cao, Q., et al.: Greenhouse temperature prediction based on time-series features and LightGBM. Appl. Sci.-Basel **13**(3), 21 (2023)
12. Bagalkot, S.S., Dinesha, H.A., Naik, N.: Novel grey wolf optimizer based parameters selection for GARCH and ARIMA models for stock price prediction. PeerJ Comput. Sci. **10** (2024)
13. Nelson, D.M.Q., Pereira, A.C.M., Oliveira, R.A.D.: Stock market's price movement prediction with LSTM neural networks. In: 2017 International Joint Conference on Neural Networks (IJCNN) (2017)
14. Zheng, W., Chen, G.: An accurate GRU-based power time-series prediction approach with selective state updating and stochastic optimization. IEEE Trans. Cybern. **52**(12), 13902–13914 (2022)

Multi-degree-Of-Freedom Shipboard Steady-State Design

Chao hui Gai[1]([envelope]), Ze yu Gao[2], Cheng Gang Wang[2], and Qian Yu Shi[3]

[1] School of Electronic Engineering, Beijing University of Posts and Telecommunications, Beijing, China
136133143@qq.com

[2] School of Mechanical Electrical Engineering, Wuhan Institute of Technology, Wuhan 430000, China

[3] School of Information and Communication Engineering, Beijing University of Posts and Telecommunications, Beijing, China
18203511586@edu.cn

Abstract. The radar stabilization system is designed to compensate the wave caused by ocean wave effectively and ensure the continuous and stable operation of shipborne radar in the changeable ocean environment. A new type of two-degree-of-freedom radar stabilization system is presented in this paper. By solving the steady-state isolation equation, we determine the relationship between the wave disturbance and the input attitude of the stabilization system, and explain its working mechanism. In order to estimate the maximum drive force required for the electric cylinder in the early stages of engineering design, we constructed the maximum drive force model in the limit state and calculated the maximum drive requirement in the extreme conditions. In order to verify the accuracy of the proposed driving force model, we use Adams software to create a simplified model and carry out kinematics and dynamics simulation according to the working principle of the system. This paper provides a valuable reference method for the design and research of radar stability system by deeply analyzing the motion characteristics and driving force characteristics of electric cylinder in different motion states.

Keywords: Multi-degree of freedom · parallel shipboard platform · Adams motion simulation · optimal design

1 Introduction

At present, radar stabilization platform plays an important role in ship applications, and its working environment is complex and changeable [1]. Because of the characteristics of environmental protection, high control precision and quick response, the electric cylinder is the first choice for driving and stabilizing platform [2]. However, under harsh sea conditions, the high strength requirement of the stabilized platform and the maximum driving force and stroke of the electric cylinder become the keys to reasonable design.

R. C. Qiu et al. (Eds.): IoTaaS 2024, LNICST 675, pp. 238–247, 2026.
https://doi.org/10.1007/978-3-032-14681-6_21

Although Adams can provide some support in the application of platform simulation, there is still room for improvement in control accuracy and response speed, and it occupies a large area, hydraulic system maintenance frequently [3].Therefore, an innovative scheme is proposed in this paper: using electric cylinder instead of traditional hydraulic system as the driving source, aiming at achieving higher control ac- curacy and real-time compensation of rolling and pitching disturbance caused by ocean waves, therefore, the high performance requirements of the stabilized platform under complex sea conditions can be met. The two-degree-of-freedom stability system constructed in this paper is mainly composed of a central pillar, a horizontal swinging electric cylinder, a vertical swinging electric cylinder and an upper and lower platform. The central pillar is located in the center of the whole system, and the horizontal and vertical electric cylinders are distributed around the central point at an angle of 90° [4].

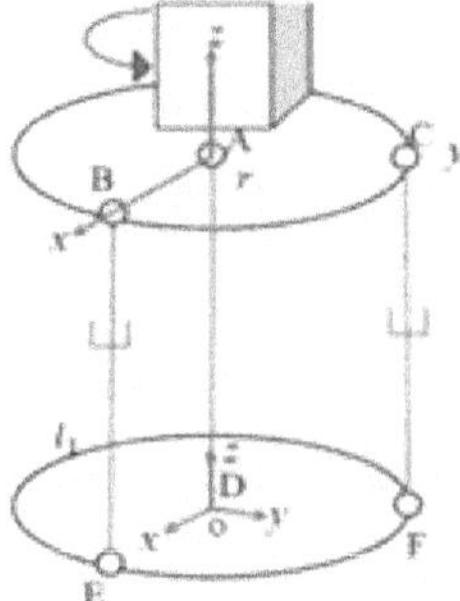

Fig. 1. Schematic diagram of the stable platform structure

The structure of the system is shown in Fig. 1, where the x-axis represents the horizontal oscillating axis and the Y-axis represents the vertical oscillating axis. According to the steady-state isolation equation, the attitude sensor and the angular velocity gyroscope can detect the angle and velocity of the disturbance when the ocean wave occurs, the upper platform rotates the same angle in reverse at a certain speed on the horizontal and vertical axes, thus ensuring the stable operation of the loaded radar [5]. According to the Euler's rotation theorem, the conversion between coordinate systems can be accomplished by rotating on three axes. The main factors that affect the radar performance are the angle of the ship's horizontal swing and the angle of the ship's vertical swing. At the beginning, the direction of the ship-borne coordinate system is consistent with that of the geographical coordinate systemb. It can be considered that the ship-borne coordinate system rotates the angle around the y axis of the geographical coordinate system B, and then rotates the angle around the x axis of the geographical coordinate system, the new shipboard coordinate system P is obtained. Its rotation matrix can be expressed as [6].

$$R_b^p = R(\gamma)R(\varphi)$$

$$= \begin{bmatrix} 1 & 0 & 0 \\ 0 & \cos\gamma & -\sin\gamma \\ 0 & \sin\gamma & \cos\gamma \end{bmatrix} \begin{bmatrix} \cos\varphi & 0 & \sin\varphi \\ 0 & 1 & 0 \\ -\sin\varphi & 0 & \cos\varphi \end{bmatrix}$$

$$= \begin{bmatrix} \cos\varphi & 0 & \sin\varphi \\ \sin\varphi\sin\gamma & \cos\gamma & -\sin\varphi\cos\gamma \\ -\sin\varphi\cos\gamma & \sin\gamma & \cos\varphi\cos\gamma \end{bmatrix} \tag{1}$$

The inverse transformation is:

$$R_p^b = (R_b^p)^T$$

$$= \begin{bmatrix} \cos\varphi & \sin\varphi\sin\gamma & -\sin\varphi\cos\gamma \\ 0 & \cos\gamma & \sin\gamma \\ \sin\varphi & -\sin\gamma\cos\varphi & \cos\varphi\cos\gamma \end{bmatrix} \tag{2}$$

A coordinate vector Sb, in a given geographical coordinate system {b}, whose coordinates are $S^p = (x^p, y^p, z^p)$ From the coordinate transformation, we can get:

$$S^p(x^p, y^p, z^p) = R_b^p S^b(x^b, y^b, z^b) \tag{3}$$

Initially, the radar coordinates are aligned with the ship coordinates pin position and in the same direction as the geographic coordinates b. The initial position of the radar coordinate system is at the center of the hinge. However, under the driving action of electric cylinder, the radar coordinate system on the upper platform rotates the angle around the y axis first, and then the angle around the new x axis, thus forming a new radar dynamic coordinate system r. Its rotation matrix can be expressed as [7].

$$R_p^r = R(\beta)R(\alpha)$$

$$= \begin{bmatrix} \cos\beta & 0 & \sin\beta \\ 0 & 1 & 0 \\ -\sin\beta & 0 & \cos\beta \end{bmatrix} \begin{bmatrix} 1 & 0 & 0 \\ 0 & \cos\alpha & -\sin\alpha \\ 0 & \sin\alpha & \cos\alpha \end{bmatrix} \tag{4}$$

$$= \begin{bmatrix} \cos\beta & \sin\beta\sin\alpha & \sin\beta\cos\alpha \\ 0 & \cos\alpha & -\sin\alpha \\ -\sin\beta & \sin\alpha\cos\beta & \cos\beta\cos\alpha \end{bmatrix}$$

In the radar coordinate system, the vector in the geographic coordinate system corresponding to a certain point. In order to ensure the stable relationship between the radar coordinate system and the geographical coordinate system, the corresponding coordinate transformation must be carried out. Combined with the formula we can deduce the following relation: where is the rotation matrix of the radar coordinate system relative to the geographical coordinate system, By combining these equations, we can get the transformation relation between radar coordinate system and geographical coordinate system [8–10].

$$S^r(x^r, y^r, z^r) = R_p^r R_b^P S^b(x^b, y^b, z^b) \tag{5}$$

$$R_{\mathrm{p}}^{\mathrm{r}} = (R_{\mathrm{b}}^{p})^{-1} = (R_{b}^{p})^{\mathrm{T}}$$

$$= \begin{bmatrix} \cos\varphi & \sin\varphi\sin\gamma & -\sin\varphi\cos\gamma \\ 0 & \cos\gamma & \sin\gamma \\ \sin\varphi & -\sin\gamma\cos\varphi & \cos\varphi\cos\gamma \end{bmatrix} \tag{6}$$

2 Stable Platform Driver Established

The maximum driving force of the stable platform is a key parameter in its design. The motor cylinder is responsible for the disturbance compensation of the horizontal swing and the vertical swing direction respectively. Therefore, in the initial analysis stage of engineering design, the two dimensions need to be considered separately. According to Fig. 2 the design specifications, the working conditions of the stabilized platform are set to five sea conditions, and the radar load should be able to rotate at a constant speed of $9°/s10$. In the working state, the radar carried by the stable platform must carry on the rotation motion besides the horizontal and vertical direction stability compensation. This process is very complex when performing dynamic analysis and calculating the driving forces required. In order to determine the maximum driving force of the stabilized platform, it must be done in the extreme condition of non-inertial condition, that is, when the load radar and the driving branch chain are on the same side, the driving force needed is the maximum [11].

$$\begin{cases} M_a = T_1 + T_2 = J_x\ddot{\beta} + mgl\cos\theta_1 + mgd\sin\theta_1 \\ \quad = F_a(\sin\theta_1\sin\theta_2 + \cos\theta_1\cos\theta_2)L_1 \\ \quad J_x = \dfrac{m(b^2+h^2)}{12} + m(d^2 + l^2) \\ \quad \tan\theta_2 = \dfrac{L_1(1-\cos\theta_1)}{L_1\sin\theta_1+H} \\ \quad F_a = M_a/(L_1 \cdot \cos\theta_1) \end{cases} \tag{7}$$

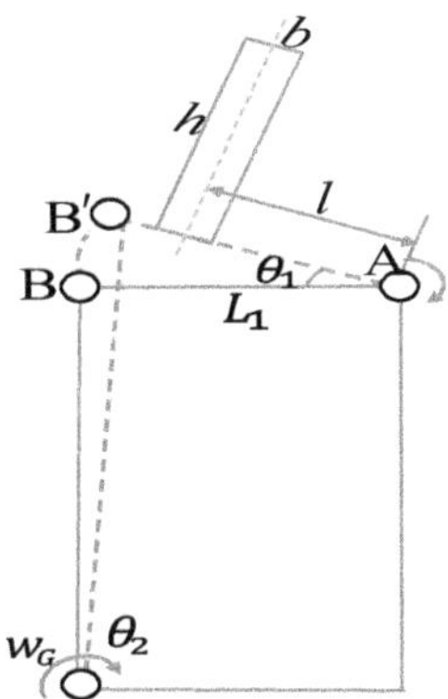

Fig. 2. Analysis diagram of driving force under roll state

3 Simulation Analysis and Establishment

3.1 The establishment of brief model

Because the mechanical structure is more complex, this paper chooses to use SOLID-WORKS software for drawing, and then the design drawings are imported into Adams software for simulation analysis. As the mechanical structure contains a large number of parts, there is a need to simplify or delete some parts that do not affect the simulation results, while assigning appropriate material properties to the model according to the design requirements.Considering the total weight of the upper load turntable and the antenna is 1800kg, the position of the center of gravity is determined based on the model of the antenna turntable, and the mass distribution of the turntable is assumed to be uniform. On this basis, the simulation model in Adams is constructed [12] (Fig. 3).

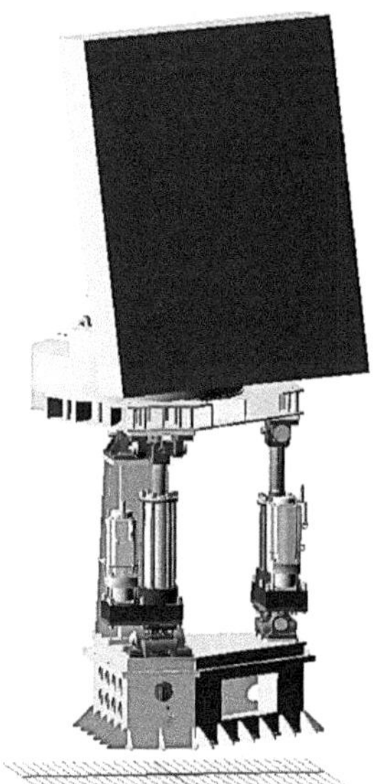

Fig. 3. ADAMS simulation model

According to the Fig. 4, Euler's rotation theorem the conversion between coordinate systems can be accomplished by rotating on three axes. The main factors that affect the radar performance are the angle of the ship's horizontal swing and the angle of the ship's vertical swing. At the beginning, the direction of the ship-borne coordinate system is consistent with that of the geographical coordinate systemb. It can be considered that the ship-borne coordinate system rotates the angle around the y axis of the geographical coordinate system B, and then rotates the angle around the x axis of the geographical coordinate system, the new shipboard coordinate system P is obtained. Its rotation matrix can be expressed as [13].

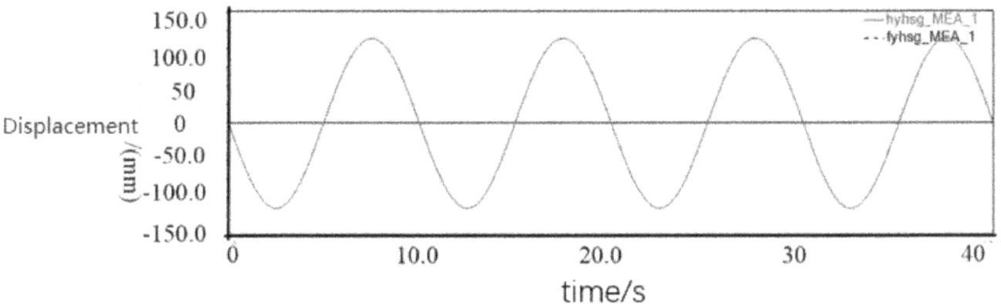

Fig. 4. Displacement curve of electric cylinder when rolling

In the radar coordinate system, Fig. 5 the vector in the geographic coordinate system corresponding to a certain point. In order to ensure the stable relationship between the radar coordinate system and the geographical coordinate system, the corresponding coordinate transformation must be carried out. Combined with the formula. we can deduce the following relation: where is the rotation matrix of the radar coordinate system relative to the geographical coordinate system, By combining these equations, we can get the transformation relation between radar coordinate system and geographical coordinate system [14].

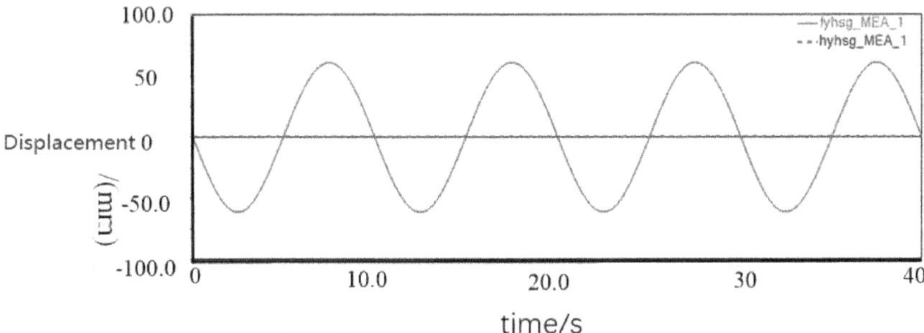

Fig. 5. Displacement curve of electric cylinder during pitching

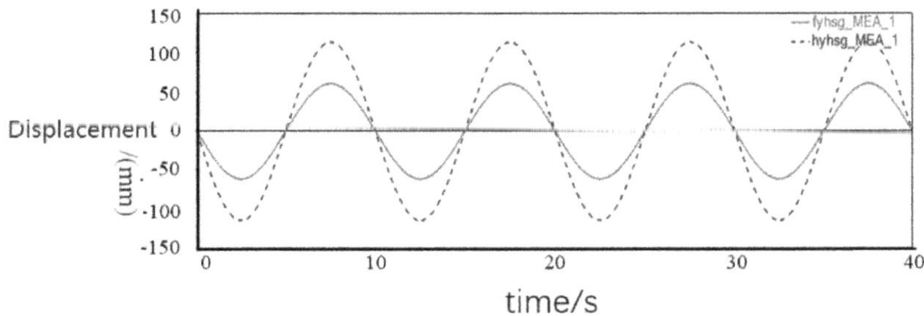

Fig. 6. Displacement curve of electric cylinder during composite Motion

when pitching alone, there is no coupling effect between the two cylinders, only the pitching branch chain is in periodic motion with an amplitude of about 125 mm. Maximum thrust of the pitching cylinder in motion, which is approximately 24209 N, while the drive force of the rolling cylinder is negligible. The accuracy of the previously established driving force Eq. (8) can be verified by comparing with the driving force curve of the electric cylinder in the figure.

In order to probe into the motion characteristics of the stable platform, the displacement of the electric cylinder under the combined motion condition is compared with that under the single rolling or pitching motion condition, the coupling effect between two branch chains in compound motion can be analyzed. Here's an enlarged graphic:

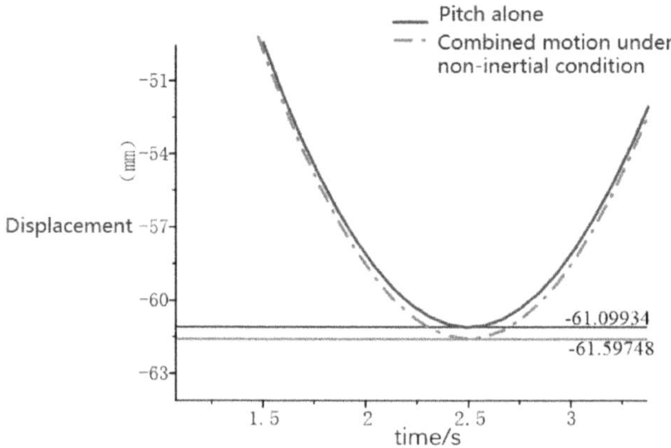

Fig. 7. Comparison of pitch strut coupling during pitch and compound

In the Euler's rotation theorem, by analyzing Figs. 6 and 7 in the rotation order of y-x-z, we can draw the following conclusion: due to the unique structural design of the stable platform, in the state of compound motion, there is no mutual coupling between rolling branch chains, but the pitching branch chain shows a certain degree of coupling. However, the maximum length of coupling is only 0.49 mm, which has relatively little effect on the branch chain displacement. Therefore, the decoupling compensation of the pitching branch chain is relatively easy to realize in the position control, whereas the rolling branch chain does not need decoupling compensation. In the 5.0 class sea condition, the two-degree-of-freedom platform not only performs the above-mentioned compound motion, but also moves with the sway of the hull. According to the steady-state isolation equation, we know that it is only necessary to apply a driving function at the spherical joint in the opposite direction of the compound motion, the displacement curves of rolling and pitching electric cylinder under inertial condition can be calculated. Furthermore, using AKISPL function, we can get the thrust change curves of rolling and pitching electric cylinders under five-stage sea conditions.

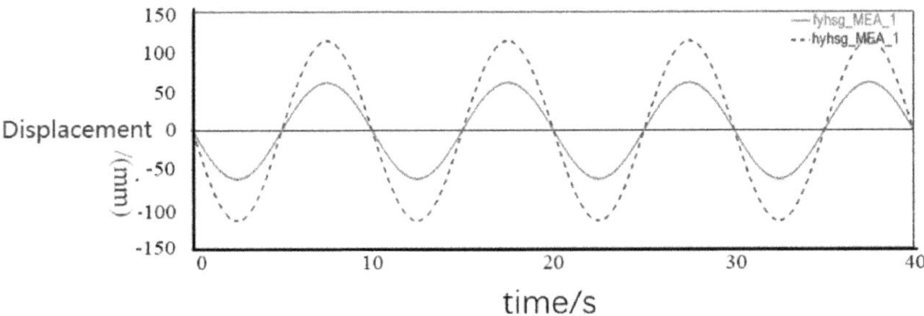

Fig. 8. Displacement curve of composite motion electric cylinder under five-stage sea state

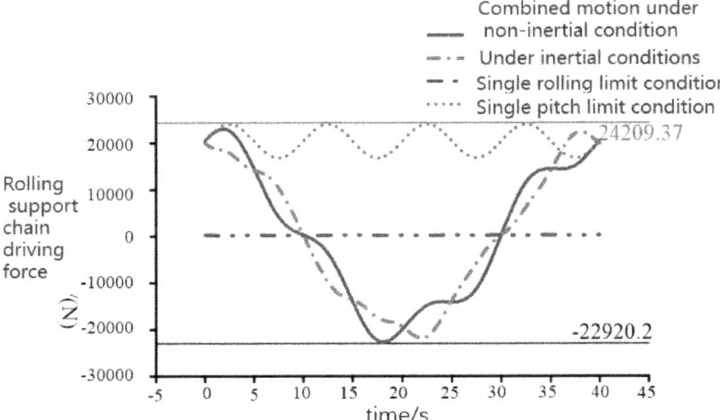

Fig. 9. Cylinder drive force curves of electric cylinders under different operating conditions

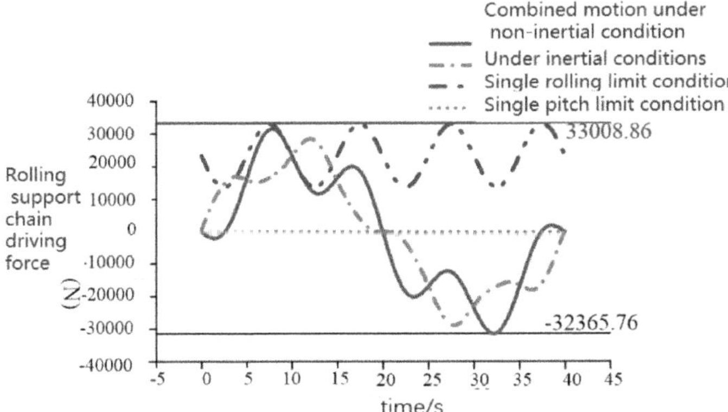

Fig. 10. Driving force curve of transverse swing motorized cylinder under each working condition

In Fig. 8, the displacement curves of the two electric cylinders are fitted and compared with the displacement curves under non-inertial conditions, a process that verifies the effectiveness of both inertial and non-inertial combined motions, the motion characteristics of the electric cylinder are consistent. This finding has important reference value for establishing the speed control strategy of the stable platform. As can be seen from Figs. 9 and 10, the maximum driving force of the two cylinders under inertial conditions is less than the maximum push-pull force under non-inertial conditions. However, under the same posture, the driving force under all working conditions is less than that under the limit state. Therefore, in the design of parallel stable platform, only the limit state under non-inertial condition should be considered, and the maximum driving force equation is used to calculate the design driving force of the driving branch chain. This provides an important reference for the preliminary engineering design of the two-degree-of-freedom stabilized platform.

4 Conclusion

In this paper, a new type of two-degree-of-freedom (2-dof) radar stabilized platform is proposed, which adopts electric cylinder as driving branch chain. The virtual prototype was built with Adams software, and the kinematics and dynamics simulation were completed. The simulation results show that there is no coupling between the two chains when the platform is rolling or pitching alone14. The roll support chain is not affected by the coupling, but the pitch support chain is affected by the coupling of roll angle, but the influence is very small, so the stable platform has high control precision. Through the dynamic simulation analysis, the driving force required under all conditions is less than the driving force under the limit state, and the accuracy of the established driving force equation is verified. This discovery has important engineering application value for the design and research of two-degree-of-freedom stable platform. Considering that the motion of radar stabilized platform is complex, and the load radar also has rotation motion, the research method based on Adams provides a feasible simulation idea and research method for the design process of radar stabilization platform, which has important reference value.

References

1. Jinqiang, G., Jiarong, L., MingFeng, G.: Design of a 3DOF XYZ Bi-directional motion platform based on z-shaped flexure hinges. Micromachines **13**(1) (2021)
2. Donglin, T., Long, L.: Simulation evaluation of underwater robot structure and control system based on ADAMS. Open Comput. Sci. **13**(1) (2023)
3. Xinjian, Y.: Motion analysis of armored vehicle suspension based on ADAMS. J. Phys. Conf. Ser. **2365**(1) (2022)
4. Yongming, L., Lei, F., Zhuanzhe, Z., et al.: Analysis of the coaxiality–geometric hystere- sis model of a rotate vector reducer based on Ansys Adams. Mech. Sci. **13**(2) (2022)
5. Hashtrudi-Zaad, K., Salcudean, S.E.: Analysis of control architectures for teleoperation systems with impedance/admittance master and slave manipulators. Int. J. Robot. Res. **20**(6), 419–445 (2001)

6. Ha, Q.P., Nguyen, Q.H., Rye, D.C., et al.: Impedance control of a hydraulically actuated robotic excavator. Autom. Constr. **9**(5–6), 421–435 (2000)
7. Johansson, R., et al.: Sensor integration in task-level programming and industrial robotic task execution control. Ind. Robot Int. J. **31**(3), 284–296 (2004)
8. Blomdell, A., Bolmsjo, G., Brogardh, T., et al.: Extending an industrial robot controller: implementation and applications of a fast open sensor interface. IEEE Robot. Autom. Mag. **12**(3), 85–94 (2005)
9. Abele, E., Weigold, M., Rothenbucher, S.: Modeling and identification of an industrial robot for machining applications. Ann. CIRP **56**(1), 387–390 (2007)
10. Brock, O., Kuffner, J., Xiao, J.: Motion Manipulation for tasks. In: Springer Hand- book of Robotics 1st ed. B. Siciliano and O. Khatib Eds. Berlin Heidelberg Germany, ch. 26 pp. 615–645, 2008
11. Matthias, B., Kock, S., Jerregard , H., et al.: Safety of collaborative industrial robots: certification possibilities for a collaborative assembly robot concept. Assembly Manuf. IEEE Int. Sympos. 1–6 (2011)
12. Ajoudani, A., Tsagarakis, N., Bicchi, A.: Teleimpedance:teleoperation with impedance regulation using a body machine interface. Int. J. Robot. Res. **31**(13), 1642–1655 (2012)
13. Kock, S., Vittor, T., Matthias, B., et al.: Robot concept for scalable, flexible assembly automation: a technology study on a harmless dual-armed robot. IEEE Int. Sympos. Assembly Manuf. 1–5 (2011)
14. Nof, S.Y., Wilhelm, W.E., Warnecke, H.:Industrial assembly. Springer Science Business Media (2012)

Design and Research of Wireless Image Systems Based on OFDM+QAM and Turbo Coding, as Well as MMSE Channel Estimation

Wang Xiaojing and Geng Jingjing[⊠]

Wuhan Vocational College of Software and Engineering, Wuhan 430205, China
20815552@qq.com

Abstract. The wireless image transmission system has a wide range of applications in high-definition video surveillance, remote medical image transmission, virtual reality, and augmented reality. With the support of 5G networks, the wireless image transmission system can achieve longer distance transmission, faster data transfer, and more stable connections, enhancing user experience and system performance. This article designs a wireless image transmission system based on OFDM+QAM and Turbo coding, as well as MMSE channel estimation. According to the basic principles and common algorithms of OFDM modulation/demodulation and Turbo coding, algorithm simulations were conducted to obtain corresponding performance curves, comparing the impact of different QAM modulation methods on the clarity of received images with SNR, summarizing the SNR requirements needed to meet the error rate for high-definition image transmission, and providing guidance for the design of 5G wireless image transmission systems.

Keywords: 5G · OFDM · Turbo · QAM · MMSE · SNR

1 Introduction

The wireless image transmission system is a system that utilizes wireless technology for image transmission [1]. It can transmit image signals through a wireless network to remote devices such as mobile phones, tablets, or computers. The wireless image transmission system can be applied in various fields such as surveillance systems, medical image transmission, camera image transmission, etc. In the context of 5G networks, the wireless image transmission system can be used in areas like high-definition video surveillance, remote medical image transmission, virtual reality, and augmented reality applications. With the support of

This research was funded by Wuhan Vocational College of Software and Engineering (Wuhan Open University) and Hubei Engineering Research Center for Intelligent Detection and Identification of Complex Parts under Research Program Grants # GCZX-XN-202409.

R. C. Qiu et al. (Eds.): IoTaaS 2024, LNICST 675, pp. 248–256, 2026.
https://doi.org/10.1007/978-3-032-14681-6_22

5G networks, the wireless image transmission system can achieve longer-distance transmission, faster data transfer, and more stable connections, enhancing user experience and system performance. Overall, the proliferation of 5G networks will bring more opportunities and application scenarios for the wireless image transmission system, offering users a superior image transmission experience.

Based on OFDM+QAM and Turbo coding as well as MMSE channel estimation, the wireless image transmission system is an efficient and reliable wireless communication system. The system utilizes Orthogonal Frequency Division Multiplexing (OFDM) technology to divide image data into multiple subcarriers for transmission, employs QAM modulation for signal modulation, enhances signal error tolerance through Turbo coding, and reduces channel transmission errors using Minimum Mean Square Error (MMSE) channel estimation technique.

2 Design and Implementation of Wireless Image Transmission System

Based on OFDM+QAM, Turbo coding, and MMSE channel estimation, the data processing flow of the wireless image transmission system is as Fig. 1:

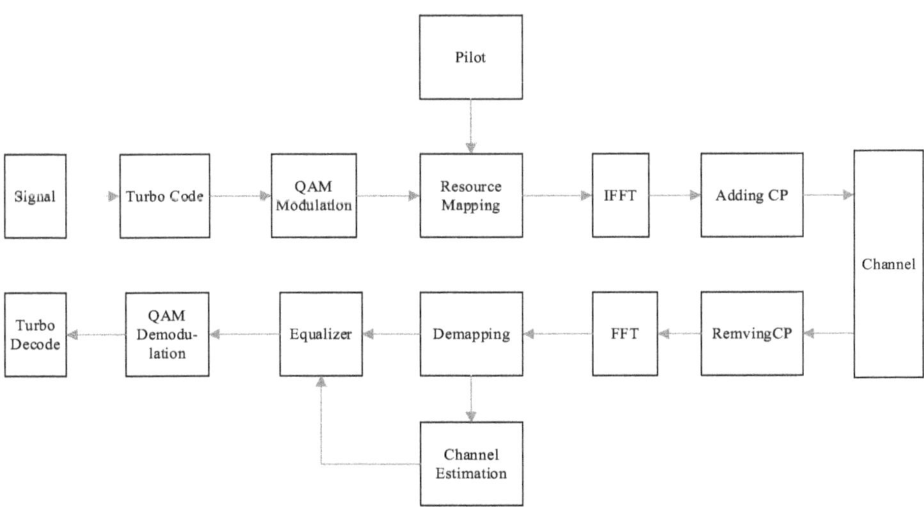

Fig. 1. Data processing flow of the wireless image transmission system.

OFDM [2] is a kind of multicarrier transmission technology that divides high-speed data into multiple low-speed subcarriers for transmission, which can effectively resist multipath fading and frequency-selective fading. In wireless image transmission, OFDM divides the image data into multiple subcarriers for simultaneous transmission, improving the data transmission rate and reliability. In

OFDM, the process of modulating the input signal $x(t)$ into the baseband signal $X(k)$ can be represented by Discrete Fourier Transform (DFT).

$$X(k) = \sum_{n=0}^{N-1} x(n)e^{-j\frac{2\pi}{N}kn} \tag{1}$$

Among them, $x(n)$ is the original input signal, and N is the number of subcarriers.

2.1 QAM Modulation

QAM (Quadrature Amplitude Modulation) is a common modulation technique used in digital communication to transmit data. It represents digital information by simultaneously varying the phase and amplitude of a signal, enabling efficient data transmission. Digital data is segmented into multiple bit groups and each bit group is mapped to a specific signal point. These signal points are located on a complex plane where the real axis represents the signal's amplitude and the imaginary axis represents the signal's phase. By changing the signal's phase and amplitude, different digital information can be represented. This paper discusses the design based on two modulation methods: 16QAM and 64QAM [3] (Figs. 2, 3 and Table 1).

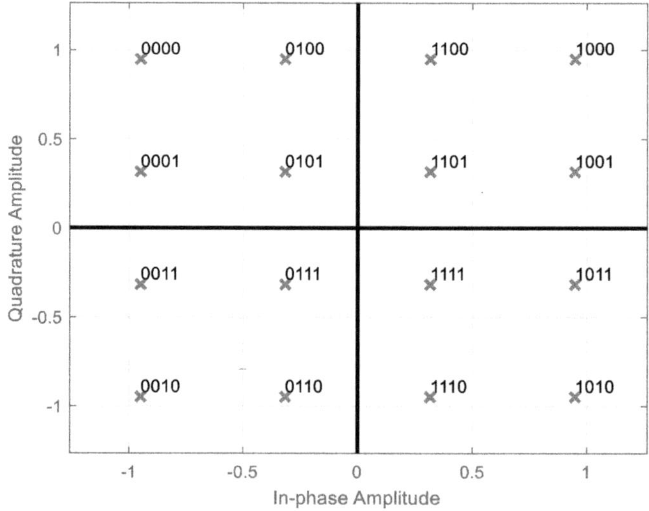

Fig. 2. 16QAM, Gray Mapping.

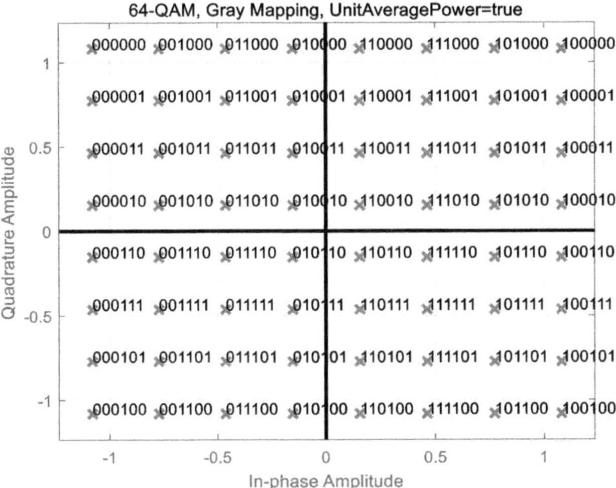

Fig. 3. 64QAM, Gray Mapping.

Table 1. 16QAM Mapping Coordinates.

4Bit	IQdata	4Bit	IQdata
0000	−0.9487+0.9487i	1000	0.9487+0.9487i
0001	−0.9487+0.3162i	1001	0.9487+0.3162i
0010	−0.9487−0.9487i	1010	0.9487−0.9487i
0011	−0.9487−0.3162i	1011	0.9487−0.3162i
0100	−0.3162+0.9487i	1100	0.3162+0.9487i
0101	−0.3162+0.3162i	1101	0.3162+0.3162i
0110	−0.3162−0.9487i	1110	0.3162−0.9487i
0111	−0.3162−0.3162i	1111	0.3162−0.3162i

In 16QAM modulation, every 4 bits are mapped to one constellation point. But In 64QAM modulation, every 6 bits are mapped to a constellation point.

2.2 Principles of QAM Demodulation

If we assume that the signal we receive is r, let's take a look at the formula for the i-th bit after demodulation:

$$L\left(b_i\right) = \ln\left(\frac{P\left(b_i = 1 \mid r\right)}{P\left(b_i = 0 \mid r\right)}\right) \tag{2}$$

This is a ratio of conditional probabilities, i.e., when the received signal is r, we infer based on the received signal's information whether the probability of this bit of the transmitted signal being 1 is greater or that of being 0 is greater (infer by reception to transmission).

$$r(t) = s(t) + n(t) \tag{3}$$

The noise superimposed on the channel is additive Gaussian white noise, so the received signal satisfies the Gaussian distribution. Then when the transmitted signal is s and the received signal is r, the conditional probability of the received signal is:

$$P(r \mid s) = \frac{1}{2\pi\sigma^2} e^{-\frac{(s-r)^2}{2\sigma^2}} \tag{4}$$

Equation (4) is a forward derivation, which is derived from sending to receiving, contrary to Eq. (2). According to Bayesian formula:

$$P(s \mid r) = \frac{P(s)P(r \mid s)}{P(r)} \tag{5}$$

Assuming that all symbols appear with equal probability, then bring Eq. (5) into Eq. (2):

$$L(b_i) = \ln\left(\frac{P(r \mid b_i = 1)}{P(r \mid b_i = 0)}\right) \tag{6}$$

When calculating $P(r|b_i = 0)$, according to the constellation diagram, calculate the distance $d = ||r - s(b_i = 0)||$ from r to each constellation point with $b_i = 0$, and then simplify it according to formula (4) when it is actually implemented.

① The constellation points modulated by QAM basically determine $b_i = 0$ or $b_i = 1$ according to rows or columns. When calculating the distance, it can be simplified to the distance from point r to a straight line parallel to the axis, that is, only the value of the real or imaginary part needs to be used.;

② The process of adding up all probabilities is simplified to finding only the largest probability value, that is, the distance value of r to the nearest constellation point when r $bi = 0$ or 1 ($b_i = 0$ or 1 for that constellation point);

③ In order to simplify the exponential operation, the probability P value is logarithmic to obtain the final LLR(log likelihood information) $= \ln(P(1)) - \ln(P(0))$.

3 Turbo Compiler Design and MMSE Channel Estimation

3.1 Turbo Encoder Design

The Turbo encoder consists of an internal interleaver and two component encoders, as shown in the figure below [4]. Except for the redesign of the internal interleaver, the component encoder structure used in the simulation is exactly the same as LTE. The role of the internal interleaver is somewhat similar to that of the channel interleaver. It is to disperse errors, which is conducive to the error correction of decoding, and has the effect of time diversity (burst errors are usually continuous in time, and the error correction code has low error correction ability for continuous errors.) (Fig. 4).

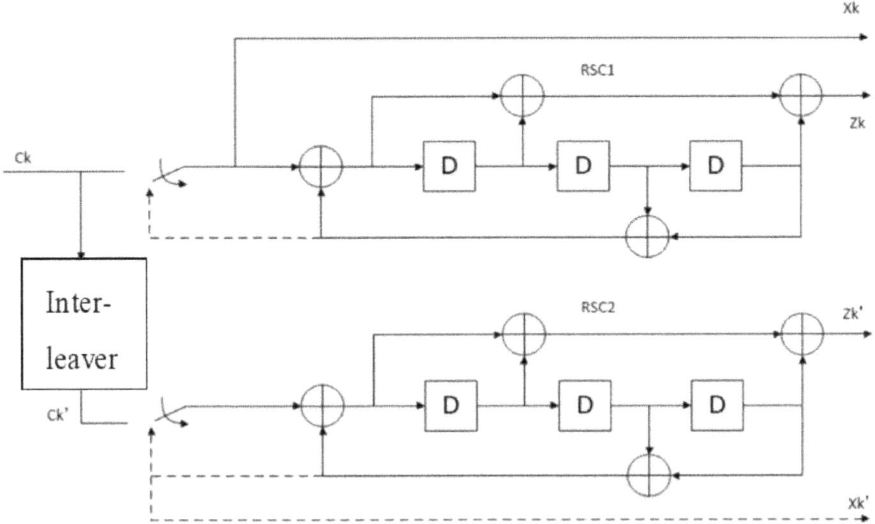

Fig. 4. Turbo encoder.

The bit rate is 1/3. It contains the system bit Xk, the first component encoder outputs Zk, and the second component encoder outputs Xk'. When implemented in hardware, multiple bits are usually input at a time, and multiple bits of output are obtained through a look-up table, and the status value is updated.

3.2   Turbo Decoding

Turbo decoding is an encoding and decoding technology that uses iterative decoding algorithms to improve the performance of bit error rate. Through the interaction between multiple encoders, it achieves better performance than traditional decoding methods. The Turbo decoding algorithm uses the Max-log-map algorithm, which is a commonly used algorithm in Turbo decoding. It combines maximum likelihood estimation and logarithmic cost function to estimate the output of the encoder by calculating the logarithmic probability, so as to achieve a more efficient decoding process. The algorithm can effectively reduce the computational complexity required for decoding and improve the accuracy and efficiency of decoding (Fig. 5).

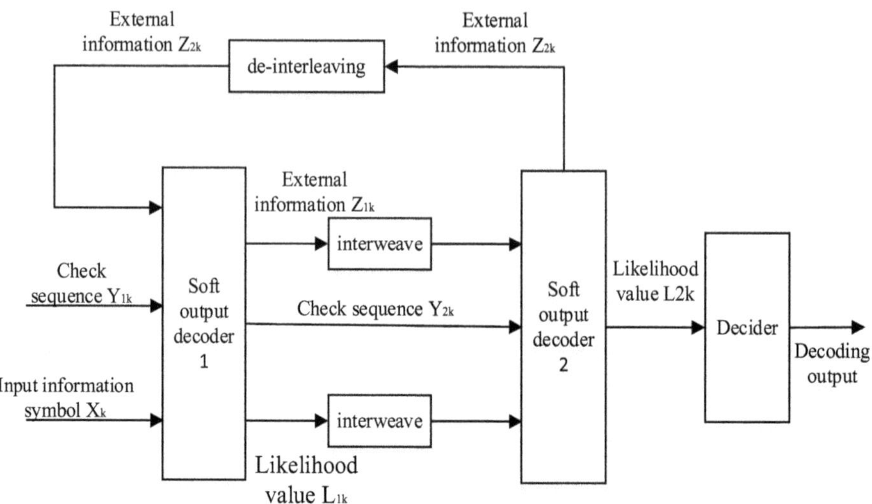

Fig. 5. Turbo decoder.

3.3   MMSE Channel Estimation

MMSE, which stands for Minimum Mean Squared Error, is an optimization criterion widely used in estimation theory, signal processing, and statistics. The MMSE estimator aims to find an estimation method that minimizes the mean squared error between the estimated values and the true values. In signal processing, MMSE is commonly used for channel estimation and equalization, signal detection, and filtering problems. For example, in wireless communications, channel estimation is a key issue due to signal attenuation, multipath propagation, and interference caused by the wireless channel. The MMSE channel estimator utilizes the received signal and known channel statistical characteristics to estimate the channel's state, enabling compensation and recovery of the signal at the receiving end [5].

An important feature of MMSE channel estimation is that it considers not only the signal noise but also the signal's prior information (if available). This allows the MMSE estimator to perform well even at low signal-to-noise ratios (SNR). Unlike the maximum signal-to-noise ratio (SNR) criterion, the MMSE criterion focuses on the variance of estimation errors rather than the SNR. Therefore, while the design and implementation of MMSE estimators may be more complex, they generally provide more accurate estimation results.

4   System Performance Analysis

Utilizing software for system simulation of 64QAM-OFDM and 16QAM-OFDM coded modulation signals, investigating the impact of baseband rate, coding algorithm, concatenation algorithm, modulation format changes on the performance of wireless image transmission systems. In the simulation system, the transmission end first converts the image into a binary data stream, then processes the signal with Turbo coding, QAM modulation, resource mapping, IFFT, serial-to-parallel conversion, and other procedures. After completing the signal encoding and modulation process, the system outputs I/Q dual signals with CP added, which then enter the channel for transmission. Upon arrival at the receiving end, the reverse operations are conducted. The signal undergoes parallel-to-serial conversion, FFT, serial-to-parallel conversion, QAM demapping, Turbo decoding, and utilizes MMSE to estimate the channel transfer function, compensating the received signal to restore the original image.

The comparison of received images under different SNRs using 16QAM and 64QAM modulation schemes is illustrated in Fig. 6 and Fig. 7:

Fig. 6. 16QAM, SNR = [4,6,8,10]dB.   **Fig. 7.** 64QAM, NR = [6,8,10,12]dB.

Under the comparison of BER under two modulation methods in Fig. 8 and Fig. 9.

From the results, it can be seen that when transmitting images of the same resolution, 64QAM requires a higher SNR; with SNR = 12, using 16QAM design, the bit error rate (BER) is approximately 0.01%; while under the same SNR conditions, the 64QAM modulation scheme has a much higher error rate, with BER greater than 1%; typically, the required BER for image transmission is below 0.1%, if using 64QAM modulation, an SNR exceeding 20 dB is needed.

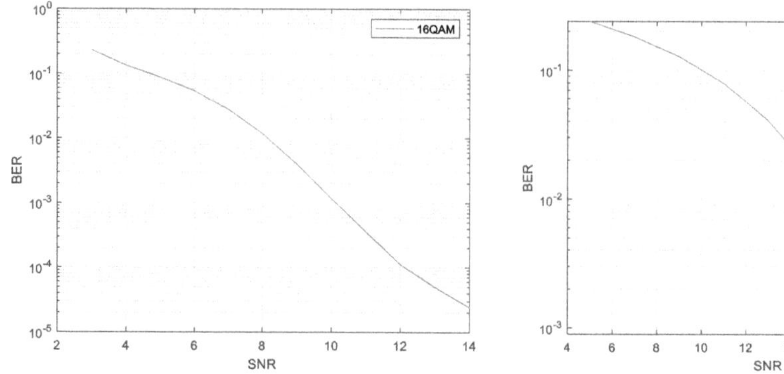

Fig. 8. 16QAM, SNR v BER.   **Fig. 9.** 64QAM, SNR v BER.

5   Conclusion

The article presents a wireless image transmission system design based on OFDM +QAM, Turbo coding, and MMSE channel estimation, investigating the impact of modulation scheme and SNR on the clarity of received images. It is observed that the higher the modulation order, the higher the performance requirements on SNR for the transmission system. Due to the higher modulation order leading to increased modulation efficiency, especially in practical applications such as 5G wireless image transmission systems, higher-order modulations are often chosen to increase system transmission rates, concurrently imposing higher demands on signal quality. The image transmission's required bit error rate is below 0.1%, and if using 64QAM modulation, an SNR of over 20 dB is needed.

References

1. Yang, L., Xuefan, Z., Miao, S., Lixu, H.: Intelligent of image transmission system based on wireless sensor network technology. Electron. Measur. Technol. **45**(08), 155–160 (2022)
2. Yue, Z., Peng, X., XiaoYv, L.: Research and analysis of channel estimation of OFDM system based on LSTM network. Comput. Inf. Technol. **30**(02), 49–52 (2022)
3. Wei, W.: Design of high order QAM demapper. Commun. Technol. **54**(03), 563–567 (2021)
4. Jiao, L., Rui, S., Na, Z.: Turbo-64qam-OFDM optical transmission. Syst. Simul. Technol **17**(02), 114–117+122 (2021)
5. Xiaoyan, W., Gaokui, G.: Pilot based channel estimation algorithm for OFDM systems. Industr. Technol. Innovation **5**(2), 16 (2018)

The Application Practice of Virtual Reality Technology for Integrating Computer Vision and Natural Language Processing

Libin Lu[✉]

School of Information Engineering, Wuhan City Polytechnic, Wuhan 430064, China
`lulibin@whcp.edu.cn`

Abstract. This paper discusses the integrated application of computer vision (CV) and computer vision (CV) technology in the virtual reality (VR) environment, aiming to enhance the sense of reality, interaction and intelligence of VR experience through the integration of deep technology. The research focuses on how to use CV to capture and understand users' non-verbal behavior, combined with NLP to analyze user language instructions, to achieve more natural and efficient user-environment interaction, so as to promote the innovative application of VR technology in education, medical care, entertainment and other fields.

Keywords: Computer Vision (CV) · Natural Language Processing (NLP) · Virtual Reality (VR)

1 Introduction

As an important branch of artificial intelligence, the computer vision system (ComputerVision, CV) automatically analyzes and understands images and video materials by simulating a human vision system. The application of CV technology with motion capture, facial expression analysis, environment modeling and recognition in virtual reality. Through CV technology, VR system can capture the user's body movements and facial expressions in real time, generate virtual characters and scenes, and synchronize with the user's movements, improving the sense of reality and interaction of the virtual environment.

NLP (Nature Language Processing, NLP) is an important field of computer science and artificial intelligence, aiming at realizing the understanding and generation of human language. It is mainly reflected in speech recognition, semantic understanding and natural language generation, etc., and NLP technology is applied to virtual reality. Through NLP technology, VR system can parse the user's language instructions and produce corresponding reactions, and realize the natural communication and interaction of language.

R. C. Qiu et al. (Eds.): IoTaaS 2024, LNICST 675, pp. 257–265, 2026.
https://doi.org/10.1007/978-3-032-14681-6_23

Systems that combine computer vision with natural language processing and apply it to virtual reality can greatly improve user immersion and interactivity – brings about entirely new applications in both education and healthcare. For example, teachers can use computer vision and natural language processing technology to analyze students 'gestures, and remotely guide students to conduct experimental operations; doctors can use computer vision and natural language processing technology to analyze patients' rehabilitation movements and feedback information, and remotely guide patients to conduct rehabilitation training – Everything in the virtual world of virtual reality.

2   Literature Review

2.1   Applications of Computer Vision Technology in VR

Movement recognition technology is an important application field of computer vision to realize natural human-machine interaction. In recent years, deep learning-based action recognition algorithms such as convolutional neural network (CNN) and long and short-term memory network (LSTM) have significantly improved their accuracy and real-time performance. For example, Microsoft's Kinect system enables natural human-computer interaction, capturing the user's body movements through a depth camera; LeapMotion and other devices capture gestures through optical sensors, which are widely used in VR systems [1].

Facial expression analysis technology can capture the user's facial expressions and identify its emotional state, thus achieve more natural and intelligent interaction in VR, such as DeepFace deep learning model, by analyzing the user's facial images to accurately identify the emotional change, in social VR application has important application value, can significantly improve the user's immersion and interactive experience, so is widely used in this field.

Environmental recognition technology makes the VR system have a great improvement in generating virtual scenes that are highly consistent with the real environment, mainly by scanning and modeling the surrounding environment. SLAM technology can build 3D environment models in real time and is widely used in augmented reality and virtual reality systems. Environmental recognition technology is an important means to help users to move and interact freely in the virtual environment, which can enhance the immersion and interactivity of the VR system.

2.2   Application of Natural Language Processing in VR

Speech recognition technology enables the system to understand the user's language instructions, which is achieved by converting the user's voice signals into text. In recent years, deep learning-based speech recognition algorithms such as Google's WaveNet and Baidu's DeepSpeech have made significant progress in recognition accuracy and response speed. The application of these technologies enables VR systems to understand and respond to users' voice commands more accurately.

3   Comprehensive Framework Design

In order to improve the application of computer vision and natural language processing technology in the virtual reality system, a comprehensive framework design is proposed, which consists of three main parts: VR content creation and real-time interactive environment adaptability adjustment.

In terms of VR content creation, the use of computer vision technology for 3D modeling and environment recognition, and combined with natural language processing technology to generate rich interactive content, is one of the current research hotspots. Specifically, the use of deep learning algorithm to identify the user's movements and expressions, and through the NLP model resolve the user's language instruction, generate the corresponding virtual environment and interactive content, using convolutional neural network for three-dimensional modeling, combined with long short-term memory network resolve the user's voice commands, generate the corresponding virtual scene and interactive content, in this way to achieve immersive interactive experience [2].

In terms of real-time interaction, the real-time response and interaction of the system is combined with natural language processing technology. To this end, this paper adopts some advanced CV algorithms for efficient action recognition and speech processing, such as convolutional neural network (CNN) and LSTM. For example, in the virtual teaching system, combined with LSTM to analyze students 'voice problems, CNN is used to capture students' gestures in real time, and provide corresponding experimental guidance and feedback in real time [3].

In terms of environmental adaptability adjustment, the system constantly monitors the user status through computer vision technology, constantly adjusts the virtual environment to improve the user experience, and analyzes the user feedback combined with natural language processing technology. For example, in the educational application, the system can dynamically adjust the difficulty and content of the virtual experiments, so as to achieve personalized learning experience according to the students' learning progress and feedback. In medical rehabilitation, the content and intensity of rehabilitation training can be adjusted dynamically according to the rehabilitation progress and feedback of patients, so as to achieve the purpose of improving the effect.

4   Technical Implementation Details

4.1   Computer Vision Algorithms

Motion capture: deep learning algorithms such as convolutional neural network (CNN) and long and short-term memory network (LSTM) are used to realize high-precision capture and real-time recognition of users' body movements. CNN is used to extract action features, and LSTM is used to capture the temporal features of the action sequence, combined to achieve efficient action recognition and real-time feedback.

Facial expression analysis: deep convolutional neural network (DCNN) and emotion classifier are used to capture users 'facial expressions in real time and identify users' emotional states. For example, the pre-trained VGG-Face model is used to extract facial features and identify emotions combined with the emotion classifier (e.g., Support Vector Machine, SVM).

Environment recognition and modeling: SLAM (Simultaneous Localization Mapping) technology is used to scan and model the environment around the user in real time to generate virtual scenes that are highly consistent with the real environment. High-precision environmental modeling and dynamic adjustment are achieved through the fusion of depth images and RGB images.

4.2   Natural Language Processing Models

Speech recognition: Using deep learning speech recognition algorithms (such as WaveNet and DeepSpeech) to convert the user's speech signals into text, so as to achieve high-precision speech recognition. Recognition accuracy and response speed were optimized by pre-trained models and speech repositories.

Semantic understanding: conduct semantic analysis of the user's language instructions, understand the user's intention, and use pre-trained language models such as BERT and GPT. For example, semantic features are extracted through BERT model and identified with intention classifier (e.g. Multi-Leveloper, MLP).

Natural language generation: Use generative models (such as GPT-3) to achieve a natural dialogue with users and produce a natural and fluent language response. Ensure the diversity and coherence of language generation, training and optimizing generative models through a large-scale corpus.

5   User Feedback Loop Mechanism

In order to continuously optimize and improve the performance and personalized experience of the system, this paper puts forward the user feedback loop mechanism, including the following three steps: user behavior monitoring-feedback analysis-system adjustment: in order to achieve the purpose of continuous improvement.

User Behavior Monitoring. Computer vision technology is applied to monitor the users 'body movements, facial expressions and environmental changes in real time, and record the user's behavior data for analysis and mining.

Feedback Analysis. Natural language processing technology is applied to analyze the user's voice feedback and text input to understand the user's intention and provide corresponding suggestions and answers. Specifically, after transcribing the speech feedback of the user, the feedback content is parsed through the semantic analysis model [4].

System Adjustment. Dynamically adjust the virtual environment and interactive content according to the user behavior data and feedback analysis results. For example, in educational applications, the difficulty and content of the experiment are adjusted according to the feedback of students; in medical rehabilitation, the content and intensity of rehabilitation training are adjusted according to the feedback from patients, etc.

6   Experiments and Application Cases

6.1   Educational Application Case

A virtual lab system for educational purposes has been developed for gesture control and voice commands to help students interact with virtual experiments. For example, in chemical experiments, students can use gestures to operate virtual experimental instruments such as a beaker or a test tube. At the same time, students can ask the system, "What is the basic principle of this chemical reaction?" The system will use natural language processing technology to analyze the questions raised by students, and give the corresponding explanations and guidance, so that students can have a more intuitive understanding of the concept of chemistry. The experimental results prove that with the help of the virtual laboratory system, students' interest and participation in learning have been significantly improved [5].

Test the system effectiveness after the results of, using the system to make students participation in chemical experiment increased by 30%, learning effect also increased by 25%, students generally reflect through gesture control and voice interaction can more effectively understand the experimental steps and principle, to make the learning experience more vivid and interesting.

6.2   Medical Application Case

A virtual training system combining computer vision and natural language processing techniques was developed in medical rehabilitation to assist patients in physical rehabilitation training. This system can capture the patient's recovery movements in real time and make posture analysis by using natural language to prompt the patient to adjust the correct movements and posture, so as to promote the improvement of the rehabilitation effect. For example, computer vision technology is used to detect the patient's arm Angle and movement trajectory, and natural language is used to prompt the patient to make corresponding movements and posture adjustment to achieve good rehabilitation effect. Some experiments have shown that this system can play an obvious role in promoting the rehabilitation progress and training effect of patients, especially in improving the accuracy and consistency of movements, so it is worth advocating the use of this system to carry out medical rehabilitation [6].

After many system test and validation, the results found that using the system of patient rehabilitation progress by 20%, training effect by more than 15%, participate in the tester think this is due to the real-time action capture and voice guidance, make the training process become more efficient and convenient, the patient's participation and training effect has significantly improved.

6.3 Entertainment Application Case

In entertainment applications, we developed a virtual role-playing game, users can through the natural language and virtual role complex dialogue, to enhance the interactive experience, through natural language virtual role-playing game, in the game, the user plays an adventurer, in the game can be with NPC (Non-PlayerPersonal) voice command dialogue. For example, a user can ask the NPC about tasks or ask the NPC for help. The system analyzes the user's language instructions through NLP technology, and interacts with the user naturally to generate the corresponding language response. The results show that the system can significantly enhance users' immersion and interactivity, making users feel truly involved in a more realistic game story and interactive virtual world [7].

User immersion and interactivity using the system have been significantly improved across multiple game companies and user groups, as tested and validated. Specific experimental data show that in virtual role-playing games, users' immersive feeling increased by 35% and their interactive ability increased by 40%. User feedback shows that through the dialogue between natural language and virtual characters, it not only makes the game story richer and more real, but also makes users feel that they really participate in the development of the game story, which greatly improves the fun and appeal of the game experience.

7 Results and Discussion

7.1 Analysis of Experimental Data

In the above experiments of education, medical and entertainment applications, we have collected a large amount of data, including user behavior data, system response data, user feedback data, etc. By analyzing these data, we can draw the conclusion:

Educational application: In the virtual laboratory system, students interact with the virtual experimental environment, through gesture control and voice interaction. The results showed that students' participation in using the system increased by 30 percent and their learning outcomes increased by 25 percent. This shows that the integration and application of computer vision and natural language processing technology can be significantly improved in the interactivity and teaching effect of the virtual education system.

Medical application: In the virtual rehabilitation training system, patients conduct motion capture, posture analysis and rehabilitation training through computer vision technology and voice prompt. The results showed that patients using this system accelerated their rehabilitation progress by 20%, and the training effect improved by 15%. This indicates that the integrated application of computer vision and natural language processing technology can be significantly improved in terms of the effectiveness and efficiency of rehabilitation training [8].

Entertainment application: In a virtual role-playing game, users talk to the virtual character through natural language, which enhances the immersion and interactivity of the game. Through the dialogue through natural language, the experimental results show that the users' immersive feeling increased by 35% and the interaction increased by 40%. This shows that the integration of computer vision and natural language processing technology can be significantly improved in terms of the user experience and interaction of virtual entertainment systems.

7.2 Technical Challenges

The experimental results are very encouraging, but there are still many challenges in the process of technology integration: first, technical difficulties may occur in the integration process; and second, the integration of different technologies may bring some incompatible aspects.

Data privacy protection: In either education or healthcare, the privacy of user data becomes particularly important. In order to ensure that users' privacy is not infringed, the system must strictly abide by the relevant data privacy protection regulations. For example, in the medical rehabilitation system, to say, the patient's action data and voice data must be kept strictly confidential to prevent leakage or abuse. Only by protecting the privacy of user data, can we ensure that users can get the best service in the process of using the system.

Computational resource requirements: Processing large amounts of image data and voice data has higher requirements on computing resources. In order to ensure the real-time performance and response speed of the system, the optimization of the algorithm and hardware configuration are essential to reduce the computing latency and improve the processing efficiency. For example, in the process of motion capture and speech recognition, it is necessary to optimize the algorithm and adopt high-performance hardware support to achieve the purpose of real-time processing and rapid response.

Cross-modal data fusion: There are significant differences between computer vision and natural language processing technologies in terms of data types, processing methods and timing synchronization, and how to effectively integrate and coordinate between these two technologies is an important topic of research. In order to achieve seamless collaboration and complementarity between different data modalities, more efficient data fusion algorithms need to be developed. For example, precise timing synchronization and data fusion techniques are required to synchronously process and respond to the user's gesture movements and voice commands.

7.3 Future Development Directions

Future developments include the application of deep learning technologies to further improve system intelligence, and strengthening interdisciplinary cooperation in VR technology applications in more fields.

Application of deep learning technology: combined with the application of advanced deep learning algorithm and the transformation and upgrading of the optimization process, a higher level can be achieved in the accuracy and efficiency of action recognition and speech processing. Specifically, a larger scale pre-training model is used as the vanguard for rapid pre-adaptation training. Then, the overall performance of the system is improved and transformed through a more efficient optimization algorithm.

Interdisciplinary cooperation: VR technology has a broad application prospect in many fields. Medical experts can work with computer scientists to develop telemedicine and rehabilitation systems. Experts in the field of education can cooperate with AI researchers to build personalized learning platforms and other innovative applications are expected to be implemented using VR technology. With the deepening of interdisciplinary cooperation. The application field of VR technology is expected to expand to more areas.

Exploration of emerging technologies: In addition to existing computer vision and natural language processing technologies, other emerging technologies applied in VR can also be explored in VR. For example, BCI (brain-computer interface) technology can directly read the brain signals of users, making the interaction between users more natural and intuitive; augmented reality technology (AdvancedReality, AR) can stack virtual information into real scenes to enhance the user's presence and interactivity.

8 Conclusion

This paper mainly discusses the fusion application of computer vision and natural language processing technology in the field of virtual reality, and analyzes the role of technology fusion in enhancing user immersion and interaction. The experimental results found that the combination of computer vision and natural language processing technology can significantly enhance the user experience of VR system, and expand its application potential in the fields such as education, healthcare and entertainment. In the future, it is necessary to pay attention to the challenges such as data privacy protection and computing resource optimization and cross-mode data fusion, and also to promote the sustainable development and innovative application of this cutting-edge technology to solve the current practical problems.

It is important for researchers and developers to continue to explore the deep integration of computer vision and natural language processing technology in virtual reality, develop more intelligent and efficient VR systems, and develop relevant standards and specifications to ensure the healthy development and wide application of technology. The joint efforts of various parties are made to realize revolutionary application of virtual reality technology in more fields, bring richer and real user experience to people, and then produce huge social and economic effects.

References

1. Zhang, M.: Research on multi-person gesture interaction based on Leap Motion in large screen environment. Hangzhou University of Electronic Science and Technology, Hangzhou, China (2023)
2. Chen, C.: Research on the influence of interaction mode on learning experience in immersive virtual experimental environment. Yangzhou University, Yangzhou, Chian (2023)
3. Zhang, E.: Research on dynamic human gesture detection and recognition technology based on computer vision. Beijing Institute of Technology, Beijing, China (2023)
4. Zhang, M.-H., et al.: Research on automatic measurement of cognitive input in immersive virtual reality environments. J. Dist. Educ. **41**(5), 76–85 (2024)
5. Xu, B.: Design and practice of chemistry teachers' workshop supported by virtual reality technology. Henan University, Zhengzhou, China (2019)
6. Zhao, J., et al.: Assessment device for limb movement rehabilitation training based on virtual reality technology. J. Jilin Univer. (Engineering Edition), pp. 1–9. (2024). https://doi.org/10.13229/j.cnki.jdxbgxb.20240066
7. Huang, C.-C.: Research and implementation of virtual reality game AI system based on reinforcement learning. Shenzhen University, Shenzhen, China (2020)
8. Yin, S.: Design and realization of walking rehabilitation training system based on virtual reality. Huazhong University of Science and Technology, Wuhan, China (2018)

LoRa Private Protocol Reversal and Network Topology Analysis Method Based on Network Trace

Weiqiang Li[1], Jiang Liu[2], Guang Hu[3], and Jin Liu[1(✉)]

[1] Wuhan University of Science and Technology, Wuhan, China
liujin@wust.edu.cn
[2] Inner Mongolia Branch of CNCERT, Hohhot, China
[3] Huazhong University of Science and Technology, Wuhan, China
huguang@hust.edu.cn

Abstract. As the LoRa communication technology is widely applied, the security issues of LoRa networks have become crucial. To detect certain non-compliant LoRa private networks and to assess the security performance of enterprise private LoRa protocols, this paper focuses on the problems of reverse engineering of unknown protocols and network topology restoration for LoRa. This paper proposes a method that combines RSSI fingerprint features with a weight-based data packet similarity calculation to differentiate network nodes, extract frequent sequences from different node information, and thereby delineate the frame format of unknown protocols, extract key protocol fields, and analyze the semantics of key fields. Through protocol reverse engineering, it discovers links in private LoRa networks, determines node identities, and restores the network topology structure. This paper improves the success rate of extracting address fields in unknown protocols and effectively identifies the number and behavior of network nodes.

Keywords: LoRa · Private Protocol Reverse · Network Topology Analysis

1 Introduction

As a long-distance communication technology, LoRa has the advantages of low power consumption and low cost [1]. More and more Internet of Things solutions will choose LoRa as the underlying communication protocol. Although the LoRa Alliance has launched a set of standard networking protocols for LoRaWAN, private protocols are still widely used on LoRa [2]. Networks with private protocols are difficult to supervise. Whether in network security maintenance or network attack and defense [3–5], reverse research on LoRa private protocols and network topology restoration of LoRa private protocols are of great research significance [6].

© ICST Institute for Computer Sciences, Social Informatics and Telecommunications Engineering 2026
Published by Springer Nature Switzerland AG 2026. All Rights Reserved
R. C. Qiu et al. (Eds.): IoTaaS 2024, LNICST 675, pp. 266–276, 2026.
https://doi.org/10.1007/978-3-032-14681-6_24

Reverse engineering link-layer protocols is difficult with limited prior knowledge. A challenge is to extract features and define formats with minimal prior knowledge, as well as to analyze key fields and semantics. Analyzing network topology involves identifying address fields to recognize nodes and their interactions [7].

In view of the physical layer characteristics of LoRa, different SF(Spreading Factor), Frequency Point and Sync Word together can form 600,000 communication channels that are not connected with each other [8], so it can be considered that all the data communicated on the same channel can be considered to use a communication protocol, or even come from the same network. Because of this feature, the work of reversing the LoRa private protocol and restoring the network topology is simplified to a certain extent.

2   Related Work

In current protocol reverse engineering research, Javad proposed a CNN-based protocol reverse engineering method CNNPRE [9], distinguishes private protocols using convolutional neural networks and employs the Needleman-Wunsch algorithm for key field extraction, but this method is suitable for the application layer and lacks relevant prior information in binary protocols, making it not well applicable to link-layer protocols. Liu proposed FEMBSC(Feature Extraction Method Base On Sequence Correlation) [10], which effectively determines the boundaries and semantics of unknown protocol fields through sequence correlation. Wang improved the FP-Growth algorithm to improve the efficiency of frequent item extraction, and extracted composite features in unknown protocols, further improving the accuracy of field extraction [11]. These methods effectively extract frequent items and their positional information. However, due to the large number of nodes in general networks, it is difficult to set an appropriate support threshold for the extraction of address fields.

Researchers have proposed automated protocol reverse engineering technologies, such as Biprominer and ProDecoder, which primarily focus on application-layer protocols. These systems are almost ineffective for binary protocols due to the lack of semantic information, making it difficult to distinguish identical binary sequences from various protocol messages [12,13]. Jiang proposed a novel field boundaries inference approach for protocol reverse engineering [14], has the good ability to infer field boundaries. Sun proposed BERRY, extracting variable-length field of binary network protocols from static traces [15].

Based on the reverse engineering of the LoRa private protocol, this article conducts identity analysis and network topology restoration of the nodes in the private protocol network. According to the current known research situation, there is no research on the direction of LoRa private protocol network topology restoration. The main work of this paper is: 1. Use the network tracking method to reverse the LoRa private protocol, use the FP-Growth algorithm to extract the composite features of the LoRa private protocol, and propose a weight-based data frame similarity calculation method combined with RSSI fingerprint features. Distinguish the communication data of different LoRa network nodes to reduce the calculation amount of FP-Growth, improve the recognition rate of key fields, and initially identify the number of nodes in the LoRa private protocol network. 2. Calculate the correlation degree of frequent sequences and determine the semantic information of key fields. 3. This article proposes a node behavior identification strategy based on the sliding window analysis method, analyzes the communication direction of data and the interactive behavior of network nodes in the LoRa private network, and restores the topological structure of the network.

3   System Design

This paper reverses and restores the network topology of LoRa private protocols based on Network trace, capturing network data with a sniffer and obtaining RSSI and timestamps as auxiliary features, as shown in Fig. 1, to simplify the analysis of private protocol networks. On the basis of protocol format division and semantic judgment, combined with the LoRa network behavior determination method proposed in this paper, the links in the private network are discovered, and the node behavior, node identity, and network type are judged. The overall flowchart is shown in Fig. 2. The system first preprocesses the sniffed data, then distinguishes the data of different nodes using the HDBSCAN clustering algorithm combined with RSSI features. After the data is distinguished, frequent items are extracted separately to obtain the longest frequent sequences. Then, by comparing the longest frequent sequences extracted from different node data, dynamic and static fields are identified, field boundaries are divided, and the address fields are mainly extracted. Finally, temporal analysis is performed on the network data to identify node behavior, node identity, and restore the network structure.

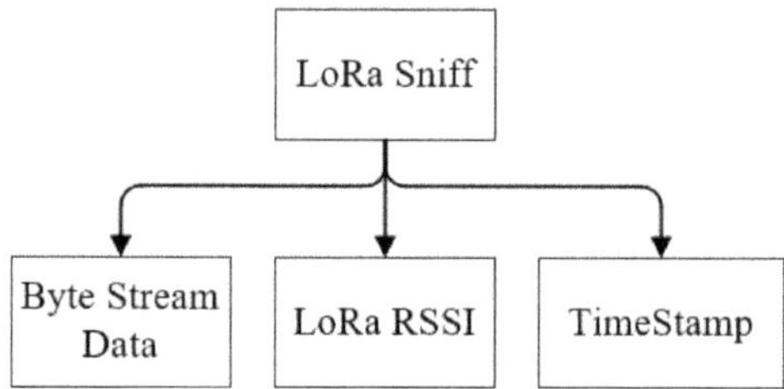

Fig. 1. Feature Information Captured by LoRa Sniffing.

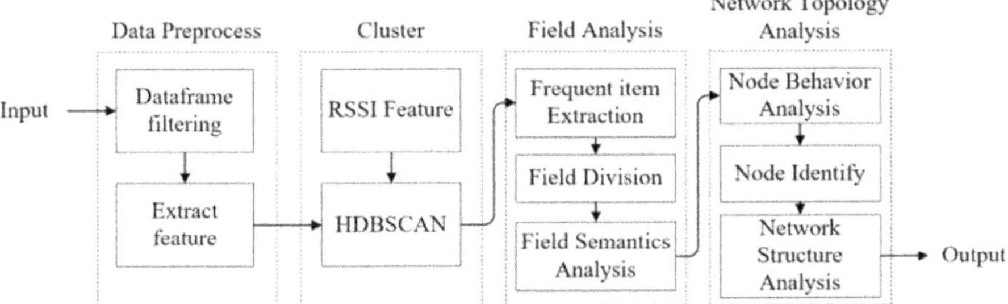

Fig. 2. Flowchart of LoRa Private Protocol Reverse Engineering and Network Topology Analysis.

3.1   Data Preprocess

According to research, essentially all wireless communication protocol data can be divided into two basic types: signaling frames and data frames. Since some wireless network protocols do not carry key fields such as address fields in their signaling frames, such as the ACK frames in Zigbee, it is necessary to distinguish between signaling frames and data frames when analyzing LoRa network data. This paper calculates the average length L_p of the network data, analyzes the length distribution status of the network data, and calculates the degree of deviation in data length:

$$Z_i = \frac{|L_i - L_p|}{L_p} \tag{1}$$

Z_i is the degree of deviation of the data length from the average length, where L_i is the length of the data item. Data with a deviation greater than 20% in the network data is statistically separated into short and long frames, with short frames considered as signaling frames and long frames as data frames in this paper.

After distinguishing the data frames, the features of the data are extracted by converting the message sequence into a hexadecimal numerical sequence, with each byte in the sequence regarded as a feature vector for subsequent clustering analysis.

3.2   FP-Growth Extract Composite Features

The key fields of a protocol are always frequent sequences, but frequent sequences are not necessarily key fields. Therefore, obtaining as many frequent sequences as possible is crucial for the candidate set of protocol keywords, making the statistics and analysis of frequent sequences essential for field segmentation.

This paper utilizes the FP-Growth algorithm to extract composite features from protocol messages, encapsulating each byte in the data sequence along with its offset as a sub-item of the sequence. If the original sequence $S_i = 1, 2, 1, 0, 5$, then the subitems of this sequence are $S_{i_0} = (1, 0)$, $S_{i_1} = (2, 1)$, $S_{i_2} = (1, 2)$,

$S_{i_3} = (0, 3)$, $S_{i_4} = (5, 4)$. This method prevents the influence of the same byte at different offsets on the extraction of frequent items, aids in field segmentation, and simplifies the identification and analysis of key fields such as control fields and addresses field in private protocols.

The concept of support is used to extract frequent items. Let the item set $\alpha = \alpha_1\alpha_2\alpha_3...\alpha_n$ and for a sequence $\beta = \beta_1\beta_2\beta_3...\beta_m$ in the network data, if $\alpha \subseteq \beta$, then the data sequence β is said to contain the subsequence α. The relationship of containment between this subsequence and all data sequences is calculated to obtain the support degree of the subsequence.

$$Sup_\alpha = \frac{\sum_{k=1}^{n}(\alpha \subseteq \beta)}{n} \tag{2}$$

$\sum_{k=1}^{n}(\alpha \subseteq \beta)$ is the total count of data sequences that contain the subsequence α, n is the total number of data sequences. When selecting frequent sequences. Selecting a Sup_min, sequences with a support greater than Sup_min are considered frequent sequences.

3.3 Node Data Discrimination Combined with RSSI Fingerprint Features

In networks, there are typically multiple nodes. When extracting frequent items of node IDs, the support of the address sequence tends to be low. This paper distinguishes the data of different nodes before extracting frequent sequences, and then extracts frequent sequences for each set of distinguished data. In this way, the support of the node address sequence is high, which allows for more accurate identification of the address fields.

LoRa is primarily applied in the IoT industry, where the geographical location of IoT devices typically does not change, so the RSSI of the devices is within a small fluctuation range in a short period of time. Therefore, by combining the idea of RSSI fingerprinting, node data is distinguished using data RSSI characteristics and frame header similarity features.

The address field is usually located in the frame header, and the frame headers of data from the same node have a higher degree of similarity. This paper proposes a data differentiation method that combines RSSI fingerprinting with a weight-based sequence similarity calculation method. Using RSSI and frame header sequence similarity as features, the HDBSCAN algorithm is employed for preliminary clustering of the data. The weight coefficient is W_i.

$$W_i = \frac{L}{1 + e^{k(i-i_0)}} \tag{3}$$

L is the maximum value of the curve, which is taken as 1 in this paper; e is the base of the natural logarithm; k is a positive coefficient that controls the steepness of the curve; i_0 is the midpoint of the curve, where the curve begins to decline. The formula for calculating the frame header distance between two sequences S_0 and S_1 is as follows.

$$D(S_0, S_1) = \sqrt{\sum_{i=0}^{n} W_i * (S_{0_i} - S_{1_i})^2} \tag{4}$$

This method can greatly optimize the clustering results, with each cluster to some extent representing a node.

3.4　Field Extraction Based on Association Rules

Based on the FP-Growth algorithm, count the frequent items with composite features in the distinguished node data. Calculate the confidence of the frequent items X and Y.

$$Conf(X, Y) = P(XY)/P(Y) \tag{5}$$

Specify a minimum confidence threshold $Conf_{min}$. If $Conf(X, Y) > Conf_{min}$ then $X rightarrow Y$ is considered a strong association rule. Concatenate frequent sequences using association rules to obtain the longest possible frequent sequence string. Analyze the offset position distribution of sub-items within the longest frequent itemsets in the network, segregate dynamic and static domains in the protocol, delineate field boundaries, and then conduct further analysis on the segmented fields.

When an address field is extracted from a frequent string, a frequent string that satisfies any of the following characteristics is added to the address sequence candidate set.

Exchangeability: Most communication protocols include target address and selfaddress fields. If there is a frequent sequence S_i of length $2n$, it is divided into two subsequences S_{i_1}, S_{i_2}, each of length n. By swapping the order of these two subsequences to form a new sequence S_{i_*}, if S_{i_*} is a subset of the frequent sequence set S, then the sequence S_i satisfies the exchangeability property. Sequences that meet the exchangeability property are selected to form a candidate set of address fields.

Continuity: If there are two frequent sequences of equal length whose offset positions are adjacent, add them to the candidate sequence set for the address field.

In some protocols, the address fields do not appear in pairs, so the aforementioned method is not applicable. By analyzing the dynamic fields within the protocol, if the sequences in the dynamic field have a high support within a cluster and a very low support in other clusters, they are judged to be unidirectional address fields.

Fields located before the address field are judged to be control fields, while fields after the address field are judged to be network identification fields.

3.5　Network Topology Analysis

This paper identifies node behavior, determines node identities, and analyzes network structures based on temporal analysis. As shown in Fig. 3, the communication time is divided into different intervals with a 0.1-second gap, and a

1-second sliding window is used to observe the message distribution characteristics within the window.

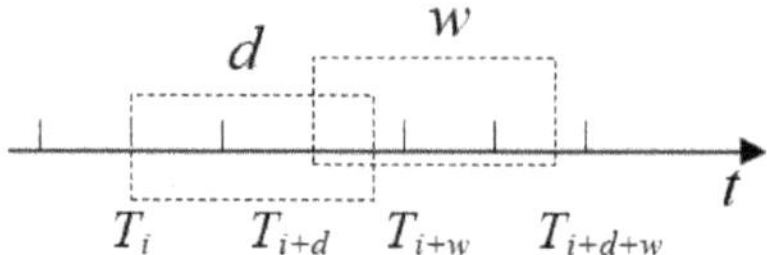

Fig. 3. Time Segmentation Chart.

Within a time window, if there are multiple communication data entries, analyze the address fields. Suppose there are nodes A and B; calculate the probability P that node B sends data immediately after node A sends data within a time window,$P = Conf(A, B)$. If $P > Conf_{min}$, it is judged that there is network interaction behavior between nodes A and B.

Compare the data with interactive behavior within the time window; if the data addresses meet the exchangeability, it is considered that an ACK interactive behavior has occurred. If the address is unidirectional, it is judged to be a relay behavior.

Analyze the directional characteristics of the network data to distinguish between chain networks, star networks, mesh networks, and tree networks.

4   Simulation

In this paper, three T-Beam LoRa development boards and one Heltec LoRa development board are used to simulate the LoRaWAN and ClusterDuck Protocol network communication environments, respectively. In the simulation, a sniffer was used to capture packets in the network, record the RSSI signal value of the packet and the timestamp when the packet was received.

4.1   Network Node Data Discrimination

The simulation first uses the ordinary Euclidean distance algorithm to cluster two sets of network data. It was observed that this method is essentially unable to effectively distinguish the data of different nodes. The clustering method proposed in this paper, which combines the RSSI feature with the similarity of packet headers, can largely separate the data of different nodes. The critical point i_0 in the weight coefficient W_i of data separation degree determines this. As shown in Fig. 4, the larger the value of i_0 in the two protocols, the lower the separation degree of the data. In these two networks, the value of i_0 is between 4-8, and the accuracy of accurately separating node data is close to 100%.

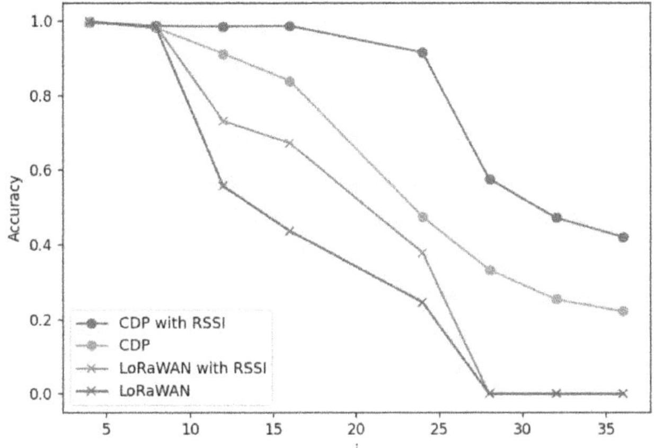

Fig. 4. Data Separation Degree at Different i_0 Thresholds.

4.2   Field Division and Semantic Judgment

The results of the longest frequent sequence extraction of each cluster in the CDP network and LoRaWAN network are shown in Table 1 and 2:

Based on the offset distribution of sub-items in frequent items from both networks, dynamic and static fields of CDP and LoRaWAN network data are extracted, as depicted in Fig. 5.

In Fig. 5(a), fields A and B are continuous and identified as address fields, while field C is a network identifier. In Fig. 5(b), fields ABC from LoRaWAN do not meet exchangeability or continuity, so field B is a unidirectional address field, field A is a control field in the header, and field C is a static field after the address, identified as a network identifier.

Table 1. The longest frequent item sets in different clusters of CDP network.

Cluster	The longest frequent item sets
0	[(72, 0), (65, 1), (73, 2), (69, 3), (64, 4), (31, 5), (31, 6), (39, 7), (00, 8), (00, 9), (00, 10), (00, 11), (00, 12), (00, 13), (00, 14), (00, 15), (10, 20), (02, 21), (00, 22)]
1	[(63, 0), (6C, 1), (75, 2), (73, 3), (74, 4), (64, 5), (63, 6), (6B, 7), (00, 8), (00, 9), (00, 10), (00, 11), (00, 12), (00, 13), (00, 14), (00, 15), (10, 20), (02, 21), (00, 22)]
2	[(4E, 0), (6F, 1), (64, 2), (65, 3), (54, 4), (65, 5), (73, 6), (74, 7), (00, 8), (00, 9), (00, 10), (00, 11), (00, 12), (00, 13), (00, 14), (00, 15), (10, 20), (02, 21), (01, 22)]
3	[(4D, 0), (41, 1), (4D, 2), (41, 3), (30, 4), (30, 5), (30, 6), (31, 7), (00, 8), (00, 9), (00, 10), (00, 11), (00, 12), (00, 13), (00, 14), (00, 15), (10, 20), (02, 21), (01, 22)]

Table 2. The longest frequent item sets in different clusters of LoRaWAN network.

Cluster	The longest frequent item sets
0	[(80, 0), (12, 1), (C3, 2), (0D, 3), (26, 4), (80, 5), (0A, 8)]
1	[(80, 0), (7B, 1), (25, 2), (0D, 3), (26, 4), (80, 5), (0A, 8)]
2	[(80, 0), (D7, 1), (22, 2), (0D, 3), (26, 4), (80, 5), (0A, 8)]
3	[(80, 0), (2A, 1), (1E, 2), (0D, 3), (26, 4), (80, 5), (0A, 8)]

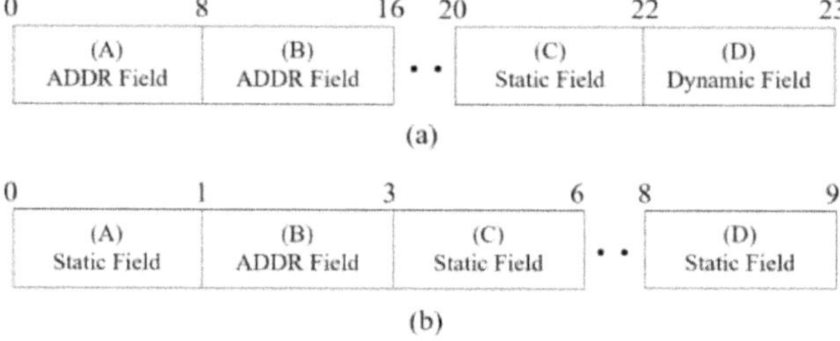

Fig. 5. CDP(a) and LoRaWAN(b) Protocol field identification results.

The simulation correctly identified address and control fields in both network protocols, but only successfully identified the network identifier field in LoRaWAN; the CDP protocol lacks this field, leading to a failed judgment.

4.3   Network Topology Analysis

The reverse-engineered address fields were used to analyze the temporal distribution of signals from various nodes. As shown in Fig. 6, both networks exhibit periodic signal transmission. In the CDP network, nodes A and B display consecutive transmission at the same time point, indicating they are relay nodes, with node B handling most of the forwarding tasks. The signal direction indicates a tree-like structure for the CDP network. In contrast, LoRaWAN node behavior analysis reveals no interaction between nodes and only unidirectional information flow, suggesting a star-shaped network topology.

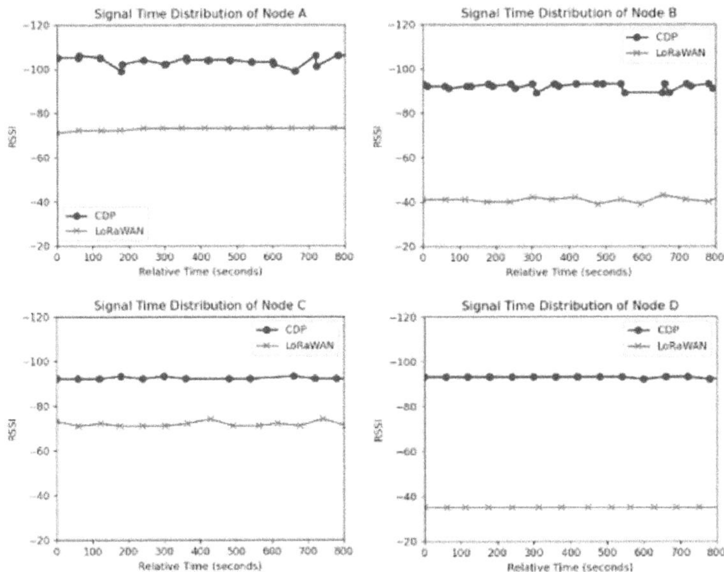

Fig. 6. Node Signal Time Distribution of CDP and LoRaWAN.

5   Summary

In this simulation, the node data with RSSI fingerprint has a good discrimination effect, and the data generated by different nodes are basically and accurately distinguished. The computational efficiency of frequent sequence extraction is improved, and the accuracy of address field extraction is improved, but due to the variability of unknown protocol formats, the accuracy of other types of field extraction may be relatively low.

After reversing the private LoRa protocol and restoring the network topology, it can be used as a model to evaluate the security of the private network in the environment, as well as network security detection and abnormal behavior capture, which is of great significance to LoRa network security.

References

1. Ghosh, A., Misra, S., Udutalapally, V., Das, D.: LoRaute: routing messages in backhaul LoRa networks for underserved regions. IEEE Internet Things J. **10**(22), 19964–19971 (2023). https://doi.org/10.1109/JIOT.2023.3281941
2. Tomar, R., Gemein, O.-G.: LoRa network for cities private and complete secured by design. In: 2018 Global Internet of Things Summit (GIoTS), Bilbao, Spain, pp. 1–5 (2018). https://doi.org/10.1109/GIOTS.2018.8534557
3. Haque, M.A., Saifullah, A.: Handling jamming attacks in a LoRa network. In: 2024 IEEE/ACM Ninth International Conference on Internet-of-Things Design and Implementation (IoTDI), Hong Kong, pp. 146–157 (2024). https://doi.org/10.1109/IoTDI61053.2024.00017

4. Huang, D., Al-Hourani, A.: Physical layer spoof detection and authentication for IoT devices using deep learning methods. IEEE Trans. Mach. Learn. Commun. Network. **2**, 841–854 (2024). https://doi.org/10.1109/TMLCN.2024.3417806

5. Rakhaine, N., Ahmed, I., Islam, T.: A comparative analysis of power consumption and security features in LoRa and LoRaWAN messaging devices. In: 2024 3rd International Conference on Advancement in Electrical and Electronic Engineering (ICAEEE), Gazipur, Bangladesh, pp. 1–6 (2024). https://doi.org/10.1109/ICAEEE62219.2024.10561782

6. Amadou, I., Foubert, B., Mitton, N.: LoRa in a haystack: a study of the LORA signal behavior. In: 2019 International Conference on Wireless and Mobile Computing, Networking and Communications (WiMob), Barcelona, Spain, pp. 1–4 (2019). https://doi.org/10.1109/WiMOB.2019.8923319

7. Ji, R., Li, H., Tang, C.: Extracting keywords of UAVs wireless communication protocols based on association rules learning. In: 2016 12th International Conference on Computational Intelligence and Security (CIS), Wuxi, China, pp. 309–313 (2016). https://doi.org/10.1109/CIS.2016.0076

8. Yu, F., Zheng, X., Liu, L., Ma, H.: LoRadar: an efficient LoRa channel occupancy acquirer based on cross-channel scanning. In: IEEE INFOCOM 2022 - IEEE Conference on Computer Communications, London, United Kingdom, pp. 540–549 (2022). https://doi.org/10.1109/INFOCOM48880.2022.9796845

9. Garshasbi, J., Teimouri, M.: CNNPRE: a CNN-based protocol reverse engineering method. IEEE Access **11**, 116255–116268 (2023). https://doi.org/10.1109/ACCESS.2023.3325391

10. Liu, Z., Zha, X., Song, G., Yao, Q.: Unknown wireless network protocol feature extraction method based on sequence association. In: 2020 5th International Conference on Mechanical, Control and Computer Engineering (ICMCCE), Harbin, China, pp. 1916–1922 (2020). https://doi.org/10.1109/ICMCCE51767.2020.00420

11. Wang, S., Guo, F., Fan, Y., Wu, J.: Association analysis and identification of unknown bitstream protocols based on composite feature sets. IEEE Access **9**, 164454164465 (2021). https://doi.org/10.1109/ACCESS.2021.3134697

12. Wang, Y., Li, X., Meng, J., Zhao, Y., Zhang, Z., Guo, L.: Biprominer: automatic mining of binary protocol features. In: 2011 12th International Conference on Parallel and Distributed Computing, Applications and Technologies, Gwangju, Korea (South), pp. 179–184 (2011). https://doi.org/10.1109/PDCAT.2011.25

13. Wang, Y., et al.: A semantics aware approach to automated reverse engineering unknown protocols. In: 2012 20th IEEE International Conference on Network Protocols (ICNP), Austin, TX, USA, pp. 1–10 (2012). https://doi.org/10.1109/ICNP.2012.6459963

14. Jiang, D., Li, C., Ma, L., Ji, X., Chen, Y., Li, B.: ABInfer: a novel field boundaries inference approach for protocol reverse engineering. In: 2020 IEEE 6th International Conference on Big Data Security on Cloud (BigDataSecurity), IEEE International Conference on High Performance and Smart Computing, (HPSC) and IEEE International Conference on Intelligent Data and Security (IDS), Baltimore, MD, USA, pp. 19–23 (2020). https://doi.org/10.1109/BigDataSecurity-HPSCIDS49724.2020.00015

15. Sun, X., Li, H., Chen, Y., Cui, J., Zhong, H.: Variable-length field extraction for unknown binary network protocols. In: 2024 IEEE 49th Conference on Local Computer Networks (LCN), Normandy, France, pp. 1–7 (2024). https://doi.org/10.1109/LCN60385.2024.10639751

Research on Digital Twin System for Intelligent Management of Dumb Resources in Optical Communication Networks

Caixiao Ouyang and Jingjing Geng[✉]

Wuhan Vocational College of Sortware and Engineering, Wuhan 430205, China
20815552@qq.com

Abstract. To accurate management the resource devices in optical communication networks that cannot automatically report their own information, this paper studies a digital twin system for intelligent management of dumb resources in optical communication networks. Firstly, the construction principles of digital twin system for dumb resource management in optical communication network are studied. Then the data capture methods of different dumb resources are analyzed to solve the problem in dumb resources. Finally, the analysis methods of dumb resource data are studied, and the isolated forest algorithm and the image detection algorithm YOLOv7 for dumb resource detection are applied to realize the analysis of dumb resource data. The application of optical communication dumb resource intelligent management digital twin system can realizes the effective management of dumb resources.

Keywords: Digital Twin · Dumb Resources · Optical Communication Networks · YOLOv7

1 Introduction

In communication networks, optical communication networks play a crucial role in the normal operation of communication network systems [1–4]. There are massive network resources that need to be managed in optical communication networks [5]. Resources that cannot automatically report their own information in optical communication networks are called "dumb resources". Dumb resources are important component of optical communication networks. During the installation process of optical communication networks [6], a large number of passive communication equipment such as fiber optic cables, splice boxes, junction boxes, splitting boxes, manhole, poles, and overhead cables [7–10]. These types of resources are called dumb resources.

With the rapid development of business markets such as 5G networks and mobile broadband by operators, the number of dumb resources is showing explosive growth [11]. Due to the inability of dumb resource facilities and equipment to autonomously transmit status information, there are significant difficulties in monitoring and managing them. At the same time, dumb resources are distributed outdoors [12], with a wide range

© ICST Institute for Computer Sciences, Social Informatics and Telecommunications Engineering 2026
Published by Springer Nature Switzerland AG 2026. All Rights Reserved
R. C. Qiu et al. (Eds.): IoTaaS 2024, LNICST 675, pp. 277–285, 2026.
https://doi.org/10.1007/978-3-032-14681-6_25

of locations, complex network structures, buried underground or overhead, and variable external environments. These feature making it difficult to inventory dumb resources in optical communication networks. Traditional dumb resource management mainly relies on the manual management and input of construction project drawings, which lacks tracking for dumb resources after project delivery is completed. Manual management will be affected by subjective human factors. In addition, design drawings often have poor intuitiveness, and various reasons on the construction site also make it difficult to fully follow the design drawings, and resulting in low accuracy of the input of dumb equipment resources.

At present, the common dumb resources among operators mainly include fiber optic cables, splice boxes, junction boxes, splitting boxes, manhole, poles, overhead cables, etc. In terms of fiber optic cable management, due to inaccurate input of dumb resources, maintenance personnel are unable to locate fiber optic cable equipment based on the resource management system. In addition, fiber optic cable belong to passive equipment, which cannot actively present the equipment status. When the optical cable is interrupted, the maintenance personnel are not clear about the routing of the optical cable. Other dumb resources are also important [13]. For example, operators are often most concerned about where the splitter box is located and whether there is still a splitter box in the target area. If the operator runs to the region without knowing where they are or cannot find them, they can only choose to cancel the order.

To address the issues of management difficulties, low accuracy, maintenance challenges, and negative impacts on user experience in optical communication networks' dumb resources [14, 15], this paper explores a digital twin system for intelligent management of dumb resources in optical communication networks. It proposes a method based on the isolation forest algorithm to diagnose optical cable fault conditions, enabling the diagnosis of the optical cable's state. A convolutional neural network (CNN) is applied to perform image detection on dumb resource devices, achieving detection and data collection of dumb resources without adding new equipment. Finally, the detection results and diagnosis outcomes are integrated into the digital twin system for dumb resource management, enabling intelligent management of dumb resources in optical communication networks.

2   The Framework of Dumb Resource Management Digital Twin Model

Digital twin system is an advanced technology that simulates the behavior of actual physical systems through mathematical models, sensor data, and simulation techniques. The core of digital twins is physical objects, real-time data, and virtual models. The construction of a digital twin system for managing dumb resources in optical communication networks requires the establishment of a close relationship between the physical objects, real-time data, and virtual models of dumb resources. Digital twin system can achieve high simulation and real-time monitoring of dumb resources in actual optical communication networks. The physical object is the dumb resource device that actually exists in the optical communication network. The goal of the digital twin of dumb resource management is to accurately simulating the information of real dumb resources. Real time data is real-time information collected from physical objects and obtained through sensors. The real-time information of the dumb resource device includes various status parameters. Real time data is used in the digital twin system of dumb resource management to update virtual models, which ensuring synchronization between the virtual model and the actual physical object. Virtual models are mathematical and computer models of physical objects, including physical models and state models. The physical model describes the real physical attribute information of dumb resources, while the state model simulates the dynamic state of dumb resource devices under different conditions. The virtual model is responsible for receiving real-time data, updating it in real-time through simulation, and mapping the actual state of physical objects. The building principles for dumb resources digital twin system is show in Fig. 1.

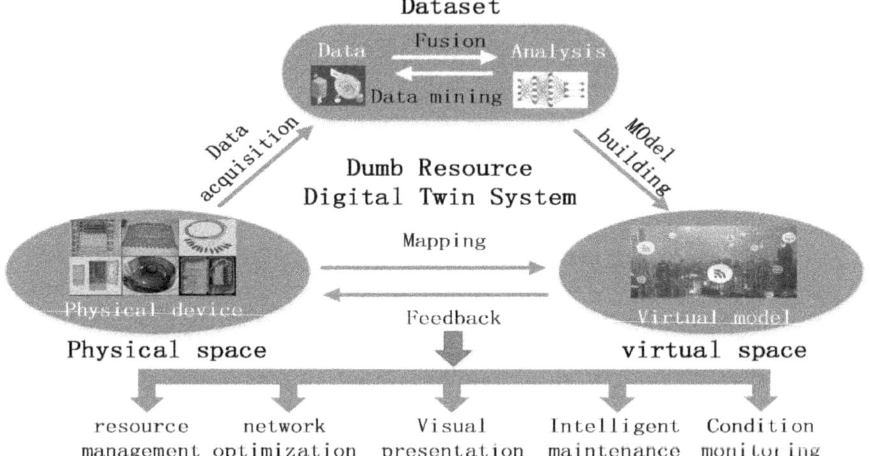

Fig. 1. Building principles for dumb resources digital twin system

The dumb resources in optical communication networks mainly include fiber optic cables, splice boxes, junction boxes, splitting boxes, manhole, poles, overhead cables, etc. Fiber optic cables are the main transmission medium of optical communication networks. The models of fiber optic cables in digital twin systems are used to monitor their transmission performance and loss in real-time, and the simulation result can provide data support for network optimization and maintenance. Fiber optic cable splice boxes are commonly used to accommodate fiber optic connectors and provide the connection, distribution, protection of fiber optic cables, and ensuring the stability and reliability of fiber optic connections. The fiber optic junction boxes is used to protect the fiber optic cable and connectors from external environmental influences. The splitting boxes is used to protect the fiber optic cable and connectors from external environmental influences. Manhole, poles, and overhead cables are mainly used for the routing of optical cables and to carry the crossing, connection, and distribution points of optical cables. The digital twin system models dumb resources and can monitor their real-time status. By modeling the splitter box through a digital twin system, it is possible to simulate the distribution of optical fibers and monitor the status of the fiber interface in the splitter box. The digital twin system models poles and overhead cables, which can simulate the crossing process of optical cables and optimize line layout.

Applying the building principles of dumb resources digital twin system for optical communication dumb resources, the architecture of a digital twin system for optical communication mute resource management is shown in Fig. 2. The overall structure of the dumb resource management digital twin system can be divided into physical network layer, perception layer, data layer, model layer, simulation layer, connection layer, management layer, and user interface layer. Each layer of the digital twin for dumb resource management bears a unique responsibility throughout the entire system, and each layers are working together to achieve comprehensive management and simulation for dumb resources.

The physical network layer is the actual physical environment in the digital twin system for dumb resources. This layer providing an accurate and reliable physical foundation for the digital twin system. The physical layer is also the main object for intelligent management of dumb resources in optical communication networks.

The perception layer is the foundation of the digital twin system for dumb resource management. It integrates various sensors and monitoring devices to sense the physical state and environmental parameters of dumb resources in real time. This includes key information such as images, locations, and connection status of optical communication devices. Data collection at the perception layer is the foundation for the digital twin system to achieve real-time monitoring.

The data layer is responsible for managing and storing the real-time data obtained from the perception layer. This includes the real-time status, historical data, performance metrics, location information, port occupancy, and other information of the optical communication dumb resource devices. Through real-time databases and other data storage systems, the digital twin system can effectively store, retrieve, and analyze a large amount of dumb resource data.

The model layer is the core of the dumb resource management digital twin system, including physical, mathematical, and state models of dumb resources. By establishing a model of optical communication equipment dumb resources, the system can more accurately simulate their attributes, characteristics, and performance to fully understand their operating status.

The simulation layer is built on top of the model layer and is responsible for performing simulations and modeling of dumb resources. Through real-time simulation, the dumb resource management digital twin system can simulate the state of dumb resources under different operating conditions and conditions, enabling intelligent management of dumb resources.

The connection layer is used to ensure the synchronization of the dumb resource management digital twin system with the actual dumb resources. The connection layer involves the connection of IoT devices, sensor networks, real-time monitoring systems, etc., to ensure the effective transmission of real-time data to the digital twin system to update models and simulations.

The management layer is the decision-making and control center of the digital twin system for dumb resource management. By using the information provided by the model layer and the simulation results executed by the simulation layer, the management layer implements real-time decision-making and management. With the management layer dumb resources can realize intelligent detection, predictive maintenance, and distribution optimization.

The user interface layer is the interface between the dumb resource management digital twin system and users. The user interface layer provides intuitive visualization tools, dashboards, and charts. Users can interactively obtain the status of dumb resources, enabling real-time decision-making and visual analysis of the system.

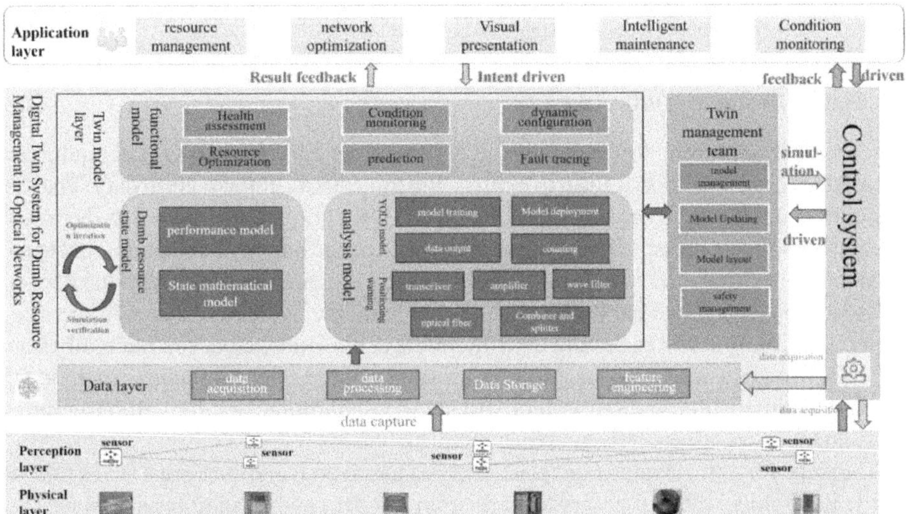

Fig. 2. Digital twin system architecture for optical communication dumb resources

3 Data Collection and Analysis for Dumb Resources

3.1 Data Collection of Dumb Resource

In optical communication networks, fiber optic cables are one of the most important dumb resources with a wide coverage area and long extension distance. Fiber optic cables are generally started from the communication room and then buried underground. Fiber optic cables data collection includes two types of data: one is the location data, and the other is the status data. The location data is collected by optical cable locators, and the position will not change after being buried underground. The method of manual inspection is used to collect data regularly through optical cable locators. For the status data, due to urban construction or other external forces, there is a risk of breakage, and it is necessary to detect the status in real time. In this paper, an optical time-domain reflectometer (OTDR) is used for fiber optic cables status data collection. Under the action of vibration environment or sound field, the optical fibers will produce small changes. Due to the photoelastic effect, the refractive index of the optical fibers will change accordingly, which causing the interference phase of Rayleigh scattering light signals in the optical fibers to change. OTDR is applied to obtain real-time data of vibration or sound wave signals in the surrounding environment of fiber optic cables.

In optical communication networks, the distribution of dumb resources such as junction boxes, splitting boxes, manhole, poles, overhead cables are widespread and the number is huge. After installation, they will not often change. Adding sensors such as RFID and WiFi modules directly for data timeliness is effective, but this collection method has high costs and requires construction and transformation of dumb resource equipment. To solve this problem of data collection, this paper uses image processing methods based on deep learning to identify images of optical communication network devices such as junction boxes, splitting boxes, manhole, poles, overhead cables. Artificial image capture is performed regularly for dumb resources, and the image processing method based on deep learning is used to detect the status of these dumb resources.

3.2 Dumb Resource Data Analysis

After obtaining different dimensional feature data of optical cables by OTDR equipment, the isolated forests method is used to analyze the fault status of the feature data. The real-time optical cable status data collected by the OTDR equipment is added to the history dataset for isolated forests. The dataset is divided according to distance to construct a decision tree. With the large number of normal data, the average distance in the decision tree is longer. For optical cable status abnormal data, the average distance in the tree is shorter. Randomly select m feature data of optical cable fault status, and randomly select a value between the maximum and minimum values of the selected features to divide the data in this dimension. Then repeatedly divide the remaining data until all observations are isolated.

The steps for optical cable fault state analysis based on Isolation Forest are as follows:
Step 1: Randomly select m points from the training data as sub-samples and place them in the main node of an iTree;

Step 2: Randomly specify a feature variable, and within the current node data range, randomly generate a segmentation point p. The segmentation point p is generated between the maximum and minimum values of the specified feature variable in the current node data;

Step 3: The selection of this segmentation point generates a hyperplane that divides the current node data space into two subspaces: placing points with less than p under the currently selected feature variable on the left branch of the current node, and placing points with p or greater on the right branch of the current node;

Step 4: Recursively apply steps 2 and 3 on the left and right branches of the node, continuously constructing new leaf nodes until there is only one data point on the leaf node or the tree has grown to the set height.

In optical cables anomaly detection, commonly used methods include: isolation forest detection, k-means clustering-based anomaly detection, and histogram-based outlier detection. Historical data containing both normal and abnormal sample points is selected to test the above three types of algorithms. Each sample point contains three feature data: wavelength, distance, and fiber attenuation. Testing was conducted on 10,000 sample points, with 100 abnormal points. The test results are shown in Table 1. In Table 1, the anomaly detection rate refers to the percentage of correctly detected abnormal points out of the total actual abnormal points, and the accuracy of detected anomalies refers to the percentage of correctly detected abnormal points out of the total detected abnormal points. The higher the two indicators, the better the detection performance. From Table 1, it can be seen that the isolation forest-based algorithm has a significant advantage.

Table 1. Detection results of different methods

Methods	the anomaly detection rate	the accuracy of detected anomalies
isolation forest detection	83.0%	92.2%
k-means clustering-based anomaly detection	43.0%	10.8%
histogram-based outlier detection	37.0%	9.25%

For other dumb resources, this article uses the YOLO v7 to detect dumb resources in images, thereby obtaining information about the type, state, and quantity of dumb resources. First, construct a dataset of dumb resource images, and manual label the images in the dataset. This article manual labels 5,000 images of each type of dumb resource. During training, data augmentation methods are used to expand the manual labeled data to obtain more image datasets, which improves the generalization ability of YOLO v7. This article mainly uses random cropping, rotation, scaling, mirroring, brightness and contrast adjustment methods to simulate different shooting conditions, ensuring that the model can make robust detections in various situations.

In practical applications, the large amount of time are required for collecting and labeling data. To improve the efficiency of YOLO v7 model applications and reduce data set preparation, this paper adopts a fine-tuning training strategy for the training of a dumb resource detection model. Applying pre-trained models, the model is fine tuned in different dumb resource scenarios to adapt to tasks such as fiber optic box port detection and dumb resource object detection. The fine-tuning process includes adjusting the model's hyperparameters, learning rate, loss function, and adapting to the characteristics of new data. The detection results of fiber splice box is show in Fig. 4. Finally, the trained model is deployed and further optimized, including model quantization, pruning, and compression techniques, to improve the inference speed of the model on embedded devices, reduce hardware resource requirements, and enhance overall performance.

Fig. 4. Detection results of fiber splice box

4 Conclusion

This study investigated the construction method of a digital twin system for optical communication network dumb resources. Firstly, the construction principles of a digital twin system for optical communication network dumb resources management were studied, and a framework for a digital twin system for dumb resources management was proposed. Then, the data acquisition method of the digital twin system for dumb resources management was studied. The Isolation Forest algorithm and YOLOv7 image detection algorithm were applied to achieve the analysis of dumb resource data. The digital twin system providing an intelligent solution for the management of dumb resources in optical communication networks. However, the development of digital twin systems is still in its infancy, and future research needs to further explore its applicability in more complex network environments, and continuously optimize the performance of the system to better meet the needs of optical communication network dumb resource management.

References

1. Guo, H., Zhang, J., Yang, X., et al.: Robust timing and frequency joint synchronization method for QNSC-enabled security optical communications system based on CO-OFDM. Optical Fiber Technol. **75**, 103144.1 (2023)
2. Amiri, I.S., Rashed, A.N.Z., Yupapin, P.: Interaction between optical sources and optical modulators for high-speed optical communication networks. J. Opt. Commun. **43**(4), 625–632 (2022)
3. Patle, N., Raj, A.B., Joseph, C., et al.: Review of fibreless optical communication technology: History, evolution, and emerging trends. J. Opt. Commun. **45**(3), 679–702 (2024)
4. Amiri, I.S., Rashed, A.N.Z., Yupapin, P.: High-speed light sources in high-speed optical passive local area communication networks. J. Opt. Commun. **44**(1), 61–67 (2023)
5. Pan, Z., Yu, C., Willner, A.E.: Optical performance monitoring for the next generation optical communication networks. Opt. Fiber Technol. **16**(1), 20–45 (2010)
6. Deen, M.J., Kumar, S.: Optical communication systems: fundamentals and applications. In: Quantum Electronics & Laser Science Conference (2014)
7. Gerasimov, V.A., Nuriev, M.G., Gashigullin, D.A.: The fiber-optic communication system in the enterprise. In: 2022 International Russian Automation Conference (RusAutoCon), pp. 75–79. IEEE (2022)

8. Huawei Technologies Co., Ltd. Cabling Engineering. Construction, Operation and Maintenance of Network System (Junior Level). Springer Nature Singapore, Singapore, pp. 21–87 (2022)
9. Gupta, M., Sinha, A.: Enhanced-AES encryption mechanism with S-box splitting for wireless sensor networks. Int. J. Inf. Technol. **13**(3), 933–941 (2021)
10. Koufos, K., EI Haloui, K., Dianati, M., et al.: Trends in intelligent communication systems: review of standards, major research projects, and identification of research gaps. J. Sens. Actuator Networks **10**(4), 60 (2021)
11. Albreem, M.A.M.: 5G wireless communication systems: vision and challenges. In: International Conference on Computer, IEEE (2015)
12. Pan, H.: NordUnet discusses ship to lay Arctic cable under Northern EU Gateways project. Submarine Fiber Optic Communications Systems (2023)
13. Morimitsu, T., Terasawa, M.: Long-distance optical fiber cable installation system using automatic control puller. Trans. Japan Soc. Mech. Eng. **62**(594), 548–553 (2007)
14. Fitzek, F.H.P., Seeling, P., Höschele, T., et al.: On the need of computing in future communication networks. Computing in Communication Networks. Academic Press, pp. 3–45 (2020)
15. Li, Y., Li, C., Liu, Z., et al.: Research and experiment on AI-based co-cable and co-trench optical fibre detection. In: 2022 European Conference on Optical Communication (ECOC), pp. 1–4. IEEE (2022)

A Low-Cost Wearable Somatosensory Control System for Humanoid Robotic Arm

Dingyi Zhao, Feng Deng$^{(\boxtimes)}$, and Xinlang Ju

Wuhan Vocational College of Software and Engineering, Wuhan, China
`81469864@qq.com`, `42200893@whvcse.edu.cn`

Abstract. This paper proposes a low-cost and lightweight wearable somatosensory controller for a robotic arm. The controller uses IMU sensors to capture the movements of the human arm and maps those movements to a remote robotic arm.On the wearable end, three IMUs are used to capture the seven degrees of freedom of the arm and send them to the remote end via a wireless network. The controller uses the space vector method to calculate the joint angles of the human arm and then performs mapping. This method effectively avoids the problems of large amount of calculation and singular points in inverse kinematics solution. It can be deployed on low-cost edge platforms. The simulation and experimental results prove the effectiveness of the controller in general scenarios.

Keywords: Motion Tracking · Robotic Arm · Wearable Sensors

1 Introduction

Remote control of robotic arms plays a vital role in many fields such as national defense, space exploration, and medical treatment, mainly to ensure the safety of users [1,2]. Among them, remote operation based on teaching is the most common application method. Such systems require a high degree of stability and precision, and are usually equipped with force feedback to enhance operational feel and accuracy. However, traditional mechanical controllers are usually bulky and susceptible to friction due to their reliance on mechanical parts, which limits their service life [3]. In order to overcome these limitations and improve the convenience of remote operation, wearable devices such as exoskeletons were later developed. They achieve the transmission of operator movements to remote robotic arms through one-to-one angle mapping. Although this method still uses the teaching method, its mechanical structure and wearing comfort are not ideal [4]. Subsequently, operations based on visual recognition became popular, using cameras to capture human gestures, postures and movements [5–7], and advances in artificial intelligence technology have significantly improved recognition accuracy [8]. Nevertheless, the visual system's susceptibility to occlusions

R. C. Qiu et al. (Eds.): IoTaaS 2024, LNICST 675, pp. 286–297, 2026.
https://doi.org/10.1007/978-3-032-14681-6_26

and the controller's lack of flexibility and limited portability remain challenges, prompting researchers to continuously seek more efficient, accurate, and user-friendly solutions.

Therefore, IMU wearable sensor controllers have recently attracted more and more attention due to their compact structure, low price and portability, and they show great potential in the field of remote-controlled robotic arms. In [9], the authors designed a controller combining IMU and potentiometer, supporting up to four degrees of freedom. In [10], the authors achieved the capture of up to four degrees of freedom motion by using two IMU sensors.

In addition to choosing the right sensors, mapping human arm motions to robotic arm joints is also a key challenge in teleoperation systems [11]. The commonly used solution is inverse kinematics. However, the computational cost of inverse kinematics is high and it often encounters singularity problems, so it usually takes a long time to get the result. To avoid these problems, inverse kinematics is often used in conjunction with other algorithms.Although this increases the complexity of the system, it can improve its stability and accuracy.At the same time, we also need to solve problems such as dynamics calculation, trajectory generation and motion planning, which further increases the complexity of the system.Currently, most of these calculations are deployed on PC platforms, which not only increases the cost of the robotic arm control end, but also affects the real-time and response speed of the system, which is often unacceptable in practical applications [12,13].

Although there are many controllers that support remote operation of robotic arms, it is worth noting that robotic arm motion control is a complete system framework, and existing controllers are not widely used in practice, such as the impact of communication delay on operation, sensor errors, and limitations of wearable controllers. These factors need to be considered during design to ensure the reliability and efficiency of the system.

Therefore, the main contributions of this paper include:

1. A low-cost wearable somatosensory controller is proposed, which can accurately capture all seven degrees of freedom of the human arm and is modular and portable for widespread use.
2. The space vector method is used to calculate the joint angles of the human arm, and the quaternion data from the IMU is used for direct calculation. Compared with the traditional inverse kinematics method, it has the advantages of small computational complexity and easy deployment on low-cost platforms.
3. A complete system framework integrating hardware design and software algorithms is designed, which not only includes the mapping algorithm but also optimizes the overall performance and adaptability.
4. Through extensive simulation and physical testing, the effectiveness and practicality of the control system in general operating environments have been confirmed.

2   Kinematic Analysis of Human Arm and Robotic Arm

The core of somatosensory control is to accurately capture the movements of the human arm and effectively map the collected joint angle data to the robotic arm. In this process, a detailed analysis of the kinematics of the human arm is essential.

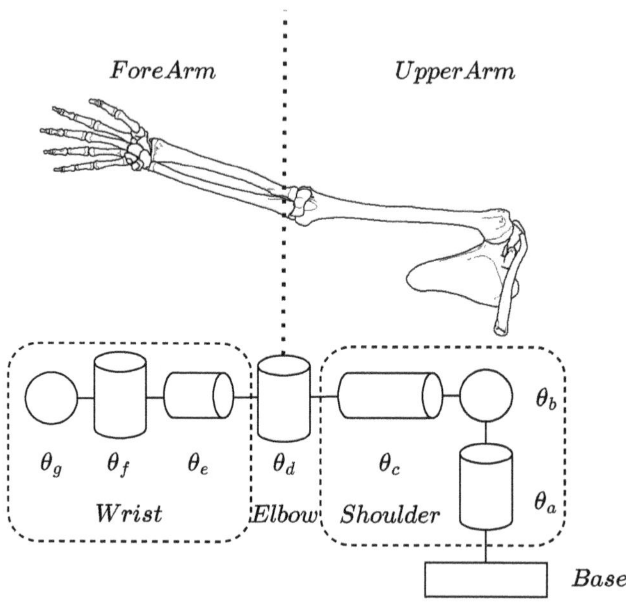

Fig. 1. Simplified physiological diagram of the human arm. Where θ_a, θ_b and θ_c are shoulder-related angles, θ_d is the elbow-related angle, and θ_e is the wrist-related angle.

2.1   Human Arm Kinematics Model

The physiological structure of the human arm is complex, involving multiple joints and parts. For ease of analysis, we simplify the human arm into three main parts: upper arm, forearm and hand, corresponding to the joints of shoulder, elbow and wrist [14]. As can be seen from Fig. 1, these parts together constitute the seven degrees of freedom of the arm.

2.2   Robotic Arm Kinematic Model

In the simulation, the robotic arm was also simplified into a complex consisting of a shoulder, elbow and wrist, with the same seven degrees of freedom as a human arm. The following Table 1 shows the mapping relationship between the human arm and the robotic arm. These mapping relationships are one-to-one, indicating that various movements of the human arm can be accurately mapped to the robotic arm.

Table 1. Robot arm angle mapping table. This table reveals a direct mapping between the joint angles of the human arm and the robotic arm, showing how each joint action corresponds in the two systems.

Human arm	RobotArm	Angles
Shoulder flexion or extension	Shoulder pitch	θ_a
Shoulder adduction or abduction	Shoulder roll	θ_b
Shoulder interior or exterior rotation	Shoulder rotation	θ_c
Elbow flexion or extension	Elbow pitch	θ_d
Forearm supination or pronation	Wrist rotatio	θ_e
Wrist flexion or extension	Wrist pitch	θ_f
Ulnar or radial deviation	Wrist yaw	θ_g

3   Robot Arm Joint Angle Calculation

In the previous section, we explored the direct one-to-one mapping relationship between the human arm and the robotic arm. To calculate the joint angles of the human arm, we installed inertial measurement units (IMUs) on various parts of the arm for detailed motion capture.

3.1   Calculation Method of Joint Angle

To describe the parts of the human arm, we use vector representation. As shown in Fig. 6, the configuration of each arm segment in the global and local coordinate systems is shown. The global coordinate system is set based on the joint angles of the upper arm. The upper arm coordinate system is used as a reference for the forearm joint angles, while the forearm coordinate system provides an angle reference for wrist motion. The action of each part is relative to its parent part. We define the global coordinate system as $[X, Y, Z]$ and the local coordinate system as $[k, u, s]$ (Figs 2 and 3).

Now we can represent these vectors directly using the IMU data. This allows the coordinate system of each arm segment to be represented by IMU data, and the joint angles of the human body are converted into the posture solution problem of the IMU. The IMU of the upper arm segment moves relative to the global coordinate system, the IMU of the forearm segment moves compared to the IMU of the upper arm segment, and the IMU of the wrist segment moves compared to the IMU of the forearm segment.

To simplify the computational model, we consider each arm segment as a revolute joint with three degrees of freedom, which allows the calculation of each part to be performed independently. In order to distinguish it from the $[\theta_{Yaw}, \theta_{Pitch}, \theta_{Roll}]$ in the Euler angle, we use $[\theta_{Pitch\prime}, \theta_{Yaw\prime}, \theta_{Roll\prime}]$ to replace the pitch, yaw and roll angles calculated by the arm segment.

Now, we only need to calculate $[\theta_{Pitch\prime}, \theta_{Yaw\prime}, \theta_{Roll\prime}]$ of each joint to realize the acquisition of human arm joints. Next, we will gradually realize the decou-

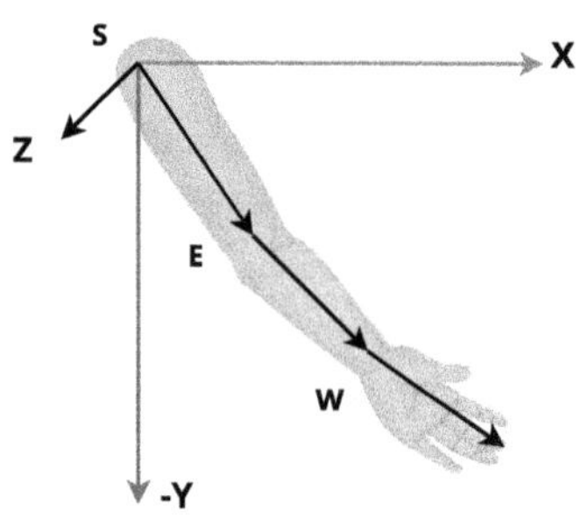

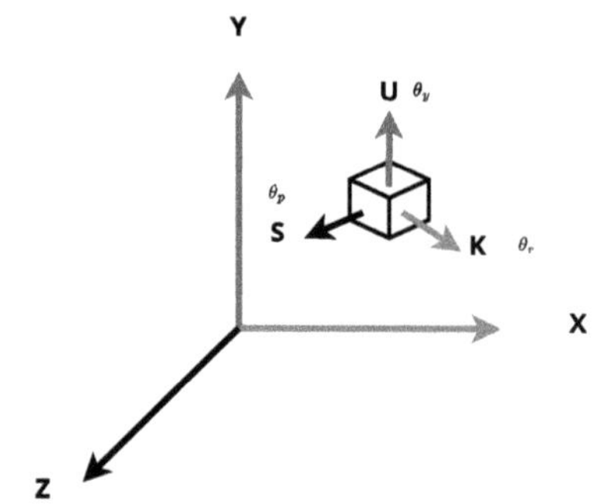

Fig. 2. Arm segment vector representation.

Fig. 3. Global and local coordinate
systems. We use a right-handed coordinate system with the Y axis pointing
upward.

pling of joint calculation through three steps: data acquisition, data conversion
and data calculation.

3.2 Data Collection

To obtain the arm segment posture, we placed three IMU sensors on the upper
arm, forearm and wrist. The acquisition end controller obtains three sets of
quaternion data from the IMU sensor to represent the direction data of the
arm segment. It is then transmitted to the remote end via the communication
network.

The quaternion obtained from these IMU sensors can be expressed as $Q_i = [q_{0i}, q_{1i}, q_{2i}, q_{3i}]$, where i represents the number of the IMU sensor, from 1 to 3,
corresponding to the upper arm, forearm and wrist respectively. To improve the
clarity of the expression, we can reformat the representation of the quaternion
as $Q_i = [q_{wi}, q_{xi}, q_{yi}, q_{zi}]$.

Considering that each arm segment i moves relative to the previous arm
segment $i - 1$, the quaternion q_i of each joint can be calculated by the inverse
of the quaternion q_{i-1} of the previous arm segment:

$$Q_i = Q_{i-1}^{-1} \tag{1}$$

3.3 Data Conversion

Next, we will convert the collected arm segment data Q_i into the corresponding
arm segment vector $[k, u, s]$.

Euler Angle Conversion. In order to better describe the rotation of the
coordinate system, we convert the quaternion into Euler angles [15]. The Euler
angle of each arm segment can be expressed as $E_j = [\theta_{rj} \theta_{pj} \theta_{yj}]^T$, representing

Roll, Pitch, Yaw respectively. Where j represents the arm segment number, from 1 to 3, then $i = j$. For Roll, Pitch, Yaw in these arm segments, they can be expressed as:

$$\begin{bmatrix} \theta_{rj} \\ \theta_{pj} \\ \theta_{yj} \end{bmatrix} = \begin{bmatrix} \arctan\left(\frac{2(q_w q_x + q_y q_z)}{1-2(q_x^2 + q_y^2)}\right) \\ \arcsin\left(2(q_w q_y - q_z q_x)\right) \\ \arctan\left(\frac{2(q_w q_z + q_x q_y)}{1-2(q_y^2 + q_z^2)}\right) \end{bmatrix} \tag{2}$$

Local Coordinate System. u_j, k_j, s_j

$$\begin{bmatrix} u_{lx} \\ u_{ly} \\ u_{lz} \end{bmatrix} = \begin{bmatrix} \sin(\theta_{yj} - \frac{\pi}{2})\sin(\theta_{rj}) + \cos(\theta_{yj} - \frac{\pi}{2})\sin(\theta_{pj})\cos(\theta_{rj}) \\ \cos(\theta_{pj})\cos(\theta_{rj}) \\ -\cos(\theta_{yj} - \frac{\pi}{2})\sin(\theta_{rj}) + \sin(\theta_{yj} - \frac{\pi}{2})\sin(\theta_{pj})\cos(\theta_{rj}) \end{bmatrix} \tag{3}$$

$$\begin{bmatrix} k_{lx} \\ k_{ly} \\ k_{lz} \end{bmatrix} = \begin{bmatrix} \cos(\theta_{yj} - \frac{\pi}{2})\cos(\theta_{pj}) \\ -\sin(\theta_{pj}) \\ \sin(\theta_{yj} - \frac{\pi}{2})\cos(\theta_{pj}) \end{bmatrix} \tag{4}$$

$$\begin{bmatrix} s_{lx} \\ s_{ly} \\ s_{lz} \end{bmatrix} = \begin{bmatrix} \sin(\theta_{yj} + \frac{\pi}{2})\cos(\theta_{rj}) - \cos(\theta_{yj} + \frac{\pi}{2})\sin(\theta_{pj})\sin(\theta_{rj}) \\ \cos(\theta_{pj})\sin(\theta_{rj}) \\ -\cos(\theta_{yj} + \frac{\pi}{2})\cos(\theta_{rj}) - \sin(\theta_{yj} + \frac{\pi}{2})\sin(\theta_{pj})\sin(\theta_{rj}) \end{bmatrix} \tag{5}$$

3.4 Calculating Joint Angles

Once we have the vector of each arm segment, we can calculate the joint angle using the space vector method.

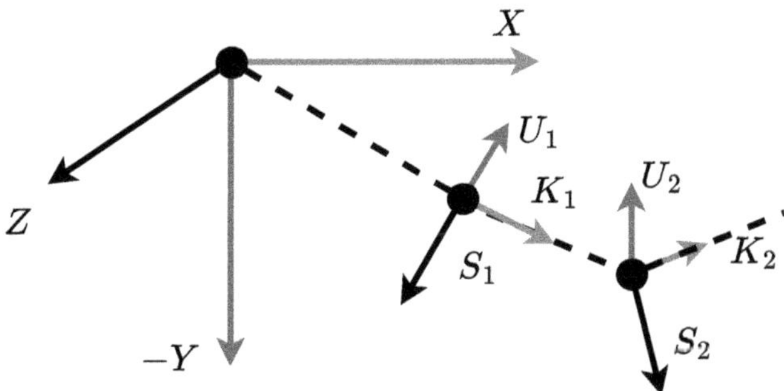

Fig. 4. Arm segment vector relative coordinate system.

In the vector diagram shown in Fig. 4, each joint moves relative to the previous joint. The angle between the projections of the global Y axis on the YZ

plane is referred to as $\theta_{Pitch\prime}$. Similarly, the angle between the vector K and the projection of the vector K on the YZ plane is referred to as $\theta_{Yaw\prime}$.

$$\theta_a = -\arctan(\frac{k_y}{k_z})\frac{180}{\pi} - 90 \tag{6}$$

$$\theta_b = -\arctan(\frac{k_y}{\sqrt{k_y{}^2 + k_z{}^2}})\frac{180}{\pi} \tag{7}$$

Similarly, the angle between vectors S_j and U_{j-1} is taken as $\theta_{Roll\prime}$

$$\theta_{Roll\prime} = \arccos(\frac{S_j \cdot U_{j-1}}{|S_j|\,|U_{j-1}|}) \tag{8}$$

4   Wearable Somatosensory Control System

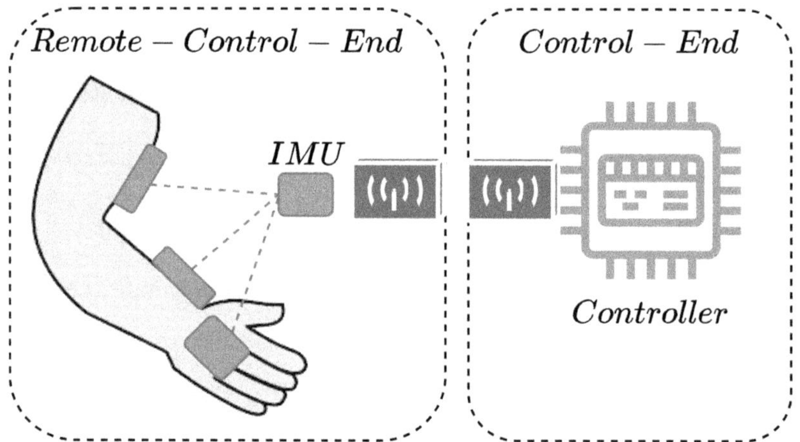

Fig. 5. Control system framework.

4.1   System Framework

The controller architecture proposed in this paper consists of a remote control end and a control end, which are connected through a wireless communication network, as shown in Fig. 5. The remote control end includes three inertial measurement units (IMUs) and a wireless transmitter, while the control end consists of a wireless receiver and a computing platform. This design allows us to decouple and expand the platform, realize cross-platform control systems and achieve diverse goals through the abstract connection level of the remote control end.

On the remote control side, we developed a low-cost wearable somatosensory device to capture the movements of the human arm. The control side is equipped with a simple robotic arm with seven degrees of freedom, whose end effector can be removed and replaced as needed. In this study, we will not involve the specific implementation of the end effector, but focus on using somatosensory control to control this robotic arm(Fig. 7).

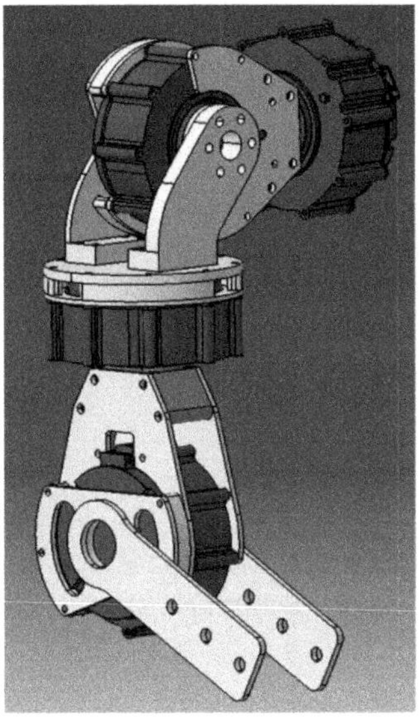

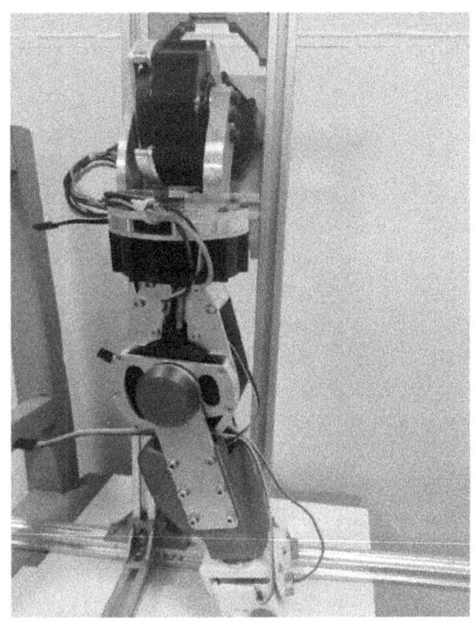

Fig. 6. Robotic arm CAD drawing.

Fig. 7. Physical picture of the robotic arm.

The remote controller receives quaternion data from the remote control end through the wireless network, performs angle mapping, and finally controls the various joints of the robot.

4.2 Mechanical Design

We designed a wearable device with a rotating mount that can stably fix the IMU and effectively prevent the offset problem during movement. As shown in the Fig. 8, the upper arm and forearm postures can be collected.

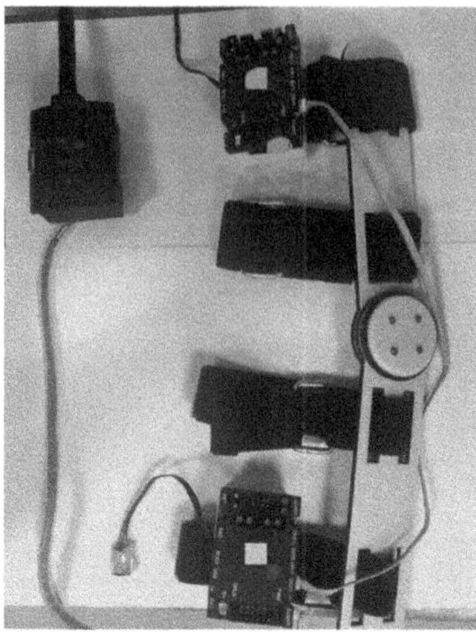

Fig. 8. Physical picture of somatosensory wearable device.

4.3 Attitude Calculation

We use a posture update algorithm based on quaternion extended Kalman filter to describe the arm segment posture. The state vector is defined as:

$$x = \begin{bmatrix} \mathbf{q} \\ \boldsymbol{\omega}^{bias} \end{bmatrix} \tag{9}$$

Among them, $\mathbf{q} = [q_w, q_x, q_y, q_z]^T$ is the attitude quaternion of the IMU coordinate system (b system) relative to the inertial coordinate system (n system). In our system, the z axis of the b system points to the sky, so it is difficult to estimate its zero bias through gravity acceleration. Therefore, $\boldsymbol{\omega}^{bias} = [\omega_x^{bias}, \omega_y^{bias}]^T$ is defined as the zero bias of the gyroscope x, y axis.

Calibrate the Coordinate System. It is worth noting that we need to align the coordinate system to the global coordinate system. In our system, BMI088 needs to be rotated $90°C$ clockwise around the X axis. The quaternion obtained by the transformation:

$$q' = r \cdot q \tag{10}$$

$$= (\cos(-\frac{\pi}{4}), \sin(-\frac{\pi}{4}), 0, 0) \cdot (q_w, q_x, q_y, q_z) \tag{11}$$

4.4   Initialization

In order to initialize the attitude solution related states, initialize from the standard T attitude. As shown in the Fig. 9, the global coordinate system and the IMU local coordinate system need to be aligned.

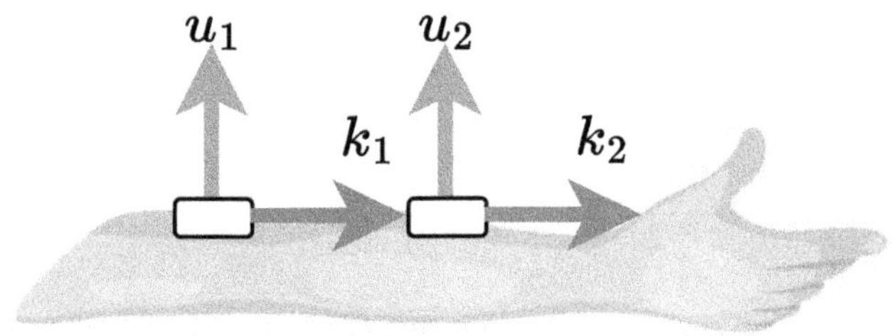

Fig. 9. IMU initialization posture, satisfying $Q_i = [1, 0, 0, 0]$.

5   Experimental Results and Future Prospects

To demonstrate the superiority of the proposed control system, we conducted a series of experiments. Figure 10 shows the robot arm returning to the mechanical zero position at the initial posture.

Fig. 10. Initial posture.

As shown in Fig. 11, we used the somatosensory device to remotely control the robotic arm and performed a series of human-like fighting movements.

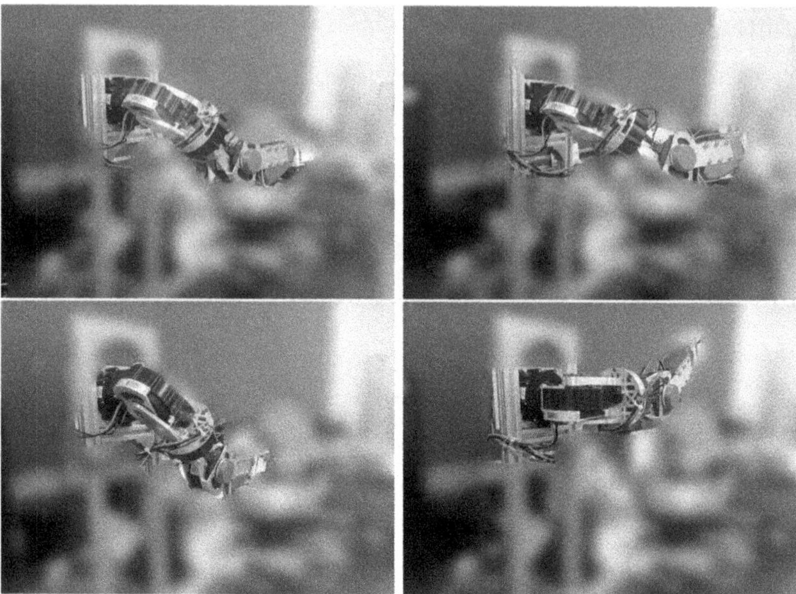

Fig. 11. Humanoid Fighting.

We used this system in the National College Students' Robot Competition (ROBOTAC) and achieved some good results. However, we encountered several issues.

1. Limited motor torque. The motor's torque is limited, which prevents achieving higher tracking angular velocities. We could only achieve better mapping performance at lower speeds, highlighting the need for a more advanced closed-loop control system.
2. Wireless communication interference. The low-cost communication device, nrf2401, suffered from interference with other wireless signals on the field, affecting communication stability.
3. Gimbal lock issue in the space vector method. After converting from quaternions to Euler angles, we encountered a gimbal lock problem, which we mitigated by setting angle limits.

This study proposes a wearable somatosensory controller for remote operation of a robotic arm, which is suitable for capturing human arm motion with up to seven degrees of freedom. The effectiveness of the controller is confirmed through simulation and physical tests, and its stability is similar to that of similar algorithms. Physical tests show that the robotic arm can successfully simulate the motion of the human arm, and the trajectory is basically the same, meeting the basic needs of real-time use.

Despite the initial results, future research will focus on improving the accuracy and adaptability of robot motion tracking. We recommend adding dynamic models and considering advanced algorithms such as adaptive control for optimization.

References

1. Nagatani, K., et al.: Emergency response to the nuclear accident at the fukushima daiichi nuclear power plants using mobile rescue robots. J. Field Robot. **30**, 44–63 (2013)
2. Laaki, H., Miche, Y., Tammi, K.: Prototyping a digital twin for real time remote control over mobile networks: application of remote surgery. IEEE Access 7:20325–20336 (2019). https://doi.org/10.1109/ACCESS.2019.2897018
3. Sin M, et al.: Development of a real-time 6-DOF motion-tracking system for robotic computer-assisted implant surgery. Sensors 23 (2023). https://doi.org/10.3390/s23052450
4. Purushottam, A., Xu C, Jung, Y., Ramos, J.: Dynamic mobile manipulation via whole-body bilateral teleoperation of a wheeled humanoid. IEEE Robot. Autom. Lett. (9)1214–1221 (2024). https://doi.org/10.1109/LRA.2023.3334677
5. Kruse, D., Wen, J.T., Radke, R. J.: A Sensor-Based Dual-Arm Tele-Robotic System. IEEE Trans. Autom. Sci. Eng. (12)4–18 (2015). https://doi.org/10.1109/TASE.2014.2333754
6. Li, S.,et al.: A mobile robot hand-arm teleoperation system by vision and IMU. In: 2020 IEEE/RSJ International Conference on Intelligent Robots and Systems (IROS). IEEE, pp 10900–10906 (2020)
7. Kofman, J., Wu, X., Luu, T.J., Verma, S.: Teleoperation of a robot manipulator using a vision-based human-robot interface. IEEE Trans. Industr. Electron. **52**(5), 1206–1219 (2005)
8. Su, H., et al.: Deep neural network approach in human-like redundancy optimization for anthropomorphic manipulators. IEEE Access **7**, 124207–124216 (2019)
9. Taunyazov, T., Omarali, B., Shintemirov, A.: A novel low-cost 4-DOF wireless human arm motion tracker. In: 2016 6th IEEE International Conference on Biomedical Robotics and Biomechatronics (BioRob), pp 157–162 (2016)
10. El-Gohary, M., McNames, J.: shoulder and elbow joint angle tracking with inertial sensors. IEEE Trans. Biomed. Eng. (59)2635–2641 (2012). https://doi.org/10.1109/TBME.2012.2208750
11. Chen, F., et al.: Sensor fusion-based anthropomorphic control of a robotic arm. Bioengineering 10 (2023). https://doi.org/10.3390/bioengineering10111243
12. Shintemirov, A., et al.: An open-source 7-DOF wireless human arm motion-tracking system for use in robotics research. Sensors **20**(11), 3082 (2020)
13. Omarali, B., Taunyazov, T., Bukeyev, A., Shintemirov, A.: Real-time predictive control of an ur5 robotic arm through human upper limb motion tracking. In: Proceedings of the Companion of the 2017 ACM/IEEE International Conference on Human-Robot Interaction, pp. 237–238 (2017)
14. Rosen, J., Perry, J.C., Manning, N., Burns, S., Hannaford, B.: The human arm kinematics and dynamics during daily activities-toward a 7 DOF upper limb powered exoskeleton. In: ICAR'05. Proceedings., 12th International Conference on Advanced Robotics, 2005. IEEE, pp 532–539 (2005)
15. Voight, J.: Quaternion algebras. Springer Nature (2021)

Lower Limb Movement Classification and Recognition Based on Surface Muscle Signals

Yanran Wang(✉)

Wuhan Vocational College of Software and Engineering, Wuhan 430205, China
447027259@qq.com

Abstract. In recent years, human-computer interaction technology has become increasingly mature, and equipment based on human-computer interaction technology, such as mechanical exoskeletons, has also begun to be used in military, medical and sports rehabilitation fields. Among them, myoelectric signal is the cornerstone of controlling human-computer interaction devices, and its feature extraction and classification recognition quality are related to the performance of such devices. Nowadays, the EMG signal processing module still has shortcomings in signal preprocessing, feature extraction and classification recognition, in view of this problem, this thesis designs a surface electromyography signal (sEMG) classification recognition system, and innovatively improves the Ensemble Empirical Mode Decomposition method(EEMD) in the signal processing process. A two-layer ensemble classifier using the support vector machines (SVM) algorithm and the gradient boosting decision tree (GBDT) algorithm built by stacking fusion strategy is designed to improve the accuracy of human motion classification recognition based on myoelectric signals.

Keywords: sEMG · EEMD · SVM-GBDT

1 Introduction

In recent years, robotics and mechanical exoskeleton technology have developed rapidly, and new technicians have continued to flow into related fields, making human-computer interaction technology increasingly mature. Among them, lower limb exoskeleton robots are increasingly used in the medical field and sports rehabilitation field.

In this paper, the motion classification and recognition based on the surface of the lower limb EMG signals was studied, and the EMG data were collected by building a EMG signal acquisition system, and a dataset of EMG signals of the lower limbs including 286 samples and 5 classifications was constructed. The wavelet hard threshold denoising was used as a preprocessing for this dataset, and the method of fusion of time domain analysis and principal component analysis was used to extract features, and the features were selected preferentially. Then, the improved EEMD signal enhancement method was introduced to enhance the signal of the EMG signal samples, and then

R. C. Qiu et al. (Eds.): IoTaaS 2024, LNICST 675, pp. 298–308, 2026.
https://doi.org/10.1007/978-3-032-14681-6_27

the feature extraction was carried out to compare and analyze the previously extracted features. Then, the SVM and BGDT algorithms were used to analyze the two sets of eigenvectors, and the results were obtained and the reasons for the errors were analyzed, and then the SVM algorithm and the GBDT algorithm were fused, and a two-layer ensemble classifier with stacking fusion strategy was designed and applied, and the resulting fusion algorithm was used to classify the dataset to seek better classification effect.

2 Collection and Dataset Construction of Lower Limb EMG Signals

2.1 Setup of the Sampling System

According to the needs of subsequent classification and identification, the workflow of the EMG signal acquisition module is to collect six-channel EMG signals through EMG sensors, wherein 1, 3, 4, and 6 channels are used in actual use, the EMG signals are amplified by amplification circuits, the detected EMG signals are output at the middle end for A/D conversion, and the output signals at the mid- end are collected by the Arduino UNO development kit matched with the six-lead EMG module at the back end. After connecting to a computer, the original signal of the sEMG can be viewed through the host computer, and the data can be recorded and exported for further processing. The first layer of the board is an analog circuit, including an EMG sensor and an amplifier circuit, and the second layer of the board is a digital circuit, including an A/D conversion module, a main control module and an output module connected to a computer.

Sensor module and muscle electricity collection wiring:

The sensor module consists of a three-lead wire, a six-lead muscle sensor, an Arduino UNO development board, and a functional block diagram of the connection schematic system (Fig. 1).

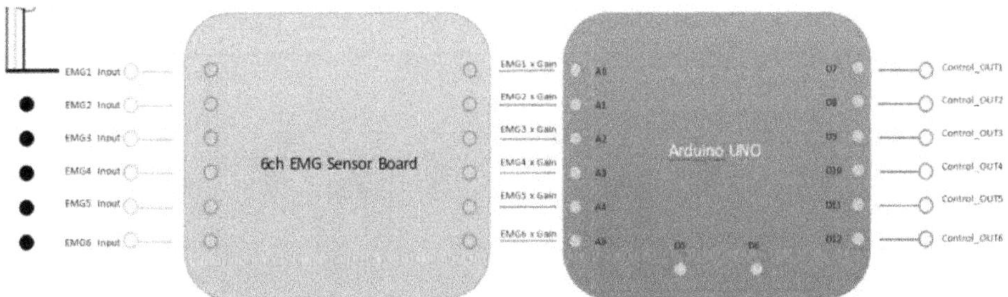

Fig. 1. System composition diagram

Introduction to the upper machine:

In the collection and output of muscle signals, the upper machine is an indispensable part. The figure below is the schematic diagram of the upper machine interface used in this article (Fig. 2).

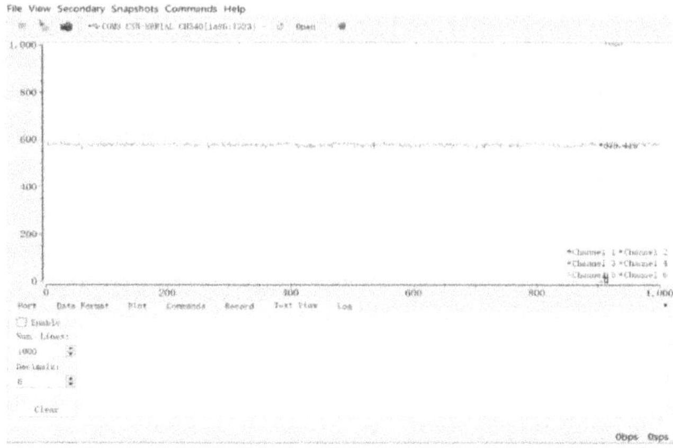

Fig. 2. Dragon of the upper machine interface

In this paper, the interface of the host computer is set to start and end the drawing of the EMG signal diagram, so that after the EMG signal is collected, the host computer can represent the EMG signal of each channel in different colors through the EMG signal data output by the acquisition module, and draw it into a waveform diagram, so that the user can understand the EMG signal more intuitively. A data saving function is also set up to collect signal samples, and a screenshot function is added to save the action waveform in real time.

Sampling action and sampling point:

There are five types of experiments, which are upstairs, downstairs, jump, walk, run.

In terms of the choice of sampling points, in order to ensure the quality of sampling, when choosing muscles, try to choose the shallow muscles close to the body surface to avoid being wrapped and covered by other muscles, causing the error of the signal, and pay attention to the choice of the sampling muscles between the sampling muscles. Differential differences in exercise, this experiment adopts a four-channel signal acquisition system. Therefore, it is selected as a sample point for rectus, biceps, gastrocnemiosus, and biochays (Fig. 3).

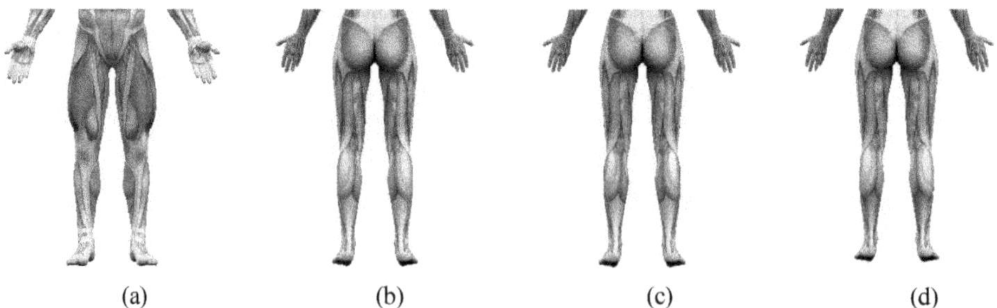

(a)   (b)   (c)   (d)

Fig. 3. Selection of leg sampling points

In this experiment, a 23-year-old woman who was a subject with a normal exercise of the lower limbs and neurotomy-free muscle diseases pasted the electrode at the four sample points of the right leg, and repeatedly repeatedly repeatedly experimented with each experimental action. Repeat the amplitude and strength of the action as much as possible when various experimental actions.

3 Pre-processing and Feature Extraction of Surface Muscle Signals

Because the surface muscle signal is relatively weak, and it is easy to mix various pseudo-trace noise during the collection process, before the subsequent classification recognition, the muscle signal is required to prepare and feature extraction. This chapter will be pre-processed with a small wave hard threshold, and the analysis of the main component analysis method of time domain characteristics is adopted for feature extraction. After that, an improved EEMD method is innovatively proposed. For the traditional EEMD method, it is easy to cause the defects of information loss. The concept of the introduction of mahalanobis distance is introduced, which makes the muscle signal be fully exfoliated.

3.1 Multi-Electrical Signals Based on Improving the EEMD Method is Enhanced

Muscle electrical signals have their own characteristics as biological telecommunications signals. For example, due to different biological individuals, muscle signals between different mobility will also cause differences, and the migration of muscle signal classification models between different people will sometimes not be high. Therefore, the classification of muscle and electricity signals is usually based on small sample data sets, so if you only perform pre-processing and feature extraction, there may be some shortcomings.

At this time, an improved collection experience modal decomposition (EEMD) method is introduced to an improved collection experience modal decomposition. Demonstrate information loss caused by the recognized noise. This method is applied to the de-noise of the muscle signal processing process before, before the feature extraction, and the preliminaries to get a better effect in the subsequent signal classification

○

EEMD is a method of noise auxiliary analysis. It is the extension and enhancement of the Empirical Mode Decomposition (EMD). This method is widely used because it does not need to set the base function in advance. Theoretically, it can, it can Adapt to the processing of any signal, especially in the non-stable time sequence signal, the advantage is obvious.

The specific steps of EEMD are:

(1) First set the average number of times as N;
(2) Set a white noise $m_i(t)$, it must be distributed for standard normal, And bring this white noise to the sample signal $x(t)$, which can generate a new signal:

$$x_i(t) = x(t) + m_i(t) \tag{1}$$

$i = 1, 2, ..., n;$

(3) For $x_i(t)$ to decompose EMD, write the form of the *IMF* and the form of each function:

$$x_i(t) = \sum_{j=1}^{J} c_{i,j}(t) + r_{i,j}(t) \tag{2}$$

Among them, $c_{i,j}(t)$ is the j th *IMF*, which is decomposed after the additional white noise of the i times. $r_{i,j}(t)$ represents the residual function;

(4) Repeat the above steps N times:

(5) To get the average operation of the *IMF* collection, you can get the final *IMF*;

$$c_j(t) = \frac{1}{M} \sum_{I=1}^{n} c_{i,j}(t) \tag{3}$$

$c_j(t)$ indicates the j n *IMF*, $i = 1, 2, ..., N, j, 1, 2, ..., J$;

From the analysis of the above principles above, it can be found that in the process of processing the signal, we have set a letter of *IMF* components of the letter and noise. For the identified noise, it will directly abandon It is caused by low accuracy of noise. In response to this situation, this article introduced the concept of Mahalanbis Distance (MD) in the signal processing process of EEMD to improve the accuracy of judgment on noise and avoid waste of information.

The decomposition signal is extracted. First, the main component analysis is performed (Fig. 4).

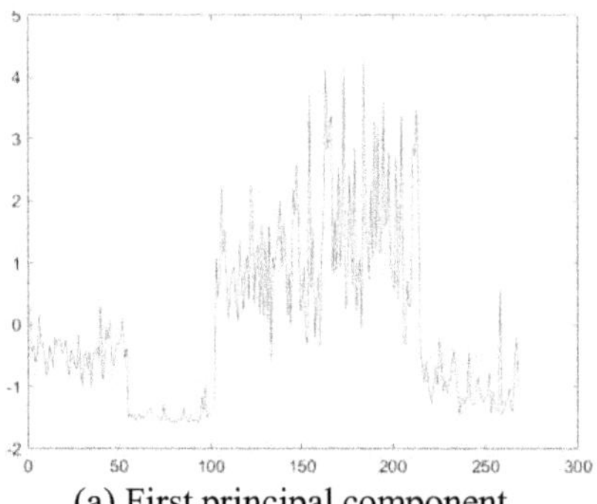

(a) First principal component

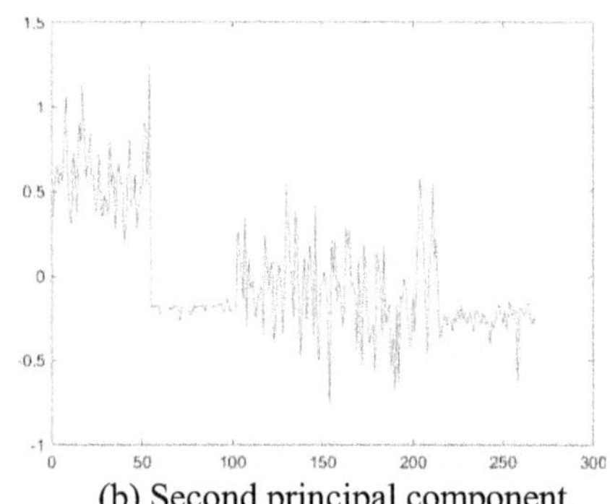

(b) Second principal component

Fig. 4. Main component analysis

Analysis of the contribution rate and accumulated contribution of the two main components (Fig. 5).

Continue to find the maximum value, strange value, coordinated, energy value, and the average value of the absolute value of the maximum value, and the average value of the muscle signal processed by EEMD.

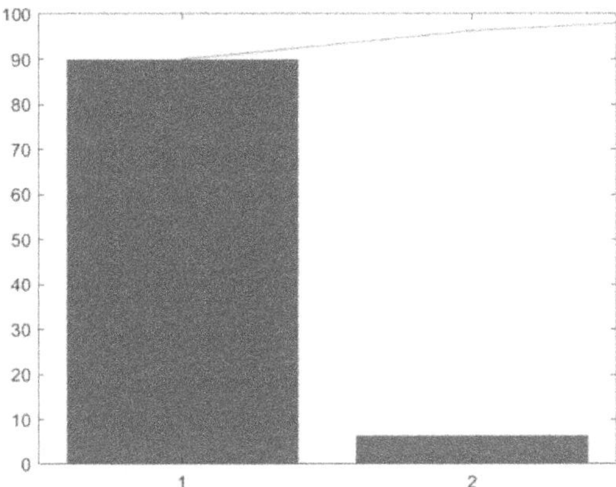

Fig. 5. The contribution rate and accumulated contribution of the main component vector

A characteristic correlation analysis of the improved EEMD-processed muscle and electricity signals, found that the correlation of several time domain features is slightly reduced in the average value of the absolute value, and the maximum value of the absolute value has also been reduced from 0.8 to 0.54, but The feature vector of the absolute value of correlation has increased, that is, the features that can be selected can be increased from 13 to 16.

4 Movement and Identification of Lower Limb Surface Muscle Signal

4.1 Classification and Identification of SVM-Based Lower Limb Muscle Electrical Signal

Support vector machine (SVM) is a kind of machine learning algorithm proposed by Russian statistician Vapnik in 1995, occupying a place in the most influential supervision machine learning algorithm. SVM is rooted in the principle of minimizing structural risk. This theory is also proposed by VAPNIK. The principle of minimizing structural risk is different from the principle of minimizing the risk to minimize the risk. Under this principle, the main tasks of the classifier are divided into two steps:

(1) Build a function subset to make this subset aimed at problems that need to be solved. It has the best and strongest classification ability.
(2) In the concentration of the construction, find a judgment function, the selection standard is the least experience risk.

Multi-classification SVM in Muscle Signal Classification and Recognition: Method of decision-making binary tree classification:

For a sample set with a class number K, if this sample set can be classified, it means that in this sample set, any two sample categories can be divided. In the set, any pair of sample classes can be classified, so this sample set with a K class is also available. Then, through a specific dual classification combination, the entire sample set can be classified. Apply this idea on the SVM of the two classifier, that is, combine the binary tree with SVM, and finally construct a multi-classifier. Then this method is called a decision-making binary tree SVM.

In this way, the classification process of the new sample is to classify from the top-level node. From this, find the next node according to the classification output value of each node until the final reaches the leaf node to achieve classification.

Not only does the decision-making binary tree SVM not only have a small number of SVMs and fast classification speeds, but also avoids the blind spots of decision-making brought by the voting mechanism, and there will be no problems that samples are not belonged to any classification. Therefore, in this experiment, the classification of SVM's lower limb muscle electrical signal will adopt this method.

Classify the muscle and electricity signals that enhance data, and find that the accuracy of classification is 89.47%. The following is a classification result map (Fig. 6):

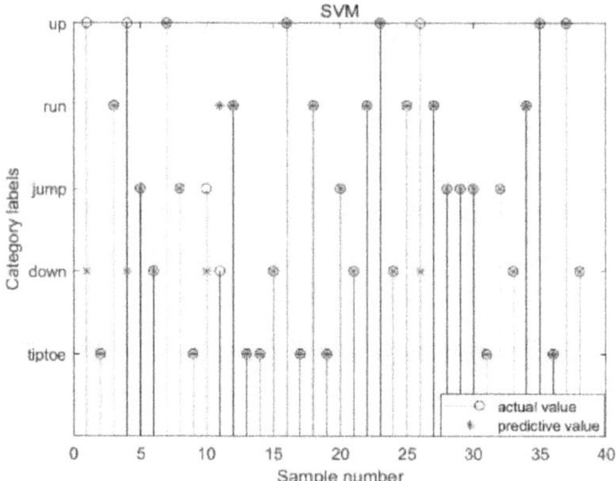

Fig. 6. SVM classification result graph-EEMD

4.2 Classification and Recognition of Surface Lower Limb Electromyographic Signals Based on GBDT

Gradient Boosting Decision Tree Principle

As an integrated algorithm, GBDT needs to set the base learning device. The CART algorithm can be applied to the classification and the regression problem. At the same time, the idea is simple and clear. The path is clear during prediction, and the operating speed is fast. Therefore, it is very suitable to become a base learning device in the integrated classification algorithm. GBDT uses the CART regression tree as a base learning device, allows the base learning device to perform linear combinations, and uses an forefront to fit the algorithm for model training. Category results. In this process, the thinking of the forefront-to-step algorithm can be understood as a step-by-step and excellence. Now a rough classification is carried out, and then gradually approach the final output in the next iteration; To train a new CART tree, we must regard the output of the tree that have been trained and the residues of the real values as input before, thereby constantly iterating and gradually narrowing the gap to accumulate the output of each round of trees. Eventually the output result.

In terms of process, the general process of GBDT is:

(1) Design a CART regression tree as a base learning device. At this time, the return tree only needs one root node。

(2) Start to improve iteration. Start calculation from the current model, find the negative gradient value of the loss function [55], which is the approximation value of the residual; the approximation value of the residue is fitted, and the area of the leaf node in the tree in the tree is estimated. Find the residual fitting value that can minimize the loss function. Generally, the linear search method is used to estimate the leaf nodes; when the best residual fitting value is found, the CART returning tree can be updated。

(3) Repeat the above process to improve and iterate, and finally you can output a model with good performance.

Experimental results and analysis of GBDT algorithm
Use the GBDT algorithm to classify the muscle electrical signal.
When a muscle and electricity signal with data enhancement is used to classify, the accuracy rate is 92.11%.The classification results are shown in the figure (Fig. 7).

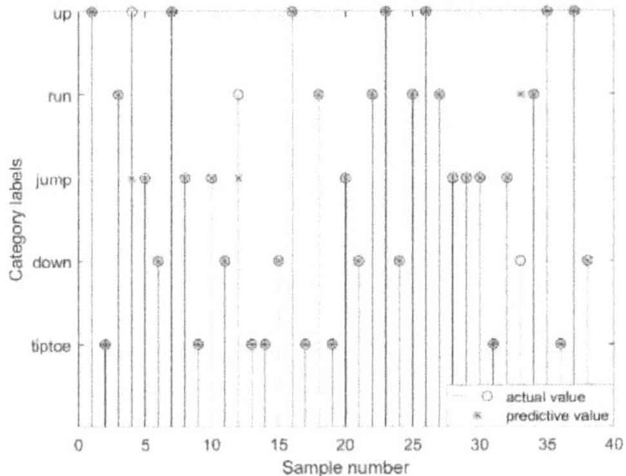

Fig. 7. GBDT classification results- EEMD

4.3 Muscle Electrical Signal Category Identification Based on Fusion Algorithm

The fusion method of SVM algorithm and GBDT algorithm.

After analyzing the two algorithms, it is found that the accuracy of a single algorithm on the classification of smaller samples is still low. Therefore, it is proposed to integrate the SVM algorithm and the GBDT algorithm to obtain a better classification accuracy rate.

In terms of algorithm fusion, this article will adopt a layered structure cross-verification method to adopt the idea of the Stacking model. The basic idea of Stacking is actually integrated the classification results of other individual individual classifiers through a classifier. The basic principle is to divide the data set to form several sub-training sets to train the base classifier to use the base classifier to use the base classifier. The result is then integrated into a training set to train the classifier on the second layer.

This article simplifies its models. The improved algorithm is divided into two layers. The first layer is a category set composed of 5 basis classifiers.

In the end, this article proposes the method of "combining the results of the GBDT as a base classifier to classify different datasets divided by the data set, and integrate the results of the SVM model's founder's founder".

In this fusion algorithm, the specific workflow is as follows:

(1) Divide the dataset and divide it into 5 sub-data sets.
(2) Set 5 GBDT models as the base classifier. For the first base learning device, the first four sub-data sets are used as a training set, the last is the test set, and the other 4 learning devices are pushed.
(3) Use 5 GBDT classifiers to classify their respective training sets, so as to obtain prediction output of 5 training sets, and integrate the prediction results of the five training sets into a new dataset.
(4) Use 5 GBDT classifiers to test classification of their respective test sets, so as to obtain prediction output of 5 test sets, and the output results are also integrated into a data set.
(5) The output dataset of the training set is used as the training set of the second-layer classification algorithm SVM model. The output data set of the test set is used as the test set of SVM models to train and test the model and output the classification results.

Experimental results and analysis of fusion models:

When the signal adopted is a muscle signal enhanced by data, it can be seen that the accuracy of the classification is 97.37%, which is the highest in the experiment (Fig. 8):

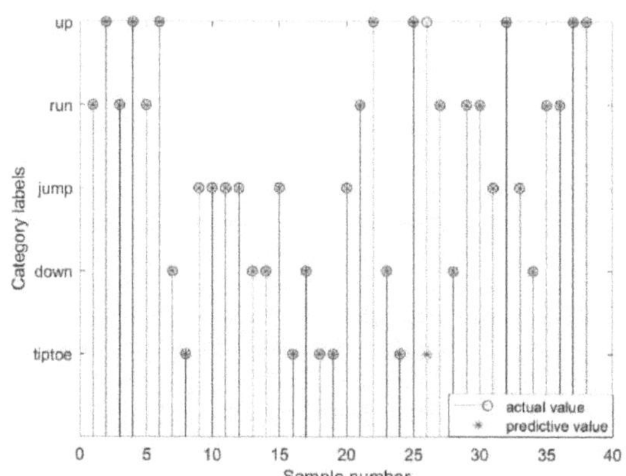

Fig. 8. SVM-GBDT classification results- EEMD

Analyze the experimental results through the form (Table 1):

Table 1. The accuracy of various algorithms in classifying and recognizing electromyographic signals

Algorithm	Signal Enhancement
SVM	89.47%
GBDT	92.11%
SVM-GBDT	97.37%

This article proposes a classification model based on the SVM and GBDT algorithm. Using the improved Stacking fusion strategy idea as a combination strategy, a integrated classifier with a two- layer structure is built, which divides the original data set into 5 sub-dataset Verification, the SVM model with a simpler structure is set as a two-layer classifier, which successfully maintains the model with high accuracy and avoids overfitting. When classification of muscle electrical signals, it is found that the accuracy of classification reaches 97.37%when this algorithm is applied to the enhanced data signal, which is excellent.

5 Conclusions

This article proposes a classification model based on the SVM and GBDT algorithm. Using the improved Stacking fusion strategy idea as a combination strategy, a integrated classifier with a two- layer structure is built, which divides the original data set into 5 sub-dataset Verification, the SVM model with a simpler structure is set as a two-layer classifier, which successfully maintains the model with high accuracy and avoids overfitting. When classification of muscle electrical signals, it is found that the accuracy of classification reaches 97.37%when this algorithm is applied to the enhanced data signal, which is excellent.

References

1. Venugopal, G., Navaneethakrishna, M., Ramakrishnan, S.: Extraction and analysis of multiple time window features associated with muscle fatigue conditions using sEMG signals. Expert Syst. Appl. **41**(6), 2652–2659 (2014)
2. Lopez, R., Salazar, S., Torres, J., et al.: Modeling and control of a lower limb exoskeleton with two degrees of freedom. In: 2012 9th International Conference on Electrical Engineering, Computing Science and Automatic Control (CCE), pp. 1–6. IEEE (2012)
3. Ghan, J., Steger, R., Kazerooni, H.: Control and system identification for the Berkeley lower extremity exoskeleton (BLEEX). Adv. Robot. **20**(9), 989–1014 (2006)
4. Anonymous, et al.: HULC exoskeleton user testing awarded to Lockheed Martin. Military Aeros. Electron. **21**(9) (2010)
5. Qi, S., Wu, X., Chen, W.H., et al.: SEMG-based recognition of composite motion with convolutional neural network. Sens. Actuators, A **311**, 112046 (2020)
6. Zhao, Z., Li, M., Deng, M., et al.: Research on a fusion gait real-time recognition algorithm[C]//Journal of Physics: Conference Series. IOP Publishing **1187**(4), 042014 (2019)

7. Khalid, S., Khalil, T., Nasreen, S.: A survey of feature selection and feature extraction techniques in machine learning. In: 2014 Science and Information Conference, pp. 372–378. IEEE (2014)

8. Galar, M., Fernández, A., Barrenechea, E., et al.: DRCW-OVO: distance-based relative competence weighting combination for One-vs-One strategy in multi-class problems. Pattern Recogn. **48**(1), 28–42 (2015)

9. Fanello, S.R., Keskin, C., Izadi, S., et al.: Learning to be a depth camera for close-range human capture and interaction. ACM Trans. Graph. (TOG) **33**(4), 1–11 (2014)

10. Song, Q., Lee, J., Akter, S., et al.: Prediction of condition-specific regulatory genes using machine learning. Nucleic Acids Res. **48**(11), e62–e62 (2020)

11. Chen, W., Wang, Z., Xie, H., et al.: Characterization of surface EMG signal based on fuzzy entropy. IEEE Trans. Neural Syst. Rehabil. Eng. **15**(2), 266–272 (2007)

12. Phinyomark, A., Campbell, E., Scheme, E.: Surface electromyography (EMG) signal processing, classification, and practical considerations. In: Biomedical Signal Processing: Advances in Theory, Algorithms and Applications, pp. 3–29 (2020)

13. Tölgyessy, M., Dekan, M., Chovanec, Ľ: Skeleton tracking accuracy and precision evaluation of Kinect V1, Kinect V2, and the azure kinect. Appl. Sci. **11**(12), 5756 (2021)

14. Shlens, J.: A tutorial on principal component analysis. arXiv preprint arXiv:1404.1100 (2014)

15. Lin, W., Zhang, B., Li, H., et al.: Short-term load forecasting based on EEMD-Adaboost-BP. Syst. Sci. Control Eng. **10**(1), 846–853 (2022)

16. Dar, L.S., Aamir, M.: Forecasting crude oil prices volatility by reconstructing EEMD components using ARIMA and FFNN models. Front. Energy Res. **1501**, 991602 (2022)

Malicious URL Classification Method Based on Feature Purification

Yuxuan Wu[✉] and Xuefang Zhang

Wuhan Research Institute of Posts and Telecommunications,
No. 88 Youkeyuan Road, Hongshan District, Wuhan, Hubei, China
xk17wuyuxuan@126.com

Abstract. With the rapid advancement of the Internet and the proliferation of Internet of Things (IoT) devices, the diversity of malicious URLs has increased. These changes are reflected not only in their increasing number but also in the escalating technological complexity, which poses significant security threats to IoT networks. Traditional detection methods relying on manual rules or specific patterns are insufficient to address these challenges. There is a pressing need for more sophisticated URL detection techniques to enhance the accuracy and comprehensiveness of malicious URL identification, especially in IoT environments. This study integrates the feature purification network FP-net into malicious URL classification and introduces the FCBA model utilizing CNN-BiLSTM-Attention as the feature extractor for FP-net. The model employs CNN for effective local feature extraction, BiLSTM for capturing sequence information, and incorporates the attention mechanism. Experimental findings indicate that the FCBA model achieves an accuracy of 94.66% in malicious URL classification, surpassing CNN-BiLSTM-Attention by 0.65%. This demonstrates that FP-net enhances the performance of the CNN-BiLSTM-Attention model, and the FCBA model excels in URL classification tasks.

Keywords: URL classification · feature purification network · BiLSTM · deep learning · IoT security

1 Introduction

In today's digital era, everything is gradually interconnected. The widespread adoption of technologies like the Internet of Things (IoT), big data, and artificial intelligence (AI) has significantly enhanced the convenience of our lives. However, the continuous emergence of malicious URLs poses a significant threat to network security. Attacks leveraging malicious URLs can not only compromise personal privacy but also potentially harm businesses and society at large. IoT devices usually have low computing power and security protection measures, making them easy targets for malicious attacks. Attackers can trick devices into accessing malicious servers through malicious URLs, thereby gaining control of the device or stealing sensitive information. The classification and identification of malicious URLs remain pivotal in the contemporary field of network security, particularly within the IoT domain.

© ICST Institute for Computer Sciences, Social Informatics and Telecommunications Engineering 2026
Published by Springer Nature Switzerland AG 2026. All Rights Reserved
R. C. Qiu et al. (Eds.): IoTaaS 2024, LNICST 675, pp. 309–318, 2026.
https://doi.org/10.1007/978-3-032-14681-6_28

Traditional machine learning approaches have significant limitations in detecting malicious URLs: they overly depend on the expertise and experience of security professionals, resulting in inherent subjectivity and constraints. This dependency allows attackers to deliberately evade or obfuscate detection systems by exploiting the features provided by experts. Furthermore, inconsistencies in feature engineering can result in unpredictable applicability across different scenarios. In contrast, deep learning, an extension of neural network algorithms, aims to emulate the structural model of the human brain. By training on extensive datasets and automatically adjusting inter-neuronal weights, it excels in feature extraction without necessitating manual feature engineering.

Wu Haibin, H.Le, and others have employed convolutional neural networks (CNNs) to process characters and words within URL strings, enabling the direct acquisition of nonlinear URL representations and capturing contextual relationships between words. This approach minimizes manual intervention [1, 2]. Zhang Ting utilized skip-gram for word vector encoding of malicious URLs and incorporated it into a Long Short-Term Memory (LSTM) network. By employing average pooling to amalgamate features extracted by the LSTM, she achieved a classification accuracy of 97.2% [3]. Zahra et al. proposed an intelligent system based on fuzzy logic and data mining to identify Covid-19-themed malicious URLs and phishing attacks. Their approach utilizes fuzzy logic to handle uncertainty and ambiguity, combined with data mining techniques to analyze URL features [4].

Continual advancements are being made by researchers building upon CNN and LSTM architectures. Zuo Wen and colleagues integrated CNNs with Gated Recurrent Units (GRUs) to extract semantic and temporal features from URLs respectively. They also employed CNN pruning and Singular Value Decomposition (SVD) to eliminate model redundancies, resulting in substantial improvements [5]. Ren et al. implemented a Bidirectional LSTM (BiLSTM) for URL classification, significantly enhancing model accuracy [6]. Liang Fei utilized N-gram for URL word segmentation, incorporated word vectors into a BiLSTM model for feature extraction, and introduced an Attention mechanism to capture intra-textual word correlations. This comprehensive approach led to improved BiLSTM model accuracy [7].

Despite the advancements achieved by deep learning in malicious URL detection, certain inherent limitations persist and necessitate further innovation. Deep learning models, while adept at capturing abstract semantic information and extracting multilayered, high-dimensional features, often encompass extraneous information detrimental to specific classification tasks, potentially compromising classification outcomes. Addressing this challenge, this paper introduces a feature purification network, enhancing the existing model to more precisely extract crucial features from malicious URLs, thereby elevating the overall classification performance of the model.

2 Proposed Method

The hierarchical architecture of deep learning models enables multi-tiered feature extraction from input data. The URL classification task necessitates feature extraction at various levels, encompassing local structures, sequential information, and global correlations. Therefore, this study selected CNN, which can effectively extract local features, and

BiLSTM, which can capture sequence information. When combined with the attention mechanism, this approach enables the model to focus more on key information while learning global correlation features, thereby enhancing the model's ability to capture global features. To enhance feature representation learning and improve the model's discriminative capability in classification, this study introduces the Feature Purification Network (FP-net). The study utilizes CNN-BiLSTM-Attention as the feature extractor within FP-net, thereby creating a novel model termed FCBA, which is then applied to the classification of malicious URLs (see Fig. 1).

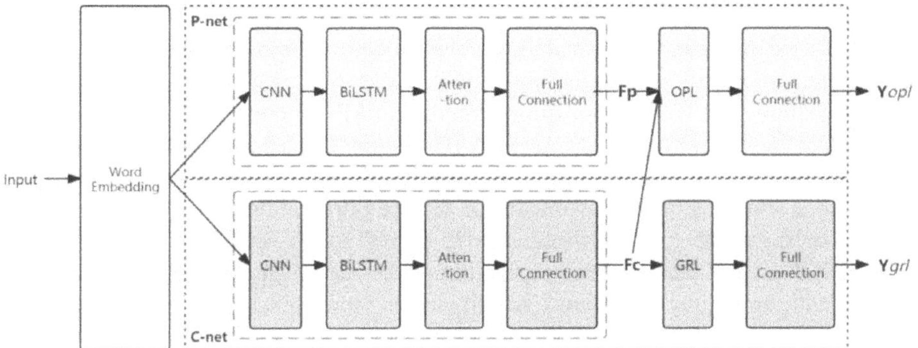

Fig. 1. FCBA model framework diagram.

2.1 CNN-BiLSTM-Attention

The CNN layer in the FCBA model employs multiple sliding windows (convolution kernels) of varying sizes for element-wise multiplication with the input data, followed by summation to produce the convolution output. The model uses 128 convolution kernels of sizes 1, 2, and 3 to capture features in the URL word vector matrix at different scales. The fully connected layer then integrates the maximum pooling results from these convolution kernels.

CNNs extract local features using sliding windows and preserve relevant information through pooling, discerning hierarchical structure and local attributes. However, CNNs can struggle with representing global features, which may impact their ability to capture long-range dependencies in text classification tasks.

To address this, CNNs are often combined with LSTM networks, which handle sequence data effectively [8]. For URL classification, this research integrates CNN with BiLSTM (bidirectional long short-term memory network). CNN extracts local features, while BiLSTM captures long-range dependencies and contextual attributes.

BiLSTM consists of two LSTM structures: one forward and one reverse, processing the input sequence from these different directions to capture both past and future contextual information. The hidden states from both directions are concatenated to yield the final representation [9]. Within a URL, the sequence of different segments may hold critical information, such as the positioning of subdomains or parameters. Leveraging its bidirectional architecture, BiLSTM simultaneously considers both forward and reverse contextual dependencies, enhancing its ability to comprehend URL sequences. The structure diagram of BiLSTM is depicted in Fig. 3.

An Attention mechanism is added after the BiLSTM layer to highlight key features. The output features are then integrated using a fully connected layer. Both sub-networks, C-net and P-net, in the model use this CNN-BiLSTM-Attention structure as the feature extractor.

2.2 Feature Purification Network

Qin et al. first proposed using the Feature Purification Network (FP-net) in 2020 to enhance feature representation learning and increase the model's discriminative ability in classification [10]. The composition structure of FP-net contains two sub-networks, namely Common feature learning network (C-net) and Projection network (P-net). The structure diagram is shown in Fig. 2. The feature extractors of the common feature learning network and projection network in the feature purification network FP-net can be replaced by any neural network that can extract text features, such as CNN, RNN, Transformer, BERT, etc.Zhang Haifeng et al. addressed issues such as inconsistent terminology, semantic ambiguity, and feature sparsity in news topic text by proposing a classification method that combines BERT and FP-net. By applying feature projection purification on features extracted by the BERT model, they were able to extract strong classification features, further demonstrating that FP-net can improve classification performance [11].

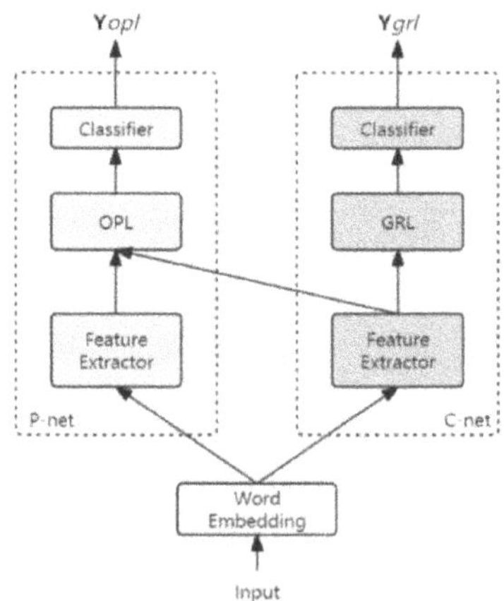

Fig. 2. FP-Net structure diagram.

C-net. The role of the C-net component is to extract common features. These common features encompass words that are overly frequent or highly generalized, such as stop words like "the", "and", "is" in text data, and terms like "www", "http", "com" in URL data. Given their ubiquitous presence across most datasets, they often lack the discriminatory information beneficial for classification. Additionally, certain overly simplistic grammatical structures or rules, such as basic word order in sentences, may offer limited contribution to the classification task. To mitigate the influence of these common features lacking discriminative power on the model's classification performance, a gradient reversal layer is appended to the conventional feature extractor of the C-net.

The function of the gradient inversion layer is to negate the original gradient during the training process, enabling the model to learn features that are insensitive to domain changes. The formula is depicted in Eq. (1). The λ value serves as the hyperparameter for GRL. During forward propagation, the gradient inversion layer does not alter the feature fc. However, during back propagation, it conveys the $-\lambda$ value to invert the loss function of the entire C-net network [11].

$$GRL(x) = x$$
$$\frac{\partial GRL(x)}{\partial x} = -\lambda I \tag{1}$$

After reshaping the feature vector obtained from gradient flipping into a one-dimensional vector, it is fed into the feedforward neural network. The output Y_{GRL} represents the feature classification result post gradient flipping. Subsequently, the cross-entropy loss function is employed to gauge the discrepancy between the predicted and actual values. Through optimizing this loss function, C-net can extract common features across different categories.

$$GRL(f_c) = \tilde{f}_c \tag{2}$$

$$Y_{GRL} = softmax(\tilde{f}_c * W_c + b_c) \tag{3}$$

$$loss_c = CrossEntropy(Y_{truth}, Y_{GRL}) \tag{4}$$

P-net. In deep learning, projection is often utilized to eliminate redundant information, extract crucial data features, or reduce dimensionality, thereby enhancing the model's performance. The original feature f_p, extracted by the CNN-BiLSTM-Attention of the Feature Projection Network P-net, encompasses the comprehensive feature details of the input data. Utilizing the Orthogonal Projection Layer (OPL), f_p undergoes a projection operation with the common feature f_c derived from the Common Feature Learning Network C-net. This step eliminates information correlated with the common feature f_c from the original feature f_p, accomplishing the goal of refining the feature f_p. This enables the model to concentrate more on learning pivotal features, consequently improving the accuracy and efficiency of URL classification tasks. The Orthogonal Projection Layer is illustrated in Fig. 3.

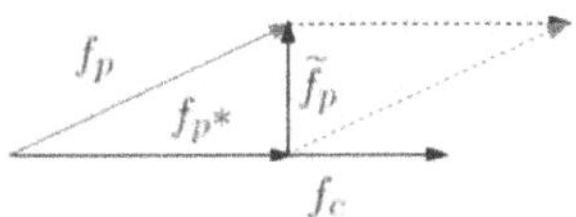

Fig. 3. Orthogonal projection layer diagram.

To accomplish this, the first feature projection is executed, projecting the original feature f_p onto the common feature f_c. The resulting projected feature vector, f_p^*, exclusively contains common feature information. Subsequently, a second feature projection is conducted, yielding a feature vector equivalent to f_p-f_p^*, which only contains features suitable for classification:

$$proj(a, b) = \frac{a \cdot b}{|b|^2} b \tag{5}$$

$$f_p^* = proj(f_p, f_c) \tag{6}$$

$$\tilde{f}_p = proj(f_p, (f_p - f_p^*)) \tag{7}$$

Finally, similar to C-net, P-net enters the feedforward neural network for classification. It uses the cross-entropy loss function to measure the difference between the predicted and actual values. Y_{OPL} denotes the classification label used for judgment after feature purification, which represents the model's final output judgment result. The final predicted classification loss function value of the entire model is termed as $loss_p$.

$$Y_{OPL} = softmax(\tilde{f}_p * W_p + b_p) \tag{8}$$

$$loss_p = CrossEntropy(Y_{truth}, Y_{OPL}) \tag{9}$$

3 Experiments and Results

To evaluate the effectiveness of the proposed method, various experiments were conducted. The experimental environment was developed using Python 3.10 and TensorFlow 1.10.0. For the online experiments, we utilized a cloud server on Google Colaboratory equipped with an Intel(R) Xeon(R) CPU @ 2.20GHz, NVIDIA-SMI 525.105.17 GPU, and 12.64GB memory.

3.1 Experimental Datasets

This study selected "Phishing Site URLs" from Kaggle as the experimental data set. After data cleaning, 60,784 pieces of data were retained, and the data set was divided into a training set and a test set at a ratio of 8:2, where the ratio of normal URLs to malicious URLs was approximately 1:1.

3.2 Evaluation Indicators

This study uses Accuracy, Precision, Recall and F1-Score as experimental performance evaluation indicators:

$$Accuracy = \frac{TP + TN}{TP + TN + FP + FN} \tag{10}$$

$$Precision = \frac{TP}{TP + FP} \tag{11}$$

$$Recall = \frac{TP}{TP + FN} \tag{12}$$

$$F1 = \frac{Precision \times Recall \times 2}{Precision + Recall} \tag{13}$$

3.3   Results and Analysis

Table 1. Experimental hyperparameters.

Batch size	128
Initial Learning Rate	0.001
Dropout	0.7
Training Epochs	30

Experimental hyperparameters are shown in Table 1.

Model Comparison Experiment.   This experiment evaluates four models: CNN, BiL-STM, Transformer, and CNN-BiLSTM-Attention, all enhanced with a feature purification network (FP-net). These models are denoted as CNN + FP, BiLSTM + FP, Trans + FP, and FCBA. The Transformer encoder uses 3 layers of self-attention, CNN has 128 convolution kernels of sizes 1, 2, and 3, and BiLSTM has 128 hidden units. Hyperparameters are set as follows: batch size of 128, initial learning rate of 0.001, Dropout value of 0.7, and 30 training epochs. Table 2 shows that all models perform well, with the FCBA model achieving the highest accuracy (94.664%) and precision (94.668%).

Table 2. Model comparison experimental results.

Model	Acc/%	Pre/%	F1/%
CNN	93.792	93.792	93.791
LSTM	93.867	93.890	93.865
Transformer	93.557	93.586	93.559
CNN + FP	94.373	94.395	94.372
BiLSTM + FP	93.900	94.002	93.895
Trans + FP	94.190	94.200	94.189
FCBA	94.664	94.668	94.663

Parameter Optimization Experiment. As an important part of the convolutional layer in CNN, the convolution kernel's shape and size directly affect the model's ability to extract features from the input data. This experiment explores the impact of different convolution kernel sizes on the FCBA model's accuracy. Combinations tested are [1–4], and [3–5].

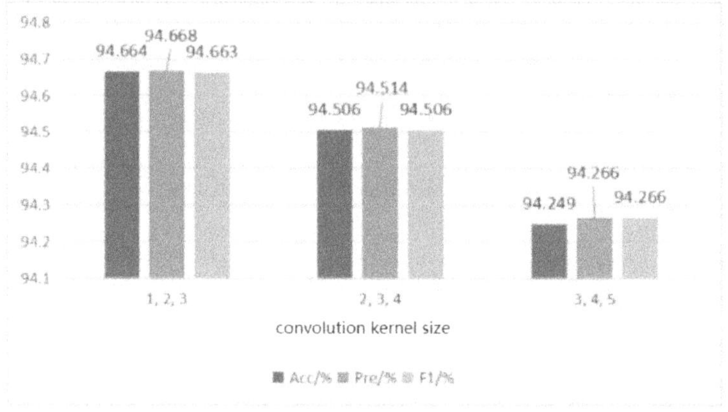

Fig. 4. Convolution kernel size experimental results.

The experimental results depicted in Fig. 4 show optimal performance when the convolution window size is [1–3], with the accuracy, precision, and F1 score reaching their peaks. As the convolution window size is increased to [2–4] and [3–5], there's a slight decline in the model's performance metrics. This indicates that, for URL classification tasks, a smaller convolution window size is beneficial for the model to capture local features within the sequence. When combined with the global information capturing capability of BiLSTM, it yields the best performance.

Table 3. FP-Net ablation experimental results.

Model	*Acc/%*	*Pre/%*	*F1/%*
FCBA	94.664	94.668	94.663
FCBA-GRL	94.008	94.070	94.005
FCBA-OPL	93.825	93.848	93.823

Ablation Experiment. Gradient reversal layer (GRL) and orthogonal projection layer (OPL) are two key components of the feature purification network. The ablation experiment removes these two parts in the FCBA model and compares various indicators, as shown in Table 3. The gradient reversal layer is located in C-net, which enables C-net to extract common features fc that are not beneficial to the classification task. FCBA-GRL removes the gradient inversion layer, and the accuracy drops by 0.656% compared to the original model. The orthogonal projection layer is located in P-net. The original features fp and fc are obtained through the first feature projection to obtain fp*, and then through the second feature projection to obtain the feature vector fp-fp*. The FCBA-OPL model removes the feature projection layer and directly obtains the feature vector fp-fc from fp and fc, and the accuracy drops by 0.839%. Experimental results indicate that the gradient reversal layer and the orthogonal projection layer each play a crucial role in common feature extraction and filtering, making them indispensable and significant components of the feature purification network (Table 4).

Table 4. FP-Net ablation experimental results.

Model	*Acc/%*	*Pre/%*	*F1/%*
CNN + BiLSTM + FP	94.506	94.514	94.506
CNN + BiLSTM + Attention	94.007	94.051	94.006
FCBA	94.664	94.668	94.663

After incorporating the attention mechanism into CNN + BiLSTM + FP, the accuracy improved by 0.158%, and the F1 score rose by approximately 0.002. The attention mechanism allows for flexible adjustment of feature attention weights to highlight the most crucial feature information among the obtained features. With feature purification, CNN + BiLSTM + Attention's accuracy increases by 0.657%, and the new model FCBA achieves 94.664%, confirming the effectiveness of feature projection in purifying URL features.

4 Conclusion

This study introduces the feature purification network into the domain of URL classification, leveraging CNN's ability to capture local semantic features and BiLSTM's proficiency in capturing long-range dependencies. A FCBA model is proposed, which employs CNN-BiLSTM-Attention as the feature extractor for FP-net. Experimental results demonstrate that the FCBA model enhances accuracy, precision, and the f1 score among other metrics in malicious URL classification tasks compared to CNN-BiLSTM-Attention. And it is better than other FP-net based models. This confirms that the Feature Purification Network (FP-net) significantly enhances the CNN-BiLSTM-Attention model, making it more suitable for URL classification tasks. Future research could explore further optimization of the model for real-time detection in resource-constrained IoT environments and extend its application to other aspects of IoT security, such as anomaly detection and intrusion prevention.

References

1. Wu, H., Zhang, D.: Malicious URL detection technology based on context information. Software **40**(01), 63–68 (2019)

2. Le, H., Pham, Q., Sahoo, D., et al.: Urlnet: learning a URL representation with deep learning for malicious URL detection. Urlnet: learning a URL representation with deep learning for malicious URL detection. arxiv:1802.03162 (2018)
3. Zhang, T., Qian, L., Wang, L., et al.: Automatic feature extraction of malicious URLs based on multi-layer convolutional models. Computer Eng. Des. **41**(7), 1821–1828 (2020)
4. Zahra, S.R., Chishti, M.A., Baba, A.I., et al.: Detecting covid-19 chaos driven phishing/malicious URL attacks by a fuzzy logic and data mining based intelligence system. Egypt. Inf. J. **23**(2), 197–214 (2022)
5. Zuo, W.: Research and design of malicious URL detection algorithm based on deep learning, Ph.D. thesis, Beijing University of Posts and Telecommunications (2019)
6. Ren, F., Jiang, Z., Liu, J.: A bi-directional LSTM model with attention for malicious URL detection. In: 2019 IEEE 4th Advanced Information Technology, Electronic and Automation Control Conference (IAEAC), pp. 300–305 (2019)
7. Liang, F.: Intelligent detection method for malicious URLs based on multi-group attention mechanism. Comput. Appl. **42**(6), 1708–1715 (2022)
8. Luan, Y., Lin, S., Research on Text Classification Based on CNN and LSTM, 2019 IEEE International Conference on Artificial Intelligence and Computer Applications (ICAICA), Dalian, China, 352–355 (2019)
9. Wankhade, M., Annavarapu, C.S.R., Abraham, A.: CBMAFM: CNN-BiLSTM multi-attention fusion mechanism for sentiment classification. Multimedia Tools Appl. (2023). https://doi.org/10.1007/s11042-023-17437-9
10. Qi, Q., Hu, W., Liu, B.: Feature projection for improved text classification. In: Proceedings of the 58th Annual Meeting of the Association for Computational Linguistics, pp. 8161–8171 (2020)
11. Zhang, H., Zeng, C., Pan, L., et al.: News topic text classification method based on BERT and feature projection network. J. Comput. Appl. **42**(4), 1116–1124 (2022)

Design and Development of Application for Owners of Intelligent Net-Connected New Energy Vehicles

Lili Quan[1]([⊠]), Tao Huang[1], and Yong Pan[2]

[1] College of Computer and Electronic Information Engineering, Wuhan City Polytechnic, Wuhan, China
quanlily@126.com
[2] NO 1 Middle School Affiliated To Central China Normal University, Wuhan, China
panyongccnu@sina.com

Abstract. The integration of intelligent technology and new energy vehicles is an important trend of future development. The further development of intelligent connected vehicle technology will improve the intelligent level of new energy vehicles and provide users with a safer, convenient and comfortable driving experience. This paper analyzes the needs of new energy vehicle owners, and develops an application for new energy owners based on intelligent network connection. The application uses uni-app technology to develop the user side, and the server side uses Java Web framework. It contains five modules: vehicle-machine linkage, data analysis, warm service, interactive community and my car, which not only meets the needs of new energy owners in terms of charging service and vehicle management and monitoring, but also provides users with a safer, more convenient and comfortable service experience.

Keywords: Intelligent network connected · New energy vehicle · Application

1 Introduction

With the increasing attention of the world to environmental protection and sustainable development, new energy vehicles, as a kind of clean energy transportation, have been widely concerned and promoted. The integration of intelligent network technology and new energy vehicles will become a trend, providing users with a more convenient and safe driving experience. New energy vehicles will gradually realize the deep integration with artificial intelligence and the Internet, so as to achieve intelligent development. Advanced functions such as intelligent driving, remote control vehicles, and data analysis will also become indispensable configurations of new energy vehicles to enhance user experience.

R. C. Qiu et al. (Eds.): IoTaaS 2024, LNICST 675, pp. 319–330, 2026.
https://doi.org/10.1007/978-3-032-14681-6_29

2 Application of Intelligent Network Technology in New Energy Vehicles

Intelligent network technology is the key to realize the intelligence and networking of new energy vehicles. The application of these technologies not only improves the safety and convenience of driving, but also provides the foundation for future autonomous driving and Internet of vehicles services.

2.1 Automatic Control Technology

The core component of the modern intelligent and connected vehicle is the automatic control technology. It realizes the environment perception, intelligent decision-making and cooperative control of the vehicle by integrating sensors, controllers, actuators and other devices, and fusing modern communication and network technology. Using advanced sensors such as radar, Light detection and Ranging (LiDAR), and cameras, connected vehicles can capture real-time information about their surroundings, including other vehicles, pedestrians, road signs, and traffic signals. This information is the basis for realizing automatic control, and the data information from different sensors is fused and processed by advanced algorithms to improve the accuracy and reliability of perception [1]. This helps the control system to make more accurate judgments and decisions.

At present, the most widely used function in new energy vehicles is the automatic parking function. Firstly, the environment is perceived through the sensors around the vehicle, which usually include cameras, radar and ultrasonic sensors. The camera can capture visual information around the vehicle to help the system identify parking Spaces and obstacles; Radar and ultrasonic sensors detect the distance and position of objects by transmitting and receiving signals, so as to accurately sense the environment around the vehicle. In addition to the perception system, the automatic parking function also relies on an accurate positioning system to determine the position and orientation of the vehicle. Positioning systems may include Global Positioning systems (GPS), inertial navigation systems (INS), and high-precision map data, among others [2]. These technologies work together to enable vehicles to know exactly where they are in space, which enables precise parking operations. Once the sensing system and positioning system collect enough information, the automatic parking system will start to plan the parking trajectory. The system will calculate an optimal parking trajectory based on the perceived size and location of the parking space, as well as the current position and orientation of the vehicle.

The system then controls the steering, acceleration and braking of the vehicle to automatically park into a parking space along a planned trajectory. In the process of automatic parking, the driver still needs to be alert and monitor the surrounding environment [3]. The driver needs to be ready to take over vehicle control at any time to ensure safety in case of an emergency or complex scenario that the system cannot handle.

2.2 Cloud Computing and Big Data Technology

Cloud computing and big data technology are important components of the core technology of intelligent and connected vehicles. They provide powerful data processing capabilities and intelligent analysis capabilities for vehicles, so that vehicles can achieve a high degree of intelligence and networking. New energy vehicles collect a large amount of real-time data through on-board sensors, cameras and other devices, including vehicle status, driving environment, driving behavior and other information [4]. These collected information is uploaded to the cloud through the connection between the vehicle and the Internet to realize remote storage and processing of data. Vehicle usage data, such as travel date, time, origin and destination locations, power consumption and other information, can be up-dated in real time and provided to users through the application, so that users can have a clearer understanding of their driving habits and vehicle status [5]. Big data analysis technology is used to perform correlation analysis and deep mining on the collected data, optimize vehicle performance, predict maintenance requirements, and improve user experience. Big data technology can also provide personalized services for users, such as according to user habits and preferences, intelligent network technology can provide personalized service recommendations, such as effective management of new energy vehicle energy, reduce energy consumption, improve driving range, etc.

The energy consumption data analysis of new energy vehicles is to collect and process various data related to energy consumption through cloud computing and big data technology, establish energy consumption model, and predict and analyze energy consumption based on the model [6]. Firstly, data collection is carried out, through the collection of various sensor data related to energy consumption, charging pile data recording the start and end time of charging, charging amount and other information, including vehicle driving distance, battery state, energy consumption data and other vehicle management system data, these data are the basis for calculating energy consumption. Then, data cleaning is performed to remove duplicate, abnormal or invalid data to ensure the accuracy and reliability of the data. Then the data analysis is carried out to analyze the battery output energy consumption, air resistance energy consumption and body electrical energy consumption [7]. Based on the collected data, considering a variety of factors, such as battery capacity, motor efficiency, vehicle weight, driving habits, etc., the energy consumption of the vehicle can be accurately predicted, and the energy consumption model of the new energy vehicle is established [8]. By comparing with the energy consumption data of actual vehicles, the accuracy and reliability of the model can be verified. If there is a large difference between the model prediction and the actual data, the model needs to be adjusted and optimized.

3 Design of Application for Intelligent Network Connected New Energy Vehicle Owners

3.1 Requirement Analysis

The demand for the application of intelligent connected owners of new energy vehicles mainly focuses on charging services, vehicle management and monitoring, user experience and social interaction, and safety protection.

Charging Service
For new energy vehicles, owners need the application to provide accurate charging station

map information and be able to navigate to the nearest charging station. This feature is essential to alleviate the "range anxiety" of EV owners. At the same time, owners want to be able to view the number of idle charging piles and charging speed of the charging station in real time, so as to make the best choice [9]. To avoid waiting for charging during peak hours, owners need to be able to plan and book charging times in advance. Convenient online payment functions and detailed charging history records can help owners better manage charging costs and understand charging habits.

Vehicle Management and Detection

Car owners hope that the application has the function of remote control of the vehicle, such as remote start, lock, air conditioning control, etc., to improve the convenience of driving [10]. For new energy owners, it is necessary to monitor the battery status in real time, including the remaining power, battery health, etc., to ensure driving safety and extend battery life.

User Experience and Social Interaction

The application interface is simple and easy to operate, so as to reduce the difficulty of use and learning costs, so that owners have a good user experience. Offering charging offers, promotions, and incentive programs at the same time can motivate owners to use electric vehicles and applications more [11]. It is better for car owners to interact, share experiences and evaluate charging stations to form a good community atmosphere and provide valuable reference information.

3.2 Main Structure Design of Application

The system has five modules: vehicle-machine linkage module, data analysis module, warm heart service module, interactive community module and My car module. The new energy vehicle intelligent network owner application can use commonly used functions such as vehicle control, intelligent charging, and online services, interact with other owners in the community, and know more new car friends. Figure 1 shows the function structure diagram of application.

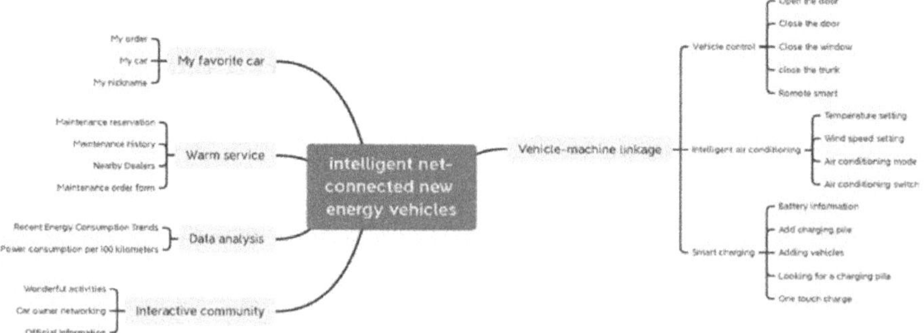

Fig. 1. Function structure diagram of application for owners of intelligent network connected new energy vehicles

The vehicle-machine linkage template is composed of three parts, which are vehicle control, intelligent air conditioning and intelligent charging. The vehicle control part can remotely control the air conditioning, doors and Windows, trunk, real-time positioning of the vehicle, etc., and also can customize the vehicle function according to your driving habits through the smart scene function. The smart air conditioning part allows users to remotely adjust the temperature in the car through a mobile application. Whether in hot summer or cold winter, users can preset a comfortable temperature environment before entering the car to ensure that the car is always maintained in a most suitable temperature state [12]. Use the cooling and heating cycle and ventilation function of the air conditioning system to help remove the peculiar odor in the car, such as the smell of smoke and the bad odor caused by food spilt. By automatically adjusting the temperature and wind speed, the decomposition and dissipation of odor molecules are accelerated, and the air inside the car is kept fresh. The smart charging part can be controlled remotely by the user through the vehicle, and the application sets a specific time to automatically start or end charging, which is usually used to take advantage of the low electricity price period at night to save costs. Real-time display of vehicle charging status, including charging progress, current power and charging amount and other information, not only can online pile, long-distance route planning, can also add household charging pile, household charging pile timing charging and other functions, improve the convenience of electric vehicle users, improve the efficiency of energy use and economic benefits.

3.3 Implementation of Key Technologies

The system is composed of client and server respectively. Uni-app technology is used for user development, so that a set of code development can be released to multiple terminals at the same time. The server is built using Java Web technology. The key technologies are introduced as follows:

Overall System Architecture

The core of the system is the intelligent network system of new energy vehicles, and the functions on the application of the owner need to be realized by the inter-face provided by this system. This system needs to be connected with the back-ground system of the new energy vehicle 4S shop to facilitate the maintenance application of the owner [13]. The intelligent cockpit application in the new energy vehicle is responsible for the control of the vehicle and the interaction with the server. The application in the smart home charging pile is responsible for the control of the charging pile and the interaction with the server [14]. The owner application controls the vehicle and charging pile and obtains data through the interface provided by the new energy vehicle intelligent network system, and makes maintenance appointments for the vehicle. Figure 2 shows the overall architecture of the system.

Uni App Development Technology

uni-app is a framework that uses Vue.js to develop all front-end application. Developers write a set of code that can be published to iOS, Android, Web (responsive), as well as various mini programs (wechat/Alipay/Baidu/Toutiao/Feishu/QQ /Kuaishou/Dingtalk/Taobao), Kua application and other platforms. In the development

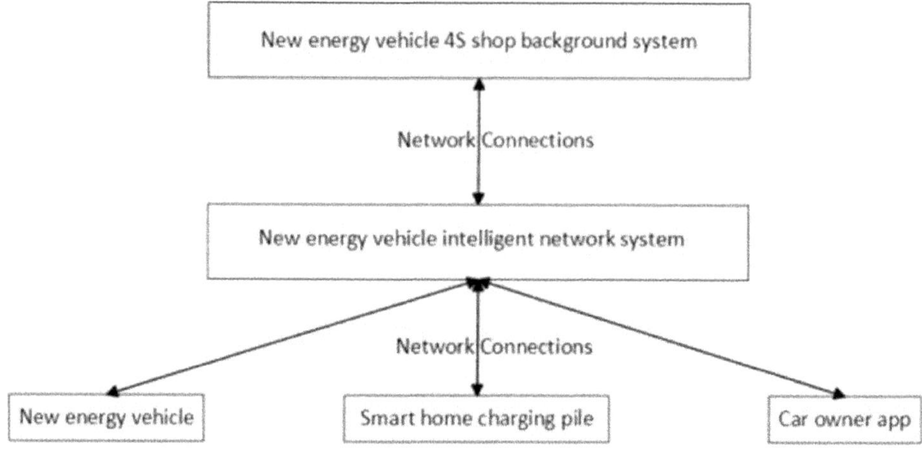

Fig. 2. System Architecture diagram

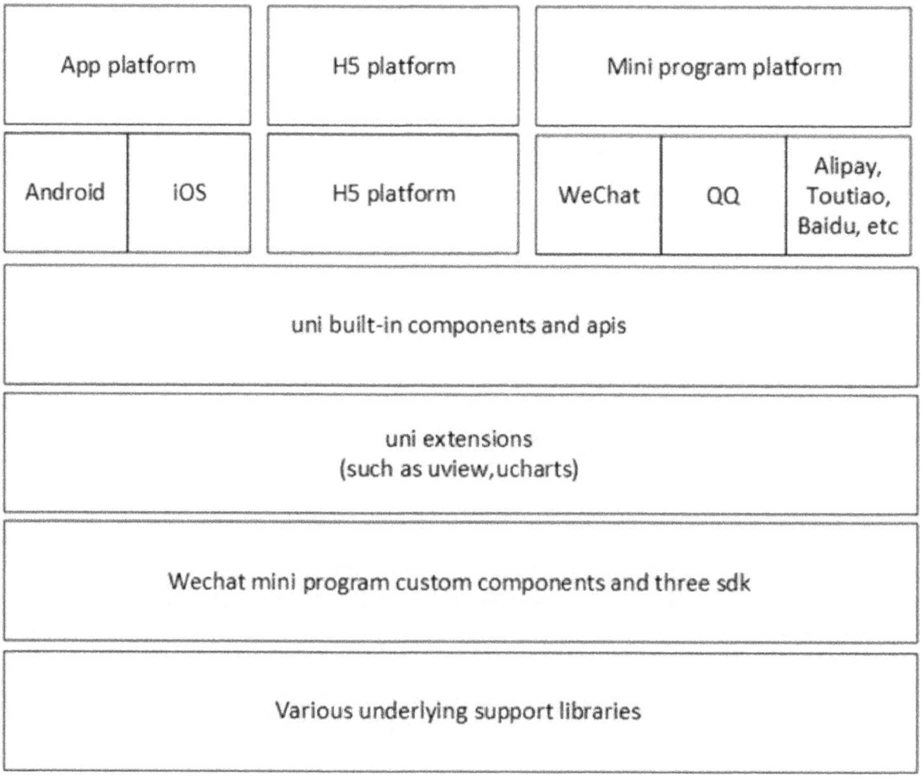

Fig. 3. Diagram of the uni-app architecture

framework of uni-app, we also use uview and ucharts third-party libraries to realize interface drawing and chart making, and Fig. 3 shows the uni-app architecture.

Java Web technologies

The server is developed using Java, using the current mainstream SpringBoot framework, the database is developed using MySql, using middleware such as Redis and ActiveMQ, the back-end management page is developed using ElementUI based on Vue, and the front-end deployment uses Nginx as a web containr, and Fig. 4 shows the technical architecture.

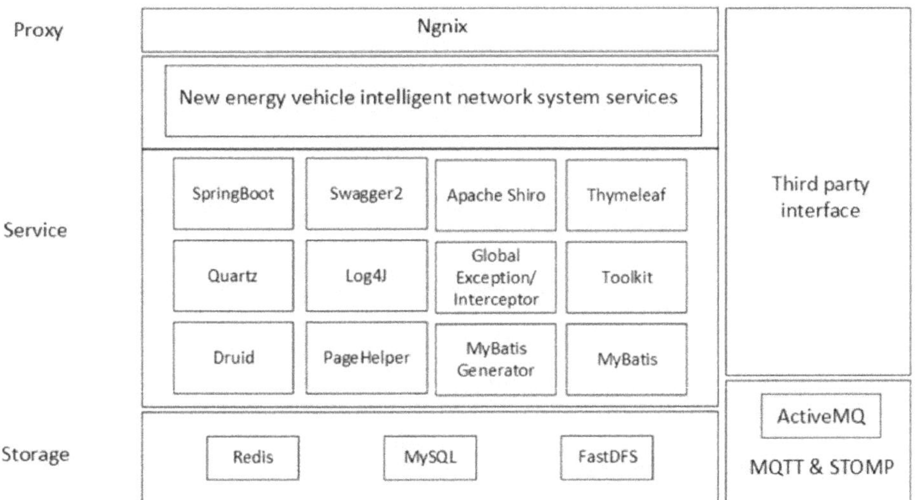

Fig. 4. Server-side architecture

4 Implementation of Application Technology for Intelligent Network Connected New Energy Vehicle Owners

4.1 Function Realization of Vehicle Control-Remote Start Module

Through the remote control software, the owner can control the vehicle at any time and anywhere, such as starting the vehicle, turning on the air conditioning, locking the car, etc., without being present in person, which greatly saves time and energy. On the home page, you can directly use the button to perform functions such as remote start, unlock the door, lock the door, close the window, close the trunk and so on. We take the function of closing the trunk as an example, and Fig. 5 shows the Screenshot of the remote boot function module.

Fig. 5. Screenshot of the remote start phone interface

4.2 Function Realization of Intelligent Charging Module

The new energy vehicle intelligent network owner application is equipped with a positioning function, so that users can quickly find the location of nearby charging piles. After the car is connected to the charging device, the vehicle battery information and the charging button are displayed. Users can view the charging information in real time, including voltage, current power, and the estimated time of battery full. Intelligent positioning services improve the user experience and provide convenience for users and Fig. 6 shows the screenshot of intelligent charging module.

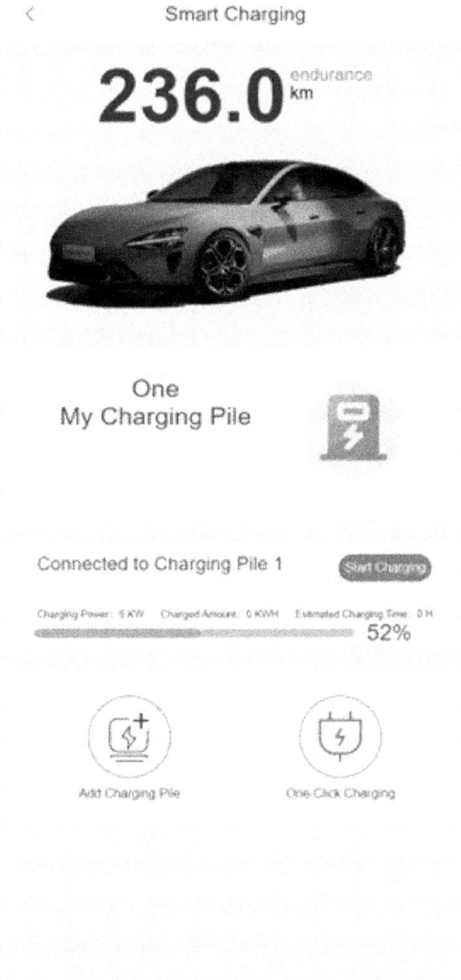

Fig. 6. Screenshot of smart charging phone interface

4.3   Function Realization of Data Analysis Function Module

Click the data analysis menu at the bottom of the home page to enter the data analysis page. You can analyze the energy consumption and the power consumption per 100 km according to the month, as shown in the figure. The data analysis page can find peaks and valleys in energy consumption, which can help determine when energy conservation measures need to be more aggressive. The monthly energy consumption helps to predict and plan the energy budget more accurately. This can help avoid energy wastage and adjust usage habits if necessary to reduce costs. The analysis of the power consumption per 100 km can provide data support for the technical improvement of electric vehicles or related devices. Developers can use this data to optimize battery management, improve energy efficiency, and even develop new energy-saving technologies. Therefore, the data analysis function not only helps to save energy and reduce emissions, reduce costs, but also provides strong support for technology improvement, policy formulation and brand image construction, and Fig. 7 shows the screenshot of data analysis function module.

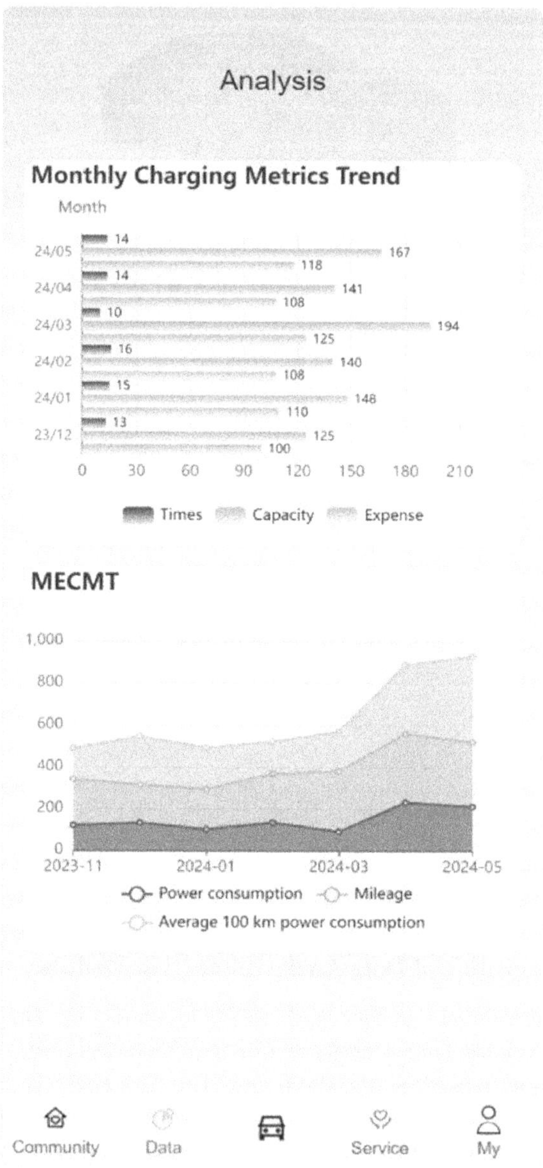

Fig. 7. Screenshot of data analysis mobile phone interface

5 Conclusions

In this paper, through in-depth research on the development and application of application system for new energy vehicles, the application of intelligent network technology in new energy vehicles, the design of application system for car owners, and the development and implementation methods are discussed. In the future, with the continuous progress of technology and the expansion of the market, the application of new energy vehicle owners will play an increasingly important role in the field of intelligent network. We look forward to promoting the rapid development of the intelligent connected vehicle application ecosystem through continuous research and innovation, providing more efficient, convenient and intelligent car use experience, and bringing a better experience to people's travel life.

Acknowledgment. Grant sponsor: Research on Strategies for Improving Higher Vocational Teachers' Digital Literacy under the Background of Professional Upgrading and Digital Transformation and Grant NO. 2023GB241.

References

1. Gu, J., Nicolescu, A.C.: A win-win relationship? New evidence on artificial intelligence and new energy vehicles. Energy Econ. 34–38 (2024)
2. Kong, C.: Research on marketing strategy and future development of new energy vehicles. In: Proceedings of 2019 International Conference on Education, Economics, Humanities and Social Sciences (ICEEHSS 2019), pp. 932–936 (2019)
3. Wei, S., Xu, H., Zheng, S., Chen, J.: Research on the impact of new energy vehicle companies' marketing strategies on consumers' purchase intention. Sustainability **16**(10), 4119 (2024)
4. Subashini, M., Abdullah, J.M.: Optimal power management for sustainable multi-purpose smart EV Charging stations. J. Phys. Conf. Ser. (26–30) (2023)
5. Răboacă, M.S., Bizon, N., Thounthong, P.: Intelligent charging station in 5G environments: challenges and perspectives. Int. J. Energy Res. **45**(11), 16418–16435 (2021)
6. Liu, Z.H., Zhang, J.W., Zhao, X., Yang, F.: The key technology research on integration between electric vehicles and smart grid. Appl. Mech. Mater. **263**, 768–775 (2013)
7. Yonis, A.Z.: Performance of ultra reliable low latency communication (URLLC) in 5G wireless networks. Przegląd Elektrotechniczny **99**(89–94), 2023 (2023)
8. Ampuero-Ruiz, P.I.: New energy vehicles and the political geoecology of China's Ecological Civilisation. Environ. Plan. C: Polit. Space **42**(8), 1317–1331 (2024)
9. Wang, Y.H., Xiong, S.S., Guo, B.S., Ren, X.S.: New energy vehicle air conditioner. Appl. Mech. Mater. **312**, 90–94 (2013)
10. Boynuegri, A.R., Uzunoglu, M., Erdinc, O., Gokalp, E.: A new perspective in grid connection of electric vehicles: different operating modes for elimination of energy quality problems. Appl. Energy **132**, 435–451 (2014)
11. Chen, D., et al.: The security technology and tendency of new energy vehicle in the future. In: Proceedings of the 10th International Forum of Automotive Traffic Safety(INFATS), School of Automobile, Chang'an University, pp. 96–98 (2013)
12. Li, Z., Xu, W., Hu, X.: Research on the development of new energy vehicle industry in China. Appl. Mech. Mater. **291**, 861–865 (2013)

13. Fan, Y., Zhang, L., Wang, K.: A new power allocation strategy of supercapacitor/battery hybrid energy storage system for electric vehicles. Adv. Mater. Res. **724**, 1389–1392 (2013)
14. Wang, Y.N., Zeng, H.M., Hu, B.X.: Economic performance model of new energy vehicles based on linear programming. Appl. Mech. Mater. **389**, 97–101 (2013)

Design of Dual-Network Redundant Ethernet Controller Based on FPGA

Houkui Fu[1,2]($\boxtimes$)

[1] Wuhan Vocational College of Software and Engineering (Wuhan Open University), Guanggu Avenue 117, Wuhan, China
826719622@qq.com

[2] Hubei Engineering Research Center for Intelligent Detection and Identification of Complex Parts, Guanggu Avenue 117, Wuhan, China

Abstract. The exponential growth in network users due to the rapid development of internet hardware and software has made Ethernet an integral part of the underlying links in today's interconnected networks after two decades of evolution. This paper introduces a design for a dual-network redundant Ethernet controller based on FPGA, aimed at improving the reliability and robustness of network systems where physical layer devices are prone to errors. The controller is capable of real-time switching between two network channels, ensuring uninterrupted data flow even in the event of a default channel failure or data transmission error. Functional simulations have demonstrated the controller's ability to switch to the redundant channel instantly when an error is detected, maintaining the integrity of data reception. The design principles, implementation techniques, and simulation results are discussed, highlighting the potential of this solution for enhancing network stability in critical applications. The paper also suggests directions for future research, including considerations for power consumption, heat dissipation, and scalability.

Keywords: Real-time Switching · Data Buffer · State Machine

1 Introduction

The rapid development of internet hardware and software has led to an exponential increase in network users. After 20 years of development, Ethernet has become an indispensable part of the underlying links in today's interconnected networks. In special application scenarios such as financial institutions, government departments, and the military, the stability of network systems is highly demanded. To enhance system reliability and robustness, dual redundancy network technology is required. Currently, the market primarily achieves network redundancy backup by using dual network cards at each network node, interconnected by two hubs or switches [1–4]. When one network card at a node fails, or a network cable is damaged, or one of the HUBs or switches fails, the system immediately activates dual redundant network card, ensuring the network continues to operate normally. Therefore, the speed of network switching is crucial for the normal

R. C. Qiu et al. (Eds.): IoTaaS 2024, LNICST 675, pp. 331–340, 2026.
https://doi.org/10.1007/978-3-032-14681-6_30

operation of the network system. Network switching with dual network cards is mainly realized through application software, resulting in slower switching speeds. Some have proposed improvements by developing corresponding network switching drivers specific to certain network cards, thereby increasing the network switching speed. However, dual redundancy network backup primarily targets the physical layer devices prone to errors within the network system [5–8]. Consequently, performing network switching within the driver still involves some delay relative to the error points in the network system. This paper proposes a method to complete dual network switching within the network controller itself, and implements it on a single chip using IP technology from microelectronics. This not only ensures real-time switching when physical layer devices fail but also allows real-time switching when data packets encounter errors during network reception.

2 Principles of Dual Redundant Ethernet Controller

The dual redundant Ethernet controller primarily accomplishes the transmission and reception of Ethernet data frames, configuration of physical layer devices, and network switching functionality when a physical device fails.

2.1 Introduction to Ethernet

In 1973, Xerox designed the first local area network system, named Ethernet. This flexible technology can operate on various network media and offers good capacity at reasonable cost. The basic characteristic of Ethernet is its use of a communication rule known as Carrier Sense Multiple Access with Collision Detection (CSMA/CD). Ethernet operates in two modes: half-duplex and full-duplex. In half-duplex mode, a station uses the same physical channel for sending and receiving information, allowing only one station to send information at any given time. Therefore, conflicts occur when different nodes compete for the same physical channel simultaneously. In full-duplex mode, the physical channels for sending and receiving information are separated, allowing two stations to send information to each other simultaneously [9–11]. The dual network real-time switching Ethernet controller discussed in this paper operates at a rate of 100 Mbit/s and functions in full-duplex mode.

2.2 Ethernet Frame Format

The signals transmitted in an Ethernet network exist in the form of frames, which are the basic units of Ethernet communication signals. The dual network real-time switching Ethernet controller described in this paper is capable of handling both IEEE frames and Ethernet frames. According to the IEEE 802.3 standard, IEEE frames are categorized into data frames and management frames.

Data Frame. Data frames are the carriers used for transmitting information between Ethernet stations, with their basic structure shown in Fig. 1.

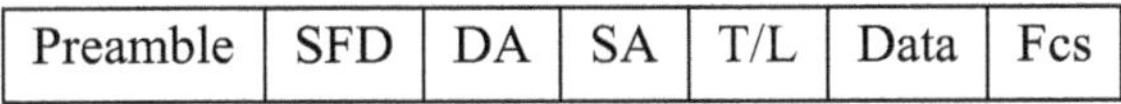

Fig. 1. Ethernet II frame format.

Each field of data frame format list below.

Preamble: Ethernet frame starts with a 7-Bytes Preamble. This is a pattern of alternative 0's and 1's which indicates starting of the frame and allow sender and receiver to establish bit synchronization. Initially, PRE (Preamble) was introduced to allow for the loss of a few bits due to signal delays. But today's high-speed Ethernet doesn't need a Preamble to protect the frame bits. PRE (Preamble) indicates the receiver that frame is coming and allow the receiver to lock onto the data stream before the actual frame begins.

Start of frame delimiter (SFD): This is a 1-Byte field that is always set to 10101011.SFD indicates that upcoming bits are starting the frame, which is the destination address. Sometimes SFD is considered part of PRE, this is the reason Preamble is described as 8 Bytes in many places. The SFD warns station or stations that this is the last chance for synchronization.

Destination Address (DA): This is a 6-Byte field that contains the MAC address of the machine for which data is destined.

Source Address (SA): This is a 6-Byte field that contains the MAC address of the source machine. As Source Address is always an individual address (Unicast),the least significant bit of the first byte is always 0.

Type/Length(T/L): Type/Length Length is a 2-Byte field, which indicates the type or the length of the entire Ethernet frame. This 16-bit field can hold a length value between 0 to 65535, but length cannot be larger than 1500 Bytes because of some own limitations of Ethernet.

Data: This is the place where actual data is inserted, also known as Payload. Both IP header and data will be inserted here if Internet Protocol is used over Ethernet. The maximum data present may be as long as 1500 Bytes. In case data length is less than minimum length i.e.46 bytes, then padding 0's is added to meet the minimum possible length.

Cyclic Redundancy Check (CRC): CRC is 4 Byte field. This field contains a 32-bits hash code of data, which is generated over the Destination Address, Source Address, Length, and Data field. If the checksum computed by destination is not the same as sent checksum value, data received is corrupted.

Management Frame. Management frames are used for communication between Ethernet and Ethernet management entities and for controlling the flow of information between network nodes. This paper implements basic management frames for configuring physical layer devices and pause frames for flow control in full-duplex communication mode. The basic structure of these frames is shown in Fig. 2.

Each field of management frame format list below.

Preamble (PRE): The first field in the MDIO protocol is indicated with Preamble. When the Preamble is sent, the MAC sends all bits as 1's in the MDIO line. The 32 bits in the preamble are always 1's.

Preamble	ST	OP	PHYAD	REGAD	TA	Data

Fig. 2. Ethernet management frame format.

Start (ST): The preamble is succeeded by the start bit which is 2 bits in size that remains 01 always in clause 22 for both read or write operations.

Opcode (OP): The next field is the opcode which gives information about whether a read or write operation is to be performed. Opcode with the value of '01' in the frame specifies the write operation. Similarly, Opcode with the value of '10' in the frame specifies read operation.

Physical Address (PHYAD): This field contains a 5-bit PHY address.

Register Address (REGAD): This field is 5 bits long indicating the register to be written or read from.

Turn Around (TA): The Turnaround field is 2 bits in size. When data is written to the PHY, the MAC will write "10" to the MDIO (Management Data Input/Output) bus. When reading data, the MAC releases the MDIO bus.

Data: This field is 16-bit wide. During the read instruction, the PHY chip writes the data read from the REGAD register corresponding to the PHYAD in Data. During the write instruction, the MAC writes the value of the REGAD register corresponding to the PHYAD in Data.

2.3 Ethernet Flow Control

Ethernet flow control is the primary means of resolving network congestion or even paralysis caused by excessive or unbalanced network load. When the receiving node's buffer exceeds a set minimum threshold, it sends a pause frame with maximum delay to the remote sending node. Upon receiving the pause frame, the remote sending node immediately stops sending the next data frame. The delay duration is determined by the control parameters in the received pause frame. When the receiving node's buffer falls below the set minimum threshold, it sends a pause frame with zero delay to the remote sending node. Upon receiving this pause frame, the sending node resumes data transmission. Since the transmission of pause frames involves uncertain delays, the minimum threshold of the buffer cannot be designed too small, otherwise, it may cause packet loss [12–16].

2.4 Principle of Real-Time Switching

The real-time switching solution proposed in this paper addresses three main issues:

Ensures that the network can operate normally even when a physical layer device fails.

When one network channel encounters a transmission error at the physical layer, it switches to the other channel, ensuring data is correctly received.

During network channel switching, due to dual-channel data backup, there is no packet loss during real-time switching.

Therefore, network switching must be synchronized with the reception of network data frames. Each network channel has its own receive buffer, as shown in Fig. 3. Under normal conditions, network channels 1 and 2 store data in receive buffers 1 and 2, respectively, with a default receive buffer set (e.g., receive buffer 2 is the default buffer for PCI to read data after power-on). The upper-layer application reads Ethernet frame data from this default receive buffer 2 via the PCI bus.

When a network channel fails, if the failed channel does not correspond to the default receive buffer 2 (i.e., network channel 1 fails), data reception continues normally. If network channel 2 fails, the other buffer 1 is immediately set as the default receive buffer, switching the PCI bus to read data from buffer 1 instead of buffer 2.

If both network channels are operating normally, and the current default receive buffer 2 encounters a CRC error during data reception, buffer 1 is immediately set as the default receive buffer. Buffer 2 will be restored as the default receive buffer once the data reception on its corresponding channel is error-free.

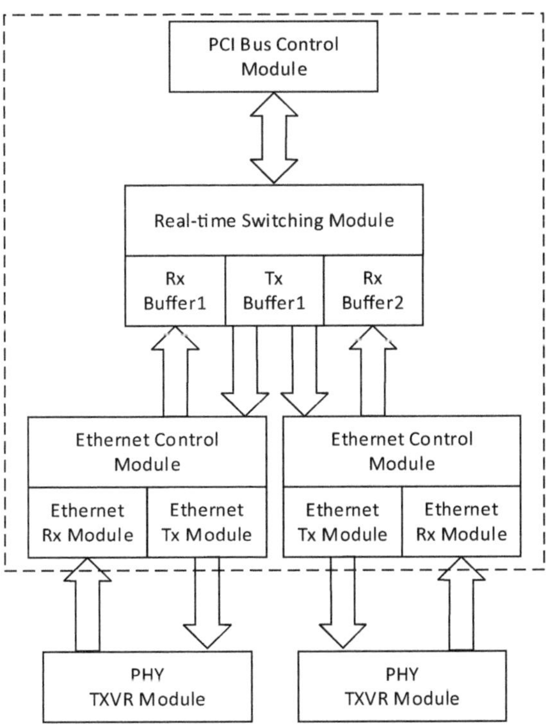

Fig. 3. Ethernet controller structure of real-time switching of dual networks

3 Implementation Technology for Dual Network Real-Time Switching

3.1 Real-Time Switching Module

This module accomplishes two main functions: isolating high-speed data from low-speed data processing modules, and real-time switching of faulty network channels to ensure normal network operation.

The PCI bus has a data transfer speed of 33 MHz and a maximum data width of 32 bits, whereas the Ethernet controller processes data at 25 MHz with a data width of only 4 bits. To isolate these two data processing modules, an asynchronous FIFO is used. The PCI module and the network controller module access data through the full and empty flags of the FIFO. During data transmission, the faster PCI rate compared to the controller ensures that the network's data transmission speed is not affected. The PCI writes data to the transmit FIFO when it is not full, then releases the bus. The controller sends out data when the transmit FIFO is not empty. Therefore, the transmit FIFO does not need to be large but should not be smaller than the maximum size of one frame, which is 1.5K bits.

For data reception, the receive FIFO should be as large as possible to prevent buffer overflow. The FIFO threshold for deciding whether to send a pause frame should also be set higher. Sending a pause frame only when the receive FIFO is empty can lead to overflow and packet loss.

Real-time switching primarily occurs during PCI data read operations, based on control signals from the receive module to switch PCI data reading from the receive FIFO. As shown in Fig. 3, since the data output from the receive module is buffered in the receive FIFO and then sent to the PCI bus by the switching module, the control signals generated by the receive module directly enter the switching module. Therefore, the control signals reach the switching module before the data signals, enabling real-time switching.

3.2 Ethernet Transmit/Receive Module

This module uses two state machines to handle the functions of the Ethernet transmit and receive controllers.

The transmit module reads data from the transmit FIFO, storing the 12-byte destination address, source address, and 2-byte length/type data in registers. It determines whether the frame is an Ethernet frame or an IEEE frame based on the length/type data, and whether the data padding area needs to be filled. Since sending one byte of data read from the transmit FIFO requires 2 clock cycles, the 7-byte preamble is transmitted while the first 14 bytes of the frame data are read out. When sending the 8th byte frame start delimiter, the length/type data has already been read from the FIFO, allowing determination of the frame type and setting the start delimiter to "10101010" or "10101011."

The transmit state machine, as shown on the left side of Fig. 6, starts from the idle state (tx_idle). When there is data in the transmit FIFO, it moves to the start state (tx_star). In the tx_star state, the 7-byte preamble is transmitted, and the 12-byte MAC address and 2-byte length/type data are stored in registers. It then moves to the frame data transmission state. The tx_l state sends the lower 4 bits of a byte, and the tx_h state sends the upper 4 bits, completing the data padding and CRC frame checksum transmission. After a frame is sent, the state machine waits for an inter-frame gap of no less than 960 ns before returning to the idle state (tx_idle) to wait for the next frame.

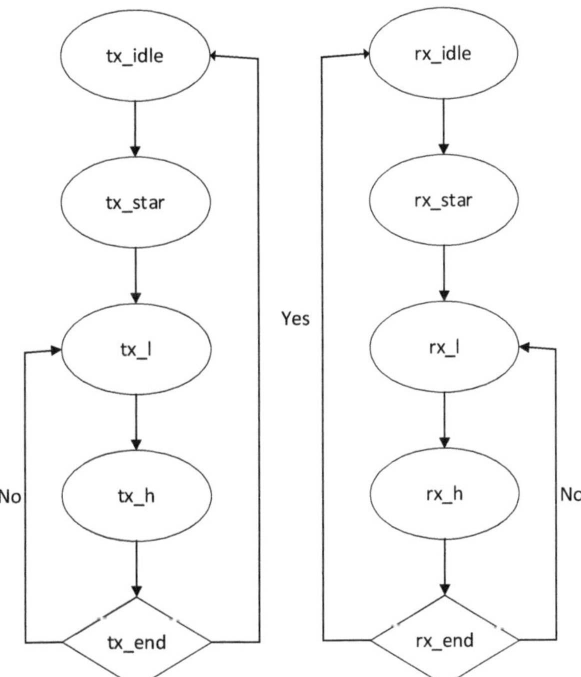

Fig. 4. Ethernet Controller TXVR State Machine

The receive module receives data from the physical layer device. Similar to the transmit module, it stores the 12-byte destination address, source address, and 2-byte length/type data in registers. It uses the length/type data to determine the frame type and length. Based on the frame length, it filters out the padding and CRC checksum data, then writes the filtered data into the receive FIFO. Concurrently, it performs CRC checks on the received frame data to determine if the received data is correct. The result of this check and whether there is a fault in the receiving channel are sent as control signals to the real-time switching module. The state machine for this process is shown on the right side of Fig. 4.

In the rx_idle state, if the receive data enable signal is active, it transitions to the rx_sfd state, receiving the low 4 bits of the frame start delimiter. If no errors occur, it then receives the high 4 bits of the frame start delimiter. If the received data is correct, the module prepares to receive the Ethernet frame data. A byte is received in two states: the rx_l state receives the lower 4 bits of the byte, and the rx_h state receives the upper 4 bits. During this process, padding and CRC checksum data are filtered out based on the length information. After receiving an entire frame, the module returns to the rx_idle state, ready to receive the next frame.

4 Functional Simulation Results

Using the ModelSim tool, the Ethernet controller IP with real-time switching was functionally simulated. The results are shown in Figs. 5 and 6. In these figures, RX_CLK1 represents the receive clock signal. RXFIFO_DATA is the data output from the receive FIFO to the PCI module. RXFIFO_DATA1 and RXFIFO_DATA2 are the output data from the buffers of channels 1 and 2, respectively. Redundance is the real-time switching control signal for the network channels, which is active high. By default, it receives data from channel 2, and switches to channel 1 when a fault occurs in channel 2. RXDV is the data enable signal for the channel, active high. RX_ER is the error signal for the channel data, with high indicating an error. RXD is the channel data signal.

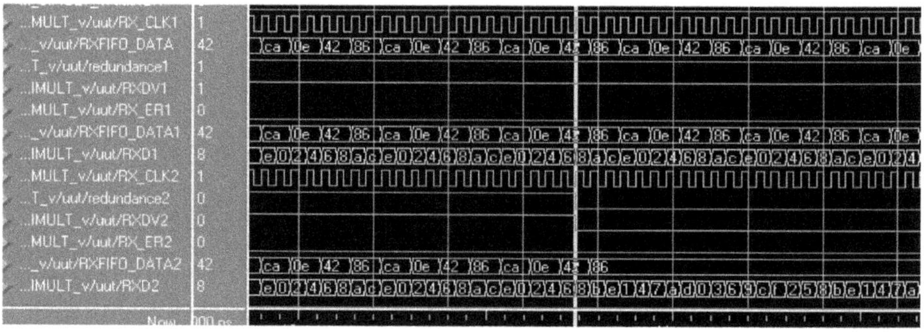

Fig. 5. Real-time switchover in the event of PHY layer fault during receiving process

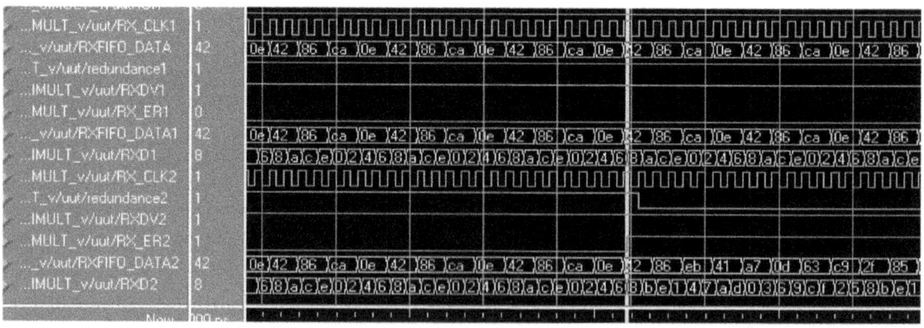

Fig. 6. Real-time switchover in the event of data error during receiving process

Figure 5 shows the real-time switching simulation waveform when a fault occurs in the network physical layer device. A vertical line marks the point in the waveform; to the left of this line is the normal receiving state, where the redundance signals for both channels are high, indicating that data is being received from channel 2 by default. To the right of the line, a fault occurs in channel 2, making the RXDV2 signal invalid. The Ethernet controller cannot receive data from channel 2, so the output data from channel 2's buffer remains as the data before the fault. The redundance signal for channel 2 goes low, and the controller automatically switches to retrieve data from channel 1's buffer in real time.

Figure 6 shows the real-time switching simulation waveform when there is an error in the network channel data. A vertical line marks the point in the waveform; to the left of this line is the normal receiving state, where the redundance signals for both channels are high, indicating that data is being received from channel 2 by default. To the right of the line, RX_ER2 goes high, indicating a data transmission error on channel 2. The redundance signal for channel 2 goes low, and the controller automatically switches to retrieve data from channel 1's buffer in real time.

5 Conclusion

This paper presents a design method for a dual-network redundant Ethernet controller based on FPGA, targeting the error-prone nature of physical layer devices in existing network systems. The design implements real-time switching functionality on a single chip, ensuring not only immediate network switching in the event of physical layer device failures but also during data packet reception errors, thereby significantly enhancing the reliability and robustness of the network system.

Through functional simulation results, this paper validates the real-time switching capability of the proposed design in scenarios of physical layer device failures and data transmission errors. The simulation data shows that when the default network channel encounters a fault or error, the controller can quickly switch to the redundant channel, ensuring the continuity and accuracy of data reception.

Furthermore, this paper discusses the design principles, implementation technology, and simulation results of the dual-network redundant Ethernet controller, providing a novel solution for the stability and reliability of network systems. Future research can further explore the practical applications of this design in terms of power consumption, heat dissipation, and scalability, as well as optimizations in network switching speed and system compatibility.

In summary, the dual-network redundant Ethernet controller design proposed in this paper effectively addresses the stability requirements of network systems in special application scenarios, offering strong technical support for network systems in critical fields such as finance, government, and military.

References

1. Kidav, J.U., Sivamangai, N.M., Pillai, M.P., Raja, S.M.: Architecture and FPGA prototype of cycle stealing DMA array signal processor for ultrasound sector imaging systems. Microprocess. Microsyst. **64**, 53–72 (2019)
2. Frazier, H.: The 802.3z gigabit ethernet standard. IEEE Netw. 12(3), 6–7 (1998)

3. Kidav, J., et al.: Design of a 128-channel transceiver hardware for medical ultrasound imaging systems. IET Circ. Devices Syst. 1–13 (2021)
4. Shamya, A., Jayaraj, U.K., Gayathri, S.: Ultrasound B-Mode back end signal processor on FPGA. Int. J. Eng. Res. Technol. (IJERT) **04**(06) (2015)
5. Yingqi, C., Kang, Y.X., Songyu, Y.: A high speed transmission/reception circuit for HDTV encoder based on parallel FIFO structure. In: Fifth Asia-Pacific Conference on... and Fourth Optoelectronics and Communications Conference on Communications, vol. 2, pp. 1023–1026. IEEE (1999)
6. Lin, T.T., Li, C.P.: Quasi-FIFO collision resolution scheme for wireless access networks. In: IEEE 14th International Conference on Personal Wireless Mobile Communications (2003)
7. Jun, X., Guan, D., Wang, Z.: Research of improved sphere decoding algorithm. In: The 31st China Conference on Control and Decision-making (2019)
8. Singh, G., Mishra, P., Vij, R.: BER Analysis of V-BLAST MIMO systems under various channel modulation techniques in mobile radio channels. In: 2012 International Conference on Computer Technology and Science (ICCTS 2012) (2012)
9. Sun, S., Ge, F.: Research of distributed synchronization and encoding-decoding technique in 34 Mbps integrated sevices digital network (double ring). In: International Conference on Communication Technology (ICCT'94) (1994)
10. Li, Y., Du, Y., Ye, X., Cai, Z.: Doppler radar real-time signal processing based on FPGA. In: IEEE International Conference on Signal and Image Processing (2016)
11. Li, L.: Design of FPGA debugging interface based on EZ-USB slave FIFO. Appl. Mech. Mater. **367**, 240–244 (2013)
12. Shi, Y.: Research and implementation of MELP algorithm based on TMS320VC5509A. In: 2014 International Conference on the Mechanics of Biological Systems and Materials (MBSM 2014) (2014)
13. Wang, G., Cheng, W.: The Optimization of G.729 Speech codec and Implementation on the TMS320VC5402. In: 2015 4th International Conference on Mechatronics,Materials,Chemistry and Computer Engineering (ICMMCCE 2015) (2015)
14. Shi, Y.: Research and Implementation of MELP Algorithm Based on TMS320VC5509A. In: Proceedings of 2014 International Conference on the Mechanics of Biological Systems and Materials (MBSM 2014) (2014)
15. Chen, X.S., Sun, Y.H., Yang, R.Z., Zhang, Y.H.: A depth-dependent derandomized sampling algorithm for lattice decoding. In: Proceedings of 2015 International Conference on Automation, Mechanical and Electrical Engineering (AMEE 2015) (2015)
16. Feng, L., Zhong, Y., Wei, W.: Design and realization based on TMS320VC5402 system. J. Simul. **3**(5) (2015)

Research on the Features of Harmony Operating System and Its Application in Smart IoT

Ding Fan[1(✉)], Zhu Rui[2], and Li Fei[3]

[1] Wuhan Intelligent Integrated Communication Technology Co., Ltd., Wuhan, China
frank@myems.com.cn
[2] Shenzhen Kaihong Digital Industry Development Co., Ltd., Shenzhen, China
[3] Shenzhen Yuyi Technology Co., Ltd., Shenzhen, China

Abstract. This paper delves into the application of the open-source Harmony Operating System (Harmony Operating System) in the fields of IoT intelligence and transportation, thoroughly analyzing the underlying connectivity technology features of the Harmony Operating System architecture. The results indicate that in-depth exploration of the Harmony Operating System architecture can be researched from the following aspects: distributed soft bus technology, distributed data management, distributed task scheduling, distributed security mechanisms, distributed device virtualization, efficient network protocol stack, automatic discovery and configuration, and low-power design. These technical features significantly enhance the connectivity, data processing capability, and intelligence level of the system, providing a solid technical foundation and broad development prospects for intelligent applications in IoT and transportation fields.

Keywords: Harmony Operating System · Smart IoT · Distributed · Low Power

Introduction

With the rapid advancement of technology, Internet of Things (IoT) technology has been widely applied globally. IoT connects various devices and systems, achieving real time data collection, transmission, and analysis, thereby greatly enhancing people's quality of life and production efficiency. In this context, the choice of operating system is crucial for the realization of IoT applications. The open-source Harmony Operating System (Harmony Operating System), with its unique technical advantages and flexible application scenarios, has become an important platform for the development of smart IoT applications [1–3]. The Harmony Operating System aims to provide a unified operating system platform for various smart terminals. Its microkernel architecture, efficient task scheduling, robust security, and support for diverse devices showcase its immense

R. C. Qiu et al. (Eds.): IoTaaS 2024, LNICST 675, pp. 341–349, 2026.
https://doi.org/10.1007/978-3-032-14681-6_31

potential in fields such as smart homes, smart cities, intelligent manufacturing, etc. Especially in IoT applications, Harmony Operating System's distributed architecture and high scalability offer developers ample room for innovation. This paper will explore the practice of the Harmony Operating System in smart IoT applications, focusing on its specific application cases and advantages in device interconnection, data processing, application development, and security.

1   Harmony Operating System

1.1   Introduction to Harmony Operating System

The Harmony Operating System aims to provide a unified platform for various smart devices. It adopts a microkernel architecture, featuring high security and low complexity, with a distributed architecture that enables multi-device collaboration. High performance and low latency ensure excellent performance on resource-constrained devices. Its key features include:

Microkernel Architecture:Simplified and secure, minimizing kernel functionality to improve system stability.

Distributed Architecture:Seamless multi-device connectivity, providing a consistent user experience.

High Performance and Low Latency:Optimized task scheduling, suitable for a variety of hardware platforms.

Robust Security:Multi-layered security protection to safeguard user data and privacy.

Developer-Friendly:Offering rich development tools and supporting multiple programming languages and environments.

Harmony Operating System is widely applied in fields such as smart homes, smart cities, intelligent manufacturing, and vehicle internet. It enables intelligent control of home appliances, efficient city management, enhanced automation in production, and efficient and safe operation of in-vehicle systems.

1.2   Architecture of the Harmony Operating System

The architecture of the Harmony operating system is designed to provide an efficient, secure, and flexible operating system solution suitable for various smart devices and IoT application scenarios. Its microkernel architecture streamlines the core functions of the operating system to the minimum, retaining only essential features such as process management, memory management, and IPC (inter-process communication). Other functionalities are modularized and run in user mode, thereby enhancing system security and stability, and reducing the risk of kernel crashes [4,5].

The distributed architecture allows multiple devices to seamlessly connect and collaborate. Through distributed soft bus technology, devices can share resources and data, achieving a unified user experience. The component-based design ensures that various functions and services exist in the form of components, which can be flexibly configured and expanded based on specific application scenarios. Developers can load or unload components as needed, improving the customizability and adaptability of the system.

Harmony Operating System optimizes task scheduling and resource management to ensure efficient operation across various hardware platforms. Its lightweight design is suitable for resource-constrained devices, achieving low-latency system response. The built-in multi-level security protection mechanisms, including Trusted Execution Environment (TEE), secure boot, encrypted storage, and access control, effectively defend against various security threats, ensuring the safety of user data and privacy.

Harmony Operating System provides a rich set of development tools and frameworks, supporting multiple programming languages (such as C/C++, Java, JS) and development environments (such as IDEs, compiler toolchains). Developers can use these tools and frameworks for application development, debugging, and deployment, shortening the development cycle and improving development efficiency. Its cross-platform nature supports various hardware platforms, including ARM and x86 architectures, allowing the operating system to run on a variety of devices, such as smartphones, smart home devices, in-vehicle systems, and wearable devices, providing a consistent user experience.

Through these architectural designs, the Harmony operating system achieves efficiency, security, and flexibility, meeting the diverse application needs of the smart IoT era and providing strong support for various smart devices. Figure 1 shows the system architecture diagram.

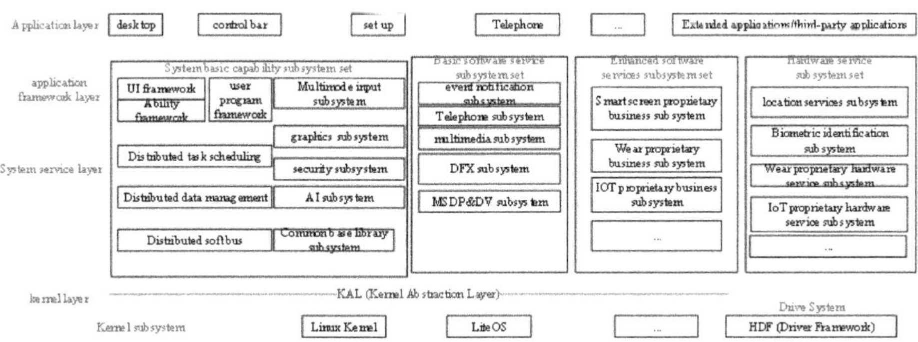

Fig. 1. Architecture of the Harmony Operating System.

2 Exploration of Harmony Operating System's Underlying Device Interconnection Technology Features

The Harmony Operating System possesses a series of innovative and advanced features in terms of underlying device interconnection technology. These features ensure seamless connection and efficient collaboration between different devices, greatly enhancing the performance and user experience of IoT applications [6]. Figure 2 illustrates the in-depth exploration of Harmony Operating System's underlying device interconnection technology features.

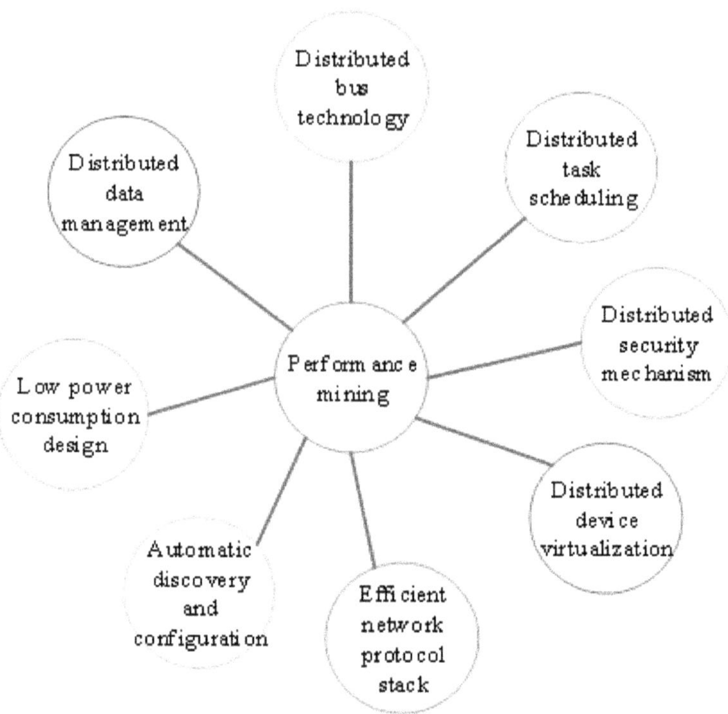

Fig. 2. In-depth Exploration of Harmony Operating System's Underlying Device Interconnection Technology Features.

Harmony Operating System achieves efficient communication and resource sharing between devices through distributed soft bus technology, supporting various transmission protocols and network environments to ensure stable operation. Distributed data management technology accomplishes cross-device data synchronization and sharing, ensuring data consistency and real-time updates, suitable for multi-device collaborative work scenarios in smart IoT applications. Distributed task scheduling technology improves the utilization of computing resources and overall system efficiency through intelligent allocation of computing tasks. To ensure the security of cross-device communication, Harmony Operating System introduces distributed security mechanisms such as identity authentication, encrypted transmission, and access control, effectively preventing network attacks and data leakage risks. Distributed device virtualization technology virtualizes multiple physical devices into a single logical device, simplifying management and operation, enhancing user convenience and system management efficiency. The efficient network protocol stack supports various communication protocols, ensuring fast and stable connections between devices, improving data transmission speed, reducing network latency, and lowering system resource consumption. The automatic discovery and configuration feature simplifies the deployment and management process of new devices, improving user experience and system scalability. Low-power design extends device battery life and enhances system efficiency in resource-constrained environments by optimizing the protocol stack and distributed task scheduling.

3 Enhancing IoT Intelligence

Harmony Operating System adopts a distributed architecture, enabling seamless connection and collaboration between different devices. Through distributed soft bus technology, devices can achieve efficient data sharing and resource scheduling, making transitions between devices almost imperceptible to users. This intelligent collaboration capability allows devices in scenarios such as smart IoT and intelligent manufacturing to work together to complete complex tasks, enhancing the overall intelligence level of the system.

Harmony Operating System is equipped with powerful data processing and analysis capabilities, capable of real-time collection and processing of data from different devices. Through distributed data management technology, data is synchronized and shared across multiple devices, ensuring data consistency and real-time updates. This allows the system to make intelligent decisions based on real-time data, improving the response speed and accuracy of IoT applications.

Harmony Operating System supports the integration of various artificial intelligence algorithms and models, endowing IoT devices with stronger intelligent processing capabilities. Through AI algorithms, devices can achieve functions such as image recognition, voice recognition, and natural language processing, enhancing device interaction capabilities and intelligence levels. For example, smart cameras can recognize and analyze video content in real-time, and smart speakers can understand natural language and execute voice commands.

Harmony Operating System's modular design allows the system to be flexibly configured and extended based on different application scenarios. Developers can load or unload functional modules as needed, optimizing system performance and resource utilization. This flexibility not only enhances the system's adaptability but also provides developers with vast space for innovation, enabling IoT applications to quickly respond to market demands.

In IoT applications, data security and privacy protection are crucial. Harmony Operating System introduces multi-layer security protection mechanisms, including identity authentication, encrypted transmission, access control, and Trusted Execution Environment (TEE), ensuring the security and integrity of data during transmission and storage. These security measures effectively prevent potential network attacks and data leakage risks, providing reliable protection for intelligent applications.

IoT devices typically have strict power consumption requirements. Harmony Operating System achieves low-power design by optimizing task scheduling and the network protocol stack, extending device battery life. This allows devices to maintain high performance while operating stably for long periods in resource-constrained environments, enhancing the intelligence level of devices.

Harmony Operating System establishes a comprehensive ecosystem, bringing together a large number of developers and partners to jointly promote the development of IoT intelligence. Rich development tools and frameworks, along with extensive community support, provide developers with strong backing, making the development and deployment of intelligent applications more convenient and efficient. Figure 3 illustrates the process of enhancing IoT intelligence with the Harmony Operating system.

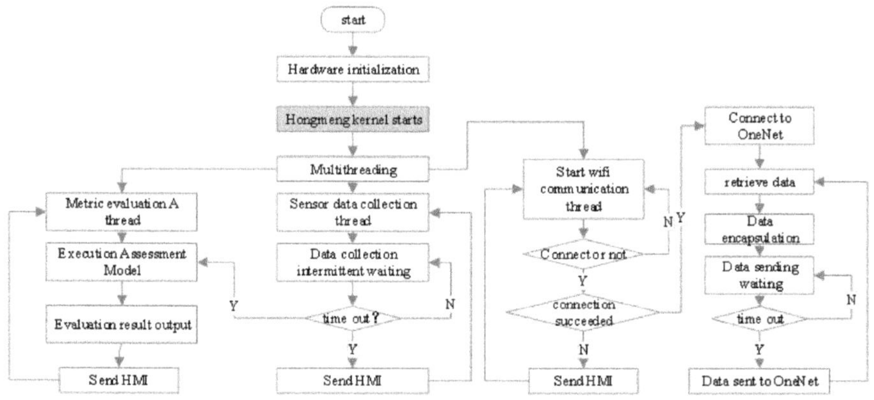

Fig. 3. Process of Enhancing IoT Intelligence with the Harmony Operating System.

4   Applications in the Transportation Sector

The Harmony Operating System's smart tunnel solution has demonstrated strong competitiveness and innovative potential in the field of transportation. The distributed architecture of Harmony Operating System allows various transportation devices to achieve seamless connection and collaboration. Through distributed soft bus technology, various devices in the traffic management system, such as traffic lights, cameras, and road condition monitoring equipment, can enable real-time data sharing and coordination, ensuring optimized traffic flow and quick response to emergencies.

Harmony Operating System's built-in efficient data processing and analysis capabilities enable the traffic management system to collect and process large amounts of data from different devices in real time. Through distributed data management technology, the traffic system can achieve data synchronization and sharing across multiple devices, ensuring data consistency and real-time updates, thereby supporting more intelligent traffic decision-making and management.

Harmony Operating System supports the integration of various artificial intelligence algorithms and models, endowing the traffic system with stronger intelligent processing capabilities. For instance, through AI algorithms, it can predict traffic flow, recognize and warn about traffic accidents, and analyze driving behavior, thereby enhancing the intelligence and safety of traffic management. Harmony Operating System's modular design allows the system to be flexibly configured and expanded based on different traffic application scenarios. Developers can load or unload functional modules as needed, optimizing system performance and resource utilization, increasing the adaptability of the traffic system, and providing developers with a broad space for innovation.

In terms of data security and privacy protection, Harmony Operating System introduces multi-layer security protection mechanisms, including identity authentication, encrypted transmission, access control, and Trusted Execution Environment (TEE), ensuring the security and integrity of data during transmission and storage, effectively preventing potential network attacks and data leakage risks. By optimizing task scheduling and the network protocol stack, Harmony Operating System achieves a low-power design, allowing traffic devices to maintain high performance while operating stably for long periods in resource-constrained environments, extending the lifespan of the devices and enhancing the overall efficiency of the traffic system.

Harmony Operating System establishes a comprehensive ecosystem, bringing together a large number of developers and partners to jointly promote the development of intelligence in the transportation sector. Rich development tools and frameworks, along with extensive community support, provide developers with strong backing, making the development and deployment of intelligent transportation applications more convenient and efficient. Figure 4 illustrates the smart tunnel solution based on Harmony Operating System realized on a highway in a certain province. Traditional tunnel devices are diverse, with many manufacturers and numerous types, requiring high maintenance and operational efficiency, and incurring high costs. Multiple subsystems are directly connected, leading to data and business silos, making it difficult for monitoring personnel to smoothly confirm events and perform linked control. Emergency handling relies on manual intervention, involving multiple devices, which is inefficient and prone to errors.

The smart tunnel solution based on Harmony Operating System achieves ubiquitous perception of tunnel operation status through a unified terminal IoT OS, a unified optical fiber ring network, and a unified digital base, breaking down the barriers of processing multi-source heterogeneous data in tunnels. The controller based on Harmony Operating System enables single control and linked

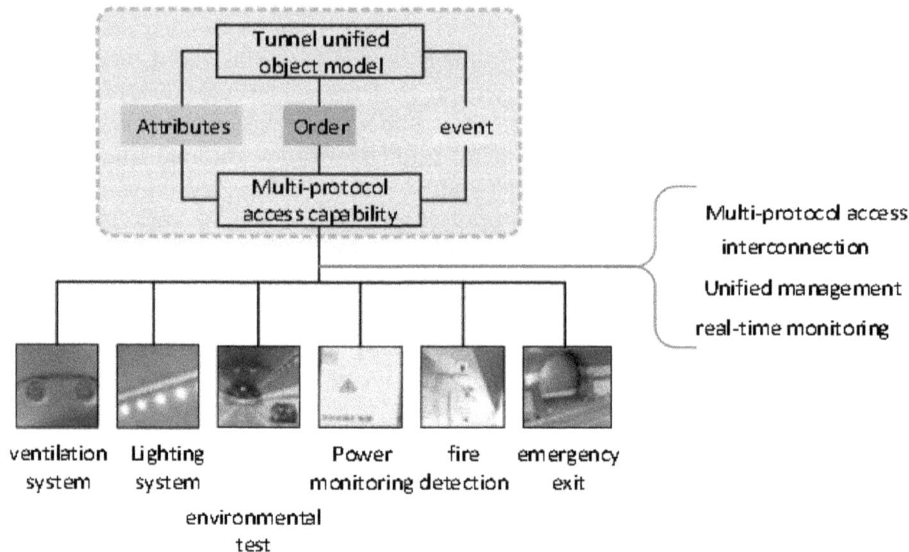

Fig. 4. Monitoring the Status of Tunnel Devices.

control of tunnel electromechanical equipment in various ways, such as in tunnel power distribution rooms and local tunnels. By integrating cross-device linkage with millimeter-wave radars and monitoring cameras, it can perceive abnormal events in the tunnel, helping tunnel administrators make corresponding decisions based on the data, effectively improving the efficiency of tunnel monitoring operations. The system can identify equipment failures at the first instance, significantly improving the operational efficiency of tunnel electromechanical equipment; it can achieve event identification and linked control with electromechanical equipment, handling potential risks at the first instance, reducing the impact of emergencies on public travel; and it can quickly handle traffic accidents, reducing the loss of life and property.

By combining Harmony Operating System's distributed architecture, efficient data processing, AI capabilities, and security mechanisms with the smart tunnel solution based on Harmony Operating System, the traffic management system can achieve more efficient device coordination, more intelligent decision support, and more reliable security assurance. This integrated application not only enhances the overall efficiency of the traffic system but also provides a solid technical foundation and broad development prospects for the development and deployment of intelligent transportation applications.

5   Conclusion

The intelligent IoT applications based on the Harmony Operating System Operating System have demonstrated their advantages in enhancing device connectivity, data processing capabilities, and system intelligence levels. Through distributed architecture, distributed soft bus technology, and efficient data management, Harmony Operating System achieves seamless connection and collaboration between devices, ensuring data consistency and real-time updates. Its modular design and AI integration capabilities enable the system to adapt to various IoT scenarios, from smart transportation to smart cities and intelligent manufacturing, providing efficient solutions. Multi-layer security protection and low-power design further guarantee the security and stability of IoT applications. Harmony Operating System, through a comprehensive ecosystem, brings together developers and partners to promote the development and application of intelligent IoT technology, fostering technological innovation and application implementation. The practice of Harmony Operating System in intelligent IoT applications showcases how it, as a powerful and flexible platform, drives the development of intelligent, interconnected, and efficient IoT devices through technological innovation and ecosystem collaboration, providing a solid technical foundation and broad development prospects for various intelligent applications.

References

1. Yiling, W., Qi, W., Junsha, A.: Porting of the lightweight harmony operating system supporting MIPS architecture. Computer Engineering (2023)
2. Keqiang, X.: Thoughts on building an ecosystem with HarmonyOS. Microcontrollers Embedded Systems Applications (2019)
3. Bin, L.: Development of remote monitoring system for fire pump APP based on HarmonyOS. Master's thesis, Donghua University (2023)
4. Haiyu, W.: Simulated consecutive interpretation practice report of HarmonyOS launch event. Bachelor's thesis, Capital University of Economics and Business (2022)
5. Houquan, M., Huajun, S.: Porting of HarmonyOS minimal system based on STM32MP1.Microcontrollers Embedded Systems Applications (2022)
6. Weihao, L.: Research on the influence mechanism of experience quality on user satisfaction and user engagement. Master's thesis, Shandong University (2022)

IoT Perception Anomaly Detection Based on Machine Learning

Qingqing Chen[1(✉)], Junfeng San[2], Zuwei Teng[2], Banli Ruan[2], and Jieyan Yang[3]

[1] Sun Yat-sen University, Guangzhou 510006, Guangdong, China
`chenqq32@chinaunicom.cn`
[2] ChinaUnicom Hubei Branch, Wuhan 430048, Hubei, China
[3] ChinaUnicom, Beijing 100033, China

Abstract. The internet of things (IoT) connectivity scenarios are becoming increasingly diverse as well as the types of connected terminals. IoT services are mainly carried on telecom operators' cellular networks, which enable applications in various scenarios while also causing significant issues in service and network perception for operators. This paper proposes an automatic detection method for IoT service perception anomalies based on machine learning. It utilizes the variational autoencoder (VAE) algorithm to encode and decode IoT service perception data, and performs anomaly detection through the different fluctuation amplitudes formed during the encoding and decoding processes. After practical verification, this technology can accurately detect IoT service perception anomalies after establishing an appropriate reconstruction error threshold. It can help operators discover IoT industry perception issues more quickly and accurately, providing a referential solution for IoT industry perception detection issues.

Keywords: Service Perception · Machine Learning · Reconstruction Error

1 Introduction

Human society has entered an era of interconnection of everything. According to a research report released by IoT Analytics, the global IoT connections reached 14.3 billion in 2022, and it is estimated that by 2027, the number of connected IoT devices worldwide will exceed 29 billion.

IoT as a service is also gradually achieving large-scale commercialization and spreading to various fields. In the future, IoT as a service will strengthen its integration with technologies such as cloud computing and big data, providing more intelligent and convenient services and decision support. However, the vast number of IoT connections and diverse business scenarios pose significant challenges to operators' network operation [1].

Constructing IoT service metrics from both NOC (Network Operations Center) and SOC (Service Operations Center) perspectives is an end-to-end indicator

R. C. Qiu et al. (Eds.): IoTaaS 2024, LNICST 675, pp. 350–358, 2026.
https://doi.org/10.1007/978-3-032-14681-6_32

system that takes into account both service perception and network performance. When evaluating relatively simple IoT services, the quality of IoT services can be monitored directly by setting Key Performance Indicator (KPI) and Key Quality Indicators (KQI) threshold values. However, with the rapid development of IoT business scenarios such as smart homes, intelligent driving, smart healthcare, and smart cities, IoT services exhibit characteristics such as rich connectivity scenarios, rapid iteration and updates of business models, and a wide variety of connected terminals [2]. Therefore, it is necessary to set threshold values for multi-dimensional KPI and KQI based on different application scenarios, which greatly increases the workload of network engineers.

Machine learning methods, through algorithms, automatically analyze and interpret data, enabling dynamic adjustment of detection model parameters to adapt to changes in system behavior and data patterns. This approach can handle non-linear and multivariate problems, demonstrating excellent flexibility and adaptability, making it suitable for KQI anomaly detection in complex systems [3].

This paper proposes an IoT service perception anomaly detection method based on machine learning. Unsupervised learning is an essential method in the field of machine learning, excelling at discovering hidden structures and patterns from unlabeled data. It is suitable for quickly identifying abnormal data points that differ from the majority in large volumes of network data. Variational Autoencoder (VAE) falls into the category of unsupervised learning, where it trains the network through encoding and decoding, and restores the output values to resemble the input values.

When VAE encodes and decodes perceived KQI data, different types of data produce varying degrees of fluctuation, enabling the identification and detection of perceived anomalies [4]. IoT services undergo service testing for different usage scenarios at the initial stage of network access to ensure good service perception. Therefore, the number of samples with normal IoT service perception in the existing network must be the majority. By inputting existing IoT service perception data into machine learning algorithms for model training, since the quantity of normal samples is much larger than that of abnormal samples, unsupervised learning methods are typically adopted for anomaly detection in such scenarios. Experimental results show that adopting an unsupervised VAE machine learning algorithm, optimizing the choice of inputs, and determining the reconstruction error threshold of the network can efficiently and accurately detect perceived anomalies.

2 Anomaly Detection Based on Variational Autoencoder for Perception

2.1 Perception Abnormal IoT Users

To detect perception anomalies, first define the concept of perception anomalies. The IoT business process generally includes four steps: network access, business access, network switching, and business switching [5]. When the KQI indicators related to network access, business access, network switching, and business usage exceed the threshold, We defined it as perception anomaly IoT users.

For example, Network access perception anomaly, IoT users with TCP second handshake delay greater than 50 ms or uplink TCP out-of-order packet ratio greater than 30% are considered to have network access perception anomaly. Service access perception anomaly, IoT users with TCP first handshake delay greater than 50ms or first packet response delay greater than 300 ms are considered to have service access perception anomaly. Network switching perception anomaly, IoT users with downlink TCP packet retransmission rate greater than 30% or downlink RTT delay exceeding 300 ms are considered to have network switching perception anomaly. Service usage perception anomaly, IoT users with both uplink and downlink RTT delays exceeding 300 ms, or with page opening success rate lower than 90%, or with service download speed below a certain threshold are considered to have service switching perception anomaly.

Based on DPI (Deep Packet Inspection) data, multi-dimensional monitoring of IoT service perception has been achieved, but the delimitation of IoT perception issues requires multi-dimensional KQI indicator correlation analysis [6], and dynamic adjustment of reference values, which is time-consuming and labor-intensive.

2.2 Variational Auto-encoder

VAE is an artificial neural network structure specifically designed for feature extraction [7]. It is mainly used to capture the potential probability distribution of a given dataset and generate new sample data. The core idea of VAE is to achieve data generation by learning the potential distribution of the data.

VAE is comprised of an encoder at the front-end and a decoder at the back-end, and they are mutually connected. The encoder is constructed in a layered manner, where the upper layers are more constricted and possess fewer nodes compared to the lower layers. In contrast, the decoder exhibits an opposite configuration, with the upper layers having a greater number of nodes than the lower ones [8].

The encoder undertakes the task of compressing the input data and carrying out dimensional reduction. Rather than directly providing the input for the decoder, the encoder generates the parameters of a probability distribution that serves as the input for the decoder. That is to say, the input to the VAE decoder is a random variable originating from a continuous probability distribution. Consequently, the decoder is presented with a diverse range of (probabilistic) inputs, even in cases where the initial input to the entire model remains unchanged.

The decoder aims to recover the compressed data to a state that closely approximates the original input data. The input for the decoder is acquired through sampling from the relevant probability distribution. As a result, it invariably generates distinct outputs even when presented with the same input. This characteristic enables VAE to function not merely as a dimensionality reduction model but also as a generative model capable of generating novel data. In the scenario of anomaly detection with VAE, it hinges on the probability of successful reconstruction of sensing data. When the VAE reconstruction is accomplished, it implies that the attributes of the input data are within the normal range. However, if there is a substantial disparity between the reconstructed data and the input data, it is probable that the input has not been part of the training set, thereby signifying that it might be anomalous data.

The VAE data processing process is shown in Fig. 1. VAE encodes the input data a into the hidden variable distribution parameters b_mean and b_log_var. Sample from N(0,1) to obtain a random number ∂ with a very small value. Obtain the hidden variable b by combining the random number ∂ with the hidden variable distribution parameters b_mean and b_log_var. Use the decoder to reconstruct the hidden variable b obtained in step 3 into the original input c.

One of the core objectives of the VAE is to model the distribution of the observed data, denoted as $p(z)$. This is accomplished by introducing the latent random variable z. The underlying principle is based on the complex theory of probability distributions, where the posterior distribution is defined as $p(x) = \int p_\theta(z)p_\theta(x \mid z)dz$,. In this expression, the latent variable z is generated from the prior distribution $p(z)$, while $\varnothing$ and θ are parameters of the encoder and decoder respectively. However, in practical situations, the parameter θ and the distribution of z are often difficult to handle and calculate precisely, which poses challenges to the implementation of the algorithm.

To overcome this predicament, the VAE adopts an ingenious strategy by representing the marginal log-likelihood of a single data point as $\log p(x) = D_{KL}(q_\varnothing(z \mid x)\|p_\theta(z)) + L_{vae}(\varnothing, \theta, x)$, where D_{KL} represents the Kullback-Leibler (KL) divergence from the prior $p_\theta(z)$ to the variational approximation $q_\varnothing(z \mid x)$ of $p(z \mid x)$, which plays a crucial role in measuring the difference between the two distributions. And L_{vae} (i.e., the loss) is the variational lower bound of the data x according to Jensen's inequality [9]. By minimizing this loss function, the VAE can continuously adjust the parameters of the encoder and decoder during the learning process to optimize its ability to represent and generate data, this allows VAE shows higher robustness than AE.

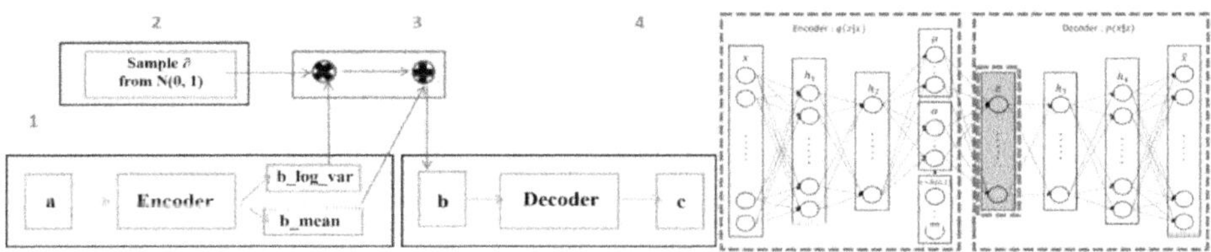

Fig. 1. Schematic diagram of VAE data processing process.

During the training process of variational autoencoders, there are two crucial loss functions that play a central role. The first is the reconstruction loss, which is used to quantify the similarity between the output data generated by the model and the original input data, usually measured in the form of mean squared error.

In order to set a reasonable threshold for the reconstruction error, we will refer to the box plot distribution of the reconstruction error, focusing particularly on its upper quartile, which can provide a conservative but instructive upper limit value. Once the threshold is set, the subset of data with a reconstruction error exceeding this threshold will be marked as abnormal, while those below the threshold will be considered normal. The second is the regularization loss, which helps the model learn a structured latent space, thereby reducing overfitting on the training data and ensuring that the model has stronger generalization ability.

2.3 Perceptual Anomaly Detection Based on Variational Auto-encoder

Using DPI (deep packet inspection) equipment to collect multi-dimensional KQI data from existing IoT users, involving network access, service access, network switching, service usage quality, etc., including: TCP link establishment success rate, service success rate, TCP link establishment one-time handshake delay server side delay, TCP link establishment two-time handshake delay (network side delay), TCP uplink disorderly packet ratio server side service switching success rate, TCP downlink disorderly packet ratio network side switching success rate, RTT uplink delay, RTT downlink delay, page response success rate, page opening success rate, page download rate, streaming media playback stutter rate, streaming media download rate, streaming media cache delay, streaming media upload rate, RTT uplink delay exceeding 300ms packet ratio, RTT downlink delay exceeding 300ms packet ratio, etc. as input data sources. Normalize the multi-dimensional KQI data to eliminate the impact of different scales on the data [10].

Create an encoder-decoder neural network, write reconstruction error and regularization loss functions, set up optimizers such as Adam, and set hyperparameters such as training epochs. Train the normalized dataset and record the training results. In each training epoch, the model iterates through the dataset, calculates the loss, and uses the optimizer to update the parameters, Then, save the trained VAE model.

Using the trained VAE model to predict the normalized IoT business perception data and calculate the reconstruction error, then set a reconstruction error threshold and compare the two values. A properly trained VAE model is expected to generate an identical output in response to each normalized input. If the calculated reconstruction error exceeds the threshold, it is determined that the perception data is abnormal.

2.4 Verification of Existing Network and Comparison of Models

Collect the multi-dimensional KQI data of Hubei Unicom's whole network IoT users for one week in one hour granularity, and obtain a multi-dimensional KQI distribution vector. Analyze the accuracy of the VAE-based perception anomaly detection method based on the distribution vector.

Randomly select the value distribution of a certain IoT user's multi-dimensional KQI perception data within 24 h of a day, and find that it has the characteristics of high dimensionality and local anomalies, as shown in Fig. 2:

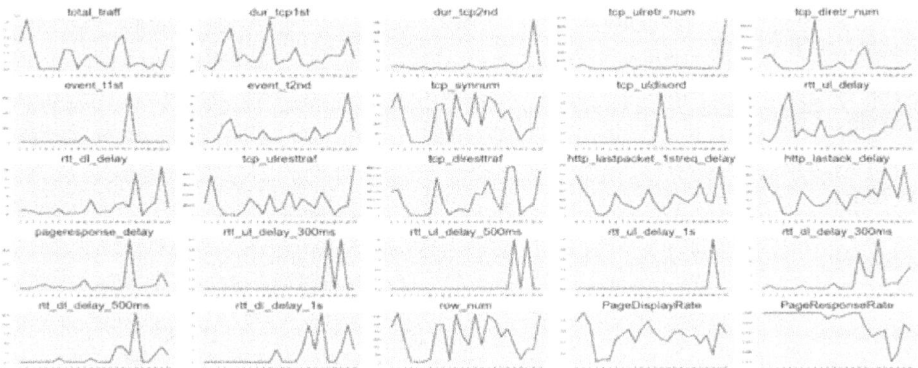

Fig. 2. Distribution characteristics of abnormal KQI perception.

According to the characteristics of KQI data, the encoder part of VAE is designed as a standard four-layer convolutional neural network structure, while the decoder part is composed of several convolutional layers. During model training, we use reconstruction loss and regularization loss functions to ensure that the model can effectively recover the original information from the encoded data and learn a well-structured latent space, thereby reducing overfitting [11].

After conducting feature engineering, the N-dimensional KQI vector data is partitioned into a training set and a test set. The training set serves the purpose of training the VAE model, while the test set is employed to assess the accuracy of the model. By setting different reconstruction error thresholds, the detection results based on AE and VAE are separately counted, as shown in Tables 1 and 2. The results show that the VAE method used in this paper for live network verification exhibits significant advantages over AE. Figure 3 is a statistical diagram of the detection results of the two methods.

The experimental results show that the accuracy of AE detection increases with the increase of the reconstruction error threshold, but the overall accuracy is lower than 90%. In contrast, the detection accuracy of VAE shows a significant improvement trend with the increase of the reconstruction error threshold. When the reconstruction threshold reaches 9.00E-17, the detection accuracy of VAE continues to be higher than 90%, and the number of detected abnormal IoT users can reach up to 12,000 (Fig. 4).

Table 1. Statistics of the accuracy rate of abnormal detection for IoT sensing based on AE

AE reconstruction error threshold	Number of users of IoT with abnormal AE detection perception	Confirmed number of IoT users with abnormal perception	Number of users of IoT with abnormal AE detection perception
5.00E-05	2361	1167	49.4%
7.50E-04	1632	867	53.1%
1.00E-04	1236	624	50.5%
1.50E-04	831	498	59.9%
2.00E-04	604	431	71.4%
3.50E-04	344	268	77.9%
8.00E-04	140	117	83.6%
1.50E-03	66	55	83.3%
3.00E-03	24	21	87.5%

Table 2. Statistics of the accuracy rate of abnormal detection for IoT sensing based on VAE.

VAE reconstruction error threshold	Number of users of IoT with abnormal VAE detection perception	Confirmed number of IoT users with abnormal perception	The accuracy rate of VAE detection
2.50E-03	2466	1394	56.5%
3.00E-03	1712	1053	61.5%
3.50E-03	1233	809	65.6%
4.00E-03	857	653	76.2%
4.50E-03	600	510	85.0%
5.00E-03	357	317	88.8%
7.00E-03	123	111	90.2%
1.50E-02	62	58	93.5%
2.00E-02	28	27	96.4%

This indicates that the VAE model exhibits high model generalization. Through comparison, due to the potential spatial data of AE being a fixed value, during the training process, as the loss function continues to decrease, the model is prone to overfitting, that is, there are samples in the training set that can be well reconstructed by the decoder, while for features that have not appeared in the potential space, the generation effect of the decoder is poor. However, VAE learns the distribution of hidden variables (allowing some noise and randomness in hidden variables), so it can have a similar regularization effect to prevent overfitting [12].

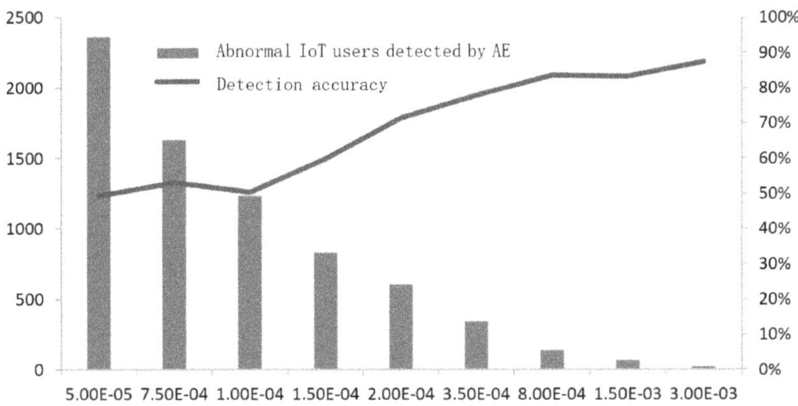

Fig. 3. IoT Perception Anomaly Detection Based on AE.

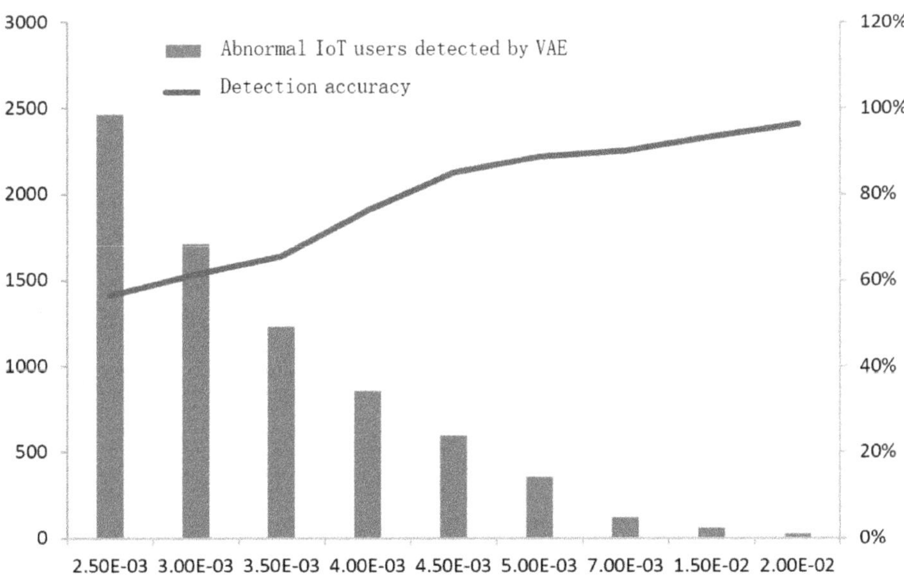

Fig. 4. IoT Perception Anomaly Detection Based on VAE.

3   Conclusion

This article introduces a machine learning anomaly detection method for IoT business perception, based on the characteristics of IoT business perception data, selecting the unsupervised VAE algorithm, and then setting a reasonable reconstruction error threshold to accurately detect abnormal IoT users.

In the future, different reconstruction error thresholds can be set for different IoT business scenarios, which can detect IoT business perception anomalies more effectively and accurately, furthermore, the LLM (Large Language Model) can also be used to intent understanding and intelligent auxiliary diagnosis thus, thus providing a reference for operators to ensure IoTaas perception more efficiently.

References

1. Malik, H., Khan, S.Z., Sarmiento, J.L.R., et al.: NB-IoT network field trial: indoor, outdoor and underground coverage campaign. In: 2019 15th International Wireless Communications and Mobile Computing Conference (IWCMC) (2019). https://doi.org/10.1109/IWCMC.2019.8766568
2. Wu, Q.H., Ding, G., Du, Z.Y., et al.: A cloud-based architecture for the Internet of spectrum devices over future wireless networks. IEEE Access **4**, 2854–2862 (2017)
3. Susanto, S.D., Arifin, M.A.S., et al.: IoT botnet malware classification using Weka tool and scikit-learn machine learning. In: International Conference on Smart Grid and Electrical Automation (2020)
4. Fathy, A.M., Ahmed, A., Aziz, S., et al.: Deep embedding data fusion scheme using variational graph auto-encoder in IoT environments. Int. J. Adv. Trends Comput. Sci. Eng. **9**(4), 4363–4372 (2020). https://doi.org/10.30534/ijatcse/2020/28942020
5. Wu, H.Q.: Technology and application progress on Internet of things. Chin. J. Internet Things **1**(1), 1–6 (2017)
6. Nooraiepour, A., Bajwa, W.U., Mandayam, N.B.: Learning-aided physical layer attacks against multicarrier communications in IoT (2019). https://doi.org/10.1109/TCCN.2020.2990657
7. Jesudurai, S.A., Senthilkumar, A.: An improved energy efficient cluster head selection protocol using the double cluster heads and data fusion methods for IoT applications. Cogn. Syst. Res. **57**, 101–106 (2019)
8. Han, K., Wen, H., Shi, J., et al.: Variational autoencoder: an unsupervised model for modeling and decoding fMRI activity in visual cortex (2018)
9. An, J., Cho, S.: Variational autoencoder based anomaly detection using reconstruction probability. Spec. Lect. IE **2**(1), 1–18 (2015)
10. Qiu, L., Wang, L.: Abnormal traffic detection method of Internet of things based on deep learning in edge computing environment. J. Circ. Syst. Comput. (2023). https://doi.org/10.1142/s0218126623502833
11. Behrouzi, T., Hatzinakos, D.: Graph variational auto-encoder for deriving EEG based graph embedding. Pattern Recognit. **121**(1), 108202 (2021). https://doi.org/10.1016/j.patcog.2021.108202
12. Liu, P., Guo, B., Zhang, Y., et al.: NB-IoT network and service collaborative optimization. In: International Conference on Signal and Information Processing, Networking and Computers (2019). https://doi.org/10.1007/978-981-13-7123-3-59

Design of Autonomous Cruise Vehicle System Based on Internet of Things Technology

Zekui Zhang(✉)

Wuhan Vocational College of Software and Engineering (Wuhan Open University), Wuhan, China
469801787@qq.com

Abstract. In order to further study the development of autonomous cruise control vehicle systems and explore their applications in environmental perception, automatic obstacle avoidance, information processing and other aspects. The autonomous cruise control vehicle system based on Internet of Things technology is a highly integrated control system. The core technology lies in the application of the Internet of Things, which connects vehicles in real-time with the surrounding environment, other vehicles, and cloud platforms through wireless communication technology, It uses the vehicle system to construct a real-time map and uses visual recognition positioning technology to perceive the surrounding environment, there by achieving automatic recognition and avoidance of obstacles. The vehicle system makes corresponding instructions that comply with obstacles based on information algorithms, Plan a cruise path for the autonomous cruise control system in the established environmental map and together completes specific tasks such as mapping, obstacle avoidance navigation, QR code recognition and machine voice of the vehicle system.

Keywords: Internet of Things · Vehicle mounted system · Autonomous navigation · information processing

1 Introduction

With the rapid development of technology, the application of Internet of Things technology in various fields is becoming increasingly widespread. Among them, the autonomous cruise control system based on the Internet of Things is gradually becoming an important innovation in the automotive industry with its unique advantages. This article will explore in detail the types, functions, operation and debugging of autonomous cruise control vehicle systems based on the Internet of Things, as well as future development trends and challenges [1].

The core technology of a cruise car based on the Internet of Things is to combine Internet of Things technology with cruise car technology. The combination of this technology enables cruise cars to flexibly cope with various challenges in complex environments, achieving a revolutionary breakthrough in traditional inspection methods. The Internet

© ICST Institute for Computer Sciences, Social Informatics and Telecommunications Engineering 2026
Published by Springer Nature Switzerland AG 2026. All Rights Reserved
R. C. Qiu et al. (Eds.): IoTaaS 2024, LNICST 675, pp. 359–367, 2026.
https://doi.org/10.1007/978-3-032-14681-6_33

of Things technology refers to the technology of connecting various equipment, machine vision, laser radar and other components through the Internet to realize the data exchange and interconnection between different equipment of the system. The Internet of Things technology enables the cruise car to obtain and process environmental information in real time, so as to achieve the purpose of completing certain tasks.

2 Overall Introduction and Architecture of the System

The autonomous cruise control vehicle system is mainly composed of an industrial computer and Ubuntu system. Utilizing depth camera modules, LiDAR modules, and ultrasonic modules to achieve automatic navigation and obstacle avoidance functions; Combining GPS module, LiDAR module, etc. to achieve positioning and navigation of the car [2]. The overall structure of this system is shown in Fig. 1.

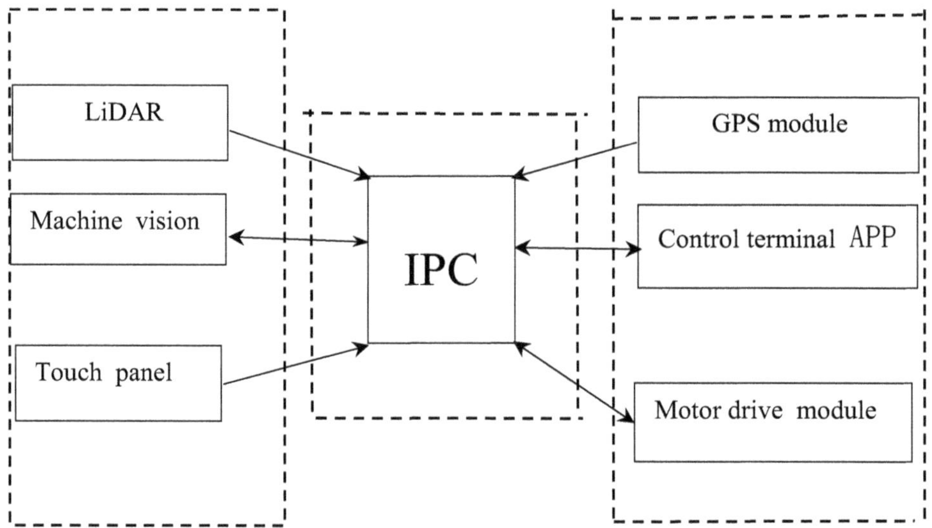

Fig. 1. Overall System Structure Block Diagram

The autonomous cruise vehicle system adopts a layered structure design, with various sensor devices such as LiDAR(Light Detection And Ranging), machine vision, and ultrasonic sensors installed on the top layer. SLAM (Simultaneous Localization and Mapping) algorithm is used to construct maps and perform self localization. In terms of hardware, the cruise car adopts high-performance cameras and sensors to obtain clear environmental images and accurate data information. At the same time, the introduction of wireless transmission modules enables the car to quickly transmit real-time video and data to remote monitoring centers, providing timely and accurate information support for decision-makers. In order to ensure the flexible and convenient movement of the cruise in car system, the chassis of the car system adopts the Mecanum wheel motion principle control [3]. The Mecanum wheel is equipped with independent small wheels with a certain tilt angle around the center wheel, which decompose the speed of the center wheel into X and Y directions. The wheels can move laterally and move forward and backward. According to the synthesis and decomposition of the forces, these forces can ultimately be synthesized in any direction that meets the requirements, generating a resultant force vector. This allows the wheels to move in the direction of the resultant force vector. In terms of software, the cruise car has achieved autonomous obstacle avoidance and autonomous tracking functions through advanced algorithms and artificial intelligence technology. It can adjust the path trajectory in real-time based on the status of the obstacle, avoiding collisions. Meanwhile, through technologies such as deep learning, the car can also intelligently analyze the environment, predict potential risks, and make early responses [4].

3 Implementation of Autonomous Cruise Control Vehicle System

3.1 Internet of Things Mobile Technology

The core technology of the autonomous cruise vehicle system based on the Internet of Things lies in the application of the Internet of Things. The Internet of Things technology connects vehicles with the surrounding environment, other vehicles, and cloud platforms in real-time through wireless communication technology, achieving information sharing and interaction, enabling vehicles to perceive the surrounding environment in real time, obtain information such as road conditions, vehicle location, speed, etc.and then issue corresponding instructions to complete tasks.

3.2 Autonomous Cruise Control Technology

In autonomous cruise control, the sensor module plays a very important role. These modules collect real-time information about the surrounding environment of the vehicle mounted system, and then convert the node data to protocol. The transmitted data is uniformly formatted and transmitted to the gateway module for network transmission of node data and management instructions. The various collected data in the system are processed and uploaded in real time. The control center calculates and processes the received data, and the control end sends instructions to control the vehicle mounted system to automatically navigate and avoid obstacles based on the instructions. By processing data, vehicles can achieve comprehensive perception of the surrounding environment and provide necessary information support for autonomous cruising [5].

3.3 Intelligent Mobile Environment Awareness Technology

The autonomous cruise control system is equipped with various sensors, such as LiDAR and visual sensors. Visual sensors refer to the use of cameras to perceive images and color information in the environment, and are used for self localization and environmental recognition in autonomous cruise control systems, using intelligent algorithms for image processing. The main function is to obtain unprocessed images required by the machine vision system, which can be driven by multiple visual sensors, including USB_cam ar_track_alver. Among them, USB_cam is one of the most commonly used drivers, which supports various types of USB cameras and provides for receiving and processing image information. LiDAR emits detection signals to the target, and then compares and processes the reflected signals with the transmitted signals to obtain relevant information about the target. This can accurately measure the state and position of the target for identification, discrimination, and tracking. Generate environmental maps to construct self positioning and environmental recognition judgments for autonomous cruise control systems. The laser measurement module processes three-dimensional coordinates and other data based on laser signals before and after launch. The onboard system utilizes visual sensors and LiDAR to monitor the vehicle's walking path and extract information on road obstacles[6].

4 System Operation and Debugging

The autonomous cruise control system needs to start from the starting point, autonomously identify obstacles based on environmental information, automatically avoid obstacles, and ultimately reach the target endpoint. Autonomous cruising first requires the construction of environmental maps, positioning of autonomous cruising systems, and planning of cruising paths. Map construction is mainly achieved by processing the spatial model obtained from the environmental information collected by LiDAR, Cruise positioning refers to the position of the autonomous cruise system in the current spatial model; Path planning is the process of planning a cruise path for an autonomous cruise system in an existing environmental map.

4.1 Construction of Environmental Maps

The construction of environmental maps is a crucial step in the operation of autonomous cruise control systems. In this step, we used the gmapping algorithm to process the environmental information obtained from LiDAR and odometry to obtain a spatial model, thereby constructing a high-precision environmental map. The construction process of this map requires manual control of the autonomous cruise control system to obtain a global prior map through LiDAR and odometer, and save the map locally. Subsequently, based on amcl autonomous positioning technology, the system compares the saved global map to determine its own position, thereby achieving precise navigation and obstacle avoidance [7]. The process of gmapping algorithm is shown in Fig. 2.

Firstly, manually control the autonomous cruise control system to obtain a global prior map through LiDAR and odometer, then save the map to the local area. Then, based on AMCL autonomous positioning, compare the saved global map with the current LiDAR and odometer to determine its own position and navigate to avoid obstacles.

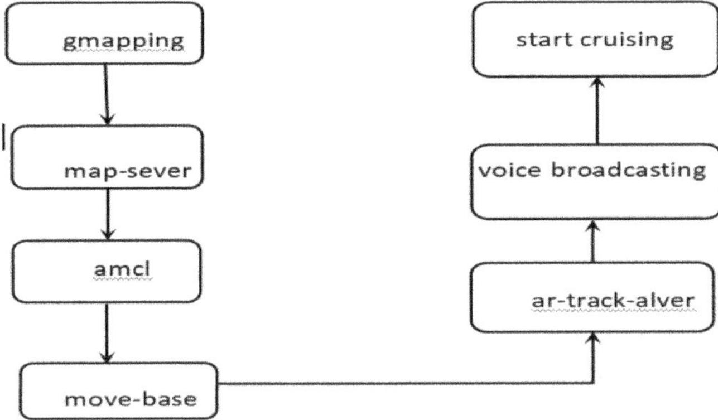

Fig. 2. Gmapping Algorithm Flow Chart

Now let's take a look at how to run this case. When entering our abot-m1-atk system, we see some shell scripts in the user directory.and the environmental map data constructed by LiDAR is shown in Fig. 3. In this case, we used this script:

Open terminal input:

$./1-gmapping.sh

You can see that the incomplete map has appeared. Select the fifth terminal on the terminal interface, and you can control the autonomous cruise control system to move forward through the "U", "I", and "O" keys on the keyboard (when the English capital is turned on, the "U" and "O" keys can control the autonomous cruise control system to move left and right in front). You can control the autonomous cruise control system to turn left and right through the "J" and "L" keys on the keyboard (when the English capital is turned on, the autonomous cruise control system to move left and right). You can also control the autonomous cruise control system to move forward through the "M", "<", ">" keys on the keyboard (when the English capital is turned on, the "<", ">" keys can control the autonomous cruise control the autonomous cruise system to move forward. The cruise control system moves left and right in the rear, controlling the autonomous cruise control system to move in the field and complete map creation. The recognition task is shown in Fig. 4.

Finally, save the map using the following command:

$ roslaunch robot_slam save_map.launch.

The following is the judgment of task information:

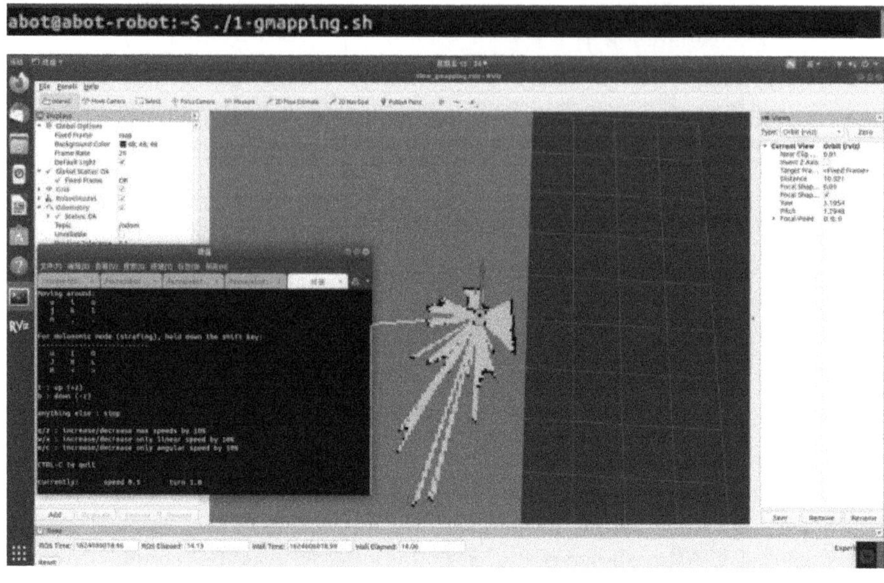

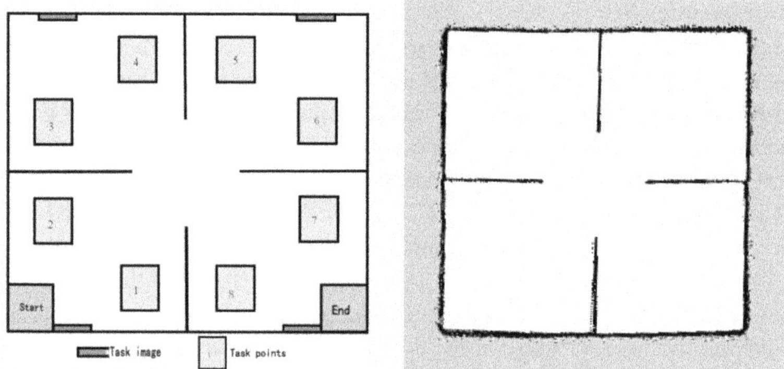

Fig. 3. Environmental Map Data Constructed Based on LiDAR

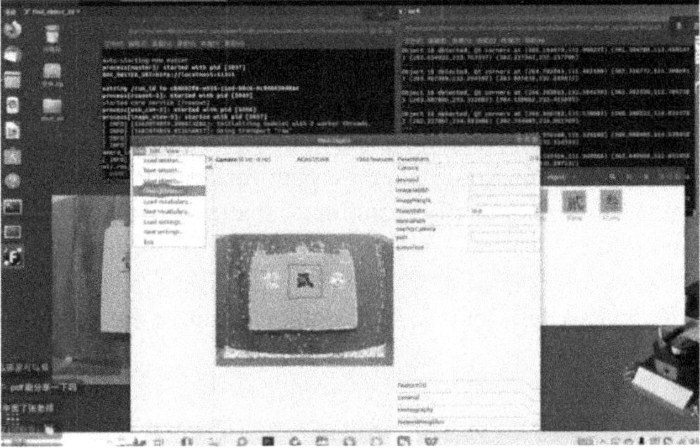

Fig. 4. Recognition Task Diagram

```
global flog0 ,flog1,flog2,count,move_flog
id=255
point_msg = data
if(point_msg.z!=255 and move_flog= =0):
if(point_msg.z>=1 and point_msg.z<=8 and flog0= =255):
    id=0
    flog0=0
elif(point_msg.z>=9 and point_msg.z<=16 and flog1= =255):
    id=1
    flog1=1
elif(point_msg.z>=17 and point_msg.z<=24 and flog2= =255):
    id=2
    flog2=2
 elif(point_msg.z!=255 and move_flog= =1):
if(point_msg.z>=1 and point_msg.z<=8 ):
    id=0
elif(point_msg.z>=9 and point_msg.z<=16 ):
    id=1
elif(point_msg.z>=17 and point_msg.z<=24):
    id=2
```

Change the scanned images to the corresponding range: for example, all images from 1 to 8 are images with the number one. In the subsequent program execution, the scanned photos and all images from 1 to 8 will be judged. If the required task information is scanned, perform operations such as broadcasting and entering the task point. If no or non task point information is scanned, go to the next task scanning point.

Finally, save the map using the following command:

$ roslaunch robot_slam save_map.launch.

4.2   Testing of Autonomous Cruise Control System

The operation and debugging of the autonomous cruise control system is a complex and meticulous process. The constructed cruise system environment map and navigation both require the environmental pose data of the autonomous cruise system. First, locate the autonomous cruise system, and then plan the path for testing based on the synthesized map. The road map for automatically planning to the target point is shown in Fig. 5.

Open terminal input:

$/ 3-mission. sh

Run this script and switch to the last terminal to achieve the following functions:

Enter 1 at this terminal.

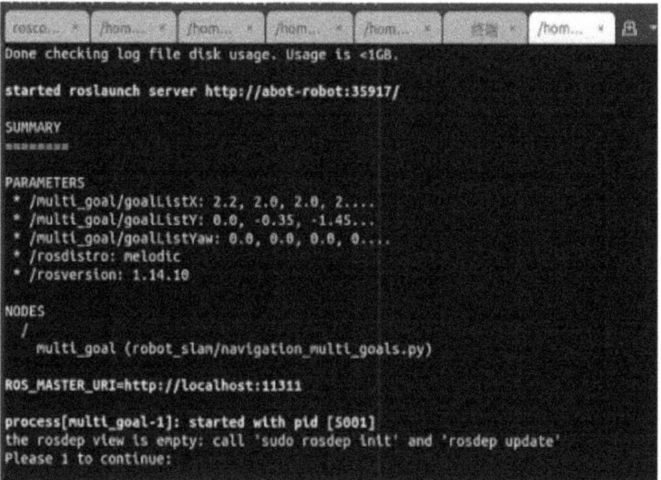

Fig. 5. Road Map for Automatic Planning to the Target Point

5   Conclusion

Overall, the autonomous cruise control system based on the Internet of Things is an important innovation in the automotive industry. It fully utilizes the advantages of IoT technology to achieve real-time connection and interaction between vehicles and their surrounding environment, other vehicles, and cloud platforms, providing strong support for improving driving safety and efficiency. We believe that autonomous cruise control systems based on the Internet of Things will play a greater role in the future, driving the automotive industry towards a more intelligent, safe, and efficient direction. In summary, the autonomous cruise control system based on the Internet of Things is a technological innovation with broad application prospects and enormous potential. By continuously optimizing system design and algorithms to solve the challenges and problems faced, it is expected to promote this technology to play a greater role in the future, bringing more convenience and safety to human life.

Although this study has achieved certain results, there are still many shortcomings and challenges that need to be addressed. For example, how to improve the endurance of small cars, ensure the safety of data transmission, and reduce manufacturing costs will help promote the further development of cruise car technology. Therefore, in the future, our research will mainly focus on continuously optimizing system design and algorithms, while combining deep information for further in-depth research on target recognition of autonomous cruise vehicle systems, in order to further enhance the system's ability to recognize complex surrounding environments and its performance.

References

1. Shi, F., Ding, Y., Shan, H., et al.: Design and implementation of smart agriculture based on internet of things technology. Netw. Secur. Technol. Appl. (01), 125–126 (2022)
2. Zeng, S., Wu, J., Ye, Z., et al.: ROS based autonomous driving intelligent vehicle. Internet Things Technol. (06), 62–63 (2020)
3. Chen, J., Lin, H., Zhang, C., et al.: Design of autonomous navigation robot based on ROS system. Comput. Knowl. Technol. **19**(23), 99–102 (2023)
4. Wu, Y., Zhang, H., Bai, X., et al.: Intelligent logistics handling trolley. Electron. Test. **36**(21), 105–107 (2022)
5. Feng, B., Gong, Y., Pan, J., et al.: Design of intelligent cruise control vehicles based on dynamic maps. Agric. Equip. Vehicle Eng. **60**(8), 124–129 (2022)
6. Wang, L., Zhang, Z., Xu, H., et al.: Design of intelligent spray trolley based on internet of things technology. Software **44**(9), 180–183 (2023)
7. Peng, L., Lu, H., Luo, Z., et al.: Research on small intelligent mobile irrigation systems based on the internet of things. Software **15**(8), 19–22 (2023)

Research and Simulation of Channel Estimation of FBMC for LEO-Satellite Internet Network Oriented by PAA

Wenjia Wang[1], Wenliang Lin[1(✉)], Ke Wang[2], Zhongliang Deng[1], Xinchen Zhang[2], and Qiushi Cui[1]

[1] School of Electronic Engineering, Beijing University of Posts and Telecommunications, Beijing, China
`Charterlin@bupt.edu.cn`

[2] School of Information and Communication Engineering, Beijing University of Posts and Telecommunications, Beijing, China

Abstract. Low Earth Orbit (LEO) satellite communication technology is set to become a cornerstone of future 6G communications, offering cost-effective and flexible deployment solutions. As mobile applications proliferate and emerging technologies like artificial intelligence, the Internet of Things, and augmented reality advance, the demand for spectrum resources is rapidly increasing. Filter Bank Multi-Carrier (FBMC) has emerged as a leading candidate waveform for 6G due to its superior spectrum resource utilization. This paper provides an in-depth investigation of an FBMC-based LEO satellite communication system, detailing the system architecture, channel estimation design, and performance evaluation. Through comprehensive simulation experiments, we rigorously analyze the performance of various channel estimation algorithms in LEO satellite communication environments, focusing on Bit Error Rate (BER) performance and practical applicability. Moreover, we propose an optimization strategy based on DMRS-Bundling to further enhance the performance of these channel estimation algorithms, ensuring the reliability and efficiency of LEO satellite communication systems.

Keywords: FBMC · Low Earth Orbit · Channel estimation · DMRS-Bundling

1 Introduction

Low Earth Orbit (LEO) satellite communications, known for their easy deployment, wide coverage, and immunity to environmental constraints, are considered the most promising candidate for global wireless communication in the 6G [1]. As 5G technology progresses, there is growing focus on integrating satellite communications (Sat-Com) with 5G, particularly in non-terrestrial networks (NTN)

Supported by National Key R&D Program of China (2022YFB2902605).

R. C. Qiu et al. (Eds.): IoTaaS 2024, LNICST 675, pp. 368–378, 2026.
https://doi.org/10.1007/978-3-032-14681-6_34

[2,5]. Orthogonal Frequency Division Multiplexing (OFDM), the fundamental waveform of 5G New Radio (NR), has strong resistance to multipath interference due to the orthogonality of its subcarriers. However, OFDM uses rectangular filters for subcarrier filtering, leading to significant out-of-band leakage of subcarrier energy. In contrast, Filter Bank Multi-Carrier(FBMC) uses non-rectangular prototype filters, resulting in lower sidelobes levels and reduced out-of-band leakage compared to OFDM.

LEO satellites, which have an orbital altitude between 500 km and 2000 km [6], have the dual advantage of low latency and path loss in satellite communication systems. However, the significant Doppler shifts caused by the high speeds of LEO satellites, reaching up to 5 to 10 km/s [7], make channel estimation in such conditions extremely challenging. The channel estimation of OFDM in LEO satellite communication has been thoroughly studied in [8,9]. Compared with OFDM, the presence of imaginary part interference due to the non-orthogonal properties of FBMC makes the channel estimation of FBMC more difficult. In order to solve the above problems, many references have proposed channel estimation methods based on pilot design for FBMC. In terms of block-type pilot channel estimation, [10] proposed two pilot-based channel estimation algorithms: Pairs of Pilots (PoP) and the Interference Approximation Method (IAM). POP makes use of the simple algebraic relationship between the two leading sequences before and after for channel estimation. IAM utilizes the method of constructing pseudo-pilot tones to emulate Least Squares (LS) in CP-OFDM systems. Simultaneously, by designing the preamble sequences, the pseudo-pilot tones' energy is maximized to minimize the impact of noise on channel estimation performance. In the channel estimation algorithm based on scattered pilot channel estimation, [11] proposed Auxiliary Pilot (AP) and Coding for channel estimation of scattered pilot channel estimation. The idea of AP is to add auxiliary pilots around the guide symbols. This arrangement ensures that the interference generated by the auxiliary pilots at the guide position cancels out with the interference generated by the rest of the time-frequency symbols. The Coding, on the other hand, encodes the data around the pilot symbols by constructing a coding matrix so that there is no interference from nearby symbols at the coded pilot position. In [12], R. Nissel designed a MMSE for CP-OFDM and FBMC, which is also based on scattered pilot channel estimation. The channels based on the above studies are flat fading channels or double selective channels, which are not the channel environment in LEO satellite communications. At present, there is not much study on channel estimation in LEO satellite communication systems based on FBMC waveforms in this area. In this background, this paper firstly describes the principle of FBMC, and provides a deep study on the pilot design and the channel estimation algorithm of FBMC system under the low-orbit satellite communication environment. And the channel estimation algorithm of FBMC system is optimized according to 5G NR. Finally, the improved algorithm is simulated and validated and the simulation results are presented.

In this background, this paper firstly describes the principle of FBMC, and provides a deep study on the pilot design and the channel estimation algorithm of FBMC system under the low-orbit satellite communication environment. And the channel estimation algorithm of FBMC system is optimized according to 5G NR. Finally, the improved algorithm is simulated and validated and the simulation results are presented [3,4].

2   System Model

In this section, in the low-orbit satellite communication scenario, the architecture of the FBMC waveform-based satellite communication system consists of satellites, ground stations, and user terminals, as shown in Fig. 1.

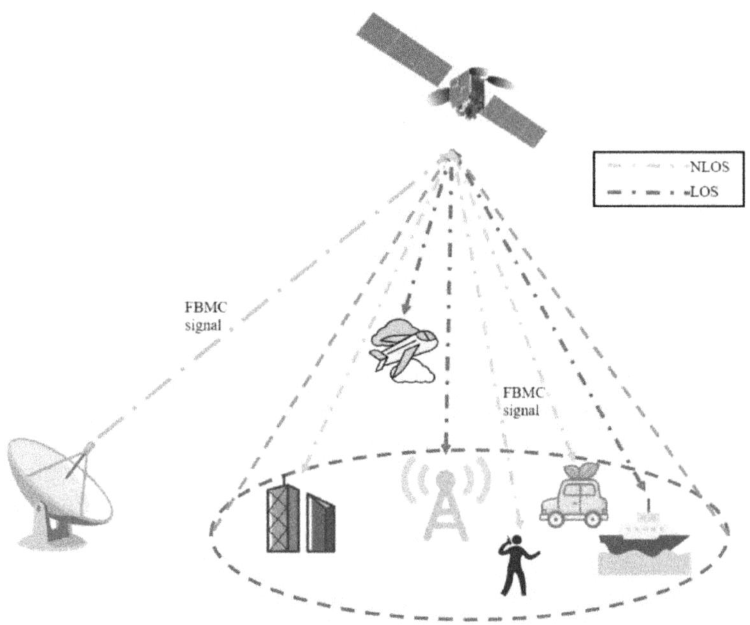

Fig. 1. Low-orbit Satellite Communication Scenario

The FBMC waveform is applied to data transmission between satellites and ground stations to support high-speed data transfer and real-time communication needs. The link model is illustrated in Fig. 2.

In FBMC transmission system, the transmitted data is $a_{m,n}$ located at the time-frequency point (m, n), which is obtained after modulation:

$$s(t) = \sum_{m=0}^{M-1} \sum_{n=0}^{N-1} a_{m,n} g_{m,n}(t) \tag{1}$$

with,

$$g_{m,n}(t) = p_{\text{TX}}(t - \Delta T)e^{\frac{j(m+n)\pi}{2}} e^{j2\pi m \Delta f t} \tag{2}$$

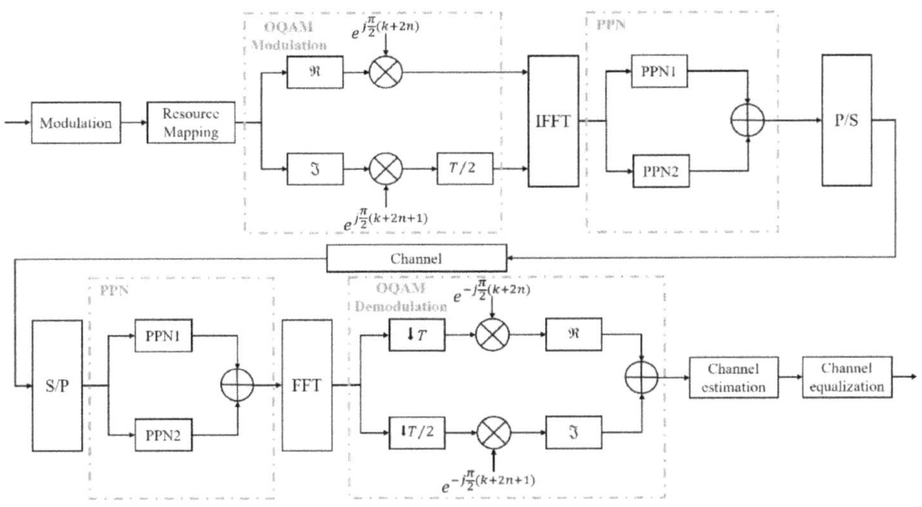

Fig. 2. Link Model

where $g_{m,n}(t)$ is obtained for the prototype filter p_{TX} after time shifting and frequency shifting. In the FBMC system, $p_{TX}(t) = p_{RX}(t)$. The received basis pulses $q_{m,n}(t)$ can be expressed as:

$$g_{m,n}(t) = p_{\mathrm{RX}}(t - \Delta T)e^{\frac{j(m+n)\pi}{2}}e^{j2\pi m\Delta ft} \tag{3}$$

The time-frequency spacing is reduced to $TF = 1/2$ to improve the spectral efficiency in FBMC. Orthogonality then only holds in the real domain, $R\left(\langle g_{m,n}(t), g^*_{p,q}(t)\rangle\right) = \delta_{(m-p),(n-q)}$.

The above signal is transmitted over a multipath fading channel:

$$r(t) = h(t) * s(t) + \eta(t) \tag{4}$$

where $h(t)$ represents the Channel Impulse Response(CIR). $\eta(t)$ represents the Gaussian White Noise, $\eta(t) \sim \mathcal{CN}(0, \sigma_n^2)$.

For the satellite channel model, the NTN-TDL model is employed, where each tap represents a collection of multiple paths with the same delay. The time-varying channel impulse response, composed of L paths, is:

$$h(t,\tau) = \sum_{l=0}^{L-1} \mu_l(t)\delta(t - \tau_l) \tag{5}$$

where τ_l is the delay of the l-th multipath signal, $\mu_l(t) = a_l(t)e^{j\theta_l(t)}$. $a_l(t)$ is the gain of the l-th path and $\theta_l(t)$ is the phase of the l-th path. Due to the high velocity of the satellite, significant Doppler effects are generated, given by $f_d = \frac{v(t)}{c}f_0$, where $v(t)$ represents the relative speed of the satellite with respect to the terminal. The NTN-TDL channel model characterizes the satellite channel for both Line-of-Sight (LOS) and Non-Line-of-Sight (NLOS) scenarios. Based on these different scenarios, the NTN-TDL model is categorized into four types: A, B, C, and D [13].

The transmission through an NTN-TDL channel can be described by the following input-output relationship:

$$r(t) = \sum_{l=0}^{L-1} \mu_l(t)s(t - \tau_l) \tag{6}$$

At the receiver, the received signal $r(t)$ is demodulated to obtain:

$$\hat{a}_{m,n} = R\left\{ \int_{-\infty}^{+\infty} g_{m,n}^*(t)r(t)\, dt \right\} \tag{7}$$

where $\hat{a}_{m,n}$ represents the demodulated signal, $g_{m,n}^*$ denotes the receiver filter, and $r(t)$ is the received signal passed through the channel. After obtaining the received signal, channel estimation is performed. Since the values at the pilot locations are known, we conducted channel estimation based on these known pilot values. x_p represents the value at the pilot location at the transmitter, y_p represents the value at the pilot location at the receiver. Using the LS for channel estimation, the result is:

$$\hat{H}_{p,\text{LS}} = \frac{y_p(k)}{x_p(k)} \tag{8}$$

However, satellite channels exhibit significant Doppler frequency shifts and delays, while the LS assumes linearity in the channel. Therefore, using the LS for channel estimation results in poor performance. On the other hand, the Linear Minimum Mean Square Error (LMMSE) takes into account the statistical characteristics of the signal and the influence of noise, minimizing the mean square error of the estimation. It can provide more accurate signal estimation compared to the LS. The estimation result is:

$$\hat{H}_{p,\text{LMMSE}} = R_{H_p \hat{H}_{p,\text{LS}}} \left(R_{H_p H_p} + I\frac{\beta}{\text{SNR}} \right)^{-1} \hat{H}_{p,\text{LS}} \tag{9}$$

where β is determined based on the modulation scheme employed. The Singular Value Decomposition based Minimum Mean Square Error (SVD-MMSE) can effectively reduce computational complexity. It utilizes the properties of singular value decomposition (SVD) to transform the complex channel estimation problem into multiple independent sub-channel estimation problems. The transformation through singular value decomposition is as follows:

$$\mathbf{R_{H_p H_p}} = \mathbf{U \Lambda U}^H \tag{10}$$

where Λ represents the diagonal matrix composed of the singular values λ_i, where $i = 1, 2, \ldots, N$ in (10). It satisfies $\lambda_1 \geq \lambda_2 \geq \ldots \geq \lambda_N$. U is a unitary matrix composed of the unit eigenvectors corresponding to the singular values at each position. Using the first-order p matrix of Λ for simplification, we obtain the estimated channel $\hat{H}_{\mathrm{SVD},p}$:

$$\hat{\mathbf{H}}_{\mathrm{SVD},p} = \mathbf{U}\boldsymbol{\Delta}_p\mathbf{U}^H\hat{\mathbf{H}}_{\mathrm{LS}} \tag{11}$$

The matrix $\boldsymbol{\Delta}_p$ in the above equation is a diagonal matrix associated with the first p singular values, with the values on the diagonal specifically represented as:

$$\delta_k = \begin{cases} \frac{\lambda_k}{\lambda_k + \frac{\beta}{\mathrm{SNR}}}, & k = 1, 2, \ldots, r \\ 0, & k = r+1, r+2, \ldots, p \end{cases} \tag{12}$$

where the choice of p value is related to the estimation performance.

3   Theoretical Deduction

In the previous section, we discussed the channel estimation model for FBMC in satellite channels. For satellite scenarios, the high mobility of satellites results in significant Doppler shifts, which can affect the performance of channel estimation. Next, we analyzed the performance of FBMC channel estimation in low Earth orbit (LEO) satellite scenarios.

We considered a discrete-time model, where sampling is performed at a rate of $f_s = \frac{1}{T_s} = F_N^{\mathrm{FFT}}$. The transmission filter is represented by the matrix $G \in \mathbb{C}^{L \times MN}$, and the reception filter can be represented by $Q \in \mathbb{C}^{L \times MN}$. In FBMC, only real orthogonality holds, i.e., $R\{Q^H G\} = I_{MN}$. The input-output relationship can be described as:

$$\mathbf{y} = \mathbf{Q}^H\mathbf{H}\mathbf{G}\mathbf{x} + \boldsymbol{\eta} \tag{13}$$

where $x = [x_{0,0}, \ldots, x_{M-1,N-1}]^T \in \mathbb{C}^{1 \times MN}$ represents the vectorized form of the transmitted data symbols, $y \in \mathbb{C}^{MN \times 1}$ represents the vectorized form of the received signal, and $\eta \sim \mathcal{CN}(0, P_n Q^H G)$ is the Gaussian white noise, and $H \in \mathbb{C}^{L \times L}$ represents the channel matrix. When the channel bandwidth is less than or equal to $5\,\mathrm{MHz}$, the fast fading channel model can be simplified to flat fading [14]. If the channel experiences flat slow fading, this indicates that $H_{m,n}$ is constant over one symbol time and one subcarrier bandwidth. Thus, the received signal can be expressed as:

$$y_{m,n} = H_{m,n}(a_{m,n} + I_{m,n}) + \eta_{m,n} \tag{14}$$

where $I_{m,n}$ represents the interference between the imaginary parts of the FBMC signal. From (14), it can be seen that for flat channels, the interference between the imaginary parts of the FBMC signal affects the received FBMC signal. If the channel experiences fast fading in a satellite broadband scenario, it can be represented as:

$$\mathbf{H} = \sum_{i=1}^{L} \mathbf{g}_i \boldsymbol{\Pi}^{l_i} \boldsymbol{\Delta}^{k_i} \tag{15}$$

374   W. Wang et al.

where Π^{l_i} represents the delay matrix of the l-th path, which is the expression of the permutation matrix Π after a cyclic shift by l_i positions and Δ^{k_i} denotes the Doppler shift matrix of the l-th path. The Doppler shift matrix is expressed as:

$$\Delta^{k_i} = \mathrm{diag}(1, w^{k_i}, \ldots, w^{k_i(L-1)}) \tag{16}$$

where $w = e^{j\frac{2\pi}{N}}$ and k_i represents the Doppler shift of different taps. The expression for each element in the matrix can be obtained as:

$$
\begin{aligned}
y_{(m,n)} = \sum_{k=-\infty}^{\infty} \sum_{l=0}^{L-1} \sum_{m=0}^{M-1} \sum_{n\in\mathbb{Z}} & \{g_i a_{(m,n)} q[k] g[k - \tau_l] \\
& e^{j(m-\bar{m})k/M} e^{-j\frac{2\pi ml}{M}} e^{j\frac{\pi(m+n-\bar{m}-\bar{n})}{2}} e^{j\frac{2\pi k_i l}{M}}\} + \eta_{(m,n)}
\end{aligned}
\tag{17}
$$

From (10), the estimated value can be obtained as:

$$
\begin{aligned}
\hat{H}_{(m,n)} = & \sum_{k=-\infty}^{\infty} \sum_{l=0}^{L-1} \sum_{m=0}^{M-1} \sum_{n\in\mathbb{Z}} \{g_i e^{-j\frac{2\pi m\tau_l}{M}} e^{j\frac{2\pi k_i l}{M}}\} \\
& + \sum_{k=-\infty}^{\infty} \sum_{l=0}^{L-1} \sum_{m=0}^{M-1} \sum_{n\in\mathbb{Z}} \{\frac{I_{(m,n)}}{a_{(m,n)}} e^{j\frac{2\pi k_i l}{M}}\} + \frac{\eta_{(m,n)}}{a_{(m,n)}}
\end{aligned}
\tag{18}
$$

From (18), it can be seen that the results estimated by the LS are affected by the interference between the imaginary parts of the FBMC symbols and noise interference. The Doppler frequency offset will affect the phase of the output signal, thereby affecting the results of the channel estimation. We used the auxiliary pilot method to eliminate interference from imaginary parts. The structure of the pilot is illustrated in Fig. 3.

For the LMMSE and SVD-MMSE, the elements in $R_{H_p H_p}$ and $R_{H_p H_p}$ satisfy:

$$E\{h_{m,n}\hat{h}^*_{\bar{m},\bar{n}}\} = E\{h_{m,n}h^*_{\bar{m},\bar{n}}\} = r_f[m - \bar{m}]r_t[n - \bar{n}] \tag{19}$$

where $r_f[m]$ represents the frequency domain autocorrelation function, and $r_t[n]$ represents the time domain autocorrelation function. For a fading channel with maximum Doppler frequency $f_{\max}$ and Jakes power spectrum, the time domain correlation $r_t[n]$ is:

$$r_t[n] = J_0(2\pi f_{\max} n T_s) \tag{20}$$

From (20), it can be observed that, for the LMMSE and SVD-MMSE, the Doppler frequency will affect $R_{H_p H_p}$ and $R_{H_p \hat{h}_{p,ls}}$. According to (9) and (11), the Doppler frequency will consequently affect the results of LMMSE and SVD-MMSE. For LS, LMMSE, and SVD-MMSE, we optimized the channel estimation algorithms by integrating DMRS-Bundling. DMRS-Bundling entails the transmitter sending the same DMRS symbol across multiple time slots, enhancing the quality of channel estimation by adding DMRS in each slot. Each group of additional DMRS constitutes repeated precoded DMRS symbols [14]. Thus, for FBMC systems, based on the concept of DMRS-Bundling, we transmitted multiple sets of FBMC signals and inserted the same pilot sequences as configured

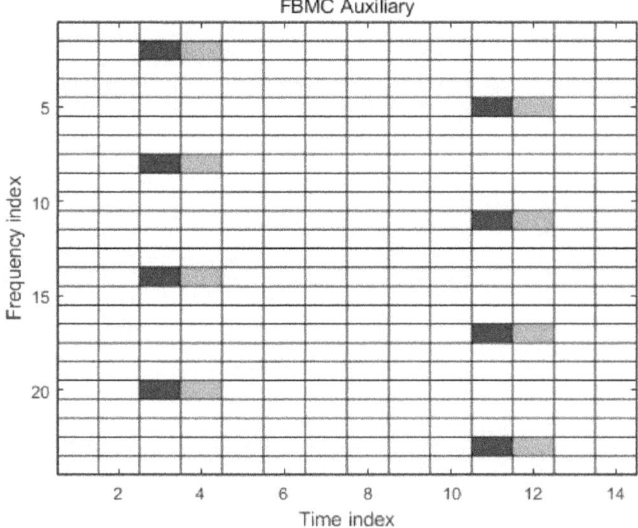

Fig. 3. Pilot Structure

above. For time-frequency selective fading, DMRS-Bundling provides diversity in both time and frequency domains by transmitting DMRS sequences at different FBMC symbols and frequencies. This approach enables better modeling and estimation of time-frequency selective fading channels, thereby improving channel estimation performance.

4 Numerical Results

In this section, we conduct simulation analysis of the channel estimation proposed for FBMC waveforms in the context of low Earth orbit satellite communication scenarios. We design the transmitted FBMC symbols based on the frame format in 5G NR, with specific simulation parameters detailed in Table 1.

Table 1. System Parameters

System Parameter	Numerical Value
Subcarrier spacing	15 kHz
SNR	0:5:40
Channel Model	NTN-TDL-A, NTN-TDL-C
Modulation Method	16 QAM
Prototype Filter	Hermite

Based on the FBMC waveform, we utilized LS, LMMSE, and SVD-MMSE for channel estimation at the receiver, and compared the BER. The receiver channel estimation algorithms are optimized using DMRS-Bundling. We then compared LS, LMMSE, and SVD-MMSE algorithms before and after optimization using DMRS-Bundling.

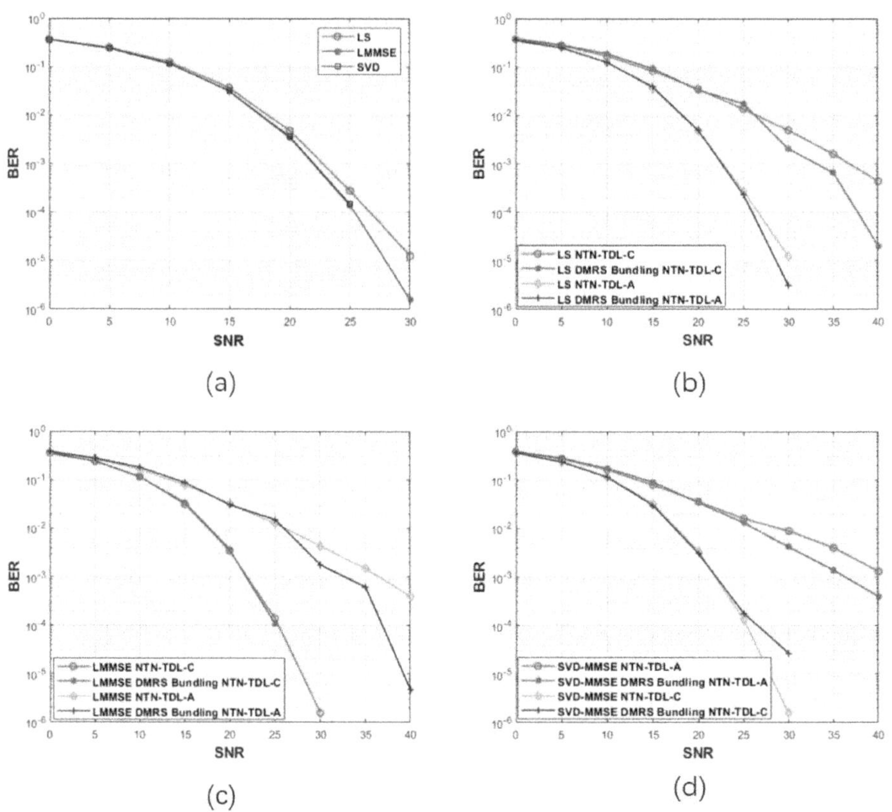

Fig. 4. Simulation Results

Figure 4(a) presents the SNR-BER curves for LS, LMMSE, and SVD-MMSE based on block-type pilots under NTN-TDL-C channel. It can be observed that the demodulation threshold for the LS is 24.2 dB, while for the LMMSE and SVD-MMSE, it is 23.4 dB. Compared to the LS, the LMMSE and SVD-MMSE consider the statistical characteristics of the channel and the influence of noise, minimizing the mean square error of the estimation. Hence, the performance of these algorithms improves by 0.8 dB. The BER performance of the SVD-MMSE is slightly better than that of the LMMSE because both algorithms are essentially MMSE. However, the computational complexity of the SVD-MMSE is lower than that of the LMMSE. This is because the computational complexity of the LMMSE mainly comes from matrix inversion, while the computational complexity of the SVD-MMSE comes from SVD, which is lower than the complexity of matrix inversion.

We compared the FBMC channel estimation algorithms with and without DMRS-Bundling through simulations. Figure 4(b) shows the SNR-BER curves of the LS algorithm with and without optimization under NTN-TDL-A and NTN-TDL-C. In the NTN-TDL-C, the demodulation threshold for the optimized algorithm is 23.8 dB, with a performance improvement of 0.4 dB. In the NTN-TDL-A, the demodulation threshold for the unoptimized algorithm is 37.2 dB, whereas for the optimized algo-rithm, it is 33.9 dB, resulting in a performance improvement of 3.3 dB. The effects of optimization for the LMMSE and SVD-MMSE under NTN-TDL-A and NTN-TDL-C are similar to those for the LS.

Figure 4(c) shows the SNR-BER curves of the LMMSE with and without optimization under NTN-TDL-A and NTN-TDL-C. In the NTN-TDL-C, the demodulation threshold for the optimized algorithm is 23.2 dB, with a performance improvement of 0.2 dB. In the NTN-TDL-A, the demodulation threshold for the unoptimized algo-rithm is 36.4 dB, whereas for the optimized algorithm, it is 34.1 dB, resulting in a performance improvement of 2.7 dB.

Figure 4(d) shows the SNR-BER curves of the SVD-MMSE with and without optimization under NTN-TDL-A and NTN-TDL-C. In the NTN-TDL-C, the demodulation threshold for the optimized algorithm is 23.1 dB, with a performance improvement of 0.3 dB. In the NTN-TDL-A, the demodulation threshold for the unoptimized algo-rithm is 40 dB, whereas for the optimized algorithm, it is 35.8 dB, resulting in a per-formance improvement of 4.2 dB.

The reason for these differences is that NTN-TDL-C represents a LOS scenario, whereas NTN-TDL-A represents a NLOS scenario. In LOS scenario, the signal propa-gation path is relatively simple, and transmission quality is better. In NLOS scenario, the signal propagation path is complex, and transmission quality is poorer. The DMRS-Bundling optimized algorithms provide more multipath samples, enhancing the ability to resist multipath interference in NLOS scenarios. Additionally, by increas-ing the number of DMRS symbols, the transmit signal power is increased, allowing the receiver to receive more amplified signals, thereby improving the SNR of channel estimation and its accuracy. However, in LOS scenarios, due to the presence of a direct path and fewer multipath effects, the signal transmission quality is usually good, hence the optimization effect is limited.

5   Conclusion

We analyzed the performance differences of channel estimation using LS, LMMSE, and SVD-MMSE for FBMC in low Earth orbit satellite scenarios. Based on this anal-ysis, we proposed optimizing these channel estimation using DMRS-Bundling. The results indicate that LMMSE and SVD-MMSE outperform the LS algorithm. Furthermore, the optimized algorithms show more significant improvements in NLOS scenarios.

References

1. Zhen, L., et al.: Energy-efficient random access for LEO satellite-assisted 6G internet of remote things. IEEE Internet Things J. **8**(7), 5114–5128 (2020)
2. Guidotti, A., et al.: Architectures and key technical challenges for 5G systems incorporating satellites. IEEE Trans. Veh. Technol. **68**(3), 2624–2639 (2019)
3. Giambene, G., Kota, S., Pillai, P.: Satellite-5G integration: a network perspective. IEEE Netw. **32**(5), 25–31 (2018)
4. Kodheli, O., Guidotti, A., Vanelli-Coralli, A.: Integration of satellites in 5G through LEO constellations. In: GLOBECOM 2017-2017 IEEE Global Communications Conference, pp. 1–6. IEEE (2017)
5. Guidotti, A., et al.: Integration of 5G technologies in LEO mega-constellations. arXiv preprint arXiv:1709.05807 (2017)
6. Leyva-Mayorga, I., et al.: LEO small-satellite constellations for 5G and beyond-5G communications. IEEE Access **8**, 184955–184964 (2020)
7. Su, Y., et al.: Broadband LEO satellite communications: architectures and key technologies. IEEE Wirel. Commun. **26**(2), 55–61 (2019)
8. Zhang, Y., et al.: Deep learning-based channel prediction for LEO satellite massive MIMO communication system. IEEE Wirel. Commun. Lett. **10**(8), 1835–1839 (2021)
9. Pu, F., Gong, J., Gan, L.: Improved channel estimation algorithm for OFDM over LEO channels. In: 2005 IEEE International Symposium on Microwave, Antenna, Propagation and EMC Technologies for Wireless Communications, vol. 2, pp. 1–6. IEEE (2005)
10. Lélé, C., et al.: Channel estimation methods for preamble-based OFDM/OQAM modulations. Eur. Trans. Telecommun. **19**(7), 741–750 (2008)
11. Nissel, R., Rupp, M.: On pilot-symbol aided channel estimation in FBMC-OQAM. In: 2016 IEEE International Conference on Acoustics, Speech and Signal Processing (ICASSP), pp. 1–5. IEEE (2016)
12. Nissel, R., Ademaj, F., Rupp, M.: Doubly-selective channel estimation in FBMC-OQAM and OFDM systems. In: 2018 IEEE 88th Vehicular Technology Conference (VTC-Fall), pp. 1–6. IEEE (2018)
13. 3rd Generation Partnership Project: Technical Specification Group Radio Access Network; Study on New Radio (NR) to Support Non-Terrestrial Networks; (Release 15), document TR 38.811, 3GPP (2020)
14. Guo, Z., Chen, D., Yuan, Y.: 5G NR uplink coverage enhancement based on DMRS bundling and multi-slot transmission. In: 2020 IEEE 20th International Conference on Communication Technology (ICCT), pp. 1–5. IEEE (2020)

Author Index

R. C. Qiu et al. (Eds.): IoTaaS 2024, LNICST 675, pp. 379–380, 2026.
https://doi.org/10.1007/978-3-032-14681-6

GPSR Compliance
The European Union's (EU) General Product Safety Regulation (GPSR) is a set
of rules that requires consumer products to be safe and our obligations to
ensure this.

If you have any concerns about our products, you can contact us on

ProductSafety@springernature.com

In case Publisher is established outside the EU, the EU authorized
representative is:

Springer Nature Customer Service Center GmbH
Europaplatz 3
69115 Heidelberg, Germany